D1001718

All for the Union

The Saga of One Northern Family Fighting the Civil War

John A. Simpson

STACKPOLE
BOOKS
Guilford, Connecticut
Blue Ridge Summit, Pennsylvania

STACKPOLE BOOKS
An imprint of Globe Pequot, the trade division of
The Rowman & Littlefield Publishing Group, Inc.
4501 Forbes Blvd., Ste. 200
Lanham, MD 20706
www.rowman.com

Distributed by NATIONAL BOOK NETWORK

British Library Cataloguing in Publication Information available

Library of Congress Cataloging-in-Publication Data

Names: Simpson, John A., 1949– author.
Title: All for the Union : the saga of one northern family fighting the Civil War / John A. Simpson.
Description: Guilford, Connecticut : Stackpole Books, [2022] | Includes bibliographical references and index. | Summary: "'All for the Union' is the dramatic story of four soldiers, all related, weaving their lives and wars into a tapestry of how one family navigated home front and battle front during the Civil War"— Provided by publisher.
Identifiers: LCCN 2021035486 (print) | LCCN 2021035487 (ebook) | ISBN 9780811770873 (cloth) | ISBN 9780811770880 (epub)
Subjects: LCSH: United States—History—Civil War, 1861–1865—Biography. | Ellithorpe, Phillip Griggs, 1843–1863—Correspondence. | Ellithorpe, Philander Doty, 1840–1915—Correspondence. | Burleson, Asa R., 1831–1917—Correspondence. | United States. Army—Biography. | Soldiers—United States—Biography. | Brothers—United States—Biography.
Classification: LCC E467 .S567 2022 (print) | LCC E467 (ebook) | DDC 973.7/410922—dc23
LC record available at https://lccn.loc.gov/2021035486
LC ebook record available at https://lccn.loc.gov/2021035487

∞™ The paper used in this publication meets the minimum requirements of American National Standard for Information Sciences—Permanence of Paper for Printed Library Materials, ANSI/NISO Z39.48-1992.

Dedicated to

Dr. Jack P. Maddex
Professor Emeritus, Department of History,
University of Oregon, Eugene, Oregon
My Civil War mentor and friend

Mrs. Rose Janke
Charter member of Lower Columbia Genealogical Society
and volunteer with Cowlitz County Historical Society,
Kelso, Washington
My genealogy consultant and friend

Contents

Acknowledgments

A General Comment about Primary and Secondary Sources

A wide range of sources were used to frame the Ellithorpe letters in context with events taking place around them. The story line is founded on official military reports in the *Official Record of the War of the Rebellion*. Public records housed in village, town, and county clerk's offices across western and northern New York, northwestern Pennsylvania, Vermont, and Minnesota heightened the sense of family economies and struggles as they moved farther away from the eastern seaboard. More than two dozen historical societies, ranging from California to Vermont, willingly provided information, photographs, and encouragement to the Ellithorpe project, as evidenced in the notes. Local newspaper accounts, although sparse, helped to round out the story.

A number of secondary sources written between 1865 and 1900 were extremely insightful regarding local affairs; many of these volumes are conveniently found online at www.archive.org. Finally, most modern secondary scholarship on the eastern theater, the Army of the Potomac, and the lives of common Civil War soldiers has been consulted in the preparation of this work, including the works of Bell I. Wiley, Peter S. Carmichael, Herman Hattaway, Stephen W. Sears, George C. Rable, Gerald F. Linderman, Ethan S. Rafuse, James M. McPherson, Gary W. Gallagher, Gordon C. Rhea, Earl J. Hess, and many others. On a related matter, the author is deeply indebted to the interlibrary loan department at Knight Library, University of Oregon, for supplying an endless stream of scholarly sources.

Photographs

The photographs of officers that appear in this study were, at the beginning of the war, almost exclusively regimental and company leaders who led the

Ellithorpes. A few of them ascended to higher ranks and led brigades, divisions, and even corps commands, but my overriding vision of a bottom-up philosophy in this narrative was maintained in the depiction of these images.

* * * * * * *

I would like to single out the following individuals who contributed in ways large and small to the finished product.

Libraries, Museums, and Archives

Gale Family Library, Minnesota Historical Society, St. Paul, MN; John Heiser (historian, Gettysburg National Military Park Library and Archive, Gettysburg, PA); Edna Smith and Dennis Northcott (Missouri History Museum, St. Louis, MO); Patricia Cummings-Witter (Archives and Special Collections, Daniel A. Reed Library, State University of New York, Fredonia, NY); Mollie Braen (research services coordinator, New England Historic Genealogical Society, Boston, MA); Stephanie Arias (Munger Research Center, Huntington Library, San Marino, CA); Shawn Purcell (senior librarian, New York State Library, Albany, NY); Sharon Thayer (Special Collections, Bailey-Howe Library, University of Vermont, Montpelier, VT); Cynthia Van Ness (director, Buffalo and Erie County Library, Buffalo, NY); Mike Sherbon (archivist, Pennsylvania State Library and Archives, Harrisburg, PA); Ronn Palm (Ronn Palm's Museum of Civil War Images, Gettysburg, PA); Tal Nadan and Susan P. Waide (reference archivist and manuscripts specialist, New York Public Library, New York, NY); Lisa DeLaurant (San Joaquin Valley Heritage and Genealogical Center, Fresno County Public Library, Fresno, CA); and Holland Land Office Museum and Library (Batavia, NY).

State, County, and Town Historical Societies

Joseph Govednik, Jim Elliott, and Bill Watson (Cowlitz County Historical Society and Museum, Kelso, WA); Rose Janke and Pam Chilton (Lower Columbia Genealogical Society, Longview, WA); Clearfield County Historical Society (Clearfield, PA); Susan Hoy (Cameron County Historical Society, Emporium, PA); Thomas S. Cook (Town of Nunda Historical Society, Nunda, NY); Caitlin Carton (Town of Hopkins Historical Society, Hopkins,

MN); Andy Bloedorn (Winona County Historical Society, Winona, MN); Ruth Covert (McKean County Historical Society, Smethport, PA); Sharon Jahn and Julie Mlinar (Spring Valley Historical Society, Spring Valley, MN); Paul Carnahan (Leahy Library, Vermont Historical Society, Barre, VT); Barbara Price (Gloucester County Historical Society, Woodbury, NJ); Mary Rhodes and Ronald G. Taylor (Allegany County Historical Society, Andover, NY); Harold L. Smith (Sheldon Historical Society, Sheldon, VT); Barb Cooper (Lawrence Historical Society, North Lawrence, NY); Laura Greene (Cattaraugus County Historical Museum and Research Library, Machias, NY); Jeannette Sawyer (Bridgewater Historical Society, Bridgewater, VT); and Katy Hogue (Fresno Historical Society, Fresno, CA).

Village, Township, and County Clerk's Offices and Historians

Amanda Forbes (town clerk of Fairfield, VT); Robert L. Christman (county clerk, Allegany County, Belmont, NY); Nancy Robinson (town clerk of Bridgewater, VT); Betty Walker (town clerk of Orwell, VT); Tracy Villnave (town clerk of North Lawrence, NY); Records Room (county clerk, Genesee County, Batavia, NY); Archive (county clerk, Livingston County, Geneseo, NY); Kim Dufresne (town clerk of Sheldon, VT); Sandra Santamoor (county clerk, St. Lawrence County, Canton, NY); Susan Eck (historian of western New York, Buffalo, NY); Cindy Amrheim (Wyoming County historian, Warsaw, NY); Rhonda Pierce (county clerk, Wyoming County, Warsaw, NY); Lorraine Wagner (town of Eagle historian, Bliss, NY); Rebecca Cole (town of Rushford historian, Rushford, NY); Mary Converse (town of Hopkinton historian, Hopkinton, NY); Craig Braack (Allegany County historian, Belmont, NY); and Lorna Spencer (town of Freedom historian, Sandusky, NY).

Photographs

Jason Martz (visual information specialist, Gettysburg National Military Park, Gettysburg, PA); Jennifer Loredo (Photographic Services, U.S. Army Heritage and Education Center, Carlisle, PA); Duane B. Miller (tech specialist, U.S. Army Heritage and Education Center, Carlisle, PA); Troy A. Hillman (family genealogist, Boston, MA); and Micheline F. Smith (family genealogist, Jamesburg, NJ).

Stackpole Staff

I would like to thank the following individuals on the Stackpole team: Dave Reisch (acquisitions editor), Stephanie Otto (editorial assistant), Patricia Stevenson (senior production editor), and Neil Cotterill (cover manager). In addition, two freelancers lent their expertise: Jennifer Rushing-Schurr (indexer) and Bruce Owens (copyeditor). I am fortunate to have had all of these professionals taking special care of *All for the Union.*

Special Recognition

I wish to thank eight individuals who were instrumental in shaping *All for the Union* over the past eight years. Three of them reside in my own community. David Freece, the retired director of the Cowlitz County Historical Society and Museum, entrusted me to be a good steward of the Ellithorpe Family Collection and also allowed me to share my findings at five community programs. Rose Janke (longtime member of the Cowlitz County Historical Society and the Lower Columbia Genealogical Society) offered wonderful insights into the pitfalls as well as successes associated with genealogical research. Finally, my health provider, Cordon Bittner, MD, patiently explained the significance of Phillip's medical chart at Gettysburg over several cups of coffee. All three of these individuals expanded my knowledge greatly in areas that were previously foreign to me.

It would be remiss on my part not to mention Ruth Covert (McKean County Historical Society, Smethport, PA). Ruth has been my boots on the ground in the heart of Bucktail country. Ruth answered all of my queries, no matter how minuscule, with cheerfulness and timeliness. She also taught me the significance of the Bucktail heritage in Smethport and its surrounding environs.

Five members of the academic community initially agreed to serve as outside readers, and three of them actually survived the ordeal. These dedicated historians are Dr. Ethan S. Rafuse (associate professor, Department of Military History, U.S. Army Command and General Staff College, Fort Leavenworth, KS); Dr. Jack P. Maddex Jr. (professor emeritus, Department of History, University of Oregon, Eugene, OR); and Dr. Lloyd A. Hunter (professor emeritus and Branigan Endowed Chair, Franklin College, Franklin, IN). I could not have been blessed with three better choices because their individual strengths complemented each other in ways that truly benefited me. One was a brilliant expert in the Army of the Potomac and the eastern theater—two subjects of vital importance to my subject. Another, a master of the English language, copyedited the material and framed it into a readable story. Prodding questions about concept, meaning, and direction improved the overall product. The third person undertook the laborious task of checking the notes for accuracy—no simple chore. I owe Ethan, Jack, and Lloyd a tremendous debt of gratitude. I also appreciate the advice and support given by Dr. Christopher W. Mackowski (professor of communications, St. Bonaventure University, Allegany, New York).

Finally, I would like to thank my wife of fifty years, Shirley. I spent six to eight hours per day, five days per week, for more than seven years on the Ellithorpes, and Shirley managed to juggle my new assignment with our other family commitments. She was the final editor of every draft and accompanied me on several research trips to the Midwest and East Coast. On various occasions, we found the graves of all principal characters, encountered an unseasonable May snowstorm in the North Country of New York while searching for Ellithorpe ancestors, visited my boyhood "dream school" (Dartmouth College), walked the path taken by the Bucktails from Little Round Top to Houck's Ridge, and spent several lovely days at the Old Library B & B in Olean, New York. Perhaps the biggest perk to our adventures, however, was meeting so many wonderful and supportive people along the way who were fascinated to learn about the complex story I was chasing. In the end, *All for the Union* gave me far more than I had ever expected.

I hope the readers enjoy my book.

John A. Simpson
Kelso, Washington

Introduction

In December 2013, Director David Freece of the Cowlitz County Historical Museum in Kelso, Washington, received a donation of 180 original Civil War letters written by two soldier-brothers and one brother-in-law to their three sisters and wife, respectively, in rural Allegany County, New York. Director Freece reached out to me to inventory, catalog, and read these family letters and then to assess their historical importance and find a permanent home for the collection. This fascinating collection of missives, stored and forgotten in a wooden attic trunk in the Pacific Northwest, is the foundation of this book, *All for the Union*.

In the late 1850s, as political storm clouds enveloped the United States over the divisive issue of slavery, the five Ellithorpe children, born between 1835 and 1845, entered young adulthood. In April 1861, eighteen-year-old Phillip Griggs Ellithorpe and twenty-year-old Philander Doty Ellithorpe answered the patriotic call to save the Union. This narrative refers to Phillip and Philander as "the Ellithorpe brothers." They would be joined during the war by future brothers-in-law Asa R. Burleson and afterward Oliver Webster Moore. Asa's and Oliver's inclusion in the extended family resulted in the foursome being collectively referred to as "the Ellithorpe boys."

The Ellithorpe "brothers and boys" miraculously served in seven different regiments from four different states throughout the entire course of the war. The intertwined stories of the Ellithorpes are told in the context of seven Union regiments in the Army of the Potomac: the 13th Pennsylvania Reserves, or Bucktails (Phillip); the 27th New York and 2nd New York Mounted Rifles (Philander); the 5th Vermont and 1st New York Dragoons (Asa); and the 1st Minnesota and Battery I, 1st U.S. Light Artillery (Oliver). Four of these units would achieve notoriety on the battlefield as well as immortality in the pages of William Fox's *Regimental Losses in the American Civil War*, a classic compendium of the top fighting regiments in the Federal army. Furthermore, the collective military experiences of the Ellithorpe "brothers and boys" embodied every branch of the northern army—infantry (including sharpshooters), cavalry (mounted and dismounted), and artillery—as well as detached duties in the commissary department, engineering corps, and ambulance corps, a broad and unique swath of wartime involvement rarely presented in a single volume of Civil War studies.

With regard to methodology, *All for the Union* recounts a bottom-up view of soldiering in the Army of the Potomac. Emphasis is placed on events at the company and regiment levels, while larger strategic decisions and army movements act as a backdrop to the group biographies. The combat timetable of the Ellithorpes spanned the first campaign into western Maryland (June 1861) through the bloody battle of Second Petersburg (June 1864). This prosopographical approach presents an unvarnished view of the daily challenges faced by these four volunteers and their shared omnipresent struggles to overcome combat insecurities and fears, serious health concerns, and home-front worries while fulfilling their obligations as members of Lincoln's legions. But make no mistake: this book is first and foremost a Bucktail story draped in family history.

All for the Union also weaves the family's home-front trials into the battlefront narrative through extensive correspondence between the Ellithorpe siblings. The principal character, Phillip, drafted almost 100 letters, and they reached out to his three sisters, brother, parents, uncle, and friends. The great majority of Phillip's epistles were addressed to his oldest sibling, Ann, and his words add substantially to the historical record about his regiment, the storied Bucktails. Similarly, the remaining seventy-five communications penned by Philander and Asa fill gaps and add new insights into our understanding of their respective regiments. It is noteworthy that Oliver did not contribute a single wartime message (because he was not yet a member of the family), but later his actions were indispensable in preserving the wartime letters of Phillip, Philander, Asa, and Ann for posterity.

The quality of the original Ellithorpe letters as they relate to modern writing conventions (such as spelling, punctuation, and basic syntax) is problematic, but therein lies their charm. For example, Phillip's semiliterate writings demonstrated a lack of understanding about the fundamental usage of commas, periods, apostrophes, and capitalization. Furthermore, he frequently misspelled words or made incorrect word choices to express his thoughts. Rather than making voluminous corrections to these errors, however, this volume chooses to retain most of Phillip's original style in order to preserve his "voice." Four spaces are inserted into direct quotations where correct punctuation is absent.

* * * * * * *

The wartime adventures and misadventures of Phillip, Philander, Asa, and Oliver resonate from the fields of glory at Bull Run, the Seven Days, Antietam, Fredericksburg, Gettysburg, Cold Harbor, and Petersburg, and the family's letters bring to life the story of one forgotten boy-soldier of the American Civil War who sacrificed his life in order to preserve the Union. Equally important, the war was, without question, the most momentous event of the lives of the survivors, and that event would cast a long shadow into the next century. More than one Civil War scholar has noted the relatively poor job done by historians in tracing the physical and mental losses caused by combat to veterans in the postwar decades. *All for the Union* is an effort to address this lacuna.

A treatment about how the family's Civil War correspondence moved across the continent from the Old Northwest to the Pacific Northwest in the mid-twentieth century is a fitting conclusion to this study, an amazing story in itself.

Whether the reader is a history generalist, a Civil War buff, or a scholar of the period, *All for the Union* will appeal to a broad audience.

Chapter One

In Search of the Ellithorpes of Western New York

Prologue

Long before the Ellithorpes and their kin arrived in Massachusetts during the Puritan Migration of the 1630s, the Seneca tribe of the Iroquois Confederation, known as "the keepers of the western door," had occupied the lands that would later be called western New York. Although a warlike people, they lived in longhouses and were closely tied to the land as farmers. With harsh winters and cool summers, the wilderness ecosystem offered a broad array of flora and fauna. Teeming with wildlife such as bears, wolves, elk, deer, raccoons, otters, and panthers, the landscape was a hunter's paradise. The region's most significant geographic feature, the Genesee River, carved a valley from south to north through a series of rugged and heavily forested mountains to fertile lowlands in the northern portion of the virgin territory. The natives called this place "pleasant valley," where "the heavens rest upon the earth." The earliest pioneer settlers labeled this region "the Genesee Country," and its natural beauty and rich bounty would appeal to hardscrabble farmers from New England. Washington Irving dubbed the expanse "Allegania."[1]

* * * * * * *

The patrilineal and matrilineal descendants of the Ellithorpes, a blend of three families, migrated across New England to northern and western New

York while those regions were still frontiers. Eventually, each side procured land from the Holland Land Company in Eagle, Allegany County, New York, and struggled as subsistence farmers for many years. By 1830, this southern tier of western New York had undergone a radical economic and social transformation. Furthermore, the decade had witnessed the union of the Ellithorpes through a marriage that would produce five children of the Civil War generation. Living on the fringe of the "burned-over district," the Ellithorpe offspring would experience major social, religious, and educational reforms firsthand in the 1840s that would shape their worldviews. By 1860, the siblings were branching out, ever mindful of the escalating sectional tensions within the United States.[2]

Puritans, Connecticut Yankees, and Vermonters: Patrilineal Descendants

In the summer of 1638, Thomas Ellithorpe boarded the *John of London* in Hull, England, and set sail for Salem, Massachusetts.[3] In his mid-thirties, Ellithorpe accompanied approximately fifty other passengers with a shared goal—to settle in Massachusetts Bay Colony. The voyage was particularly noteworthy as the ship's hold transported the first printing press to the British colonies. One year later, Thomas established himself as one of sixty charter households in Rowley, Massachusetts, thirty-three miles north of Boston and close to the present border of New Hampshire. There, the Ellithorpe family lived for three generations.[4]

For most of the eighteenth century, several generations of Ellithorpe progeny migrated to different locales because of the thin soil base that had played out, growing population pressure, or the enticement of cheap land to veteran soldiers. Family tradition placed great importance on lucrative saw and grist mill industries, participation in civic affairs, service in militias, and membership in the Congregational Church. Such travels led them to settle Thompson and Pomfret, Windham County, Connecticut; Worthington, Hampshire County, Massachusetts; and Hungerford (renamed Sheldon), Franklin County, Vermont, to be closer to a sizable Ellithorpe enclave.[5]

To Vermont

In 1796, Jacob Ellithorpe married Huldah Fisher of Burlington, Vermont. The newlyweds immediately took up residence in the town of Orwell, a few miles east of Lake Champlain. Originally called Wood Creek, Orwell had doubled in size in the decade after statehood in 1791. Jacob's property was bounded on the west by a swift-running stream called Lemon Fair. Early residents set up sawmills along its banks and engaged in potash production. In Orwell, Huldah gave birth to four sons. The youngest, Lyman, was destined to play a major role in Ellithorpe family affairs as the father of the Civil War generation.[6]

To the North Country of New York

Shortly after the Panic of 1819, Jacob's family uprooted from Orwell in response to new opportunities opening in the North Country of upstate New York. In St. Lawrence County, the federal government was offering tracts of public land at the rate of $1.25 per acre in an effort to stimulate population growth. Two aggressive land agents, Nathan Ford and Lewis Morris, targeted Vermonters, and their canvass paid big dividends. "If any region in America deserves the name of New Vermont, it is the northern counties of New York State."[7]

The Ellithorpes' decision to purchase land in Nicholville, St. Lawrence County, New York, coincided with a wave of Orwellians into that northern New York community. In those days, the journey to Nicholville was made easier because of the recent completion of the St. Lawrence Turnpike, which connected Plattsburgh and Carthage, New York. Originally known as "Sodom," the hamlet of Nicholville was situated on the banks of the St. Regis River, across from Hopkinton. Danforth's marriage to Paulina Phelps, the daughter of a prominent Orwell clergyman who had proceeded the Ellithorpes to St. Lawrence County, likely solidified the brother's decision to relocate unencumbered. Following the sudden death of his father, Danforth deeded his widowed mother thirty acres in Orwell. In 1825, Huldah sold her property and moved to Nicholville to be closer to her sons.[8]

The Ellithorpes left an impressive entrepreneurial footprint in Nicholville. The 1830 census listed both Danforth and William as farmers, but the former also built the town's first sawmill in 1828 and operated it for fifteen years. He also opened a blacksmith shop. Both brothers dabbled in land speculation, quadrupling their holdings over the next thirty years, and became members of the local Methodist church.[9]

Less is known about the younger brothers, Charles and Lyman. Although Charles lived in the township at least until his wife's death in 1842,

Lyman is even more of an enigma. Still a young teenager when his brothers moved to northern New York, Lyman lived with and labored on Danforth's farm until the late 1820s. The 1830 census lists Lyman as residing next to his three brothers and a neighbor named Sanford. His household included two women: one in her sixties and another in her late teens. The older woman was likely Lyman's mother, and a genealogical report states that he had married a woman named Marinda. Whether or not they became a couple, his household produced a child, Danforth Sanford Ellithorpe, on July 14, 1833. Then Lyman's alleged spouse disappeared.[10] Later, Danforth chose the original spelling of the family's surname without the final "e."

Puritans, Connecticut Yankees, and Vermonters: Matrilineal Descendants

The matrilineal line of the Ellithorpes followed a similar migratory pattern, whose ancestors arrived during the Puritan Migration of the 1630s, and later descendants trekked across Massachusetts, Connecticut, and Vermont in the seventeenth and eighteenth centuries. En route, they forged important social and economic alliances before uniting with the Ellithorpes through marriage in western New York at the dawn of the nineteenth century.

The Griggs Clan

In the spring of 1636, Thomas Griggs, a fifty-year-old English patrician, arrived in Massachusetts Bay Colony; purchased twelve acres of land in Roxbury, Massachusetts (now Brookline); and signed the town registry as a founding father. But the accomplishments of Thomas's son (Joseph) and grandson (Benjamin) surpassed his own financial successes as proprietors, selectmen, deputies to the General Court, and surveyors of new roads and settlements in Woodstock and Pomfret, Windham County, Connecticut. Their penchant for surveying and land speculation remained a strong Griggs tradition and contributed to their growing influence in society and politics.[11]

During the Revolutionary War, the twenty-two-year-old Ephraim Griggs Jr. responded to the call of Gen. George Washington for Connecticut to raise an emergency force of two regiments to protect against an expected Redcoat invasion of New York City. When his term of service was completed, he returned to Windham County and married Hannah Eastman of Ashford, the daughter of the affluent Timothy and Easther Eastman.[12]

The Griggses made Pomfret their home for twenty years, raised eight children, and made frequent visits to Hannah's parents, who had moved to east-central Vermont. In the 1790s, more than forty villages had sprung up around the hamlet of Barnard, and many of them adopted names from Connecticut townships and villages (i.e., Pomfret and Woodstock) in a region unofficially dubbed "New Connecticut." The draw of the Eastmans on the Ellithorpes had always been keen, so shortly after the birth of their last child in 1797, Ephraim and Hannah decided to escape their exhausted soil and join the post-statehood migratory boom to Vermont. The promise of inexpensive land and living closer to the Eastmans undoubtedly made their decision much easier. In addition, the oldest Griggs child, Philip, was approaching his majority, and he would prove to be a great asset to his parents during the relocation.[13]

In February 1799, the Griggses purchased fifty acres from Hannah's wealthy father. The parcel lay just across the southern border of Barnard in the extreme northeast corner of Bridgewater township. Bridgewater was heavily timbered and required intensive labor to clear, although many open fields made it practical for the planting of winter wheat and grazing livestock. The township was aptly named because of the seventy bridges built over many small but swift-flowing tributaries of the Ottauquechee River.[14]

Philip Griggs

The Griggs family was in transition shortly after settling in Bridgewater when twenty-two-year-old Philip met the love of his life, Rebecca Cain. On December 26, 1800, the couple married in the mountain village of Ely, Vermont, on the Connecticut River. The idyllic, fjord-like setting of nearby Lake Fairlee would become a favorite family vacation spot. Their household burst at the seams over its first twelve years with the addition of seven children, the norm for young families living in frontier Vermont. Much later, the couple would become grandparents to the five Ellithorpe children of the Civil War generation.[15]

In 1803 and 1805, Philip and Rebecca purchased eighty-five acres adjoining his father's property in Bridgewater township. Twice, they added acreage, and Philip remained active in the local real estate market. But unforeseen economic problems arose. In 1805, a prolonged summer drought severely damaged the harvest. Low crop yields caused by inadequate fertilization and crop rotation sapped the soil of its nutrients. Then the Embargo Act of 1807, designed to force Great Britain and France to honor American neutrality during the Napoleonic Wars, backfired. The legislation devastated winter wheat farmers in Vermont who relied on a robust trade with Montreal, Canada. The ensuing Panic of 1807 and subsequent collapse of the state bank in 1811 ruined many hardscrabble farmers.[16]

In 1811, the difficulties multiplied when an outbreak of spotted fever coincided with a disastrous freshet in July that knocked out two-thirds of the mills and bridges in Windsor County. Perhaps the last straw occurred one year later when war hysteria swept throughout the region with the outbreak of the War of 1812. But where would Philip find economic and political security for his large family? One possibility lay in the vast and undeveloped land in western New York.[17]

The Holland Land Company of Western New York

In the late 1790s, after the Senecas were officially evicted from their ancestral homeland in western New York, the Genesee Country was thrown open to large land companies hoping to satisfy the appetites of land-starved New England farmers. In 1792 and 1793, a Dutch investment syndicate gobbled up the territory west of the Genesee River. Known as the Holland Land Company (HLC), the firm would play a major role in developing western New York and financing mortgages to farmers for more than forty years.[18]

In 1797, Theophilius Cazenove, the overseer of HLC interests for the absentee landlords, hired Joseph Ellicott, a skilled surveyor with a national reputation, to conduct an extensive survey of the Genesee Country. Ellicott devised a unique boundary system that departed from the prevailing grid method as outlined in the Northwest Ordinance of 1785. His "long lotting" of land parcels was particularly popular in the southern tier of the Holland Land Purchase, where low mountains, hills, narrow valleys, and many creeks dominated the landscape.[19]

In March 1798, Ellicott ordered twelve chief surveyors and 130 laborers into the wilderness of western New York to map more than three million acres of land. Each survey party was armed with a special portable transit designed by Ellicott's brother and a new brass ruler that ultimately standardized the unit measure of one foot at twelve inches in the United States.

Miraculously, "The Great Survey" completed its task in only thirty-one months, and the HLC opened western New York for settlement.[20]

Ellicott's other major responsibility throughout the survey had called for the collection of massive amounts of data on the physical landscape of each individual lot. As a result, his crews generated large ledgers known as Field (or Range) Books. These tomes were indispensable aids to sales agents and prospective buyers. They not only commented on contours of terrain and drainage patterns but also included invaluable observations on the quality of soil, species of trees, types of vegetation, and wildlife. Finally, the Books offered suggestions for the placement of villages, roads, and mills.[21]

Ellicott's surveyors concluded that the best farmland lay along the northern tier, where an abundance of fertile soil blanketed a lowland plain.

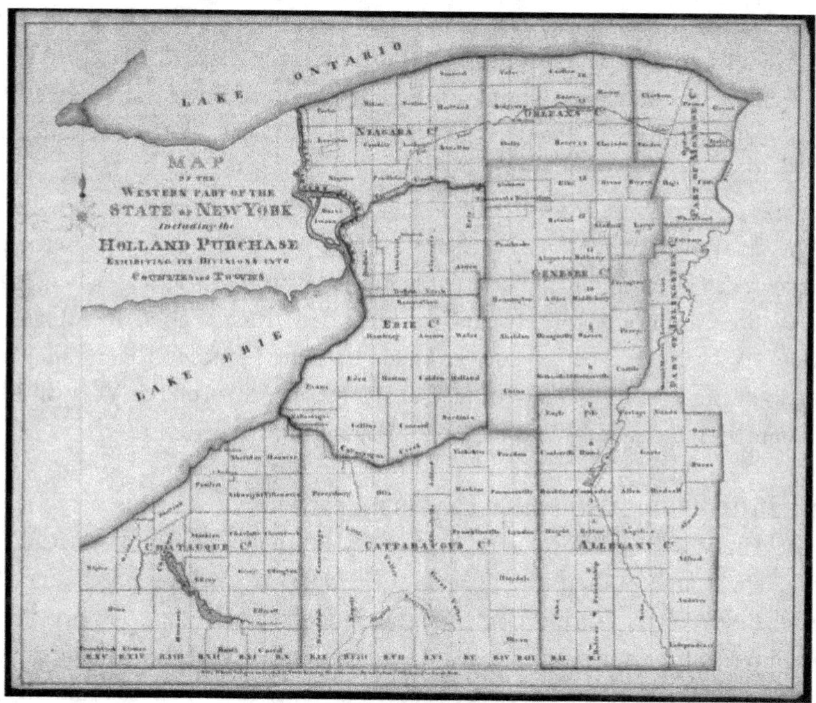

Historic Holland Land Company map of counties and townships of western New York, 1825.

SOURCE: DANIEL A. REED LIBRARY, ARCHIVES AND SPECIAL COLLECTIONS, STATE UNIVERSITY OF NEW YORK, FREDONIA, NEW YORK; MUNICIPAL ARCHIVES OF AMSTERDAM; NEDERLANDSE DOCUMENT REPRODUCTIE B.V.

Elsewhere, they were skeptical of the thin layer of shale and sandstone. Thus, the "southern tier" was deemed ill suited for growing staple crops like corn and wheat, and the subregion was considered an economic backwater for decades.

In 1800, the new general agent for the HLC, Paul Busti, made a major personnel decision when he appointed Ellicott as resident agent to oversee land sales from company headquarters in the new village in Batavia, New York. Ellicott assembled an energetic sales staff stationed in Albany and devised a sound marketing strategy targeted specifically at Vermonters. They wrote glowing newspaper articles, distributed advertising handbills, prepared maps of western New York, and organized "spirited speaking tours" from a field office in Danby, Vermont. Struggling farmers in Vermont were receptive to this intense propaganda campaign, and HLC promotions generated a great deal of excitement, which onlookers dubbed "Genesee Fever." Perhaps the most persuasive arguments in favor of relocation came in letters from friends and family members who had already ventured into western New York. Nor would Philip Griggs have been oblivious to the HLC campaign or ignored his own instinct to leave Vermont and seek financial security for his family.[22]

Hardy Vermonters normally began the journey to western New York in the dead of winter, attaching sleigh runners to their wagons and crossing frozen Lake Champlain in order to avoid the summer months when roadways were commonly muddy and overcrowded. They tended to follow old Indian "traces," the Mohawk River valley, and the Genesee River valley and its tributaries to mark their route. Growing concern over the War of 1812 then precipitated a second wave of emigration from Vermont.[23]

The Philip Griggs Family Lands in Eagle, New York

In February 1813, Philip and Rebecca sold their substantial acreage in Bridgewater and joined the "Yankee Exodus" of Vermonters bound for western New York. During that time, Eagle township in the southern tier of Allegany County was part of the William Willink Tract, which had earned a notorious reputation as a haven for squatters. It is entirely possible that Griggs was among the freeloaders because there is no extant evidence of his signed Article of Agreement. In any case, Griggs occupied the southern third of lot 50 in Range 1, township 7, a 115-acre plot. Thirteen months later, Rebecca gave birth to their eighth child in the Eagle wilderness.[24]

At first, Griggs's parcel was under the authority of the township of Nunda, where its *Record Book* listed him as the "path master" for District 14, a road maintenance position. He held the post until administrative jurisdiction for his neighborhood in Eagle was transferred to the township of Pike in 1823.[25]

Adapting to frontier life in Eagle was a challenge for Philip, Rebecca, and their ever-increasing brood of children. Pioneer families in the Genesee Country learned much from the previous occupants of the land—the Senecas. After building a crude log cabin, they burned off as much underbrush as possible and spent the cold winter months girdling trees. These actions complied with HLC regulations, which required new tenants to erect a small dwelling and clear a minimum of four acres per year. In the first spring, the farmers would cut down the dead trees and float them downstream to mills in Rochester or burn them in large piles in order to manufacture potash. The practice of unauthorized "woodchoppers," who had no intention of making improvements to the land, aggrieved the HLC. These clandestine operators remained a presence in the region into the 1830s and practically denuded the countryside a decade later.[26]

Engraving of a typical frontier farm in western New York (ca. 1820).

SOURCE: ORSAMUS TURNER, *PIONEER HISTORY OF THE HOLLAND LAND PURCHASE OF WESTERN NEW YORK* (BUFFALO, NY: JEWETT, THOMAS & CO., 1850), 582.

Equally important to the survival of the Griggses and other transplanted Vermonters, the local Native Americans taught the newcomers how to harvest maple sugar in late March. Famished settlers consumed large quantities of the sweet syrup for its nutritional value and wonderful taste. Over time, the practice of "sugaring" evolved into an elaborate social occasion when winter-weary neighbors gathered, harvested, consumed, and frolicked prior to the arduous planting season in the spring. The tradition would become a popular pastime for two of Philip's future grandsons.[27]

Economic Troubles in the Genesee Country

The first mention of Philip Griggs in official public documents occurred on May 31, 1819, when he witnessed a land transaction in the Allegany County Clerk's office. Then, on December 22, 1819, Philip signed a reversion to his HLC contract, or Article of Agreement, indicating that he had, indeed, purchased his Eagle homestead legally from Ellicott in the past.[28]

The timing of Philip's emergence into public life coincided with the Panic of 1819. The economic downturn had driven many farmers to amend their original contracts in order to avoid foreclosure. Homesteaders in the southern tier were mortgaged to the hilt, and they despaired in light of the

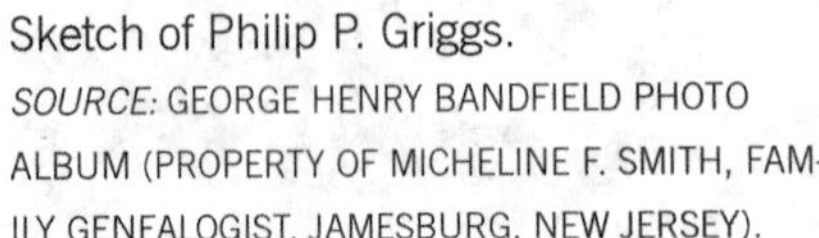

Sketch of Philip P. Griggs.
SOURCE: GEORGE HENRY BANDFIELD PHOTO ALBUM (PROPERTY OF MICHELINE F. SMITH, FAMILY GENEALOGIST, JAMESBURG, NEW JERSEY).

growing agricultural depression. Sensing this anxiety, the HLC agreed to accept payment in kind. Griggs took advantage of this readjustment, often using cattle to make mortgage payments. The financial crisis did not abate in western New York until after 1825.[29]

In 1821, the absentee landlords in the Netherlands had lost patience with the drop in revenue and suddenly replaced Jacob Ellicott with Jacob S. Otto, a successful salesman in the Allegany County field office. Otto was specifically detailed to restore and enforce strict mortgage payment schedules in order to recoup the company's $4.4 million debt. In this post-Panic era, holders of more than one-fourth of all Allegany County contracts, approximately 8,000 families, had defaulted. The amount of indebtedness increased to the point where the rate of interest on delinquent balances exceeded the total valuation of the property, a situation ripe for foreclosure. Some families simply abandoned their land and departed for the Ohio Country.[30]

Otto understood his hard-line instructions. Shortly after taking over company operations, he reexamined delinquent contracts and implemented a policy of "detachment" to remove trespassers from company land. Otto's unpopular action fueled anger among impoverished farmers. Although harsh, Otto's policy of accountability comported with growing pains associated with the nation's fledgling commercial market economy. During the decade, Philip made four trips to the Allegany County Clerk's office in order to restructure his real estate obligation.[31]

Agrarian Unrest and Glimmers of Economic Prosperity in Western New York

In 1827, the first signs of organized agrarian dissatisfaction surfaced in western New York when disgruntled farmers held town hall meetings in Lockport and Buffalo to raise grievances against the HLC. Known as the Agrarian Convention, the gatherings attracted a potpourri of special interest groups, including anti-masons, evangelicals, and future supporters of the Whig Party. Especially upsetting to the farmer element was the growing number of evictions in the southern tier authorized by Commissioner Otto. Although the HLC made a token effort to reduce payment schedules and renegotiate more than 13,000 contracts, the anti-rentism sentiment boiled over in two short-lived armed rebellions in the early 1830s. Such radicalized unrest would affect Philip's household at mid-decade.[32]

Wedlock

Despite the volatile nature of frontier economies, there were indicators of Philip's growing prominence in the community as the southern tier slowly transitioned from subsistence to commercial agriculture. The bellwether social events were the marriages of his five oldest daughters. In May 1825, the series of nuptials began when Maria Griggs married William Webster Mills, the son of Roger Mills. The Mills family were among the first pioneers to settle in Allegany County. In search of a suitable mill site, they founded the village of Hume, named for Scottish philosopher-historian David Hume, and shortly thereafter the village of Mills Mills, on the upper falls of the Genesee River. The diversity of enterprises in Mills Mills—a saw and grist mill, a tavern, a distillery, a log schoolhouse, and a "pioneer hotel"—added to the family's social and economic prominence. The marriage of William and Maria not only established a marital bond between the two families but also foreshadowed the growing reputation of the Philip Griggs family.[33]

Over the next twenty years, Philip and Rebecca observed the marriages of four other daughters. These nuptials included Lucinda and Edward Van Dyke (January 1838), Rebecca and David O. Sessions (September 1840), and Eleanor and Carlos Leonard Stebbins (May 1845). But the critical union regarding this narrative was the marriage of their second daughter, Fannie, to Lyman Ellithorpe (ca. 1833 or 1834) in Pike.

On last account, Lyman had been living in Nicholville with his mother and a young female. Between the year of the federal census (1830) and the birth of his son, Danforth (1833), however, his whereabouts were unknown. In the meantime, the HLC had been inundating St. Lawrence County with handbills describing fertile land selling for discounted prices in Allegany County. It was during a period when the bankrupt company was in the process of liquidating its massive landholdings in western New York, and some North Country residents had taken up the call to relocate. It is not known how long Lyman had been present in the Genesee Country, but on October 23, 1833, he signed an Article of Agreement with agents of Wilhelm Willink for fifty acres in Eagle township.[34]

Here, Lyman and Fannie Ellithorpe would farm the land and raise five children, the principal characters of the Civil War generation. Their fourth child, Phillip Griggs Ellithorpe, was named for his maternal grandfather, and he would later emerge as the centerpiece of family wartime correspondence.[35]

Lyman and the Patriot Hunters' Lodge

The anti-rent crisis was running stronger than ever in the southern tier of Allegany County after the marriage of Lyman and Fannie. The root of the controversy lay, it will be recalled, in poor communication between farmers, company agents, and absentee landlords. And agrarian anger continued unabated after two American financial institutions assumed ownership of HLC liens. Then, in May 1837, another national financial crisis, this time caused by the issuance of the Specie Circular, created widespread panic in rural communities such as Eagle.[36]

These events coalesced in the creation of a secret society known as the Patriot Hunters' Lodge. Founded in St. Albans, Vermont, to address agrarian grievances, the Hunters' Lodge attracted thousands of members from all walks of life—professionals (physicians, clergymen, lawyers, and military officers), middle-class farmers and merchants, working-class urban workers, and landless rural laborers. The clandestine organization was particularly strong in western New York.[37]

The organizational structure of the Hunters' Lodge utilized a military format with tiered wilderness titles. New recruits were assigned to the entry level, or Snowshoe; the Beaver class was made up of commissioned officers; Grand Hunters raised funds and sought new enlistees; and the Patriot Hunter administrated local affairs. The rank-and-file members employed secret verbal and nonverbal oaths, signs, handshakes, and passwords. Lodges gathered in secluded locations at late hours of the night to listen to inflammatory speeches and partake in symbolic induction ceremonies. In 1838, Lyman was initiated into the body at an officer's grade of second lieutenant, a Beaver.[38]

By 1842, public sentiment for the Hunters' Lodge was beginning to wane as the American economy showed signs of revitalization and an international treaty settled the U.S.–Canada border dispute. Although membership was still strong enough in western New York to influence the outcome of several local elections, the paramilitary career of Lyman Ellithorpe came to an abrupt end.

Carlos Leonard Stebbins

At this time, the Griggs–Ellithorpe family was about to add a significant person to the fold. In July 1834, Elijah and Harriet Leonard Stebbins of

Carlos Leonard Stebbins and Eleanor Griggs Stebbins (1872).
SOURCE: GEORGE HENRY BANDFIELD PHOTO ALBUM (PROPERTY OF MICHELINE F. SMITH, FAMILY GENEALOGIST, JAMESBURG, NEW JERSEY).

York, Livingston County, New York, purchased fifty acres in the northeast corner of lot 50 in Pike, next to Philip Griggs. Elijah was the product of three generations of Stebbins cloth and woolen workers, who had played important roles in the formation of Northampton, Deerfield, and Conway, Massachusetts, three villages at the center of the energizing textile industry in pre-Revolutionary America. Elijah, who had worked in a woolen factory in Manlius and York, New York, was likely drawn to Allegany County by the opening of a new cloth factory in Eagle as well as the prospect of an expanding woolen industry countywide.[39]

Elijah and Harriet had two sons, Carlos Leonard and Sylvester. The young brothers became playmates to the Griggs children because of the nearness of both households and the closer proximity of their ages. Carlos's mother, reputedly of Italian ancestry, allegedly trained him in artistic endeavors, at which he proved quite adept. On May 22, 1845, Carlos Leonard Stebbins married Eleanor Griggs in Pike, establishing an important new relationship with five Ellithorpe nieces and nephews.[40]

The Burned-Over District

When the Ellithorpe siblings—Ann, Mary, Philander, Phillip, and Permelia—were still infants, the tenets of humanitarian reform were introduced throughout the Genesee Country in a subregion dubbed "the burned-over district." By the time several of the children reached adolescence in the late

1840s, they were exposed to and affected by the ferment of change that was crisscrossing their village and county: revivalism, temperance, abolitionism, free public education, and woman suffrage.[41]

In the 1840s, the vestiges of the Second Great Awakening lingered in western New York, and revivalism maintained a particularly strong foothold in the southern tier of the Genesee Country. Since the appearance of Presbyterian, Methodist, and Baptist missionaries forty years earlier, the region bore witness to emotion-laden camp meetings as well as other forms of spiritual expression. At this moment, many revivalists were reacting to the perceived crassness of commercialism and materialism in American society and its corresponding loss of piety and moral direction. In the Genesee Country, these evangelists forged alliances with other reform groups, most notably abolitionists and temperance crusaders. From an early age, Lyman's children absorbed these principles of godliness and social improvement, as evidenced in later Civil War correspondence among them.[42]

The greatest change agent to directly benefit the three Ellithorpe sisters, however, centered on educational opportunities for young women. The notion of creating a system of free public education in western New York was not a new idea. Indeed, one cornerstone of mid-nineteenth-century American thought included the establishment and maintenance of a literate society in order to preserve democratic principles. But the inclusion of equal opportunities for young women was a fairly revolutionary thought. Yet a number of academies and seminaries were opened to female students between the ages of seven and sixteen in western New York in the 1840s. Ann and Permelia took advantage of this opportunity to differing degrees, but there is no extant record of Mary's formal education or academic interests.[43]

When the Ellithorpes moved to Rushford in the early 1850s (to be discussed shortly), the children honed their skills in the classroom. Ann, in particular, developed a keen intellectual aptitude in reading, writing, and public discourse. She benefited greatly from her enrollment in Rushford Academy, which had opened in September 1852. "The institution," claimed two local historians, "greatly advanced public education in northwestern Allegany County."[44] Ann sought perfection in her studies and in the writings of others.

In 1858, Ann joined with thirty-six other young ladies to found a self-improvement society. The primary goal of the Mystic Association of Rushford sought to refine the lives of young women through tasteful studies in "eloquence, reading, and literature." The sorority held a public debate once each year as well as a dramatic literary production with musical accompaniment. On November 21, 1860, Ann participated in a recital for the village titled "United We Stand," an anti-secession and antislavery program. Through her academic studies and postgraduation activities, Ann demanded high standards when it came to the proper use of grammar, spelling, and penmanship.[45]

In stark contrast to Ann's scholarly pursuits, the Ellithorpe brothers acquired only semiliterate skills. Phillip and Philander would later confess that they had squandered classroom opportunities and possessed only rudimentary skills in areas where Ann excelled. Permelia, a sickly child who suffered from bouts of encephalitis, enjoyed music. Later, she took advantage of piano courses offered at Vickery's Music School, held in the Rushford Methodist Church.[46]

The Ellithorpe children absorbed enough from their school and church lessons to provide a foundation from which to formulate later opinions about antislavery, temperance, and women's rights as well as secession and emancipation. They were surely aware of Rushford's chapter of the Sons of Temperance and the village's station on the underground railroad.

The Economic Transformation of the Southern Tier

In the early days of the HLC settlement of western New York, the State Assembly offered its own enticement to attract newcomers to the region. In 1802, they created Genesee County, which was eventually subdivided four more times as the population swelled—Allegany (1806), Cattaraugus (1808), and Monroe and Livingston (1821). Then, in May 1841, the New York state legislature created Wyoming County from the southern portion of Genesee County. Five years later, approximately 120 square miles of northern Allegany County was ceded to the fledgling county in order to provide additional territory, revenue, and population. That boundary adjustment affected the Griggs–Ellithorpe–Stebbins homesteads because it now placed Eagle and Pike under the jurisdiction of Wyoming County.[47]

By the early 1850s, Wyoming County farmers profited from increased access to distant markets due to completion of the Erie Canal, expansion of a network of east–west turnpikes, and culmination of the Genesee Valley Canal and Erie Railroad. These transportation innovations fostered favorable shipping rates for farm commodities and transformed the southern tier from subsistence to commercial agriculture. Increased yields in traditional grain products, such as corn, winter and spring wheat, oats, and rye, were supported by the introduction of fruit varieties, such as apples, cherries, plums, and pears, as well as the appearance of sheep and hogs. Moreover, more attention was being given to dairy production, specifically the manufacture of butter and cheese. Diversification and stability had finally come to previously impoverished farm communities. As a result, the economic fortunes of the Ellithorpes and their kin gradually began to show signs of improvement.[48]

Perhaps the best indicator of this economic progress as it affected the Lyman Ellithorpe household is found in the *Agricultural Census of 1850*. Consider the following comparative chart:

Agricultural Census of 1850
Wyoming County, New York
(Production figures in parentheses represent the county average)[49]

	Ellithorpe (Eagle)	*Griggs (Pike)*	*Stebbins (Pike)*
improved acres (67)	76	115	100
unimproved acres (38)	50	50	93
total acreage (105)	126	165	193
value of farm ($2,500)	$3,000	$3,325	$5,000
value of machinery ($112)	$50	$200	$300
horses (2.5)	4	8	3
milch cows (4.3)	1	6	6
beef cattle (11)	0	6	12
sheep (39)	0	140	18
swine (4.6)	2	4	3
value of livestock ($385)	$425	$670	$600
bu. of wheat (99)	ww20	50	70
bu. of Indian corn (54)	10	75	50
bu. of oats (163)	500	280	200
lbs. of wool (108)	0	125	100
bu. of peas/beans (6)	40	8	0

(*continued*)

Agricultural Census of 1850 (*continued*)

	Ellithorpe (Eagle)	*Griggs (Pike)*	*Stebbins (Pike)*
bu. of potatoes (64)	300	250	0
bu. of barley (14)	60	60	0
bu. of buckwheat (8)	0	0	25
Value of orchards ($6)	$0	$10	$5
lbs. of butter (340)	630	500	600
lbs. of cheese (286)	1,000	600	1,250
tons of hay (21)	50	40	50
lbs. of maple syrup (163)	$50	0	400
Value of homemade manu. ($8)	$5	$30	$20
Value of slaughtered animals ($44)	$87	$66	$120
lbs. of beeswax/honey (11)	0	0	1,000

These production figures indicate that Lyman and Fannie operated a thriving farm based largely on two dairy commodities: 630 pounds of butter and 1,000 pounds of cheese, supported by 500 bushels of oats and 50 tons of hay (for milk cows). These production yields surpassed countywide averages. They also harvested significant amounts of potatoes and beans and likely bartered these vegetables with relatives and neighbors for foodstuffs they lacked. Conversely, Griggs and Stebbins relied heavily on herding sheep and selling fleece to local woolen mills. There is no doubt that the Ellithorpes and their extended family prospered due to expansion of the market economy in western New York.[50]

In the 1850s, farmers faced one decades-old problem in the southern tier: a severe labor shortage. The Griggs–Ellithorpe–Stebbins clans employed a pragmatic solution to alleviate the scarcity: Each family often hired one or two adult males to assist with farm chores. But they also utilized a system called "binding out," or lending out young offspring to provide labor on a relative's farm. Accordingly, Lyman often sent his two oldest sons, Danforth and Philander, to work for Uncle Carlos and Grandfather Philip. Carlos and Eleanor were childless, so they extended the same opportunity to two other nephews from nearby North Dansville, Edwin and James K. P. Stebbins. The older Ellithorpe brothers engaged in this practice as late as 1860, and, over time, it is conceivable that the brothers grew more attached to their cousins, uncle, aunt, and grandparents than to their own parents and siblings. This observation is based on Philander's distant tone to his siblings in future wartime correspondence and Danforth's disappearance from family affairs.[51]

Rushford

In March 1853, an unexpected bombshell dropped when the Ellithorpes suddenly left their productive farm in Eagle for the village of Rushford in Allegany County. The family's new dwelling, a two-story house with shed dormers, sat on a half-acre lot located a few blocks above the village and situated between Dr. Jesse P. Bixby and the village cemetery. The dwelling on Lewellen Street would be near a new pineapple cheese factory. There is no extant reason to explain why the Ellithorpes abandoned their lucrative farm in Eagle.[52]

The settlement of the village of Rushford was similar to other Allegany County hamlets, such as Pike and Eagle. In 1808, the first settler, Eneas Gary, arrived from Vermont, and others soon followed him. These pioneers originally named their community "Windsor" but changed it in honor of the famous Philadelphia physician, Dr. Benjamin Rush. Rushford township adopted Ellicott's growth model, and by 1820, the village boasted an inn, a general store, a saw and grist mill, and a church. The local economy graduated from timber-related activities to winter wheat production, and then to more diverse endeavors such as the flourishing dairy spin-offs, cheese and butter.[53]

By the time the Ellithorpes unpacked in Rushford, the hamlet had shaken off its frontier persona and emerged as a thriving commercial center. Its twelve stores prompted the claim that Rushford was "the liveliest place in the county" and a place where industry, thrift, and morals of its citizenry had contributed to its moniker, "the second New England." Rushford had surpassed Pike and Eagle in population, commerce, and economic livelihood.[54]

Phillip Griggs Ellithorpe

By his own admission, Phillip Griggs Ellithorpe was a spirited lad. As a youth, he would sneak out of the second-floor dormer window when everyone in the house was asleep and frolic around the neighborhood. He devoured raw maple sugar at spring harvest time and reveled in winter sleigh rides with his new friends in the village. He was versed in the fiddle and delighted in impromptu sessions, or "jaw boning," with fellow musicians and family members adept at the guitar, piano, and harmonica. Phillip absorbed enough from his formal schooling to appreciate poetry, although he struggled with the basic rules of capitalization, punctuation, and spelling. His penmanship was excellent, and he expressed his thoughts effectively. In later correspondence, Phillip would convey deep reverence to God, great fondness for his oldest and youngest sisters (Ann and Permelia), and tremendous loneliness for his older brother (Philander), whom he admired greatly but from whom he had been separated for much of his life. By all accounts, Phillip was a typical American boy.

In December 1859, sixteen-year-old Phillip purchased personal toiletry items and writing supplies from the Rushford dry goods store and laid plans to cross the state line to Smethport, Pennsylvania. There, he would apprentice as a "moulder" and learn the blacksmith trade. Perhaps he had acquired an interest in ironworks from the foundry in nearby East Rushford. "Cousin Edwin" (Stebbins) accompanied Phillip on his fifty-mile journey to Smethport, where he secured temporary lodging with Edward and Lucy Griggs Van Dyke, his aunt.[55]

One week before his seventeenth birthday in April 1860, Phillip wrote his first letter to sisters Ann and Permelia in Rushford. The young apprentice bragged about his successful work experience thus far in the McKean County seat. "I am well to and have to work pretty hard," he stated matter-of-factly. "The Boys seem to be very much pleased with me [and] say that I will make a first rate molder."[56] Phillip noted that his wardrobe was threadbare, however; there were holes in his socks, shirts, and "overhalls," and his boots were worn out. He bartered with a peddler to upgrade the quality of his garments, but he also requested that his sisters send a package of supplies from home.[57]

Proud of his progress as a molder's apprentice, Phillip's benefactor, Mr. Yarlis, offered him a three-year contract with free room and board and promises of annual salary raises. But Phillip was irritated by the incessant snoopiness of "moriah Yarlis," who regularly inspected his room. Another blacksmith, Mr. Krans, tendered a competing bid for Phillip's services. One of Krans's trainees, Thomas Barnes, recommended that Phillip accept the latter offer.[58]

Phillip accepted Krans's terms, and his new mentor proved to be a generous and benevolent employer. Once, the master craftsman represented his young tenderfoot in small-claims court and won a case against a former customer who had refused to pay Phillip for services rendered. "I thank God for my fortune so far," he closed.[59]

Despite long hours of physical labor, Phillip led an active social life. He attended several "fancy dress balls" and assured Ann and Permelia that he associated with "the best company." He went on horseback outings with young ladies and enjoyed one of his favorite pastimes, eating "warm sugar." Then Phillip made a stunning admission regarding one particular dalliance: "I never was so sagged [depressed?] but once in my life," he confided. "I never commit such a sin again. For since I came here to Smethport to work I married on molly My finnigin."[60] The revelation appeared to be a clumsy mea culpa of sexual offense. Phillip, likely admonished by his sisters, wished to soften the admittance by explaining that he had been attending Wednesday evening church services and promised "a change" (in behavior).[61]

In March 1861, Phillip had been away from Rushford for more than a year, and he admitted to feeling "very lonesome" despite still living with his aunt. In one letter, he implored father, mother, brother, and sisters to write soon. He censured Permelia, in particular, for ignoring him. "Now let me give you a little advice," Phillip scolded his fifteen-year-old sister: "dont be so sparing of your pens and paper . . . do as I do write some news." However, Phillip often wrote without having anything significant to report. "I Just set a trapping for rats here in the store," he once noted. "I'll go and look and sure enough thar in the trap is a large Rat. I hit the Rat in the head with the stove poker and come bak and sit down to write but hark what is that[?] the trap springs again and I have another Rat." In another missive, he complained, "I am alone in my room but I can't think of anything more to write." Boredom hung in Phillip's words. More and more, he reminisced nostalgically about past boyhood days, such as the time he had visited Mr. Benjamin's place and ate warm sugar.[62]

When Phillip first arrived in Smethport, he was well aware of a significant economic development taking place in northwest Pennsylvania. Indeed, the public's elation over the discovery of petroleum in Titusville may have attracted Phillip to Smethport in the first place. "Thare is some excitement here about the Oil that appears to be floating on the water [and] a company is coming to sink a Well . . . I think they will find oil here," he predicted. "The prospects are very favorable and if they succeed in doing so times will be better."[63] The growing sectional conflict, however, interrupted Phillip's further exploration of a career in this booming new industry.

Conclusion: Colonial Ancestry

The union of the Ellithorpe and Griggs families in western New York in the 1830s had its origin during the Puritan Migration of the 1630s. As generations of matrilineal and patrilineal kin crossed the New England frontier, the similarities of their experiences painted a picture of an ancestral Yankee heritage steeped in the principles of self-reliance, orderliness, religious and moral piety, productiveness, industriousness, and literary competence.

Ellithorpe and Griggs genealogies are filled with accounts about middle-class proprietors of significant social prominence. In most of the colonial communities in which they lived, they undertook roles as public servants: constables, assessors, judges, delegates on town councils, and legislative representatives. They were usually among the first settlers into a region, taking advantage of land speculation and other commercial ventures fueled by an insatiable land hunger. The common occupational thread in both families, surveying, offered a steady income unavailable to typical yeoman farmers.

They were also steeped in the frontier proclivity of hard work, large families, and a willingness to uproot and move westward once the soil gave out or climatic conditions threatened their prosperity or political-military circumstances demanded their relocation. Both families adhered to the industrious philosophy ingrained in frontier individualism and the Puritan work ethic.

Finally, Griggs–Ellithorpe men did not shy away from military service. Whether they joined formal armies during the American Revolution or the War of 1812 or less formal associations such as community militias to meet specific threats (usually Native American uprisings), they willingly accepted this obligation of military service. Much later, these family martial traits would be passed along to the Ellithorpe brothers of the Civil War generation.

Conclusion: The Civil War Generation

By the time the fifth (and last) Ellithorpe child was born to Lyman and Fannie in 1845, the cauldron of "freedom's ferment," as well as the economic transformation of the southern tier of western New York, was well under way. Yet within ten years, four important questions arose about the financial, medical, and emotional stability of several family members.

First, why did the Ellithorpes leave their productive farm in Eagle and move to Rushford? Explanations differ based on the individual needs of each family member. For forty-seven-year-old Lyman, a major producer of dairy products, the opening of a cheese factory in Rushford probably provided a major draw.[64] In 1860, the Ellithorpes churned 130 pounds of butter from their lone cow, underscoring the family's continued, if minimal, contact with the industry. In addition, Lyman may have grown weary of battling against the farm labor shortage in Wyoming County, especially after binding out his two eldest sons, Danforth and Philander. Fannie may have approved the move since Rushford was closer to her parents and siblings in Pike. Suffering from an undisclosed ailment, Fannie would find comfort in the presence of Dr. Bixby next door. The physician could also address the medical needs of Permelia. Ann, a budding scholar with a yearning for knowledge, embraced the opening of Rushford Academy as a wonderful learning opportunity as well as fellowship with like-minded young women. Finally, Phillip secured odd jobs delivering timber to sawmills and driving herds of cattle to market in Franklinville and Farmersville. The move to Rushford, therefore, seemed like a good "fit" for everyone.[65]

Second, something unexplained had occurred to cause the Ellithorpes to struggle financially once they relocated to Rushford. Two years later, in January 1857, the Allegany County sheriff was ordered to auction off their household items to pay an undisclosed debt. In a later wartime missive, Phillip recalled these hard times with shame because school chums often teased him for his ragamuffin appearance. The decision to bind out Mary to Uncle Carlos at this moment was yet another example of the family's desperation. Whatever the root cause of the Ellithorpes' economic distress, the Panic of 1857 later in the year exacerbated their impoverished condition.[66]

Third, there is mystery surrounding Lyman's oldest son, Danforth. Two nagging questions emerge: Where was Danforth's birthplace, St. Lawrence County or Allegany County? And who was Danforth's natural mother, Marinda or Fannie? Public records, destroyed by courthouse fires, are lost and therefore not helpful in shedding light on these queries. Yet the answers are important because they would establish whether Danforth was the natural brother to the five Ellithorpe children or their half brother.

Fourth, the unfolding close relationship between Uncle Carlos and the Ellithorpe children is critical to unraveling the family dynamics. In young adulthood, the multitalented Carlos was pulled in directions other than farming. His giftedness in portrait painting and compassion as an educator received praise from the Pike community, where he offered free art lessons to the children. In 1856, he was selected a trustee for the newly chartered Pike Seminary, taking an active role in picking the building site, surveying its premises, and overseeing construction of the three-story structure. Stebbins taught painting and drawing there for decades. Beyond his renown as an accomplished artist and educator, Carlos was respected in the community for his superior intellect, inventiveness, and mechanical aptitude. "A gentleman of superior mental endowments, blameless morals, and pleasing social qualities, Mr. Stebbins stands high in the estimation of his fellow citizens," boasted one Pike observer. Moreover, the Ellithorpe children held Uncle Carlos and Aunt Eleanor in high esteem and considered their welcoming household a second home.[67]

* * * * * * *

The Ellithorpe brothers of western New York, Phillip and Philander, absorbed a strong sense of family and community, and they would carry it into their Civil War experiences. The internecine struggle might have been caused by national issues, but it would be fought on distant fields by brothers, friends, and neighbors. The Ellithorpes would explain their participation in the cataclysmic struggle simply as a patriotic act to preserve the Union. In April 1861, when the call to arms finally sounded, the Ellithorpe brothers felt equipped to meet the challenge.

Chapter Two

Duty, Honor, Country

The Ellithorpe Brothers Prepare for War

In April 1861, neither of the Ellithorpe brothers resided in Rushford; Philander lived in Pike with Uncle Carlos, and Phillip moved in with his aunt in Smethport. Almost immediately after hostilities broke out between the North and South following the bombardment of Fort Sumter, each one volunteered in a local infantry regiment. In their missives to sisters at home, the trainees expressed commonly held motivations for their eager enlistments, centering on patriotic themes of duty, honor, and country.[1] They shared similar training camp experiences at Camp Curtin in Pennsylvania and Camp Elmira in New York, and after six weeks of preparation devoted largely to marching commands and exercises on the parade ground, the Ellithorpe boys readied themselves to engage the enemy on the field of battle. The defining event of their lives had begun.

In November 1860, Philander (age twenty) and Phillip (age seventeen) had not expressed political opinions in extant letters, and neither was of voting age during the presidential election. Still, if local politics and individual identity were intertwined, they favored the Republican candidate, Abraham Lincoln. Although Lincoln carried the state of New York by winning a majority (54 percent), much of his strength came from western New York, where he swept Allegany (72 percent), Wyoming (66 percent), and Cattaraugus (62 percent) counties. The Ellithorpe brothers were living through critical events that increased sectional tensions throughout that decade and marked the nation's steady descent into civil war. If each incident was portrayed metaphorically as a point on a thermometer, the ten-year span registered increased temperatures caused largely by irreconcilable differences over the peculiar institution of slavery. These flash points culminated in the presidential election of Abraham Lincoln and the secession of South Carolina (1860) that followed. Within three months, six more southern states had followed the Palmetto State out of the Union. By the spring of 1861, public emotions on both sides of the Mason-Dixon Line had reached the boiling point.[2]

Phillip

Phillip Griggs Ellithorpe celebrated his eighteenth birthday on April 8, 1861, but the real fireworks occurred four days later when Brig. Gen. Pierre Gustave Toutant Beauregard orchestrated the Confederate bombardment of Fort Sumter in Charleston Harbor. Two days later, the Federal garrison surrendered, and one week after Phillip's birthday, President Lincoln called for 75,000 three-month volunteers to put down the rebellion. The initial response was overwhelming, and the Ellithorpes were caught up in this groundswell of northern enthusiasm. Indeed, this spirit of volunteerism reached a feverish pitch across communities both North and South, large and small, partly because many recruits on both sides believed the war would be short lived.[3]

Renowned Civil War historian Bell Irvin Wiley states in his seminal study, *The Life of Billy Yank*, that Beauregard's bombardment of the Federal installation was perceived in the North as "an affront to the flag" and, as a consequence, unleashed a tidal wave of nationalism and patriotism. But this spontaneous release of emotion in western New York was insufficient to totally explain the complex range of motivations that drove young men to enlist in such massive numbers.[4]

Enlistment

Lincoln's call for 75,000 troops on April 15 placed the onus of recruitment on northern state governors, such as Andrew Gregg Curtin of Pennsylvania. In a surprisingly short period of time, Curtin demonstrated great acumen in mobilizing twenty-five regiments, almost double the national quota set for his state by Secretary of War Simon Cameron. Just one day after the surrender of Fort Sumter, a prominent Philadelphia lawyer and district judge, past Utah frontiersman, and currently resident of northwestern Pennsylvania wrote to the governor and offered his services to assemble "a company of horse" (cavalry) from McKean and Elk counties. However, the War Department was accepting only infantry and sharpshooter units into Federal service at that time, so Curtin adjusted Thomas Leiper Kane's original petition to assemble a regiment of "rifles."[5]

Standing only five feet, four inches, the diminutive Kane was filled with boundless energy and abolitionist zeal. The son of a federal judge and an ardent abolitionist and lawyer, Kane sent representatives to comb through McKean, Elk, Cameron, and Potter counties, a rough frontier logging region known as the Wildcat District. Kane invited its hardy outdoorsmen to a public meeting to be held at the Bennett House in Smethport on April 18, 1861. A now famous handbill was printed in Olean, New York, and distrib-

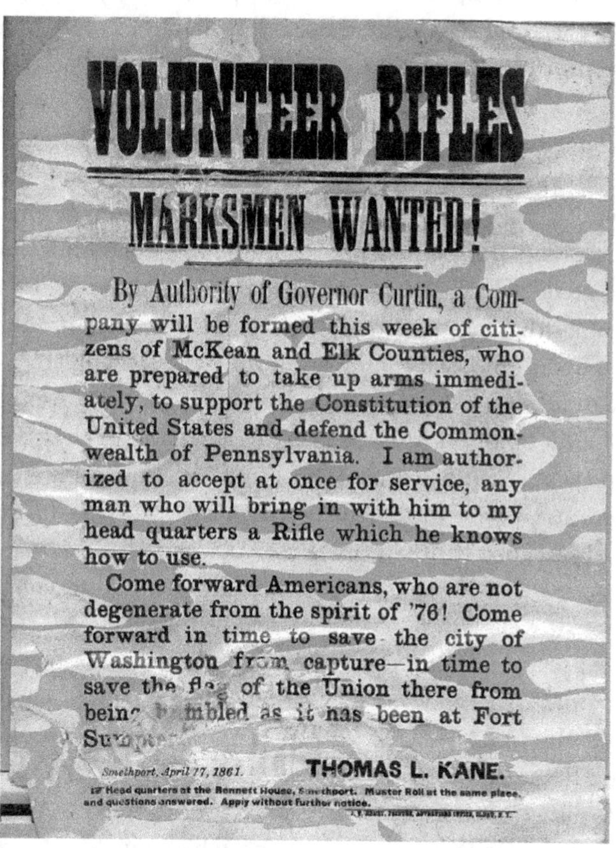

VOLUNTEER RIFLES

MARKSMEN WANTED!

By Authority of Governor Curtin, a Company will be formed this week of citizens of McKean and Elk Counties, who are prepared to take up arms immediately, to support the Constitution of the United States and defend the Commonwealth of Pennsylvania. I am authorized to accept at once for service, any man who will bring in with him to my head quarters a Rifle which he knows how to use.

Come forward Americans, who are not degenerate from the spirit of '76! Come forward in time to save the city of Washington from capture—in time to save the fla[illegible] of the Union there from bein[illegible] [illegible]mbled as it has been at Fort Su[illegible]

Smethport, April 17, 1861. THOMAS L. KANE.

☞ Head quarters at the Bennett House, Smethport. Muster Roll at the same place, and questions answered. Apply without further notice.

Recruitment handbill for Company I, 13th Pennsylvania Reserves.
SOURCE: MCKEAN COUNTY HISTORICAL SOCIETY AND OLD JAIL MUSEUM, SMETHPORT, PENNSYLVANIA.

uted in public places to advertise the gathering. An overflow crowd of spirited lumberjacks showed up on the appointed evening and listened to Kane as he outlined a long list of grievances against the rebellious South, a standard practice among recruiters. Many men wore the attire of their trade—red woolen shirts, black felt hats, and high-topped boots. They received Kane's address with great passion. A musical band whipped the audience into a frenzy.[6]

As elsewhere across the Keystone State, the surge of manpower swamped Kane's recruiting station at the McKean County courthouse. In the first twenty-four hours following the rally, two of Kane's diligent lieutenants, William Thomas Blanchard (a railroad promoter) and Frank J. Bell, registered fifty-six men in Bradford and Smethport, Pennsylvania, and Ceres, New York (just across the state line). Local lore identifies the brother of Phillip's friend from the blacksmith shop, Joseph Barnes, as the first signatory on the roster sheet. Phillip affixed his signature to the document as well.[7]

Kane selected twenty-three-year-old Blanchard to become his chief scribe to record personal and physical data about each volunteer. Over the next few days, Blanchard diligently collected valuable data on time and place of enlistment, occupation, and age. In addition, he entered information such as height, color of hair and eyes, and shade of complexion. Phillip's enlistment card reveals that he shared Kane's short stature and dark black hair and eyes. A rudimentary physical examination followed the enlistment euphoria for all of the inductees. On the afternoon of April 22, 1861, Kane assembled his seventy coarse followers outside the McKean County courthouse, which served the dual purpose of registration center and company headquarters, and told them to prepare to march to war in the morning. In this fashion, Company I of the 13th Pennsylvania Reserves was born.[8]

Phillip sensed that his spur-of-the-moment decision to enlist in Company I did not sit well with his mother back in Rushford. "Mother," he later wrote, "I asked your advise as to whether I should go or not but the start . . . came before any answer and so I enlisted for three months [with] 50 young men with red shirt and Rifle. . . . I am verry sorry that I could not have time to come home and bid you fare well." He continued, "I trust you will forgive me for leaving on short notice, but I have resolved to bring back . . . the stars and stripes as the flag of our union which our fore Fathers fought for and gained."[9] It was difficult to argue with Phillip's patriotic ardor, but his reasoning fell on deaf ears. In an effort to ease his mother's anxiety over

Colonel Thomas Leiper Kane, 13th Pennsylvania Reserves.
SOURCE: CIVIL WAR PHOTOGRAPHS, 1861–1865, LIBRARY OF CONGRESS, PRINTS AND PHOTOGRAPHS DIVISION.

his enlistment, Phillip acknowledged that his fellow comrades in arms were "tough and good looking Soliders." Likewise, he comforted his sister to "be of good cheer for I intend to put my trust in God and keep my Powder dry."[10]

Birth of the Bucktails

Prior to Phillip's departure from Smethport, a defining episode in the future regiment's history took place. One of the enlistees, James Landregan, who had walked twenty miles from Bradford to enlist, noticed a dead deer hanging outside a butcher shop across the street from the McKean County courthouse. Caught up in the exhilaration of the moment, Landregan contemplated sprucing up his appearance. So he proceeded to cut off the tail from the dead animal and pin it to his cap. His comrades in arms approved of the fashion statement, and within a short period of time, the entire contingent had acquired their own white-tailed headgear. Kane intuitively recognized the significance of Landregan's action and dubbed his new recruits the "Bucktails." The selection of an acceptable company nickname was an important first step toward establishing a sense of camaraderie among the men and second only to the presentation of a battle flag representative of home. A soldier's personal honor was directly interconnected with his pride in company, regiment, state, and nation. Thus, Kane's label stuck.[11]

At 6 a.m. on April 23, the men gathered in the McKean County courtroom with rifles, coats, and blankets in hand. There they listened to their first military instruction as Kane outlined the marching schedule for the next several days. Then the commander dismissed the unit to the Bennett House for breakfast. At 8 a.m., they reassembled in front of the courthouse, where they listened to several patriotic speeches delivered by local dignitaries. At the conclusion of the remarks, Kane permitted the men a few moments to say good-bye to family and friends. Phillip consoled his sister, relating that Mrs. Krans had given him "a farewell kiss." "It made me think of my home and friends that I was leaving," reflected Phillip sentimentally. Now, he prepared "to camp out to war."[12]

To Camp Curtin

At 9 a.m., Kane barked a command, and his citizen-soldiers fell into formation. Then they filed out of town to loud huzzahs from the local citizenry. The Bucktails intended to rendezvous with other recruits in Emporium, the county seat of Cameron County, twenty-seven miles to the south. Kane's undersized company plodded along but did not reach their destination until well after dark. Still, the townspeople welcomed the footsore marchers with a torchlight parade and served them "delectables." Early the next morning, Kane's enlarged force moved farther southward to Driftwood at the junction of Sinnemahoning Creek and the West Branch of the Susquehanna River, where they united with a third group of volunteers from Elk County.[13]

Because of the slow progress that three companies of men would make over land, Kane opted for an innovative alternative to quicken the pace. He would use the skills of his lumberjacks to construct three log booms to float the recruits down the West Branch to one of the railheads at Lock Haven or Sunbury, where the men could transfer to railcars for the remainder of the trip to Harrisburg. "The orders are to build a large float of slabs and move . . . down the River," reported Phillip to his sister.[14]

The loggers took to their assignment with great relish. The design called for three sixteen-foot log squares to be lashed together to produce a craft measuring sixty-four by sixteen feet. They completed the task in only two days. On the lead raft, the Smethportians mounted a hickory pole and nailed a bucktail atop it for ornamentation. Kane's solution to use log booms to convey his men downstream was certainly a bold one but befitting his risk-taking personality.[15]

The enlistees cheered as Kane nudged his horse, Old Glencoe, onto the flagship, and once everyone was aboard, the three flat booms pushed off from the bank and started their hazardous journey. Several portages loomed ahead through a series of gorges, canyons, and rapids. As a result, Kane's navy made slow progress the first day and camped several miles south of the village of Sinnemahoning at Rattlesnake Falls. Phillip was enthralled by this great adventure.[16]

Meanwhile, Kane's unexpected departure from Smethport had caused an official stir in Harrisburg. Curtin had been dealing with a mounting crisis since the third week of April: a multitude of fresh recruits were daily descending on the state capital from around the Commonwealth, and he had not made any arrangements to house, feed, or clothe them. Furthermore, Cameron, a fellow Pennsylvanian, contributed to the chaos by stating that the War Department would not provide any relief for this growing manpower dilemma. In his first major decision as a war governor, Curtin ordered the state militia to prepare the Dauphin County Agricultural Fairgrounds to receive an estimated influx of 5,000 men by early May. The facility was eventually called Camp Curtin.[17]

Curtin's second major decision turned out to be unsuccessful. Since Kane had not been authorized to proceed to Harrisburg, the governor sent a wire to intercept him en route. The official dispatch instructed Kane to turn around at Lock Haven and return to northwestern Pennsylvania. But the telegram was never received. Consequently, Kane's amphibious expedition pushed ahead to Sunbury, where they boarded cattle cars for the remainder of the trek to Harrisburg. Kane's three undersized companies were the last three segments of his future command to arrive at Camp Curtin on May 4, a miserably cold and windy day when crusted snow covered the ground.[18]

Inclement weather did not dampen the enthusiasm of the Bucktails, however, as they detrained at the Harrisburg depot. Phillip's comrades made an unfavorable first impression with their backwoods garb and overt exuberance as they fired rifle volleys into the air at the station to announce their arrival. This unruly behavior contributed to the public's perception of them as uncouth "wildcats."[19]

Kane formed his men and marched one mile up a tree-lined avenue to the front gate of Camp Curtin, which was in various stages of completion. A two-story wooden administrative building sat in the middle of the spacious and partially fenced eighty-acre compound and was encircled by a racetrack. Several smaller buildings and sheds lined the perimeter. The location possessed adequate drinking water but poor drainage in the lower eastern and western corners of the camp. Ridge Road, which led to Harrisburg, bisected the parade ground and complicated military drill exercises. Camp Curtin benefited from exceptional rail and river transportation just beyond its walls.[20]

Turning Civilians into Soldiers

Until the middle of May, the Smethport men and their colleagues from around the Commonwealth received little instruction, discipline, or guidance about military life. Bored and frustrated with the lax situation, Kane conducted marching drills devised by himself, but without formally trained company commanders, the enlistees ran amok. Writing shortly after his arrival at Camp Curtin, Phillip revealed to his sister his great pleasure in being partnered with Joe Barnes in one of the two-man A-frame, or wedge, tents.[21] The brother of Thomas Barnes, Joe was a likable nineteen-year-old immigrant born in Nottinghamshire, England. The pair hit it off immediately, and they would be reassigned a large tent with two other friends from home, John K. Haffey (a civilian chaplain, company recruiter, and sergeant of Company I) and William J. Kibbe. This cramped living arrangement forged a strong bond between these four comrades that rivaled the ties of kin and friendships at home.[22]

One day after their raucous display at the Harrisburg train depot, a number of Bucktails slipped past the untrained camp guards on the southern and eastern end of camp, where a number of sheds offered cover and a low fence provided no hindrance. The call of cheap whiskey and prostitutes a short distance away was too great a temptation. Once in Harrisburg, these rugged woodsmen and river men from the Pennsylvania outback created quite a sensation. They made it clear to the local constables through their rowdiness that they did not care much for discipline of any sort. As a result, the rabble-rousers got drunk and fought with the police, and a near riot ensued. A contingent of sober soldiers from Camp Curtin escorted the

Corporal Joseph D. Barnes, Company I, 13th Pennsylvania Reserves.
SOURCE: MCKEAN COUNTY HISTORICAL SOCIETY AND OLD JAIL MUSEUM, SMETHPORT, PENNSYLVANIA.

guilty "miscreants" back to camp, where Kane threw three of the instigators into the guardhouse. Phillip drew one of the watches, but the motley crew escaped with the help of friends, and they returned to the tavern to continue their revelry.[23]

The episode on May 5 received widespread newspaper coverage in Harrisburg, and Kane took quick action to punish the disorderly conduct. "We are confined to rather close quarters right now," Phillip later confided to Ann. "We are not allowed to go out of Camp without a pass from our Captain [unidentified] the reason why we are kept so close is on account of some of the Soldiers going to town and getting drunk which creates a great deal of hard feelings on the part of the citizens. The punishment for this offense is 14 hours in the gard house which is not a very desirable place."[24] Unfortunately, more displays of insubordination popped up among Kane's men throughout the first half of May.

Serious food shortages, the lack of uniforms and inferior military equipment, and an outbreak of childhood diseases added fuel to the discomfort and the disgruntled attitudes of some Bucktails. At first, the Ladies Aid Society in Harrisburg attempted to remedy the demand for quality foodstuffs and proper eating utensils, but as the soldier population swelled each day, their efforts were insufficient. The daily consumption amounts soon topped 6,500 pounds of beef along with 4,000 loaves of fresh bread and 100 boxes of hardtack. Commandant Washington H. R. Hangen had originally contracted with local butchers and bakers in Harrisburg, but there was no quality inspection process in place. Thus, the meat tended to be rancid, and the bread was moldy or infested with bugs. However, there were surpluses of coffee and pork, and a black market flourished in the camp's commissary department.[25]

Multiple Disappointments

For many young recruits, the ultimate sticking point centered on the failure of the state or federal government to issue a standard military uniform and musket or deliver a paycheck in a timely manner. As a result, the Pennsylvanians were ill clad and penniless. Phillip groused when a smartly dressed and equipped regiment arrived from Michigan and bivouacked right next to his own.[26] These shortages took more than two months and one military campaign to resolve.

A variety of health problems abounded at Camp Curtin and plagued soldier morale. Exposure due to a shortage of tents and blankets and an outbreak of childhood diseases caused increased suffering among the men. Sanitation conditions worsened as more and more men crammed into Camp Curtin, and overused latrines started to malfunction. Careless soldiers littered the ground with trash and garbage and exacerbated the health threat. In early June, an outbreak of measles suddenly struck the camp, devastating Phillip and the Bucktails. At this time, Phillip also dealt with a second malady; one of his hands trembled uncontrollably. Both conditions resulted in Phillip's hospitalization.[27]

Phillip experienced pangs of homesickness in his first month away from Rushford. The eighteen-year-old penned no fewer than six letters to family members, and his angst increased when he received no replies. He hypothesized about the silent treatment: "I suppose you would like me to have had come home and went from thare," he confided to his sister. "Think not hard now of your Brother who has been called upon to enter the field of action which call he will try to meet like a man although he is not a man in stature will try to act the part of one which I know is your most earnest wishes." A letter arrived from Ann two days later, and it confirmed Phillip's suspicion; his mother was upset because he hadn't returned to Rushford to enlist with his brother, cousins, friends, and neighbors. "I felt I had to leave," explained Phillip, "and have felt bad since I first came here [to Camp Curtin]."[28]

Leisure Activities

Phillip shook off the doldrums and tediousness of camp life in a variety of ways. Shortly after his regiment arrived at Camp Curtin, he attended an athletic contest taking place on the parade ground. "I have just come in from a little Sport in the way of Ball," Phillip explained. "The Regiment has three large rubber balls and all [of the participants] form a line in the Shape of a Square with a party inside to kick the ball and the one that can kick it the highest is the best fellow. Many times in trying to kick it before it comes near the ground the one who tries to be the Smartest falls to the ground and then gets up." Other competitions would take place throughout the history of the Union army. One sutler, hoping to drum up business with the troopers, set up a target at 200 yards and challenged soldiers coming off guard duty to hit the mark and win a prize. Phillip won twice and earned one dollar.[29]

Letter writing also helped to keep Phillip from feeling "the blues." He thirsted for any news about his Allegany County chums and two cousins in Pike. In fact, he asked for missives from everyone in the family. "I dont care who," he snapped. Tent mate Joe Barnes got into the act, too. He cut a locket from his "very long hair" and asked Phillip to send it to Ann, who should braid it and keep it until the end of the war.[30] Feelings of loneliness, nostalgia, and sentimentality and the strong need for family approval crept into Phillip's correspondence as Kane's companies settled into a more vigorous martial routine as the month of May wore on.[31]

Military regimentation alone would not completely pacify every restless or intemperate Bucktail spirit. Although many McKean County men had been around firearms their entire lives, some careless mishaps occurred. "We had scarcely arrived in Camp," Phillip remembered, "when we were requested to march to the Cemetery . . . to accompany a fellow soldier who was shot by accident."[32] A second firearm accident occurred one month later when a soldier was wounded in the knee because of another soldier's careless discharge of a pistol while reposing in camp. Unauthorized shooting contests also took place.[33]

The Pennsylvania Reserves

About the time the command presence was beginning to assert itself in training camp, Curtin was taking executive action to address the federal government's steadfast refusal to accept responsibility for Pennsylvania's volunteers. The chief executive was especially apprehensive about a potential Confederate invasion launched from the Shenandoah Valley. On May 15, a special session of the State Assembly requisitioned $3 million in emergency funds to operate Camp Curtin and give financial assistance to the Commonwealth's military organization. Curtin immediately appointed Brig. Gen. George A. McCall to lead the state troops. Not only would Pennsylvania's recruits not be sent back home, but Curtin's foresight also led to the formation of thirteen regiments known as the Pennsylvania Reserve Volunteer Corps. Seven companies from northwestern Pennsylvania and three companies from the more heavily populated southeast corner of the state combined to create the 13th Pennsylvania Reserves.[34]

Protocol dictated that the new Pennsylvania Reserves take the oath of allegiance and listen while an officer read the Articles of War. Shortly thereafter, some regiments were issued white "duck" trousers and a blue woolen blouse, but much of the soldier's attire was still supplemented with civilian garments. At the conclusion of the induction ceremony, Curtin ordered an inspection of his new creation. "We were all formed in to rank double file and marched through the gate of the Camp," recalled Phillip. "Then the order was given to form into sections of 8 which was obliged," and the Bucktails marched to the statehouse. "I will not attempt to describe the beautiful aspect of the capitol yard but . . . we halted several times and were [admired] by the ladies of Harris Burg."[35] Now the 13th Pennsylvania Reserves could commence drilling in earnest, though not until officers had been elected.

In mid-May, Kane and his principal recruiters—William T. Blanchard, Frank J. Bell, Roy Stone, Langhorne Wister, Alanson E. Niles, and Charles F. Taylor—were slowly getting a handle on discipline. Military exercises involved instruction on the proper handling and care of firearms and the correct response to various marching commands as outlined in Hardee's *Manual of Arms*. Phillip harped on about the repetitious nature of military drill in "doing the same thing over and over every day," but he agreed that the activity gave the men in his mess a hearty appetite. "We have plenty of

Pennsylvania Reserves Training at Camp Curtin, Harrisburg, Pennsylvania.
SOURCE: HARPER'S WEEKLY, MAY 11, 1861.

Pork Beef Bread [and] Beans," he boasted. "We can cook for ourselves if we choose although we have a tolerable good cook. I like to get up early in the morning and roast my beef stake on the coals and roast my own bread and . . . coffee we have plenty of crackers to chaw upon."[36] Showing his puckish nature, Phillip crowed about the "good cook" in his unit—himself!

Selection of Officers

The process of selecting officers in the Pennsylvania Reserves was laid out in Hardee's *Tactics*. Field, or grade, officers at the regimental level consisted of a colonel, a lieutenant colonel, and a major and staff officers with the title of adjutant, quartermaster, chaplain, and surgeon. Junior grade officers at the company level included a captain, first and second lieutenants, and an orderly sergeant.[37] On June 12, the men elected the following regimental officers of the 13th Pennsylvania Reserves:

Colonel: Thomas L. Kane

Lt. Colonel: Charles J. Biddle

Major: Roy Stone

Adjutant: John T. A. Jewett

Quartermaster: Henry D. Patton

Surgeon: S. D. Freeman

Chaplain: Rev. W. H. D. Hatton

Phillip and Company I welcomed two familiar faces to leadership roles—Capt. William Thomas Blanchard and First Lt. Frank J. Bell. The company also assumed a special "title" through which to preserve its unique geographic identity, foster unity within the ranks, and remind the soldiers of home: "McKean Rifles."[38]

Phillip remained upbeat throughout the selection of officers. He expressed great pride to Ann in belonging to the "Buck Tails" and "McKean Rifles," his regimental and Company I monikers, respectively. And he greatly admired the leadership qualities of "Kernal Thomas L. Cane." Kane, a father figure to Phillip, was "one of the smartest men that I ever new. Thare is not a man in the Whole 10 companies that can say that they dont like him, beamed the youthful recruit."[39]

Still, the selection of regimental and company officers did not put an immediate end to disenchantment among some rank-and-file Bucktails because most of the leaders chosen were not trained professional soldiers but simply prominent citizens. Thus, most of the officers, regardless of rank, needed to master the new craft of military leadership on the fly just as the enlisted men were learning their new roles. In time, almost every company officer in the 13th Pennsylvania Reserves would play an increased role in regimental affairs because of promotion based on attrition and merit.[40]

One of the first official directives given to the 13th Pennsylvania Reserves caused serious consternation when the men were ordered to stack their personal weapons and receive an 1837 Harpers Ferry smoothbore musket that had been stored in the state's militia arsenal for years. Humiliated, the Bucktails saw this order as an insult. After all, the antiquated muzzleloader was not an appropriate firearm for a sharpshooter regiment. Simultaneously, Kane was pressing McCall to formally endorse his regiment as the "1st Rifles." Phillip barely disguised his contempt about both matters in a missive to his sister. Four men deserted from Company I, and one asked Phillip to join him, "but something whispered in my heart and not in my ear."[41] The weapon controversy, like the clothing debacle, took several months and one military mission to sort out.

In comparison, Phillip's complaints were minor: tight sleeping quarters because of cramped space in his tent and shortages of ink, writing paper, and stamps. A cracker (hardtack) box served three purposes as a chair, table, and desk. Despite these little inconveniences, "I feel proud . . . that I am able to serve in a cause," noted Phillip, " and I will never consent to leave until . . . the stars and stripes shall wave throughout the Southern States."[42] Phillip's patriotic ardor, partially developed as a civilian, had emerged full blown at Camp Curtin. He was one of "a nation of innocents."[43]

Phillip enjoyed his role as cook for his mess and tent mates, and his duties soon expanded to other, related assignments. For example, he worked as a hospital cook and nurse while convalescing from his illnesses in May and June. Then, in early June, Phillip was detailed to the commissary, where he prepared meals for the staff in addition to his clerical and distribution responsibilities. He must have been good at his job because the young Alleganian was chosen to prepare and serve dinner to officers of a visiting Michigan regiment along with their wives and children, seventy-five people in all.[44]

"Kane's Rifles" and Rumors of Military Action

Shortly after the election of officers in mid-June, rumors circulated that the Pennsylvania Reserves would soon be deployed in a reconnaissance, and Kane began to second-guess his own merits as colonel of the regiment. Thus, he assembled his company captains and informed them that he wished to step aside and elevate the more experienced Biddle to command the regiment.

The company leaders accepted Kane's proposition on condition that another election should be held, McCall must act on their petition for sharpshooter status, and future official military reports should identify the 13th Pennsylvania Reserves as "Kane's Rifles" in honor of its founder. McCall accepted these terms, and, following a second vote, Kane and Biddle exchanged ranks. The 13th Pennsylvania Reserves were in good hands with the no-nonsense Biddle at the helm. Three days after Biddle's promotion, Curtin named the strict disciplinarian in charge of the entire operation at Camp Curtin. At first, the rank-and-file soldiers of the 13th Pennsylvania

Colonel Charles John Biddle, 13th Pennsylvania Reserves.
SOURCE: MOLLUS MASSACHUSETTS COLLECTION, U.S. ARMY HERITAGE AND EDUCATION CENTER, CARLISLE, PENNSYLVANIA.

Reserves resented his penchant for drill and obedience, but eventually they grew to respect his authority and leadership.[45]

On June 18, Phillip drafted separate letters to his mother and father. The missives were prompted by rumors of the imminent departure of the Bucktails into the field to flush out the "Rebbels." Not wishing to cause alarm, Phillip sought to console his parents and relieve their anxieties. "Our Regiment will be formed in a few days," he informed his mother, "and sent to some Camp where thare will be a chance to prepare for War by drilling so that we can handle our Arms and do it up in stile in case we are called upon to fight which prospects are quite slim." Phillip lied; he was trying to ease his mother's worry over the impending movement. Then he switched to a subject sure to elicit comfort—religion. Phillip informed his mother that he was reading one chapter from his "testament" every night, attending midweek prayer meetings, and worshipping on Sunday mornings. One of his messmates, John Keenan Haffey, was a universalist minister. "I like to hear him preach. He gives good advice," Phillip revealed. He concluded with a heartfelt prophesy: "I take much pleasure in writing for . . . you must know that you have a son that is going to try to be somebody." In time, Phillip would fulfill his promise.[46]

The tone of Phillip's missive to his father was more informative than consoling. Here, Phillip found the need to describe his manly duties as a soldier and detached duty in the commissary department. "I am working [as a] second clerk," Phillip told his father. "I help to deal out the Provisions. . . . This occupies most of the time in the forenoon and in the afternoon we . . . prepare Provisions for the next Day." Phillip's specific responsibility was to receive, inventory, prepare, and distribute hardtack to each company orderly sergeant to be parceled out to the soldiers. Specifically, he received shipments of sixty-pound "cracker boxes," broke the brick-like "bread" into prescribed three-inch squares, and allotted the correct amount per company. Like many of his comrades, Phillip soaked his own "biscuits" in hot coffee to soften them and make them more palatable. The young soldier proudly mentioned to his father that his new assignment in the commissary meant a four-dollar raise to his monthly salary. In closing, Phillip confided in his father on a matter of personal concern: since his arrival at Camp Curtin, he had written to each of his siblings, but he had sadly received only one reply.[47]

In regard to leisure and social activities at Camp Curtin, Phillip enjoyed playing his fiddle with other musicians in the evening to serenade his company. "Thar are several fiddles in the camp and we get together and have a break down by ourselves," he said. In addition, Phillip performed at "stag" dances in camp that entertained the lonely and homesick men. He informed his father, almost in passing, that the Bucktails were preparing to march to the Maryland state line in a few days.[48]

In fact, General in Chief Winfield Scott had ordered McCall to send two regiments from Camp Curtin on a mission to rescue Col. Lew Wallace and the 11th Indiana, who feared an enemy attack at Cumberland, Maryland. McCall passed Scott's instructions down to Biddle, who chose his own 13th Pennsylvania Reserves, and the 5th Pennsylvania Reserves commanded by Col. Seneca G. Simmons. On the morning of June 22, the 1,500-man force, including artillery battery, boarded a train for Hopewell, Pennsylvania, on the first leg of its journey. Phillip headed off to war.[49]

Philander and War Fever in Wyoming County

For Philander Doty Ellithorpe, the enlistment fervor in northwest Allegany County and southwest Wyoming County, New York, equaled the frenzied scene taking place in McKean County, Pennsylvania. "The people were alive with zeal," recalled one historian. "They held public meetings, adopted patriotic addresses, raised money and enrolled men in every corner of the State. . . . All was animation and a state of peace had suddenly been transformed into a condition of war."[50] Philander fell under the same patriotic ardor as Phillip during his recruitment.

On April, 19, 1861, the community of Nunda hosted a meeting eleven miles east of Pike to respond to Lincoln's call to arms and to raise a company of volunteers from Livingston and Wyoming counties. New York Gov. Edwin D. Morgan encouraged such spontaneous gatherings. In Pike, Carlos Stebbins ran the recruiting station along with local tailor Henry Runyan. Two of Carlos's nephews, eighteen-year-old James K. P. Stebbins and twenty-year-old Edwin Stebbins, inked the Company F roster of the 33rd New York (Ontario Regiment), while Carlos's third nephew, Philander, returned to Rushford.

In the third week of April, a public meeting was hosted in Angelica, New York, by local attorney Curtiss Crane (C. C.) Gardiner, with a focus identical to the one called by Kane in Smethport. It is unknown whether Philander attended this gathering, but the event set the tone for other such meetings springing up throughout the county. On May 3, Philander attended such a turnout at Rushford's Academy Hall, where he signed up along with seventy-five men from the adjoining villages of Pike, Eagle, Hume, Belfast, and Centreville.[51]

Gardiner sent word to the recruits registered in Rushford to spend the next few days taking care of personal matters at home before reporting to Angelica on May 11. On the appointed date, he welcomed his new volunteers and immediately began to drill them. One week later, Gardiner assembled his company in the village park, where they listened to fiery speeches by local dignitaries and administered the oath of allegiance. Each trooper was issued a blanket and tin mess kit and told to prepare for a noontime departure to Camp Elmira.[52]

Philander took advantage of the brief respite to scribble his first wartime letter to sister Ann in Rushford. His generic remarks mentioned reasonably comfortable sleeping quarters and adequate food. Philander also admitted to taking his recent four-day homecoming furlough to Pike and Mills Mills with an unidentified travel companion to visit his sister, Mary, and an aunt.

Captain Curtiss Crane (C. C.) Gardiner, Company I, 27th New York.
SOURCE: CIVIL WAR PHOTOGRAPHS, 1861–1865, LIBRARY OF CONGRESS, PRINTS AND PHOTOGRAPHS DIVISION.

His missive concluded with thoughts about a stirring sermon he heard on the meaning of life, thus confirming his own religiosity.[53]

To Camp Elmira and Exile

On May 21, Gardiner's men marched through the gates at Camp Elmira, where 809 men from seven New York counties were organized into the 27th New York. Philander and his Rushford companions made up Company I, "the color company of the regiment," because Gardiner's boys had brought a battle flag from home. The fledgling regiment adopted the "Union Regiment" as its nickname because of its broad geographic representation of seven different counties in western New York. Field officers were promptly confirmed: Col. Henry W. Slocum, Lt. Col. Joseph J. Chambers, and Maj. Joseph J. Bartlett. Slocum, a career West Pointer, and Bartlett, a Binghamton lawyer, would be destined for a greater roles in the Union army.[54]

The first official duty of the new regiment did not meet with favor from the rank and file of the 27th New York. Because of the overcrowded conditions at Camp Elmira, Slocum's unit was exiled across the Chemung River to Southport. There, the regiment was assigned quarters in "a shanty" and detailed to collect stones to prepare a hard marching surface for a makeshift parade ground. The men grumbled over the menial labor and became incensed by the poor quality of rations they were being fed. Once, Company E held a mock burial for a piece of tainted beef complete with a funeral procession to the cemetery to the refrain of "The Rogue's March." Pvt. Albion W. Tourgée delivered a eulogy, and someone fashioned a wooden headstone. Slocum reprimanded the future Carpetbagger and celebrity author for his role in the protest. Then, on June 1, a more serious incident occurred when a group of indignant men from Companies B and D kicked over their dining tables and stormed off in protest. Philander defended Company I to a Rushford friend on the grounds that it had maintained the cleanest table in the regiment.[55] Within the hour, Slocum ordered his agitated regiment to form on the uneven parade ground. He announced that the Federal quartermaster corps would soon replace the local food contractors from Elmira. He also vowed to personally inspect the kitchen on a regular basis to ensure the quality of the food and its proper preparation. The food revolt presented Slocum with an excellent opportunity to inform the men about the impending muster of the 27th New York into Federal service.[56]

Comrades and Leisure

Philander stood almost six inches taller than his younger male sibling, but the Ellithorpe brothers shared the same dark eyes and dark hair and complexion. Coincidentally, Philander drew the same initial duty as his younger brother in the Company I cookhouse. And, just as Phillip forged close friendships with fellow messmates and tent mates, so, too, did Philander cultivate similar bonds with hometowners, such as Willis Kendall, Romain Benjamin, Ira Worthington, Charley Wilson, and Tim Charles. Philander also dealt with camp problems such as measles and dysentery; low-quality food; inexperienced officers, lack of pay, uniforms, and weapons; and repetitive exercises on the parade ground.[57]

Philander described moments of bucolic camp life, too. On one quiet afternoon, he jotted down his surroundings: "Romain is on his bed and Tim is siting by his side reading his bible. Ira Worthington is on the next bunk reading. . . . Charley Wilson is plugging on the fiddle." And, like Phillip's Bucktails, the enlistees of the 27th New York enjoyed dances and sing-alongs.

Philander and his comrades even pooled their money to purchase "glee [song] books." To this point, the war was a lark for Philander and his chums.[58]

Philander's 27th New York mirrored Phillip's regiment in other respects—too many New Yorkers had responded to President Lincoln's initial call for volunteers. In New York, Gov. Morgan answered the limited Federal quota in the same manner as Pennsylvania Gov. Curtin; he requested and received a special appropriation from the State Assembly to operate five training facilities. In so doing, Morgan welcomed thirty-eight regiments into state service for a period of two years. But the ongoing silence over incorporation into Federal service rankled many of the men. This particular drama unfolded at the ground level in the first week of June when Philander observed the sudden disappearance of several men from Company I. They had taken French leave. New York trainees, like those in Pennsylvania, were becoming increasingly agitated over their nebulous status outside the national military system.[59]

Acceptance into Federal Service and the Dunn Incident

On June 12, the War Department finally accepted all New York (and Pennsylvania) regiments into federal service, but later that evening, a major brouhaha spilled over between two sister regiments, the 27th and 33rd New York. These units had drawn volunteers from many of the same towns, villages, and neighborhoods along the Allegany–Wyoming county line, so they were naturally keen rivals. The flap started when an intoxicated Pvt. Gibson Dunn of Company B, 27th New York, publicly insulted the leadership abilities of Col. Robert F. Taylor of the 33rd New York. Dunn was immediately tossed into the guardhouse of the 33rd New York for insubordination.

That night, a rescue mission was hatched by a number of men from Philander's regiment, but the party was met en route by a body of soldiers from the 33rd. "Soon the two regiments were in battle array and armed with cobblestones," observed one eyewitness. Some of the men were armed with loaded muskets and revolvers, bowie knives, and clubs. A great deal of posturing was taking place on both sides. "With great difficulty the few officers in camp prevented an attack," claimed one eyewitness.[60] Indeed, it took another stern lecture from Slocum to avert violence, but order was not fully restored until after dark. Meanwhile, Dunn escaped from his confines during the heated exchanges.

It is not known whether Philander took part in the melee or whether he encountered his cousins Edwin and James Stebbins of the 33rd New York. Nor is it known whether Philander personally knew the perpetrator, though he was acquainted with one of Dunn's relatives in Company I. While Philander provided few details about the incident in a letter to his sisters and friend, he confided that "a great deal of drinking" takes place in camp and confessed, "I have a great deal to contend with here."[61] Two recent murders in camp also unsettled him. Philander noted that the tense situation deescalated several nights later when the 27th New York busied itself cleaning "the shantes" in Southport and moving into "new Baracks" in Camp Elmira. "We have a nice place now," a relieved Philander told his sister.[62]

Like Phillip's comrades, Philander's comrades continued to grouse about their lack of uniforms, pay, equipment, or weapons. Impatient New Yorkers watched with irritation as a fully outfitted and paid regiment bivouacked beside them. The elevated level of disaffection reached Company I when Philander noted that "a boy from Rushford should leave [left] the Company in whitch he inlisted." Philander penned a patriotic response to this type of behavior. "I shall not leave. I volunteered to serve my contry and shall [not] discharge before I see it through," he told Ann.[63]

At the end of June, the 27th New York finally received its accoutrements. Now, Philander posed an important question to Ann: How soon "shall we march directly for the land of cotton?"[64]

* * * * * * *

The Ellithorpe Brothers and the Early Military Experience

Despite the fact that Phillip and Philander approached military service in different regiments belonging to different states, they shared common experiences.

The Recruitment Process

The writings of Phillip and Philander describe similar recruiting experiences. Regarding their motivation to enlist, each one expressed a deep obligation to preserve the Union. And such conviction contributed to a huge bottleneck at their induction sites in Smethport and Angelica. The day they embarked on the experience of a lifetime, Company I of the Bucktails and the future 27th New York had listened intently to fiery oratory and martial music and heard the cheers of adoring crowds. The emotional troopers were filled with pride and a sense of purpose. The Ellithorpe brothers recognized their manly duty, repudiated the act of secession, and expressed an eagerness to march into Dixie and teach "secesh" a lesson. They did not mention any concern for ending slavery in their letters.[65]

The Ups and Downs of Camp Life

Once in training camp, Phillip and Philander complained incessantly about the poor quality of rations, shanty-like accommodations, and seemingly endless hours spent in squad, company, and regimental formations on the parade ground. The repetitive nature of military life quickly bored them. And the brothers and their comrades were further frustrated with the federal government's failure to officially recognize them and provide uniforms, pay, weapons, or decent rations.

In camp, the new recruits struggled with illnesses such as measles, pneumonia, and dysentery as well as exposure to the elements and overtaxed sanitary facilities. It is entirely possible that Phillip was physically unfit for active duty. Had he slipped through the perfunctory physicals administered at the recruiting station in Smethport? Exhibiting a weak constitution, he visited the hospital on two occasions while at Camp Curtin. In his defense, several later studies assert that one-third of all Union recruits were sick in May and June 1861 and that the vast majority suffered from childhood or weather-related illnesses.[66]

Both brothers enjoyed idyllic moments of camp, especially on Sunday afternoons. Each bonded with comrades whom they identified by name in their letters and forged lasting friendships, some of which would transcend the wartime years. Phillip and Philander also pledged to religious principles through nightly reading of the scriptures, participation in midweek prayer meetings, and regular attendance at Sunday worship services. They likewise voiced moral indignation on the abuse of alcohol in camp.[67]

The Ellithorpe brothers demonstrated a fondness for music—Phillip with his fiddle and Philander through song. Both seemed to possess outgoing personalities. It was serendipitous that both secured jobs in the company cookhouse and that both were assigned to Company I of their respective regiments. Despite the busy lifestyle of these fledgling citizen-soldiers, they left a poignant record of homesickness within a few weeks of their departure.

The Lack of Obedience and Self-Control among Comrades

Similarities existed between the 13th Pennsylvania Reserves and 27th New York in the formative months of organization. At first, the Pennsylvania and New York regiments acted disobediently and challenged military authority. The 13th Pennsylvania Reserves, for instance, descended on the state capital like hillbillies from the backcountry. They resented any exercise of discipline, and their unruly behavior increased as their unofficial status as a Federal unit dragged on. A lack of bread and bullets became the theme of complaint for dissenters in both regiments. Several demonstrations against poor quality of provisions, one near riot, and the Dunn incident solidified Philander's New Yorkers as a regiment of rabble-rousers. On these episodes, Phillip and Philander remained largely nonjudgmental in their homebound letters.

While a sense of localism strengthened the bond between company leaders and rank-and-file enlistees, the same could not be said about the Ellithorpes' regiments as a whole. In fact, the ten companies making up the Bucktails and 27th New York drew from different counties in nearby regions around their respective states, thus lacking overall homogeneity as a 1,000-man unit. Consequently, the concept of group loyalty was much more evident at the company level, whereas regimental pride would develop only after it had been tested as a fighting unit in battle.[68]

Military Regulations concerning Regimental Size

On their unit's enrollment in federal service in June 1861, Phillip's Bucktails and Philander's 27th New York faced blowback from top commanders. Philander's regiment accounted for only 800 men at its first muster call, and Phillip's Company I reflected manpower deficiencies in most other Bucktail companies when only seventy-seven soldiers answered the first roll call. This issue would become the subject of tense discussions shortly.

The Letters

On June 22, the Ellithorpe brothers were on the verge of marching toward the signature event of their lives. In their preparation for war, Phillip and Philander maintained a steady correspondence with older sister Ann from the moment they first enrolled. In the two-month period beginning April 20, 1861, Phillip penned at least eight letters to family and friends, while Philander drafted five. And there is strong evidence in surviving epistles to suggest that they drafted even more. Averaging one missive per week, the boys reinforce an understanding among Civil War historians that letter writing was a popular activity among the soldiers because it established an outlet to boredom and helped them cope with new and stressful situations. "A soldier never put pen to paper," notes one, "without considering how he might be perceived by his loved ones."[69] The Ellithorpe brothers usually folded one piece of paper to create four equal squares, and they wrote on practically every inch of surface area, including perpendicularly on the margins of both sides of the sheet.

Each of Phillip's and Philander's semiliterate letters contained a scripted introduction, another common practice of Civil War soldiers. The tidings usually began with an apology for two specific shortcomings—having failed to write sooner and admitting in advance to any grammatical errors to follow. Phillip expressed great pleasure in receiving any news from Rushford and Pike and tendered heartfelt feelings of goodwill, good health, and good fortune to all family members. Almost 90 percent of Union soldiers could read and write, and their best cure for homesickness was to send and receive mail from home. The body of each Ellithorpe letter provided information about camp life, ranging from mundane topics to stirring events. A more sober tone would filter into the Ellithorpe brothers' correspondence once the war heated up and they were confronted with life-and-death subjects, such as combat, battlefield landscapes, troop movements, illness, injury, death, and inclement weather.[70]

The writing mechanics of the Ellithorpes differed greatly. Phillip usually wrote in ink on heavy-bond stationery or sheets torn from accounting ledgers. His penmanship was legible, and his characters assumed a vertical posture with appropriate spacing between each character. Phillip's most common writing faux pas were run-on sentences and lack of proper punctuation and capitalization. Philander, in contrast, often used thin paper and wrote in faded pencil. His penmanship flowed diagonally in a slanted lower-left-to-upper-right configuration, bunching individual words and making it more difficult to read. It was Philander, however, who provided more compelling descriptions of camp life. Phillip seemed overwhelmed or else oblivious to events taking place around him. Sometimes the writings of both brothers lacked cohesion, and their thought processes often rambled in "streams of consciousness."

Many soldiers often wrote in pencil because ink was difficult to obtain, and the quality of their penmanship ranged from beautiful to crude, depending on their skills and the setting from whence they wrote. The semiliterate letters of the Ellithorpe brothers, like many of their comrades, did not always conform to the rules of grammar, so there were frequent errors in spelling, punctuation, and capitalization.[71]

Finally, the letters composed by the Ellithorpe brothers clarified a number of questions regarding family relationships. The vast majority of extant letters written by the brothers were addressed to Ann or Permelia in Rushford, who were living alone. Sister Mary still resided in Pike with Uncle Carlos along with half brother Danforth. In 1861, Danforth had moved to Buffalo, married a Canadian woman named Martha, crossed the international border to live in Ontario, and raised three children born between 1861 and 1864. He did not return to the United States until 1866. This unusual behavior raises a red flag: Was twenty-eight-year-old Danforth a draft dodger? It is noteworthy that Danforth was never mentioned in the siblings' correspondence before, during, or after the war. Finally, the peculiar living arrangements of Mother and Father remain an anomaly. They bounced back and forth between Rushford and Pike with regularity for unknown reasons, and they were sometimes separated.[72]

Enlistment Misunderstandings

The enlistments of Phillip and Philander raise a few questions about their behaviors and family dynamics. In a letter to Ann, Phillip revealed that he had learned about a letter sent by Mother, imploring her son to return to Rushford in order to enlist. Her message had arrived too late in Smethport because Phillip had already joined the Bucktails and shipped out to Camp Curtin. This understanding of his mother's wishes would plague Phillip for some time.[73]

Philander had been a resident on Uncle Carlos's farm as late as 1860. Why hadn't he signed up in the Pike recruitment station and accompanied Edwin and James Stebbins into the 33rd New York, which was heavily recruited in southern Wyoming County? Why did he travel, instead, to

Rushford to enlist? To placate his mother's wishes for both of her sons to sign up together in their hometown? After signing his enlistment papers at Rushford Academy and reporting to Angelica, why did Philander opt to visit Pike and Mills Mills while on furlough instead of returning to see his family in Rushford? There are no clear answers to explain any of Philander's actions in the extant material, but they cast a shadow on Ellithorpe family dynamics.

Participation in the Civil War would greatly accelerate the maturation process of Phillip and Philander. For the Ellithorpe brothers and their comrades, the enlistment process was "a rite of passage into manhood" filled with complex real-life, adult challenges. "Soldiers," states one modern historian, "were never just cogs in the proverbial military machine; before they donned uniforms, they were husbands and sons and brothers, and so they remained."[74] At times, the transformation would be traumatic because of their new military setting.

The Ellithorpe brothers' letters embodied the family's traditional commitment to public and military service, willingness to sacrifice, and love of country. Their writings were blunt, unsophisticated, uncensored, and rough around the edges, but they also evinced a sentimental romanticism indicative of mid-nineteenth-century American values. "Convictions of duty, honor, patriotism, and ideology functioned as the principal sustaining motivations of Civil War soldiers," words that adequately represent the motives of the Ellithorpe brothers.[75]

In the summer of 1861, Phillip and Philander would face the enemy on the battlefield albeit in two different locations. For the Ellithorpe brothers of western New York, the Civil War was about to become quite personal.

Chapter Three

The Road to Bull Run

Practicing the art of soldiery for less than two months, the Ellithorpe brothers were deemed ready by their trainers to meet the enemy on the battlefield. One headed from Pennsylvania to western Maryland and northwestern Virginia, while the other traveled from New York to the nation's capital, where they engaged in skirmishes, scouting forays, picket duty, and the first major combat of the Civil War. During each of these forays against the Confederates, whether major or minor, the Ellithorpes stayed connected through spotty correspondence with Ann. By the time the first season's campaigns had drawn to a close in the fall of 1861, the lads had been "baptized in blood" and changed in many ways.

On June 18, Phillip had erred on the departure date of the Bucktails from Harrisburg by nearly one week, when he penned those consoling letters to his parents. McCall had been busy finalizing plans to implement General in Chief Scott's order to send two regiments from Camp Curtin to reinforce Col. Lew Wallace's 11th Indiana who were stationed in Cumberland, Maryland. Politicians in Washington and Harrisburg were mutually fearful of a possible Confederate incursion from the Shenandoah Valley that might threaten the Baltimore & Ohio Railroad, southwestern Pennsylvania, and even the nation's capital.[1]

Phillip

McCall turned the assignment of checking the Rebels over to Biddle, who selected his own 13th Pennsylvania Reserves and 5th Pennsylvania Reserves led by Col. Seneca G. Simmons for the task. Biddle was hoping to gratify his own regiment, which was still upset for receiving neither uniforms nor rifles befitting a sharpshooter's title. The colonel promised his testy men that he would personally ensure their proper equipage as soon as they would return from the field. Having narrowly averted a regimental showdown, Biddle marched his undersized force to the Harrisburg train station early on the morning of June 22 to board a westbound train. The ladies of Huntingdon met the troop transport with baskets of "delectables," and the hungry men filled their stomachs and haversacks. Pushing on, the travelers arrived in Hopewell after dark, but the local citizens hosted them to a fine supper before they retired for the evening.[2]

Flushing Out the Enemy in Western Maryland

The next morning, Biddle's column marched toward the state line. After a hot and dusty trek of twenty-three miles, the footsore troops arrived in Bedford Springs, where they were greeted with another sumptuous banquet. Since seasoned troops normally marched twelve miles per day, the men required a couple days to recoup their strength before proceeding to their primary objective in Cumberland, Maryland, more than thirty miles to the south.[3]

While the regiment rested at Bedford Springs, Phillip landed a plum assignment. "I have the honor of being Kane's orderly and clerk," Phillip bragged to Ann, "which required a good second [recommendation] from the Comesary at Camp Curtin." A benefit of this new detail meant "I dont have to stand or gard or drill." Phillip was allowed to sleep in Kane's tent, guard the officer's personal belongings while the regiment was away in the field, and care for his "high spirited bay" whom the Bucktails had renamed "Bob Tail." Kane promised to reward Phillip's dependability and loyalty with a tent and horse of his own once the mission to Cumberland was over. Even Biddle knew Phillip's name.[4]

On June 26, Biddle's reconnaissance resumed down the Bedford Valley Road. He halted one-quarter mile from the state line and approximately five miles north of Cumberland. Here, an interesting debate broke out among the officers. Were Pennsylvania troops legally allowed to cross into Maryland? After all, these Pennsylvania Reserves had sworn allegiance to the Commonwealth, had mustered into state service, and still awaited official federal recognition. Did Biddle's soldiers have the authority to enter a neighboring state? While the officers discussed the merits, some Bucktails planted a flag only yards away from the Maryland line. Biddle decided to hold his command in position and await further instructions.[5]

Meanwhile, what became known as "Camp Mason and Dixey," or "Dickinson" according to Phillip, would be home to Biddle's force for almost two weeks. The feisty disciplinarian drilled his charges three times every day, but the marshy environs proved quite unhealthy. Foul drinking water and inadequate supply of rations contributed to an outbreak of sickness, so the soldiers renamed the site "Camp Misery and Despair."[6]

On June 29, Phillip started a letter that took several days to compose but made little mention of his journey to the Maryland state line. Writing with a faded pencil, he assured Ann that he was "in good health," but the repose fostered opposite feelings of camaraderie and homesickness. He complained to his sister about the failure of Mary, Permelia, and Philander to answer his letters since his induction. "I . . . would like to get a letter to cheer me up," noted the private to Permelia.[7] He also wanted to hear from a Rushford chum, Henry Hyde, with whom he had once driven a herd of beeves to market.

Joe Barnes sympathized with his comrade's loneliness. "My friend Joe . . . says he will be my Father and mother to[o] if he can fill the offices although he dont think I am much of a Baby for it is all he can do to keep up with me on doubbl marches," declared Phillip. Joe made it a point to visit his battle buddy every day at Kane's tent. The fact that Phillip had not yet been paid and wore "the same old rags" from Smethport also grated his spirits. Indeed, his pants and only shirt were already dirty and threadbare. Phillip promised to send Ann a picture as soon as he would receive a crisp new blue uniform.[8]

The military situation in the upper Potomac region was intensifying at this very moment. Consequently, Wallace was ordered to march to Romney and Martinsburg, Virginia, to assist Brig. Gen. Robert Patterson in recapturing Harpers Ferry. Wallace's departure left a void in the Federal presence in western Maryland, and the citizens of Cumberland were justifiably concerned that they had been left unprotected. Thus, on July 7, Biddle took discretionary action, crossed the state line, and occupied Wallace's former campsite in Cumberland after nightfall.[9]

Once the two Pennsylvania regiments had entered Maryland, Phillip reported several spirited clashes with Confederate pickets. In one encounter, a southern soldier had been captured and taken to "jail whar he awaits his fate which will probably end with dancing at the end of a hemp or light rope," boasted Phillip. Filled with manly bravado, Phillip told Ann how he intended "to whip the Rebbels."[10]

Meanwhile, the commander of the newly created Army of Northeastern Virginia, Brig. Gen. Irwin McDowell, was developing a battle plan on Confederate positions defending Manassas Junction, about twenty-five miles southwest of Washington. Manassas Junction had become the focal point for both Union and Confederate strategists because of its close proximity to both national capitals as well as its intersection with two major railroads (the Orange & Alexandria and the Manassas Gap) and three roadways (Braddock Road, Centreville Road, and the macadamized Warrenton Pike). Bull Run, a shallow and mucky creek with steep banks, meandered on the north and east sides of town.[11]

If Phillip knew about the impending clash near Manassas Junction from his vantage point in Cumberland, he did not reveal it. He was not even aware of Scott's scheme to clear the upper Potomac River region of all enemy forces, a plan that ensured that Biddle's force would remain in western Maryland and northwestern Virginia for the foreseeable future. The Pennsylvanians remained vigilant as Confederate troops and sympathizers tested their perimeter in several nighttime raids. Disparaging these hit-and-run tactics, Phillip chided that "they have played the Coward . . . and dare not come and face [us] like men." The stratagem offended Phillip's sense of chivalry and masculinity.[12]

Phillip spent his days foraging for cream and butter to supplement the officer's dinner table. He also informed Ann about the death of a young soldier from the town of Cuba in Allegany County from exposure or pneumonia. The news of this first wartime fatality evidently jogged Phillip's sense of mortality because he signed off his missive cryptically: "when I come home if God should spare my life."[13] Suddenly, the war had turned into a life-and-death matter.

Biddle's men continued to contend with the harassing hit-and-run tactics of Capt. Angus W. MacDonald's 7th Virginia Cavalry. Charged with guarding the bridges and fords across the North and South branches of the Potomac River above Harpers Ferry, MacDonald's cavalrymen were extremely active between Romney, New Creek Station (Keyser), Piedmont, and Cumberland. Itching for a fight, Kane requested and received permission from Biddle to launch an advanced scouting expedition to the North Branch, occupy Piedmont, and protect a bridge of the Baltimore & Ohio Railroad. This decision effectively split Biddle's command. Sixty men from four companies volunteered for the mission, including Blanchard of Company I and Kane's orderly, Phillip. The vanguard left Cumberland by rail on July 12.[14]

Kane made decent progress, halted several miles from the North Branch, and spent a rainy night at an old gristmill. Phillip's band set up pickets in the rain, an unpleasant duty. Early the next morning, Kane sent out feelers toward Piedmont, where it was rumored MacDonald's men had bivouacked the previous night. Reaching the North Branch across from Piedmont, Kane discovered that the rail trestle had been destroyed. He ordered Blanchard to take some volunteers and track down the arsonists. The rest of his command spread out on the riverbank to locate a shallow ford.[15]

Phillip accompanied Blanchard's reconnaissance. He recounted a story to Ann about filing past "two Beautiful and amiable young ladies" who were allegedly guarding a store from foraging Confederates. Indeed, they uncovered an abandoned wagon loaded with stolen letters and dry goods. The women offered to lead the party of Pennsylvanians to a suitable spot in which to cross the river. Suspecting an ambush, Blanchard refused to cross over to the Virginia side. One of the female guides taunted Blanchard for his apparent lack of courage and boasted that the Confederates "would not have escaped if she had been Captain."[16]

As Kane entered Piedmont, he was disappointed to discover that MacDonald had slipped away to New Creek Station, about six miles distant. Leaving ten men in town, he hastily assembled his remaining fifty soldiers and double-quicked in pursuit of the elusive Rebels. When they arrived at New Creek Station, the Federals set up headquarters in the majestic Armstrong House on the road leading to Romney. He dispatched several officers to check the surrounding area and sent a message to MacDonald (through a Confederate sympathizer) with a challenge to show up and fight.[17]

Early the next morning, the gray-clads accepted Kane's invitation. Phillip mused that the Virginians "rode into town with the intention of some Buck tail soup for breakfast." They killed a youth from Cumberland who had served as a guide to Kane. Phillip recounted the deadly event to Ann and his cousin: the lad had fallen asleep on the steps of a warehouse when he was shot. For good measure, a sword-wielding Confederate officer split open the head of the unfortunate lad. Such gruesome stories were designed to brutalize and dehumanize the enemy, and Phillip responded accordingly.[18]

Kane sent a detachment into New Creek Station to investigate the clatter, but fearing possible encirclement by MacDonald's attackers, he ordered the party to fall back to his brick headquarters and prepare for the expected onslaught. In the pell-mell retreat, a few Bucktails had become separated and hid in tall grass behind one of the estate's stone walls. Kane waited patiently as the enemy horsemen galloped toward the house, announcing their arrival with a piercing "rebel yell"; he told his soldiers not to shoot until given the command.[19]

When Kane gave the instruction to open fire, the attackers were stunned by the unexpected firepower. Falling back, the southerners passed beside the field where other Pennsylvania Reserves hid, and they were met by a second fierce volley. A familiar name provided the heroics here. "James Landergan [sp.?] . . . after fireing and killing one of the Rebbls . . . jumped over the fence and sit down in the grass bullets falling or whistling by his head . . . [he] was soon fireing again none of Kane's party got even a scratch," crowed Phillip. "This is the way they came out with their Breakfast."[20] Landregan was credited with killing two Confederate horsemen.

On June 13, while "Kane's Scouts" were engaging MacDonald's cavalry at New Creek Station, Biddle was preparing to cross the North Branch and enter Piedmont. But the commander fretted that an open river crossing might expose his men to sharpshooters who still lurked in buildings on the other side. Thus, Biddle directed a small group to sweep enemy defenses from the opposite bank, enter Piedmont, and establish a defensive perimeter. The mission succeeded; on the morning of July 16, Biddle began the task of fording his two infantry regiments and one artillery battery across the river, an event that took all day.

After dark, Biddle received an untimely message from Kane, who had overzealously pursued MacDonald to Romney, the Confederate stronghold. Impetuous in temperament, Kane had overextended his force and thereby placed it in extreme peril. Likely upset by Kane's ill-advised chase, Biddle immediately ordered a forced night march to rescue Kane from his exposed position. The next morning, Biddle's tired command reunited and promptly returned to Piedmont, where he spent the next ten days drilling his rusty troops.[21]

Biddle's ten-day occupation of Piedmont served other useful purposes. Beside achieving most of its original goals, the 5th and 13th Pennsylvania Reserves lent a Federal presence in the upper Potomac region that might have played an indirect role in the future creation of the pro-Union state of West Virginia. By contrast, Biddle's Pennsylvanians were still legally state militia and, strictly speaking, not acting on behalf of the Federal government. To complicate the matter, the other eleven regiments of the Pennsylvania Reserves that Biddle had left behind at Camp Curtin were sworn into Federal service as the 42nd Pennsylvania Infantry Regiment and sent to guard Washington during operations at Manassas Junction. Biddle's absence in Piedmont unintentionally delayed official Federal recognition for his two detached regiments.[22]

Meanwhile, the new head of the Department of the Ohio, Brig. Gen. William S. Rosecrans, not knowing the official status of Biddle's regiments, assigned them to the Cheat River District. Rosecrans's order was never carried out. On July 27, Curtin recalled Biddle to Harrisburg. Phillip's first exposure to combat, albeit limited, was over.[23]

Philander

The day Biddle entered Piedmont, the wheels of war were spinning quickly in the capital city of Washington. One month earlier, McDowell was under increasing pressure from the Lincoln administration to launch an attack and defeat the Rebel scourge. Prompt action was essential because three-month volunteers were scheduled for discharge in late July. In turn, McDowell designed a three-pronged offensive against Confederate forces under the direction of Beauregard that were posted along an eight-mile front near Manassas Junction. Energetic and capable, some of McDowell's critics viewed the Union tactician as humorless, rude, and temperamental, but he was adept at military organization. McDowell's newly constituted Army of Northeastern Virginia began a series of precursory probes, resulting in the seizure of Alexandria and Arlington Heights.[24]

Philander Prepares for Battle

In the early months of the war, the majority of troops defending Washington came from the states of Pennsylvania and New York. Yet Philander and his comrades in the 27th New York remained at Camp Elmira, where they received daily drill instruction under Slocum. Camp life was uneventful, and some men actually received short furloughs over the Fourth of July. When everyone had returned from the holiday, Philander's outfit received new blue uniforms, a knapsack, haversack, and canteen. On July 9, Gardiner's Company I was the first company in the regiment to be sworn into Federal service for two years. The next day, the other nine companies followed suit.[25]

On July 10, railcars carried Slocum and his regiment through Williamsport, Harrisburg, and York—past "excellent farmland and beautiful homes," according to Philander. In Baltimore, the regiment marched through the city with fixed bayonets and then transferred to a second train for the final leg of their journey. Once they reached the nation's capital, the New Yorkers were assigned to makeshift wooden barracks erected in Franklin square. The men called their new home "Camp Anderson," and soon the entire square was jammed with shelters of all description. The five-acre site also boasted several natural springs that had serviced the White House since 1816.[26]

Philander and two of his tent mates, Tim Charles and Will Robinson, visited the major attractions in Washington. First, they walked five blocks to see the Executive Mansion. Next, they viewed "the ante chamber of the House of Representatives," and outside they plucked small flowers from the Capitol lawn to send them home. The trio also visited the Smithsonian Institute, where they examined displays of "fishes and animals of all kinds" as well as the popular gallery where portrait paintings of Native Americans were exhibited. Finally, Philander and his friends ended their self-guided walking tour at the Patent Office and Old Post Office. Some soldiers were disappointed in the muddy streets and unfinished Capitol dome, but most were impressed by the famous government buildings, which they visited in droves.[27]

On July 15, Franklin Square was abuzz as the 27th New York received the latest in rifled weaponry, the .58-caliber Model 1861 Springfield muzzleloader. The regiment took live ammunition practice immediately, which was a rarity by Civil War training standards. Little did the enlistees realize they would be using their new firearms on live targets in less than one week.[28]

In the meantime, McDowell had added another layer to the command structure of the Army of Northeastern Virginia: the division. It was a clear sign that a large campaign was about to be unleashed. To fill these new roles, McDowell promoted current brigade commanders to fill them. Using the same logic, he would elevate regimental colonels with regular army experience to fill brigade vacancies. Career officers such as Slocum would be tabbed shortly. The 27th New York would be attached to Col. David Hunter's Second Division in the 1st Brigade commanded by Col. Andrew Porter.[29]

March to Bull Run

On the morning of July 16, Philander's 27th New York stood in formation for three hours, then crossed the Long Bridge into Virginia with Hunter's division. The ebullient soldiers broke into singing "national airs," such as "The Star Spangled Banner." Their route took them past the Custis-Lee Mansion in Arlington, the home of Confederate general Robert E. Lee. The first day's objective of Hunter's middle prong, a march to Annandale, was achieved but not without hardship. Still, McDowell's grand scheme was strategically impressive on paper.[30]

Most of the soldiers had been instructed to travel lightly—three days of cooked rations, a coat, a pair of socks, a blanket, and forty rounds of ammunition. Some packed sixty pounds of gear. Regardless of the load they carried, the hot and muggy day quickly sapped their energies as their feet kicked up massive volumes of dust that parched their throats. Furthermore, the line of march was led by officers with little training about how to time and coordinate such a massive movement. The accordion-like pace of the Army of Northeastern Virginia quickly degenerated into a sluggish crawl.[31]

When the march resumed on July 17, a new set of obstacles arose. First, Hunter's division had tightened the noose around Fairfax Court House, but they discovered that the Confederates had already vacated the area. Angry and frustrated, some soldiers in the 27th New York participated in looting Fairfax Court House and Jermantown before resuming their pursuit of the enemy. Then, as Philander's unit cautiously approached Centreville, many comrades broke ranks in search of berries, water, and rest.[32]

Late on the evening of July 17, the retiring Confederates slipped inside Beauregard's line behind Bull Run, so McDowell altered his operational plan in favor of using Centreville as the staging area and pivot point in a "turning movement" along an eight-mile front. The next morning, McDowell put his large force in motion on the macadamized Warrenton Pike, and later that afternoon, he halted his footsore troops three miles east of town while his staff gathered intelligence on enemy positions.[33]

Prior to launching the attack, McDowell desired to learn more about the nine fords and two bridges that spanned Bull Run between Union Mills and Sudley Ford. The best crossings were over Stone Bridge and Blackburn's Ford because macadamized roads led up to them. McDowell hoped to ascertain how strongly these points were being defended. Thus, he sent one division from Centreville to the ford but *not* to engage the enemy. Foolishly, a brigade under Col. Israel B. (Fighting Dick) Richardson made solid contact with a Confederate brigade led by James Longstreet and sustained significant casualties. Despite the disobedient act, the reconnaissance provided valuable information; any assault on the enemy downstream from Stone Bridge was ill advised. Thus, McDowell focused on the crossings north of the bridge in the hopes of gaining the Confederates' rear.[34]

On July 19 and 20, the Federal army rested outside of Centreville as its chief engineer, Maj. John Gross Barnard, surveyed the fords north of Stone Bridge for a suitable crossing. These two days were quiet, and many men became reflective and introspective in letters they wrote home, perhaps their last ones. Philander's faded missive to an unknown friend was brief and mentioned only "little battles" (skirmishes) over the previous three days. He did not let on that a major battle was in the offing.[35]

Hunter's division headquarters lay across the road from the encampment of the 27th New York, and the Marine Band of Washington serenaded the troops at night. The men listened intently to the sweet melancholy strains of the finale, "Home Sweet Home." This two-day interlude would cost McDowell's army dearly, however, as Confederate brigadiers Joseph E. Johnston and Thomas J. Jackson were hurrying to reinforce Beauregard.[36]

On July 19, one of the harshest and most widely publicized examples of military discipline occurred outside Centreville and was witnessed by the 27th New York: two deserters were marched into a square of volunteers representing all of the regiments in the division, given fifty lashes, and branded with the letter "D" on their hip—"a sickening and disgusting site." Witnesses included men from the 1st Minnesota and 27th New York. The grisly scene made a lasting impression on many of the observers who wrote about the incident in their letters and diaries. Afterward, the 27th New York elected its color-bearer, Pvt. Burton Freeman of Philander's Company I. The selection of this high honor went to the soldier whom his comrades considered the most courageous. The regimental flag, a symbol of home, was to be protected at all costs, and its presence on the battlefield always attracted enemy gunfire. Thus, the color-bearer's job was extremely hazardous.[37]

McDowell reprised his original three-prong campaign strategy. Richardson's brigade would be deployed as a smokescreen at Blackburn's and Mitchell's fords, while the rest of the division would proceed to Stone Bridge and carry out an artillery diversion set for 6 a.m. In the meantime, Hunter's division was slated to tail them down Warrenton Pike, turn right at a blacksmith shop just beyond Cub Run Bridge, and proceed along the narrow path for six miles until they reached a fork in the road. At this crossroads, Hunter was to merge to the right and proceed to Sudley Ford and cross Bull Run once the artillery sounded at the bridge. If all went according to plan, the Federals would outflank the Confederates and collapse their defenses.[38]

Philander's Baptism of Fire

Most soldiers learned how to fight through firsthand experience on the battlefield, and their letters described combat situations from the vantage point of their own confined sector; this was precisely the case of Philander. At 2 a.m. on July 21, the 27th New York awakened with the rest of the Army of Northeastern Virginia and formed within thirty minutes. They waited for the advance division to pass, but it moved with extreme caution along Warrenton Pike. Logs and other debris blocked the roadway and took time to clear away, resulting in a fierce bottleneck on the narrow Cub Run Bridge.[39]

Philander's 27th New York, positioned at the rear of Porter's brigade, waited impatiently for the Federal vanguard to push through the quagmire. Finally, at 5:30 a.m., Hunter's divisions pulled forward. Unfortunately, McDowell's timetable for engagement was hours behind schedule. But Beauregard inadvertently played into McDowell's hands, placing the majority of his troops below Stone Bridge and leaving exposed his extreme left wing above the bridge at Sudley Ford.[40]

The morning sun beat down mercilessly on the marchers, and Hunter struggled to make good time on the farm road because it, too, was choked with fallen trees. His vanguard, the brigade of Col. Ambrose E. Burnside, did not reach Sudley Ford until 9:30 a.m., four hours behind schedule. The Yankees waded into the stream immediately and, once across, began a purposeful march toward Matthew's Hill. While waiting their turn to cross the creek, Philander's 27th New York fell to the ground hungry, tired, and exposed to an intense sun. Some thirsty soldiers filled their canteens with the muddy water of Bull Run. About the time the 27th New York had queued up to wade across Bull Run, Confederate commanders had taken the initiative to confront the Union threat at Sudley Ford. On the southern slope of Matthew's Hill, they collided with the Federals.[41]

Matthew's and Henry Hill

As Burnside's brigade engaged the enemy on Matthew's Hill, Porter's brigade traversed the stream. Half an hour later, they were on the other side, heading at the double-quick toward the sounds of battle. According to Philander's lieutenant in Company I, Samuel M. Harmon, the regiment arrived winded at a position on the west side of Sudley-Manassas Road about one mile from Dogan Ridge. Several hundred yards away stood a prominent stone house on Warrenton Pike.[42]

By 11 a.m., the Rebels' line on Matthew's Hill cracked under the pressure of a Federal pincer. They fell back over Buck Hill and across Young's Branch in the general direction of Henry House. During the retreat, both sides charged and counterattacked, creating mass confusion and increasing the number of casualties. Early in the firefight for control of Matthew's Hill, Hunter was wounded, and command of his division passed to Porter. Although the Federal command structure was being severely tested, a victory seemed in plain sight.[43]

The 27th New York and 2nd Rhode Island were thrown into the fray to nip at the heels of the retreating Confederates. The Rhode Islanders shouted a throaty battle cry as they pursued the enemy, a phenomenon adopted by the 13th Pennsylvania Reserves while in training camp. The Bucktails shouted their unique "wildcat serenade" throughout the war. "The overture opens with a solo mew from the grand maestro wild-cat," stated one Pennsylvanian. "A responsive y-e-o-w on the octave below comes from a remote corner of the quarters. These two performers serve the purpose of guides in a military movement on the right and left. They give the key notes . . . but the whole feline chorus break in with a mewing tune to the characteristic refrain of the wild-cat."[44]

The 27th New York repulsed several halfhearted rearguard actions, but as soon as they approached the stone house, the Staunton Light Artillery atop Henry Hill shelled them with grape and canister projectiles (balls and bent iron). That was where the regiment sustained its first casualties of the war. In a post-battle letter, Philander told Millie, Father, and Cousin Ell, "I am in good health," but supplied no details about the fight. Forty-three years later, he would vividly recalled the moment of Rushford's first fatality, Albert Babbitt.[45]

Hoping to shelter his command from the intense artillery barrage, Slocum moved his men obliquely 200 yards to the left along the base of Henry Hill. The regiment struggled to execute the maneuver, however, and it quickly became disorganized. Moreover, the inexperienced warriors had overextended themselves in the heat of battle and occupied an exposed salient. Philander's regiment collided with the 4th Alabama, whom they mistakenly identified as the gray-clad 8th New York Militia. A fierce fight erupted. When Wade Hampton's Legion of South Carolinians joined the contest, the 27th New York momentarily panicked, and Slocum ordered a withdrawal to Buck Hill. As soon as the New Yorkers entered an oak stand, a bullet struck Slocum in the thigh, and command fell to Bartlett, a Binghamton lawyer who had no military experience but was known as "a man of good character." Gardiner of

Captain/Major/Colonel Joseph J. Bartlett, Company C, 27th New York. *SOURCE:* CIVIL WAR PHOTOGRAPHS, 1861–1865, LIBRARY OF CONGRESS, PRINTS AND PHOTOGRAPHS DIVISION.

Company I later referred to the route as "a trap," but the Confederates did not have time to contrive such a surprise attack in the mayhem.[46]

In the relative safety of the woods, Bartlett faced a difficult task in rallying his disheartened regiment for an impending counterattack. When the order to advance did not arrive, Bartlett guided his dazed column from Buck Hill to the brushy valley along Young's Branch, where the regiment sat out the remainder of the battle. Some of Philander's comrades melted away in the direction to Sudley Church, where a field hospital had been set up. Later, regimental historians would claim that Bartlett's leadership, courage under fire, and sound judgment had kept his demoralized men out of harm's way in the "needless stampede" that followed. Philander made only brief reference to these events.[47]

Philander's regiment was knocked out of action at the same time the opening phase of the battle was drawing to a close, after which an ominous two-hour interlude descended over the field. McDowell used the time to shore up his lines in preparation for a knockout punch directed at Henry Hill. "In retrospect," claims one historian, the delay was "an error of monumental proportions." Essentially, the failure of the Army of Northeastern Virginia to maintain pressure on the reeling Confederates allowed them to reinforce Henry Hill. One of the most notable southern arrivals on the hill was five regiments of Virginia troops and thirteen pieces of artillery. When the Union attack resumed around 2 p.m., the Confederates were ready.[48]

The Second Phase of Battle

In preparation for the final phase of the battle, McDowell repositioned his two batteries (Ricketts and Griffin) across Sudley-Manassas Road, within 300 yards of the Confederates on Henry Hill. At 2 p.m., an intense artillery duel lasting for half an hour and directed at Henry House signaled the resumption of hostilities. It was apparent to McDowell that an infantry assault would be necessary to dislodge Jackson's smoothbores. Given this task, the 11th New York (Fire Zouaves) and 1st Minnesota made several advances to within 150 yards of the western summit. Believing the blue-clad 33rd Virginia to be friends, the Minnesotans were ordered not to shoot; his was a grave mistake. When Col. J. E. B. Stuart's cavalry burst from its concealed position behind Bald Hill, the Fire Zouaves and 1st Minnesota were caught in a deadly crossfire. The Federals raced back down the same hillside they had just ascended and did not stop until they reached the woods across Sudley-Manassas Road on Bald Hill. There, many men from a variety of units milled about in stunned disbelief. Nevertheless, the extreme right of the Yankee line had collapsed.[49]

Sensing that they now held the upper hand, the Confederates atop Henry Hill sought to silence the Federal artillery. Over the next two hours, the guns of Ricketts's and Griffin's batteries changed hands three times as fifteen Union regiments and thirteen Confederate regiments slugged it out; strangely, never more than two or three Union regiments were ever engaged at any one time. Vicious hand-to-hand fighting erupted as fragments of Federal regiments provided cover support from the woods. The fight for Henry Hill had produced an intense cacophony of sounds, including the piercing rebel yell for the first time.[50]

Retreat

About 4 p.m., the Confederates pushed the last disorganized resisters from Henry Hill and decisively turned back two relief brigades. The Rebels controlled the field, and the rout was on. Federal soldiers, organized at first, fled to the rear in droves. The battle of Bull Run was over.

While historians debate whether the Federal retreat was unnerving and disgraceful or an orderly withdrawal, it certainly was chaotic. Covered by the U.S. Regulars, most soldiers in Hunter's division reversed their morning steps from Sudley Ford to Cub Run Bridge. Because of its advantageous position behind Young's Branch, Bartlett's 27th New York provided rearguard protection as hundreds of distraught comrades raced through its formation. Three times, Harmon lined up Company I in open ground, attempting to stem the flow of withdrawal and protect the retreating army from enemy attackers. Intense combat had created chaotic conditions, and linear formations quickly disintegrated, but given the opportunity to reorganize once they had reached relatively safe positions, many commands did so.[51]

Once Philander's unit and his brigade approached Cub Run Bridge on the choked arterial, Warrenton Pike, all semblance of military discipline vanished when a well-placed Confederate artillery shell landed amid the human logjam, overturning a wagon and effectively blocking the span. Then the presence of Confederate cavalrymen in the rear pushed the frayed nerves of the Federal infantrymen over the edge and into full-scale panic. One of

Philander's comrades in a later recollection stated that "the floodgates of Pandemonium had been thrown open."[52] The Yankees discarded weapons, clothing, packs, and all sorts of miscellaneous material. The presence of civilian observers riding in carriages added to the confusion. Seeing the unfolding danger on the bridge, Harmon led Company I into the stream in order to avoid the structure that was obviously being targeted. Racing through Centreville, the harried soldiers and civilians proceeded to Fairfax Court House, where they were instructed to keep moving to the nation's capital.[53]

The Costs of War

In the early morning hours of July 22, a driving rain fell on the bedraggled soldiers, an apt metaphor for the gloom and despondency of Yankee spirits. Shaken, the 27th New York partially regrouped at Fort Corcoran and proceeded to Franklin Square around noontime. The beleaguered Army of Northeastern Virginia had been awake and unfed for more than thirty hours and marched approximately sixty miles. Many official battle reports would make a point to explain how their regiments, brigades, or divisions had left the field at Bull Run in an orderly fashion, but few mentioned how they had arrived in Washington.[54]

McDowell's losses at Bull Run stunned the nation (460k/1,124w/1,312m), and the 27th New York paid an especially heavy price. Slocum's regiment suffered 26k/44w/60m for a total of 130 casualties, or eighth for the army as a whole. Regarding fatalities, the 27th New York ranked first in Porter's brigade and fifth in McDowell's army overall. Suffering a casualty rate higher than 18 percent, Bull Run would prove to be the second-bloodiest engagement ever waged by the 27th New York in the entire war.[55]

The short-term psychological impact of Bull Run on the Army of Northeastern Virginia was significant. "Pennsylvania Avenue was gorged with panic-stricken citizens and soldiers," noted the observer of the 27th New York.[56] The mental distress was not caused entirely by the stinging defeat. Rather, soldiers had witnessed the grisly scenes of battlefield carnage firsthand; these images would not be easily erased from their minds. "As you pass along you will see one [soldier] gasping for breath, another crying for water, another begging for you to blow his brains out, and put him out of his misery," recounted one private of the 27th New York. "Some have their limbs blown off, others part of their faces off, then you will pass by one already in the cold embrace of death. You may read but you cannot imagine a thing about it."[57] Philander and his comrades had "seen the elephant," and he chose to shelter his family from such realities.[58]

Quick Rebound and Reassignments

One week after the battle, someone in a position of authority had to be held accountable for the disastrous turn of events. McDowell proved to be the most available scapegoat. President Lincoln wasted no time in summoning thirty-four-year-old George B. McClellan to Washington to offer him command of the Army of Northeastern Virginia. McClellan was considered by many political and military observers to be the brightest young mind in the regular army, with a penchant for organization.

On July 27, the "Young Napoleon" arrived at Union Station (with considerable personal baggage as well). He quickly surmised that many units lacked military discipline, and some soldiers were roaming the city streets like packs of lawless thugs foraging for food and fighting with each other. The Federal military structure appeared to teeter on the edge of collapse. McClellan understood the important connection between pageantry and high morale, so in mid-August, he scheduled the first of many troop reviews. On August 20, "Little Mac's" new Army of the Potomac was born.[59]

The failures of McDowell's command filtered down in the form of personnel changes at the brigade and regimental levels. At Bull Run, Slocum and Bartlett earned high marks as positive role models with the 27th New York—the former for his steely handling of the regiment during the initial phase of the engagement and subsequent flesh wound while confronting the enemy and the latter for his cool reorganization of the unit under dire circumstances, tempered involvement of the regiment in the later phase of the rout, and deft handling of the rearguard action from Sudley Ford to Cub Run Bridge. For their efforts, Slocum and Bartlett each received post-battle promotions to fill vacancies at the rank of brigadier general and colonel, respectively. Consequently, the 27th New York petitioned for assignment to Slocum's brigade, a request that was granted.[60]

Whenever command openings occurred, it was usually filled from the ranks below, so when the 27th New York lost its colonel, lieutenant colonel, and major through promotion and retirement, it created opportunities in the lower echelon. When Bartlett assumed command of the regiment, Capt.

Alexander D. Adams (Company B) became lieutenant colonel, and Capt. Gardiner (Company I) became its major. In turn, Lt. Harmon was elevated to captain of Company I. Only time would tell whether these fluid changes from top to bottom might impact military performance. Nonetheless, Philander's Company I was significantly impacted.[61]

Phillip and the Confines of War

In his first few months with the Bucktails, Phillip wore many hats as a cook in the mess and hospital, a clerk in the commissary, and an orderly for Kane. He appears to have received preferential treatment from not only Kane and subsistence director Capt. James B. Clow but also his company leader, Blanchard. Why? Did Phillip's short stature, youthful appearance, innocence, and polite demeanor play a role in his being given such favors? Another possible explanation is the Civil War stereotype of the "mama's boy," a fellow perceived as helpless, sensitive, and vulnerable. In addition, his ragamuffin appearance projected an image of the "poor soldier," one whose poverty and depravation elicited sympathy from comrades and superiors alike. Did these labels apply to Phillip and result in his securing "bombproof jobs"?[62]

The letters written by the Ellithorpe brothers on the events of mid-July are silent on the combat they experienced. It was customary for soldiers to write letters home following major engagements in order to ease anxieties of family members as well as to soothe their own frayed nerves. Typically, soldier missives detailed the buildup, the fight itself, the role played by the individual, the horrors witnessed, expressions of relief for the survival of self and friends, and a closing statement hoping for a quick end to the horrible war. But Philander offered none of these talking points in his letters of August 1 and 7, and Phillip was equally tight lipped. In fairness to the brothers, they may have intentionally withdrawn in silence and suppressed their emotions, or they may have written to others on these subjects that are now lost.[63]

A persistent disconnect materialized between the perception of war by the Ellithorpe siblings on the civilian front and the realities of military life faced by Phillip and Philander in the ranks. For example, Ann flustered Phillip during the Piedmont campaign by criticizing his writing mechanics. He asked for compassion and more understanding of his primitive living conditions in the field. "Please consider how I am situated," he implored his older sister. Unfortunately, none of Ann's letters from home to the front have survived, a typical circumstance of Civil War correspondence in general.[64]

At the same time, Phillip and Philander were juggling several family issues back in Rushford that were not spelled out in correspondence in the days leading up to the battle of Bull Run. These worrisome subjects dealt with unresolved questions of finance, residence, and health. Regarding the first point, Ann dropped multiple innuendos about an undisclosed financial need, perhaps concerning home ownership. A second concern centered on the family's living arrangement. Did Ann and Permelia dwell alone in the house on Lewellen Street? Was Mary still living in Pike? And where was Father? The third misgiving, on health, was a real bombshell dropped by Philander: Mother was "unwell." What was her ailment? Had she gone to Pike to be nursed by her sisters? If these uncertainties were correct, they raised a number of important questions that went unresolved in surviving correspondence.[65]

Clearly, the Ellithorpe brothers were receiving the wrong kind of letters from their family, ones that emphasized home-front hardships and placed unexpected stress on them. These dilemmas over money, residence, and health were problematic, and Philander and Phillip would discuss them once their regiments moved into closer proximity around Washington over the winter of 1861–1862. Meanwhile, McClellan was at work consolidating his newly constituted Army of the Potomac, retooling and revitalizing it into an efficient fighting machine.[66]

* * * * * * *

As summer turned to autumn, the Yankee army slowly put the disaster of Bull Run behind them. Indeed, the resilience of the soldiers shone through: "Love of country, a sense of duty, grim determination, and even personal honor survived regardless of complains, pessimism, and despair."[67] Under new leadership, Phillip and Philander would bounce back along with their comrades, develop a renewed spirit of determination, and train hard to avenge the stinging Union defeat. In September, a third character known to the Ellithorpe brothers would enlist and soon become a member of the family: Asa R. Burleson of Freedom, New York.

From September 1861 to March 1862, the threesome would prepare for their first full year of combat. Interrupting their preparations in winter quarters, Phillip's Bucktails would fight in a highly publicized skirmish, and Philander would learn how to construct fortifications to protect the nation's capital. Despite facing health challenges, the Ellithorpe boys of western New York (though serving in three different regiments representing four different states) were far better equipped to wage war in April 1862 than they had been one year earlier.

Chapter Four

Retooling the Army of the Potomac

On July 27, 1861, George Brinton McClellan inherited a poorly trained army and an inefficient command structure in desperate need of reorganization. Generally, the rank and file were not defeatists, but some malcontents roamed the streets of the nation's capital. The new commander accepted the challenge to retool, reshape, and reorganize his Army of the Potomac. The Ellithorpe brothers embraced the reforms of "Little Mac," and they gradually developed into effective soldiers after long hours of daily drills and frequent inspections at the company, regiment, brigade, and division levels. Live encounters with the enemy also occurred while on picket duty and one engagement that made national headlines. The Federal recruitment push in the aftermath of Bull Run would add a volunteer from Cattaraugus County, New York, a character of great importance to the family. Although the three "boys" worked in "bombproof jobs" as orderly, commissary clerk, cook, and musician, these tasks did not protect them from a most dangerous enemy—disease. Yet, by the next spring, they were ready, willing, and able to face the Confederate army to test their mettle.

McClellan's first act called for the restoration of order in Washington, and he made two appointments to achieve this goal. First, he chose Brig. Gen. Andrew Porter to serve as provost marshal with instructions to put an end to the mayhem in the streets. Second, he selected Brig. Gen. Silas Casey to supervise the instruction of inexperienced lower-grade officers by instilling ways to establish military discipline in the ranks and educating the civilian officers in the art of military drills.[1]

Phillip

Although Biddle's campaign in western Maryland and Virginia was limited in scope, it provided the strict disciplinarian with an opportunity to drill his green outfit. The field experience had also offered "valuable practical experience" to the 5th and 13th Pennsylvania Reserves. Then, on July 27, Biddle's force suddenly broke camp and retraced their steps to Harrisburg. Rumors circulated among the Pennsylvanians in light of McDowell's rout at Bull Run that the federal government was finally amenable to absorbing all fifteen regiments recruited from the Keystone State. Indeed, during the aftermath of hostilities in Manassas, the War Department had pulled six of McCall's regiments from Harrisburg to defend Washington. In the meantime, Curtin lobbied successfully to ensure that all Pennsylvanians would enter Federal service as one division under the command of McCall. But many Pennsylvanians feared that the Confederates might follow up their shocking victory and march on the North. To address the latter concern, Biddle was recalled from his distant outpost.[2]

On July 31, the Bucktails returned to the state capital but in an agitated frame of mind. The lack of pay, uniforms, adequate food, tents, and the latest model of rifles caused grousing and permeated every company. Several other unresolved issues fueled the soldier's discontent. The men were dirty and ill clad from living outdoors for more than a month, and the summer heat and humidity added to their discomfort and lowly personal hygiene. While drafting a letter, Phillip noted that "the flies are so thick and they bother me." A near riot was narrowly averted after hundreds of disobedient soldiers from various regiments bathed in the Susquehanna River within sight of Front Street. The mayor closed down a popular saloon, and the governor called out the 12th Pennsylvania Reserves to maintain order.[3]

Another issue centered on the eagerness of the ninety-day enlistees to be paid before they were scheduled for discharge the following day. Staying out of the discussion, Phillip boasted to his parents that he planned to have his photograph taken as soon as he received his dress blues, but he, too, complained about not receiving a sharpshooter's musket. He had also been returned to "the comesary."[4]

On August 1, Curtin scheduled an inspection of the Bucktails. Biddle's soldiers did not disappoint the large civilian crowd in a flawless demonstration of the manual of arms and precise responses to Kane's unique bugle call commands. One week later, the bulk of McCall's division reported to Tenallytown, a neighborhood in northwest Washington, to formalize its organization and continue to train[5]—but not the all-Philadelphia 2nd Pennsylvania Reserves or 13th Pennsylvania Reserves; instead, these two regiments were detached and sent to the Shenandoah Department commanded by Brig. Gen. Nathaniel P. Banks, who was currently stationed on the north bank of the Potomac River across from Harpers Ferry.[6]

On August 14, McClellan scheduled the first grand review of the Army of the Potomac with President Lincoln in attendance. Regrettably, Phillip and the Bucktails were privy to neither this morale-building pageant in Washington nor the formal acceptance of McCall's Pennsylvania Reserves into Federal service. Instead, the 13th Pennsylvania Reserves bivouacked in Sandy Hook, Maryland, for nearly two months, where they were normally confined to camp because of the hostility their presence elicited from local citizens. Their status as a federal entity still remained in doubt.[7]

One exception to the quarantine order occurred on August 17, when the Bucktails were sent on special assignment to Hyattstown, Maryland. There, more than 200 members of the 19th New York demanded their immediate discharge on the grounds that they had served more than their ninety-day obligation. The War Department was equally adamant that they convert to the new standard length of enlistment—two years. The 1st Rifles guarded the mutinous New Yorkers at the point of a bayonet, but a serious outcome was averted when twenty-three ringleaders were arrested and sent to the Dry Tortugas.[8]

Phillip was beginning to adjust to military life. He understood the dangers posed in the regiment's assignment in Piedmont, and he began to verbalize a stronger martial spirit. In Harrisburg, he had asked Kane to release him from his duties as orderly "because I could not fight in a Battle and it was very confining for me to stay in Camp when the rest of our Company was out fighting."[9] He wanted to prove his bravery and loyalty by toting a rifle in defense of his country. At the same time, Phillip sought to alleviate his family's anxieties about the current hazards he faced. "Tell mother not to worry about me," Phillip cheered to Ann. "I am fat and as tough as a bear and I am going to fight like a tiger when I get a chance . . . [and] distance cannot change the heart," he concluded.[10] Phillip enclosed "an artifact," a wooden sliver from the scaffold on which John Brown had been hanged. Such relics helped soldiers to place themselves in the historical moment and signify their manly resolve to see the war through to its conclusion.

On August 29, the Bucktails were directed to Darnestown, Maryland, to guard the Chesapeake and Ohio Canal as well as two major turnpikes. They spent an idyllic month in "Camp Union," where Clow's commissary built a brick oven to bake soft bread. Phillip enjoyed the natural surroundings while encamped in a pine grove. "Thar is plenty of squrrels and Partiges in the Woods," he exclaimed, "and plenty of eels in the Creek which makes it very pleasant."[11] The war seemed far away, and Phillip was starting to adapt to his new life by mastering the art of scavenging.

Ever since the Bucktails had been recruited, McCall, Biddle, and Kane had known that some of their companies were substantially less than the army's regulation of 101 men. When Banks inspected his command, he deemed that half of the companies in the 2nd Pennsylvania were deficient in manpower and recommended to disband them, sending a shock wave through the 13th Pennsylvania Reserves. In response to this situation, Bell and Haffey (Phillip's messmate) left immediately for McKean County to conduct a second round of recruitment. Together, they signed up 120 new enlistees, increasing the fighting force of the 13th Pennsylvania Reserves to an acceptable level of 960 men. Company I grew to 126 men. "Three cheers for the Wild cat or Buck Tail company," shouted Phillip as he welcomed a familiar Smethportian, Thomas Barnes, the brother of Joe.[12]

Philander

In the aftermath of Bull Run, Philander and the 27th New York reached the safety of "Camp Anderson" on Franklin Square. Their nerves were severely shaken, and a medical inspection of New York enlisted men in late July concluded that one-third of them suffered from demoralization. Philander noted that some reluctant warriors were taking French leave in his regiment, while others suffered from fevers and an outbreak of diarrhea. He was also opinionated about the rumored extension of service to three years. "It is . . . too much to expect," complained the Alleganian to his sister. With military exercises temporarily suspended, the 27th New York spent many nights guarding Franklin Square, Chain Bridge, and newly constructed installations and foraging across the Potomac River.[13]

When the war first broke out, Brig. Gen. Joseph K. Mansfield had assumed command of the Department of Washington and set out to create a defensive network around the city, including its bridges and main roadway approaches. Mansfield was particularly concerned to occupy Alexandria and Arlington Heights, Virginia, in order to keep Confederate batteries from setting up there and shelling the city. Along with chief engineer Barnard, Mansfield personally supervised the erection of six fortifications on three main arterials that crossed the Potomac River at three principal bridges—Chain, Long, and Aqueduct. His efforts ultimately produced an intricate system of forty-eight forts, earthworks, and battery installations along a thirty-seven-mile ring around the capital.[14]

In mid-August, the 27th New York was temporarily detached to provide labor under the direction of Barnard to complete a timber and earthworks fortification that had been started before the battle of Bull Run. Fort Ellsworth, a large installation west of Alexandria, sat atop high ground with a sweeping vista to the south. Its twenty-seven cannon controlled the approaches to the Orange & Alexandria Railroad and Little River Turnpike. Once they wrapped up construction on August 26, McClellan reviewed his pick-shovel-and-ax regiment and then reassigned them to a new project south of Hunting Creek. The appearance of the paymaster and issuance of new Springfield rifles boosted the spirits of Philander and his calloused comrades.[15]

The 27th New York spent several weeks on Ballenger's Hill cutting down "magnificent oaks" on the estate of George Mason and clearing thick underbrush for a new post. Fort Lyon was one of the largest in the system with a 937-yard perimeter and nine-acre enclosure. Abatis and rifle pits ringed the outer walls, giving the appearance of invincibility. The fort's thirty-one cannon and sixteen mortars overlooked Telegraph Road, Columbia Pike, Little River Turnpike, and the Orange & Alexandria Railroad.[16]

The 27th New York finished Fort Lyon in only one month despite battling an outbreak of typhoid fever. The fortress was a showplace of military engineering and anchored the extreme left of the capital's defensive line. For several months, Fort Lyon would become home to the 27th New York and four other regiments from the Empire State. Philander took pride in the massive accomplishment, but he also lamented that comrades were misbehaving under the influence of alcohol. The teetotaler "wished justice would come here and rain on this Camp. it would be so plisant," he confided to Ann.[17]

Burleson Family Background

Asa R. Burleson's ancestry followed paths similar to those of the Ellithorpe–Griggs–Stebbins clan. Edward Burleson had been part of the second wave of Puritan colonists arriving in New England in the 1650s in the turbulent aftermath of the English Civil War. He had established himself in Suffield, Massachusetts (later Connecticut). A flax dresser by trade, Edward eventually owned a forty-acre tobacco estate along the Connecticut River, and three generations of his progeny farmed in the region into the 1740s. A strict Congregationalist, Edward is recognized as the patriarch of the Burleson line in America, which eventually split into northern and southern branches. After the American Revolution, a large contingent of northern Burlesons departed for the northwest corner of Vermont, where they established a large enclave in Franklin County communities such as Fairfield, East and West Berkshire, Sheldon, and Franklin.[18] But, as the land played out, Asa's grandparents followed some of their neighbors from Pownal, Vermont, to "the howling wilderness" of West Burlington, Otsego County, New York.

In 1824, Asa's father, Owens, married Mary Bedell of Junius, New York. Seeking a fresh start, the newlyweds opted to push into the alluring Genesee Country. Although the best farmland had already been scooped up in the northern tier, there was still a decent amount of affordable acreage available in the timbered southern tier. The village and township of Freedom, located in the northeast corner of Cattaraugus County, suited them. In 1828, Owens and Mary purchased thirty-five acres on lot 37 in Range 3.[19]

Owens built a house and a sawmill next to Clear Creek on the road between Freedom and Sandusky, a perfect location for the aspiring carpenter and millwright. In time, Burleson Pond became a well-known fixture for locals. Here, Asa was born on September 4, 1831.

The Formative Years of Asa R. Burleson

Asa received an academy education in nearby China (today Arcade), New York. In 1855, he left Freedom and taught at Franklin Academy in Franklin, Vermont, where he was surrounded by a multitude of uncles, aunts, and cousins. But the studious Asa was also drawn to read law at the firm of Fitch and Newton in Highgate, Vermont. Then, in 1858, the collector and inspector of customs for the Port of Burlington tendered him an appointment as a deputy customs agent. Asa's selection reflected the political importance of the Burleson name in northwestern Vermont. One year later, he passed the Vermont bar exam but chose to remain in his civil service post. Based on future correspondence, Asa had courted Ann Ellithorpe in the mid-1850s, but his marriage proposal had been rejected.[20]

War Clouds in Vermont

In the summer of 1861, Asa had been monitoring military developments in Virginia from his post as deputy customs agent in Burlington. Post–Bull Run recruitment was taking place at a blistering pace throughout the Granite State, and the thirty-year-old Asa heeded the president's second call for manpower just as Thomas Barnes had done in Pennsylvania.

A native Vermonter and career officer trained at West Point, Brig. Gen. William Farrar "Baldy" Smith envisioned the creation of an all-Vermont brigade similar to the all-Pennsylvania division being fashioned by McCall. In response to Lincoln's proclamation and Smith's declaration, the 5th Vermont was formed largely from communities in the northwestern corner of the state. Asa affixed his name to the three-year roster in Burlington. On September 15, a twenty-piece band welcomed the volunteers to the staging grounds in Smith's hometown, St. Albans. The next day, they shipped out to the nation's capital with little fanfare and with no formal military training. Urgent times called for urgent actions.[21]

On September 25, after making two transfers to railcars and linking up with a steamship, the 5th Vermont arrived in Washington. They spent two days at Soldier's Rest, a reception center where each enlistee drew the standard government issue of a dark blue jacket, blouse, cap, light blue pair of pants, haversack, cartridge box, a pair of heavy black shoes derisively referred to as "gunboats," and an Enfield Rifle. Col. Henry A. Smalley was selected to lead the 5th Vermont.

Originally commissioned as "state principal musician" and drill master, Asa was reassigned to Company F & S (Field & Staff) as chief drum major at the rank of lieutenant.[22]

Colonel Henry A. Smalley, 5th Vermont.
SOURCE: CIVIL WAR PHOTOGRAPHS, 1861–1865, LIBRARY OF CONGRESS, PRINTS AND PHOTOGRAPHS DIVISION.

In the early days of the war, musicians were recognized as an integral part of the military experience. Drum, bugle, and fife bands had been highly visible entertainers at most recruiting stations, and they were deemed essential to soldier morale in camp. In battle, the sounds of these three instruments signaled the infantry into formation and set the cadence for marches. Although musicians were technically noncombatants, they provided valuable service by removing the wounded from the field. Furthermore, they often expressed military élan and patriotic ardor. For instance, one fifer in Burleson's company, Jonathan Remington, heaped violent epithets on the enemy, wishing the "rebbels burn in hell," and hoped his 5th Vermont would "vomet death and destruction" on the Confederacy.[23]

On receiving their equipage, Asa and his fellow Vermonters in "the Old Brigade" moved to an outpost near Lewinsville, Virginia, to guard the road leading to Chain Bridge. Here, at Camp Advance, they spent the autumn and winter learning military drills, cutting down trees, and standing on picket duty. The site was renamed Camp Griffin.[24]

Home

In early August, Philander received a message from Ann about Mother's illness, but his reply neglected to mention specific details about her condition or its seriousness. One month later, the Ellithorpe brothers acknowledged guarded optimism from home that she was showing signs of improvement.[25]

Then bucktailed Capt. Leander Weaver Gifford of Company C delivered a message to Phillip that Mother had taken a turn for the worse. The distraught private immediately asked Kane for a furlough to go home, but the Bucktails were currently preparing to unite with McCall's division in Tenallytown. "I wondered if I should go home to see her on Earth," stated Phillip in desperation. "I was afraid I would not and had resolved to act in such a way as to meet her in Heaven . . . and we might all meet her thar." Then the gut-wrenching news arrived: Mother had passed away on September 13.[26]

"I had lost the best friend in the world," Phillip wailed in disbelief. In an effort to comprehend his deep sense of loss, the eighteen-year-old second-guessed his decision to enlist away from home and fretted that, somehow, he had "caused her sickness" to worsen. He showed sincere compassion for his father, too, concluding that her passing away "will allmost kill him."[27]

Phillip coped with the death of Mother in a most heartfelt way. In the first of several poems and songs he would send to Ann during the war, Phillip enclosed a slightly altered version of "Faded Flowers," a popular parlor song written in 1851. Phillip's version, titled "Gone Home," was a touching tribute to his recently deceased mother:

The flowers I Saw in the wildwood
Have since dropped there beautiful leave
And that Mother I left in my childhood
Now slumbers alone in her grave

But the bloom on the flowers I remember
Though their smiles I may never more see
For the cool gentle breese of September
Has stole my dear Mother from me
The roses may bloom on the morrow
And the many dear friends I have won
But my heart can part with but sorrow
For I know my dear Mother has gone

Tis no wonder that I'm broken hearted
And stricken with sorrow should be
We have lived we have loved but have parted
My Mother my sisters and me.

How dark looks this world and how dreary
When we think of the ones that we love
But theres rest for the faint and the weary
And friends meet with lost ones above.

Phillip later purchased the sheet music and enjoyed singing this ballad, an activity that brought him some degree of comfort. The sentimentality and emotionalism of the lyrics revealed how deeply hurt and vulnerable the young Bucktail was over the death of Mother. It is not an overstatement to say that the event forever changed him.[28]

Phillip was fortunate to be surrounded by sympathetic and consoling battle buddies, particularly "Brother Haffey" and Joe Barnes, who were especially touched by his sorrow. "I have many friends here who take an interest in my welfare," admitted Phillip. "For the past week I have sent up many thoughts Praise to God that I might be cleansed and be pure and holy I feel as though my Prayers had been answered. I have felt better," he concluded with religious conviction. But, under the stressful circumstances, Phillip implored Ann not to worry about him: "be of good cheer your brother will come out at the top of his beef. . . . I love to carry [a gun] in this case especially," he added. "I feel more as though I should like to Die in the Battle Field than ever."[29] A certain fatalistic tone had filtered into Phillip's lines, counter to his usual cheerfulness.

The death of Fannie struck Philander like a thunderbolt, too. In fact, Philander was more than a little miffed because Ann had taken more than two weeks to relay the information. By the time Philander received the tragic news, his mother had already been laid to rest in Rushford Cemetery, within sight of the Ellithorpe house on Lewellen Street. Feeling helpless and homesick for being so far away from home, he chastised Father, Mary, Permelia, and cousin Edwin (Stebbins) for failing to respond to any of his recent missives. Philander admittedly struggled to find appropriate words to convey his grief and apologized to Ann for not writing sooner. He "did not know how to begin," he apologized. Philander closed with a curious request to share the family's bad news with Asa R. Burleson.[30]

Prior to hearing from Philander, Asa had begun composing a letter to Ann on October 9. "For God sake, why don't your write?" the drum major pleaded. He apologized for not traveling to Rushford prior to his enlistment, claiming that, afterward, he had been denied a furlough. Asa took exception to Ann's blunt accusations that he had acted selfishly and lacked devotion and affection toward her. "I have five hundred men to make into Soldiers," he quipped.[31] Asa demanded, "How and where have I ever given cause for Suspicion or doubt . . . your doubts are without foundation."[32] Asa reminded Ann that "many years ago I asked for the right to be always with you," but his proposal had been rebuffed. Clearly, a degree of insecurity on the part of Ann and oversensitivity on the part of Asa had driven a wedge between the couple.[33]

Asa's frustration softened the next day when he finally received a missive from Ann. Its contents revealed the death of Fannie. "Oh how joyful my heart bounded at the sight of the precious messenger [postman]," exclaimed Asa on receiving word from Ann. "And tears filled my eyes ere I broke the seal. . . . [and] how my heart saddened when I read the Sad news which you had written. Gladly would I have flown to you had it been possible to soothe your heart and Share your Sorrows, but now I have the pain of thinking that you, my heart's idol, is in grief."[34] Clearly, Asa still loved Ann.

Foraging

In late September and early October, Asa's 5th Vermont ventured into enemy territory in search of firewood and provisions. The environs of Camp Griffin were plentiful, and the Vermonters prided themselves in plundering nearby plantations of hogs, chickens, ripe corn, and hay. The Yankees not only were astonished at the bountiful harvests but also marveled at seeing slave huts and contrabands for the first time.

Likewise, Philander explained to Ann that the 27th New York often crossed the Potomac River and foraged as far south as Mount Vernon. Despite warnings from officers, they pillaged and looted the properties of wealthy southern sympathizers. One night on picket duty, Philander stole a pail of milk and some potatoes. On another occasion, he witnessed the ransacking of "Dr. Mason's" plantation house, including the theft of the "famus Rebels" piano by another regiment. While on yet another reconnaissance, the 16th and 27th New York jointly looted the farm of John A. Washington, confiscating several hundred bushels of wheat and corn and a team of fine horses. Several other raids on local plantations netted large quantities of herring, cattle, and smokehouse hams.[35]

5th Vermont at Camp Griffin.
SOURCE: CIVIL WAR PHOTOGRAPHS, 1861–1865, LIBRARY OF CONGRESS, PRINTS AND PHOTOGRAPHS DIVISION (GEORGE HARPER HOUGHTON).

The living conditions of Asa and Philander were strikingly different. Philander's 27th New York benefited from the comforts of Fort Lyon, "the grandest camping ground the regiment ever occupied," claimed one comrade. From its lofty elevation, the soldiers could see the Capitol's dome and many vessels plying the Potomac River. Asa's Camp Griffin, in contrast, was not desirably situated. Located on Smoot's Hill, the Vermont Brigade had to cope with "nightly alarms" of Confederates infiltrating their lines, and the frequency of picket and fatigue duty had fostered "a nostalgic element" among the men. Spongy soil became contaminated, which caused "an extraordinary amount of sickness" in camp.[36]

Crisis and Rebirth in Tenallytown

On September 25, the Bucktails rejoined McCall's division in Tenallytown, but they were still in a foul mood. Basically, the 13th Pennsylvania Reserves had been paid only once since being deployed to western Virginia, and those funds had been authorized by Curtin and the Commonwealth of Pennsylvania. Biddle immediately requisitioned a federal paymaster to provide three months of back pay for his regiment, but he was refused. The army clerk could find no record showing their date of muster. His only accommodation was to send for a superior officer to formally administer the oath of allegiance and officially register them. Incensed, Biddle threatened to return the Bucktails to Harrisburg and disband if they were not compensated. Only the intervention of Cameron and the War Department staved off a full-scale mutiny. In this manner, the 42nd Pennsylvania was duly born. History would remember them by their more colorful nicknames—the 1st Rifles, Kane's Rifles, and the Bucktails.[37]

On October 9, McCall's fully restored Pennsylvania Reserves, led by the 1st Rifles, crossed Chain Bridge into Virginia to the strains of "Dixie's Land." They halted near Langley, Virginia, and set up a new headquarters called Camp Pierpont.[38]

Repositioning the Pennsylvania Reserves to Camp Pierpont, the Old Brigade of Vermonters to Camp Griffin, and the 27th New York to Fort Lyon suggests that McClellan was planning an action on the upper Potomac River northwest of the capital. On October 19, McCall was ordered to make a reconnaissance to Dranesville, Virginia, about twelve miles southeast of Leesburg, as part of a larger demonstration at Edwards Ferry in order to test Confederate resolve. Phillip's regiment investigated, discovered that Dranesville was deserted, and were recalled to Camp Pierpont. The other Federal force at Ball's Bluff was not so fortunate.[39]

Phillip: Winter Quarters and Illness

From the end of October until March 1862, the lives of the Phillip, Philander, and Asa followed a predictable routine. Their activities revolved around trying to stay warm and dry, dealing with sickness, foraging, participating in dress reviews, and fighting in one stiff skirmish that attracted national attention.

On one frosty autumn morning shortly after the battle of Ball's Bluff, "Little Mac" reviewed McCall's Pennsylvanians at Camp Pierpont. For weeks, the weather had been unseasonably warm during the day, but nighttime temperatures dipped, causing considerable discomfort. A relentless taskmaster, Biddle continued to exercise his regiment several times per day (except Sunday) and conducted numerous inspections on the parade ground per army regulations despite the arrival of steady rainfall in November. Not surprising, exposure to these conditions resulted in outbreaks of typhoid fever, pneumonia, diarrhea, dysentery, and measles; one-tenth of the Army of the Potomac was listed on sick call.[40]

Hospitalized twice during training camp, Phillip was now placed on sick call two more times in late August and October. At this time, the 1st Rifles accounted for the largest percentage of sickness in the Pennsylvania Reserves. Claiming to be "very sick," Phillip received visits in the hospital from a host of comrades. Philander and some hometown friends from the 27th New York stopped by to make him a bowl of "grule." Of course, messmates Haffey and the Barnes brothers were frequently present at his bedside, too. Clergyman-Sgt. Haffey wrote to Ann, explaining that "the Drum Major of the 5th Vermont" had "never been absent from his [Phillip's] cot." Philander confirmed Phillip's illnesses but made an important observation, saying that his younger brother was "a good soldier."[41] Roll call records indicate that Phillip made productive use of his time in the hospital as a cook and nurse, but these numerous trips to "Company Q" were raising questions about his physical and mental well-being.

At his lowest point in mid-November, Phillip applied for a medical discharge, but Blanchard denied his request. Instead, the captain ordered Phillip to return to Company I. He rationalized the rejection to one sweetheart: "I don't think I should enjoy myself much away from war."[42]

Meanwhile, one of Phillip's visitors in the hospital had been the newly appointed director of subsistence for McCall's three-brigade division. Recall that Phillip had worked sporadically under Clow in the first commissary system at Camp Curtin and after Bull Run. Now, Clow extended a generous offer to Phillip, a "pleasant" clerk's position with "light" duties in the massive food distribution center. The debilitated soldier would have his own bunk in a warm and dry building out of the winter weather. Clow insisted that Blanchard must sign off on this arrangement, however.[43]

Phillip was discharged from the hospital, but rather than returning to Camp Pierpont, he convalesced with Asa. But the location of his recovery at Camp Griffin was ill advised. At that moment, the Vermont Brigade had nearly one-fourth of its men incapacitated by illness, and the 5th Vermont led the way with 250 men out of action. The regiment posted the highest ratio of illness in the entire Army of the Potomac until February 1862. The principal culprit was measles. Thus, it was not surprising when Asa caught the contagious disease, too.[44]

Phillip was granted a pass to visit Philander at Fort Lyon to regain his strength, but the young Bucktail would not be healthy enough for active duty for some time. Despite his slow recovery, Phillip's physical energy and mental outlook improved markedly as the Christmas season approached. He greatly appreciated the "nut cakes and cheese box" sent by Ann, and he generously shared these holiday treats with the Barnes brothers and Clow, who deemed them "first rate." Such packages, normally about the size of a shoe box, were delivered to soldiers in the field by the Adams Express Company. Generally, these care boxes were filled with much-needed clothing items, such as woolen or cotton shirts and socks (depending on the season), gloves, and boots, as well as fresh fruits, sweets, and money. It was not uncommon for parcels to be damaged, opened, or even stolen, as was, unfortunately, the case for Phillip on several occasions. A special guest, Curtin, arrived on Christmas Day to inspect the Pennsylvania Reserves and offer remarks of holiday cheer.[45]

In winter quarters, Phillip spent a great deal of leisure time with acquaintances in the 27th, 33rd, and 64th New York. These units were sprinkled with hometown pals. The amount of interregimental networking within the Army of the Potomac was truly remarkable. Asa commented during a visit to the Ellithorpe brothers how glad he was "to see thar I [Phillip] was a favorite among the Boys." As Phillip gradually regained his strength, Philander took him on a tour of Washington, where they visited the unfinished Capitol building. As the New Year approached, it was time for Phillip to get back to work. But a problem arose.[46]

Clow had lost patience waiting for Phillip to report to the commissary and wrote out his discharge papers. The prospect of going home tempted Phillip, but the director rescinded the order at Phillip's request and promised him instead a furlough to visit Rushford in February. The timing of Phillip's return to Camp Pierpont was impeccable, as cold rain and snow struck the Army of the Potomac, and the nasty weather did not abate until March. Mud clung to everything, and Phillip complained that the goo was ten inches deep in places, which made walking and travel by wagon difficult.[47]

The 13th Pennsylvania Reserves personalized their sector of Camp Pierpont, naming it Bucktail City. The men constructed small log dwellings covered with a shelter tent. Company streets were decorated with cedar boughs, but green firewood filled the damp air with thick clouds of smoke. The men passed the time playing cards, writing letters, and inventing games for entertainment. Once, a snowball fight broke out between Companies A and G. Catching rabbits bare-handed was another popular diversion to the dreary days.[48]

Philander: Winter Quarters and Drudgery

Perhaps the least favorite activity in winter camp was the loneliness associated with picket duty. "Thare we sit," Philander explained to Ann, "hour after hour watching while our mind wanders back to the friends we have left behind. I sometimes wonder if this is war."[49] In mid-October, the 27th New York and Slocum's brigade were reassigned to Fairfax Station. The amount of picket duty increased dramatically to four straight twenty-four-hour shifts every sixteen days. Once, Philander and his Company I chums took residence in an abandoned plantation with four fireplaces. These solitary moments on the edge of the Federal army's extreme right flank provided opportunities for introspection, too. "I have thought more of my Future life and the life after death and I hardly know what to think," he told Ann. "I hope the Lord will teach me and enable me to see . . . write me a long letter full of god."[50] Philander ached for some words of comfort from home.

Philander accepted a new position as cook and orderly for the captain of Company I, Harmon. It meant extra pay, but three months later, he sang a different tune regarding his culinary responsibilities. "Women's work is never done," complained the disgruntled cook, "and I am tired of it."[51] His dissatisfaction grew when his workload increased to drawing rations for Company I and dividing the portions among the men. On a personal note, Philander mentioned making the acquaintance of a candy peddler from Elmira, a person of future importance to the Ellithorpe family. Philander's "season of inactivity" was interrupted only by special details to cut down trees to make corduroy roads in camp.[52]

The Grand Review

In the winter of 1861–1862, rain, snow, and mud might have dampened the Ellithorpes' spirits, but they experienced morale-building activities in the Army of the Potomac, too. Perhaps the greatest example was the Grand Review held at Bailey's Crossroads. On November 20, McClellan invited President Lincoln and several members of his cabinet to inspect the troops. An estimated civilian crowd of 20,000 came out to witness the spectacle despite the cold weather and muddy grounds. Seven divisions comprising more than 75,000 soldiers formed a four-mile-long semicircle standing at attention as the president conducted his inspection. McCall placed his colorful Bucktails at the head of the Pennsylvania Reserves.[53]

The pageantry of the Grand Review and the pride it generated was not lost on the rank and file. Philander complimented the appearance of Kane's Rifles, "a smart regiment" that had made a favorable impression on everyone in attendance. Clearly, the Pennsylvanians were one of the most recognizable units in the entire formation because of its uniquely decorated kepis. Philander also praised the good account of "the Vermont Brigade," which "made the green mountain state proud." As for himself, Philander "had the Pleasure of dofing my hat to Old Abe and George B. Mc." After the event, he told Ann, "My courage is strong."[54]

Photographs in the form of *carte de visites* helped to improve morale of soldiers on the battle front and family members on the home front. While stationed in western Virginia, Phillip had had a likeness taken and sent home. Then, when the 13th Pennsylvania Reserves received its official designation as the 42nd Pennsylvania, he sat for a second portrait in his new blue uniform. The only surviving image of Phillip was captured at Camp Griffin, however, when he substituted for a sick fifer in Asa's drum corps. With the battle flag of the 5th Vermont serving as a backdrop, with its two concentric

Drum and fife band of the 5th Vermont at Camp Griffin.
SOURCE: CIVIL WAR PHOTOGRAPHS, 1861–1865, LIBRARY OF CONGRESS, PRINTS AND PHOTOGRAPHS DIVISION (GEORGE HARPER HOUGHTON).

circles of stars and a single star in the middle, Phillip's bucktail-adorned visage is clearly visible in the center of the front row. On the receiving end, Phillip shared a photo of Ann with his comrades, who admired the "smart looking woman."[55] The Ellithorpe sisters were justifiably proud of their soldier-brothers and vice versa.

Leadership Changes Affecting the Ellithorpes

Neither of the Ellithorpe brothers seemed particularly fazed by army politics, although they often mentioned by name their leaders at the regimental level. Beginning in early November, three important changes occurred at the highest levels of the army that would have an impact on the lowliest enlisted men. First, McClellan succeeded Scott as general in chief, a decision widely applauded by rank-and-file soldiers. Second, Edwin McMasters Stanton was chosen to replace Cameron at the War Department in January 1862. Together, Lincoln and Stanton would push an ambitious timetable to set the Union armies in motion. Third, the Army of the Potomac was reshaped in March into four corps because of its sheer size. The creation of this new organizational model promised to streamline top-to-bottom decisions and improve the performance of the entire army.[56]

On December 12, Biddle suddenly resigned his commission from the Bucktails to take his seat in Congress, representing his home district in Philadelphia. A regimental election was scheduled for mid-January to select his replacement, and the leading choice, Kane, assumed temporary command and awaited results from the election. Then a spirit of military action interrupted regimental politics.[57]

Dranesville

A week later, the Bucktails played a significant role in a larger engagement at a small crossroads village twelve miles from Camp Pierpont. The skirmish was initiated in response to rumors that Rebel cavalryman J. E. B. Stuart was leading a sizable foraging force toward Dranesville on the extreme right flank of the Army of the Potomac. In response, McCall ordered a brigade of Pennsylvania Reserves under Brig. Gen. E. O. C. Ord to reconnoiter the area. Kane's 1st Rifles were detached to act as advance skirmishers. The rumors turned out to be correct. On the frosty morning of December 20, the Federals approached Dranesville from the east on Alexandria Pike, and Stuart's advance horsemen opened fire from a concealed position behind a tree line. The Bucktails found themselves exposed on the extreme left flank.[58]

When the shooting began, Ord feared the enemy's cavalry would attempt to outflank Kane's Rifles and capture his only section of artillery. Indeed, both sides exchanged artillery rounds of grape and canister, and three Confederate regiments had extended beyond the left of Kane. Frantically, Kane dispatched Companies E and I under the combined command of Capt. Alanson E. Niles to double-quick at the left oblique across Centreville Pike, take possession of a brick house, and defend the position to anchor the Yankees' left wing. An intense firefight ensued, and Hezekiah Easton's battery lent significant support. The entire engagement lasted less than two hours, and Rebel resistance broke after Kane ordered a fixed bayonet charge.[59]

The blue-clads' victory at Dranesville was, in large part, because of Kane's heroics. Ord's command inflicted four times more casualties than Stuart's Virginians, captured sixteen wagons of hay and twenty-two wagons of corn, and held the field while the enemy skedaddled. But the victory came at a cost—7k/61w/3m. Kane suffered a painful wound to the roof of his mouth, and Niles was shot during the assault to secure the brick house. Quite understandably, the 1st Rifles accounted for almost half of the fatalities (three) and wounded (twenty-six). Not only was the engagement at Dranesville "the first measurable victory for the Army of the Potomac," but its favorable result had also captured the attention of the northern press, which was thirsting to report on *any* Federal victory.[60]

Phillip was still recovering with Philander at Fairfax Station when the Bucktails saw their first major action, but it did not prevent him from sharing secondhand battlefield stories. Writing to Friend Nell and his sisters, Phillip regretted his absence from the field of glory. "I am sorry to say that I was not thare," he admitted. Phillip shared news of the injuries to Kane and Niles and described the bravado of his old tent mate. The standout performance of Joe Barnes was "distinguished for Coolness and bravery while the enemy were briskly upon us," he reported. When Kane had ordered the bayonet charge, Barnes sprinted ahead of the Bucktails and took cover behind a stump. Seeing a parlay of Confederate officers partially hidden behind some trees, Barnes took careful aim and felled one of them. "Joe was loudly cheered by all" when he retired to his company, establishing his reputation as a brave soldier.[61]

In the month leading up to his return to the commissary shortly before January 6, Phillip's letters confirm his Christmas season wanderlust. In addition to visiting friends in other New York regiments, he made time to stay with Philander at Fairfax Station (December 22 and 27) and with Asa at Camp Griffin (November 13 and December 31). He had also reappeared with the Bucktails (December 8 and 26). When Phillip finally reported to Clow at the commissary, he penned an interesting self-assessment of his evolving role in army life. Basically, he conceded to "playing soldier" and "peddling beef." "I have very good times here in the Commissary," Phillip chimed. "I have as good a Bed as I wish for."[62] But he also confessed to speculating on his earnings, buying high-demand items, such as matches, watches, and newspapers, and reselling them to the men. In his black market shenanigans, Phillip often netted $17 per week, and Clow locked his growing nest egg in the commissary safe.[63]

Election

After the Bucktails had returned to Camp Pierpont, partisanship about the vacant colonelcy dominated the conversation throughout the month of January. Some soldiers openly distrusted Kane's battlefield judgment in western Virginia and Dranesville, alleging that he took unnecessary risks. Kane remained extremely popular in the companies he had recruited in northwestern Pennsylvania, however, and Phillip predicted his victory. But a serious challenger emerged.

Capt. Hugh Watson McNeil of Company D was a college-educated banker and lawyer whose calm and contemplative demeanor resonated with many Bucktails in contrast to the more impulsive Kane. When the ballots were counted on January 22, McNeil garnered 223 more votes than Kane in a resounding upset. Phillip was usually apolitical in his letters, but the outcome of the McNeil–Kane campaign and election had rankled him. "You have no doubt heard of the election of Captain McNeel over Kane," Phillip told his sisters and father in disgust. "The men feel bad."[64] The election results drew attention to a potential rift between those companies hailing from the Wildcat District of northwestern Pennsylvania and those recruited from the urban centers of eastern Pennsylvania. Kane retained his rank as second in command of the 1st Rifles.

Captain/Colonel Hugh W. McNeil, Company D, 13th Pennsylvania Reserves, 13th Pennsylvania Reserves. *SOURCE:* CIVIL WAR PHOTO COLLECTION, UNITED STATES ARMY HERITAGE AND EDUCATION CENTER, CARLISLE, PENNSYLVANIA.

Prepping for the Spring Campaign

In an attempt to prod McClellan to put his Army of the Potomac in motion and raise soldier morale, President Lincoln called for every regiment to assemble on February 22 and listen to a reading of George Washington's Farewell Address to the troops. As it turned out, the event had a second purpose—to celebrate the Union victories of Brig. Gen. Ulysses S. Grant at Forts Henry and Donelson in Tennessee. "We are having very good news," Phillip exclaimed to Ann. "Thare was loud cheering when we read [in *Frank Leslie's Illustrated*] . . . about the capture of Fort Donelson." After the regiments were dismissed, Phillip and Asa were treated to a large party at their respective campsites. The carnival-like celebrations included foot and sack races, a greased pig scramble, and "a rousing game of ball." These recreational activities signaled the end of winter camp and the resumption of campaigning. Caught up in the euphoria, Phillip bragged to his sisters in several missives that "this Rebellion will be crushed . . . by the 4th of July."[65]

The Urbanna Plan

McClellan was hard at work in February 1862 perfecting his plan for an amphibious assault on Richmond. His scheme called for transporting his

100,000-man army down Chesapeake Bay and fifteen miles up the Rappahannock River to a small town on the south bank. Known as the Urbanna Plan, the campaign required a diversion on the upper Potomac in March 1862 to remove the Confederate presence and secure the right flank of the Army of the Potomac. The Ellithorpe brothers had become weary of wet weather over months of sedentary living. They yearned for action. In accordance with McClellan's timetable, the 13th Pennsylvania Reserves, 27th New York, and 5th Vermont swung into motion with their respective corps on March 10.[66]

At the appointed hour, McCall led his Pennsylvania Reserves to Hunter Mill, eighteen miles away. A cold drizzle dampened the spirits of the marchers, and the latest issue of equipment—oil cloth raincoats—were ineffective throughout the ten-day show of force. The poncho-like design was intended to double as a tent while in the field. A significant number of Pennsylvanians straggled, however, and sarcastically dubbed their new destination "Smoky Hollow." Some nabbed plump chickens from local farmers, so McCall set up a special provost guard to prevent further thievery. When news came that the Confederates suddenly abandoned the Manassas line and retreated southward to the Rappahannock River, McCall was instructed to fall back to Falls Church and await further instructions.[67]

Back at Camp Pierpont, Clow had ordered Phillip to remain behind to guard the commissary along with Clow's younger brother. Together, they split six-hour shifts around the clock. Then, during a downpour on the evening of March 15, Clow sent new directions "to pack up things and prepare to take a trip on Water."[68] Based on intelligence reports, McClellan had been forced to revise the Urbanna Plan. The Army of the Potomac would, before long, move by sea to the tip of the James Peninsula in Virginia.

The day before his departure, Philander penned a melancholy note to Cousin Ell as the regimental band played "The Girl I Left Behind" in the background. "It cheers a Poor soldier to hear from home often" stated the homesick lad, but "with God's help I will do my duty leaving the results in [H]is hands." Recently promoted to sixth corporal of Company I, Philander mentally geared up to face the enemy and lay a final blow on "Secesh." On March 10, the New Yorker sloshed fourteen miles and waited out the current storm underneath a "dog house." Four days later, Slocum's rain-drenched troopers retraced their steps back to Fairfax Station, following an evening of beer-infused revelry, and spent the next three weeks in a heightened state of military preparedness.[69]

Asa and the 5th Vermont contended with the same rainfall as Phillip's Bucktails and Philander's 27th New York on their trek to Flint Hill north of Fairfax Court House. There, the Vermonters hunkered down for four miserable days in wet surroundings. Then, on March 15, the Old Brigade countermarched to Alexandria. The drum major did not indicate that he would be among the first soldiers in the Army of the Potomac to board transports bound for the James Peninsula.[70]

None of the men in the ranks seemed to know where they were headed next. One thing was certain: their recent diversionary marches in northern Virginia were over.

* * * * * * *

The Ellithorpe brothers discovered simple joys in their army experiences. Philander counted many "True and Deer friends" in his unit but agreed that brotherly love topped the list. When Phillip succumbed to illness for a third time since training camp at Camp Pierpont, Philander consoled his sisters at home. "[Phillip] is just the same as when he left us full of fun," he mused.[71]

In his quest to seek out friends and family members in other regiments, Phillip frequently visited hometown buddies who were bivouacked nearby. He especially enjoyed the companionship of Asa and cousin James Stebbins. Phillip was fortunate on another count; he developed an abiding friendship with Joe Barnes, who "said he would come home with me when the War is over," and a strong spiritual connection with civilian chaplain John K. Haffey. When Phillip misplaced his fiddle, the men of Company I pooled their money to buy him another so they could continue to enjoy "fine times." But Phillip assured his loved ones that his friendly nature was not the product of stimulants. "I dont drink whiskey nor use Tobacco in any way," he testified.[72] By most indicators, Phillip was a clean-cut soldier with few vices.

Childhood diseases like measles, fevers, and pneumonia affected the Ellithorpe boys in the first year of the war, especially Phillip. Without hard medical evidence to firmly identify Phillip's exact ailments, which included an unexplained hand tremor, it is possible that the youngster was simply unfit for the physical and mental demands placed on him. There were extenuating circumstances that likely contributed to Phillip's "debilitis," the term used by physicians to explain his weak constitution.[73] These include threadbare and unwashed clothing, exposure to the elements, poor diet, unsanitary camp conditions, and contaminated water. Muster records and sick call data confirm that Asa, too, was plagued with a bout of measles. It is highly doubtful that any of the Ellithorpe boys were completely recovered when active campaigning resumed in March 1862.

Positive military role models remained a constant for the Ellithorpe brothers at the end of their first year of service. Good leadership spelled effective discipline and high morale, and this formula proved effective for Phillip through Kane and Biddle and for Philander through Slocum and Bartlett. Enlisted men tended to scrutinize their company leaders with a harsher eye, but soldiers typically accepted the importance of military order, obedience, and discipline to their own survival, especially following their "baptism of fire" on the battlefield. Furthermore, the resistance of the rank and file to military order gradually dissipated as camaraderie increased.[74]

The Ellithorpe home front was laden with unanswered questions in the first year of the war. Judging from the letters of Phillip and Philander, it is safe to say that Father, Mary, and Danforth had left the Lewellen Street address at different times before the death of Mother in September 1861. Once, Phillip revealed that Father was living and working in Geneseo (about forty miles northeast of Rushford) and on another occasion placed Father as residing in Pike. Thus, Ann and Permelia were left alone to manage the household. The Ellithorpe family seemed to be disintegrating, especially after Mother's death. As a result, these mysterious living arrangements placed great stress on Phillip, Philander, and Asa so far away from home.[75]

* * * * * * *

In the months between August 1861 and March 1862, the Army of the Potomac benefited from McClellan's methodical retooling process. The commanding general had restructured the military hierarchy from top to bottom, trained the inexperienced lower officer corps in the techniques of leadership and military exercise, and drilled the rank and file to move with efficiency in formation from the corps to company levels and to execute battlefield orders. As a result, Little Mac's soldiers gained confidence to survive under the challenges of modern warfare. McClellan took great pride in his new creation, and the volunteer army responded with unflinching devotion to its dashing commander.

The morale of the Ellithorpe brothers skyrocketed, too, as their letters reflected the importance of comrades in addition to the previous emphasis on family and friends. One unforeseen vice lurked in the near future, however: the temptation to corruption.

By March 15, 1862, McClellan had committed to unleashing the largest amphibious military campaign ever staged in North America, one that would deliver the Army of the Potomac "to the gates of Richmond."[76] From their soggy campgrounds in northeastern Virginia, the Ellithorpe boys were ready, willing, and able to test their newfound skills against the dangerous foe.

Chapter Five

The Fight for Richmond

The Peninsula Campaign and the Seven Days

On the stormy night of March 15, 1862, rain and snow continued to fall across northern Virginia, and the Ellithorpe brothers could only speculate about their futures. With the Rebels withdrawal from Manassas Junction and the obsolescence of the Urbanna strategy, McClellan changed his strategy to an amphibious assault of the James Peninsula, a ten-mile-wide lowland framed by the James and York rivers. The deployment of the Ellithorpes beginning in late March would take them into a series of battles fought over seven days within sight of Richmond. No one could have foreseen the carnage they were about to witness.

The terrain of the James Peninsula was low, flat, swampy, and prone to flood when heavy spring rains turned the dirt roads into muddy quagmires and waterways into raging torrents. McClellan made two significant alterations to his original Urbanna Plan regarding the new campaign. First, he called for transporting the Army of the Potomac by sea using hundreds of public and private vessels from Alexandria and consolidating his force at Fortress Monroe, a Federal garrison at the tip of the James Peninsula. Second, McClellan selected the small community of West Point, Virginia, as the new base of operations once the fighting had begun. Situated on a narrow spit between the Pamunkey and Mattaponi rivers, the location was also the terminus of the Richmond & West Point Railroad, making it an ideal transportation hub for any army on the move against Richmond, only seventy miles away.

The magnitude of logistical issues confronting McClellan's grand scheme was impressive. The War Department chartered more than 400 vessels to transport 120,000 men, 15,000 animals, 1,250 wagons, 44 artillery batteries, and 110 heavy siege guns as well as mountains of ammunition, forage, rations, and miscellaneous items, such as tents. The transfer of one division per day would take a month to complete. The Lincoln administration's skepticism centered on an obsession to protect the nation's capital during the absence of the Army of the Potomac.[1]

Indeed, the president had seriously questioned the commanding general's arithmetic in regard to the number of troops he promised to leave behind in Washington. Critics claimed that McClellan's estimation of 75,000 was greatly inflated. Then, in an action sure to anger McClellan, President Lincoln pulled McDowell's corps from the transport line and created an independent command called the Department of the Rappahannock, answerable only to Stanton. The Bucktails and 27th New York, among the last units slated for departure from the Alexandria wharves, found themselves reassigned to McDowell.[2]

Phillip

Phillip had embraced the upcoming amphibious campaign as one to end the war and deliver him safely home. A month earlier, he had actually anticipated the approaching offensive. "Everything is in our favor and we hope soon to see this Rebellion crushed," stated the commissary clerk to his sisters, "and the time . . . when we would meet the dear ones at Home . . . I look forward to happier times." Clow had revoked the February furlough promised to Phillip; on March 15, the commissary was abuzz, boxing provisions for a sea voyage. While the final destination remained unclear, the mode of transportation was generally understood by Phillip.[3]

While McClellan bickered with the Lincoln administration in late March, Phillip and the 1st Rifles dealt with two leadership problems. The first issue resulted from the absence of McNeil because of a case of typhoid fever. As a result, McCall temporarily elevated Maj. Stone to lead the 13th Pennsylvania Reserves.[4]

The second issue stemmed from the recent regimental election held on January 22. Still smarting from the rebuff at the ballot box, Kane now petitioned McClellan to detach the three companies he had personally recruited, C, G, and I, as well as Company H, and allow him to train them in a series of nontraditional skirmish maneuvers initiated by bugle sounds he himself had invented. Kane had been deeply moved by the destructiveness of concentrated firepower on close order infantry formations as well as the inefficiency of communicating with troops in the din of battle. His solution, inspired by Native American tactics he had observed while living in Utah before the war, called for the soldiers "to pick out a target, fire, scatter, reload behind whatever natural protection was available" and then repeat the process. Kane inserted a written copy of his innovative program, titled "Indian Drill," with his petition, and McClellan approved it. Phillip reaffirmed his ongoing loyalty to Kane, claiming "he has done more for the benefit of the Regt than any other man." Comrades who hailed from the Wildcat District of northwestern Pennsylvania agreed.[5]

As McCall's division awaited orders, Phillip addressed back-to-back letters to Father, to whom he rarely wrote. Despite the fact that constant rain, wind, and cold had hindered him, Phillip mentioned pleasant meetings with Philander. The brothers engaged in several of their favorite pastimes. "We just came in from playing a game of Ball," Phillip exclaimed, "the first time [since] we were in Camp Curtin." They also made sightseeing visits to Washington. On one occasion, they listened to several bands on the steps of "The Old Gothic" building. Phillip especially enjoyed a lampooned rendition of "Dixie," "a tune thar seacesh dont like to hear." Phillip also admitted to Father to having lent money to officers and comrades and charging 10 percent interest. He did not reveal the source of this newfound wealth, but Phillip sent some money to the Van Dycks in Smethport, his aunt's family who had boarded him in the prewar days.[6]

Asa Leads the Way

On the evening of March 16, the Army of the Potomac began its monthlong transfer to the James Peninsula, so Asa was the first Ellithorpe boy to ship out. Smalley's 5th Vermont queued up at the Alexandria dock with the rest of the "Old Brigade" for the short trip by water. They encountered heavy rain and rough seas on the way to Fortress Monroe, causing much seasickness because the men lay on open decks. When they made landfall, Asa's regiment camped in a marsh on the outskirts of Newport News and awaited the arrival of the rest of the invasion force. On March 27, the Vermonters conducted a short reconnaissance, and four days later, the commander of IV Corps, Brig. Gen. Erasmus D. Keyes, inspected them. Otherwise, Asa and his comrades spent a leisurely week basking in sunshine, swimming, and gathering and eating oysters.[7]

McClellan scheduled his two-prong invasion up the James Peninsula for April 4. Keyes was selected to conduct the advance up the Great Warwick Road on the west side of the peninsula; the James River flowed to his immediate left. The other corps were instructed to advance on the east side of the peninsula in the direction of Yorktown, their principal objective. The York River lay to their immediate right.

Phillip and Philander in Manassas Junction

On April 4, after much haggling between the Lincoln administration and McClellan, McDowell swung his independent corps toward Manassas Junction with Philander's 27th New York in tow. Phillip's 13th Pennsylvania Reserves followed several days later. The objective was to repair burned bridges and damaged sections of the Orange & Alexandria Railroad and provide a viable Federal presence on McClellan's extreme right flank.

The Bucktails arrived in a nasty storm of sleet and snow, and the chilled Pennsylvanians stumbled on a mountain of Confederate supplies at the depot that had been hastily left behind, including several casks of whiskey. Reminiscent of the 27th New York's lager fest several weeks earlier, the fatigued soldiers broke into the barrels of food and drink. Sadly, two Bucktails died from an overdose of medicinal laudanum.

McCall's division bivouacked near the Bull Run battlefield amid the debris of war, and Phillip boasted to his sisters that "we aint going to run back this time." The brothers camped near each other for almost a week, and they were able to spend some leisure time together. Phillip attached a melancholy addendum, admitting to having spent "a very lonesome [nineteenth] birthday" on April 8.[8]

During his stay in Manassas, Phillip demonstrated an awareness of recent history through the collection of artifacts. In a large box, he sent Ann a Confederate revolver, a fragment of grapeshot, and a yellow flower plucked from the Bull Run battlefield. Phillip also made space for his winter gear: a heavy jacket, blanket, pair of boots, gloves, and mittens. "I will want them if ever I come home," he commented. Phillip would be concerned over the safe delivery of this package for the next few months because of the new policy instituted at Fortress Monroe, where most boxes were opened for inspection. He promised to forward an assortment of cones and "shells from way down south in Dixie" once the Bucktails reached the coast of Virginia.[9]

To the Peninsula

On April 12, Philander left Manassas with Bartlett's regiment and countermarched to Alexandria. Five days later, the 27th New York boarded the steamer *S. R. Spaulding*, where they spent several miserable days at sea. Many New Yorkers succumbed to seasickness and fell victim to exposure because they had not been issued any protective gear from the relentless wind and rain. They sailed to Ship Point at the mouth of the York River, about ten miles south of Yorktown. Kept aboard ship for a few days, they eventually went ashore and set up camp in a lush grove of trees overlooking an inlet of the Poquosin River. There, they spent ten days eating clams and oysters, bathing, dodging raindrops, and awaiting further instructions.

On April 17, the 1st Rifles marched out of "Menses," as Phillip misspelled "Manassas." The commissarian had been instructed to bring only items he could fit into his haversack. The objective of McCall's Pennsylvania Reserves was to march to Catlett's Station while McDowell's larger force demonstrated against Falmouth. They hoped to push the Confederates out of Culpeper but met with stiff resistance. The weather did not cooperate either; Phillip complained that "the mud is hub deep and we can hardly navigate." Still, the Confederates withdrew, and McDowell entered Falmouth at the end of April, where his Department of the Rappahannock spent nearly one month in relative seclusion.[10]

The Bucktails bivouacked a mile from Falmouth in a pleasant spot. The soldiers decorated their "company" streets with garlands, boughs, and evergreen arches. Some wrote home to the Wildcat District requesting a fresh supply of bucktails. Phillip settled into a routine at Clow's soft-bread bakery; he even had time to go fishing for eels with Joe Barnes in a swift-flowing stream. Fragments of information about Asa's Vermont Brigade on the James Peninsula also began to surface at Falmouth.[11]

The Brief Military Career of Asa

Asa accompanied the 5th Vermont only a short distance up the west side of the James Peninsula. After the battle of Bull Run, a debate had raged among departments of the federal government regarding the assigned role of army musicians. The original policy of May 1861 was now under attack. While no one disputed the important role played by music in uplifting soldier morale, some questioned the need for every regiment to support one such band. An independent survey concluded that 143 regiments currently supported bands, which translated into more than 3,700 men being withheld from combat. In an equally damning report, the paymaster general implied that regimental bands were merely "ornamental," and they drained the military budget of $5 million. As a result, the adjutant general and inspector general agreed to eliminate all bands from units mustered after January 1, 1862, and discharge all nonplaying musicians assigned to current regiments. Asa's position as "principal musician" of the 5th Vermont was in serious jeopardy.[12]

On April 4, Keyes's corps approached the swollen Warwick River. At Young's Mill, the 5th Vermont collided with Rebel pickets. The next day, the Vermonters advanced cautiously to the south bank of the river "in a violent thunderstorm." Here, they encamped in front of Lee's Mill and awaited further orders. On the north bank, behind a network of earthworks, lay the undersized Confederate command of Brig. Gen. John Bankhead Magruder. The perceived strength of the Rebels had caught McClellan off guard, and the Federal advance stalled. For the next two weeks, the 5th Vermont was employed felling trees and building corduroy roads.

On April 11, Asa's commission was formally revoked at Lee's Mill. It would appear one Ellithorpe boy had been knocked out of the war without firing a single shot. Asa would miss the unmitigated disaster at Dam No. 1 five days later when the 5th Vermont was cut to pieces in an enemy crossfire during a botched rescue mission. Smalley's regiment suffered eighty-three casualties with nothing to show for it. Moreover, Asa was erroneously listed among the dead. Their repulse convinced McClellan to drop his plan for a direct assault on Yorktown on the other side of the peninsula in favor of a siege.[13]

Philander

Philander's 27th New York brought up the rear of the tri-corps advance up the eastern flank of the peninsula. As part of Brig. Gen. Edwin V. Sumner's

II Corps, they were expected to support a ground assault of Yorktown following the end of the siege. But when the Confederates vacated their trenches, the Yankees reboarded their vessels and steamed up the York River to Brick House Point. The process took two days to accomplish because of the many cumbersome artillery pieces as well as the sheer size of brigades being loaded. Philander's flotilla had heard the siege guns at Yorktown and the din of battle from Williamsburg.

On May 6, Bartlett's 27th New York was the first of Slocum's brigade ashore, and they were immediately posted on picket duty. The next morning, the pickets were driven in by the enemy, and a stiff skirmish ensued. The division of Brig. Gen. William B. Franklin lacked aggressiveness, however, and allowed the smaller Rebel force to slip away. One eyewitness to the fight from Philander's regiment later claimed that his company's captain was drunk during the entire episode at Eltham's Landing and that the casualties incurred were the result of "rum and imbecility." The lackluster "peninsular campaign" was over.[14]

McClellan utilized the lull to reorganize his army prior to its next major push against "the johnnies." The changes in leadership affected Philander from top to bottom. Franklin was elevated to the new rank of major general and placed in charge of the newly created VI Corps, Slocum to the helm of the First Division, Bartlett to the 2nd Brigade, and Alexander D. Adams to the 27th New York.[15]

Bartlett's brigade welcomed three new regiments: the 5th Maine, made up of hardy foresters from the northeastern corner of the state and bearing a resemblance to the Wildcat District loggers in Phillip's regiment; the 16th New York, whose unusual headgear—straw hats—distinguished itself much like the Bucktails; and the 96th Pennsylvania from the coal district of Luzerne County, led by their jovial 200-pounder, Col. Henry L. "Johnny-cakes" Cake. The composition of Bartlett's brigade remained intact until the 27th New York mustered out of service.[16]

Philander cheered these promotions, especially Slocum and Bartlett, whom he held in high esteem. He remained mum on the selection of Adams, however. One critic later opined while Adams was an educated and refined man, he "lacked dash." These remarks from the rank and file were typical of criticisms often leveled at lower-grade officers of the 27th New York.[17]

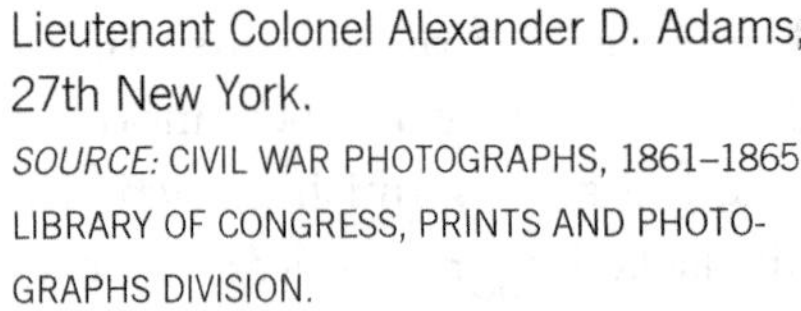

Lieutenant Colonel Alexander D. Adams, 27th New York.
SOURCE: CIVIL WAR PHOTOGRAPHS, 1861–1865, LIBRARY OF CONGRESS, PRINTS AND PHOTOGRAPHS DIVISION.

Preparing for the Seven Days

McClellan spent until the end of May solidifying his supply base, consolidating his six corps, and detaching troops to cut down trees, build corduroy roads, and erect bridges across the Chickahominy River, all in preparation for a spectacular ground assault against Richmond. The principal supply depot shifted three times and ultimately settled on a mammoth facility at White House Landing. Philander and the rest of Slocum's division guarded this expanding site until May 26.[18]

Shortly before resuming operations, McClellan sought to extend his right flank by bringing McDowell's corps down from Falmouth. Together, these forces would demonstrate against Richmond from the north while McClellan's main force would advance from the east. On May 22, half of Bartlett's brigade (including cavalry and artillery) conducted a reconnaissance-in-force to Mechanicsville, a small village north of the Confederate capital. The Yankees dug rifle pits upslope from the Chickahominy and skirmished twice with Confederates on May 23–24. Philander's 27th New

York fronted Meadows Bridge and avoided combat taking place farther to the south at New Bridge.

From this elevated vantage point, Philander told Permelia he could see church spires in "the Capitol of Jeff" (Richmond) only five miles away. He also commented on a rising flood of contrabands entering their camp. He utilized three runaways to cook for the captain. On the morning of May 27, Bartlett's expedition expected to reconnect with McDowell's force, but they had doubled back to Fredericksburg; a major showdown seemed imminent.[19]

Fair Oaks (Seven Pines)

Halfway between McClellan's supply depot at White House and the Confederate capital lay the crossroads community of Fair Oaks. Confederate Maj. Gen. Joseph E. Johnston had withdrawn to this locale, but with his back literally against Richmond, he felt his force could not withstand a lengthy siege like the one orchestrated by McClellan at Yorktown. Thus, he decided to strike a blow on the two Federal corps isolated south of the Chickahominy.

The weather benefited neither Yankees nor Rebels, as torrential rains had fallen between May 20 and 30, so both sides postponed several scheduled attacks. As a result of the spring runoff, some of the eleven bridges meticulously erected by McClellan's engineers had washed away as the raging Chickahominy approached flood stage. More important, the river had driven a natural wedge between McClellan's five corps.

Johnston's plan nearly worked. On May 31, the initial surge of the Rebels pushed back the Federals for over two miles, but McClellan conducted a controlled retreat, and the blue line did not break. At 3 p.m., "Little Mac," in a crucial decision, ordered reserves north of the swollen river to cross the damaged Grapevine Bridge to bolster his endangered right flank. Brig. Gen. John Sedgwick's division made the "perilous" crossing in spite of the danger of the wooden span being swept away and splendidly saved the day. In his tour of the battlefield afterward, McClellan was revolted by the carnage.

Philander and Malaria

Beginning on June 2, the 27th New York changed its position from Mechanicsville to picket at Grapevine Bridge. For four nights, they dealt with a series of ferocious thunderstorms. On their "off" days, they chopped logs for corduroy roads and laid them across White Oak Swamp. Then the New Yorkers were sent to repair washed-out roadways approaching New Bridge and Woodbury Bridge. Philander commented to his sisters, tongue in cheek, that the sweet melody of drum and bugle had been replaced by the repetitive sound of pick, ax, and spade. On a more serious note, he had contracted malaria.[20]

Philander's illness was not unusual. Almost one-tenth of the Federal army was on sick call, and the number of deaths resulting from dysentery, chronic diarrhea, typhoid fever, and malaria almost equaled the combat casualties sustained at Fair Oaks. He was sent to a hospital housed in White Oak Church near Falmouth.[21]

Separation

Throughout April and May, Phillip had been exceedingly busy in the Falmouth bakery. The ovens produced 2,000 loaves of soft bread per day, and the brick facility doubled as the camp post office. Said Phillip to Ann at the end of April, "The only excuse I have to offer for not writing more is the numberous duties I have to perform." The local citizenry did not impress the young Alleganian, either. "The people of this Town have a very bad opinion of the Yankeys," Phillip explained. "We call them the ignorant class[;] they thought that the yankeys were coming here to butcher them and destroy their Property." As McDowell's command launched its aborted mission to protect McClellan's right flank, Phillip knew his older brother was somewhere in the Mechanicsville–Fair Oaks theater of operations. He was exceedingly worried about Philander's well-being.[22]

On May 15, in response to a growing threat posed by "Stonewall" Jackson in the Shenandoah Valley, McCall was instructed to detach Kane's four companies of Bucktails to assist the "Flying Brigade" of Brig. Gen. George D. Bayard in an attempt to bottle up the Rebels in a pincer movement. The six remaining companies of 1st Rifles would remain under Stone in Falmouth. Many Bucktails were incensed that their regiment had been split up. Furthermore, the detachment of Kane's companies resulted in the separation of Phillip from Company I. After all, his primary duties were tied directly to the expanded commissary needs of the entire division and not to his own regiment.[23]

On May 28, Bayard and his bucktailed sharpshooters departed for the valley. The Flying Brigade sought to destroy Jackson's wagon trains and draw out Confederate cavalryman Brig. Gen. Turner Ashby, the "Black Knight." Kane's crack outfit displayed remarkable stamina throughout the monthlong campaign by keeping pace with Bayard's cavalry on five marches up and down the valley.[24]

On the afternoon of June 6, Bayard's 1st New Jersey rode into a Confederate ambush in a wooded area about one mile south of Harrisonburg. Four dozen Yankee horsemen were captured, and many wounded were left on the field because of the hasty retreat. Kane asked for and received permission to mount a relief mission to rescue the injured. As darkness approached, Kane's Rifles stumbled into the 58th Virginia, a rear guard led by the Black Knight himself. The first Federal volley felled Ashby, killing him instantly. The firefight carried on for an hour, and the number of wounded started to mount up. Shot through the leg, Kane was propped against a tree where he continued to direct his men in the unique skirmish tactics he had taught them. During the close-quarters fight, he sustained a second injury, a Confederate rifle stock to the chest. After dark, the 1st Rifles slipped away but not before they sustained fifty-two casualties, almost half of the rescue party, and the capture of Kane himself.[25]

Bruised and bloodied, the Bucktails resumed the chase the next day under the temporary command of Capt. Hugh McDonald (Company G). On June 8, they caught up with the gray quarry at Cross Keys Tavern. The Confederates quickly enveloped the small band of Pennsylvanians, and desperate hand-to-hand fighting broke out for the second time in as many days. Bayonets were burnished on both sides. Company I was particularly hard pressed. Blanchard sustained gunshot wounds to both legs, and he was superseded in command by Bell. As the valley campaign wound down several days later, Kane's battered Bucktails were returned to guard McDowell's headquarters in Manassas and armed with enough war stories to establish themselves as a fighting unit.[26]

Dispatched to Dispatch Station

Meanwhile, on the day Kane's Rifles fought at Harrisonburg, McCall received orders in Falmouth to prepare for immediate departure to reinforce McClellan. Two days later, June 8, the Pennsylvania Reserves boarded six steamers; Stone's six companies of Bucktails loaded onto the *South America*, and Phillip's commissary followed on the *Eagle*. The flotilla sailed down the Rappahannock and up the York and Pamunkey rivers to White House Landing. Along the way, they witnessed a family of slaves on the riverbank who hailed them, "Oh! glory! glory!" and implored "Masa Lincoln's" flotilla to stop and pick them up. When their pleas were disregarded, the family waded into the water up to their necks in pursuit of the vessels as they disappeared around the bend.[27]

On the morning of June 12, Phillip heard musketry coming from the direction of Tunstall's Station where J. E. B. Stuart was starting his infamous three-day ride around the Army of the Potomac. Phillip predicted to Ann that "thare is going to be a fight or a Foot Race before long."[28] It must have unnerved Phillip on his arrival at White House Landing to see the dock stacked with pine coffins filled with dead soldiers and countless wounded men waiting for transport aboard hospital ships. This horrible impression inspired Phillip to begin an intense but unauthorized search for Philander. Obtaining the location of the 27th New York ten miles away, Phillip set out on foot "through the swamps" to determine his brother's fate. He found the bivouac of Philander's unit, but his brother was out on picket duty. Relieved, he returned to the Bucktails, who were preparing to "ride the cars" to the Chickahominy.[29]

The Seven Days

Day 2: Mechanicsville

In the third week of June, McClellan resumed his cautious advance toward Richmond. The offensive began when Maj. Gen. John Fitz Porter's new V Corps marched to Mechanicsville with orders to protect McClellan's right flank, guard the Richmond & York River Railroad, and protect the army's supply depot at White House Landing. On June 25, the lull in combat ended with an inconclusive encounter at Oak Grove, the first day of the Seven Days battles.

Stone's 1st Rifles entrenched with McCall's division behind Beaver Dam Creek and in front of a large swamp that flanked both sides of the Chickahominy. This natural stronghold on Old Church Road anchored the extreme right flank, and the Bucktails were situated on the outermost edge with the 2nd Pennsylvania Reserves and a section of ten-pound parrot guns. Despite the network of Federal rifle pits, redoubts, and artillery bunkers sprinkled throughout its length in this sector, the Rebels and Yankees were separated only by the width of the Chickahominy.

Here, Phillip echoed Philander's earlier observation about seeing Richmond's church spires. There were some casual moments in the hours before battle, however, when the blue and gray bartered for the usual products: newspapers, coffee, and tobacco. Phillip noted that each night his regiment was serenaded by "a Reb Band playing several fine peases," including "Home, Sweet Home!" But Phillip also complained to Ann about contracting Father's old ailment, rheumatism.[30]

The new Confederate commander, Gen. Robert E. Lee, recognized the vulnerability of the Porter–McCall line on the Chickahominy, and he formulated a battle plan for his newly constituted Army of Northern Virginia. He called on Maj. Gens. A. P. Hill and James Longstreet to demonstrate in front of the Pennsylvanians, while "Stonewall" Jackson's command, which had arrived from the Shenandoah Valley, would deliver the decisive blow on McCall's flank. Lee's plan had merit.

Since their arrival in Mechanicsville, three companies of Stone's Bucktails had been impressed to establish a picket presence about one-half mile

Captain/Colonel Roy Stone, Company D, 13th Pennsylvania Reserves.
SOURCE: CIVIL WAR PHOTO COLLECTION, UNITED STATES ARMY HERITAGE AND EDUCATION CENTER, CARLISLE, PENNSYLVANIA.

west of the village at Meadows Bridge under the overall direction of Col. Seneca G. Simmons (5th Pennsylvania Reserves). Situated only 100 feet from the Chickahominy, the marksmen would be the first line of defense against any enemy incursion toward the Beaver Dam Creek line.[31]

The late morning stillness on June 26 was interrupted by sustained small-arms fire coming from north of Mechanicsville. There, the 8th Illinois Cavalry, on patrol in Atlee Station and Shady Grove Church, had been attacked by Hill's vanguard. Impatient with Jackson's tardiness, "Little Powell" had taken it on himself to initiate the Confederate assault. Unaware of the Rebels' intentions, McCall instructed Stone to lead three companies of Bucktails and investigate the clatter. Three captains important to future regimental history were selected for this mission: Langhorne Wister (Company B), Edward A. Irvin (Company K), and John T. Jewett (Company D). The investigators were about to step into a gray buzz saw.[32]

Around 3 p.m., Stone's small force had barely reached an important rural crossroads south of Atlee Station when portions of the Federal scouting party came racing pell mell down Atlee Station Road with the enemy in hot pursuit. The blue and gray horsemen overran and scattered Jewett's company, who were marching unwittingly up the road. Wister was able to briefly set up a defense at the crossroads, but soon all three companies were acting independently of one another and melting into the Virginia landscape. The Bucktail relief expedition had been caught completely off guard.[33]

Stone realized they could not reassemble and retrace their steps in an orderly fashion. They were completely cut off. So the inventive Stone opted for a forced retreat northward to try to outdistance his command from the Confederates. He eventually made it back safely with most of Companies B and D. Company K was not so fortunate. Irwin led his men into the woods and swamps when they were dispersed, and they hid for almost a week before surrendering because of hunger and thirst. Approximately seventy-five Bucktails spent the next two months in a Richmond prisoner-of-war camp.[34]

By late afternoon, Lee concentrated his energies on the Federals behind Beaver Dam Creek. But he faced a natural obstacle: the creek itself was nearing flood stage, and advancing Confederates would have to wade in chest-deep water to traverse it. The spongy terrain not only impeded a direct infantry assault but also challenged the mobility and placement of short-range artillery. The approaches were wide open for 200 yards, and while the stream was not very wide, its banks were quite steep and slippery. Meanwhile, the Union rifle pits commanded a spectacular view from their earthworks seventy-five feet above the waterway. Still, the Confederates were so optimistic about success that President Jefferson Davis and members of his cabinet came out to witness an expected victory.

During the five-hour conflict at Mechanicsville, the bucktailed sector withstood three successive enemy charges. The Pennsylvanians laid down a withering rifle fire while one section of artillery dispersed more than 800 rounds of shot, shell, and canister on the Rebels. On their right, the aggressive Col. William McCandless and the 2nd Pennsylvania Reserves performed with equal valor. Together, they successfully defended the extreme right of the Federal line. At one point, the remaining three companies of Bucktails rebuffed the only Confederate regiment to reach Union trenches, the 35th Virginia. Both sides burnished bayonets, and fierce hand-to-hand fighting ensued. Then, after dark, the field fell relatively silent except for the pitiful wails of the wounded who lay on the marshy ground. Lee's army had been repulsed by a determined foe, solidly entrenched soldiers, and well-placed artillery batteries. The battle of Mechanicsville was a shining moment for McCall's Pennsylvania Reserves.[35]

Day 3: Gaines' Mill

Late on June 26, McClellan, fearing that the Rebel force was still capable of turning his flank, called a late-night retreat to Boatswain's Creek, a swampland near Gaines' Mill. McCall was incensed by the directive: "This order, I must confess, gave me some concern," he confided in his official report.[36] McCall was justifiably concerned that the movement would not get under way for several hours, and he worried that daylight would expose his column to the enemy. His assessment was correct. No sooner had his first brigade departed than the Confederates opened up with grape, canister, and small-arms fire.

At sunrise on June 27, the 1st Rifles and one battery were among the last to leave the field, and they formed the rear guard of the Pennsylvania Reserves. The three-mile withdrawal was disorganized, however, and because of the resumption of Confederate shelling, some Bucktail companies had not received the order to fall back. Thus, Capt. Alanson E. Niles and Company E became separated from the main body, and several soldiers were captured, but not before they buried the regimental battle flag in the

Captain/Major Alanson E. Niles, Company E, 13th Pennsylvania Reserves. *SOURCE:* CIVIL WAR PHOTO COLLECTION, UNITED STATES ARMY HERITAGE AND EDUCATION CENTER, CARLISLE, PENNSYLVANIA.

swamp. Some of Niles's men, acting independently, were able to sneak back piecemeal to the regiment.[37]

By noon, most of McCall's Pennsylvania Reserves had arrived at Boatswain's Creek, where they were assigned to the second line of defense 600 yards back in front of the Adams House on Turkey Hill. McClellan intended to use the Pennsylvanians as reservists since they had been so heavily engaged at Beaver Dam Creek. Stone's bedraggled companies of Bucktails counted only 131 men present for duty.[38]

The topography at Boatswain's Creek exhibited similar natural attributes to those of Beaver Dam Creek—a sluggish stream, elevated and steep banks, thick stands of timber, and dense underbrush. An open marsh extended for several hundred yards to the west. Unlike Beaver Dam Creek, Boatswain's was marked by steep ravines. The Federals felt that both positions were highly defensible.

Heeding the Call for Reinforcements

During the hurried retreat to Boatswain's Creek, McClellan was preoccupied with shifting reinforcements to the north side of the Chickahominy. The latter concern affected Philander's 27th New York, which had bivouacked with the division since June 23 on Garnett's farm. The New Yorkers were so close to enemy lines that they could clearly hear the southerners as they answered to morning roll call. Early on June 27, Philander's unit heeded the call for reinforcements and headed for Boatswain's Creek with the rest of Slocum's division.[39]

On the afternoon of June 27, the Confederate infantry attack on Boatswain's Creek commenced, but it lacked coordination and clear communication between its commanders. Despite these shortcomings, the southerners had set on the Federal right wing held by the U.S. Regulars of Brig. Gen. George Sykes. In response to the possible breakthrough, the Pennsylvania Reserves abandoned their reserve location, traversed the field from left to right, and plugged holes wherever they appeared. In this manner, the 1st Rifles fought where a 500-yard gap precariously opened to their right. McCall rode furiously along the entire front in a futile attempt to control events. His division was fighting for their lives; ammunition was running low, and the Federal cause hung in the balance. Reinforcements were vital.[40]

Slocum's division had been on the march since early in the day but found Duane's Bridge on the Chickahominy clogged with military personnel and equipment, so they countermarched to Woodbury's Bridge. Once they crossed the bridge, Philander recalled in his first post-campaign letter that his comrades followed the roar of musketry and artillery to Boatswain's Creek. Bartlett's brigade was the last one to reach the battlefield, and Adams's 27th New York brought up the rear.[41]

When Slocum entered the field of combat, he occupied the same ground held earlier by the Pennsylvania Reserves. But Federal reinforcements were still desperately needed to bolster Sykes's sagging right flank. Accommodating this change in placement would require Bartlett's brigade to replicate the Pennsylvanians route and double-quick parallel to and within range of Confederate marksmen. They accomplished the dangerous maneuver but sustained significant casualties.[42]

The brigade reached its destination downslope from the McGehee farmhouse, and Bartlett ordered Adams to take his 27th New York to seek cover in a nearby ravine. A corporal remembered "half spent balls from the enemy's guns . . . pattering down all about us like big drops of rain on a dusty road."[43] When enemy artillerists sized up the brigade's location, they peppered the Yankees with canister. Their position appeared untenable.

Consequently, Bartlett barked to his men to fix bayonets and double-quick uphill to a brick farmhouse and engage the Confederates who were assembled there. The 27th and 16th New York screamed "the unearthly yell that we had learned to give" as they collided with North Carolina troops in front of McGehee House, where Maj. Gardiner fell, concussed by an exploding shell. At one point in the close-quarters melee, the 27th New York mistakenly opened fire on their Straw Hat allies. The ebb and flow of combat lasted for two hours. The regiment held a critical position in Bartlett's line, and Adams skillfully realigned his regiment under extraordinarily chaotic conditions on three separate occasions.[44]

The coup de grâce occurred in the evening when the Confederates launched a stunning assault of sixteen divisions with fixed bayonets. The sheer magnitude of the attack spread panic down the two-mile-long Yankee line, and the soldiers began to run to the rear. Both the Bucktails at Adams House and the 27th New York at McGehee House were swept away by the immense volume of blue-clad stragglers racing for the Chickahominy. Here, Philander recalled the capture of messmate Will Robinson, and Phillip's brigade lost its commander, Brig. Gen. John F. Reynolds, to a prisoner-of-war camp.[45]

Days 4 and 5: Savage Station

In a midnight war council with his corps commanders and some division leaders, McClellan was convinced to fall back from Boatswain's Creek and reorganize his shattered force. The retreat would demand the destruction of massive stores at Dispatch Station and White House Landing and a shift in the supply base to Harrison's Landing on the James River. McClellan's decision would require half of the Army of the Potomac to serve as rear guard to ensure the safe passage of all soldiers and materiel across White Oak Swamp. The change also meant that the massive field hospital at Savage Station could no longer transport the wounded to safety through White House Landing. The overall operation promised to be a logistical nightmare with only one road leading through Savage Station, which quickly became clogged with infantry, artillery, commissary wagons, quartermaster wagons, and a large herd of beeves. Phillip's wagon of regimental stores was caught in the bottleneck.

During the retreat on June 28, McCall's overworked division escorted thirteen batteries comprising nearly 300 conveyances. Consequently, the

Pennsylvanians slipped one regiment from one division between each battery and placed the other two divisions along the flanks of the column, which extended for seven miles. A steady rainfall hampered the sluggish marchers, and the one-lane road turned into a muddy morass. After midnight, Stone camped his exhausted Bucktails in a field within sight of the large Federal field hospital.[46]

A psychological drama was playing out at Savage Station during the evacuation of the Army of the Potomac. Some units were testy, believing that they had not been allowed to follow up the perceived victory at Fair Oaks and the decided victory at Mechanicsville. Their angst was fueled by the fact that many of them had neither slept nor eaten for at least two days. Many haversacks were left behind at Gaines' Mill in the rapid retreat. When Philander's 27th New York reached the station, the destruction of massive stockpiles of ammunition, foodstuffs, clothing, silage, and other equipment was well under way. Some of Adams's troopers added to the surreal scene, even helping themselves to new items of clothing before torching the crates and railcars.[47]

At the field hospital, 2,500 sick and wounded men were told to either follow as best they could the retreating army or surrender to the advancing Rebels. Most of the injured were uncharacteristically left behind, contrary to American military tradition to never leave a wounded comrade to the enemy. One corporal of the 27th New York recalled the scene vividly: "Scores of mangled men lay upon the ground around the hospital tents: their wearied, haggard and smoke-begrimed faces . . . appealed . . . not to be left [behind]. Certainly these scenes were more trying to the spirit of the soldier than the combat they endured."[48]

Day 6: Glendale

On June 29, delays in crossing White Oak Bridge were horrendous as the Federal horde jammed the single avenue of retreat on Willis Church (aka Quaker) Road. McCall's Pennsylvanians were among the first to arrive at the bridge, but it took five hours to traverse the swamp. McCall was instructed to lead his advance division to a crossroads west of Glendale, halt, and set up a buffer for the blue column as it filed past to Harrison's Landing. The tousled Pennsylvanians did not arrive on-site until midnight, and Stone reported considerable straggling along the route.[49]

In the meantime, Slocum's division set up pickets on the south side of White Oak Swamp to guard against Confederate encroachments at Long Bridge and then redirected to Charles City Road to block Brackett's Ford. The stage was now set for the decisive battle of the campaign, Glendale, and Phillip's Bucktails and Philander's 27th New York would see crucial action in different sectors of the field.

Slocum's position on Charles City Road connected with another division and resembled an inverted right angle. They dealt with constant Confederate artillery shelling from across White Oak Swamp throughout the morning and several piecemeal infantry sorties in the afternoon. Philander and his comrades spent the next twenty-four hours constructing abatis and rifle pits amid the din of battle.[50]

On June 30, no one in the Pennsylvania Reserves expected to play a major combat role in light of the heavy casualties they had sustained at Mechanicsville and Gaines' Mill. Yet McCall unwittingly posted two brigades in a salient on Long Bridge Road, uncomfortably close to woodlots that might disguise enemy movements. That placement would become the epicenter of the impending battle. McCall also erred when he positioned his five artillery batteries in the forefront of his infantry. The Bucktails were placed in reserve on Willis Church Road.[51]

In the late afternoon, the Rebels launched a massive nine-brigade assault on the center of the Pennsylvania Reserves. The attack could not have come at a less desirable time for the Federals because a 500-yard gap yawned to McCall's left. This was a recipe for disaster. McCall's difficulties multiplied when Rebel infantrymen popped out of the dense woodlot at Whitlock's farm, dispatching the Yankee pickets, overrunning two batteries, and driving back two regiments of Reserves. Shortly, the blue and gray lines locked in a back-and-forth struggle on Long Bridge Road, where hand-to-hand fighting broke out.[52]

In an attempt to stem the gray onslaught, McCall ordered a counterattack, rushing two regiments obliquely to the left while simultaneously moving two regiments forward. Stone directed his reserve 1st Rifles into a woodlot on the left to defend six endangered parrot guns. As they reached a clearing on Nelson's Farm, they were greeted by an immense throng of panicked blue-clads running toward them in full retreat.

Unable to stem the rout, a situation reminiscent of Philander's regiment at Bull Run, Stone frantically ordered the Bucktails to hit the ground, using the technique Kane had taught them. When the blue mob cleared from view, Stone instructed his Bucktails to stand, deliver two quick volleys, and then retreat at the double-quick. More than 400 yards to the rear, Stone was able to rally only sixty-three Bucktails. Other commands were not so fortunate.

McCall's advance not only failed to check the southerner's attack but also created a new breach on the right. Pandemonium reached its peak when the upper command of the Pennsylvania division crumbled. All three brigade commanders were incapacitated: one killed (Seneca G. Simmons), one seriously wounded (George G. Meade), and one missing (Truman Seymour). Regimental officers were equally decimated, with four of them killed or wounded.[53]

Facing mounting pressure to his front and hearing the clatter of musketry to the south, Slocum pulled back toward Glendale. The timely arrival of Slocum's force, along with the appearance of Sedgwick's division from Savage Station, stabilized McCall's shattered center.[54]

Despite cracking McCall's line, the Confederates failed to carry Willis Church Road, prevent the Union withdrawal, or destroy the Army of the Potomac. As darkness descended over the killing ground, an inglorious end to a long and eventful day for the Pennsylvania Reserves occurred when McCall and Stone undertook a reconnoitering mission to determine enemy positions and gather missing men. Instead, they stumbled into a Virginia regiment, which captured McCall and wounded the colonel of the Bucktails. Again, Philander supplied no details of Glendale, and Phillip and McCall's commissary wagons were presumably headed south to rendezvous with the Army of the Potomac at Harrison's Landing.[55]

Before midnight, Seymour had been found, and temporary command of the Pennsylvania Reserves fell to him. He gathered what few officers he could scramble and told them to form those men present for duty and filter them into the line of march to Malvern Hill. His second order, to leave the wounded on the battlefield, was not received well in the ranks, and the retreat lacked both order and discipline. It was hard to imagine how the overworked division could possibly function if hostilities were to resume the next day. Despite the fact that the Pennsylvanians had bought precious time to save

McClellan's army, several corps commanders painted a negative picture of them in their official reports.[56]

Day 7: Malvern Hill

Malvern Hill was an elevated plateau measuring one square mile about 130 feet directly above the James River. The slope leading to the summit was bare and free of obstructions. The eastern side of the plateau angled down sharply to Turkey Island Creek and Western Run, and two Yankee gunboats and one ironclad on the James River blanketed the western slope. The centerpiece of the defensive plan was the thoughtful placement of 171 artillery guns throughout the Federals' lines.

At daybreak on July 1, most of the Federals had reached Malvern Hill, where they occupied formidable defenses thrown up by the first corps to arrive. Any attempt by the southerners to challenge this position would be foolhardy. Coincidentally, the regiments of Phillip and Philander were assigned to noncombat roles in close proximity to each other. The Pennsylvanians guarded Malvern House, Brig. Gen. Fitz John Porter's headquarters, along with the reserve artillery. Some who saw their depleted ranks were shocked and believed the Reserves would need to be either refitted or dissolved.[57]

Philander and the rest of Bartlett's brigade marched completely through the defenses to an impregnable hilltop on the extreme right, forty feet above Turkey Island Creek. There, they busied themselves building breastworks and abatis for batteries in their sector. They were among seven divisions placed in the southeastern corner of the field, within a mile of Haxall's Landing on the James River. Consequently, Philander was not in harm's way on the afternoon of July 1.[58]

The Rebels fought valiantly in three unsupported infantry assaults in the late afternoon, but they were turned away with heavy doses of grape, canister, and deadly rifle fire from behind entrenched positions. Unfortunately, McClellan was not present to witness the exemplary performance of his army. Instead, he had boarded the ironclad *Galena* and steamed off for a second inspection of Harrison's Landing.[59]

The four-hour battle of Malvern Hill turned out to be the concluding chapter of McClellan's march on Richmond. Federal casualties at Malvern Hill paled in comparison to Confederate losses. Consensus in the trenches wanted to hold the hill and even use it as a base to launch a counterattack on the southerners the next day. But the only voice that mattered was that of McClellan, who ordered the retreat to resume to Harrison's Landing. The Pennsylvania Reserves pulled out at midnight and Slocum's division shortly thereafter. The movement was executed during a torrential downpour, and the roadway turned into a sloppy mess.

There was no sense of celebration in the blue ranks. The wet, hungry, and exhausted victors were thoroughly demoralized. Some soldiers threw away their guns in disgust, and straggling was widespread. "Shame, deep sorrow and patriotic indignation filled the hearts of many of the . . . men," claimed one historian of the Pennsylvania Reserves.[60]

Summarizing the effect of the entire campaign on the spirits of the troops, perhaps Cpl. James A. Wright of the 1st Minnesota stated it best: "Each day of the Seven Days added a full year to our ages and . . . not one of them was the rollicking noisy boy he was before. And he *never was afterwards*."[61] Philander had "seen the elephant" for the second time, and Phillip hung around its edges. The Seven Days were over.

Gains and Losses

The Ellithorpe brothers were present with the Army of the Potomac on the road to Richmond—the Peninsula campaign (April 4–June 1) and the Seven Days (June 25–July 1). Throughout these two campaigns, McClellan had employed the most modern military theory in his planning—a balance of the tactical defensive and the strategic offensive. The Union forces were clear victors in the first and last battles of the Seven Days and modestly successful from a tactical standpoint in holding the ground in two others. The Yankees failed, however, to achieve their great prize—the capture of Richmond.

The number of casualties stunned the North. The greatest blow had fallen on McCall's Pennsylvania Reserves, taking the brunt of the action in three consecutive battles (Mechanicsville, Gaines' Mill, and Glendale) and sustaining casualties of more than 20 percent (253k/1,240w/1,581m). The Bucktails were a microcosm of this sacrifice. Stone's six companies had started with 450 men, but the first muster at Harrison's Landing listed less than 100 present for duty. Kane's four companies in the Shenandoah also suffered casualties out of proportion to their original size. It might be suggested that the Pennsylvania Reserves and the Bucktail never recovered from the numerical losses sustained in the spring of 1862. Not to be outdone, the 27th New York recorded 151 casualties at Gaines' Mill on the bloodiest single day in its history.[62]

Family Hardships Continue

The spring campaigns of 1862 were ones of mobility. As such, there were gaps in the brothers' letters to loved ones. Phillip was unavailable between June 21 and July 1 and Philander between June 19 and July 6. In any case, their letters came to a household in turmoil.

For months, Ann had pleaded with her brothers to send home money, and her tone became increasingly desperate. Philander responded generously, but Phillip was less receptive. Before the outbreak of the war, the Ellithorpe family was showing signs of falling apart, and the situation escalated after the death of Mother in September 1861. By early 1862, Father and Mary were living with Uncle Carlos in Pike, and sometimes Father's whereabouts were unknown to all of the relatives. Once, a flurry of Ellithorpe correspondence speculated that he had run off and remarried an unidentified woman.[63]

Now that Ann and Permelia resided alone in the "brown gothic" on Lewellen Street, the question of legal ownership of the property resurfaced. Recall that the Ellithorpes had purchased the house in March 1853, failed to meet its mortgage obligation four years later, and auctioned off personal property to pay the debt. In March 1862, the same problem resurfaced.[64]

In correspondences among the Ellithorpe siblings, an unlikely savior appeared in the person of Oliver Hazard Perry Griggs, the tenth child of Grandfather Philip. Uncle Perry made overtures to purchase the house (and perhaps sell it), but Ann strenuously objected. Writing from the commissary bakery in Falmouth, Phillip vowed to support his sisters: "Perry wont get the House without some trouble." Instead, the young Bucktail boldly promised to pay the lien against the house. The matter had not been resolved when the Ellithorpe brothers left for the James Peninsula. It gravely concerned Phillip and Philander because they were unable to return home and settle the dispute.[65]

Writing a letter at Ship Point prior to his march toward Yorktown, Philander warned his sister that he well knew "the other party," and he possesses "a selfish disposition." Philander, like Phillip, disputed the efforts of "our Noble uncle [Perry]" to sell the family dwelling, although he admitted that somehow they had defaulted on the rightful owner. The time had come, Philander concluded, for Phillip to pony up cash to help his destitute sisters.

At the end of July, the younger brother responded with $100, an astronomical amount for a private's salary. But the family narrowly averted foreclosure.[66]

ASA AND ANN RECONCILE

One of Phillip's missives brought up another important family question: Where had Asa been living since his discharge in April—in Rushford or Freedom? Previous missives between the Ellithorpe siblings had intimated that Asa might resume his courtship of Ann. Philander, in particular, took exception to this possibility. Drafting a letter written in pencil on coarse blue paper, he implored Permelia, "Dont let that Fellow Cary Ann off until I get home." That was not exactly a ringing endorsement. Yet the wedding announcement of Asa and Ann in the Rushford Methodist Episcopal Church on June 2 reached the brothers after the fact. They were not initially pleased.[67]

Philander confided in Permelia that the newlyweds might have shown more consideration and waited until he returned from the war, but he softened his disappointment in hoping "to see that old Maried Woman."[68] If Philander was surprised by the nuptials, Phillip was downright dumbfounded. Shortly after his arrival at Dispatch Station, the commissary clerk scolded the new Mrs. Burleson: "You did not write [that] you were married I wish that you would tell a fellow."[69] Phillip and Philander probably struggled to separate their feelings about family difficulties from the impending deadly work of soldiering in Virginia.

Not all Ellithorpe-related news from home was controversial or emotional. Take the inventive genius of Uncle Carlos, who, on March 25, 1862, received a patent for his original design to improve the functionality of the sewing machine. He had devised a mechanism to apply tension to the fabric as it crossed the "feed dog" and needle plate. This improvement ensured that stitches were uniform in size and distance, a feature that would contribute to clothes and household manufacturers—an industry embedded in his family's colonial heritage. Phillip learned about the achievement from Mary, and he eagerly informed Father and Philander that he desired to become a sewing machine salesman after the war.[70]

THE MYSTERIOUS WHEREABOUTS OF PHILLIP

While preparing and dispensing rations to the Bucktails, Phillip learned secondhand about the actions of Kane's Rifles in the Shenandoah Valley and firsthand about Stone's companies on the Chickahominy. The commissary worker provided a reasonably accurate, if disjointed, timetable of events as they unfolded around him.[71] Phillip offers a description of Stone's reconnaissance to Atlee Station, Niles's haphazard retreat into the swamp, and the secret burial of the regimental colors during the hasty retreat from Boatswain's Creek. In separate missives to Ann and Permelia, he confided that he had narrowly escaped capture, but it is unclear whether he was referencing the clashes at Atlee Station or Gaines' Mill. But he assured both of them that "in the fight before Richmond . . . I was in the whole thing."[72]

Phillip's statements confirm his presence with his bucktailed comrades, but his responsibilities in safeguarding the regiment's commissary wagon while on the frantic retreat to Harrison's Landing afterward make his direct participation in military action highly unlikely. On the contrary, Phillip offers no evidence in his writings about this frantic journey to the James River. Of course, it is possible that forward commissary workers and their wagons were recalled to destroy the stores at Dispatch Station before taking an alternative route to Harrison's Landing. Using Phillip's own words (and lack of words), it is impossible to unravel his role in Bucktail movements after Gaines' Mill.

Contemplating the Future

By the summer of 1862, Phillip and Philander often expressed feelings of nostalgia and homesickness in their writings. Both New Yorkers hoped that the war would be over as soon as possible, and they wishfully predicted their homecoming by the Fourth of July. In a more somber moment, Philander second-guessed the wisdom of his enlistment and blamed the governor of New York for "exiling" him to the South.[73]

A growing sense of disillusionment filtered into the thoughts of Phillip and Philander at Harrison's Landing as they complained about boredom, frequent shifts on picket duty, and sedentary camp life in a swampy environment. Phillip bemoaned his separation from Smethport friends in Company I, who were still guarding McDowell's headquarters in Manassas. His "unsteady hand" and nervousness returned, and he hoped for the anticipated reunion of Kane's Rifles and Stone's Bucktails so that he could ask the captain of Company I for a medical discharge. "I dont think there is any help for [me] now," exclaimed the sickly lad.[74] Phillip's enthusiasm for the cause seemed to be waning.

Regarding the future, Philander pledged to Ann to buy a farm in order to keep the family together, but he added a frightening forecast: "I may come Home . . . with one arm and perhaps I may not be alowed to come at all."[75] Phillip contemplated studying law under Asa or his aforementioned interest in selling sewing machines. The war was slowly changing men's attitudes, and Phillip and Philander typified this psychological transformation. In the back of their thoughts, each brother contemplated his own mortality.[76]

* * * * * * *

McClellan's troops gradually mended from the stresses and strains associated with the recent bloody campaigns. The six-week interlude at Harrison's Landing not only witnessed another reorganization in leadership but also highlighted changes in the military lives of the Ellithorpes: one would be tempted by corruption and reassigned to a new department, and a second would respond to patriotism and rejoin the war in a brand-new regiment. Regarding his future, Phillip explained to Asa, "I will trust in Providence and await my destiny."[77] This was no time to sit around and do nothing, however. Another major fight was waiting for the brothers at the end of August.

Chapter Six

Watchful Waiting and Second Bull Run

For nearly two months, the Army of the Potomac languished in the sultry swampland of Harrison's Landing. Hot temperatures, fetid water, and mosquitoes created unhealthy conditions for many of the soldiers. McClellan utilized the interlude to refit units decimated by the previous months of combat, promote new commanders to fill vacancies, and create new departments. These changes filtered down to the company levels of Phillip and Philander. Lincoln's second call for volunteers after the Seven Days resulted in the return of Asa to military service, now officially an "Ellithorpe boy." A dark story of corruption blemished Phillip's career in the commissary, and then an opportunity of a fresh start presented itself. By late August, the watchful waiting on the James River came to an abrupt end as another major battle loomed on familiar soil. The story line was not so much about the battle itself as it was McClellan's procrastination in lending assistance, which directly affected the movements of the Ellithorpe brothers.

Medical Reforms

In April 1861, the Medical Department of the U.S. Army had been woefully unprepared for war. At that time, eighty-year-old Surgeon General Thomas Lawson oversaw fewer than 100 surgeons and assistant surgeons. Overwhelmed, he was replaced one month into hostilities by Dr. Clement A. Finley, who appointed Dr. Charles S. Tripler to a new position: medical director. Finley's system of care relied on surgeons, usually political appointees with a broad range of abilities, to administer to wounded soldiers in field tents placed directly behind each regiment on the battlefield. As the war progressed, many enlisted men came to disdain regimental surgeons as quacks and butchers too willing to resort to amputation. The rank and file also viewed the regimental hospital with derision and fear.

In the earliest engagements, the job of removing wounded men from the battlefield fell to regimental musicians, comrades, or shirkers. Those diverse attendants were untrained and unreliable. In an attempt to remedy the situation, Tripler assigned the Quartermaster Corps to clear the wounded and transport them to hospital stations, but his innovation failed to improve care. There was a shortage of qualified handlers and wagons, too. The earliest ambulances, known as "Finley's" or "gutbusters," were two-wheeled wooden conveyances, rickety, uncomfortable, and prone to breaking down. The Federal program of care for and transportation of wounded soldiers under Finley and Tripler was understaffed, untrained, and untested.[1]

As cracks began to appear in the Army Medical Department after Bull Run, informed civilians increasingly criticized its operation. Led by Massachusetts abolitionist Dr. Henry I. Bowditch and New York Unitarian clergyman Henry Whitney Bellows, these philanthropists lobbied for an independent aid society to unite charity groups across the North to supplement the military's system of care. Their brainchild was known as the United States Sanitary Commission, and it received Lincoln's endorsement in an executive order signed on June 13, 1861. At first, the commission was viewed with suspicion and jealousy by army doctors, the secretary of war, the general in chief, and high-ranking officers.

The objectives of the Sanitary Commission were straightforward: to improve sanitation conditions (broadly defined); to coordinate, prepare, collect, and transport necessary medical supplies; to transfer the wounded efficiently from the battlefield to the hospital; and to improve the diet of the troops with fresh fruits and vegetables. Commission investigators entered army camps and encouraged officers to weed out physically unfit soldiers, offered advice on food preparation to regimental cooks, taught proper hygiene to hospital nurses, and lobbied for litter-free grounds. A national headquarters was established in an old warehouse in Washington along with the creation of a reception center for newly arriving troops.[2]

The disastrous treatment of the wounded in the aftermath of Bull Run was the result of a breakdown in Finley's "regimental system," whose undermanned and poorly trained stretcher bearers could not keep up with the carnage. The Quartermaster Corps incurred special censure by its botched transportation of the wounded during the retreat. Many injured soldiers were abandoned and told to fend for themselves. The energized voices calling for change now became a roar.

On April 25, 1862, the executive secretary of the Sanitary Commission, Frederick Law Olmsted, persuaded Lincoln to replace Finlay with thirty-four-year-old Dr. William A. Hammond as surgeon general. Less than two months later, Hammond selected Dr. Jonathan K. Letterman to replace Tripler as medical director of the Army of the Potomac. Together, Hammond and Letterman hoped to relieve the Quartermaster Corps of its responsibility to transport the wounded and assume that duty themselves. The key to this reform was the creation of a trained ambulance corps. Unfortunately, these goals were not operational in time for the Seven Days, but Letterman proceeded to formulate his vision, which would have a profound impact on one of the Ellithorpe brothers.[3]

Harrison's Landing and Sickness

Harrison's Landing was an inhospitable environment where humid summer temperatures often hovered at 100 degrees Fahrenheit and the 100,000-man Army of the Potomac was packed into a four-square-mile parcel along with thousands of animals and tons of war material. These conditions placed unbearable stress on the sanitation system, and the overcrowded living quarters, marked by inadequate shelter and inconsistent delivery of rations, became a breeding ground for disease and discontent. At the end of July, the health crisis reached epidemic proportions when thousands of soldiers were reported ill from dysentery, diarrhea, typhoid fever, and scurvy.[4]

Part of the problem centered on the medical treatments of patients in the United States up to the war, which had been mightily influenced by Benjamin Rush (1745–1813), a physician with an impressive public résumé. The Philadelphian, an exemplary Renaissance man, was also the most well known physician in the United States and generally acknowledged as the father of American medicine. He based his homeopathic treatments (termed "heroic remedies") on three basic procedures—bloodletting, blistering, and purging—designed to remove impurities from the body. For decades, physicians were trained almost exclusively through apprenticeships, so Rush's treatments were dutifully applied to almost every known physical ailment.[5]

By 1861, Rush's concepts were beginning to be challenged by a younger, university-educated class of doctors trained in modern scientific principles (allopathy). There were enough caregivers, however, who still practiced homeopathy, and a showdown loomed between the old and new ways of delivering quality medical care to the rank and file once the war was under way. All three Ellithorpe boys would experience the conflict between the two competing methodologies in their individual military medical histories.

Phillip continued to suffer from illnesses first diagnosed in 1861–1862. In his third bout with the crippling effects of rheumatism since training camp, Phillip also complained to his sisters about an "unsteady hand." He contemplated asking the Bucktails' surgeon, Dr. S. D. Freeman, for a medical discharge, but the thought of leaving his comrades caused Phillip mental angst and general depression, so he did not pursue the request.[6]

Drudgery

At Harrison's Landing in July, McClellan's first order of military business was to erect a defensive perimeter to secure his army from enemy attack. Within the first week of their arrival, the Federals had dug eight miles of trenches, built artillery emplacements, and started construction on a bridge. On July 8, Lincoln paid a visit to the commanding general and spent time with each division. Philander thought that "Little McC" looked haggard and "quite careworn" as he accompanied the commander in chief.[7]

The 13th Pennsylvania Reserves and 27th New York were quickly put to work. The army's engineers faced unique challenges from the numerous streams in the James River drainage system, which were affected by tidal currents and susceptible to flooding. These narrow appendages presented transportation and communication problems. To remedy the situation, the 13th Pennsylvania Reserves were detached to build a bridge across Herring Creek. Stone ordered his lumbermen to denude the surrounding landscape of trees, and, miraculously, the Bucktails took less than eighteen hours to erect a 500-foot span over water that was more than ten feet deep in places.[8]

The 27th New York spent much of their time conducting similar construction projects, and Philander recalled this moment as living with a spade in his hand while digging wells, entrenchments, redoubts, and artillery emplacements. And, of course, there was endless picket duty, where the New Yorkers sometimes conversed with unseen Rebels across the water. Philander's regiment received a new issue of clothing and a visit from the paymaster, which lifted their spirits. Other pleasures involved picking wild blackberries, swimming, and bathing in the swollen James.[9]

Yet morale wavered. "The men would drink commissary whiskey until they were half drunk, or swallow quinine till their heads buzzed around like a top," one regimental historian confided. "The living rotted faster than the dead. . . . The once jolly mess tables at Elmira, that used to sing with jests and laughter, and glow with wit and good humor, is exchanged for the continuation of low, peevish growls that resound through the camp," the veteran concluded.[10]

The Ellithorpe brothers expressed differing opinions about soldier morale from the banks of the James. Philander complained to Asa about the repetitious nature of picket duty in the swamp where the Yankees battled "flies" (mosquitoes), sweltering heat, and shared disappointment in the generals for not capitalizing on the victory at Mechanicsville and Malvern Hill.[11] Phillip spun a different message in regard to the leadership: "We still have the utmost Confidence in General McLellan," he confided to Asa, "and still believe that he is the Man that can lead us through the Storm and bring us out."[12] Phillip's views about McClellan were much more in step with the opinions of rank-and-file soldiers, but he also yearned to be reunited with Company I, and he felt somewhat out of place. The brothers shared in one pleasure at Harrison's Landing: they were able to visit each other frequently.

McClellan Reorganizes the Officer Corps . . . Again

In the dog days of summer, death, illness, retirement, reassignment, and/or promotion had taken a toll on the officer corps. In one sweeping decision, McClellan increased the rank of all corps commanders and several division commanders to major general, including Slocum. Bartlett joined a dozen other newly minted brigadiers. That realignment also created an artillery corps under Brig. Gen. Henry J. Hunt and a cavalry corps directed by Brig. Gen. George Stoneman. These changes underscored McClellan's penchant for organization.

Structural change filtered down to the company and regiment levels, where a serious manpower shortage existed. At the bottom of the army's reorganization, Philander was elevated to sixth (later second) corporal of Company I.[13] In mid-August, Phillip would also be affected by McClellan's alterations.

The Return of Asa

On June 3, the day after the marriage of Asa and Ann, Gov. Edwin D. Morgan of New York released a statement seeking to replenish his state's fighting force. Anticipating the call for a second wave of federal government recruitment a month later, Morgan ordered "an enrollment to be made of all persons within the State liable for military duty" and attached a $50 bounty to lure prospective new volunteers. On July 25, young men gathered at recruiting stations in Allegany, Livingston, and Wyoming counties, New York, and listened to the pitch of two civilian promoters, William S. Fullerton and Asa R. Burleson, and Capt. Thomas Jones Thorp (85th New York). Over the following weeks, their efforts bore fruit with the creation of the 130th New York regiment, and Asa was awarded the second lieutenancy in Company H.[14]

Changes to the Bucktails

The announcement in July calling for more troops also affected Phillip and the Pennsylvania Reserves. When McNeil finally caught up to his 1st Rifles after a long illness, he was shocked to learn that so few Bucktails were present to answer the first roll call. The six companies were in such desperate condition that representatives from the Ladies Aid Society of Philadelphia and the Sanitary Commission paid special attention to their needs. Moreover, the recent campaign had greatly weakened the division's officer corps. Only Seymour remained from McCall's general staff, and eight field officers and eighty-one company officers had been casualties. The Pennsylvania Reserves needed to be rebuilt from top to bottom, especially the Bucktails, who had been shorthanded even before their appearance on the James Peninsula.

In early August, Seymour authorized McNeil to send captains Roy Stone and Langhorne Wister to Pennsylvania and recruit replacements for the recent losses sustained in the Seven Days. McNeil envisioned an all-Bucktail brigade, and he shared his idea with Pennsylvania's governor. Because of the shortness of time and the need to assign new regiments to defend the state capital, Stone and Wister successfully raised two full regiments, the 149th Pennsylvania and the 150th Pennsylvania, respectively. Thus, none of these recruits were funneled to the 13th Pennsylvania Reserves, but rather made up thirty-six new regiments mustered in September 1862. They brazenly adopted the bucktail as part of their uniform.[15]

Corruption in the Commissary

Phillip's role in the Bucktails had evolved since his enlistment—soldier, orderly, cook, nurse, and commissary worker. While his exact duty at Harrison's Landing was unclear, it was about to be clarified.

In late April, Phillip had crowed to his sisters about a new but undisclosed source of income. He explained how Clow would keep his earnings in the commissary safe, which often totaled three figures. Shortly, Phillip engaged in loaning money to enlisted men and officers alike. His company captain, Blanchard, in particular, signed a promissory note for $140 at 10 percent interest. "It is strange," Phillip boasted, "how money will find its way into my hands."[16]

Ann and Permelia were shocked to learn about Phillip's admission. How, they asked, did he obtain the funds? How reliable were those indebted to him? Was his "business" legal? Was it dangerous? Phillip brushed off his sisters' legitimate worries.[17]

The real answers were complex. At the beginning of the war, the method of food distribution was straightforward: company cooks and/or orderly sergeants reported to the commissary to receive their company's daily ration. As commissary workers discovered surpluses, they sold extra food to orderlies or civilian sutlers who had been approved by the regimental officer. In this way, these sutlers resold food to hungry soldiers and marked up popular items, such as sweets (cakes, pies, and cookies), to extort greater profits. Then the sutler would skim off a portion of his earnings to pay off his commissary contact. Another version of this black market scheme found commissary workers in cahoots with company officers who reinvested the unused portion of their generous meal allowance in the scam to achieve greater profit. Thus, the key to profitability was the working relationship between the commissary worker, on one hand, and the company officer or civilian sutler, on the other. Phillip solidified such a relationship in Falmouth and continued this operation to a lesser extent until the end of July 1862.[18]

Once Phillip was ensconced in the unprincipled system, he advised Asa to apply for a job overseeing the division bakery. Then he encouraged Asa to acquire a sutler's license and connect with him at the commissary. Phillip informed Asa that Clow's brother was in partnership with a sutler, and, together, they were hauling in $150 per week. The suggestion was dishonest, and Asa would have nothing to do with the illegal racket.[19]

In late July, Clow assembled his staff at the commissary to issue "very strict orders against speculation." "I dont know how to content myself," stated a distraught Phillip, "as they wont alow me to speculate anymore."[20] Clow's new policy was directed squarely at the corrupt practice of selling excess stores for self-gain. On the basis of Phillip's nefarious activities, it seemed likely that his days at the commissary would be numbered. Then another opportunity opened up.

Phillip and the Ambulance Corps

Dr. Letterman's concept to speed delivery of wounded from the battlefield to the hospital was really quite novel. He would replace the inefficient regimental system with a mobile triage unit that would accompany the soldiers into battle. The field surgeon would attend to the wounded immediately, followed by the rapid transfer of the injured on stretchers to a comfortable four-wheeled ambulance parked nearby. Each wagon was stocked with an assortment of medical supplies and equipment. The ambulance driver would then transport the wounded to the division hospital farther to the rear, where a team of surgeons and assistant surgeons, nurses, and orderlies awaited.[21]

In early August, McClellan adopted Letterman's dream of an ambulance corps in General Order No. 147. A mounted sergeant supervised each ambulance wagon comprising three privates: a driver and two stretcher bearers. The privates wore a two-inch green band around their cap and a two-inch green half-chevron on their sleeve so they would be easily recognizable on the battlefield. McClellan's directive welcomed strong, fit, and committed soldiers to apply and train for this vital lifesaving assignment. Certainly, Phillip would be challenged to meet these stringent requirements, but he was selected, nonetheless, to become a stretcher bearer for the Bucktails on August 12.[22]

Meanwhile, the Sanitary Commission had been struggling to remove wounded soldiers from hospitals on the James Peninsula to Washington. By mid-August, the situation had reached a crisis. Health officials warned about a shortage of qualified nurse attendants and disparaged at the large number of unauthorized soldier-volunteers who had not been detailed to hospital duty. Within one week of his new appointment, Phillip found himself at Fortress Monroe two weeks after his appointment to the ambulance corps, separated once again from his bucktailed comrades, who were marching toward Aquia Creek.[23]

The evacuation of 12,000 sick and wounded men was no small order. That mission of mercy shared a river channel jammed with troop transports, naval ships, and cargo tenders. As the Army of the Potomac slowly pulled back from the James Peninsula, Phillip revealed to Ann that he had contracted "Yellow Jandus," and he required another stay in the hospital. Despite being sick, he still managed to load wounded and sick soldiers aboard Sanitary Commission vessels as well as ambulance materials left behind during the surge to Washington.[24]

In early September, Phillip prepared to depart in one of the last ships from Hampton Roads, and he pined over not receiving missives from family or friends. His ongoing failure to receive a steady stream of mail since his induction fostered a sense of neglect and abandonment. Phillip reasoned that correspondence addressed through Company I might not have reached him at his posts in the commissary and ambulance corps, being sent to the Shenandoah Valley instead. Furthermore, he was clearly agitated at "those Patriots who stayed Home," young men who chose not to enlist. He peppered Ann with questions about "whether People [in Rushford] feel as Patriotic as when this Rebellion broke out," fretting that civilian morale was wavering. Many in the Army of the Potomac and northern society were beginning to express comparable feelings of "the blues" over the direction of the war.[25]

Problems of Independent Command

During the fight for Richmond, Lincoln reiterated his perception about a lack of security in the nation's capital. His solution resembled the earlier plan to create McDowell's independent Department of the Rappahannock. Now, on June 27, the president created another separate command, the Army of Virginia, under the aggressive Maj. Gen. John Pope. Pope's new force combined smaller western departments led by three familiar generals—Frémont, Banks, and McDowell—whose divisions were spread out in a large arc from Falmouth in the south to Fairfax in the north. Pope's consolidation would affect Kane's Rifles, McNeil's Bucktails, and Philander's 27th New York to varying degrees.

On July 8, Lincoln pressed for a quick follow-up to the victory at Malvern Hill in a meeting held at McClellan's headquarters. Yet the army remained entrenched along the James River. On August 3, after losing patience with McClellan's "slows," the president sent newly appointed General in Chief Henry W. Halleck to order the commanding general to shift his base to Aquia Creek, transport the Army of the Potomac via rail or ship to Alexandria, and march to support of Pope in northern Virginia. Lincoln's dual decisions to elevate Halleck and Pope had infuriated "Little Mac," and his departure proceeded at a painfully slow pace beginning on August 14. He had no intention of rushing to assist Pope.[26]

Surprised

McNeil's Bucktails were issued new Sharps rifles prior to leaving for Aquia Creek, a decided improvement over the muskets they had shouldered until then and sure to come in handy. The recently exchanged Reynolds replaced McCall at the head of the Pennsylvania Reserves and assigned McNeil's Bucktails to Meade's Brigade. Kane's Rifles continued to guard McDowell's headquarters at Catlett's Station. On August 27, the Pennsylvania division bivouacked in Gainesville, about seven miles west of Groveton-Manassas, where they would be in perfect position to intercept enemy forces that might try to slip through Thoroughfare Gap to reinforce the Confederates facing Pope. A foreboding thought: the Bucktails were poised to enter a major fray without the benefit of Phillip's ambulances.[27]

Several days earlier, on the dark and exceedingly foul night of August 22, Kane and his four Bucktail companies were guarding Pope's baggage at McDowell's headquarters in Catlett's Station. The train consisted of 300 wagons, and one of them contained Pope's personal papers and dress uniform. Fifteen men from Company I stood on evening picket duty as rain fell in sheets.

At dusk, J. E. B. Stuart's 1,500 horsemen fell on the unsuspecting Federals while probing their right flank. Kane's dazed troopers rushed from their tents and headed for cover in the woods, but they were heavily outnumbered. The Rebel horsemen ransacked the camp—burning wagons, pilfering stores, and setting tents ablaze. Night fighting was always chaotic, but Kane was able to rally his men and resist the Virginia cavalry as they attempted to plunder the train depot.

Kane quickly determined that the main objective of the mounted raiders was to destroy the railroad trestle running over Cedar Run. In the midst of the violent thunderstorm, one group of Confederates was already struggling to bring down the bridge with torch and ax. Resisting, Kane's plucky Bucktails laid down a withering fire from concealed positions behind trees and rocks on the opposite bank. The attackers recoiled and withdrew before they could bring down the span, failing in their strategic mission. But the southerners did capture 200 prisoners, 500 horses, a payroll chest, and, most embarrassing of all, Pope's dress uniform.[28]

The Battle of Second Bull Run

Pope faced an unanticipated problem at Manassas when two of McClellan's largest corps (Franklin's VI Corps and Sumner's II Corps) had failed to materialize due to unexplained delays. Within the 27th New York, there was considerable grumbling and straggling as they retraced their steps through Williamsburg, Yorktown, and Newport News. Humiliated, the men felt that they were running away from an enemy they had twice defeated, but on August 22, they set sail on the steamer *John Brooks* for Alexandria. On the eve of impending battle six days later, McClellan inexplicably halted Philander and his comrades at Annandale after only a seven-mile march and at Centreville the next day, where the regiment dug breastworks at Cub Run Bridge. In doing so, McClellan's procrastination had denied Pope 25,000 men. Consequently, it took them two days to march twenty miles; by then, the battle was over.[29]

On the morning of August 28, the day Philander's force disembarked in Alexandria, the Pennsylvania Reserves were involved in a significant precursor to the main battle fought over the following two days when Pope instructed McDowell's corps to proceed eastward on Warrenton Pike to the concentration site at Manassas Junction. No sooner had the Federals pushed through Gainesville than they encountered enemy batteries lodged two miles away on a ridge above Groveton. Their menacing barrage of grape and canister temporarily halted McDowell's march, so he ordered the Pennsylvania Reserves to remove the Rebel obstacle. Meade's brigade formed to the left of Warrenton Pike in an open field with McNeil's Bucktails thrown in front as skirmishers. Rebel sharpshooters, lodged in a farmhouse on the extreme left flank, added another challenge, so Meade told McNeil to split his band of marksmen to create pincers and silence the enemy. In a matter of minutes, the new Sharps rifles employed by the 1st Rifles had dispersed the southerners, and the Pennsylvanians resumed their trek.[30]

Having pushed through Groveton, Reynolds pulled his division off Warrenton Pike and started cross-country to Manassas Junction but not before detaching three companies of Bucktails under the combined command of Capt. Edward A. Irvin to tail the fleeing "johnnies" down Groveton-Sudley Road and possibly determine the location of the larger Confederate force. Irvin found a sizable body entrenched in an unfinished railroad cut at the base of Stony Ridge and reported his discovery to Reynolds. Skirmishing continued around Groveton and north of Warrenton Pike throughout the day, but it did not involve McNeil's Bucktails, who had performed well. The hot, muggy, and laborious two-hour off-road march ended at Bethlehem Church, where Reynolds's foot-weary division was ordered to return to Groveton via Warrenton Pike and prepare for a morning attack.[31]

Before dawn on the morning of August 29, Pope still struggled with pinpointing the exact whereabouts of Lee's Army of Northern Virginia, even theorizing that they were in full retreat toward the Shenandoah Valley. And where were McClellan's two missing corps? They would be indispensable to his strategy for the impending battle. The Pennsylvania Reserves straddled Warrenton Pike on the extreme left flank of the Army of Virginia. Before they headed toward the roar of musketry and shelling ahead, Meade ordered the thinned Bucktails to fan out in front to span the length of his entire brigade. As the 13th Pennsylvania Reserves pushed through Groveton, they were greeted by intense rifle fire from a house and thicket south of Warrenton Pike and artillery shelling from the north. Reacting instinctively, the Bucktails dove to the ground and engaged the enemy in the fighting style familiar to them. Once again, the new Sharps rifles hit their mark, and a bayonet charge dislodged the Rebels.

At the house just vacated, the 1st Rifles attempted to liberate almost forty wounded Federal soldiers from the Brawner's Farm encounter the previous day. As fighting intensified, however, it became apparent that McNeil's small force would not be able to hold its position. Accordingly, Reynolds ordered the advance party of Bucktails to fall back to Lewis Lane, where the division re-formed out of harm's way until late in the afternoon.[32]

Unbeknownst to the Federals, Longstreet's Confederates were pressing vigorously to turn their extreme left flank, and a gap similar to the one experienced by McCall at Glendale threatened Reynolds now. At dusk, the Pennsylvania Reserves regrouped near the crest of Chinn Ridge and awaited the morning, while the southerners were strengthening to deliver a frightening blow south of Warrenton Pike.[33]

On the morning of August 30, Pope rejected intelligence shared by Irvin and preferred to believe that Longstreet was not even present on the field but in full retreat. In mid-afternoon, Pope launched his forces toward Sudley Springs, with Reynolds's three brigades on the south side of Warrenton Pike in a supportive role. McNeil's Bucktails took their customary place in advance of Meade's brigade. After crossing Young's Branch, the 1st Rifles retrieved approximately thirty wounded soldiers, underscoring the terrible reality that they lacked ambulances to gather the wounded from the field. As the Federals engaged the enemy north of the roadway, the 1st Rifles cleared Groveton of Confederates but soon found themselves pinned down.[34]

In fact, Lee's Confederates launched a devastating counterattack south of Warrenton Pike with the objective of capturing Chinn Ridge and Henry House Hill. In response, Pope repositioned the Pennsylvania Reserves atop Dogan Ridge as a precaution to prevent the loss of Warrenton Pike. It was a calculated risk that further weakened the extreme left flank of the Federal line.

Watching as danger unfolded, Pope repositioned Reynolds (for a second time) to Henry House Hill at 5 p.m. Meade placed the 1st Rifles on his right with an unobstructed view of the junction of Warrenton Pike and Manassas-Sudley Road. As the Confederates rushed down Bald Hill and flooded both roadways, the bucktailed sharpshooters controlled every movement, and Meade ordered a bayonet charge down the slope. The fight was intense but short, and the southerners backed down. The Pennsylvania Reserves had performed admirably and preserved the army's main avenue of retreat. Arguably, the Pennsylvania Reserves provided the firepower and courage necessary to turn the southern aggressors away and prevent an undisciplined Federal rout similar to First Bull Run. Afterward, the Bucktails received special mention in Meade's official report.[35]

Aftermath

Throughout the Second Battle of Bull Run, Kane's Rifles had performed valuable service as McDowell's infantry escort, and McNeil's Bucktails were repeatedly called on by Meade to exercise their skills as marksmen and skirmishers. The successes of both branches of the regiment added significantly to their storied history, a story to which Phillip can lay partial claim.

During the retreat in a steady drizzle, Kane noticed that Stone Bridge was undefended, and he received permission to set up a picket on the east bank to protect the span from enemy capture. Only after the entire Army of Virginia had crossed the structure on their way to Fairfax Court House in the early morning hours of August 31 did Kane destroy it and fall back. Several days later, however, a genuine celebration broke out on Munson's Hill near Arlington, where McNeil's Bucktails and Kane's Rifles were reunited after a four-month separation. The 13th Pennsylvania Reserves were once again a ten-company outfit (sans their ambulance corps).[36]

In similar fashion, Philander's 27th New York offered protection at Cub Run Bridge and Centreville during the retreat, but the vanguard of his corps behaved disgracefully, hurling obscenities at Pope's defeated force as they trudged along Warrenton Pike. On September 2, Philander temporarily occupied a familiar post: Fort Lyon.[37]

Absence from Second Bull Run

In early September, Phillip was counted among the last soldiers in the division's ambulance corps to evacuate the James Peninsula. Once aboard and stricken with jaundice, he spent five uncomfortable days anchored off Old Point Comfort being tossed around by heavy wind, high seas, and rain. Only with great difficulty was he able to keep his ambulance equipment and himself on the open deck from being swept overboard. On September 6, Phillip's hospital ship docked at the wharves in Washington.[38]

In a larger sense, Phillip's nonattendance in the recently concluded campaign is further evidence of McClellan's shortsightedness and pettiness in refusing to act promptly in response to Halleck's directive to send aid to Pope. In this regard, Phillip was a pawn in the highest levels of military intrigue. McClellan should also be censured for making the ambulance corps the lowest priority on the eve of battle.

War of Words and Command Changes

A war of words was just heating up over McClellan's inexplicable behavior in holding back his largest two corps from the James Peninsula. His shameful role "represented one of the sorriest chapters in the history of the war."[39] In the nation's newspapers, there were "whispers of treason," and four cabinet members petitioned Lincoln to remove McClellan from command of the Army of the Potomac. Congress was in an uproar, and investigations were sure to follow. But Philander remained a McClellan loyalist: "The Army has not lost any of their confidence in him," the corporal reassured his sister, "if the Papers and Old Greely in Particular would Stop their Blowing we should get done more."[40] The reference was critical of Horace Greeley, founder and editor of the *New York Tribune*, an anti-McClellan newspaper.

On September 2, having nowhere else to turn following the defeat, Lincoln consolidated the commands of Pope and McClellan under duress. He placed "Little Mac" in overall command and transferred Pope to Minnesota to head the Department of the Northwest to quell the uprising of the Santee Sioux led by Little Crow.[41]

In the same flurry of command changes, Kane was promoted to brigadier general for meritorious service rendered to McDowell. Phillip was under the impression that Kane, too, was headed to Minnesota, so he asked his sisters, "Should I get the chance to go with Kane and fight the Indyans shall I go?"[42] Joe Barnes had already gone to Washington to interview as Kane's orderly, and the new brigadier asked about Phillip's availability for one of the "honorable positions." Nothing came of the inquiry; Kane remained in the Army of the Potomac, and his promotion opened the way for McNeil to assume undisputed command of the reunited Bucktails. Because of the shortage of company officers, Frank Bell continued to lead Company I in Blanchard's absence, and a hospital steward, R. Fenton Ward, was promoted to second lieutenant. Ward knew Phillip's medical history intimately.[43]

Lieutenant R. Fenton Ward, Company I, 13th Pennsylvania Reserves.
SOURCE: CIVIL WAR PHOTO COLLECTION, UNITED STATES ARMY HERITAGE AND EDUCATION CENTER, CARLISLE, PENNSYLVANIA.

Unpleasant Discovery

The 13th Pennsylvania Reserves, the "old" Bucktails, were horrified when they discovered the two untested regiments of Stone and Wister wearing bucktails on their kepis in the nation's capital. The original Bucktails felt strongly that they had earned their distinctive headgear (and stellar reputation) through sacrifice, perseverance, and hard fighting. Many of them harbored deep resentment toward the "bogus" Bucktails, feeling that the volunteers of 1862 had not earned the privilege of wearing this symbolic accessory. Furthermore, the two "new" regiments filled only three of twenty companies from original wildcat districts of northwestern Pennsylvania. Bitterness would linger for decades.[44]

Highs and Lows

The main feature common to the Ellithorpe brothers in the month leading up to Second Bull Run focused on health challenges. Basically, Phillip and Philander suffered from mental and physical exhaustion at Harrison's Landing. Despite the visitation by Lincoln to each division's camp on July 8 and the grand review orchestrated by McClellan on July 22, the Ellithorpe brothers continued to deal with bouts of "the blues," homesickness, and nostalgia caused by the magnitude of death and destruction they had witnessed in Virginia. Both young men pined to be back home working civilian jobs and reintegrating into Rushford society. "I shall have many stories to relate when I see my friends," Phillip explained. Even so, Phillip parroted Philander's steadfast loyalty to "McLellan."[45] At their lowest points of despondency, both brothers discussed the unpleasant possibility of becoming an amputee or, worse yet, coming home in a pine box.

Commissary versus Ambulance

It is unfortunate that the ambulance system was not yet ready for implementation at Second Bull Run. The commander and brigade leaders of the Pennsylvania Reserves regretted the lack of ambulances on the battlefield. Instead, Dr. S. D. Freeman of the Bucktails and other physicians followed the men into battle and cared for the wounded as best they could. Unfortunately, some of the wounded lay on the ground untreated for days before it was deemed safe enough to recover them, and one can only speculate about the number of men who died of their injuries because they did not receive prompt medical attention. Yet Letterman's greatest reform, the ambulance corps, would emerge from the nadir of unnecessary human suffering at Second Bull Run and achieve a level of functionality within several weeks on another battlefield.

So why did Phillip engage in corrupt activities in the commissary, and how did he secure his appointment with the ambulance corps?

In regard to the commissary, many opportunities to circumvent the system of distribution opened doors for Phillip and his accomplices to engage in black market practices to supplement their military salaries. Phillip mentioned receiving only two paychecks—one from the Commonwealth of Pennsylvania in July 1861 and the other from the U.S. government paymaster in July 1862. His fellow Bucktails were paid more frequently, and Phillip's pay situation was shrouded in a series of complex factors. The questionable military status of the 1st Rifles as a Federal regiment contributed to initial delays in regimental payments, and the money shortage caused Phillip great hardship in purchasing basic writing necessities, such as stationery, pencils, and stamps. Phillip's frequent illnesses and detachments from Company I further hampered his availability to meet the paymaster and exacerbated his impoverished situation.

The commissary worker conceived a pragmatic solution to obtaining capital—selling commissary foodstuffs for personal gain and loaning his profits at high rates of interest. Finally, there may have been a personal inducement to explain Phillip's dishonesty. Shortly after arriving at Harrison's Landing, Phillip revealed to his sisters that he might apply for a medical discharge and come home, and he had definite plans for how to use his extra earnings: "When I do Come [home]," he stated, "I will have enough [money] to Buy some of those Boys who used to laugh at me because I was poor."[46] It was a touching revelation about the family's prewar poverty, and Phillip used it to rationalize his mercenary activities to cheat the commissary.

The loans Phillip consummated were problematic from a collections standpoint as well. Take the $140 note at 10 percent interest to Capt. Blanchard of Company I. The lead officer had been sent home to convalesce from his two leg wounds after the battle of Cross Keys in June 1862. Blanchard would never return to active duty with the Bucktails, and Phillip complained vociferously for months that his repeated requests for repayment went ignored. Eventually, Phillip learned a hard lesson about deceit and human failings. Long afterward, two Bucktail veterans would challenge Phillip's high interest charges: "There were many in the regiment who made no charge for loans." The authors seemed intent on fostering an image of goodwill among the Bucktails rather than providing an accurate accounting of such financial interactions.[47]

At any rate, commissary director Clow was under increasing pressure at Harrison's Landing to clean up "speculation" in his department, and it is likely that Phillip's participation was a matter of common knowledge. So Phillip had a reason to angle for a job with the ambulance corps. To rid himself of one potentially unreliable and double-dealing worker, Clow may have recommended Phillip to the ambulance corps despite the strict qualifications for new corpsmen. He was particularly pleased to surrender his commissary apron for the "green bands," which designated his new relationship with the 1st Rifles. "Each one of us has our green band . . . one for each Arm," Phillip explained to his sisters with pride.[48] Phillip's inglorious stint with the commissary was over.

* * * * * * *

By September 1862, Phillip was shaping up to be a young man who desperately wanted to prove himself loyal to the Union Cause. Now he would carry a stretcher onto future battlefields and expose himself to great dangers as a member of Letterman's ambulance corps. Time would tell whether Phillip would accept the challenge of aiding fallen comrades in the heat of battle.[49]

The period of watchful waiting was over for the Ellithorpe brothers. The Army of Northern Virginia had slipped across the Potomac River, and McClellan's primary objective was to track them down. What would follow was the bloodiest single day in American military history in the lush farmland of western Maryland. "Youths who have dreamed only of glory," concluded one historian, "will be appalled by the realities."[50] For the Ellithorpe brothers, the price they paid was steep—namely, their loss of innocence.

Chapter Seven

The Loss of Innocence in Maryland

Concern in the ranks over the defeat at Second Bull Run lasted for less than a week because their savior, McClellan, was once again restored to command the Army of the Potomac. Yet Pope's failure encouraged Lee to advance the Army of Northern Virginia across the Potomac River into Maryland, alarming the North. Less than one week after their arrival in Washington, the Yankees were once again in motion in search of the Rebels. In another week's time, the regiments of both Ellithorpe brothers distinguished themselves in stiff engagements at South Mountain and the momentous battle of Antietam. Meanwhile, Asa resumed his military service in a different theater of operations in southeastern Virginia. The physical and psychological impact of the Maryland campaign hardened the minds of the main characters, as their post-battle letters to Rushford would testify.

Immediately after Second Bull Run, Lee's Confederates seized the initiative and crossed the Potomac to force another battle with the Army of the Potomac before it would have time to regroup. The Confederate venture into the rolling hills of Maryland was filled with high stakes for the South: shock value as well as promising military, political, and diplomatic gains. Indeed, Lee's aggressiveness on northern soil sent shivers through the national press and society. On September 5, separate wings of the Rebel army began to consolidate around Frederick, Maryland. McClellan's army responded to Lee with uncharacteristic speed.[1]

On September 5–7, the Bucktails marched out of Arlington and the 27th New York from Fort Lyon along with their respective corps to pursue the elusive Army of Northern Virginia. Philander was energized when his regiment passed through cheering crowds on the streets of Washington and filed past the home of McClellan. The experience rekindled his support for "Little Mac."[2] Army morale had rebounded nicely from its recent setback.

As the vanguard to McClellan's force marched toward Frederick, only a small portion of the ambulance corps was in tow. Unfortunately, not all of the ambulances had arrived from Fortress Monroe; thus, Dr. Letterman had only 200 wagons properly outfitted for the upcoming campaign. Logistical problems arose where a railroad trestle over Monocacy Creek was destroyed by the enemy, and trains full of medical supplies were placed on side tracks to allow for the passage of quartermaster and commissary railcars. Some medical supplies were hastily transferred to wagons and transported over roads. When the last of the hospital vessels docked in Washington, Letterman ordered the ambulance wagons stocked and forwarded. Phillip was part of this contingent.[3]

As the Army of the Potomac was en route to Frederick, Gov. Curtin made a panicky decision to recall Reynolds to take control over the Pennsylvania militia, which was in disarray. He genuinely feared a Confederate invasion of his state. McClellan, in turn, promoted Meade to command the Pennsylvania Reserves. In battles on the James Peninsula and northern Virginia, Meade had built a respectable reputation as a thoughtful, yet aggressive, general. He was not as well known to the enlisted men, but he promised to be an acceptable replacement to the highly respected Reynolds. In preparation for their departure, McNeil's Bucktails received a new issue of clothing, and Kane's four companies received new Sharps rifles.[4]

Asa and the 130th New York

As the Ellithorpe brothers filed northward toward a monumental showdown with the Army of Northern Virginia, Asa and his untrained 130th New York mustered for three years at Camp Williams near Portage, New York, and headed in the opposite direction. The fledglings were placed under the command of Col. Alfred W. Gibbs, a cavalryman and West Point classmate of McClellan. Gibbs had notched more than twenty years of service in the dragoons and had recently been paroled after being captured during the battle of Mesilla in New Mexico Territory. On September 6, prior to boarding a train that would carry 2nd Lt. Burleson and his Company H comrades to Elmira, the regiment stood "at parade rest" and witnessed the marriage vows of Lt. Col. Thorp to Mandana Major.[5]

Colonel Alfred W. Gibbs, 130th New York/19th New York Cavalry/1st New York Dragoons.
SOURCE: CIVIL WAR PHOTOGRAPHS, 1861–1865, LIBRARY OF CONGRESS, PRINTS AND PHOTOGRAPHS DIVISION.

Riding in smelly cattle cars from Elmira to Harrisburg, Gibbs's command transferred to dusty coal cars for the next leg of the journey and again to railcars in Baltimore. When they reached Washington, Gibbs delivered the 130th New York to the new "Soldiers' Home," where, according to an eyewitness, the men were provided "an unappetising meal of army bread [hardtack], boiled pork, and coffee."[6] Many fresh regiments were arriving daily from around the North, and Halleck earmarked approximately one-third of them to serve in a department called the Defenses of Washington. The remaining two-thirds were sent into the field; the 130th New York drew the latter assignment.

Without delay, Gibbs boarded his regiment on the steamer *New York* for a short and "invigorating" sea voyage to Fortress Monroe. As the regiment disembarked on September 13, Gibbs cheerfully led his men in singing "John Brown's Body." A short train trip brought the "very raw" unit to Suffolk, Virginia, its home for the next nine months.[7]

The 130th New York had been an organized military entity for only one week, had received no military training in the Manual of Arms, and now found themselves on active duty south of the James River near the Virginia coast. Suffolk, the county seat and largest town in the region, held strategic importance at the headwaters of a narrow, crooked, and marshy river, the Nansemond, which was partially navigable by gunboat. A major tributary of the James, the Nansemond contained large quantities of fish and oysters, an attraction to unauthorized Federal foragers. To the south of Suffolk lay the Great Dismal Swamp, an inhospitable region of dense underbrush, thick forests, and swampland that extended into North Carolina. With natural, jungle-like vegetation, the Dismal was an ideal landscape for small hit-and-run raiders. To the west flowed the Blackwater River. By constructing fortifications around Suffolk, the Federal occupation force would control both land and sea approaches to Norfolk, Portsmouth, and Hampton, Virginia.[8]

Suffolk lay within striking distance of Richmond, only eighty miles to the northwest. The junction of two railroad lines, the Norfolk & Petersburg and the Seaboard & Roanoke, added to the region's strategic military importance. Thus, the Federals laid out a defensive perimeter around Suffolk in a fourteen-mile arc that would include eight forts, many rifle pits, breastworks, and artillery emplacements and eventually manned by 17,000 soldiers.

After nearly two months of nonstop pick and shovel work, the extensive system of ramparts was completed. Asa had been detached from Company H to work as an "assistant engineer" in the layout and construction of Fort Nansemond in the northwest corner of the Suffolk line. It is unclear where he gained the construction knowledge necessary to tackle this task. Here, Asa's regiment bivouacked alongside the 99th New York, its constant companion for the ensuing months.[9]

Unwittingly, the popular Gibbs alienated the men by his mishandling the vacant position of regimental chaplain. Refusing to accept any applications, the colonel had approved a sign that read, "No chaplain needed here." Pious soldiers were incensed. The flare-up reached New York newspapers, spawning legions of complaints to the War Department. For the time being, the issue remained unresolved, and Gibbs did not regain his favorable rating with the rank and file until the regiment had participated in its first combat months later.[10]

In the fall of 1862, the coastal weather around Suffolk turned very rainy. Unfortunately, the 130th New York was not outfitted with pup tents or rubber blankets, so many men fell ill from exposure. Poor drinking water and proximity to the Great Dismal Swamp compounded the health crisis in Gibbs's regiment, where sickness struck with a vengeance. As Asa was acclimatizing to his new surroundings in southeastern Virginia, Phillip and Philander were closing in on the elusive gray quarry in western Maryland.[11]

Battle Plans North and South

To this point, McClellan was oblivious to Lee's motives, so he formulated a three-pronged movement designed to probe a large geographic area and collapse on its main objective, Frederick, from three different directions. Meanwhile, Lee finalized his battle plan, too. Basically, he intended to utilize a physical feature called South Mountain, fifteen miles northwest of Frederick, as a buffer to disguise his northward movements.

Calling South Mountain a "mountain" is something of a misnomer. An extension of the Blue Ridge Mountains, it more closely resembled a fifty-mile-long ridge reaching elevations no greater than 1,300 feet. It ran in a northeast-to-southwest direction, bisected two large valleys, and offered the perfect cover for the Army of Northern Virginia to advance into southern Pennsylvania. The rugged terrain was steeply sloped, heavily wooded, blanketed with dense underbrush, and carved by many deep ravines. Where the land had been cleared in the lower approaches, many productive farms dotted a pleasing landscape etched by low stone walls and split-rail fences. Three "gaps" no more than ten miles apart traversed the ridge: the National Road crossed at Turner's Gap on its way to Boonsboro, Old Sharpsburg Road was at Fox's Gap, and Burkittsville Road meandered up to Crampton's Gap and spilled into Pleasant Valley.[12]

On September 10, the Confederates left Frederick to implement Lee's design, Special Order No. 191. The directives to Rebel commanders were wrapped around three cigars and stuffed into an envelope. Two days later, McClellan's vanguard entered the Maryland town. There, two soldiers found Lee's "Lost Orders" lying on the ground in a vacated Rebel campsite. If McClellan acted promptly, he might catch the divided enemy unaware and defeat them. Unfortunately, the Army of the Potomac remained in place for eighteen crucial hours while the Federals consolidated their lines.[13]

The mountain passes of South Mountain provided McClellan with the key to a simple strategy that, if effective, would drive a wedge between the disjointed Rebels on the west side of South Mountain. On September 13, he settled on a plan to storm the three gaps simultaneously.

McClellan's scheme held promise. His 100,000-man army should steamroll over the 3,000 gray-clads who provided a shadowy line of defense at the crests. These directives would deliver Phillip and the Bucktails to Turner's Gap and Philander and the 27th New York to Crampton's Gap.[14]

Bucktails at Turner's Gap

On the morning of September 14, McClellan's orders reached the Pennsylvania Reserves camped along the Monocacy River about two miles east of Frederick. McNeil's Bucktails assembled at 3 a.m., assumed their customary place at the head of the 1st Brigade, and were on the march an hour later. Turner's Gap lay ten miles ahead, and their corps stretched out for four miles. When Meade's vanguard reached Bolivar, they turned onto Mount Tabor Church Road. Pausing about one mile down the road, the Pennsylvanians encountered Rebel resistance at Mount Tabor Church.[15]

As the batteries unlimbered, Meade formed his three brigades in an open field within sight of Confederates concealed farther up the mountainside. Two soldiers from Company I were mortally wounded there by enemy grapeshot. The 1st Brigade assumed the extreme right of the division, and six companies of Bucktails, more than 250 men, were thrown out as skirmishers with four companies held in reserve. The 1st Rifles intended to flush out the enemy defenders while at the same time protect the extreme right flank of Meade's advance. This would be dangerous duty for infantrymen and ambulance men alike.[16]

The Bucktails started up Frostown Road at 5 p.m., but in less than half a mile, the road forked. Seymour's 1st Brigade angled to the right as Meade's other two brigades, led by Col. Thomas F. Gallagher and Col. Albert L. Magilton, advanced on the left on Dahlgren Road. A deep gulley separated the two wings. The Bucktails traversed inhospitable ground, a series of rolling hillocks and steep ravines strewn with boulders, which offered the southerners natural breastworks and concealed hiding places. In contrast, the Gallagher–Magilton brigades passed through open pastureland and meadows broken by stone fences. These physical barriers inhibited Meade's ability to coordinate the advance, and the terrain quickly broke down regimental cohesion.[17]

The Pennsylvanians advanced cautiously, and when the road split again, the Bucktails turned right onto Zittlestown Road while the rest of Seymour's brigade remained on Frostown Road. Here, the Confederate commanders understood the gravity of the situation. If the 1st Rifles continued on the road, they would turn their left flank, just as Meade had intended. An intense firefight broke out between the Bucktails and the 6th Alabama led by Col. John B. Gordon, forcing McNeil to call forward his four reserve companies.[18]

The 2nd and 6th Pennsylvania Reserves were sent to reinforce the 1st Rifles, and the combined Federal charge broke the Rebel line near Widow Main's house. Firing their Sharps rifles on the run and diving on the ground to reload, they managed in opening Zittlestown Road all the way to the summit, capturing eleven prisoners along the way. In the meantime, Meade's other two brigades put enormous pressure on the Confederate defenders on Frostown Road, whose resistance crumbled at approximately the same time as the assisted Bucktail breakthrough.

Downslope, behind the bucktailed sharpshooters, were strewn sixty-three wounded and killed comrades. Phillip and fellow stretcher bearers worked feverishly until after nightfall, clearing almost 400 wounded soldiers from Meade's division, including twenty-three line officers. Dr. Letterman had set up a hospital station in Middletown about four miles from Turner's Gap. One of Phillip's good friends, Sgt. William J. Kibbe, was among those mortally wounded. The ambulance man shared neither his personal loss nor specifics about his dangerous work in correspondence.[19]

That evening, the victorious Yankees spent a chilly night at Mountain House atop Turner's Gap, sleeping beside their weapons. The bigger picture showed that the Federals had succeeded in driving a wedge between Confederate forces in Boonsboro, Pleasant Valley, and Harpers Ferry. Having accomplished McClellan's first objective, attention shifted six miles to the south toward Crampton's Gap.[20]

Philander at Crampton's Gap

On September 14, Philander and his corps broke camp at Buckeystown at 5:30 a.m., but unlike the vigorous Federal push to Turner's Gap, the Yankees approached Crampton's Gap with extreme timidity. They arrived in the village of Jefferson several hours later, about seven miles short of their goal, and halted to await the arrival of the reserve corps. After an hour's delay, with no reinforcements in sight, the march resumed. About noon, Cake's 96th Pennsylvania in Bartlett's brigade proceeded through the picturesque village of Burkittsville at the base of South Mountain. Philander and the 27th New York were not far behind.[21]

As soon as the Pennsylvania regiment cleared the settlement, they discovered a fortified butternut presence aligned behind a stone wall that extended along Mountain Church Road perpendicular to Burkittsville Road and Arnoldstown Road. The appearance of the 96th Pennsylvania touched off an immediate response from the Rebels. The intensity of musketry, grape, and canister signaled to division commanders that a frontal assault would be necessary to dislodge the southerners from their strong defensive position.[22]

Slocum placed his brigades on the extreme right flank of the Federal line with Bartlett's brigade occupying the outermost edge. A meandering creek, Burkitt's Run, separated Bartlett from the rest of the blue-clads. Once deployed, Slocum's three-brigade division extended for a mile. They halted and awaited further instructions. They outnumbered their foe ten to one.

Indecision

At an impromptu and seemingly informal council of war, the corps commander asked for advice from his division and brigade commanders, specifically, who should initiate the attack? Slocum offered Bartlett's brigade, whose troops already held the extreme right and stood the greatest chance of turning the Confederate left and opening Arnoldstown Road, the main roadway to Crampton's Gap. The alternative, a direct frontal assault on the enemy's center, would result in high casualties. Meanwhile, gray-clad reinforcements were racing toward Crampton's Gap from Rohrerville in Pleasant Valley. When Bartlett arrived at the powwow in the yard of the Shafer House, he was angered by the cavalier posture of the cigar-smoking officers in attendance. Still, he accepted their decision for his brigade to spearhead the attack. Bartlett would lead his five regiments parallel to Arnoldstown and Burkittsville roads and target two prominent buildings: the Tritt House and a small church that stood at the center of the Rebels' line. He would form two columns of two regiments each, space them 200 yards apart, and throw out Philander's 27th New York to skirmish 100 yards in advance of the brigade. It took an hour to align his men, so the assault did not begin until well after 4 p.m.[23]

Bartlett's soldiers viewed the stone wall that protected the enemy at the base of South Mountain with trepidation. As they prepared to double-quick across the rolling terrain divided by many stone and wooden fences, Bartlett pulled Adams aside, pointed his sword toward Crampton's Gap, and dramatically instructed the commander of the 27th New York to "take your regiment to the top of that mountain."[24]

As Bartlett's attackers emerged from their concealed position in the creek bed ravine, Confederate artillery opened on their lines. Adams encouraged his skirmishers onward, but the 27th New York broke into a run and quickly lost cohesion as its extreme left and right flanks rushed forward much quicker than its center. As they scaled the last stone wall and entered a clover field, the 16th Virginia opened fire from about 300 yards away. The New Yorkers dropped to the ground and fired their muskets from a prone position, but their ammunition ran out after twenty minutes. Then the Straw Hat Boys and the 5th Maine charged through their ranks to take the lead, but the assault had stalled. Adams pulled the 27th New York back to a cornfield to reorganize, receive more ammunition, and await new orders.[25]

Consequently, the brigades of Col. Alfred T. A. Tolbert and Brig. Gen. John Newton double-quicked to the rescue. Slocum's three brigade commanders conferred briefly on the field, agreed to launch a frontal bayonet assault involving the entire division, and pledged to not slow down until they would reach Crampton's Gap. The courage of these field officers to seize the initiative superseded the fumbling, indecisive leadership at corps headquarters.[26]

The cobbled plan called for Tolbert's brigade to lead the charge, to be followed in waves by Newton and then Bartlett. Cake's 96th Pennsylvania, the sister regiment of the 27th New York, was positioned on the extreme right flank of Bartlett's force and now amassed on Arnoldstown Road. The Yankee attack that followed was a numbers game—the heavily outnumbered Confederates behind the stone wall eventually crumbled but not before Cake's regiment battled regiments of Virginians, North Carolinians, and Georgians in hand-to-hand combat along a 150-yard stretch of the stone wall. By evening, the Rebels were in full retreat toward Pleasant Valley with Bartlett's brigade in hot pursuit. Philander's 27th New York was kept in reserve during the race up Arnoldstown Road, but they had been bloodied, sustaining thirty-three casualties in the three-hour engagement. For the next two days, Bartlett stationed his former regiment at brigade headquarters atop Crampton's Gap.[27]

Prelude to Hard Fighting

By nightfall on September 14, McClellan's forces controlled Fox's Gap and Turner's Gap and had extended beyond Crampton's Gap, the most complete Federal victories in the eastern theater to date. The Army of the Potomac was in high spirits as they prepared to descend the western slope of South Mountain the next morning.

McClellan had issued specific follow-up instructions to his corps commanders. Franklin was to disperse the Confederates in Pleasant Valley, lift the enemy siege on Harpers Ferry, and anchor the left wing of the Army of the Potomac. In the meantime, Maj. Gen. Joseph Hooker should also descend into the valley, proceed through Boonsboro, and occupy Keedysville, where Dr. Letterman planned to set up a large field hospital. The former movement would include Philander; the latter movement would include Phillip.

In typical form, Franklin advanced at a snail's pace, so only portions of his command occupied the valley by nightfall. Although Hooker rested his command in the morning and fought through a determined Rebel rear guard, he achieved his objective by late afternoon. From a perch west of Keedysville, the Federals could see Antietam Creek meandering through the countryside in the distance. They halted; there would be no more fighting on that day or the next. In the peaceful interlude, the stealthy Jackson took advantage of the lull to transfer troops to Lee.

On the foggy morning of September 16, Lee's Army of Northern Virginia occupied a ridgeline running north to south between the Potomac River and Antietam Creek on the west side of a prosperous village called Sharpsburg. Antietam Creek was neither deep nor wide, and it offered suitable fording spots for infantry, but the cavalry, artillery, quartermasters, commissary, and ambulance corps required bridges on which to operate. Three stone bridges extended across the creek from north to south: Upper Bridge, Middle Bridge, and Lower Bridge. Two main arterials entered the town from north to south: Hagerstown Pike and Smoketown Road. Productive farms at harvest time filled the countryside with ripened corn, grain, and fruit. Open meadows and three principal woodlots, North Woods, East Woods, and West Woods, completed the topography. Here, the Ellithorpe brothers would forge a lifetime of wartime memories in the next forty-eight hours.[28]

McClellan's strategy was quite simple. At dawn on September 17, Hooker's corps would "open the ball" at the north end of the field, seek out the enemy on the west side of Antietam Creek, and keep the Rebels occupied between Hagerstown Pike and Smoketown Pike. If the diversion succeeded, the Yankees might even occupy the Dunker Church plateau, where both pikes converged. The attack would be a signal for hostilities to commence in the south. Together, these coordinated actions should trap the Confederates in a double envelopment. Once the Rebels would be totally engaged on both extremities, two Federal corps would move forward from their center position. McClellan's strategy was theoretically sound, but it would require pinpoint execution by several moving parts over long distances. Phillip would enter the field in the north and Philander from the center.[29]

The Bucktails at Antietam

Needing to be in place on Hagerstown Pike north of Sharpsburg on September 16, Hooker began crossing Antietam Creek at Pry's Mill Ford and Upper Bridge about 2 p.m. Once across, Meade's Pennsylvania Reserves was instructed to advance on two woodlots adjacent to both pikes and flush out Confederate resisters. The Pennsylvania Reserves were destined to take in a preview of the battle that very afternoon.

At George Line's farmhouse, Meade held a brief meeting with his brigadiers and ordered 1st Brigade commander Seymour to continue down Smokehouse Road and explore the East Woods while he took the rest of the division cross-country toward the North Woods, where the Confederates were believed to be lying in wait.[30]

At 4 p.m., McNeil assembled the Bucktails as skirmishers to lead the brigade in the direction of the East Woods. He placed two companies on either side of Smoketown Road and held his remaining six companies in reserve. No sooner had the marchers departed than they were exposed in an open field and peppered with rounds of grape and canister from enemy howitzers masked by the woodlot.[31]

The 1st Rifles reached a rail fence on the northern edge of the East Woods with the rest of the brigade and Phillip's ambulance corps approximately 600 yards in the rear. At this place, McNeil signaled forward his six reserve companies and told the small regiment to anticipate extremely hazardous duty ahead once they entered the foreboding woods to clear out the Rebels. No sooner had he stood up, shouting encouragement to advance and leading from the front, than McNeil was shot in the chest. He died almost instantly.[32]

The enraged Bucktails, aflame with fury, stormed into the timbered abyss without command. Beneath the canopy of trees, the ground was surprisingly open, and numerous rock ledges and fallen logs offered ample protection. Here, the 1st Rifles employed their familiar fighting style with great effectiveness. For nearly two hours, the Pennsylvanians fought against Texans in very tight quarters, sometimes only twenty paces apart. Casualties mounted on both sides.[33]

The fight for the East Woods became protracted once the entire brigade moved forward to reinforce the Bucktails. Fiery flashes from musket barrels went on long after sunset, and several heated exchanges with a North Carolina brigade erupted in the hours after midnight. Since retreat was impossible, the leaderless Bucktails hunkered down for an uneasy night as light rain began to fall. Phillip and his colleagues in the ambulance corps were able to remove some dead and wounded comrades only after the Confederates pulled back in the predawn hours, including the wounded Capt. Bell of Company I.[34]

The stiff resistance faced by the Pennsylvania brigade convinced Hooker, whose corps stretched from Hagerstown Pike above the North Woods to the East Woods, that the Dunker Church plateau held the key to success in the battle about to be waged the next day, and he planned accordingly. The opponent, Lee, who held the advantage of interior lines of defense, shared that suspicion.

The Battle of Antietam

At dawn on September 17, Hooker launched the Federal assault down Hagerstown Pike, and the roar of artillery on both sides shook the ground, announcing the commencement of the battle. Meade's shorthanded Pennsylvania Reserves followed in support, while his 1st Brigade was still locked in sporadic combat and pinned down in the East Woods.[35]

Hooker's attack showed promise of turning the Rebels' left flank, but the Federals faced growing opposition as they approached Miller's thirty-acre cornfield. He called for reinforcements, but they responded slower than the Confederates under the command of Brig. Gen. John Bell Hood, who poured into the field in a vicious counterattack. The fighting was ferocious, and the desperate sounds of mortal combat lasted for more than two hours, during which time "the Cornfield" changed hands six times and witnessed some of the most savage close-quarters fighting of the entire war.[36]

One participant recalled that the fighting among the ripened cornstalks was so intense that the sheer volume and surreal sound of lead balls, grape, and canister zipping through the air sounded like "the whisper of eternity." Regardless of uniform color, blue or gray, the combatants fell in clusters. Another eyewitness later claimed that a person walking the length of the Cornfield would step on corpses of dead soldiers and never touch the ground.[37]

Some Bucktails were likely witnesses to the pandemonium from their precarious position in the East Woods behind a snake-rail fence that bordered the soon-to-be-infamous landmark. They were busy inflicting damage with their Sharps rifles on a group of Confederate infantrymen occupying an open field on the Mumma farm, but the crack riflemen were running dangerously low on ammunition. In addition, the regiment still contended with enemy batteries near Dunker Church and Nicodemus Heights. It remained a definite "hot" spot.[38]

Desperate Work to Save Lives

As expected, Phillip's ambulance corps was exceptionally busy. The field hospital for the brigade was laid out at the George Line farmhouse, but other locations popped up at the Miller and Morrison farmhouses, north and east of the Cornfield, respectively. The principal staging area for ambulances in this sector congregated on Poffenberger's Lane. Everywhere on the field, stretcher bearers were conducting dangerous work because the novelty of their assignment attracted enemy fire.[39]

One week after the battle, Phillip provided his first-ever graphic portrayal of actual combat and his personal experience in a four-page missive to his sisters. "The worst of all is after the Battle is over and the wounded have been brought from the field," he informed them, "to see a poor fellow Shot through in almost every place some with a foot leg or arm Shot off." Phillip also recorded his compassion for the enemy. "I dressed one Rebs wounds. He was shot in the back of the neck," he recounted. "The Ball came out under his left ear. He [said] one of them d——d bucktails done it . . . the best men I have met [in battle]. . . . I treated him with respect for we like brave men."[40] By donning the green armbands and a half-chevron insignia on his sleeve, Phillip had finally discovered his appropriate niche in the war.

Disaster in the West Woods

By 9 a.m., Hooker's advance had been stymied by Hood. The battlefield in the north turned unnaturally quiet as the second phase of the struggle shifted to the center of McClellan's line. Meanwhile, Sumner's corps had completed its tedious crossing of Antietam Creek at Upper Bridge and Pry's Mill Ford, and his centerist march proceeded toward the West Woods. En route, Sumner made several crucial mistakes. First, he neglected to provide specific marching orders to his two trailing divisions, and they drifted off course in the direction of the Sunken Road, a serious miscommunication. Second, Sumner failed to take the time for a thorough reconnaissance, and he was about to unleash his force blindly. Three blue-clad columns, bunched only seventy yards apart, were easy targets for enemy grape and canister fired from Hauser's Ridge—Sumner's third error of the morning. He had unwittingly delivered his largest division into a Confederate trap that crushed his left flank. The stunned Yankees fled northward, and they did not regroup until they reached the relative safety of the North Woods. The collapse had been as complete as anything witnessed at First Bull Run or Glendale, and it would impact the placement of Philander's tardy corps shortly.[41]

Philander: Too Little, Too Late

After a four-hour march from Pleasant Valley, Franklin's vanguard reached the Upper Bridge and Pry's Ford about the time Sumner was entering the West Woods. McClellan immediately ordered Slocum's division forward. Bartlett's brigade occupied the rear and stood in readiness for two hours, slowly inching forward while under heavy enemy shelling. Once across the creek, Bartlett assigned his favorite regiment, the 27th New York, to protect a battery near the Cornfield as the battle shifted to the center and south. Adams's regiment spent an unnerving night surrounded by corpses. But they were fortunate for not being used in combat.[42]

As the din of battle ebbed in the East Woods, Cornfield, and West Woods at noontime, the battle shifted to the center, where the fight for the Sunken Road, or Bloody Lane, took place. Here, Phillip's friend from Rushford, Pvt. Charles Van Dusen of the 64th New York, participated in, arguably, some of the fiercest action of the entire war. Farther to the south, waves of Federal soldiers advanced across Lower Bridge, an attack designed by McClellan to coincide with the early morning movement to the north.

It partially succeeded, though with tremendous loss of life. By nightfall, the bloodiest single day in American military history was over.[43]

Loss

The next day, the contesting armies held their ground during a twelve-hour cease-fire to collect the wounded and begin the arduous task of burying the dead. The vast accumulation of corpses overwhelmed stretcher bearers, surgeons, and burial parties alike. The 27th New York stayed in the Cornfield for four days, dug large trenches, and interred 100 South Carolinians. "The bodies of the dead," stated one of Philander's comrades, "having lain so long exposed to the sun, were rapidly decomposing, and the stench was almost unendurable." In the surreal silence after the battle, the sheer magnitude of slaughter had a lasting shock, changing the lives of some men forever. The war had lost its allure. On September 18, under the cover of darkness, Lee and the Army of Northern Virginia slipped back across the Potomac River.[44]

On October 1, President Lincoln traveled to Sharpsburg to review the troops, visit hospitals, tour the battlefield, consult with the generals, and prod McClellan to follow up on the victory and pursue the Rebels into Virginia. Lincoln left four days later without having received guarantees, but he acknowledged genuine concerns about shortages of food, shoes, blankets, clothing, ammunition, horses, wagons, and staggering casualties.[45]

Where Were the Bucktails?

In the aftermath of battle, two conflicting versions about how long the Bucktails remained in the East Woods emerged. One account claims that, at about 7 a.m., an unidentified officer in the 13th Pennsylvania Reserves, perhaps Adjutant W. Ross Hartshorne or Capt. Dennis McGee, took advantage of the melee in the Cornfield to extricate the regiment and withdraw along the same path they had entered the East Woods the previous evening. Hartshorne and McGee were two of the few line officers not missing during the struggle.

A second version suggests that the scattered and isolated 13th Pennsylvania Reserves remained in the woodlot longer and fought on as independent warriors. What is clear is that the Bucktails were in disarray as a result of the chaos and absence of clear leadership in the East Woods. Similarly, many units would lose regiment and company officers the next day, and generally, the responsibilities of command often fell to sergeants, enlisted men, or individual discretion. In sum, the precise movements of the Bucktails on the morning of September 17 is a historical blur, although it was well known afterward that much straggling occurred in their sector.[46]

Revamping from Top to Bottom

The Pennsylvania Reserves underwent a drastic reshuffle after Antietam. First, Curtin released Reynolds from state militia duty to resume command of I Corps, which would bump Meade back to division command once he had recovered from his wound received in the battle. One brigade vacancy was filled by the forceful Col. William McCandless of the 2nd Pennsylvania Reserves. Phillip's Bucktails fell beneath the commands of these three officers.

The greatest impact on Phillip's bucktailed compatriots, however, was the shocking loss of McNeil. Although McGee, an Irish immigrant and civilian grocer from Mauch Chunk, Pennsylvania, assumed control of the Bucktails in the East Woods, he was as "green" as the Antietam cornstalks. Thus, during the Indian summer interlude in western Maryland, three other company captains were promoted to regimental positions: Col. Charles Frederick Taylor, Lt. Col. Edward A. Irvin, and Maj. W. Ross Hartshorne. Reminiscent of Kane–McNeil electioneering squabbles, some soldiers complained about these appointments, believing that company captains Niles

Captain/Colonel Charles F. Taylor, Company H, 13th Pennsylvania Reserves. *SOURCE:* THOMSON AND RAUCH, *HISTORY OF THE "BUCKTAILS,"* 245.

and McDonald were more deserving leaders based on their demonstrated valor since Mechanicsville. The regiment also lost Chaplain W. H. D. Hatton through resignation, and he was not replaced. Closer to Phillip and Company I was the wounding of officers Bell and Ward, the death of good friend and messmate Kibbe at South Mountain, and the nonlethal shoulder injury to his cousin, James Stebbins.[47]

On September 30, Curtin requested Lincoln and McClellan to return the Pennsylvania Reserves to Harrisburg to be refit because of their decline in manpower to 4,000 men. Phillip engaged in this debate: "Thare is a story afoot in Camp that Governor Curtin wants to get us back into the State," he explained to Ann. "I only hope that he will succeed. I think we have done our part of the Fighting and ought to have rest."[48] In the days after Antietam, McClellan found Curtin's request untimely and ultimately denied it. In a compromise, however, he assigned the freshly recruited 121st Pennsylvania to McCandless's brigade.

Such a decision highlighted several fears among the Bucktails that they might be assimilated into other units, and some veterans petitioned the governor to veto such action. At the same time, many "old" Bucktails harbored equally strong feelings about *not* accepting new "bounty" recruits into their ranks because such enlistees were believed to be fighting for bonus money rather than higher principles, such as patriotism. The Bucktails simply did not want to lose their hard-fought identity or see it diluted.[49]

Indian Summer

In the weeks following the battle, the Army of the Potomac recuperated in Sharpsburg, and a number of charitable groups visited the Pennsylvania Reserves. Representatives of the Pennsylvania Relief Society, the Patriotic Daughters of Lancaster, and the U.S. Sanitary Commission administered to the needs of the infirm in hospital wards. During the unseasonably warm and dry autumn, the soldiers took advantage of the downtime to write letters home, welcome family visitors, and meet up with hometown friends in nearby regiments. Phillip and Philander spent time together and saw cousins Ed Stebbins in the 33rd New York and his wounded brother, James, who was recuperating in the Smoketown Road (Keedyville) hospital. These visitations to field hospitals often exposed the soldiers to distressing conditions. Reflecting on his own good fortune, Phillip told Permelia, "I was a pretty

Lucky Fellow to get through this far." Gripped by homesickness, Philander yearned to come home "to enjoy the peasefull quiet of home amongst the hills of Allegany." Both brothers hoped for an early start to winter quarters and an end to the war.[50]

Repairs to the 27th New York

Like Phillip's regiment, Philander's 27th New York underwent significant post-Antietam command changes. First, Slocum was promoted to lead XII Corps, and Bartlett was rewarded for his leadership at Crampton's Gap with a brigadiership. Adams was awarded a full colonelcy along with the advancement of two captains, Lt. Col. Joseph Bodine and Maj. George G. Wanzer. It should be emphasized that Philander's New Yorkers were completely in awe of the valor demonstrated by Slocum and Bartlett since First Bull Run, but the rank and file were lukewarm to these regimental and company selections and sorely disappointed in not being assigned to Slocum's new corps. In the first week of October, there were fewer than forty men present for active duty in Company I, but Philander informed Ann that most of the "Rushford boys were healthy and in good spirits."[51]

Dismissal

Despite Lincoln's protestations and prods from Halleck for McClellan to commence operations, the Army of the Potomac remained in Sharpsburg for seven weeks following the battle, although the marvelous weather was ideal for military campaigning. Philander and the 27th New York enjoyed the respite and bivouacked in Bakersville, a hamlet about four miles north of Sharpsburg. There, Philander observed "a Thriving Villidge" surrounded by "well cultivated farms." The New Yorker was "enjoying a few weeks of quiet rest in one of the finest valleys in the world."[52]

One episode disturbed the quietude when several contrabands were caught stealing Slocum's wine and cigars. The guilty parties were herded through camp, each one wearing only a barrel, a common army punishment for thievery. "As they were marched along," recounted one eyewitness, "they were met at each Company's street by handfuls of flour from the men which was thrown into their faces." The volunteers also tossed the "darkies" in a blanket before releasing them. Clearly, the white-face incident points to a much more disturbing example of racial prejudice.[53]

During the autumn interlude, Philander and the 27th New York broke the monotony with numerous shifts on picket duty. They routinely patrolled around Shaffer's Mill and often exchanged musket fire with Rebels across the Potomac River at Dam Nos. 4 and 5, six miles northwest of Sharpsburg. In more fraternal moments, the combatants exchanged newspapers, coffee, and tobacco in clandestine nighttime visits. On October 9–12, the friendly atmosphere abruptly changed when the brash Confederate cavalryman J. E. B. Stuart rode completely around the Army of the Potomac for the second time in four months.[54]

Lincoln's patience with McClellan's inactivity was wearing out. Finally, on October 26, the Army of the Potomac started a slow and painstaking crossing of the Potomac River. It took more than a week to transfer the army to Virginia soil and advance less than fifty miles. Phillip complained about the daily routine of short marches and occasional skirmishes. On November 2, the expert forager quipped that "12 Chickens near the road had to suffer" on one march.[55]

Unamused with the lack of progress, on November 7, the commander in chief ordered the general in chief to remove McClellan of his duties. The rank and file were stunned as well as exasperated. Phillip overheard soldiers "grousing" in camp over the removal. Some hardened veterans of many battles cried openly, while others spoke of mutiny. The 27th New York learned about the disconcerting news while patrolling Thoroughfare Gap.[56]

Three days later, the deposed commanding general reviewed his former legions along a three-mile route near Warrenton. Some brigades stood in deep mud and waited for two hours in blustery weather to have one last glimpse of "Little Mac." Philander's corps marched six miles to reach the site of the farewell. It was an emotional gathering. Soldiers frequently broke ranks and surrounded their bareheaded ex-commander as he strode past on horseback. Some shouted unabashed praise; others uttered profanities in frustration. Cannons fired, and regimental bands filled the air with patriotic music. The scene was one of mass pandemonium. Said Philander to Cousin Ell, "I never saw him look sad until then. The men crowded around so that he could hardly get along and Cheer after cheer went up for our Beloved Commander. Meny saw the Tears steel down his cheeks." The next day, November 11, McClellan boarded a train, never to return to command Union troops.[57]

The prospect of going into winter camp without McClellan appealed to very few soldiers. Commenting on McClellan's successor, Philander wrote to Cousin Ell, "He [Maj. Gen Ambrose E. Burnside] is a good man . . . he will do everything in his Power for our Country but the men have not the confidence in him as they have in Little McLellen." Phillip stated the situation more forthrightly: "Thar is no news in Camp [except] the growling about McLellons being superseded by Genl Burnside." The answer to the brothers' doubts would be given very shortly.[58]

Asa and the 130th New York

Since the conclusion of the battle of Antietam, Ann had fretted to her brothers that she had not heard from Asa since the 130th New York had left Portage in mid-September. Philander attempted to console her. "Be of good cheer," he encouraged her. "All will yet be well. I do not think the 130th will see any fighting this fall." Except for occasional exchanges on the picket line, Philander's observation proved correct.[59]

In fact, Asa and his regiment had settled into a routine in southeastern Virginia. Almost immediately on their arrival in Suffolk, they had begun daily military drills consisting of company exercises in the morning, regiment formation in the afternoon, and full dress parade in the evening. These daily exercises coincided with increased picket and fatigue duty and spade and pick labor to build fortifications. Beginning in October, the 130th New York took part in extended reconnaissance marches, one per month, that often resulted in skirmishes with the Rebels near the towns of Franklin and Zuni on the Blackwater River, about twenty miles west of Suffolk. During this hectic time, Asa did not write a single letter to Ann, and the silence caused her to fret over his well-being. It would not be long before Confederates would challenge the Yankees' presence.[60]

* * * * * * *

Perhaps the most consequential development to touch the lives of the Ellithorpe brothers during the Maryland campaign was the transfer of Phillip to the ambulance corps. Letterman's new corps did a commendable job in removing approximately 1,800 men from South Mountain and 9,400 more from Antietam in little more than one day, and the green-banded corpsmen practiced daily to improve their skills. Their task was dangerous: "these noncombatant medics risked their lives to reach the wounded in the midst of battle and evacuate them as quickly as possible," and most of the stretcher bearers behaved "with conspicuous bravery under fire," stated one historian. A common characteristic among many of these caregivers was the fact that they wished to serve the Union Cause but simply lacked the ability to kill another human being.[61]

Widespread trauma associated with canvassing the battleground searching for wounded among the dead and dying also affected the psyche of ambulance men. One freshman ambulance man in Philander's sister regiment, the 16th New York, described the horrors of a nighttime lantern search for the wounded at Crampton's Gap: "This was my first experience in gathering the wounded from a battlefield after it was won. Many have visited such a place and reported the sickening sights, but I cannot describe their ghastly realities. Later I became more familiar with such scenes . . . [but] the memories of what I saw there will remain with me to the end."[62]

Phillip felt similarly, but like many other soldiers, he was unable to express himself on the brutal pictures in his mind. One week after Antietam, he wrote to sisters Ann and Permelia, "I have much to tell you that I cant find words to explain," he confessed. "I might give you a fair idea of how a Battle field looks, but I cant describe the horror of it." The cries of the wounded and dying haunted his recollection. Mirroring a haunting thought conveyed earlier by Philander, Phillip informed his sisters, "I may come Home with but a Leg or an Arm."[63] The optimist and exuberance of 1861 had evolved into pragmatic fatalism in 1862. The Ellithorpe brothers of western New York had lost their innocence.

* * * * * * *

Phillip and Philander had witnessed firsthand the brutality and inhumanity of modern warfare as it unfolded in western Maryland; each one had become acutely aware of the cruelty, violence, and suffering they faced. While Phillip honed his new skills in the ambulance corps, Philander was counting down the days until his anticipated discharge in April. Yet before either brother would be able to move beyond the morbid scenes of destruction they had witnessed at Antietam, another brutal event would transpire within a month at Fredericksburg.

Chapter Eight

The Saddest Hour at Fredericksburg

The selection of Maj. Gen. Ambrose E. Burnside to lead the Army of the Potomac on November 7, 1862, was received with mixed feelings since a majority of officers and enlisted men knew relatively little about their new commander; moreover, they worshipped the deposed "Little Mac." Moving quickly, Burnside reorganized the Army of the Potomac into three grand divisions comprising two corps apiece and moved his base of operation from Warrenton to Falmouth on the Rappahannock River across from the prosperous colonial city of Fredericksburg. This geographic shift took place during the onset of winter; the troops suffered from exposure, shortages of food, increased sickness, and uncertainty over their future. Most soldiers anticipated settling into winter quarters in mid-November; instead, they would fight a major battle several weeks later with dire consequences in what one eyewitness termed "the saddest hour" in the history of the Army of the Potomac.[1] The battle would mark the nadir of Yankee spirits, a depressing sentiment shared by the Ellithorpe brothers of western New York.

Three Grand Divisions

Before the start of military operations, Burnside assigned leadership to his three grand divisions. The Right Grand Division was led by Sumner (II Corps and IX Corps), the Center Grand Division by Hooker (III Corps and V Corps), and the Left Grand Division by Franklin (I Corps and VI Corps). For the first time in the war, Phillip and Philander found themselves serving in the same command, Franklin's Left Grand Division, but in different corps (Reynolds and "Baldy" Smith, respectively).[2]

Pressure for a Winter Campaign and Costly Delays

Succumbing to pressure from the president and secretary of war to open an offensive before the end of the year, Burnside formulated a battle plan. The new commander intended to surprise Lee by sending his three grand divisions on a forced march to Fredericksburg as pontoon bridges were to be shipped simultaneously to that location. The logistics involved in transporting the portable wooden bridges was a huge undertaking, requiring many wagons to carry the bulky spans and supplemental hardware necessary to assemble them. Burnside intended to use the pontoons to cross the Rappahannock River and pressure the Confederates to retreat from their advanced line. Using a steamboat landing on the south bank of the Potomac, the Federals built a massive supply depot at Belle Plain.[3]

To many southerners, the Rappahannock and Rapidan rivers represented the proverbial line drawn in the sand that had to be defended at all costs since so much of importance to the Confederate war effort lay below them—the capital city, rich food resources, transportation hubs (railroads and roadways), and navigable waterways reaching across southern Virginia to the foothills of the Blue Ridge Mountains. Burnside's strategy had merit, but it depended on stealth and speed, precise coordination of the attack, and careful attention to minute details. Having one principle in place without the other two would seriously jeopardize the entire operation. And there was another problem: "the thought of a Winter Campaign," chirped Phillip, "is what I dont like."[4] Many blue-clads shared Phillip's opinion.

Beginning on November 15, the three Grand Divisions departed for Fredericksburg, with Franklin's Left Grand Division trailing as far as Rappahannock Station. Sumner's lead miraculously covered forty miles in only two days through a driving rainstorm and sloppy road conditions. When the Federals reached Falmouth, they discovered that Fredericksburg across the river was only lightly defended by the Rebels, but the pontoons had not yet arrived. Whether the fault resided with General in Chief Halleck or the head of the Engineer's Brigade, the fact remained that the bridges were barely under way from Washington, and any delay of their shipment was cause for alarm regarding Burnside's strict timetable. Another unforeseen difficulty arose when the wharves and the rail line from Aquia Landing on the Potomac River needed to be rebuilt. Still worse, the commissary wagons had not arrived, so the Federals went hungry for days.

Not to be discouraged, Hooker wired Burnside for permission to ford the Rappahannock upstream from Falmouth while the weather cooperated and the river remained reasonably low. His request was nixed, however, and thereby a golden opportunity was missed to occupy Fredericksburg before the Confederates would learn their true intentions. While the Grand Divisions waited for the pontoons, a cold and heavy rain began to fall, the Rappahannock started to rise, and Federal morale began to drop.[5]

On November 21, the element of surprise had been lost when the Army of Northern Virginia appeared on the southern bank of the Rappahannock on an elevated ridge extending from Marye's Heights to Prospect Hill. Perhaps the only thing that went right for the Yankees occurred when 147 artillery pieces were placed behind Falmouth on Stafford Heights, giving the artillerists an unobstructed view of Fredericksburg on the far bank.[6]

Phillip the Forager

A week after the battle of Antietam, Phillip confided to his sisters, "I am so glad that I came out when the war first began." Phillip explained, "I have learned how to take Care of myself and can stand the hardships so much better than those [volunteers] coming out now." But he regretted the human cost of that early learning—namely, the depletion of the Bucktails. "Whare are they?" he asked rhetorically in reference to the absence of familiar faces at roll call. "Some have found rest in their silent Grave."[7]

In October, the young Alleganian frequently took his ambulance into the countryside to forage for food. Once, he found an unharvested field of corn five miles away and shucked a wagonload. On the way back to camp, he stopped to visit some of the Rushford boys in the 64th New York, including his Lewellen Street next-door neighbor, Dr. Bixby, and several boyhood chums. When he prepared to leave, the Rushfordites warned him to avoid the provost guard stationed on the outskirts of camp. Phillip solved the problem with practical cunning. He borrowed a piece of paper and pencil, drafted a pass authorizing himself to search for food, and forged the general's signature at the bottom of the sheet. He also removed his "Plume" to avoid detection as a Bucktail. The ruse worked.[8]

The food crisis did not abate when Meade's Pennsylvania Reserves moved to Rappahannock Station. "I have just finished my breakfast this morning of Crackers and Coffee," he teased, "and for supper we expect to have Coffee and Crackers." Phillip also told Ann and Permelia in a composite letter spanning several days about a rabbit that had hopped in front of his tent. After a brief chase, he caught his prey and roasted it over an open fire. It was a welcome supplement to his bland diet of hardtack and coffee. Phillip had elevated the act of foraging to an art form, explaining to Ann, "We have fresh meat when we go out and catch a Pig or Sheep and that is very often." Of course, his scavenging behavior ran counter to army regulations.[9]

On the clear and frosty morning of November 16, Meade instructed his Pennsylvania Reserves to prepare to leave Rappahannock Station within two days. That night, the skilled forager Phillip procured "6 Beeves Tails" and served his messmates a tasty dish of oxtail soup. His chums devoured the meal and teased Phillip that he "was worth saving" after all. Afterward, Phillip generously shared an extra portion with Clow and his wife. Apparently, he was still on good terms with his former boss at the commissary.[10]

Another Example of Resourcefulness

Phillip confided to his sisters that he desperately needed paper, stamps, ink, and pen tips. Lacking stationery, Phillip had resorted to tearing sheets from a hospital ledger, and pen tips were especially important to him. "I dont like to write with a Pencil and that aint the worst of it. I wont write another letter with one," he threatened. "Now if you want to hear from me again . . . Just send me a Pen of Some kind."[11] The threat did not work; within a week, he had drafted three more missives in pencil on thick sheets of blue packaging paper probably procured from the commissary.

The resourceful ambulance man learned a creative trick to solve his shortage of ink. He gathered "Polk berries" growing along a creek bed, mashed them, and used the juice to serve as ink. Now, armed with a dull pen tip, coarse paper, and a fresh supply of "nature's" ink, Phillip sat down to draft an evening letter. He marveled at the expanse of the army in bivouac: "I cant tell you how beautiful the camp fires look as far as one can see," he beamed, "it looks like the Lights of the City."[12]

Guarding Belle Plain

During these cold mornings prior to his departure with the Bucktails, Phillip grumbled to his sisters about the persistence of the "Virginia cold snap."

But he appreciated the luxury of being able to sleep in his ambulance wagon instead of on the frozen ground. As snow gently fell, he teased Ann about whether she had yet taken a sleigh ride. Then he hitched up his conveyance in anticipation of an early departure the next morning, November 18.[13]

As the Left Grand Division marched toward its separate assignments, Philander's 27th New York bivouacked at Stafford Court House while Phillip's Bucktails would push through to Brooke Station. On November 22, the Federals hunkered down in both locations to await further instructions. The stoppage placed Phillip and Philander only a couple of miles apart. Rumors spread through the Pennsylvania ranks that they were going to go into winter quarters, so they began to cut logs to build permanent huts. After all, the weather had turned unbearably cold with intervals of wind, sleet, and snow. Less pleasing hearsay predicted a Federal consolidation of the grand divisions for an impending battle.[14]

By the time Philander's regiment had reached Belle Plain, they were bitterly cold and wet from a sleet storm. Here, Bartlett detached Philander's hungry 27th New York to guard the supply depot and unload ships at Aquia Landing. After another freshet, they tried and failed to start fires with green wood; discomfort was everywhere. The precipitation turned to snow and lasted intermittently for three more days.[15]

Phillip complained about the relentless ten-hour marches on the road and stiffness in his hips. Philander, too, fussed about the nonstop pace of the movement. At Stafford, food shortages continued to plague the army, so Phillip relied on his formidable foraging skills. One evening, he slipped past the pickets and engaged a young female vendor who sold him four "Ho cakes" for fifteen cents apiece in Federal currency and the balance in Confederate scrip. Struggling with privation, Phillip's messmates did not even have any hardtack to eat. And they were not alone.[16]

Burnside's three grand divisions would require roughly 800 tons of food per day to sustain their numbers, but regular deliveries would not commence until early December. Some members of the Pennsylvania Reserves staged a hunger protest, and Meade punished the entire division by standing at attention in a field during a fierce downpour. Once, Meade caught a bucktailed lieutenant in the act of stealing a pig. Incensed, the commander asked the officer why he was disobeying the latest regulation against such behavior.

The officer defiantly answered that he had no respect for any directive that required him to go hungry while protecting the property of Rebels. Meade had him arrested and then promptly released.[17]

On the eve of the nation's first celebration of Thanksgiving, the short-handed Bucktails were in an ungrateful mood because they had drawn picket duty. Ironically, Philander's 27th New York endured the same duty at Stafford Court House. "The boys are thinking much of home," reported one New Yorker.[18]

Nostalgia and homesickness were running amok in both units during the holiday season. "I have been washing my Ambulance inside and out," Phillip told Ann. "The soft rain on the Wagon cover makes music that charms me and once in a while . . . my thoughts wander back to the loved ones at Home." He teased his sister, claiming that she was probably reading this letter in front of a toasty fire, eating baked apples, and sipping "Sider." In contrast, Phillip sat in front of a smoky fire with some of his comrades, "amusing themselves telling some of the old trials through which they have passed."[19]

Phillip's "blue" moods often reflected his health struggles with rheumatism and the grippe caused by sleeping in wet clothes. His complaint reached Fent Ward, the former hospital steward and current second lieutenant of Company I, who offered him a medical discharge. Ward likely sized up Phillip as a deadbeat because of his frequent earlier trips to the hospital and recent inconsistent attendance because of his detached service in the commissary and ambulance corps. Phillip shrugged off Ward's tender: "if this thing is ever going to be settled," he postulated to his Father, "I want to be there to see the end of it."[20]

In early December, Phillip witnessed an astronomical rarity while on guard duty at Brooke Station. "Thare was an eclipse of the Moon and I think it was one of the nicest things I ever Saw. I watched it for three long hours. The weather is very Cold and clear," he concluded.[21] A couple of days later, the thermometer plunged to sixteen degrees Fahrenheit as snow blanketed the ground and a thick layer of ice turned the corduroy road into a slick thoroughfare.

Consolidating the Grand Divisions

On December 4, Franklin finally received orders to consolidate his grand division and rendezvous with Sumner and Hooker. On December 7, Meade placed the 1st Rifles in advance as skirmishers in the vanguard of the Pennsylvania Reserves as they slid toward Falmouth. Blizzard-like conditions halted the advance at White Oak Church, about six miles short of its goal. There, each man was issued sixty rounds of ammunition, cooked rations for three days, and waited out the blustery nor'easter. When Philander's 27th New York caught up, some disgruntled men stormed a sutler's tent and made off with a large stock of supplies. The next morning, "the men could be seen exchanging right hand gloves for left, etc."[22]

The Plan

On December 9, Burnside summoned his three grand division commanders to a council of war to present his battle plan. It had been more than three weeks since the Army of the Potomac had arrived in Falmouth, and Sumner's and Hooker's troopers were itching for a fight. Burnside proposed to lay pontoons, which had finally arrived, at three sites across the Rappahannock: two at the upper end of Fredericksburg, one at the lower end of town, and two more about a mile downstream across from Deep Run.

The commanding general laid out the following assignments: Sumner's Right Grand Division would cross the two northern bridges and occupy Fredericksburg. Then Franklin's Left Grand Division would cross the two bridges below the town, secure the Old Richmond Road (aka Bowling Green Road), and cut off the anticipated Rebel escape route. In doing so, Franklin's advance might also turn the Confederate right flank. Next, Sumner should demonstrate against Marye's Heights to occupy Lee's left wing and prevent it from reinforcing the principal point of the Federals' attack in the south. Finally, Hooker's Center Grand Division would be held in reserve on the west side of the Rappahannock to protect the bridgeheads leading into the city. Such a plan foretold major roles for the Ellithorpe brothers in the upcoming hostilities.[23]

Burnside's strategy was risky. Two formidable elevations anchored opposite ends of the Confederate line running along a long ridge, Marye's Heights in the north and Prospect Hill in the south. From these locations, Rebel infantrymen would be protected by a stone wall and thick woods with artillerists well positioned in their rear. Burnside's initiative relied on precise timing, but if his subordinates carried out their instructions as he designed, it might result in the destruction of the Confederate army.[24]

The erection of the 400-foot wooden spans over the Rappahannock would expose the engineers to Confederate sharpshooters in the city. Therefore, several Federal batteries and a detachment of sharpshooters would be needed to lend support from concealed positions along the eastern riverbank. Accordingly, after dark on December 10, the 10th and 13th Pennsylvania Reserves were to accompany the batteries of Capt. James H. Cooper and Lt. John G. Simpson on the mission. The infantrymen and artillerists fully understood their furtive assignment: to protect the pontoon construction crews from enemy sharpshooters lodged across the river. The rest of Meade's division filed out of White Oak Church several hours later with Phillip's ambulance corps in tow.[25]

The morning dawned foggy on December 11, and as the mist lifted, a ferocious artillery exchange erupted along the Rappahannock. Cooper's and Simpson's batteries "engaged in a raking crossfire of the enemy," mixing their charges between solid shot intended to collapse structures on the other bank and canister to discourage Rebel infantrymen from repositioning themselves amid the rubble. Upstream, Federal cannons barked from Stafford Heights.[26]

Facing relatively light Rebel opposition at the southern crossing, the engineers completed two bridges by 11 a.m., but Burnside kept Franklin's Left Grand Division from crossing until the middle and upper bridgeheads had been secured. The northern crossing of the Rappahannock and occupation of the town proved to be infinitely more difficult, where the first large-scale amphibious assault and ferocious urban warfare in American military history broke out. In the center, Adams's 27th New York had crossed one of the bridges only to discover that the rest of the brigade had remained behind on the eastern shoreline with the rest of the corps. Once the overeager New Yorkers had discovered their error, they retraced their steps across the pontoon without incident. With all pontoon crossings finally secured, Burnside spent most of December 12 transporting his force across the Rappahannock.[27]

Phillip and Philander Cross the Rappahannock

On the chilly morning of December 12, Meade led his 4,500 Pennsylvania Reserves, the smallest division in the smallest corps (Reynolds's) in the army, across the southernmost pontoons with little enemy opposition. They marched briskly down Old Richmond Road to Smithfield, a plantation built in 1814. Col. William Sinclair, the new head of the 1st Brigade, brought up the rear. When they reached their destination, the 1st Rifles set up a picket line facing south between the road and the river to protect the extreme left flank of the Left Grand Division. The rest of Meade's force assumed a position behind Old Richmond Road and unlimbered four batteries in front of the infantry. Less than 1,000 yards across an open plain lay Prospect Hill (elevation 1,100 feet) and, in its forefront, the rail bed of the Richmond, Fredericksburg & Potomac. The assault of Meade's Pennsylvanians the next morning would signal to the rest of Burnside's army the opening round of the battle. Every commander in the Left Grand Division understood that Meade's tiny force would need prompt relief if they successfully breached the Rebel defense and carried Prospect Hill. It remained to be seen whether Franklin would implement Burnside's battle plan. Phillip's ambulance corps assembled in the plantation yard.[28]

Once across the Rappahannock, Philander's corps extended beyond two creeks, Deep Run and Hazel Run, and connected with the right wing of Phillip's corps. They were instructed to behave as reservists, protect the middle and lower bridges, and undertake the rear guard in case of a Federal retreat. The 27th New York occupied a ravine near Deep Run and hugged the ground as Confederate shells rained down. By the evening of December 12, the Ellithorpe brothers were positioned only 300 yards from the Rebel lines and less than two miles apart. The following morning, they were positioned to unleash the dogs of war on unfavorable ground against formidable Rebel defenses recently strengthened.[29]

The Bucktails at Prospect Hill

On the morning of December 13, the thermometer plunged to thirty degrees Fahrenheit, and a thick fog blanketed the Fredericksburg landscape as Meade organized his Pennsylvania Reserves for the assault. It took an hour to trim the three brigades, which were stacked 300 yards apart, but by 9 a.m., all was in readiness. William Sinclair and Conrad Feger Jackson were relatively new to brigade leadership, and the Bucktails, too, were breaking in twenty-two-year-old Col. Taylor to regimental command, the youngest colonel in the Army of the Potomac. The batteries of Simpson and Cooper were parked directly in front on a slight knoll. Meade's blue lines extended a mile and a half, an impressive array.[30]

Near Smithfield plantation, Capt. Patrick J. O'Rourke hurriedly assembled Meade's ambulance corps for last-minute instructions. Keep up with the front of the charge, he directed, and carry away the wounded as soon as they fall. Letterman's grand design of battlefield retrieval was about to be put to a severe test, and O'Rourke fully understood his duty. He would lead his green-trimmed corpsmen into battle by example from the front.[31]

Shortly before advancing his brigade toward Prospect Hill, Sinclair pulled the 1st Rifles from the line to guard the Simpson–Cooper batteries, perhaps because Bucktails had been on picket duty all night, exchanging rifle fire with the Rebels. This decision was a rare instance in which the depleted regiment did not lead the brigade into battle.

Meade gave the order to set the Yankee line in motion. His division advanced only 200 yards when a hidden Confederate horse battery, including one long-range 12-pound Napoleon, enfiladed them from the extreme left and wreaked havoc with the advance. So the Simpson–Cooper batteries were frantically repositioned to respond. There, on the open field, the stalled Pennsylvania Reserves sustained their first casualties, and it took an hour to drive off the gray-clad artillerists. The all-out attack resumed with the addition of the reserve brigade.[32]

As soon as the Pennsylvania Reserves came within range of forty Confederate artillery stationed atop Prospect Hill, they were hit with grape, canister, and solid rounds. Again, the Pennsylvanians hugged the ground about 150 yards from the railroad grade that protected southern infantrymen, caught in a merciless cross fire of shot and shell. The Federals responded with a cannonade of their own; Simpson's exposed battery, moved twice, received heavy casualties, including sixteen horses. The artillery duel lasted for more than two hours, and casualties mounted among the pinned-down Yankee infantrymen.[33]

At one point during the attack, Meade caught sight of the 1st Rifles dug in around Cooper's battery. The short-tempered commander galloped over to Taylor, demanding to know why his regiment was not participating in the infantry advance. Once informed of Sinclair's order, Meade countermanded it. Taylor hurriedly organized his 250 Bucktails, and they double-quicked toward the railroad grade at the base of Prospect Hill.[34]

O'Rourke's ambulance men were hard pressed on the plain in front of Prospect Hill. At one point, an enemy bullet struck the handle of Phillip's stretcher; he told his sisters in a letter that the impact "nocked me so flat that

I was thought by my mate to be dead but I was only sleeping." Phillip quickly revived and proceeded to collect wounded comrades on the open field. Then there came a surprise no novelist could imagine: "who should I meet but my old companion Joseph Barns he was Struck with a spent ball and was only slightly injured but I was content with him for my next load."[35] Carried to Smithfield for initial treatment, Barnes was then transported to a hospital in Falmouth.

About 1 p.m., a Federal shell struck a Rebel ammunition chest on Prospect Hill, and the explosion stirred the Pennsylvania Reserves into action. Spontaneously, Meade's brigades leaped to their feet and crashed into the Confederate defenders behind the railroad grade. The hand-to-hand fighting was intense, and all semblance of unit cohesion quickly broke down as they chased the Rebels up the hill.

Amid the confusion on Prospect Hill, the Bucktails soon found themselves commingling with members of the 5th and 11th Pennsylvania Reserves at the epicenter of the fight. Inadvertently, they had stumbled into the Achilles' heel of the Confederate defense with others—a 600-foot gap in a marsh that southern leaders considered impassible. They were wrong. Exploiting the hole, Meade's men flooded into it and sprinted toward the crest of the hill. At one point, McCandless of the 2nd Pennsylvania Reserves turned to see O'Rourke nearby and questioned why the ambulance officer

Colonel William McCandless, 2nd Pennsylvania Reserves.
SOURCE: CIVIL WAR PHOTO COLLECTION, UNITED STATES ARMY HERITAGE AND EDUCATION CENTER, CARLISLE, PENNSYLVANIA.

had advanced so far. The Irishman replied wryly, "Colonel, will I find the wounded in the rear?" Commenting on O'Rourke's bravery after the war, one Bucktails historian stated that "the troops . . . never before saw an ambulance corps so ably commanded during battle."[36] Somewhere in the melee, Phillip operated his stretcher with the broken handle.

The Confederate line had been not only breached but also split wide open. Near the summit, the momentum of the blue wave swept over an unsuspecting South Carolina brigade and scattered them. The surging Pennsylvania Reserves had opened Military Road with the freshman 121st Pennsylvania leading the way. A complete victory seemed within Meade's grasp. The proud Pennsylvania division had accomplished the near impossible. All that he required now was the arrival of reinforcements to preserve the gain.[37]

For some unknown reason, Franklin refused to throw his other corps into the fray. Without support, Meade now had no alternative but to signal a retreat to the railroad grade and then to Old Richmond Road. During the hasty withdrawal, the right wing of the Bucktails was enveloped by Confederates, and they added more casualties to their battle total of 161, which led the brigade. When the Pennsylvanians reached the relative safety of Smithfield, the 1st Rifles were justifiably frustrated. Even the lowliest private knew that victory had been within their grasp.[38]

Philander at Deep Run

Since December 12, Bartlett's brigade (under the temporary command of Cake) had been stationed behind Old Richmond Road near Deep Run. The next morning, Cake ordered two companies from the 27th New York to make a reconnaissance up the roadway toward Fredericksburg. Near Hazel Run, they encountered stiff resistance, and Adams's patrol promptly fell back to their original position. Their rebuff signaled that the enemy was lurking only a few hundred yards in front of their line. Prudently, the reservists dug in behind a low ridge that protected them from rifle fire but not from the constant Confederate shelling, which included railroad irons that whistled through the air and lasted for the remainder of the day. On one incoming round, an officer shouted, "Lie down! Another blacksmith shop is coming." The men complied.[39]

Addressing a letter to "Friends" the day after the battle, Philander recounted his comrades' harrowing experience from their vantage point in the middle of the action: "We were hard pressed fighting upon the right [Marye's Heights] and left [Prospect Hill]. The Rebs have yet a Strong position." The corporal of Company I was surprisingly mindful of previous command blunders in the campaign regarding the unnecessary wait for pontoons and related delays in crossing the river. Now Philander added to his list of grievances the inability of his corps to reinforce Prospect Hill. "So much for the Removal of Mclellan," he concluded bitterly. "There has been many lives lost within the last day."[40] Remarkably, the 27th New York escaped one of the bloodiest battles of the war without a single casualty.

The Saddest Hour at Marye's Heights

The battle of Fredericksburg now shifted to the northern sector for the final phase opposite Marye's Heights. The hill rose 130 feet on the western edge of town and across an open plain of 900 yards. Rebel defenders clustered behind a four-foot stone wall at its crest. A millrace, five feet deep and fifteen feet wide, meandered midway between the opposing forces. The Right Grand Division would utilize three narrow and rickety bridges to funnel troops over the man-made obstacle. Tucked into the ravine at Deep Run, Philander's regiment could hear the horrific sounds of battle as events unfolded.[41]

In all, seven divisions made fourteen separate charges against Marye's Heights, but never more than one brigade was committed at a time. No Yankee soldier made it to within twenty-five yards of the stone wall. The end result was devastating. Federal casualty figures for the entire battle surmounted 12,650, and the northern nation was aghast. It was simply murder, as many commented then and later.[42]

Fraternization

On December 14, the high commands of both armies considered the possibility of resuming the battle, but Burnside ultimately opted to withdraw his battered army over the Rappanhannock after dark the next evening. A surreal aurora borealis colored the sky, and Yankees and Rebels alike sought divine meaning in it.

In the cold retreat, both Ellithorpe regiments were detached to picket their respective bridgeheads on the east side of the river. Both sides initially viewed each other suspiciously from opposing riverbanks, exchanging rifle fire and hurling insults. "We could see the yung rebel Bucks upon the opisit side of the River," Philander noted in a Christmas Eve correspondence to Ann. "Soon one of [them] came down to the water and halowed us." This gesture led to increased fraternization between the "johnnies" and "yanks."[43]

Members of two familiar foes of the 27th New York since First Bull Run, the 8th Georgia and 4th Alabama, forded the Rappahannock to exchange tobacco, coffee, and newspapers. Philander singled out one college-educated Rebel whom he nicknamed "The Professor." These goodwill ambassadors pledged to look out for one another in case of capture and enjoyed swapping lighthearted banter and stories before they dispersed. The next day, the New Yorkers pulled away from the river to White Oak Church.[44]

Clearing the Battlefield and Missions of Mercy

On December 14–15, Phillip himself had remained extremely busy during a truce, accompanying his ambulance onto the battlefield, picking up its human cargo, and delivering them to the division hospital in Falmouth. The work was intense, as many Pennsylvanians lay prone on the approach to and the slope of Prospect Hill. Despite flying a yellow flag to signify peaceful intentions, some ambulance workers attracted enemy rifle fire. To make matters worse, the regimental surgeon of the 1st Rifles, Dr. Freeman, had transferred to the U.S. Volunteers weeks earlier. Phillip verified his participation in it. "I went through the fight safe and I was under a heavy fire for 3 hours and 37 minutes," he revealed to Ann in incredibly fine detail.[45]

On December 17, Dr. Jonathan J. Comfort, an assistant surgeon with the previously untested 121st Pennsylvania, was promoted to full surgeon of the Bucktails. Overwhelmed by the task of caring for 227 wounded from his former and current regiment, the Quaker physician instructed Phillip to assist in the loading and transporting of them from the division hospital "to the Cars" for the four-hour trip by rail to Aquia Landing. There, the wounded would be boarded onto steamers bound for hospitals scattered throughout Washington, Philadelphia, and Baltimore.[46]

Comfort specifically asked Phillip to accompany the seriously wounded Pennsylvanians on the rail and sea journey. One incapacitated comrade who had suffered a leg amputation pleaded with Phillip not to leave his side once they arrived in Washington. Phillip submitted to both requests.[47]

Nurse

On December 23, Phillip was scheduled to depart with ten of the most seriously incapacitated patients from Meade's division hospital in Falmouth, but the humanitarian journey was delayed for almost a week because of railroad bottlenecks and cluttered docks. During the interlude, the young corpsman attended to his patients, and he was deeply touched by the severe level of hardship they had to endure. "Thar is one man," he informed Ann, "that was Shot in the left Breast and the ball is in his Lungs yet . . . I wont sleep much because he sleeps so heavy I wish I could help the poor fellow I am afraid he wont get over it."[48] Such scenes of human distress burned in his mind. The holidays were an especially lonely time for the New Yorker. "I think if I were Home," he told his sisters, "I would hang up my stocking butt it is of no use now for old Santa Claus dont come in the Army."[49] Phillip longed to be home.

Phillip's attitude regarding the war changed drastically after Fredericksburg. "I have seen enough of the battlefield," he divulged to Ann, and dubbed the once-glorious Union Cause as "wicked" and "accursed." He fretted over the cost of victory and compiled a list of dead or wounded men from Company I. He estimated that only 100 Bucktails were present at the first roll call after the battle.[50]

Phillip laid out possible scenarios for his immediate future: to either commandeer a set of "Citizen Clothes" and spend the winter in Rushford or work in a warm and clean hospital ward in Washington. One thing was certain: Phillip was adamant about not living in a tent for another cold winter, exposed to snow, rain, and mud. "I am tired of the country life in winter," he stated emphatically. On New Year's Day, Phillip removed his option of taking French leave. Clearly, the thought of desertion had occupied him for several weeks. It was not a decision to be taken lightly and certainly not one to be made impulsively.[51]

On December 30, Phillip boarded the steamer *Mary Washington* at Aquia Landing with his ten invalids and made the eighteen-hour journey up the Potomac to the Sixth Street wharf in Washington. Once they docked, Phillip assisted the soldier whose leg had been ripped off below the knee to quarters at Trinity Episcopal Church, less than a mile from the U.S. Capitol building. The sanctuary of the "gothic" cathedral had been converted into a 200-bed hospital with raised planks nailed onto the top of the pews.[52]

Trinity Episcopal Church, Washington, D.C. Glass negative taken by George N. Barnard (1862).
SOURCE: BRADY-HANDY PHOTOGRAPH COLLECTION, LIBRARY OF CONGRESS, PRINTS AND PHOTOGRAPHS DIVISION.

A ward master offered to fill out the paperwork necessary to detach Phillip from the Bucktails to work in his wing as a nurse. Although the transfer was never officially consummated, Phillip instructed Ann to direct future letters to him at the church, despite the fact that Trinity Hospital closed in mid-February and its patients were sent to larger pavilion hospitals operated by the U.S. Army. In a rare letter to sister Mary, Phillip boasted that his new surroundings were kept "neat as a Parlor and as still as a mouse." He asked both sisters for a box of fruit along with the boots, socks, and mittens he had sent home the previous spring through the Adams Express Company. They lovingly complied despite the fact that many Christmas boxes addressed to soldiers from home in the winter of 1862–1863 had been opened, damaged, or pilfered at inspection stations.[53]

Phillip's extended tenure in the hospital ward was not altogether unpleasant. He noted that the elevated location of the church offered a stunning view of the unfinished Capitol dome and the surrounding city. In his spare time, Phillip visited the Smithsonian, which had become his favorite tourist attraction. He also purchased a gilt-edged diary in which to record upcoming events in 1863. He even felt moments of gaiety. On January 20, the staff and patients joined in "a Theatrical," but the sing-along soured when an oil lamp overturned on a bedridden patient and severely burned him.[54]

Working the night shift, Phillip appreciated the quietude to reflect on his recent experiences in the ambulance corps while nursing his one-legged patient, the most serious case in the entire ward. In these peaceful hours, Phillip observed many men occupying themselves by copying popular verses and writing acrostic poems. Phillip transcribed two renditions that held special meaning to him and mailed them to Ann. One, "The Maid of Monterray" (1848), written by J. H. Hewitt, described the brave action of a Mexican senorita who comforted mortally wounded soldiers from both sides during the battle of Monterrey in the Mexican War. The sentimental lyrics were extremely popular among Civil War soldiers. Phillip related the pathos and self-sacrifice of "the bright beauty" to his own hazardous ambulance service at Fredericksburg.[55]

Phillip's second poetic transcription was "The Dream of Napoleon" (1813), a romanticized account of Napoleon's betrayal and downfall, written by Mary Russell Mitford. Phillip may have seen parallels between this topic and the recent dismissal of McClellan. He still yearned for the return of "Little Mac," his favorite commanding general. "Just as long as the Union Stands I am a McLellon man," he stated with sincerity.[56]

The most personal piece of verse shared with his sisters, however, was written about Phillip by a convalescing soldier in his hospital ward. Pvt. George Steiner joined the 10th Pennsylvania Reserves shortly before First Bull Run. Wounded at Gaines' Mill and Fredericksburg, Steiner dictated his lyrics to Pvt. Henry O. Pardeye, another wounded warrior and member of the 99th Pennsylvania.[57] The acrostic addressed the close bond of friendship between the caregiver, Phillip, and the incapacitated Steiner:

G – eorge his best love to relative and friends
E – ager he is to tell them that he mends
O – f this they may be certain, care most kind
R – eceiving his daily from friends true touch to mind
G – ently to nurse him, and to tend his wound
E – ver at call at his bedside they are found

S – teiner to Ellithorpe his comrade true
T – ells all his friends, great gratitude is done
E – Evening and morning constant is his care
I – n willing kindness he'll no labour spare
N – ever was friend more constant or more true
E – ver should he be remembered by you
R – emember, write to him the great thanks that are due

Steiner's acrostic is a touching tribute to Phillip's caring nature and sincere devotion to debilitated comrades.

Phillip's decision to spend months away from the 1st Rifles without being granted formal permission was hardly an isolated incident. Indeed, the number of soldiers away without leave from the Army of the Potomac in the winter of 1862–1863 had reached staggering proportions. Some estimate the number of men absent at more than 25 percent. The state of turmoil for those who remained in the ranks at winter camp was exacerbated by boredom, wet and cold weather, and disillusionment fostered by the magnitude of deaths at Fredericksburg. Some displayed mutinous behavior. The Bucktails, for example, had not been paid for months, and their frustrations mounted. Similarly, there was much "croaking" in the 27th New York about the perceived failure of army leadership. On December 26–30, the third Confederate cavalry raid orchestrated by J. E. B. Stuart on the supply lines of the Army of the Potomac exacerbated the surly attitude of despair. Emotions ran the full gamut, from defeatism to resignation to homesickness to surliness to insubordination.[58]

The Ellithorpe Brothers and the Worst of Times

As soldiers like Phillip and Philander began to digest the senseless slaughter and lost opportunities they had witnessed at Fredericksburg, a distinct change in attitude overcame the general psyche of the Army of the Potomac. No longer did the traditional mores and sentimental tenets of courage hold up to the new realities of modern warfare. Definitions of bravery and cowardice began to blur; a paradigm shift was under way.[59]

Some soldiers were being worn down by civilian defeatism. Phillip eagerly read a Christmas letter from his Rushford chum, Henry Hyde, but the contents were not comforting. "I do not wondor Phillip that you feel somewhat discouraged as regards to war matters," Hyde began, "for that seems to be the prevailing sentiment here at the North." Phillip's friend admonished public negativity from his fellow citizens and encouraged them to "be more united than at the present." Hyde claimed that the town was practically devoid of young men because they were "gone to war," and he harbored plans to leave for Oregon in the springtime.[60]

Hyde's analysis of the decline in home-front support for the war effort bothered Phillip. In fact, nothing aggravated soldiers more than civilian war weariness and defeatist commentaries in the northern press. For Phillip and thousands of AWOL enlistees, the easiest way to deal with the mounting mental stresses was to desert temporarily. Indeed, many quasi deserters left the army on multiple occasions and not always for the same reason. Illness, privation, and battlefield trauma topped Phillip's list.[61]

Within the Ellithorpe family, Philander tried to ease Ann's discouragement over the "dark outlook." His thoughts showed an amazing understanding of current domestic affairs, military decision making, and international diplomacy: "I do hope this Rebellion will be crushed before France Shall have interfered," he concluded.[62]

Recalling the carnage after Antietam, Phillip had confided to Ann that he could not find words to describe the confusion of battle, a problem he shared with countless other comrades. Now, after Fredericksburg, the corpsman repeated the same confession: "what a change has taken place [in me] since leaving home. Just wait until Peace is declared and I will come [home] and tell you what my pen cannot write," Phillip promised.[63] The war was transforming sentimentalists into battle-hardened warriors, and the carnage at Prospect Hill had completed Phillip's conversion.

Home-Front Concerns

While Phillip worked at Trinity Hospital and Philander occupied a log hut in winter quarters near White Oak Church, both brothers were forced to contend with ongoing problems at home. A surprising development occurred when Lyman proposed selling the Lewellen Street house to his children, with Ann to act as principal buyer. Such a transaction should have stabilized the family's living arrangement, but it only presented another example of Lyman's mysterious behavior. In one missive, Philander wrote, "Oh Ann I am sory that Father is making so much trouble. . . . Who is the woman he would bring to our home?"[64] For the time being, the soldier-brothers were forced to cope with their father's unharmonious and indiscrete actions from long distance.

In the new year, Ann's personal insecurities over the whereabouts and well-being of Asa created additional angst in the family, and she frequently shared these fears with her brothers. After all, she had received no word from Asa since the 130th New York had departed for Suffolk in September. Phillip, too, mentioned that Asa had failed to reply to any of his earlier missives. In fact, at the time of Ann's marriage, Phillip had erroneously thought Asa was still serving in the 5th Vermont. The lanky Asa was definitely guilty of poor communication with his new family, including his young wife.[65]

Combat Fatigue

Philander and the 27th New York were minimally engaged at Fredericksburg, but they still endured mental stress from their close proximity to the enemy. Huddled in a ravine near Deep Run and kept out of the fight, the 27th New York suffered no casualties at all in a battle practically synonymous with massive death and destruction. Nonetheless, prolonged exposure to enemy shelling and spent musket balls while lying prone instilled great anxiety in disengaged soldiers. The Rebel cannonade was particularly "unnerving" because the artillerists had used railroad irons, which tumbled through the air, making a terrifying whistling sound. The unorthodox ordnance had introduced a new component to warfare—psychological. Philander would replay the memories of Fredericksburg in the future, but for now, he focused exclusively on his own survival and anticipated discharge in the spring.[66]

In contrast to his brother, Phillip witnessed horrific combat scenes at Fredericksburg. Entering the field to pick up mangled bodies, Phillip was not only exposed to fierce enemy fire but also once the specific target. He was fortunate that a musket ball merely shattered his stretcher handle and threw him, momentarily unconscious, to the ground. It took newfound courage for Phillip to enter the fray as a noncombatant, rescue his closest friend, and nurse other disabled comrades. In doing so, Phillip played a role in something much bigger than himself: the successful implementation of Dr. Letterman's ambulance corps and hospital system.[67]

However, the deadly action and its consequences had unnerved Phillip. Whether because of the carnage he witnessed firsthand on the battlefield or its consequences in the hospital wards later, Phillip was emotionally spent, a casualty himself of posttraumatic stress, a psychological condition unknown to Civil War soldiers.[68]

One might extrapolate beyond the individual, Phillip, on the condition of the Bucktails and the Pennsylvania Reserves after Fredericksburg. In the course of the battle, the Bucktails had lost to injury every regimental officer—Taylor, Irvin, Niles, and Hartshorne. At the brigade level, Sinclair was inactivated by a foot injury before his men had reached Prospect Hill, and Jackson was killed in action. Company I fought without its wounded leader, Ward; many other leaderless regiments and companies banded together in small packs of enlisted men to carry on the fight. And Meade's division, the smallest in the Army of the Potomac, reported 40 percent casualties. One thing was certain: the Pennsylvania Reserves and the 1st Rifles, in particular, were fought out.[69]

Phillip's Unresolved Relationship with Capt. Blanchard

The protracted refusal of Capt. Blanchard to repay Phillip's loan became a major sticking point that fostered his growing loss of faith in the goodness of humanity. Indeed, Phillip became increasingly obsessed with Blanchard's delinquency, and it further agitated his state of mind. Between December 6 and March 25, Phillip would mention Blanchard's failure to make restitution eight times in letters to his sisters. Twice, he had sought out the former captain of Company I, first at Brooke Station before Fredericksburg and afterward in winter camp at Belle Plain. Now a sutler, Blanchard agreed to sign a new IOU, promising to send the amount owed directly to Rushford. The former captain neglected to do either. Phillip had grown increasingly skeptical, divulging to Ann on New Year's Day, "I am a little fearful that I wont get the money." Three weeks later, he added, "I have learned a good lesson and Paid a good price" for having trusted the captain. The entire episode of Blanchard's deceitfulness made Phillip acutely aware of the dark side of human nature and jaded his outlook on life to his dying day.[70]

* * * * * * *

The promise of the new year would offer more gloom as the Ellithorpe brothers contemplated a wide range of thoughts, such as French leave, discharge, and even mutiny and intrigue at the highest level of command that added to their degree of uncertainty. An ill-advised mud march in the dead of winter would fuse all of these grievances, resulting in the promotion of another new commander of the Army of the Potomac, which would translate into another major campaign. Sweeping reforms improved morale, but time was running out as one Ellithorpe brother prepared to leave the service and the other struggled with his deteriorating sense of patriotism.

Chapter Nine

"I Have Seen Enough of This Unjust War"

The Ellithorpe Brothers and the Limits of Patriotism

The Ellithorpe brothers, chastened by the Fredericksburg fiasco, must have looked forward to spending the upcoming months in combat-free locations: Washington (Phillip), White Oak Church (Philander), and Suffolk (Asa). Alas, the army's malaise during the winter of 1862–1863 had not been limited to the enlisted men, as intrigue was brewing at the highest level of command, too. A disastrous mud march in the dead of winter sealed the level of sullenness and cynicism, as insubordination broke out in some regiments. The Army of the Potomac appeared on the brink of mutiny, and desertion had reached epidemic proportions. The selection of a new commander offered hopeful reforms to rebuild morale, restore health, and seek solutions affecting manpower shortages, three areas of importance to the Ellithorpes. Beginning in early February, Asa's 130th New York saw significant action in Suffolk that would continue for months, and Phillip's Bucktails and the Pennsylvania Reserves appeared headed for deactivation. Philander's 27th New York focused on their impending discharge in April when another bloody campaign interrupted their plans. By May 1863, the lives of Philander and Phillip had been raked increasingly by war weariness and revealed serious limitations to their patriotism.[1]

As the Army of the Potomac was shuttered in place in January, a staggering number of soldiers were reported away without leave, a figure estimated at more than 25 percent, which included Phillip. But the army's displeasure was not limited to the enlisted ranks. The center of dissension resided in

Franklin's Left Grand Division, where Phillip and Philander yearned for the return of "Little Mac." Some officers openly verbalized no confidence in the leadership of Burnside, and on December 30, two brigadier generals secretly visited President Lincoln to share their concerns. The meeting was one of the worst-kept secrets in the army, and news of it leaked out. As the blame game unfolded in the officer corps, one bright spot centered on the promotion of Meade on Christmas Day to command V Corps. The advancement would have direct repercussions for his former division, the Pennsylvania Reserves.

Resuming the Campaign

On December 26, Burnside seriously considered resuming the offensive as the weather turned unseasonably mild, but his soldiers appeared restive as they prepared three days' rations. The general's strategy was quite inventive. It called for a cavalry ruse to the north and a faux crossing at Kelly's Ford, while the Right Grand Division would demonstrate south of Fredericksburg. Simultaneously, Burnside would lead the bulk of the Army of the Potomac across the Rappahannock at Banks' Ford, turn Lee's left flank, and then march on Richmond. The subterfuge of the plan had merit, but, while the favorable temperatures held, a series of unforeseen events delayed implementation of his plan for more than three weeks.[2]

The Ellithorpe brothers were appalled by the unconventional call for a midwinter campaign. Sending a letter to his sister several days before the movement, Philander lamented, "Oh Ann how I long to be at home with my sister the term of my Enlistment draws to a close. I feel more uneasy more anksious for time to pass."[3] Clearly, he was focusing on his mustering out in three months rather than on facing the Confederate army in late January. Despite his relative isolation in Trinity Hospital, Phillip twice compared his current situation as a soldier to "slavery."[4]

Meanwhile, on January 19, twenty-three insubordinate Bucktails stacked their weapons and refused to budge unless they received their back pay. Col. Taylor tried to intimidate the demonstrators, but his use of colorful language and threats to arrest the surly troopers failed in its desired effect. Changing tactics, he promised to pay the men once the current mission was over in much the same way that Biddle had cajoled the 1st Rifles in June 1861. Sixteen Bucktails remained steadfast in their defiance, however, and they were arrested.

The Mud March

On the evening of January 20, the weather turned for the worse, and the Army of the Potomac was caught at the end of its first day's march in a severe downpour accompanied by howling winds. The storm dropped several inches of rain, and by the next morning, the Rappahannock swelled into a raging torrent. Hooker's lead Center Grand Division churned up tremendous volumes of mud, and Franklin's trailing Left Grand Division floundered. Philander and the 27th New York sloshed at the extreme rear of the march; wagons sank to the hub as hundreds of men tugged on ropes to dislodge them. Animals and humans slipped and struggled for solid footing.[5]

By this time, Burnside's element of surprise was lost, and Rebel pickets across the swollen river hooted at his mud-spattered and rain-soaked Yankees as they retraced their steps to White Oak Church on January 23. Disconsolation and humiliation was complete as the number of stragglers and deserters skyrocketed. Delivery problems caused food shortages in the commissary, making the miserable trek of thirty-six hours even more unbearable. In all ranks, the Army of the Potomac was in a foul and dangerous mood.

The Rise of Hooker

Among the officers, the blame game was now in full stride. Infuriated with the perceived disloyalty of his officers, Burnside met with President Lincoln on January 24. Armed with General Order No. 8, the general pressed the commander in chief to cashier a number of generals, a list that included the heads of all three grand divisions and most of the upper echelon of the Left Grand Division. Burnside threatened to resign if the president refused to approve the mass firings. Lincoln accepted his resignation and elevated Hooker to be the third head of the Army of the Potomac in less than three months.[6]

In the short term, Hooker proved to be an excellent choice to restore morale in the army. A friend of the Radical Republicans in Congress and agreeable to President Lincoln because of his aggressive impulses, Hooker instituted a series of structural and personnel changes aimed at restoring the pre-Burnside command system while, at the same time, improving the spirit of his army. Yet "Fighting Joe" possessed plenty of negative baggage; he was a womanizer, a heavy drinker, an arrogant and abrasive person, and an archenemy of General in Chief Halleck. However, these flaws did not matter because Hooker was an acceptable choice among top army leaders, the rank and file, and President Lincoln.[7]

Despite Hooker's promotion, the army was still honeycombed with officers and soldiers who expressed loyalty to "Little Mac," and the Ellithorpe brothers belonged to that persuasion. Still, they were minimally impacted. Philander and the 27th New York welcomed the new head of VI Corps, the likable Maj. Gen. John Sedgwick. "Uncle John" was cautious, and his division commanders were competent. In regard to Meade's departure to head VI Corps, the Pennsylvania Reserves were momentarily leaderless, which left nagging doubts about its future. While the Bucktails remained in McCandless's brigade, the regiment went through slight revisions albeit with familiar faces. Alanson E. Niles replaced Irvin, who had resigned as lieutenant colonel, and W. Ross Hartshorne was commissioned major.[8]

The Unsettled Future of the Bucktails and Pennsylvania Reserves

A more permanent decision regarding the status of the Pennsylvania Reserves was pending. The once-storied division had lost well over 60 percent of its manpower since the beginning of the war, and since Meade's published appraisal of its weakened condition on Christmas Day, rumors had swirled in camp. Would they remain with Reynolds? Would they be reassigned to Meade? Would they be pulled entirely from the line in order to be refitted? The answer came shortly.[9]

On January 29, five inches of snow fell in Belle Plain, but it did not dampen the spirits of the Bucktails because they had just received four months' back pay. Then, on February 6, the three Pennsylvania brigades boarded a rickety canal barge, transferred to a steamer before the scow sank, and ferried upriver to Washington. Once there, they were assigned to the Department of Washington, an assortment of commands who were either fought out or freshly recruited on their way to the front.

Having just been paid, some bucktailed hijinks broke out in Alexandria, where some of the men attended a circus but others sought to spend their paychecks on the kind of revelry that only saloons and brothels could provide. That evening, a contingent of Bucktails ended up fighting with a patrol of the 2nd District Regiment in a well-publicized fracas at the Light house. The Light family and their three promiscuous daughters were well-known transients with a "noisy, quarrelsome, and outrageously profane" reputation. They operated out of a shanty near Cliffbourne Hospital, and their outlandishly bawdy behavior was so infamous that an alley in the city bore their name. The near riot was reminiscent of the civil disruption in Harrisburg during the regiment's training camp days. The local newspapers printed details of the sordid affair, and the unruly "wildcats" were escorted out of town and told never to return.[10]

The brigades of the leaderless Pennsylvania Reserves were sent to three different locations around the capital at Munson's Hill, Upton Hill, and Fairfax Station. McCandless's brigade, which included the 1st Rifles, drew the latter place and were ordered to guard a supply depot on the Orange & Alexandria line. Shortly, they would engage with a pesky band of Confederate guerrillas.[11]

Phillip claimed that he had expected to be recalled to the Bucktails before the Mud March but instead learned of the regiment's recall to Fairfax Station while on a sickbed at Trinity Hospital. Doctors labeled his condition "debilitis," a sketchy medical term used to describe exhaustion. Despite his weakened condition, Phillip showed generosity toward other patients. When a belated Christmas box arrived from Ann, he shared its contents of apples, preserves, cheese, and butter with the wounded warriors in his ward. He gifted a pair of slippers to one of his patients, "Mr. Gibbels," a particularly needy fellow with a marvelous singing voice. Why Phillip chose not to return to his regiment, which was camped only eighteen miles away, once he recovered or after the hospital closed on February 14 is suspicious.[12]

Asa and Deserted House

Since Asa's arrival in Suffolk in September 1862, his 130th New York had been put to work erecting fortifications under the watchful eye of Maj. Gen. John J. Peck. They endured the same discomforts posed by snowy weather, food shortages, exposure, and illness. Yet there was an endless amount of pick and spade work to be done, and Asa explained to Ann and Phillip that his tedious workload would not be finished until May. In the meantime, there were worrisome signs that the Rebels were becoming more daring to the west. Indeed, the Yankees had skirmished more than thirty times with small enemy forces, and they were targeted by civilian bushwhackers who employed hit-and-run tactics and disappeared without a trace into the Great Dismal Swamp.[13]

On January 10, Peck ordered what became known as "the Windsor March," a harbinger of Burnside's Mud March, which would occur ten days later. The event started in bright sunshine, but the weather turned foul toward evening when heavy rain began to fall. For the next few days, the marchers covered twenty-four miles and trudged through sand trails and muddy roads. Finally, the unsuccessful patrol was ordered to make a forced thirteen-mile night march back to Suffolk. Some unfortunate fellows fell out of line from exhaustion and were killed by southern sympathizers.[14]

The Federals' suspicion about a Confederate buildup was justified. On January 25, 1863, a force of 1,800 butternuts crossed the Blackwater River to forage, advanced to Kelly's Store about eight miles from Suffolk, and set up pickets. Five days later, Peck ordered a reconnaissance-in-force commanded by Brig. Gen. Michael Corcoran. Corcoran's division consisted of seven infantry regiments, an artillery battery, and a squadron of cavalry, or 8,000 men. With Gibbs in charge of the infantry, Thorp assumed the reins of the 130th New York. It can only be assumed that Asa rode with Company H.[15]

The ensuing three-hour engagement between Pryor and Corcoran on January 30, known as the battle of Deserted House, was actually a series of three separate skirmishes. At the beginning of the hostilities, Corcoran and Gibbs argued about the proper placement of the infantry. At a pivotal point in the fight, Gibbs, who had been placed under arrest by the temperamental Corcoran, grabbed the regimental flag of the 130th New York and personally led his men into the woods, routed the enemy, and repulsed several spirited counterattacks. Eventually, the action forced the withdrawal of the Confederates behind the Blackwater River. Corcoran's force held the field at a cost of 143 casualties. The 130th New York was particularly bloodied with twenty-nine casualties, and Thorp was singled out in the official reports of Peck and Corcoran for valorous leadership.[16]

In February, Longstreet's Confederate corps and Hood's division arrived in the region of the Nansemond and Blackwater rivers, signaling an escalation in hostilities. The Rebels' objectives boiled down to defending Richmond, foraging for food to sustain a spring offensive, and harassing Peck's network of fortifications around Suffolk. In a rare letter to Phillip, Asa sensed that another movement was afoot but explained that the renewal of hostilities was not necessarily a bad thing. "[The 130th] does not like to be Shut up inside a line of fortifications," he confided. A major showdown loomed ahead.[17]

The no-man's-land between the Federal and Confederate armies in Southampton County, Virginia, remained tense with frequent skirmishes throughout the snowy months of February and March. In one nonmilitary action, some enlisted men in Asa's regiment kidnapped several runaway slaves and sold them back to their southern owners. The illegal activity was, perhaps, their angry response to Lincoln's announced Emancipation Proclamation. Apparently, some soldiers in the 130th New York disapproved of the president's new war aim.[18]

Finally, Ann had received a letter from Asa dated on the eve of the fight at Deserted House. The missive did much to clarify the communication problem between husband and wife, but it also revealed the presence of unresolved tension. In the lengthy correspondence, Asa responded to Ann's criticism, which had charged him with neglect. Asa was offended by her insinuation, claiming that he always replied to every one of her letters despite overbearing responsibilities building forts and fighting against Confederate guerrillas. Furthermore, he had applied for a one-month furlough, but Peck denied it. He asked rhetorically, "Would you have me resign my position and forsake my countries cause and come home. Would you feel as though I was doing my duty?" Then the lieutenant softened his language. "I may be dilatory about writing," he said apologetically, "but for heaven Sake get it into your head that my feelings are not changed toward you." Writing to Phillip, Asa reaffirmed that he had "no time to loaf around."[19]

Hooker's Reforms

Hooker devised an innovative list of programs to assist in improving soldier morale and health in the Army of the Potomac, and the Ellithorpe brothers directly benefited from three of them: the creation of distinctive corps emblems to be sewn onto caps and flags and representations painted on conveyances for easier identification during battle, the introduction of dietary and sanitary regulations to improve overall health, and the magnanimous offer of amnesty to deserters. Actually, on March 10, President Lincoln added the latter as an amendment to Hooker's reforms, offering an unconditional pardon to any deserter who would report back to his regiment by March 31.

Phillip stood to benefit from these reforms, especially the generous addition of amnesty to deserters at Lincoln's insistence.[20]

Hooker's embroidered cloth badges, unique to each of the eight corps in the Army of the Potomac, was designed for the practical purpose of allowing for easier recognition of each corps during battle. Within each corps, the insignias were color coded to signify the 1st (red), 2nd (white), and 3rd (blue) divisions. These symbolic representations were eventually painted on ambulances, ammunition wagons, and artillery caissons and flown on flags at headquarters. The badges were met with almost universal approval, and they supplied a beneficial psychological purpose. Phillip had taken immense pride in the green cloth markings on his uniform that identified him as a member of the ambulance corps. Now every soldier could take similar gratification in wearing a comparable badge of recognition. Hooker succeeded in restoring camaraderie and élan through this most basic and pragmatic art form.[21]

Hooker's new health reforms might have had a positive effect on the sickliest Ellithorpe, Phillip, but it came too late. At the end of January, health problems had risen, and related desertion rates reached 30 percent, major concerns to army officials. Half of the missing men in the ranks were wounded, detached, or sick, with the remainder being healthy but away without leave. At Trinity Hospital, Phillip's physical condition deteriorated during one of the harshest winters in recent memory when he spent four stints in the hospital, not as a nurse but as a patient.[22]

Then, in mid-February, Ann shared some sad news: the death of Phillip's eighty-five-year-old namesake, Philip Griggs, of Pike. Saddened, the grieving lad had hoped to share stories with his grandfather one day after the war. Phillip intended to return to the Bucktails in March, but his trembling hand and anxiety had returned. Besides, his regiment was currently dealing with an outbreak of smallpox in Fairfax Station, and two companies had been quarantined at Convalescent Camp. Phillip's prolonged and unauthorized absences made him less and less of a Bucktail with each passing day.[23]

The Bucktails versus Mosby's Rangers

For most of February and March, while McCandless's brigade encamped at Fairfax Station, a Confederate partisan cavalry band under the command of Maj. John Singleton Mosby, the Gray Ghost, was conducting hit-and-run raids in north-central Virginia, much to the frustration of Federal commanders. On March 1, Mosby's Rangers audaciously struck the 1st Rifles at midnight and then disappeared into the darkness. On heightened alert, the Bucktails doubled their pickets and sent out daily patrols. One week later, Mosby raided the headquarters of Brig. Gen. Edwin H. Stroughton, commander of capital defenses in Fairfax, capturing three Union officers (including Stroughton) and thirty enlisted men. The incident was an embarrassment.[24]

The next day, the Federals hatched a plan to apprehend Mosby. Bucktailed volunteers from each company were hidden in the beds of four forage wagons and guarded by a small cavalry detachment. Their goal was to enter the nearby woods and lure Mosby to attack the undersized party. The 1st Riflemen made contact with the elusive Rangers two days later, but Mosby refused to take the bait to assault the suspicious caravan. The expedition returned to camp but not empty-handed; they procured a number of chickens and wild ducks for the evening meal from various farms and fields in the outlying area.

Winter of Despair

As Phillip's bucktailed comrades struggled with inclement weather, smallpox, and the apprehension of Mosby, the sickly ambulance man continued to use Trinity Hospital as his mailing address despite the institution's being closed since mid-February. At this moment, Phillip had reached a crossroads in his life: whether to rejoin his regiment or rejoin his sisters in Rushford. The choice was not an easy one. He expressed these options in three letters to his sisters, and Ann shared their contents with Asa.[25]

On March 14, as Phillip struggled with his decision, Asa drafted a letter offering his struggling brother-in-law some heartfelt advice. "Phillip I am and I believe always have been independent yet have never failed to Show respect to my Superior Officers," he began. Asa recommended that Phillip put aside personal feelings of anger and disappointment for the good of the Union cause for which they were both fighting. "Dont do anything to give those who are appointed over you any cause whatever to complain of your conduct," Asa counseled. "Retain your place there as long as you can and be faithful and honest and you may yet occupy a higher position ere your term of Service expires. God Speed the close of the war, but I had rather Stay in the field twenty years than to purchase peace which would be dishonorable to the Federal cause. I dont want the d——d rebels to have anything more than traitors deserve."[26] Asa's advice to Phillip contained a subliminal suggestion, based on personal honor, not to desert.

On March 23, Asa wrote a second letter to Phillip that was equally insightful and practical. First, he encouraged Phillip to resume his association with the ambulance corps once he returned to the 1st Rifles and to use that labor as a basis to request an honorable discharge. Then Asa offered a most remarkable observation: "I know you are not fit to do the duty as a Soldier."[27] This powerful statement contains the full realization of Phillip's limitations as a combat soldier.

On March 25, less than a week before Lincoln's amnesty for deserters was scheduled to expire, Phillip wrote to Ann. "I am going to my regiment," he proclaimed, but "my nerves are unsteady." His journey would not be easy. Phillip would have to be processed first at Convalescent Camp, a facility on the outskirts of Alexandria designed to accommodate deserters, stragglers, soldiers too weak to return to active duty, and wounded men recently released from hospitals for repatriation to their former outfits. "Camp Misery," as soldiers derisively called it, was a squalid facility with shortages of food, clothing, shelter, and military discipline. The heterogeneous population included many unsavory characters, and considerable idleness allowed resourceful individuals to blend in with the rabble to avoid detection. There, Phillip spent a undisclosed length of time under a surgeon's care for his unsteady hand, which could not grip a pencil.[28]

On April 25, Phillip notified Ann that he just rejoined the Bucktails at Fairfax Station after a five-month separation. The thinned ranks of the regiment surprised him, and he noted many of his enlisted friends were now officers. His reception given from old comrades was unknown, and precisely what role Phillip would play in future Bucktail adventures was yet to be determined.[29] Meanwhile, the war had found Asa's relatively quiet corner in Suffolk.

Asa and the Siege of Suffolk

Confederate general Longstreet had plenty of manpower to protect Richmond while foraging behind the Blackwater River line, but he lacked sufficient resources to launch a direct assault on the fifteen-mile, horseshoe-shaped ring of Federal forts protecting Suffolk. Asa and the 130th New York occupied their familiar position at Fort Nansemond in the northwest corner of the Federal perimeter on the South Quay Road, a sector strengthened by eleven naval gunboats, converted packet boats, and armed steamers on the Nansemond. On April 11, Lee's "Old War Horse" opted to lay down a siege.[30]

The siege of Suffolk (April 11–May 4) produced very few casualties because its particular style of combat consisted of sniper fire by day and artillery exchanges by night. The southerners employed guerrilla tactics using the Great Dismal Swamp as a natural haven and hiding place. The 130th New York was particularly vulnerable to sharpshooters across a log pond at Kirby's Mill. On April 17, several companies from the regiment launched a preemptive strike to dislodge the Rebels.[31]

Thorp had conducted the Kirby's Mill raid since Gibbs was incapacitated by a bout of angina pectoris. The regimental surgeon had performed a Dr. Rush remedy of purging Gibbs's system of impurities. Placing a newspaper on Gibbs's chest, he doused it with whiskey and set it ablaze. The treatment formed a large blister, and his prognosis was for a full (if painful) recovery.[32]

On April 24, the Federals conducted a reconnaissance-in-force similar to the Deserted House operation but this time directed at the Blackwater River. Again, Corcoran assembled a substantial force of 5,000 infantry, 500 cavalry,

Lieutenant Colonel Thomas J. Thorp, 130th New York/19th New York Cavalry/ 1st New York Dragoons.
SOURCE: CIVIL WAR PHOTO COLLECTION, UNITED STATES ARMY HERITAGE AND EDUCATION CENTER, CARLISLE, PENNSYLVANIA.

ten pieces of artillery, and a regiment of sharpshooters. About four miles down the Edenton Road, the Yankees ran into a Rebel brigade. The surprise collision resulted in a brief skirmish, followed by a mutual withdrawal without inflicting serious damage to each other. The foray had accomplished absolutely nothing other than tallying several casualties, including four missing officers from the 130th New York. An unconfirmed rumor reached Ann in Rushford that Asa was one of the men lost.[33]

It rained in Suffolk for almost half of the twenty-three-day siege, adding to discomfort and causing a sharp uptick in sickness on both sides. The blue and the gray engaged in much fraternization as well. Nighttime rendezvous included the usual swapping of stories, telling jokes, singing, and exchanging tobacco, coffee, and coat buttons. Regimental bands serenaded the sedentary soldiers, and most "concerts" concluded with the wildly popular "Home, Sweet, Home."[34]

When Lee recalled Longstreet in early May, Peck's command, including the 130th New York, remained in Suffolk for the next forty-seven days, dismantling Yankee fortifications. Thus, Asa was out of harm's way as storm clouds built along the Rappahannock. Philander was not so fortunate.

Ramping Up the Army of the Potomac

By mid-March, a number of promising signs indicated that Hooker had succeeded in restoring confidence and élan of his troopers. Two large celebrations honoring St. Patrick's Day and an outdoor festival illustrated how Hooker's goals were being achieved. Throughout the blustery months of February and March, some regiments held impromptu snowball fights. When the weather improved, the Army of the Potomac became smitten with the game of "base ball." Once again, Bartlett displayed his athleticism in a pair of contests representing the 27th against the 32nd and 34th New York. In addition, the number of soldiers given medical discharges during this time dropped significantly.[35]

These morale-building exercises convinced Hooker that his reinvigorated men were ready to resume the campaign trail. The general commanding shared two relevant but contrasting concerns with the president: all but 2,000 deserters had returned to the ranks, and thirty-four regiments were scheduled for discharge in mid-April. These indicators encouraged Hooker to resume hostilities shortly. Congress attempted to remedy the manpower shortage by passing a conscription law, but it would take time to recruit and train such a large number of raw conscripts.

Meanwhile, Philander and his comrades in the 27th New York had been counting down to their anticipated discharge, targeting the date of their enlistment in Angelica in April 1861 and not the date when the regiment had been officially accepted into federal service in Elmira one month later. In the coming weeks, expectations surrounding the faux date would cause great consternation for Philander and his comrades.[36]

A different problem, specific to the 27th New York, appeared. In early April, Philander's comrades had been thrown into a fit of frenzy over the delay of the U.S. Senate to confirm Bartlett's nomination to brigadier general. Instead, it was widely rumored that the popular commander would soon be replaced. On April 14, the entire brigade turned out to wish Bartlett good-bye as he prepared to board a train for Binghamton. At the eleventh hour, Hooker summoned Bartlett to his headquarters, where a telegram was read: "Tell General Bartlett to put on his [uniform] again, and return to his command, Signed, A. Lincoln." The 27th New York soldiers were greatly relieved that they would continue to take orders from their beloved leader.[37]

Hooker's Plan

In concept, Hooker's battle plan was remarkably similar to Burnside's Mud March. It called for the bulk of the 120,000-man Army of the Potomac to deploy with lightning speed in three separate phases in order to surprise the Confederates and turn their left flank. Hooker's double envelopment strategy had merit, although it shared basic flaws with Burnside's, as will be seen.[38]

Phase 1 of Hooker's grand design called for the cavalry corps to create a ruse by crossing the Rappahannock, demonstrate against Richmond, and disrupt enemy lines of communication. The horsemen also hoped to draw Lee's attention to the southeast while the rest of the Army of the Potomac slipped out in a northeasterly direction. Encamped at White Oak Church, Philander and his comrades in the 27th New York were totally aware of the military buildup, which started at mid-month.[39]

Phase 2 relied on three corps to march with stealth to Kelly's Ford and cross the Rappahannock, proceed to Ely's and Germanna fords and cross the Rapidan, and concentrate near the crossroads of Plank Road and Orange Turnpike to the west of Fredericksburg at a dense setting called

Chancellorsville. The triumvirate of Meade–Howard–Slocum would then be in perfect position to launch a surprise attack against the Confederates.

Phase 3 involved the largest and smallest corps in the Federals' arsenal, Sedgwick's and Reynolds's corps, respectively, to cross the Rappahannock south of Fredericksburg, demonstrate against Prospect Hill and Marye's Heights, and push the Rebels down Plank Road toward Salem Church. This alignment would include Philander's 27th New York. If Hooker's instructions were carried out on time and with sufficient vigor, the Army of Northern Virginia would be enveloped on both flanks. The Yankees held the element of surprise, but a one-day delay cost their offensive dearly.

Chancellorsville was not a village. It was simply a spacious house owned by the Chancellor family since 1816 and located in the center of a seventy-square-mile region of impenetrable thickets, rolling terrain, and dense stands of trees. Known as the Wilderness, this physical barrier of overgrown foliage and irregular topography posed serious challenges to any army's mobility, coordination, and communication.

Handicaps

Hooker's army operated under two handicaps. First, the upper officer corps had been stripped by combat deaths, resignations, and reassignments. Out of ninety-four pre-Fredericksburg brigade and division officers, only twenty held the same level of command at present. Second, the attrition of qualified officers at the regiment and company levels was even more stark, although Philander's 27th New York was an exception to the norm regarding turnover. In April 1863, the regiment still took orders from its post-Antietam staff officers, Adams, Bodine, and Wanzer, as well as Company I captain, Burton Freeman, who had replaced Philander's friend (Harmon) after Antietam. Philander, too, was progressing up the chain of command; he became the sergeant of Company I on March 1, 1863.[40]

Rebelliousness

Then the War Department made its decision affecting the status of the 27th New York. The regiment would not be mustered out until May, the month they had been formally enrolled in federal service. The reaction was instantaneous. A spirit of rebellion swept through the New York regiments led by the 1st, 18th, 20th, 27th, 31st, 32nd, and 34th New York. Philander felt "[en]raged" when he was told to turn in his winter clothing for summer garb, draw sixty rounds of ammunition, and cook rations for eight days.[41]

On April 23, the mutiny grew when the 1st New York threatened to leave camp en masse along with the 7th New York, which had just departed for home. The 20th New York staged a similar walkout in Falmouth, and the 34th New York flatly refused to cross the Rappahannock, reluctantly forming at the point of a bayonet. Hooker disarmed these tense situations, advising his brigadiers to position all short-term troops at the rear during the upcoming campaign. Not every commander would comply.[42]

During the commotion, Philander wrote a letter to his younger brother, the only missive to have survived the war. His calm tone on the eve of battle was tempered by his deep spiritual devotion. "I do not know whare we are going," said Philander, "but I will Put my Trust in God and Joe Hooker." Philander described his camp at White Oak Church as "relaxed"—some of the boys occupied their time reading, while others played whist. Philander closed with an age-old soldier complaint: "I have not heard from home in a long time," he lamented. "Perhaps I do not write often enuf I will try and do better if the Rebs do not get me." He also mentioned receiving a magazine from an acquaintance, the Elmira candy maker's sister, Christena O. Walker.[43]

On the drizzly morning of April 27, Bartlett formed his legions and told them to be ready for action the following morning. He also made a personal plea for individuals soon to be discharged to reenlist. No one stepped forward. Some men replied that they did not want to be used in another battle but instead wanted to go home. Then, in a calculated moment, Bartlett announced that the 27th New York was slated for discharge on May 21. Spontaneous jubilation consumed Philander and his comrades.[44]

Once Bartlett dismissed his brigade, Philander returned to his tent and composed his final letter as a member of the 27th New York. To Ann, the recently minted sergeant of Company I confided, "I have got the inflamation of the eye prety bad [conjunctivitis]." Earlier in April, he had spent a total of nineteen days in the hospital but asserted that he was prepared to do his duty in the impending fight.[45]

Philander Crosses the Rappahannock

The next afternoon, Adams's regiment filed out of White Oak Church with the rest of Sedgwick's corps during a light rain shower. In the evening, the mammoth party halted about one mile from the Rappahannock and waited for twenty-three state-of-the-art canvas boats as well as some standard wooden pontoons. When the watercraft finally arrived, Bartlett detached the 27th New York to lift, drag, and carry the burdensome 1,250-pound wooden spans to the river's edge. It took multiple trips and many hours to complete the laborious task while encountering resistance from Confederate sharpshooters across the river.[46]

Meanwhile, some of Philander's comrades fretted that they would be pressed into action against Marye's Heights. They had heard stories about the last bloody attempt to scale the heights, and those images were fresh in their minds. None of the New Yorkers were in a happy mood. When the time arrived to cross the river, forty men were wedged into each boat. Said one eyewitness of the 27th New York, "I dont pretend to know where rests the responsibility of delaying us until it was light enough for the enemy to use us for target practice, but it looks like criminal imbecility. . . . By the time we reached the top [of the bank] we were the maddest set of men the Army of the Potomac had ever set loose." By noon, Sedgwick's corps was safely across the river and spread along Old Richmond Road between "The Bend" and Smithfield plantation.[47]

After the crossing, the 27th New York deployed on the extreme right flank of the corps, where they dug rifle pits near the same Deep Run ravine they had occupied during the battle of Fredericksburg. Bartlett placed the 27th New York in the second row, per Hooker's instructions, to protect those regiments scheduled for imminent decommission. For three days (April 29–May 1), the men ducked for cover under a relentless Confederate barrage of shot and shell because conflicting orders from Hooker had kept their corps locked in place. Unknown to the Federals, they faced only a skeleton force under Confederate Maj. Gen. Jubal Early.[48]

On the evening of April 30, the 27th New York advanced on patrol up the Deep Run ravine, a major conduit for Confederate sharpshooters who were harassing any movement on the Old Richmond Road. Instead of a firefight, however, a round of fraternization broke out similar to the post-Fredericksburg encounters along the Rappahannock with exchanges of coffee, tobacco, and good-natured humor. Philander did not comment on this activity, a clear violation of Hooker's new policy against such interaction.

The Battle of Chancellorsville

As fog lifted on the morning of May 1, Sedgwick's corps heard the sounds of battle in Chancellorsville twelve miles away. Holding an indefensible salient, Hooker ordered a retreat at the end of the day, a major blunder, leaving the Federals' right flank unprotected. The next morning, Hooker was incapacitated for several hours after being struck in the head by a fallen beam at his headquarters. As a result, the separate corps of the Army of the Potomac functioned without direction. Ultimately outflanked, a furious fight ensued, and the Federals panicked. Only the onset of darkness prevented a total disaster on the magnitude of First Bull Run. Here, "Stonewall" Jackson was mortally wounded by friendly fire while on a late night reconnaissance.[49]

Late on May 2, the majority of Early's Confederate defenders had departed from Prospect Hill, so Hooker sent a series of dispatches ordering Sedgwick to immediately pursue the retreating Rebels along Plank Road and crush Lee's rear at Chancellorsville. Sedgwick felt that he was embarking on a fool's errand: to launch his 24,000-man corps late in the day, march twelve miles in the dark, and attack the rear of the Rebel army before dawn appeared ludicrous to him. In all fairness, Hooker assumed that Sedgwick had already stormed Marye's Heights, which was not the case. Still, Sedgwick obediently set his corps in motion toward Fredericksburg. In compliance with these instructions, Bartlett's brigade was repositioned to Mansfield plantation and given a special directive to protect the vital left flank of the corps, as it would march *en column* to Fredericksburg. Adams's 27th New York occupied the back row, and Philander's comrades sensed with trepidation that a larger movement was afoot.[50]

On the Jump to Second Fredericksburg

At the tail end of the line of march, the Federals would contend with an aggressive enemy brigade. Concealed behind a railroad embankment that ran perpendicular to Deep Run, the Louisiana Tigers could easily disrupt any movement along Old Richmond Road. Thus, Bartlett's brigade was dispatched to drive the lurking enemy from the field. Philander's regiment joined the 96th Pennsylvania on the right bank; together, they pushed the Rebels back, but not before an enemy shell tore a gaping hole in the battle flag of the 27th New York, neatly removing its single star. Adams's skirmishers doggedly held the ravine until early the next morning while "hugging the ground" for protection from Confederate sharpshooters, who were lodged in trees.[51]

At daylight on May 3, as Sedgwick's vanguard pushed into Fredericksburg, Bartlett realigned the 27th New York to the rear of the division as protectors. His decision was justified, as the regiment exchanged musket fire with the Rebels all the way into town. On the march, Philander's unit had "a splendid view" of Sedgwick's two-division assault on Marye's Heights, which broke Confederate opposition on the third charge. Intercepting a few deserters and stragglers, Adams's regiment maintained its defensive posture in the rear.[52]

Normally a cautious commander, Sedgwick resumed his push down Plank Road toward Chancellorsville but not before he brought his reserve division forward to lead the corps since they had not participated in storming Marye's Heights. The 27th New York slipped to the tail end of Sedgwick's column and continued its rearguard support, ostensibly at the behest of Bartlett. A serious bottleneck developed on Plank Road, slowing the blue-clad advance to a crawl as it headed into an ambush three miles down the road at Salem Church.[53]

Salem Church

As the reserves pressed on with excessive caution, Lee accurately assessed the inactivity along his front and seized an opportunity to challenge the developing threat on Plank Road. Thus, he began skimming off troops to block the Yankee advance at Salem Church. The eastern approach to the churchyard was wide open, while the west was covered by a dense woodlot on an elevated ridgeline. From this location, every move made by the Yankees would be clearly visible while the Rebels were masked behind the tree line and hillside.

An Alabama brigade took up a defensive position on the ridge about halfway between Chancellorsville and Fredericksburg and 500 yards west of Guest House. Later in the morning, reinforcements arrived to lend support. By early afternoon, Federal skirmishers reached a toll gate on Plank Road where they engaged a small force of southerners who fell back. From his headquarters at Guest House, Sedgwick meticulously began to deploy two brigades on either side of the roadway, with Bartlett's forming on the left. The 16th New York (the Straw Hat Boys) stood in reserve, while the 27th New York was still pushing from behind the throng on the road in front of them.[54]

The Yankees were not ready to attack until late afternoon. The fight at Salem Church would be conducted largely by the infantry, without artillery support or cavalry reconnaissance. When Bartlett gave the command to double-quick, he used Salem Church, fifty yards away, as a visual marker. No sooner had the blue-clads burst from Jones Woods and bowled over two Rebel regiments than they were met by an explosive volley of musketry from the front. The 96th Pennsylvania and 121st New York took the brunt of the deadly blast, and Bartlett was forced to call on the soon-to-be-retired 16th New York to shore up his faltering line. Smoke filled the air, and the fighting became desperate. The Straw Hat Boys gained control of the churchyard around Salem Church but only for a short while and at a frightful cost of 142 casualties. Elsewhere, the Federal assault lacked élan, and the blue line reeled back to the toll gate. The surging Confederates recaptured Salem Church, but the onset of darkness and the Rebels' own fatigue saved the tattered Yankee line from complete collapse.[55]

Defense of Scott's Ford and Banks' Ford

On the evening of May 3, Sedgwick faced a dilemma. He could not retrace his steps eastward toward Fredericksburg because the Rebels had reoccupied it following the surprise withdrawal of Federal defenders who had been left on Marye's Heights. Likewise, his corps was unable to travel westward toward Chancellorsville because it was successfully blocked. Lee understood Sedgwick's desperation, and he hoped to crush him before the Federals had an opportunity to refortify. The only avenue of escape left open to the blue-clads was to withdraw northward, set up a tight U-shaped perimeter, and protect Scott's Ford and Banks' Ford. After dark, the 27th New York arrived on the scene with the other two divisions.

Bartlett positioned his former regiment on the extreme left of his brigade, where they formed at a sharp angle with the 5th Vermont, Asa's old regiment. One officer described this corner as "two [connecting] sides of a parallelogram." Hazel Run meandered in front of them, a natural obstacle for attacking southerners. There, Philander and his comrades waited anxiously for dawn and the anticipated Rebel attack.[56]

Philander and his comrades marked time for most of the day because the Confederate commanders experienced communication difficulties. The gray-clads finally materialized before 6 p.m., but their charge was neither well coordinated nor well executed. The 27th New York had been placed in front of the brigade as skirmishers, where they intercepted a Georgia unit, but a meandering gully separated the combatants and funneled the attackers toward the 5th Vermont, who absorbed the brunt of the assault. The lackluster chargers were repulsed; the battle for control of Scott's Ford and Banks' Ford was over.[57]

Retreat

About midnight on May 4–5, Sedgwick ordered a withdrawal to the two fords. The 27th New York, the last of Bartlett's brigade to reach the field at Salem Church, was an ideal selection to cover the rear of their division. Adams's soldiers fulfilled the task under a shower of grape and canister, and they were among the last to leave the field. There was much straggling on the withdrawal to the river, however, and some disgruntled soldiers in the 27th New York complained that they had, once again, "been made dupes of bad generalship."[58] On the retreat, Confederate infantrymen peppered the regiment from half a mile away, but Sedgwick's entire corps safely forded the river early on the morning of May 5. Confederate pickets chided the losing army from the south bank, shouting, "We have a new commanding officer here, 'General Starvation,' but we also have a new quartermaster, 'Joe Hooker.'" Hooker had no choice but to retire across U.S. Ford the next evening.[59]

Heading for Home

By May 8, Philander's regiment was back in its familiar campground at White Oak Church. Three days later, the 16th New York assembled for the final time as members of the Army of the Potomac. The 16th and 27th had been battle buddies since the Peninsula campaign, serving in the same brigade. They usually entered scrapes together, and their bivouacs generally adjoined one another. They were truly a band of brothers who identified so strongly with each other that they often saw themselves as one unit. The appointed hour of send-off for the Straw Hat Boys had arrived. A speech by Bartlett was followed by hearty handshakes and three huzzahs, and then they were gone to their homes in the North Country of upstate New York. In camp later that evening, a sense of melancholy swept over the 27th New York.[60]

Three nights later, on May 14, the 27th New York formed on the same parade ground to hear parting words from its beloved brigadier. There, Bartlett read Special Order No. 120 from Sedgwick, informing the regiment that they would muster out of service the next day. Bartlett's fondness for his former commands ran deep: "I have purposely reserved until the last all mention of . . . the 16th and 27th New York Regiments," he stated in his official report of Second Fredericksburg and Salem Church. "The terms of service of these regiments had nearly expired before the campaign commenced; yet, true to the instincts of the soldier, both officers and men have elicited the warmest admiration for their gallant conduct throughout. . . . They deserve well of their country and will be received with honor."[61] Then a surprise guest appeared: the present commander of XII Corps and the first leader of the 27th New York. Slocum, too, thanked the men for their service and wished them well in the future. Then they were dismissed.

On the morning of May 15, the 27th New York assembled for the final time. Bartlett's other regiments turned out to give them the same good-bye they had tendered to the 16th New York. Then Adams marched his command to Falmouth, where they caught a train for Aquia Creek and boarded a steamer bound for Washington. On May 18, the Union Regiment reached Elmira, where the men received back pay and a bonus allowance for extra service. Perhaps the sergeant of Company I made time to visit Christena O. Walker, the sister of the candy maker whom Philander had befriended during his training camp days. The 27th New York was officially disbanded on May 31.[62]

In the first week of June, joyous ceremonies were held for each of the companies in the local communities where the men had been originally recruited. In Rushford, the ladies of the community prepared a sumptuous dinner for their returning heroes of Company I. Sgt. Philander D. Ellithorpe was, once again, a civilian.[63]

Metamorphosis

The battles of early 1863 had completed the transformation of the lives of the Ellithorpes, and the life-changing events had become fully transparent in their correspondence in the months leading to Chancellorsville. Phillip,

Philander, and Asa had been spurred to action in 1861 out of sentiments of loyalty, patriotism, and defense of the Union. While not fully repudiating those earlier goals, their personal attitudes were now tempered by new military realities, which were quite different from the sentimental ones they had originally held at their enlistments. By May 1863, each one of them had acquired an altered worldview, pragmatic and cathartic, based on diametrically opposite feelings of camaraderie and man's inhumanity to man. And this life-altering metamorphosis was not limited to the individual soldiers but extended to their family members as well. Consider the journeys taken by each of them in the opening months of 1863.

Phillip

Phillip had served the ambulance corps with distinction at Antietam and Fredericksburg, where he witnessed firsthand the horrors of modern warfare. But the amount of carnage and human suffering had nauseated him. He wrote to Ann on December 22 explaining that he intended to find comfortable winter lodgings in Washington or else desert to Rushford. After Fredericksburg, the opportunistic fellow landed satisfactory relief work at Trinity Hospital in Washington, but he learned that that facility was scheduled for closure in mid-February; thus, the prospect of his desertion was, once again, under consideration.

In the two months following the closure of Trinity Hospital, Phillip resurfaced as a patient at Finley Hospital, a 1,000-bed facility located on Kendall Green in the northeast corner of the capital.[64] An examination of Phillip's health history is worthwhile during this period. In a later letter to his sisters written at Fairfax Station, Phillip explains, "I have had father's old complaint . . . I am very tired."[65] He consistently reported on the same symptoms throughout his military life, including anxiety, fatigue, and involuntary hand shakes (tremors). These manifestations, in combination, are frequently associated with emotional stress. And the timing of Phillip's afflictions usually flared on the eve of impending battle. The fact that Phillip's father also suffered from this condition suggests that the ailment might have been hereditary. Judging Phillip's traits, modern medical experts might conclude that Phillip suffered from a neurological disorder called essential, or familial, tremor. Of course, lacking this medical knowledge at the time of the war,

Phillip's surgeons and attendants likely shrugged off his frequent hospitalization as malingering behavior.

Two consequential events interceded in March, causing Phillip to reexamine his future. First, Lincoln's generous proclamation of amnesty to soldiers who had deserted was about to expire on March 31. Second, Asa's timely letters dated March 14 and 23 provided sage advice to Phillip: do not desert, do your duty, and seek a discharge. This call to honorable action inspired Phillip to disregard the possibility of taking French leave and instead return to the Bucktails to fulfill his obligation. Time would tell whether this was a wise decision.

While recouping at Finley Hospital, Phillip was robbed of $40 and spent his twentieth birthday there. When he arrived at Convalescent Camp on April 25, Phillip did not care for his surroundings, calling it "a Prison." Although he was enrolled there to be reassigned to the Bucktails, he drafted a cryptic line to Ann: "I am of no use in this dirty camp."[66] Since Phillip's most recent service at Trinity Hospital had involved nursing, it is plausible, based on his own words, that Phillip had initially gone to that camp to pursue the same kind of work. If so, the foul conditions caused him to pause.

Despite all the weaknesses in Phillip's character and physical constitution, he never deserted outright but chose to return to his duty station. The option of deserting was the single most momentous decision faced by soldiers during the war, and the thought of abandoning his comrades was odious to him. In fact, many hardened veterans were beginning to shed their idealistic preconceptions of bravery and to appreciate a soldier's loyalty based on factors other than battlefield valor. The thin line between cowardice and bravery was beginning to blur, so some soldiers came to view any demonstration of an individual's devotion to the regiment as acceptable behavior, which led to forgiveness of other shortcomings.[67]

Philander

Philander and the 27th New York had occupied a sheltered ravine near Deep Run at Fredericksburg, guarded the rear of Sedgwick's corps at Second Fredericksburg, missed Salem Church, and faced the enemy late in the defense of Scott's Ford and Banks' Ford. The regiment had been minimally exposed to harm throughout the campaign largely because of the magnanimous treatment of Bartlett, who repeatedly placed the 27th New York at the rear of every march. Throughout the period between the two Fredericksburg engagements, however, Philander began to express more negativity and cynicism in his letters home. While he, like Phillip, still believed marginally in the principles that had originally inspired his enlistment, he pushed his impending discharge to the front of his thoughts of survival. Philander had become weary; he was especially disenchanted by the lack of support on the home front, and he lacked confidence in the latest recruits to join the army. Although Philander did fight out of a strong sense of duty, he had lost the will to fight.[68]

Asa

Asa was not a very good communicator. He took his military responsibilities seriously, but he dealt with laxity when it came to drafting correspondence to Ann, Phillip, and Philander. And the siblings were stung by his oversight. Without question, the building and dismantling of fortifications in Suffolk, the engagement of Deserted House, and the siege of Suffolk had occupied an enormous amount of Asa's time in the first four months of 1863. He did, however, scold Ann, claiming that he had written more frequently than she had received, and consoled her that he had remained loving and faithful throughout their rocky courtship and marriage.

Serving in a far-off theater of war, Asa penned two of the more significant letters in the entire Ellithorpe wartime collection. His recognition that Phillip lacked the soldier's basic instinct to kill another human being had been liberating. Thus, Asa's intervention had delivered Phillip from psychological angst and allowed the young ambulance man to move forward in a positive direction. Asa had provided a noble act.

Ann

Ann, perhaps, had changed more than any Ellithorpe. At the beginning of the war, she had been a finicky critic of both brothers' writing styles and wrote in a haughty tone. But Ann matured quickly, as she was forced to deal with the death of her mother, dalliances of her father, mortgage concerns, household maintenance, and financial shortages. Her marriage to Asa in June 1862 offered some security, but he had gone away far too soon with the 130th New York.

In Asa's absence, Ann had developed a closer bond with her younger sister and housemate, Permelia. Phillip and Philander had written more letters to their oldest sister than to any other family member, including each other. It is highly questionable whether Ann sought the title, but she was *the* glue that kept the Ellithorpe family together.

Because of these increased responsibilities, it is, perhaps, permissible to excuse Ann for her insecurities in regard to Asa's self-described "dilatory" behavior. He might have contributed to her anxious feelings, but she was forced by circumstance to cope with the absences of one husband, two brothers, and several cousins who were doing deadly work in the Union army. When Ann received unofficial word that Asa had been killed at Deserted House, she spent a couple of months as a grieving widow. A second message corrected that mistake, but by 1863 the war had radically changed Ann from the innocent intellectual she had been in 1861.

* * * * * * *

On May 31, 1863, only Phillip and Asa remained on active duty. Three days later, as Phillip and the Bucktails camped at Fairfax Station, the Army of Northern Virginia was once again on the move, headed for Pennsylvania. In less than a month, the defining moment of the war had arrived for the North, the South, and one of the Ellithorpes of western New York.

Chapter Ten

"Death before Dishonor"

Gettysburg

The Army of the Potomac spent much of May 1863 licking its wounds from the missed opportunities at Chancellorsville. Despite the usual accusations and subsequent transfers within the officer corps and rising disenchantment in the enlisted ranks over the quality of generalship, the Federals itched for another confrontation with the Army of Northern Virginia. They did not have to wait very long. On June 3, the Confederates marched northward with plans to tap the rich resources of southern Pennsylvania. The Rebel invasion of the Keystone State affected two Ellithorpe boys, Phillip and Asa, still in military service. The end result, the battle of Gettysburg, decisively changed the direction of the war and profoundly tested the courage and loyalty of one Ellithorpe boy from western New York.

Phillip and the Battered Bucktails

Except for their failed mission to bag Mosby's guerrillas in early March, the 1st Rifles spent an uneventful period at Fairfax Station under the banner of the XXII Corps. Having missed the battle of Chancellorsville, the regiment joined the chorus who condemned top officers for bungling and yet welcomed another opportunity to crush the Rebels.[1]

Phillip found much to appreciate about the clean campsite of the regiment "in a green meadow" and whose streets were lined with cedar boughs. He painted an idyllic picture of the spot where he drafted his letters: "in the Shade of the old Oak whare I often go when it is to warm to sit in my tent."

He bantered lightheartedly with his sisters about his sweetheart back home and regretted not "be[ing] in Rushford for the [annual] Ball at the Washington House" but teased cryptically that his tent mates had recently "danced to the music of Hades Band." He "shouted for joy" on learning that Philander had been discharged and hoped Ann and Permelia would greet him warmly with "a heroes welcome."[2]

Of course, a question arose concerning Phillip's return to the Bucktails. While the reception he received from his comrades is unknown, it is clear that the officers were not particularly pleased. For one thing, the new head of the Pennsylvania Reserves, Brig. Gen. Samuel W. Crawford, did not reassign Phillip to the ambulance corps because that branch demanded dependability and dedication to service. So Phillip was returned to Company I to serve as an infantryman, and Dr. Comfort cleared him for military duty within a couple of weeks. Yet by this point in the war, the officers in the army were becoming increasingly weary and wary of dealing with stragglers

Brigadier General Samuel W. Crawford, Pennsylvania Reserves.
SOURCE: CIVIL WAR PHOTOGRAPHS, 1861–1865, LIBRARY OF CONGRESS, PRINTS AND PHOTOGRAPHS DIVISION.

and shirkers.[3] Now Phillip had resurfaced, once again, but the Bucktails desperately needed to fill their depleted ranks.

On May 15, the carefree mood of the battered regiment suddenly turned dark when Stone of the 149th Pennsylvania and Wister of the 150th Pennsylvania, the "new Bucktails," presented the "old Bucktails" with a new silk battle flag to replace the one lost at Gaines' Mill. Although the Stone–Wister gesture was sincere, the original Wildcats were resentful of the gift because they felt the new recruits had not yet earned the right to wear the distinctive headgear. Phillip jokingly acknowledged the flag presentation to Cousin Ell: "I fear that it will get smoked not a little if we join Hooker."[4]

Confederate Threat and a Botched Federal Diversion

On June 3, the Federals did not comprehend Lee's motive as his graybacks consolidated at Culpeper and headed north toward the Potomac. Instead, Hooker bickered with his nemesis, Halleck, over troop allotments for almost two weeks before recognizing the Confederates' actual intention. Three parallel ridges, extending from central Virginia to southern Pennsylvania, effectively shielded the Rebel movement. Yet there was no disguising Lee's goal when, on June 15, the Army of Northern Virginia crossed the Potomac. This bold thrust panicked the citizenry of Harrisburg, Philadelphia, Baltimore, and Washington.[5]

As Lee's troops marched northward, Asa and the 130th New York were completing their assignment to dismantle fortifications in the Suffolk area. Then, on June 12, the War Department detached Peck's command to Maj. Gen. Erasmus D. Keyes, the inept left-wing commander of McClellan's early Peninsula campaign in 1862. Keyes was ordered to set up a diversion on the James Peninsula to threaten Richmond, hoping that such a demonstration would divert some Confederate divisions from advancing farther into Maryland.[6]

The 130th New York spent six days marching, riding the cars, and taking river transports to Yorktown and White House Landing. From this base, Keyes proceeded with excessive caution toward New Kent Court House and spent three weeks near the Pamunkey, conducting "a masterly inactive campaign." They fought two insignificant skirmishes at Bottom's Bridge (July 2) and Baltimore Crossroads (July 4) against Virginia state militia; thus ended Asa's unceremonious role in the campaign, labeled by officers and enlisted men alike "a total farce" during the battle of Gettysburg.[7]

Reactivation of the Pennsylvania Reserves

On June 17, seventeen officers of the 2nd Pennsylvania Reserves signed a petition asking their former commander and current brigadier, McCandless, for permission to defend their own state from the invaders. Their request echoed two previous attempts made by Meade and Reynolds to reactivate the Pennsylvania Reserves. The next day, Phillip sounded relaxed and satisfied with himself in a letter to Ann, perhaps a sign that his wildcat comrades had forgiven him for past indiscretions. "I am Just as happy as a Clam," he confided, "and content with my lot." He signed off using "Kane's Rifles, Co. I"—an outdated reference, to be sure. Phillip asked Ann an important question in closing: "What do you think of the invasion of Pa [?]"[8]

Then, on June 25, the southern vanguard slipped over the Mason-Dixon Line. The Confederates were targeting not Washington, the War Department finally surmised, but Harrisburg. Thus, all opposition dropped to holding the Pennsylvania Reserves in the nation's capital. But Halleck instructed Crawford to leave behind one of his brigades for added security. Thus, the two reinvigorated brigades under Col. Joseph W. Fisher and McCandless made hasty plans to catch up to Meade's corps in Frederick. Some soldiers were overheard cheering, "McClellan, Give us McClellan."[9]

The news to mobilize reached Phillip, but it caught him a bit flat-footed as he accompanied his closest friend, Joe Barnes, "down to the creek and took a wash." Then the camp of the 1st Rifles was thrown into a heightened state of activity, and all was in readiness in the early evening of June 25. Before departing, Phillip scrawled a quick note to Ann. Its patriotic tenor was unmistakable. Now he eagerly welcomed his new role in the liberation of Pennsylvania, and "The Boys . . . will do all they can," Phillip promised Ann, "to put a star on the Cols [McCandless] Sholdier."[10]

Meade Replaces Hooker

Hooker's Army of the Potomac had been shadowing Lee's Army of Northern Virginia for ten days, but an important subplot continued to be the ongoing feud between the commanding general and the general in chief. When Halleck denied Hooker's request for 10,000 additional troops stationed at Harpers Ferry, "Fighting Joe" tendered his resignation. Perhaps to everyone's surprise, President Lincoln accepted it on June 27, and he promptly promoted Meade to lead the Army of the Potomac into his native Pennsylvania.

Brig. Gen. George Sykes, a capable and methodical tactician, assumed command of V Corps. On the day of Hooker's removal, Crawford's two brigades were given new badges for their kepis, the Maltese Cross of V Corps, a final vestige of Hooker's influence on the Pennsylvania Reserves.[11]

From Fairfax Station, Crawford had set a ferocious pace to catch up to Sykes's corps, which was still in Frederick. His frantic clip covered sixty miles in the first four days, twelve to sixteen hours each day, causing much straggling because of leg weariness and foot sores. After all, Crawford's two brigades had been relatively sedentary since Fredericksburg. Bell of Company I later recalled the importance of the regimental band during these marches as the men "sang in chorus to keep ourselves awake."[12] On entering Maryland, the band struck up "Maryland, My Maryland," and some Bucktails even sang the hated "secesh chorus." Morale was high. Once Crawford caught up to Sykes, the Bucktails were formed toward the rear of a seven-mile-long caravan headed to York, Pennsylvania, to protect Meade's right flank. It is worth remarking that Phillip kept up with that demanding pace.[13]

Following is the marching schedule of Crawford's Pennsylvania Reserves:

June 25 to Vienna, Virginia, nine miles

June 26 to Goose Creek, Virginia, twenty-one miles

June 27–28 to Edwards Ferry and Frederick, thirty miles

June 29 to Libertytown, Maryland, fifteen miles

June 30 to Union Mills, Maryland, twenty-three miles

July 1 to McSherrytown, Pennsylvania, fifteen miles

July 2 to Gettysburg, Pennsylvania, twelve miles

In the meantime, Confederate Lt. Gen. Richard S. Ewell, or "Old Baldy," was closing in on Chambersburg, Pennsylvania, and the bountiful Cumberland Valley.

On June 30, Sykes halted his exhausted corps at Union Mills, Maryland, about six miles from the Pennsylvania state line. Despite the hardships resulting from the twenty-three-mile march, the Pennsylvania Reserves did not lack resolve. In fact, they were highly motivated to rebuff Lee's advance onto northern soil. Early on the afternoon of July 1, Crawford's division reached the Maryland–Pennsylvania line. There, the strict and aloof disciplinarian gathered his men together to deliver impassioned remarks to inspire them for the desperate work that lay ahead. He said, "Our native state is invaded by the ruthless horde of plunderers who desire to spoil our rich valleys, our homes . . . and our fields. . . . Let the sights of the mountains and our native plains free your hearts and nerve your arms in the hour of battle. . . . Remember you are Pennsylvanians. Let no breach of discipline mar the glory of the past."[14] Then the Pennsylvania Reserves filed into the Keystone State for the first time in more than two years.

Meanwhile, the Confederates had extended in a long arc between Chambersburg and the outskirts of Harrisburg. Portions of a division had been sent out to search for shoes in Cashtown on the Chambersburg Pike, only seven miles northwest of Gettysburg. In response to this presence, Meade ordered a division of cavalry under Brig. Gen. John Buford to conduct a reconnaissance-in-force in Gettysburg along with the corps of fellow Pennsylvanian Reynolds. The sheer magnitude of the number of blue and gray soldiers descending on the southern Pennsylvania town was staggering. The pieces were now in place for a cataclysmic collision. The fate of two countries and the lives of thousands of common foot soldiers hung in the balance.

Gettysburg

The picturesque town of Gettysburg had been laid out in the 1780s and settled by German immigrants noted for their large barns, neat fences, and well-manicured fields. In 1863, the burg was the seat of Adams County, boasted a population of 2,400 people, served as a transportation hub for ten roadways (including three major turnpikes), and prospered as a regional trade center. Two small colleges and several manufacturing firms were also located in Gettysburg.

The topography and man-made obstacles in and around Gettysburg—numerous fences, stone walls, streambeds, woods, brambles, rock outcroppings, orchards, and farm buildings—would impede large-scale mobility and disrupt military cohesion. Four ridgelines split up the countryside: two ran northwest of town (Herr and McPherson), and two extended south of town (Seminary and Cemetery). To the south of town, two peaks anchored the bottom of Cemetery Ridge. The smaller one was known locally as Sugar Loaf Mountain, but history would call this hillock Little Round Top.

July 1

Early on the morning of July 1, exploratory forces of the contesting armies met head-on three miles northwest of Gettysburg on Herr Ridge. From the outset, the combat was intense, and after approximately two hours, the Federal cavalry gave up ground to the numerically superior Confederates. Meanwhile, Reynolds's corps had arrived on the field and deployed on Chambersburg Pike and offered stiff resistance. There, one of the saddest chapters of Pennsylvania's proud Civil War heritage occurred when Reynolds was mortally wounded. To the north, a second Federal corps also arrived, but this line was caught in a pincer and enveloped. Around 4 p.m., the outnumbered and outmatched Yankee infantrymen fell back through the streets of Gettysburg. The timely arrival of Maj. Gen. Winfield Scott Hancock and his placement of his corps on Cemetery Ridge stalled the Confederate advance, stabilized the retreat, and prevented a complete rout.[15]

At approximately the same time, the vanguard of Sykes's corps reached McSherryville after another long, hot, and dusty march. There, they halted to eat and rest. Some soldiers dined on ripe cherries growing in nearby orchards. McCandless's brigade brought up the rear, and they could hear the sound of combat being waged only twelve miles to the west. Phillip and his comrades were eager to reach the battlefield.

After dark, a courier from Meade arrived imploring Sykes to head out immediately on a midnight march to Gettysburg. The messenger also carried the tragic news about the death of Reynolds. Crawford's brigades reacted with expected rage. Although they were exhausted, the Pennsylvania Reserves fell in, infused with renewed vigor and urgency. The Federal column advanced cautiously in the dark because large numbers of Confederates lurked north and south of Hanover Pike. Around 4 a.m., they reached Bonnaughton (today Bonneauville), about four miles east of Gettysburg. There, Capt. Bell witnessed the warm greetings of local citizens to family members who were serving in Company K, 1st Pennsylvania Reserves.[16]

July 2

Sykes received updated instructions to form in reserve behind Little Round Top. So he veered off Hanover Pike at E. Deardorff's farm and followed Brinkerhoff Ridge cross-country until they came to Baltimore Pike about noon. Here, Sykes ordered a break at the farm of G. Musser on the west side of Rock Creek near Power's Hill. Weary men spoke in muted tones, napped, made coffee, received ammunition, and waited in the late morning heat for Crawford's two brigades to arrive. Fortunately, the Confederates in front of Little Round Top had been largely quiet throughout the morning hours. Unfortunately, this sector was about to be fraught with danger.[17]

On that same morning of July 2, Lee had decided on two simultaneous assaults against the extreme left and right flanks of Meade's army. The desired objectives at the southern end of the field would be to carry the Peach Orchard, Wheatfield, Devil's Den, Houck's Ridge, Little Round Top, and Big Round Top and roll up the Federals' flank to secure a Rebel victory. The two Round Tops were not defended at the moment, exposing Meade's vulnerable southern flank. Still, the Confederate command was stricken with indecision.

Sickles's Debacle

In the afternoon quietude at the southern end of Cemetery Ridge, Maj. Gen. Daniel E. Sickles, a political appointee, had taken it on himself to reposition his two divisions from low ground to a more elevated prominence along Emmitsburg Road. The new placement caused a serious tactical problem: it was 1,500 yards beyond the line of defense Meade had laid out in his battle plan. Sickles had unwisely created an indefensible salient as well as opening a half-mile gap on Cemetery Ridge. Most egregiously, however, Sickles had neglected to inform Meade about his westward move toward the Peach Orchard.

The short-tempered Meade exploded when he learned of Sickles's unauthorized decision. In an emergency meeting of corps commanders at his headquarters, Meade ordered Sykes to hurry and reinforce Sickles. Phillip and almost 300 Bucktails hastened toward Little Round Top, but they encountered delays once they reached Taneytown Road because the thoroughfare was jammed with ambulances, ammunition wagons, sections of artillery, and infantrymen. Then, at 4 p.m., Rebel cannons sounded the attack and waves of southerners stepped forward to rip holes in Sickles's poorly designed deployment. The collision of forces reached a level of intensity seldom witnessed in the war. Sykes was seemingly too late.[18]

On his arrival on the northern flank of Little Round Top, Sykes dispatched two divisions to aid Sickles in the Peach Orchard and the Wheatfield. He also detached the brigade of Col. Strong Vincent to occupy the undefended western summit of Little Round Top, a move that ultimately set up the famous fight between the 20th Maine and the 15th Alabama. Despite all of the efforts to save Sickles, however, his line broke, sending the panicked Yankees into full retreat.[19]

To Little Round Top

Crawford's Pennsylvania Reserves reached the back side of Little Round Top at approximately the same time the Confederates were chasing disorganized Federals across Plum Run Valley. McCandless hurried his brigade up Cross (today Wheatfield) Road to an elevated vantage point between Little Round Top and Weed's Hill, where he had a partial view of Plum Run Valley, Houck's Ridge, and the Wheatfield. Here, the Pennsylvanians piled hundreds of knapsacks; a few of Phillip's comrades in Company I were whispering in low tones, but one Bucktail later commented that "the silence [in the ranks] was deafening." Veteran campaigners agreed, however, that this was the best defensive ground they had seen since Malvern Hill. Crawford detached the brigade of Col. Fisher to bolster Vincent on Little Round Top and then to push forward to fortify Big Round Top.[20]

Two Union batteries arrived on the scene. The first, Lt. Charles E. Hazlett's Battery D, 5th U.S. Artillery, was immediately forwarded to the summit of Little Round Top. The second, Capt. Frank C. Gibbs' Battery L, 1st Ohio Light Artillery, unlimbered two sections on Weed's Hill on the right side of Cross Road and rushed two guns under Lt. H. F. Guthrie to the northwest flank of Little Round Top. Guthrie beheld a panoramic, albeit worrisome, view of retreating Federals and advancing Confederates.[21]

Gibbs and Guthrie trained their 12-pound Napoleons on the Rebels as they burst from Rose's Woods, Houck's Ridge, and the Wheatfield. As the southerners drew nearer to the base of Little Round Top, Guthrie depressed the barrels of his two pieces in order to drop double rounds of canister into Plum Run Valley. The cannons became overheated, and the artillerists could not even touch the barrels. The late afternoon sun hung like "a dull red ball of fire wrapped in drifts of lurid and acrid smoke," one soldier later claimed, and it had become difficult for the defenders to differentiate between the retreating blue-clads and the attacking gray-clads. Sunset was rapidly approaching, and the battle for Little Round Top hung in the balance.[22]

At this critical moment, Sykes ordered Crawford to move his one remaining brigade of Pennsylvania Reserves obliquely across Cross Road and form beside Guthrie's two pieces on Little Round Top. McCandless executed the instructions flawlessly and arranged his five regiments accordingly.

Once in place, the 11th Pennsylvania Reserves immediately affixed their bayonets. Everyone comprehended the significance of this action. As Taylor's Bucktails stood in relative silence and waited for the inevitable command to charge, panicked soldiers filtered through their ranks. Rebel sharpshooters from Devil's Den were attempting to pick them off, which placed McCandless's command in greater danger. Several Bucktails were hit, including one company captain. Thus, the Pennsylvanians were ordered to lie down in the style originally taught by Kane and used frequently by them throughout the war.[23]

"In the Name of Pennsylvania, Charge!"

When the first southerners reached the base of Little Round Top, McCandless's men delivered two volleys, which temporarily staggered the attackers. Then Crawford grabbed the flag of the 1st Pennsylvania Reserves and shouted his command: "In the name of Pennsylvania, charge!" The fiery brigadier personally led his lone brigade, whose members "screamed their special Reserve [wildcat] yell." Some throaty Bucktails shouted, "Remember Reynolds!" as they streamed down the hill. Passion and rage had consumed the undersized brigade.[24]

Meanwhile, ambulances and stretcher bearers stood behind Little Round Top in readiness to retrieve the wounded and deliver them to nearby collection stations. The organizational network of medical staff on the battlefield was absolutely amazing. The medical director had assembled 650 physicians, an ambulance corps of 1,000 wagons and drivers, and 3,000 stretcher bearers. Each division was responsible for setting up its own field hospital staffed by three surgeons and three assistant surgeons. The only glitch in the system was delays in the delivery of medical supplies and hospital tents.[25]

Two hundred yards north of the Cross Road–Taneytown Road junction sat the 100-acre farm of Jacob Weikert. The Weikert farmhouse, barn, outbuildings, and orchard had been assigned the primary aid station for Sykes's corps. Two acting assistant surgeons would leave firsthand accounts of the horribly overcrowded conditions there, Drs. John S. Billings and Cyrus Bacon. Dr. Louis W. Read (aka Reed), the U.S. Volunteer surgeon assigned to Crawford's division, and Bucktail surgeon, Dr. Comfort, were part of the staff.[26]

Into the Valley of Death

Small-arms fire and rounds of artillery blistered the thin blue line of Pennsylvanians as they sprinted toward Plum Run. Within thirty yards of the stream, the ground became spongy from recent rainfall, and the attack briefly stalled. Rebel sharpshooters lodged in Devil's Den were particularly bothersome, so Crawford detached two regiments from the second row of his brigade for a special mission. He ordered the 1st Rifles and 2nd Pennsylvania Reserves to veer by the left oblique and silence the enemy lying among the boulder-strewn hillside. The remaining three regiments would proceed straight to the Wheatfield. Crawford's decision placed the Bucktails and thirty-six members of Company I on the extreme left of the thin blue line, exposing them to enemy cross fire. The Bucktails held one important advantage in this deadly assignment, however. They were one of the few Federal regiments that carried new Sharps rifles into the battle.[27]

As Taylor and the 1st Rifles waded across Plum Run, the Federal batteries on Little Round Top and Weed's Hill lobbed double rounds of grape, canister, and single solid shot onto the crest of Houck's Ridge and Devil's Den. This was inexact work, especially because of the poor visibility caused by the thick smoke and approaching sunset. Yet, on the valley floor, Phillip and his comrades were overcome with élan as they started up the low ridge. The tricky oblique maneuver created "a most irregular line," recalled Bell, as his small regiment struggled to maintain its cohesion.[28]

Houck's Ridge and a Less Famous Stone Wall

As the Bucktails approached the crest line, a low stone wall materialized that ran the length of a woodlot on the other side. Rose's Woods, approximately seventy-five yards deep, did not offer much concealment since local swine had denuded practically all of its undergrowth. But the attacking Pennsylvanians halted there; it was impossible to determine the strength of the Confederates on the other (west) side of the trees in the Wheatfield. Accompanying the attack the entire way, Phillip and his comrades were exposed to heated enfilade rifle fire from Devil's Den to their left and Rose's Woods to their front. In this hot spot, Phillip had finally reached the point where he would function as an infantryman on the battlefield.[29]

Waving his sword, Taylor and a handful of Bucktails, including Ward of Company I, leaped over the stone barrier and entered the woods, isolating

Captain/Major/Colonel W. Ross Hartshorne, Company K, 13th Pennsylvania Reserves.
SOURCE: MOLLUS MASSACHUSETTS PHOTOGRAPH COLLECTION, UNITED STATES ARMY HERITAGE AND EDUCATION CENTER, CARLISLE, PENNSYLVANIA.

themselves from the rest of the regiment. The small advance party stopped briefly once they discovered their predicament. From this advanced position, Taylor and his associates could see through the stand of trees into the Wheatfield. Then the unanticipated happened: Taylor was cut down by a Confederate bullet to the chest and died almost instantly. Ward helped to carry Taylor's lifeless body back to the stone wall, from which soldiers carried his remains to the rear. At the far right end of the Bucktails' line, the dependable Hartshorne assumed temporary field command of the regiment for the third time in as many battles.[30]

Hartshorne's overwhelming concern was the steady stream of enemy musketry coming from Devil's Den into his flank, which was "up in the air." All the while, artillery shells were ripping through the canopy of Rose's Woods to the front. As the new commander conferred with the leaders of Company I, Bell and Ward, an errant Federal missile suddenly burst into the stone wall, injuring eight members of Companies B and I. One of the fallen was Phillip, whose left knee had been struck.[31]

Adjusting his expectation for a quick solution to the ongoing Confederate threat to the left, Hartshorne ordered four companies to form a right angle with the end of the stone wall and face Devil's Den. Bell and Company I formed the apex. There, the blue and the gray exchanged sporadic gunfire until well after dark. But this was no longer Phillip's fight. He would engage in a different kind of life-and-death struggle.[32]

July 3

Now, the matter of clearing the injured from the field proceeded at a feverish pace. Capt. James A. Bates, the chief ambulance officer for V Corps, and his eighty one-man crews scoured the fields. By 4 a.m. on July 3, they had transported approximately 1,300 wounded to various stations along Taneytown Road while sustaining only one injured corpsman. A red flag flew outside Weikert's farmhouse signifying its use as a hospital, where more than 750 wounded soldiers overwhelmed the surgeons. Many late arrivals were simply laid in the orchard to await treatment. Phillip reached Weikert's in the wee hours of July 3, when he was formally admitted but not treated.[33]

While the ambulance corps was transporting Phillip and others to Weikert's, his comrades in the 1st Rifles spent an uneasy night, leaning against their weapons and listening to the wails of the wounded and dying. Bell later commented, in disgust, that many of his company's picketers had disappeared during the night. At dawn, Hartshorne had grown frustrated with the southern sharpshooters in Devil's Den, and he asked Bell a rhetorical question: "Are you going to let those fellows pick us off?" Shortly thereafter, Company I and Company F of the Bucktails left on patrol, but when they reached some boulders, a sudden blast from the Rebels sent the Yankees scurrying back. Bell had been hit in the right ankle. The impact of the shot had blown away his boot heel, throwing him onto the ground and shattering his tibia and fibula. Several comrades raced their longtime company leader to Weikert's, where he, like so many others, was propped against a tree and left in the yard. At noon, Hartshorne ordered a second demonstration against the rocky bastion, but Lt. John Kratzer and Company K were similarly repulsed.[34]

Bombardment, Evacuation, and Victory

Since daylight on July 3, several Confederate batteries behind the Wheatfield and Peach Orchard had been shelling Houck's Ridge and Little Round Top. Some of the ordnance overshot its intended target, exploding on Taneytown

Road near Weikert's farmhouse. The cannonade was designed to disguise the shift of Rebel troops to the center of their line on Seminary Ridge, where Maj. Gen. George E. Pickett was setting up for an all-out assault on the center of the Federals on Cemetery Ridge. The brisk artillery barrage put the lives of wounded blue-clads at risk.

As soon as Confederate shells began to fall, the wounded at Weikert's farm were painstakingly evacuated to smaller makeshift hospitals several miles from the battlefield. Crawford's division hospital was assigned to Jesse Worley's farm near Little Run, about two miles southeast of Little Round Top and in the general direction of Two Taverns on Baltimore Pike. As it turned out, Worley's was "the most remote field hospital" at Gettysburg.[35]

Phillip, Frank Bell, and other prime candidates for amputation made the uncomfortable journey along with many others. Beginning on July 4, a steady rain started to fall and continued through July 8, adding to the discomfort of those incapacitated soldiers who had to lay on the open ground and seek shelter under rubber mats. Eventually, eighteen canvas hospital tents were assembled in a semicircle facing Worley's farmhouse along with a number of shelter tents. There, Drs. Read and Comfort and nine other physicians cared for 181 patients. But within days, eight of the physicians had fallen ill, likely from exhaustion caused by the excessive workload.[36]

As Phillip was being transported to Worley's, the massive southern artillery bombardment suddenly ceased, and 15,000 Rebels emerged from the woods on Seminary Ridge and traversed 1,400 yards of open ground toward Cemetery Ridge. On Houck's Ridge, McCandless's brigade had a perfect view of the grand spectacle only one mile away. A few Confederates momentarily breached the Yankees' line at the soon-to-be-legendary stone wall near the copse of trees on Cemetery Ridge, but the assault known later as Pickett's Charge had failed.[37]

Now Meade saw an opportunity to turn the enemy's right flank at Little Round Top. Accordingly, Crawford's Pennsylvania Reserves were given the task to clear out pockets of Confederate resistance from the Wheatfield. In another stand of trees on the western edge of the Wheatfield, a brief but fierce firefight broke out between the 1st Rifles and 15th Georgia and resulted in the southerners losing their regimental battle flag, an important war trophy. Thusly, Crawford's Pennsylvania Reserves earned the distinction of leading the final charge at the battle of Gettysburg. Back in the Wheatfield, Phillip's friend, Pvt. Thomas Barnes, lay on the ground with a non–life-threatening wound. On the evening of July 4, Lee began his withdrawal from Gettysburg.[38]

Phillip and Medical Indecision

The day after the battle, Gov. Curtin made the hospital rounds to visit wounded Pennsylvanians, and he was visibly shaken by the level of carnage and human suffering. Once, he spoke with Bell and several other critically wounded officers in a tent reserved for field officers. Then Bell's shattered limb was promptly amputated. He spent ten days recovering on the floor of Worley's barn, using his blanket as a mattress and his jacket as a bedsheet. The amputee propped his stump onto a small wooden milking stool covered with a child's doll pillow, but he could find no physical relief. Bell's bare wound turned purple and then black. But the surgeon determined that the captain of Company I was strong enough to be transported to the Gettysburg train station, where he was loaded onto a cattle car and shipped to a hospital in Washington. Phillip was not as fortunate.[39]

On July 7, the quality of medical care declined markedly once the Army of the Potomac left Gettysburg to pursue the Rebels. Letterman took most of the U.S. Volunteer surgeons and regimental doctors with him and left only a skeleton crew of 106 doctors behind to care for more than an estimated 14,000 patients. The medical director sent out an emergency appeal for civilian "contract physicians" to assist with the unfathomable caseload. These hired physicians were to be paid at the rank of first lieutenant, and their primary function was to track each patient's medical case and conduct light nursing duties. Eventually, more than 250 doctors answered the call, and many hailed from Philadelphia.[40]

Another significant decision made by Letterman that would profoundly affect Phillip was the creation of a central hospital in Gettysburg to deal with patients who were too weak to be transferred to other facilities in Washington, Philadelphia, and Baltimore. In less than three weeks, such a hospital was erected on George Wolf's farm, on the rail line one mile east of Gettysburg's town square. It was a naturally favorable spot: it possessed a spring, good drainage, and ample trees for shade. The design was symmetrical, with 400 tents holding twelve cots in six rows between two stands of oak trees.

Camp Letterman

On July 22, the staff of Camp Letterman braced to welcome almost 1,400 patients who still remained in and around Gettysburg. Dr. Henry J. Janes, the regimental surgeon of the 3rd Vermont, was chosen to be the chief administrator of the hospital. The hospital's opening caused excessive traffic jams on the pikes leading into town, and the final transfer of patients was not completed until August 8. Crawford's division hospital at Worley's farm was among the last to be vacated. Phillip later admitted to Ann that the six-mile trip by wagon had "used me up," an indication of his frail condition.[41]

The medical staff at Camp Letterman was instructed to minimize the number of amputations, using the procedure only as a last resort. Most Civil War physicians, though, had learned that the greatest chance of patient survival depended on removal of the shattered limb within forty-eight hours of incurring the injury. A skilled surgeon could lop off an appendage in two minutes, and Bell had received just such a "primary amputation."[42] But Phillip had not.

Phillip lay in his tent at Worley's farm for almost a month with his shattered leg still attached, and his level of care was dubious. Then, on August 1, he was admitted to Camp Letterman and assigned to a ward consigned to two contract physicians with completely different backgrounds. Dr. Ellis P. (E. P.) Townsend had recently graduated from the Jefferson Medical College of Philadelphia in March 1863 with a specialty in variola (smallpox) infections. The twenty-three-year-old Townsend benefited from a world-class medical education that emphasized scientific principles as the foundation of the medical profession, or allopathy. The second physician, forty-four-year-old Dr. Charles Stockton Gauntt, had graduated in 1844 from the University of Pennsylvania Medical School in Philadelphia, and the date of his education indicates he was trained in homeopathy, or "heroic remedies," developed by Dr. Rush. Since Townsend and Gauntt were assistant surgeons as well as civilians, they would be held in low esteem by wounded soldiers.[43]

At Camp Letterman, Phillip was diagnosed with a "gsw," or gunshot wound, to the left knee, which had fractured his thighbone, a condition that normally required instant attention and immediate amputation. But such surgical procedures in the vicinity of the knee were considered delicate operations, requiring great skill on the part of the surgeon. On August 7, Phillip's attendant deduced that his wounded knee was "a very hard case."[44]

The next day, on August 8, in his first letter to Ann since the Bucktails had left Fairfax Station, Phillip painted a worrisome image of himself: "I dont like to tell you now but I am wounded. I am shot through the bottom of the left knee joint the bones are shattered [and there] is some discharge it makes me very weak. I have not been off my bed since I came to this Camp [Letterman] on the 1st. . . . My bed sore troubles me much laying all the time in the same position."[45] By his own admission, Phillip was beginning to waste away.

One doctor had prescribed morphine, and Phillip confided to Ann that he took "a great deal of Stimulants . . . but I dont think it does me any good." He admitted rather after the fact, "I might better had my leg off in the Start but the Drs thought they could save it." Phillip now yearned for Rushford's Dr. Bixby to take care of him. But, in the same breath, he implored Ann not to travel to Gettysburg to care for him because Camp Letterman was not a place for her.[46] Phillip's protectiveness toward his sister was admirable in light of the pain he was enduring.

Amputation and Complications

August 10 was a special day at Camp Letterman. The Ladies of Gettysburg had teamed with the Sanitary Commission and Christian Commission to sponsor a picnic for the patients and staff, Union and Confederate alike. The meal featured chicken, ham, and oysters prepared on the kitchen's "five large boiler stoves, six cooking ranges, and immense ovens." The attendees were served ice cream for dessert. Entertainment consisted of footraces, climbing a greased pole, and a "negro minstrel show." But not all patients were in a festive mood. Phillip had undergone surgery earlier that day. By mid-September, he was incapacitated and disinterested.[47]

Phillip was in the throes of a life-and-death struggle, and a detailed account of his treatments illustrates the prolonged suffering he endured.[48]

Date: August 10

Symptoms: Ball passing through left knee joint fracturing condyles of femur

Treatment: Amputation at juncture of upper and middle third

Modern analysis: Phillip's operation was termed a "secondary amputation."

By definition, a "secondary amputation" is performed more than forty-eight hours after the initial injury. The mortality rate for such a procedure of the thigh ranged as high as 70 percent. The surgical technique used on Phillip was called a "flap," in which a long piece of skin was used to cover the exposed stump. It required sutures to attach the flap to healthy surrounding tissue. Unfortunately, the flap often required future sloughing of discolored or distended tissue. Inexperienced surgeons often bungled this operation, leaving either too little flap to cover the wound—resulting in a bone protruding from the stump—or too much flap—causing putrefaction and infection (unknown at the time) of the bone, or erysipelas.

> Date: August 14
>
> Symptoms: Left the bone portruding [and] the integuments [flap] not reaching over it
>
> Treatment: Sloughing of stump
>
> Modern analysis: Civil War physicians believed that sloughing would assist in drying the wound site by removing cankered and discolored tissue. It is called "granulation." In nonmedical circles, it was often misidentified as a "third amputation." Sloughing frequently led to pyemia, a deadly infection that spread through the bloodstream.

> Date: September 3
>
> Symptoms: Patient in fine spirits, but bedsore redness on back is 10" in diameter, and redness on side of stump, which is discharging profusely. Feverish.
>
> Treatment: Stump dressings. Administered quinine bitters, herbal tonics, and iron acitate of lead applied topically.
>
> Modern analysis: Infection from bedsore and/or stump. Possible presence of gangrene and emission of pus. Feverish. Serious cases of gangrene had a 46 percent mortality rate.

Dr. Ellis P. Townsend took charge of Phillip's case.

Date: September 10

Symptoms: Night sweats and fever

Treatment: Acidum Sulphoricum, Pulsetilla, Aromatic Sumac administered

Modern analysis: These homeopathic remedies were designed to combat gangrene, lethargy, and nasal congestion. Phillip may also have been dehydrated. There is no mention of dysentery, but Phillip was symptomatic.

Date: September 19

Symptoms: Diarrhea and hemorrhaging

Treatment: Camphonated opium pills (paregoric)/poultice compress on stump

Modern analysis: The poultice kept the site of the wound damp. Civil War doctors believed that the moisture was healthy. In reality, it greatly increased the spread of infection. Hemorrhaging at the wound site was often caused by infection or imperfect or overly tight ligations. Phillip's condition deteriorated during the next week, but no treatments were administered. Phillip's case file was devoid of physician's notes during this critical time.

Date: September 26

Symptoms: Diarrhea, fever

Treatment: Prescribed Sumac, Morphine, and Capsicum

Modern analysis: Those were medications designed to deal with pain, fever, and digestive issues.

On September 28, Dr. Townsend was promoted to assist Dr. Janes. Phillip's case was turned over to Dr. Gauntt.

Date: October 2 and 4

Symptoms: Night sweats, fever, severe hemorrhages from wound, excessive exhaustion

Treatment: Compression by tourniquet

Modern analysis: Attempt to remedy the discharge from the protruding stump. Phillip had contracted either pyemia (a blood infection with a mortality rate of 97 percent) or erysipelas (a bone infection with a high mortality rate). Severe fever and discharge of pus.

The Last Full Measure of Devotion

On October 5, 1863, two days after President Lincoln declared a national day of thanksgiving to be celebrated in November, Pvt. Phillip Griggs Ellithorpe of Company I, 13th Pennsylvania Reserves, passed away at the age of twenty. His remains were placed in a makeshift graveyard at Camp Letterman along with more than 400 of his fallen comrades in arms after having given "the last full measure of devotion" to preserve the Union. Then, beginning on October 27, Pennsylvania's governor authorized the disinterment of all Federal soldiers scattered around Gettysburg for reburial in a central location near the battlefield. The daunting task would take six months. In the meantime, on November 20, 1863, Camp Letterman closed, one day after the dedication of the Soldier's National Cemetery in Gettysburg.[49]

Four Questions

Phillip's nonsurgery, injury, treatment, and interment require additional examination.

Nonsurgery

Why had Phillip's attending surgeons at Weikert's, Worley's, and Camp Letterman waited for more than a month to amputate his leg? There are several plausible explanations. First, on July 2–3, the doctors at Weikert's field hospital were clearly overwhelmed. Likewise, beginning on July 7, the surgeons at Worley's were overburdened and understaffed. Second, Phillip was probably under the care of Bucktail physician Dr. Comfort, at least for the short term. If Comfort balked at performing an amputation, he would have opted for the standard alternative procedure: clearing the wound of shattered bone and foreign objects, such as cloth, dirt, and metallic debris. Third, when the Army of the Potomac pulled out of Gettysburg on July 7 and took more than 500 doctors with them, it created serious personnel shortages in field hospitals such as Worley's. Consequently, the physician-to-patient ratio later ballooned to 1:150 at Camp Letterman. Fourth, Phillip might have argued persistently to keep the limb at all costs. Certainly, the one-time stretcher bearer, hospital attendant, and frequent patient was familiar with the gruesome amputation process. Finally, if Phillip's primary caregiver was at all tentative about performing an amputation in the first place, there was no other authority present to raise questions about the efficacy of such a delay. In hindsight, the doctor's procrastination, for whatever reason, cost Phillip his life.

Injury

The accepted version of Phillip's injury is that one enlisted man from Company I had been mortally wounded (or killed outright) at the stone wall on Houck's Ridge by friendly artillery fire. The source of this round was likely from one of Guthrie's guns on Little Round Top, which was firing double rounds of grape and canister into Rose's Woods. Jagged metal fragments and flying shards of stone could easily produce deadly results, especially if the explosion landed among a crowd of soldiers.

Yet, on August 7, when doctors examined Phillip's wound at Camp Letterman, they determined the cause of injury as "gsw." Is it conceivable that Phillip's doctors could have confused a shrapnel injury with a gunshot wound? These conflicting medical and historical accounts are baffling. One fact is certain: Phillip was the only enlisted fatality listed in Company I at the battle of Gettysburg.[50]

Circumstantial evidence based on geographic proximity supports another hypothesis that Phillip could have been taken down by a minié ball. The Bucktails' assault on Houck's Ridge had moved across Plum Run Valley in a southwesterly direction, and Devil's Den was to their immediate left, positioned at a right angle from the stone wall. Thus, the profiles of the bucktailed attackers were exposed on their left side and, therefore, susceptible to Confederate sniper fire. It is possible that Phillip was struck on his lower left knee by a musket ball at the moment the shell exploded among his comrades at the stone wall. Still, Phillip's wound itself is shrouded in mystery.

Treatment

If Phillip's doctors misunderstood the nature of his injury, it is conceivable that they might have erred in his treatment as well. For example, did Phillip have a case of diarrhea (and accompanying dehydration), or did he contract dysentery? The symptoms he exhibited beyond diarrhea included fevers, stomach ailments, and mucus discharge, all manifestations of dysentery. Yet if Phillip's doctors had suspected the disease, he would have been given a prescribed set of medications, which did not happen.

Phillip may have suffered from dehydration. If so, the weather in Gettysburg might have contributed to this condition. During the tipping-point week of his convalescence, September 19–26, the weather in southern Pennsylvania turned unseasonably warm and humid, but there were no entries in Phillip's medical log. Could this lack of professional care and the stretch of Indian summer have adversely affected Phillip?[51]

It is difficult, if not impossible, to determine the precise cause of death of hospitalized Civil War soldiers on the basis of records kept by contemporary physicians who lacked understanding about bacteria. Observations made by attending physicians of Phillip's case often overlapped and drew an array of conclusions; thus, he was administered an equally broad array of treatments that sometimes conflicted with each other.

In Phillip's case, it is likely that the area around his reddened stump had been overrun with bacteria, staphylococcus, and/or streptococcus, causing a bone infection known as erysipelas (St. Anthony's fire) or pyemia (an infection caused by bacteria that had entered the bloodstream). The oozing bedsore on Phillip's back may have exacerbated the spread of germs to his open wound, and the sloughing procedure of tainted soft tissue around the wound might have produced similar dangers. So what caused Phillip's death? It was likely a combination of several factors working in tandem.[52]

Interment

Phillip's interment presents the final mystery in his end-of-life story. Two contemporary reports prepared by Dr. Janes and the U.S. Sanitary Commission and one plot map of the Camp Letterman graveyard prepared by the Gettysburg National Military Park Commission present contradictory information about Phillip's burial site. Janes reports that, on Phillip's death, his body was placed in section 9, grave 4, at Camp Letterman. The Sanitary

Commission, however, listed the occupant of that grave as Sgt. Samuel Lesage of Company A, 147th New York, who was wounded on July 1 and passed away at Camp Letterman on September 8. The National Park Commission map shows the grave completely empty, and later research conducted by a park historian notes that the final disposition of Phillip's remains, along with more than fifty others, is unknown.[53]

Whoever occupied the aforementioned grave might be simply explained. Lesage's date of death, which predated Phillip's by one month, suggests that he occupied the grave from his death until his disinterment and reburial in the Soldier's National Cemetery after October 27. A reasonable supposition is that Phillip was temporarily buried at Camp Letterman for a few days and that his remains were then shipped home. Indeed, an embalmer's station was set up adjoining Camp Letterman, and the business thrived.[54]

In the fall of 1863, no one in the army seemed to have any information about Phillip. Roll call records show that the adjutant general of the 13th Pennsylvania Reserves did not know Phillip's whereabouts for months, and Ward had not filled out a Final Statement report until the following March. In September 1863, Philander wrote to the Philadelphia Agency of the U.S. Sanitary Commission to request information on the status of his brother from its hospital directory system. The commission was unable to make a definitive determination until the end of the year. Then, on October 30, Permelia received a letter of condolence from Sgt. A. Gillman Foster of Company I.[55] For Phillip's youngest sister, this was old news.

In Search of "The Good Death"

It was only natural for the Ellithorpe family to seek as much information as possible regarding Phillip's final three months: where and when he had been wounded, what kind of care he had received, and how to retrieve his body for reburial at home. The war had permanently altered the traditional manner in which the American people grieved, and the Ellithorpes reflected this evolving process.[56]

In antebellum America, "the good death" was a highly developed mix of traditions, customs, and conventions; the death of a family member had been very much a family affair. Individuals usually died at home surrounded by their loved ones, and the death scene took on a ritualistic tone. Its goal was not only to celebrate "the good life" of a dying relative but also to provide the family with a sense of closure. In addition, "the good death" was vitally concerned with religious conventions regarding salvation and repentance. But when fathers, husbands, brothers, and cousins perished on distant battlefields, it altered the notion of death as an integral aspect of domestic life.[57]

In the new ways that families were forced to cope with a soldier's death, the condolence letter took on added significance. The correspondence was designed to lessen the family's anxieties caused by lack of information. Custom dictated that the deceased soldier's best friend write this important missive. The substance was formulaic. It contained details of the soldier's death on the field of honor or in the hospital, some evidence of patriotism or loyalty to the Union Cause, and a record of last spoken words. Above all, the epistle must reference the spirituality of the dying soldier and his commitment to Christian principles before he entered God's Kingdom.[58]

Regarding Phillip's death, his best friend, Joe Barnes, did not pen the all-important message to Rushford. That may have been because the Bucktails and the Pennsylvania Reserves had been tracking the Army of Northern Virginia since July, fought several skirmishes between the Rappahannock and Rapidan rivers, and participated in the Bristoe Station and Mine Run campaigns in October and November, respectively. Instead of Barnes, the duty fell to Sgt. Foster of Company I, a McKean County lumberjack.

So did Foster's condolence follow the protocol set by "the good death"? The sterile tone and dearth of details about Phillip's life and role in the 1st Rifles indicate that the sergeant of Company I lacked sufficient knowledge about his subject. His words read like an official notice, devoid of any feeling or empathy, and the impersonal matter-of-fact style raised additional concerns. Foster began with an appropriate patriotic compliment—"Your brother lost his life in the defence of his Country"—but proceeded to explain that he had "had Friends," a lukewarm reference lacking any compassion. Several soldiers owed Phillip some money, but Foster did not know their names. Then the missive abruptly ended without meeting most of the guidelines of a model condolence letter. Strangely, Foster's letter was addressed to Permelia.[59]

Going Home

Why had the condolence letter been sent to Permelia? In his final letter to Ann, Phillip had tried to dissuade his older sister from traveling to Gettysburg to be at his bedside. But Phillip's revelation of his untreated, month-old wound and subsequent amputation caused Ann to disobey his wishes. Boarding a train for the first time in her life, the distraught Ann had gone to Camp Letterman, where she served as a surrogate nurse through Phillip's declining days and eventual death. She was, in all probability, the family member who made arrangements to have Phillip's body embalmed and shipped to Rushford shortly after his passing on October 5.

Governor Curtin had assisted such efforts when he created the Pennsylvania State Agency, which provided state funds to pay the cost of disinterring and transporting roughly 1,500 deceased Yankees from Gettysburg to their Pennsylvania hometowns for reburial. The Adams Express Company and the Staunton Transportation Company assisted in this humanitarian endeavor. It is probable that the Pennsylvania State Agency had paid for the transport of Phillip's casket at least as far as Smethport, the site of his enlistment in the Bucktails, and that Ann paid $20 for the remainder of the journey to Rushford.[60]

A proper burial for Phillip in the Ellithorpe family plot in Rushford Cemetery was central to "the good death" ideology, and Ann ensured that this would happen. Thus, Phillip was laid to rest in "a soldier's grave" next to his mother. Afterward, Ann's three-month participation as a volunteer nurse became a life-altering experience. It remained etched in her memory for the rest of her life, and Asa would inscribe this episode on her tombstone. The consequences of the war, fully comprehended by the Ellithorpe brothers of western New York, had, in turn, finally come to rest on Ann.

* * * * * * *

On the afternoon of November 19, President Lincoln traveled to Gettysburg to take part in the dedication of Soldier's National Cemetery. Using only 274 words, the president delivered his famous Gettysburg Address, one of the most eloquent speeches in American history. He reminded the nation of the sacrifices made by the many Federal soldiers who had given "the last full measure of devotion" on "this hallowed ground" to the cause of freedom. The commander in chief exhibited great compassion and depth of understanding about the changing principles of "the good death," and he elevated its tenets to the regeneration and rebirth of the nation.[61]

As the president wrapped up his two-minute speech in front of an immense throng of the living and the silent graves of the fallen, there was an inconspicuous bucktailed absentee. The least likely Ellithorpe to live out the noble words of Lincoln's famous address had already gone home.

So an eighteen-year-old boy from rural Allegany County, New York, who loved wintertime sleigh rides, springtime sugaring, summertime dances, and sneaking out of his second-story home on Lewellen Street for an evening of hijinks, was overcome with patriotic ardor when he enlisted in the 13th Pennsylvania Reserves with other young men he barely knew. In less than thirty months, Phillip had undertaken various official roles in the Bucktails as an orderly, commissary clerk, stretcher bearer, and infantryman. On a personal level, he demonstrated compassion and loyalty to those closest to him as a cook, musician, nurse, friend, and brother. The one military aspect to which he never became accustomed was his dread of killing another human being.

Once wounded during his singular act of heroism at Gettysburg, Phillip demonstrated admirable qualities under great duress. His wound proved his courage, his death proved his sacrifice, and both gained him admission to the Bucktails' brotherhood of warriors. On Houck's Ridge, Phillip made the ultimate sacrifice when he lived up to the oft-repeated soldier's adage of the day: "death before dishonor."[62]

In the spring of 1864, President Lincoln would appoint another new commander to head the Army of the Potomac, and his arrival foretold a new strategic style of unrelenting warfare. Such a grand "overland" design required a massive recruitment of new volunteers, previously discharged veterans, and reassignment of existing servicemen. Ultimately, these changes would affect Asa and Philander, who exchanged their infantry boots for riding saddles but would incur life-altering injuries in the process.

Chapter Eleven

In and Out of the Saddle

The Overland Campaign

After the battle of Gettysburg, the Army of the Potomac cautiously shadowed the Army of Northern Virginia southward into Virginia, but there was no significant contact between the two forces until October. In August 1863, Asa and the 130th New York embarked on a historic transfer to the Cavalry Corps, and the new year witnessed the reenlistment of Philander in a mounted unit. Together, the duo participated in most of the bloody Overland campaign under a new commander with a new strategy. The relentless nature of the combat produced increased levels of carnage and human suffering in less than six weeks. "The ornamental latticework of chivalry and righteousness had been seared completely away," stated one historian. "Battles in which winning and losing seemed to be important were no longer a part of the scheme of things [but] were filled with hard-fought, desperate battles [and] in the end, the places themselves meant nothing."[1] In this final episode of the Ellithorpes in wartime, there was limited personal correspondence because of the mobile nature of that campaign. By June 1864, after spending months in and out of the saddle, Asa and Philander would be knocked out of the war but grappled with new postwar challenges in adapting to its consequences.

From Infantry to Cavalry

Following the removal of Keyes because of his inept advance on Richmond in June 1863, his command was split up among different corps in the army.

In early July, the 130th New York was pulled back to Washington, where it spent two weeks, and Asa scoured the local hospitals in search of his wounded brother-in-law. Not knowing the seriousness of Phillip's condition, Asa tendered him the position of bugler in his own Company H after he would recover.[2]

On July 12, Gibbs's regiment was transported by rail to Frederick, Maryland, to guard Meade's headquarters. Two weeks later, a rumor that the 130th New York would be transferred to the Cavalry Corps proved correct. At the time, there were only 174 horse regiments in the entire army. For a brief period, Asa's newly constituted regiment was known as the 19th New York Cavalry.[3]

The creation of the 19th New York Cavalry was more than the simple transfer of one infantry regiment to the cavalry. It was part of a widespread reform to form a Cavalry Bureau within the War Department. The goal of this new agency was to streamline expenditures, procure healthy horses, establish proper training procedures, and build a reception center for incoming cavalry recruits in Washington. Maj. Gen. George Stoneman was selected chief administrator of the new cavalry depot housed near Giesboro Point. The facility bore the name Camp Stoneman, but it was more commonly known as Dismounted Camp. The first cavalry recruits to arrive were often inactive because they lacked both mounts and lessons in horsemanship. To partially rectify this situation, Thorp was immediately sent on a recruiting trip to western New York to sign up more recruits and gather more horses.[4]

The horse shortage in the army was a serious matter. In October 1863, there were 16,000 horses stabled at Giesboro Depot, but they were mostly broken-down or reissued mounts that lacked physical endurance. At one point, Secretary Stanton seriously considered mounting the blue-clad cavalry on mules. Forage also was in short supply because the contesting armies had been tramping over roughly the same ground in northern Virginia for two years, and natural grasses and pasturelands had become scarce. Some animals, inexperienced in combat, would bolt at the first sounds of battle.[5]

Mastering the Art of Horsemanship

On August 13, the dismounted 19th New York Cavalry reported to Manassas Junction to stand guard at the headquarters of the Cavalry Corps commander, Maj. Gen. Alfred Pleasonton. At this time, the cavalry command was in flux, and Gibbs, experienced in horsemanship, often juggled responsibilities as head of his regiment and brigade. In early October, the State of New York approved a name change for the 19th New York Cavalry to the 1st New York Dragoons (hereafter identified as the 1st Dragoons), perhaps in recognition of Gibbs's expertise. For the remainder of the war, official reports of other commanders often used the federal and state designations interchangeably.[6]

Gibbs was well equipped to lead a detachment of dragoons. The career cavalryman had graduated from West Point as part of the famed Class of 1846. He fought in a regiment of mounted riflemen in the Mexican War and later battled Native Americans on the western frontier in the 1850s. Now Gibbs faced major challenges. His 1st Dragoons were inexperienced, and Confederate sympathizers and Mosby's partisans were active around Manassas Junction.

On September 13, a shipment of emaciated horses arrived, and Gibbs began to train his men in earnest on the basics of horsemanship: how to mount, dismount, and handle horses as well as the proper use of sabers and sidearms while mounted. In the beginning, some ill-behaved trainees were prone "to circus antics with the horses," but Gibbs, a strict disciplinarian, demanded "no monkeyism."[7]

The 1st Dragoons received much on-the-job training. Two primary tasks were patrolling the Orange & Alexandria Railroad and protecting the Federal supply depot at Manassas Junction. On September 22, Gibbs took his horsemen on their first mounted patrol between Warrenton and Centreville, when the Rebels ambushed them, resulting in the loss of six men and ten horses. Once the firing had commenced, chaos ensued. "My horses are too green to be serviceable as cavalry," Gibbs concluded.[8] The commander laid partial blame for the embarrassing incident squarely on unseasoned cavalrymen, and he lobbied for his regiment to be integrated with veteran riders.

Incident in the Saddle

In early October, Meade kept the Army of the Potomac at a safe distance from the enemy but regularly utilized the cavalry to probe Rebel positions. Then, on October 9, Lee's Confederates crossed the Rapidan and attempted to maneuver around the Federals. The surprise caught the Federals flat-footed, resulting in the ten-day Bristoe Station campaign.

That morning, Gibbs ordered Capt. Russell A. Britton to take his Company H on a reconnaissance in search of a notorious "guerrilla scout" in the vicinity of Brentsville, about nine miles west of Manassas Junction. While instructing Company H to "close up" ranks prior to heading out, Asa wheeled his mount too sharply, and the spooked horse dashed out of control toward the head of the line. Horse and rider approached a ditch, but both misjudged the distance. The horse stumbled, taking the full impact of the opposite side of the ditch to its chest and catapulting Asa forward "with great force into the pommel of the saddle."[9]

Undoubtedly shaken and stunned, Asa was escorted to the field hospital. The regimental surgeon examined his swollen testicle and tender lower abdomen and found a scrotal hernia. Three days later, the surgeon transferred the injured equestrian to Seminary Hospital in Georgetown for further treatment. There, a specialist diagnosed Asa's condition as orchitis, an abnormal swelling in the veins of the scrotum. A bout of "acute diarrhea" added further to his misery. In his absence, Asa missed the attachment of the 1st Dragoons to the Reserve Brigade of Brig. Gen. Wesley Merritt. Merritt held Gibbs's regiment in reserve for the remainder of the Bristoe campaign despite several cavalry clashes.[10]

In early November, Asa returned to Company H and found them repairing torn-up railroad tracks near Culpeper, but it was clear that he was in no condition to ride a horse. At the end of the month, Meade made one last effort before the onset of winter to push the Confederates out of their twenty-mile network of trenches south of the Rapidan at Mine Run. On November 26, the operation swung into motion during a fierce rainstorm, and Asa rode in an ambulance behind the cavalry. Merritt assigned the 1st Dragoons to surveil river crossings along the Rapidan, where they engaged in dismounted clashes. On December 1, Meade's army recrossed the Rappahannock and went into winter quarters.[11]

The Third Winter Camp of the War

From December until May, the opposing blue and gray forces faced each other along a no-man's-land behind the Rappahannock and Rapidan rivers. Merritt's Reserve Brigade bivouacked in front of the infantry at Mitchell's Station, about seven miles south of Culpeper Court House. The regiment laid out a "cozy camp" along several corduroy avenues they named Main,

Broadway, and First. The log cabins they erected were considered "architectural marvels," and the abode of Asa's captain was especially "pretentious," so that some called it "Britton's Ranch." During periods of relative inactivity, the 1st Dragoons spent time picketing, scouting, guarding river crossings, and riding herd over the commissary's "Bovine Corps."[12]

In the first six weeks of 1864, the 1st Dragoons rotated picket duty with other regiments and made more frequent contact with the enemy. Several noteworthy skirmishes broke out on January 20 and February 6–7 near Barnett's Ford on the Rapidan. Such clashes, however, were less frequent than the "nocturnal conversations" with Rebels and the welcome habit of exchanging newspapers, tobacco, and coffee.[13]

Capt. Britton limited Asa's soldierly activity to desk work as assistant adjutant general for the 1st Dragoons. Excused from daily drill and other physical activities, he later mused to Ann, "I have gone from being a fighting to a writing man." Commenting for the first time on the seriousness of his injuries, the dragoon admitted to his wife, "[Your] Soldier Boy . . . is disfigured and . . . maimed for life." He also mentioned to Ann that while he had convalesced in Washington back in October, he had searched for the elusive Blanchard and hoped to involve the provost marshall's office in his dishonest dealings with Phillip. "He [Blanchard] has played a mean part to Say the least," Asa concluded. Then, in mid-January, he applied for and received a fifteen-day furlough to take care of an unspecified personal matter in Vermont.[14]

Asa found diversions from his clerical duties, too. He partook in the popular winter camp ritual of visiting friends in other regiments, especially the 5th Vermont, who bivouacked near the "Rapid Ann." His cavalry comrades also constructed a large multipurpose building made from logs that they dubbed "Canterbury Hall." It served as an entertainment center and social gathering point for a glee club, a brass band, "stag" dances, and biweekly minstrel shows performed by local contrabands. Asa expressed joy, informing Ann that twelve musical instruments had recently been delivered and that the regiment was in the process of forming a band. He had exhibited strong musical inclinations since his Vermont days, but it is not clear whether he participated in the procurement or organization of the troupe.[15]

Meanwhile, in Rushford, Ann dealt with familiar unpleasantries, exchanging "harsh words" with her father over some undisclosed matter. Following the "unnecessary trouble," Lyman threatened to move to Denver.

It is plain that Asa's father-in-law used harsh language and had intimidated his wife. Asa felt helpless being so far away from home and unable to protect Ann from such abuse. He admitted to experiencing moments of "the blues," too. On one occasion, he explained that he wanted to take piano lessons and learn French but only "when this cruel war is over," thus echoing Phillip's post-Fredericksburg language from the previous year. Ann busied herself during the winter, procuring headstones for Fannie and Phillip's graves, while Asa's 1st Dragoons were sent to guard a mountaintop signal station until the end of March.[16]

Philander Returns to the War

After his discharge from the 27th New York, Philander returned to western New York and secured a job constructing a pineapple cheese factory in Rushford. Meanwhile, the war raged on, and a manpower shortage, aggravated by the expected discharge of many three-year regiments in 1864, plagued the army. Consequently, several northern states began proactive campaigns to attract new recruits by making special appeals to discharged veterans. Accordingly, John Fisk, the postmaster of Niagara Falls, was appointed to recruit an infantry regiment and later changed to a mounted rifle unit. Fisk faced difficulty in filling even one company with local Erie County men, so he expanded the range of recruitment to include other counties in western New York.[17]

In Pike and Rushford, fifty-year-old Henry Runyan and twenty-two-year-old Watson W. Bush scoured Allegany and Wyoming counties looking to sign up interested volunteers for Company B, 2nd New York Mounted Rifles (hereafter identified as the 2nd Mounted Rifles). State and federal signing bonuses, exceeding $700, enhanced the incentive for first-time volunteers and veterans alike. On January 4, 1864, Philander was persuaded to join up in Gainesville at the rank of corporal. It must have comforted Philander to know personally his two superior officers, recruiters Runyan and Bush. Eight days later, Company B took the Oath of Allegiance at Fort Porter in Buffalo, and Philander was promoted to fourth sergeant. On March 4, the "Governor's Guard," the regimental nickname, departed for Washington.[18]

The New Yorkers were temporarily assigned to XXII Corps and housed at Dismounted Camp. The late winter grounds were muddy, and the idle New Yorkers groused over inactivity as well as the failure of the government to supply horses promptly. Maj. Nahum Ward Cady, something of a lightning rod for controversy, vocalized to superiors his men's growing concern about the rumor that the 2nd Mounted Rifles was about to revert to an infantry regiment. They also had not been paid.[19]

The Arrival of Grant

On March 8, while Asa sat atop Pony Mountain near Culpeper and Philander sloshed about in Dismounted Camp, President Lincoln summoned Maj. Gen. Ulysses S. Grant from the western theater to the White House. Two days later, the president conferred on him the rare military rank of lieutenant general and bestowed on him the office of general in chief. The new commander retained Halleck and Meade as chief of staff and commanding general of the Army of the Potomac, respectively.

Grant's promotion signaled reducing the number of corps but expanding the number of regiments serving in each brigade. He also eliminated or reassigned underperforming commanders and promoted others with proven combat records. The 1st Dragoons celebrated Grant's elevation with a massive snowball fight against their antagonists, the 5th U.S. Cavalry, that nearly degenerated into an all-out brawl.[20]

In point of fact, Grant had inherited a cavalry corps in disarray. Beginning in December 1863, the cavalry had lost arguably its most accomplished officer when Buford suddenly died from an illness. Three weeks later, Stoneman resigned from the Cavalry Bureau. Then the embarrassing Kilpatrick raid in early March precipitated the demotion and transfer of Pleasonton from head of the Cavalry Corps.[21]

Grant envisioned a more inclusive and vigorous role for the Cavalry Corps in military operations, where they would serve as an independent extension of the infantry. The traditional use of horsemen had been limited to guarding supply trains and river crossings, reconnaissance, and protecting infantry flanks during active engagements. Meade subscribed to this model, and for that reason, some critics in the 1st Dragoons derisively nicknamed him "Grandmother Meade."[22]

On April 4, Grant rectified the cavalry dilemma with the selection of Brig. Gen. Philip H. Sheridan to head the Cavalry Corps. Unimpressed with Grant's choice, some of Asa's dragoons were overheard asking, "Who is Sheridan?" Another chuckled that "Little Phil's" boots were too long for his short legs. Still another critic compared his appearance to "a rat terrier." It would not take long for attitudes to change.[23]

Preparing the Cavalry Corps for Action

Sheridan wasted no time in assessing the prowess of his new command. He ordered Capt. F. C. Newhall, the acting inspector general, to investigate the condition and preparedness of each division and regiment. On April 17, Sheridan received Newhall's report, an unflattering indictment of Merritt's horsemen. The inspector took offense to the untidy campsite of the Reserve Brigade, describing it as the most unhealthy in the entire army. He believed that "the horses are used up" and that the troopers in the 1st Dragoons were poorly groomed and sloppily dressed, a direct slap at the fastidious Asa. In fairness to Merritt, the brigadier had suggested that the regiment be permanently dismounted because of the "emaciated" condition of their horses, but Gibbs had lobbied against such a drastic recommendation. Newhall further observed that the undersized New York regiment was armed with outdated Joslyn carbines. "In my opinion," Newhall concluded, "these troops are not in condition to perform active duty." He recommended pulling the Reserve Brigade out of line and completely reorganizing it.[24]

Sheridan used the unflattering inspection as an opportunity to defend his corps to Meade. "Little Phil" placed the blame for unpreparedness squarely on incessant guard duty and scouting forays. Meade listened and then issued ten days of rest for the Reserve Brigade. The horsemen were also refitted with the latest in weaponry, the Spencer repeating rifle, a decided improvement in firepower according to Asa.[25]

Less than a week after assuming command, he appointed Brig. Gen. Alfred T. A. Torbert to head the division, which comprised Merritt's Reserve Brigade. The choice of Torbert was a curious one. A trained infantryman, Torbert was inexperienced in the rapidly changing realm of horse combat, but there was no questioning his aggressive spirit in battle. Torbert's selection might have owed something to the growing belief of using the cavalry as an offensive weapon.[26]

Unfortunately, Torbert would develop an abscess at the base of his spine in early May, causing him great discomfort while riding horseback. He would be unavailable for the opening salvo of the new campaign.

Grant's Strategy for the Overland Campaign

Meanwhile, Grant had perfected a strategy involving five "simultaneous advances" to begin on May 4. His plan called for Maj. Gen. William T. Sherman to advance from Chattanooga to Atlanta, Maj. Gen. Nathaniel P. Banks to march from New Orleans to Mobile, Maj. Gen. Franz Sigel to create havoc in the Shenandoah Valley, and Maj. Gen. Benjamin F. Butler to pressure the Confederate capital from Bermuda Hundred. To Meade and the Army of the Potomac fell the task of forcing Lee out of the Rapidan line through a series of flanking movements. Central to Grant's synchronized operation was placing maximum pressure on multiple locations in order to eliminate the enemy's ability to resupply and/or reinforce. In addition, the Federal forces must be doggedly committed to the offensive even in the face of tactical defeat. The Overland campaign would be so mobile that Asa did not pen a single letter to Ann during its operation.[27]

On the evening of May 4, Sheridan's cavalrymen were set in motion. The two cavalry divisions of James H. Wilson and David M. Gregg led the largest infantry columns to Ely's Ford and Germanna Ford, respectively, while Merritt's Provisional Brigade was in position to guard the massive supply train as well as the rear of the army, an assignment sure to rankle Sheridan. If everything went according to plan, Grant's troops would steal through the dense foliage of the Wilderness before the Confederates even knew they had given up the Rappahannock line. In Torbert's absence, Merritt assumed the reins of the division, Gibbs took control of the Reserve Brigade, and Thorp was elevated to head the 1st Dragoons. These last-minute changes on the eve of impending battle remained intact for the next three weeks. Asa accompanied the 1st Dragoons, but it is unknown whether he rode on horseback with Company H or sat in an ambulance as he had done at Mine Run.[28]

The Wilderness

On May 5, Grant intended to cross the Rapidan undetected and control three east–west arterials and one north–south pathway leading to the Wilderness. The plan went awry from the start when the Federals bumped into a Confederate corps. A ferocious fight broke out at a clearing known as Saunders Field, and Grant's strategy rapidly unraveled as the army bogged down in the dense foliage of the Wilderness. Eventually, both sides disengaged in order to dig breastworks and prepare for a major clash the next day. In the meantime, Merritt's cavalry escort had been plodding toward Wilderness Tavern but then were redirected eastward to Catherine's Furnace to address a rumor that J. E. B. Stuart's horsemen were attempting to harass Grant's rear. Lacking a meaningful role in the next day's combat, Sheridan's divisions shifted to Todd's Tavern to protect the left flank at the junction of Brock and Catharpin roads.[29]

The outcome of the second day at the Wilderness would depend on whichever side would respond the quickest with reinforcements. The Federals held their own, and victory was within their grasp provided that the reserves reported promptly. But they did not. Instead, the timely appearance of Confederates recently arriving from Tennessee determined the outcome of the day's fight. After dark, the battlefield grew eerily quiet. In places, the dense undergrowth caught fire, adding to the suffering of the wounded, an element of horror never before witnessed in the war.

Todd's Tavern

On the morning of May 7, Sheridan's horsemen faced a major test at Todd's Tavern. Ordered to disperse Confederate cavalry, Merritt deployed his three brigades at the Brock–Furnace crossroads, with Gibbs in reserve. Before they reached the tavern itself, the Yankees collided with their Rebel counterparts. Both sides dismounted and engaged in close quarters for fourteen hours. The Confederates grudgingly gave way, and Merritt called up Gibbs to lead an afternoon counterattack down Brock Road. The 1st Dragoons lined up to the right of the roadway and charged. Adrenaline outweighed sound judgment, however, as Thorp's center outran its flank protection, creating a salient, and they were in danger of being surrounded by the enemy. The presence of reinforcements rushed forward by Gibbs stabilized their line, however. The new Spencer carbines may have given the dismounted blue-clads the edge at Todd's Tavern. Both the longest and the largest dismounted cavalry engagement of the war had just been waged.[30]

Todd's Tavern is often treated as an afterthought to the battle of the Wilderness, but Sheridan's cavalry acted with true bravado. Leading the Federal counterattack, the 1st Dragoons performed a major role in forcing the Rebels to retreat from the strategic crossroads. In the process, Thorp's men had accrued ninety-one casualties, the largest in Gibbs's brigade and the highest single-day loss in regimental history. As Grant contemplated his next move, the Army of the Potomac calculated astronomical losses at the Wilderness, almost 18,000 killed, wounded, missing, or captured.[31]

Relentless Advance

Grant's next move called for disengaging from the Wilderness and turning the Confederates' right flank at Spotsylvania Court House. The plan would require stealth as well as a cavalry presence to sweep the Rebels from Brock Road and screen the infantry's movement. Accordingly, Meade instructed Sheridan to set the cavalry in motion no later than 5 a.m. on May 8, which would allow the Federals to reach Spotsylvania unencumbered. But there was a problem. Apparently, Meade's directive had never reached the horsemen. When the first infantry corps reached Todd's Tavern at approximately 8 a.m., they discovered the cavalrymen asleep and the Confederates still blocking the road. Gibbs had his division in motion first, and he threw out the 1st Dragoons as skirmishers. They encountered "very stiff resistance" in the vicinity of Hart's House and Block House Bridge on the Po River. The regiment added twenty-two more casualties to the total it had accumulated the day before.[32]

Showdown

Later on May 8, when Meade and Sheridan met face-to-face, both commanders were in a foul mood. The commanding general accused the Cavalry Corps of failing to cover the movement of the army, and the cavalry chief accused the infantry branch of handcuffing his horsemen when they could be of greater service attacking Confederate targets. Their disagreement became so heated that Grant intervened and granted Sheridan permission to launch an independent strike to disrupt the Confederate rear. Although Sheridan's departure would leave Grant without cavalry protection, the same could be said for Lee if Stuart should follow the Yankees. The best scenario would produce an epic showdown between Stuart and Sheridan for cavalry supremacy.[33]

Sheridan's Raid

In the predawn hours of May 9, Sheridan's three divisions hoofed down Telegraph Road with more than 10,000 troopers as well as six horse batteries.

The thirteen-mile column and supply train kicked up considerable dust, and the mounted riders took four hours to pass any particular point. Sheridan hoped to cross all four tributaries of the Mattapony undetected, secure the bridgeheads over the North Anna River, and attack a major Confederate supply depot at Beaver Dam Station. The Yankees would be in the saddle for the next two weeks.[34]

The Federal horsemen had reached the north bank of the North Anna River, where they bedded down for the evening except for Brig. Gen. George A. Custer. The Michigander promptly led his brigade across the river, attacked the Rebel depot, and burned a warehouse. The raiders captured three locomotives with cars containing 1.5 million rations and 200,000 pounds of bacon plus flour, ammunition, and medical stores. Before they recrossed the river, they tore up ten miles of track and liberated nearly 300 prisoners of war who had just been captured at the Wilderness. Meanwhile, Gibbs posted Thorp's 1st Dragoons at Davenport Bridge near Goodall's farm, where the picketers were bloodied for the fourth consecutive day. As the regiment's assistant adjutant, Asa would chronicle the mounting casualties for official reports.

The next morning, Sheridan's force headed to the South Anna River, where they encountered more resistance at Ground Squirrel Bridge. The fight was intense and lasted for two hours before the southern horsemen retreated, but they had succeeded in slowing the blue wave on its relentless march.

From Yellow Tavern to Haxall's Landing

On May 11, the stage was set for a collision of blue and gray cavalrymen at Yellow Tavern. The abandoned inn, six miles east of Richmond, was situated at the junction of three roads. Around noon, the clash commenced with Gibbs's Reserve Brigade in the lead. Both sides initially fought mounted, but they all eventually dismounted. The Confederates were outnumbered, and the new Spencer carbines laid down a withering fire. The tide of battle slowly turned in mid-afternoon when the Rebels' left flank was turned and Stuart, "the Bold Dragoon," was mortally wounded.[35]

In the early morning hours of May 12, Sheridan camped along the Chickahominy across from Meadows Bridge. It was imperative to storm the bridge and clear out the lightly defended enemy on the opposite bank. Accordingly, the 1st Dragoons marched four abreast over the bridge, charged with their repeating rifles blazing, and extended Sheridan's right flank. The Rebels retreated, and after another brief skirmish, Sheridan proceeded to Haxall's Landing on the James River, where he hoped to connect with Butler's Army of the James, resupply, and give his men and horses a much-deserved rest.

Sheridan's six-day raid was over at a cost of 625 men and 300 horses. Its strategic accomplishments were minimal, but morale soared within the Cavalry Corps. They had faced the challenge, battled the elite southern horsemen on an equal footing, and killed the legendary Stuart. Ever present, Asa probably welcomed a ten-day respite on Malvern Hill regardless of his mode of transportation or level of engagement in Sheridan's bold venture.

Spotsylvania

In the meantime, Grant was engaged in a cat-and-mouse chase to reach Spotsylvania Court House ahead of the Confederates. By dawn on May 10, the Federal and Confederate armies faced each other along a four-mile front extending from the Po River to Spotsylvania Court House. There was nothing irregular about the placement of troops except for a bulge in the center of the Confederate line called the Mule Shoe.

Grant scheduled a simultaneous full frontal assault in the evening along the entire Confederate line to test for weak spots in the formidable defense. The most dramatic movement was performed by Col. Emory Upton, who assailed the Mule Shoe with twelve regiments in a silent bayonet charge. The inaudible attack caught the Rebels off guard and routed them. But Upton could not hold the breakthrough without reinforcements, and his force withdrew after dark. The bold attack had given Grant new inspiration, however, to launch the exact same kind of attack against the Mule Shoe but on a much more massive scale.

Before 5 a.m. on May 12, the brigade of Col. John R. Brooke departed from the Brown farm with his corps and one company of boys from Rushford and Allegany County, Company D, 64th New York. They struck the east side of the Mule Shoe like a sledgehammer, driving the Rebels back several hundred yards from the salient. Hand-to-hand combat broke out almost immediately, all sense of formation was lost, and the vicious struggle lasted for fourteen hours in a driving rainstorm. "Never during the war have I seen such desperate fighting," commented Brooke. "The bayonet was freely used on both sides."[36]

After replenishing their ammunition at the Landrum farm, Brooke's men were repositioned on the other side of the apex and fought at a place forevermore known as the Bloody Angle. After dark, Grant's line held the outer parapets of the Mule Shoe but at a terrible cost of 18,400 casualties. One of the Federal fatalities that day was Pvt. Charles Van Dusen, the boyhood chum of Phillip and frequent companion during the early part of the war. The staggering losses would impact Philander and the 2nd Mounted Rifles shortly.[37]

The bloody battle was over, and the combined Federal casualty figures for the Wilderness and Spotsylvania totaled more than 36,000 in little more than a week. In order to address this sudden manpower shortage, Grant called on Halleck for the immediate release of all able-bodied soldiers currently stationed in Washington to the battle front. Accordingly, the chief of staff authorized 21,000 servicemen, mostly from XXII Corps, to report directly to Grant. The Defense of Washington would be left with a skeleton force.[38]

Stirring the 2nd Mounted Rifles

Halleck's order reached the disgruntled 2nd Mounted Rifles, who were still stationed at Dismounted Camp, impatiently awaiting their mounts. Fisk marched his reluctant warriors to the wharves, boarded a steamer, and arrived the next morning at Belle Plain. Then the regiment exchanged its cavalry gear for infantry equipment and departed on foot to Fredericksburg. The journey of fourteen miles over muddy roads and clogged thoroughfares strained these sedentary troopers. On May 15, they crossed the Rappahannock in a driving rainstorm and briefly rested atop Marye's Heights before proceeding to Grant's headquarters later that evening. The next morning, Fisk reported to Burnside for assignment, an underperforming commander in the recent campaigns.[39]

The Unique Provisional Brigade

On May 16, Burnside assigned the 2nd Mounted Rifles to the new Provisional Brigade of Brig. Gen. Elisha Gaylord Marshall. A career officer, Marshall had served on the American frontier in the 1850s and earned a reputation as a strict disciplinarian. Meade's aide-de-camp, Theodore Lyman, opined that he was an exemplary leader. In 1861, Marshall recruited the 13th New York (Rochester Regiment) and served as colonel until the two-year

Colonel Elisha G. Marshall, 14th New York Heavy Artillery, Provisional Brigade.
SOURCE: CIVIL WAR PHOTOGRAPHS, 1861–1865, LIBRARY OF CONGRESS, PRINTS AND PHOTOGRAPHS DIVISION.

unit discharged in May 1863. Then he recruited the 14th New York Heavy Artillery, primarily from Rochester and St. Lawrence County.[40]

Marshall's patchwork brigade was composed of two dismounted cavalry regiments—the 2nd Mounted Rifles and 24th New York Cavalry—and two artillery regiments—the 14th New York Heavy Artillery and the 2nd Pennsylvania Provisional Heavy Artillery. This unique combination made Marshall's the only infantry brigade in the army composed entirely of dismounted cavalry and heavy artillerists. Grant's veterans typically greeted such "heavies" with contempt, considering them "soft and untested," and dubbed dismounted cavalry without horses a laughingstock. Only time would tell whether these biases would affect the prowess of Marshall's brigade.[41]

The soldiers of the 2nd Mounted Rifles were upset in their allocation, and once again, Maj. Cady stepped forward as their spokesman. Cady charged that the War Department had been duplicitous in recruiting them as a mounted regiment and assigning them instead to Marshall's ragtag brigade. He censured Secretary Stanton for "willfully breaking faith with our soldiery." Feeling deceived, Cady pointed out that the morale of his men had dropped noticeably at Dismounted Camp, and much straggling occurred on their march from Belle Plain to Spotsylvania. The major sensed that his grievance was being ignored, so he registered his complaint up the chain of command, demanding the reinstatement of his regiment to the horse brigade. His fiery criticisms went unanswered but were not forgotten.[42]

After spending two days within sight of Spotsylvania Court House, Marshall's Provisional Brigade was shifted to Landrum House. There, armed with pick and shovel, the brigade was instructed to dig a double row of entrenchments. This assignment was not inconsequential; Confederate artillery played havoc with their work, and the 14th New York suffered fifty-four casualties, although the 2nd Mounted Rifles were practically unscathed. Incidentally, the next day, seven regiments of "heavies" fought valiantly in an impressive stand against a Rebel counterattack at the Harris farm, dispelling the thought that artillerists would run at the first sign of battle.[43]

To Hanovertown

Grant's failure to budge the Confederates convinced him to return to the flanking stratagem, so he refocused his attention on Hanover Junction on the North Anna River, where several rail lines converged. Sheridan's cavalry corps had just rejoined the army, and Torbert resumed command of his division, a move necessitating the return of Merritt to the brigade and Gibbs to the 1st Dragoons. On the march, Marshall's Provisional Brigade detached to protect Burnside's corps, and they clashed several times against spirited Confederate patrols all the way to Hanovertown. So, it seems, Philander's regiment and brigade were continually being relegated to such backyard duty. This time, however, the 2nd Mounted Rifles were bloodied.[44]

Before dawn on May 27, Torbert's horsemen reached the Pamunkey near Dabney Ferry and began erecting two pontoon bridges. At mid-morning, they crossed with Asa in the saddle. Pushing forward one mile to Hanovertown, a colonial tobacco center with several fine plantations, Merritt posted the 1st Dragoons in reserve. The ultimate objective of Sheridan's force was to secure the small community of Haw's Shop, where five roads converged. Custer's brigade detached up the Hanover Court House Road to protect the right flank against elements of southern cavalry. The Wolverines ran into heavy resistance, indeed, and dug in behind Crump Creek.[45]

The brisk cavalry skirmishes at Hanovertown and Crump Creek are noteworthy because historians often considered them the first actions of the battle of Cold Harbor. But Asa recalled it with greater urgency. While riding with Company H into Hanovertown, he reinjured himself in the same manner at Brentsville. As the 1st Dragoons advanced toward Cold Harbor, a surgeon evaluated Asa's deep contusion and confirmed that he had aggravated his orchitis.[46]

On June 1, the 1st Dragoons fought the opening round at Cold Harbor in breastworks while the regimental band played behind them. Meanwhile, Asa had made the nine-mile journey to the General Hospital of the Cavalry Corps in City Point, Virginia. He spent a couple of days in the tent city and then transported by ship to the Officer's General Hospital, Division No. 1, in Annapolis, Maryland, the largest facility dedicated specifically to the care of wounded officers. On June 9, Asa arrived at the Naval Academy grounds, where his case was assigned to Dr. B. A. Vanderfieft. A weekly newsletter written by the patients, *The Crutch*, welcomed Asa and others to the facility. Fortunately, Letterman's medical system had become streamlined by this time, and the wounded at Cold Harbor were treated expeditiously.[47]

Ann was informed about Asa's second accident less than a week after it had occurred, and she felt deep compassion for his condition. "When I think what you have been through and what you may have to suffer and endure[,] every nerve in my body quivers," she wrote.[48] Ann disclosed that many of their acquaintances in Rushford were asking about Asa's "particular case" and thirsted for details about his hospitalization. "My answers cannot be very satisfactory," she added about the delicate subject.[49]

While convalescing, Asa later confessed to Ann that "I shall never be fit for field duty again." One thing was certain: "I cannot stand it in the saddle."[50] Pondering his future, Asa hoped to secure a desk job in the draft bureau, Invalid Corps, or War Department. In the worst case, he would apply for a medical disability discharge and begin to teach in Rushford.

Both Ann and Asa came to understand that his kind of injury would prevent them from having children of their own. Ann took the high road: "The future may not be as bright and joyous as anticipated," she admitted, "but I know there is much happiness in store for you and me, My husband." Then she pleaded with Asa: "Oh! come back to me Asa with your heart in the right place." Asa responded pragmatically: "If there are only two of us we can manage to cloth and feed ourselves . . . I am glad that there are no little ones to Suffer."[51] For Asa, the war had come to an abrupt end.

Philander at Cold Harbor

One day before Asa's injury, Philander and the rest of Burnside's corps departed from the North Anna and plodded toward Hanovertown. Many soldiers, including those in the 2nd Mounted Rifles, complained about the "insufferable stench" of dead horses as they tramped over the same ground Sheridan had taken to and from Haxall's Landing. At daybreak on May 30, Burnside's corps and Marshall's Provisional Brigade started across the Pamunkey and proceeded to Haw's Shop and then to Totopotomoy Creek. But many of Philander's comrades had fallen out of these extended marches.[52]

On June 1, Merritt's brigade occupied a doglegged line near Cold Harbor, straddling Shady Grove Road and bending at an awkward right angle to face Magnolia Swamp. Their exposed left flank was in the Confederate crosshairs. When Rebel forces struck this undefended sector, the blue line was pushed back. The Federals rallied, however, but only after a bitter counterattack aided by Bartlett's reliable brigade from across the swamp.[53]

After dark, Grant repositioned his army, leaving Burnside's corps to cover the leftward movement. In reserve near Bethesda Church on June 2, Philander's comrades endured intense Rebel artillery barrages and one enemy sortie, which caused a "real skedaddle" among the 2nd Mounted Rifles on picket duty. At one point, Marshall placed Philander's friend and captain of Company B "in arest" for running to the rear instead of moving forward to meet the enemy. Order was restored, however, but Grant's nighttime shift and proper troop placement were woefully behind schedule. The misfires forced the lieutenant general to reschedule his full-frontal assault for June 3.[54]

On June 3, Grant's brief attack on entrenched southerners supported by artillery proved to be a costly defeat reminiscent of Fredericksburg. Some soldiers had pinned name tags to their blouses before entering the attack, which may count as the first "dog tags" in American military history.[55] Philander and his regiment, brigade, and corps were much more fortunate; they remained in reserve and out of harm's way during the bloodbath in a relatively quiet sector.

Since May 5, the Army of the Potomac had sustained approximately 55,000 casualties, an astronomical figure widely condemned in the northern press. It bears noting that the 2nd Mounted Rifles were bloodied in multiple rearguard actions, accruing sixty-eight casualties. The Overland campaign was officially over, but the bloodletting would continue as Grant diverted his attention to a major rail center six miles south of Richmond.[56]

Reassignment

During an eight-day interlude, Grant repositioned Burnside's corps to the northernmost location and farthest from enemy lines. Both armies probed each other frequently during this time, and Philander's unit skirmished twice with gray-clads determined to turn "Old Burn's" right flank. But this was also a critical moment in the history of the 2nd Mounted Rifles, as important news broke on June 7: Philander's division commander, Brig. Gen. Thomas L. Crittenden, abruptly tendered his resignation. Speculation abounded in the ranks about his untimely departure in the midst of an active campaign. One story claimed that the Kentuckian opposed the designation and use of seven African American regiments in one of his brigades. Another rumor claimed that Grant intended to revamp Burnside's underperforming corps.[57]

Crittenden's departure did initiate a modest reshuffle. On June 9, Marshall's Provisional Brigade was stripped of its two dismounted regiments, reducing it to only two "heavy" regiments. Grant kept Fisk's 2nd Mounted Rifles in Burnside's corps but reassigned it to the division of Brig. Gen. Robert Brown Potter in the brigade of Col. John I. Curtin, the cousin of Pennsylvania Gov. Andrew Curtin and former leader of the 45th Pennsylvania. Curtin was a "green" officer at the brigade level, having been promoted to colonel in the field less than a month earlier.[58]

Potter barely disguised his contempt for the 2nd Mounted Rifles while evaluating them in reports to superiors. He derided the fact that his newest regiment was "mostly made up of new . . . and old men," a slap at their abilities

Captain/Major/Lieutenant Colonel John I. Curtin, 45th Pennsylvania. *SOURCE:* CIVIL WAR PHOTOGRAPHS, 1861–1865, LIBRARY OF CONGRESS, PRINTS AND PHOTOGRAPHS DIVISION.

as soldiers. "In my opinion," the brigadier concluded, "the 2nd Mounted Rifles will never be effective as an Infantry organization." There was no secret that the regiment had been outspoken in its disappointment about serving as footmen. And Marshall had responded, showing little confidence in the regiment and relegating it to picket duty at bridges, protecting the corps' rear, and digging breastworks. Rarely were the New Yorkers used as skirmishers or on the front line. Maj. Cady took umbrage with Potter's appraisal and sent a letter of complaint to Meade, outlining the "unmerited insult."[59]

PHILANDER AND THE BATTLE OF SECOND PETERSBURG

On June 12, the Army of the Potomac conducted a night march to disguise its movement and ultimate destination, Petersburg. Grant gave Burnside the longest and most circuitous route of march so he would not slow down the other corps. Grant's subterfuge worked; Lee was stunned when he discovered that the Federals had vacated the trenches at Cold Harbor. On June 14, the first blue-clads crossed a 2,100-foot pontoon bridge at Weyanoke Point, the longest in American military history, and arrived on the outskirts of Petersburg.[60]

On June 15, the first Federal corps launched an attack on the eastern face of an outer ring of entrenchments called the Dimmock Line. Ten miles in length, the line was defended by a small force of militiamen and conscripts. Still, there was not enough support in place to capitalize on a modest two-mile breakthrough. Burnside's corps arrived the next day, but it took until nightfall for his divisions to deploy, entrench, and participate in a brief skirmish. To the front of Curtin's brigade, on the extreme left flank of the division, stood Shand House and, slightly to its left, Battery No. 15.

Grant selected Burnside to conduct a predawn attack on June 17, and Potter's division was chosen to initiate first contact with the Rebels. The assault would then roll up Burnside's line. With bayonets fixed and rifles uncapped, Curtin arranged his brigade in two lines, with the 2nd Mounted Rifles on the left end of the second row and initially earmarked as reserves. They moved out after midnight and focused on Shand House, approximately fifty yards away. The silent advance would be aided by a ravine leading to the base of the Rebel trenches on Hickory Hill. Here, the Yankees waited for first light. Stealth held the key to success.

* * * * * * *

Philander's 2nd Mounted Rifles advanced, but in the dark, they lost cohesion and inadvertently veered toward Baxter Road. Now Fisk's men faced a greater danger: his left wing was up in the air and, as such, was vulnerable to enfilade farther down the Dimmock Line. When the shooting started, the New Yorkers were riddled in a cross fire.[61]

The surprise attack initially pushed the Confederate defenders back to a second line of parapets. The Federals had captured several field guns, four stands of colors, more than 300 prisoners, and 1,500 small arms. One eyewitness claims the 2nd Mounted Rifles had been responsible for capturing two of the flags and 100 prisoners. Then they anxiously waited for assistance, but none was forthcoming, forcing a withdrawal in the evening after running out of ammunition. During the heated engagement, the 2nd Mounted Rifles tallied 102 casualties, the most in Curtin's brigade and the most in regimental history. One of the wounded was the fourth sergeant of Company B, who received a gunshot wound to the left arm, shattering bone.[62]

The arrival of Lee's Army of Northern Virginia on June 18 signaled both the end of the battle of Second Petersburg and the start of a prolonged nine-month siege that would ultimately bring about the end of the war. Yet the three days of fighting added 10,000 Federal casualties to the monumental numbers already accrued in Grant's Overland campaign. But this was no longer a concern for Philander D. Ellithorpe. He was already bound for a surgeon's tent in City Point. He would miss his regiment's bloody participation in the Crater at the end of July.

Asa and Jubal Early's Raid

On June 12, the day the Army of the Potomac left Cold Harbor, Lee dispatched Maj. Gen. Jubal Early's corps to Lynchburg to deal with a Federal presence and secure much-needed foodstuffs from the Shenandoah Valley, a daring plan that would affect Asa. Early quickly drove away his adversary, Maj. Gen. David Hunter, who retreated to the Ohio Valley. Now the Rebels had free rein in the Shenandoah Valley. At first, the Federals responded tepidly, believing that Early's march was merely a cavalry diversion. By July 5, the thoughts in the capital changed significantly, as the Confederates crossed the Potomac, sowing widespread panic in the North. Early occupied the Maryland cities of Hagerstown and Frederick and boldly extorted cash ransoms. The closeness of the enemy set Washingtonians aflutter as large numbers of refugees from Silver Spring poured into Tenallytown. The Department of Washington swept through hospitals in Washington, Philadelphia, and Baltimore to impress convalescing soldiers who might be able to offer some resistance. Once again, the hot war had found Asa.[63]

Brig. Gen. Lew Wallace marched 7,000 troops out of the District of Annapolis to challenge Early. In the Maryland state capital, Asa and 100 debilitated comrades manned a rifle pit dug by contrabands and "secesh sympathizers" under the direction of Col. Adrian R. Root. Before his departure, Wallace had instructed Root and his invalids to protect the state archives from Early's torches. Two artillery pieces and an offshore gunboat bolstered Root's line of defense. No Rebel force ever came close to Annapolis, so Asa felt quite relieved. Nevertheless, Early's bold demonstration had frightened Ann, who sought permission to travel to Annapolis to administer care to Asa. Her request was denied.[64]

Asa attempted to ease Ann's worries with stories about pleasant conversations he had had in Annapolis with wounded comrades from the 1st Dragoons. He had listened intently to firsthand accounts of the regiment's bloody encounter at Trevilian Station on June 11–12, which had resulted in a large number of casualties and the capture of the highly respected Thorp and the loss of Gibbs's personal records. Asa shared a new aspiration with Ann to study for the New York bar exam when he returned to Rushford. Turning Ann's thoughts away from the war seemed to lessen her anxieties. Of course, the rejection of Early's raid on July 11 at Fort Stevens, the northernmost installation in the capital's extensive network of forts, ended the Rebels' threat to Washington. Asa was safe.[65]

When Asa Came Marching Home

An unexpected natural event played a role in Asa's ultimate decision to seek a medical discharge. On the evening of August 16, torrential rains had breached the banks of Rush and Caneadea creeks in Rushford. By the time the sky had cleared the next day, a disastrous flood had rampaged through the small downtown business district. This was the last straw. On August 22, the Medical Board at Annapolis approved Asa's application for discharge. On September 1, Asa was coming home.[66]

When Asa returned to Rushford, he stepped into a teaching position in the public schoolhouse on Lewellen Street. At the same time, he brushed up on New York State law and prepared to take the bar exam. But the war struck one final blow to the Burleson household. On March 14, 1865, Cpl. DeWitt C. Pelton, a former comrade of Philander's in the 2nd Mounted Rifles, was on picket duty near Appomattox when a Confederate sharpshooter took his life. Pelton left behind a widow and three small children in Rushford. In circumstances that are not well known, Asa and Ann, who would remain childless, adopted one of the children, a three-year-old girl named Cora.[67]

Philander's Hospitalization

Philander experienced a far different kind of closure to his soldierly life. After being shot in the left arm on June 17, the wounded sergeant was carried to a field hospital and quickly transferred to City Point, only nine miles away. There, he was put aboard a steamship bound for Washington, where he arrived within hours of receiving his wound.[68]

Unlike his younger brother, Philander received prompt medical attention and decisive treatment. His entry wound was on the lower left forearm, and the bullet had fractured his humerus. So the surgeon performed an amputation above the midway point between the shoulder and the elbow. The procedure left a raw stump, but it was simple and quick. It seldom had to be sloughed and hopefully allowed for fitting a prosthetic limb.[69]

On June 19, Philander was admitted to U.S. General Hospital at Mount Pleasant in Washington and transferred to Christian Street Hospital in Philadelphia one month later. Situated in Moyamensing Hall, the small 220-bed facility was located across the street from St. Paul's Catholic Church, and nuns from the Sisters of Charity volunteered at the hospital. This was a stroke of good fortune. The Sisters were excellent caregivers and extremely popular with their patients.[70]

Word of Philander's injury spread quickly through the Ellithorpe–Stebbins families. On June 28, Ann fired off a letter to Annapolis, informing Asa about Philander's condition. "Oh! My husband," she lamented. "My heart is full of fear and anxious for you and my dear noble brave brother."[71] Several days later, Philander sent a note to Asa making light of his amputation: "I think I shall not . . . make any more flank movements."[72] Capt. Runyan had contacted Philander and extended to him the second lieutenancy of Company B. The offer, while flattering, seemed impractical to the empty-sleeved veteran.

In early September, Philander received a two-week furlough to go home. He spent short stints with Ann and Permelia in Rushford and with Uncle Carlos and Mary in Pike. He journeyed to Buffalo, where he crossed into Canada, an indication that he was in contact with his older half brother, Danforth. "Philander's arm is healed," Ann explained to Asa, "but it is not a very nice stub, a rather bungling piece of work." Before he returned to Philadelphia, Philander squeezed in a brief visit to Elmira for unknown reasons.[73]

At the end of September, Philander was moved to the less nurturing Broad and Cherry Street Hospital. Its bawdy neighborhood featured many saloons, Catherine Lewis's whorehouse, and frequent street crime. This dangerous street culture bothered the recuperating Alleganian. He was especially agitated that he could not be fitted for a prosthetic limb that attached comfortably to his shortened stump. He also felt deprived because his former residence at the Sisters' hospital had offered a U.S. Christian "commission college" to train amputees in new lines of work. In another letter, Philander regretted not having taken his childhood education more seriously, and the sleeveless one was coming to the realization that his physical disability would affect his future livelihood. "I have the blues," he opened up to Ann. "I never had them at the front."[74] He hoped to enroll in Asa's classes in the future.

Finding God

In the coming months, Philander's depression rebounded gradually during his hospitalization. The one-armed veteran drew strength from a previously unmentioned source: "I will be something yet," he promised his sister, "with God's help."[75] The Sisters of Charity had done their work well. Shortly before Christmas, while brooding in his dismal surroundings, Philander penned a heartfelt religious testimony to Ann: "With Gods help I will be a true man and a Christian . . . [and a person cannot become a Christian] unless we confess before the world must we not seek Heaven through Christ he is the way it is not sufisent that we live as honest upright men and women for is it not said 'to whomsoever confesseth [will] . . . be for Christ or we are against him.'"[76] One month later, Philander shared his reborn faith with Asa: "It has been growing up within me for a long time. It is the striving of the spirit within me and it is my earnest prayer that it will continue to strive with me and enable me to lead others in the right path."[77] Many soldiers such as Philander, who had been nominal Christians in 1861, became devout by 1865.[78]

Shortly after the new year, the medical authorities in Philadelphia were beginning to consolidate some of the smaller nonmilitary hospitals into the mammoth pavilion models, which operated under the broad label of "U.S. Army General Hospital." Consequently, Philander was transferred to South Street Hospital on January 25, 1865. Nonetheless, he did not report to that facility but instead returned to the Sisters of Charity on Christian Street. There, he worked in the laundry room washing bedding and clothes in exchange for being allowed to attend occupational and Bible classes. He also continued to draw $20 per month in salary. "We are established in the best Place that I know of," he confessed to Asa, and he informed Ann not to expect him home anytime soon.[79]

On February 25, 1865, Philander acted on his affirmation of faith to spread the Gospel in his last extant wartime letter. To young Permelia, he shared, "Your Dear Brother has been led to seek God and find true peace that passeth all understanding . . . if you knew how much better I feel you would not hesitate to come forward and stand for Christ."[80] Philander proudly announced to his sister that he has been "baptized and confirmed in the Protestant Episcopal Church."

Philander's living arrangement at Christian Street was not unusual. Although his wound had healed sufficiently, Philander felt more secure being connected to the sisterhood. Thus, he cultivated a quasi-convalescent status while engaging in helpful tasks such as nursing, cooking, housekeeping, and laundering services. Wounded warriors such as Philander were caught in limbo between active duty and physical incapacitation and simply had nowhere else to go. His volunteerism was a pragmatic solution to a difficult situation.[81]

After Lee's surrender at Appomattox, the Christian Street Hospital closed. On May 10, 1865, Philander was sent to the 1,300-bed U.S. Army General Hospital in Chester. Then, on July 21, Sgt. Philander D. Ellithorpe received his medical discharge. The physician signing his release misspelled his name "Ellithorp," an error that would later cause him hardship.[82]

* * * * * * *

The Ellithorpes of the Civil War generation are all gone now: Phillip, Philander, Asa, Permelia, and Ann, the keeper of the family's correspondence. These ordinary foot soldiers and horsemen lived through extraordinary times and did their duty to preserve the Union. Yet their stories of sacrifice, which resonated from the fields of glory at Bull Run, the Seven Days, Antietam, Fredericksburg, Gettysburg, Cold Harbor, and Petersburg, were lost to history—that is, until a trove of family letters were uncovered in the Pacific Northwest in late 2013.

Chapter Twelve

A Trunkful of Letters

There is one piece of unfinished business regarding the Ellithorpe narrative: How did their Civil War letters journey from western New York to western Washington State, and how were they discovered? The answers are steeped in the family movements of the descendants of Oliver Webster Moore of Minnesota.

Background

On May 31, 1869, Mary Ellithorpe married widower Oliver Webster Moore in Pike, New York. An early territorial settler of Rushford, Winona County, Minnesota, a community dubbed "the New England of the West," Oliver was an experienced wagon maker by trade and a veteran of the 1st Minnesota. His Civil War trials and tribulations would rival the medical sufferings of Philander and Asa.

By coincidence, Oliver's frontier neighbor was Sylvester Stebbins, the younger brother of Carlos Stebbins. It is possible that Sylvester had introduced Oliver to thirty-two-year-old Mary Ellithorpe during his monthlong layover in western New York in March 1863 following his medical discharge. At the time, she was unmarried and still living with her uncle and aunt in Pike. Oliver left neither extant Civil War letters from his wartime experience nor an explanation of his prenuptial courtship of Mary, but he would eventually play an indirect role in preserving Ellithorpe family history.[1]

The Fourth Ellithorpe Boy

The opening salvo fired at Fort Sumter struck a patriotic chord in Rushford, Minnesota, just as it had done in Smethport, Pennsylvania, and Rushford,

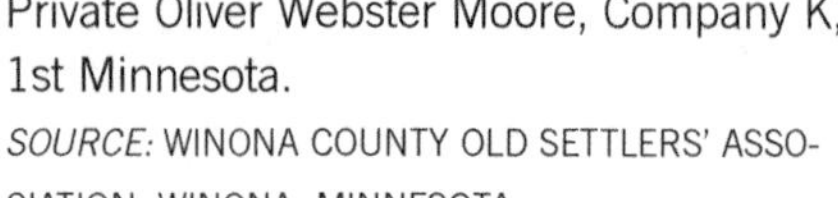

Private Oliver Webster Moore, Company K, 1st Minnesota.
SOURCE: WINONA COUNTY OLD SETTLERS' ASSOCIATION, WINONA, MINNESOTA.

New York. In April 1861, Gov. Alexander Ramsey pledged to raise an infantry regiment of 1,000 men for the Union Cause, and Minnesotans, not surprisingly, responded with enthusiasm in towns along the Mississippi River, such as Red Wing, Hastings, Wabasha, and Winona. Within one week of Ramsey's call to arms, Oliver and his younger brother, John, along with eight Norwegian and two German immigrants and eighty others, had signed the roll of the "Winona Volunteer Company." At Fort Snelling, the state's rendezvous and training site, the Winonans were organized into Company K, 1st Minnesota, a regiment destined for future greatness. With only one month of training, the Minnesotans headed off to war; the inauspicious military career of Oliver was under way. When asked fifty years later why he enlisted, Oliver replied simply, "To save the Union."[2]

While Company K provided valuable scouting services to the Army of the Potomac at Ball's Bluff and Yorktown, Oliver's regiment performed well at First Bull Run and magnificently at Gettysburg. Because of their civilian skills as lumbermen, the regiment was frequently tasked with building or repairing bridges, outposts, and corduroy roads and clearing away roadway obstructions felled by Rebel forces. But between March and June 1862, Oliver was stationed in one damp and inclement location after another, and later depositions from former comrades indicate that his exposure to incessant rainfall, swamp-like and unsanitary bivouac sites, and riverine construction jobs had caused him to contract chronic diarrhea and debilitating rheumatism.[3]

Once the Seven Days campaign came to a close, the Federals recouped at Harrison's Landing on the James River, where, on July 15, Oliver was detached to Battery I, 1st U.S. Light Artillery. The 1st Minnesota and Battery I were not strangers; they had fought alongside one another and belonged to the same brigade since the first campaign of the war. Oliver's transfer to Battery I made total sense. He brought significant expertise in the repair of wooden artillery limbers, caissons, and wagons. There was always need for qualified artificers.[4]

Oliver and Battery I participated in Antietam, firing double rounds of canister from Wilson's and Mumma's fields to cover Sedgwick's fateful assault on the West Woods. Afterward, Oliver's physical afflictions worsened once the weather turned bitter cold.

Then, on the same day of Sumner's Right Grand Division entrance into Falmouth at the onset of the Fredericksburg campaign, the War Department issued an order to return all detached servicemen to their original units. Thus, Oliver's stint with the artillery came to an abrupt end.[5]

On November 25, Oliver reported back to the 1st Minnesota, but his physical condition had deteriorated to the point that his weakened immune system battled new infirmities—weight loss, loss of teeth (scurvy), and pneumonia. The Mud March in mid-January and continuous exposure to frigid temperatures in February and March only aggravated his growing frailty. As a result, he was totally incapacitated for the last sixty days of his enlistment. Thus, on March 25, 1863, Oliver received a certificate of medical discharge signed by regimental Asst. Surgeon Jonathan LeBlond, Lt. Col. William Colvill, and 2nd Lt. William Lochren. He would miss the battle of Gettysburg by three months, where the 1st Minnesota perhaps saved the Army of the Potomac and the Union itself. The Minnesota wagon maker was once again a civilian.[6]

Move to Spring Valley

After their marriage in 1869, Oliver and Mary returned to Minnesota. Oliver went back to work building and repairing wagons for the Rushford Wagon and Carriage Company, but he wanted to open his own shop. Thus, the Moores stayed for only a couple of years before pushing west approximately forty miles to the community of Spring Valley. There, they raised three children. Perhaps, the sudden and unexplained death of Oliver's thirty-two-year-old brother on May 16, 1871, had spurred this move.[7]

In Spring Valley, the Moores purchased several lots in the Warner and Griswold addition and built a home. Oliver rented space in a building on the south end of Main Street for his wagon shop, sharing the space with blacksmith James Sears, the father of Richard Warren Sears (future founder of Sears & Roebuck). He supplemented his income by selling land and moonlighting as a peddler for Hanker Notions.[8]

The Moores' decision to settle in southern Minnesota proved a good one. In July 1873, the Burlesons picked up stakes in western New York and joined them. At that time, the plains community was on the cusp of unprecedented economic growth. In less than twenty years, the town boasted sixty businesses, including two banks, three weekly newspapers, six churches, one school, a library, an opera house, two hotels, two railroads, seven fraternal lodges, and a stable population of 1,500 citizens. Together, the Moores and Burlesons called Spring Valley their home for the rest of their lives. In time, Oliver and Asa were recognized as pillars of the community.[9]

The Moore Grandsons and the Ellithorpe Letters

In the 1890s, Oliver's son, Burton, lived in Stewartville, about fifteen miles north of Spring Valley. In 1920, Burton's two sons, Ronald and Maxwell, graduated from Carlton College in Northfield, Minnesota, and Stewartville High School, respectively. After World War I and graduation, Ronald enrolled in the University of Minnesota law school, and Maxwell matriculated from Carlton as well. The paths taken by Ronald and Maxwell from the Old Northwest to the Pacific Northwest are inextricably linked to the Ellithorpe letters, as will be seen.[10]

From the Old Northwest to the Pacific Northwest

In the first half of the nineteenth century, the subregion later known as southwest Washington State experienced the typical frontier cycle of fur traders, missionaries, and independent adventurers. In 1847, Peter Crawford, a surveyor from Kelso, Scotland, became the first settler to file a land claim on the east bank of the Cowlitz River above its confluence with the Columbia River. His settling there generated a small land rush to the area, and in

1853, Cowlitz County became one of eight original counties in the newly formed Washington Territory. Crawford's "Kelso" grew slowly but steadily for the remainder of the century, and many based their livelihoods on different aspects of lumber production.[11]

When Ronald and Maxwell Moore were mere toddlers, Frederick Weyerhaeuser was operating one of the largest timber concerns in the nation from his headquarters in St. Paul, Minnesota. When timber reserves declined in his southern and midwestern lands, Weyerhaeuser purchased 900,000 acres of virgin old-growth forestland from James H. Hill, owner of the Great Northern Railway and proprietor over Northern Pacific landholdings. The sale was one of the largest transactions in American financial history up to that time. Big things were about to take hold in southwest Washington.[12]

In the meantime, a second lumber entrepreneur was drawn to the untapped resources of the Pacific Northwest for the same reasons that attracted Weyerhaeuser. Headquartered in Kansas City, Missouri, the wood products company of Robert A. Long and Victor Bell had faced the same dwindling southern pine forests in Louisiana and Texas, forcing Long-Bell Company to consider relocation at the end of World War I. By 1920, Weyerhaeuser and Long-Bell had become two of America's top lumber producers.[13]

Long was a visionary with plans to build a huge mill somewhere in southwest Washington, but he had concerns. The town of Kelso, on the Cowlitz River, was already an established community, but Long considered its population too small to provide an adequate labor force, and it was several miles from the Columbia River with its deep-harbor potential. Long, a southerner by birth, also worried about Kelso's radicalized workforce (Wobblies), and he prudishly disapproved of its rowdy reputation. Consequently, Long opted to build a new city on a floodplain between Kelso and the Columbia River, known locally as Cowlitz Valley. In January 1922, Long's agents purchased the necessary property and began to construct "the planned city."[14]

Long had surrounded himself with a young and energetic staff who shared his vision in the creation of the model city that they named Longview. They erected a sawmill dubbed "the biggest . . . on Earth," a quarter of a mile long and containing ten-foot single-cut band saws capable of trimming logs fourteen feet in diameter. The urban planners also laid out a residential grid, providing temporary housing for the mill workers and a shantytown called

Skidville, and built a school, community church, library, and classical brick hotel, the Monticello.[15]

Ronald Moore

In the spring of 1923, Long's henchmen undertook a nationwide advertising campaign to attract a workforce to the planned city. The boosters took out full-page ads in the *Saturday Evening Post*, *The Literary Digest*, *National Business*, and other publications around the country. One recent law school graduate from the University of Minnesota responded to Long's appeal. Ronald Moore was counted along with 3,723 other residents in the city's first census taken in December 1923. Three years later, he purchased a house on Old Kelso Hill, not far from Crawford's original homestead. By 1926, Ronald had established a successful partnership with Howard J. Atwell, and their law practice thrived in downtown Kelso. He was justifiably proud of his new enterprise and involvement in civic boosterism. Ronald's professional legacy remains secure with the continuation of his law firm under the partnership of Walstead and Mertsching, the largest of its kind in Longview today.[16]

In 1938, Ronald's father, Burton, a traveling salesman and casket maker by trade, moved from Minneapolis to Kelso to work as an office manager in Ronald's firm. The move would have major implications regarding the safe storage of the Ellithorpe letters.

Maxwell Moore

Maxwell Moore took a different route to reach Kelso. After graduation from Carleton, he tired of his clerk's position with the Northwest Bell Telephone Company in Minneapolis. So, in 1927, he turned to a new career as an "embalmer." Within a year, he owned his own funeral parlors.[17] At the height of World War II, Maxwell sold his establishment in Hopkins, Minnesota, and relocated to Kelso, where he soon became the business manager and part owner of Ditlevsen-Moore Funeral Home. Mirroring his brother's social résumé, Maxwell joined many of the same fraternal groups in Kelso and served one term as president of Kelso's Chamber of Commerce.[18]

Together, Ronald and Maxwell made substantial contributions to the city of Kelso, but their time was growing short. Their father, Burton, passed away on May 5, 1953, and his remains were shipped back to the Spring Valley Cemetery Mausoleum. Then, on February 7, 1968, Ronald died from a heart attack. Finally, Maxwell perished on June 19, 1991.[19]

The Moore brothers may never have given a thought to their role in preserving the family's Civil War heritage. It is not a reach to suggest, however, that the Ellithorpe family missives had passed through the hands of the Burlesons to the Moores, from Oliver and Burton to Ronald and Maxwell (the last steward of the letters). Each one had been responsible for keeping the cache of correspondence safe. After all this, as a result of their custodianship, the correspondence, carefully bundled and tied with fringed red ribbon, was stored in a wooden trunk in Kelso and left undisturbed for more than two decades.

The Ellithorpe Family Letters Today

In early May 2021, the Cowlitz County Historical Museum, Kelso, Washington, donated Oliver's mahogany-framed photograph of the 1896 reunion of Company K, 1st Minnesota, and his eight-page memoir of pioneer life in territorial Minnesota to the Winona County Historical Society, Winona, Minnesota. Simultaneously, the CCHM turned over 180 letters of the Ellithorpe Family Collection to the McKean County Historical Society, Smethport, Pennsylvania. Phillip's epistles are now back where they belong—in Bucktail Country.

Postscript

Bivouac of the Dead

Philander, Asa, and Oliver required ongoing medical treatment for injuries incurred during the war, and each of them sought comfort from the memories borne on bygone battlefields. A partial resolution to their shared physical dilemmas would take place with the creation of a military pension system committed to alleviating some of the pain and discomfort associated with their wartime injuries. Then the creation of a veterans' organization would provide camaraderie, an important foundation for improved mental health and socialization. The association coincided with the birth of regimental reunions and the construction of granite memorials, which validated their sacrifices of 1861–1865. This process of revitalization would be bittersweet; one Ellithorpe boy would become ensnared in a national case of pension fraud and another all but forgotten to history. In the end, the war cast a long shadow, but it did not consume every aspect of their lives.

* * * * * * *

The following postwar vignettes of Ellithorpe family members appears below in order of date of death, except for the final entry.

Lyman Ellithorpe

In the immediate postwar years, Ellithorpe family dynamics continued to revolve around the strange behavior of Lyman. Asa's undisguised animosity toward his father-in-law had only deepened after the war, and one event in particular illustrated their rancorous relationship. On July 17, 1867, Lyman filed for a federal pension based on the military record of his deceased son,

Phillip, and supported by language contained in Section 12 of the Pension Act of 1862. Two depositions described Lyman's condition as having been gravely ill for the past year, unable to secure a job, leaving him destitute. His only personal property was the clothes on his back, and he frequently shuttled back and forth between relatives in Buffalo, Pike, and Rushford. A pension examiner made two requests for additional documentation to build a case for Lyman, having been dependent on his son for his livelihood in the prewar years. At this point, Lyman asked Asa for a character reference.

On March 4, 1871, Asa drafted a scathing rebuke to the Pension Office. "I feel it my duty to inform the department of the facts in this case," Asa began. "I have been acquainted with the family of Ellithorpe and their circumstances for sixteen years, and [I] know that before the beginning of the late rebellion . . . Lyman Ellithorpe was not dependent upon his Son." Rather, "Lyman Ellithorpe was a Strong, healthy man." Asa mentioned that Lyman currently had two healthy sons living in Buffalo (Danforth and Philander), and they should assume "as much duty and obligation to Support and maintain . . . their father." In sum, Asa would not support Lyman's application "in good conscience," and "it is useless to pursue the matter any further."[1]

Lyman never did receive the benefit he sought, and Asa exacted his revenge for past misdeeds inflicted by the father on his children. It is not altogether clear that other members of the family fully shared Asa's harsh tone.

On March 6, 1873, Lyman passed away in Rushford. On hearing the news while visiting Mary in southern Minnesota, Permelia experienced a long bout of "the blues." And Mary poignantly wrote to Ann asking, "Did Father mention any of us before he died[?]"[2]

Danforth Sanford Ellithorp

In 1861, Danforth, the enigmatic half brother of the other four Ellithorpe siblings, lived in Ontario with his Canadian-born wife and three children: Helen (b. 1861), Phillip (b. 1862), and Sadie (b. 1862). When the Civil War ended, the Ellithorps returned to Buffalo, where Danforth found steady work over the next fifteen years loading vessels as a "weighman" and "watchman" for grain elevator companies on the Buffalo River.[3]

In 1874, the family was lured briefly to the Black Hills of Dakota Territory, where their fourth child, Ida, was born. They returned to Buffalo almost empty-handed but yearned to return to South Dakota Territory.[4]

In the early 1880s, an influx of homesteaders had begun settling in the James River valley of South Dakota Territory. These hardy pioneers lived in houses constructed from sod, farmed at the subsistence level, and battled severe droughts, floods, and blizzards. In those days, wheat was king in the Valley of the Jim, but commercial production would be hampered until the development of mechanical farm implements helped to tame the wild prairie.[5]

In 1881, the Danforth Ellithorp family disappeared from the Buffalo city directory and reappeared in Belmont Township, Spink County, South Dakota Territory, amid a rush of land-hungry farmers. On December 15, 1888, Danforth applied to the U.S. Department of the Interior for a homestead patent for the quarter section of land he occupied. As misfortune would have it, the deadliest blizzard in Great Plains history struck only one month later.[6]

The Ellithorps' relocation to Belmont township was actually a solid fit. It combined Danforth's earlier experiences as a farmer while living with Uncle Carlos and his later connection with grain elevators in Buffalo. Danforth lived on his spread until his death on April 7, 1904, at the age of seventy. He is buried in Altoona Cemetery, Hitchcock, South Dakota. A quick afterthought: There is no surviving correspondence between Danforth and the Ellithorpe–Moore–Burleson families before or after the war despite the fact that they lived only 350 miles apart.

Carlos Leonard Stebbins

When Carlos Leonard Stebbins married Eleanor Griggs in 1845, they became uncle and aunt to the Ellithorpe siblings. In the 1850s, the Stebbinses graciously opened their Pike farmhouse to Danforth, Philander, Mary, and two other nephews.

By the end of the war, Carlos had amassed a significant résumé in several fields. An artist who never signed his portraits, the public deemed his works "of exceptional excellence," and his canvases sold in faraway places, such as New York City, Buffalo, and Rochester. Carlos stayed connected with Pike Seminary after its construction, where he instructed art and served as a trustee for many years. He also enjoyed ironwork and silversmithing as an artistic medium. His mechanical inventiveness extended to repairing violins, the workings of the sewing machine, and his slight modification to the oper-

Carlos Leonard Stebbins.
SOURCE: GEORGE HENRY BANDFIELD PHOTO ALBUM (PROPERTY OF MICHELINE F. SMITH, JAMESBURG, NEW JERSEY).

ation of the steam engine. The Rushford (New York) Museum displayed his personal sewing machine for years.

Carlos was a businessman, surveyor, and civic leader in the Pike community, too. In the 1870s, he was the junior member of Blodget and Stebbins Bankers and later presided over the State Bank of Pike. For a time, he worked as treasurer of the Tonawanda, Wiscoy, & Genesee Valley Canal and Railroad, a venture that was never completed. In politics, he voted the Democratic ticket.

A longtime member of the Masons and the Odd Fellows, Carlos held high offices in each group. In 1876, he keynoted the Pike community centennial celebration for the Declaration of Independence. By every measure, Carlos led a busy and productive life.

On January 23, 1914, "death removed the oldest and most highly respected citizen in the vicinity," said the *Fillmore (NY) Observer*. The Pike Baptist Church hosted the funeral for the distinguished nonagenarian, where eulogists described him as "serene, cheerful, honest, honorable, sincere, earnest, humble and unassuming." Carlos Leonard Stebbins, "the gentleman of superior mental endowments" and uncle to the Ellithorpe children, is buried in Pike Cemetery, Pike, New York, along with his wife.[7]

Mary Ellithorpe Moore

Mary Ellithorpe Moore appears to have led a happy and contented life centered on domesticity. While little is known of her activities outside of the home, she did belong to the Spring Valley Woman's Relief Corps #38. Beginning in 1908, local newspaper accounts reported on Mary's declining health. Then, on April 26, 1914, Mary Ellithorpe Moore answered the call "to cross over the river" at the age of seventy-seven. Her passing made front-page news in Spring Valley, and it left a hole in Oliver's life.[8]

Philander D. Ellithorpe

When Philander "came marching home," he was greeted by no formulaic celebrations—no parade, speeches, banquet, or local mustering-out ceremonies. He had left Philadelphia's Chester Hospital almost four months after Lee's surrender, during a period when most soldiers simply wanted to go home and reintegrate into peacetime society, but the bureaucratic process of demobilizing a million men was slow and cumbersome. The system of release appeared to overlook thousands of men convalescing and working in hospitals.[9]

On December 15, 1865, Philander married Christena O. Walker of Elmira. Born in Edinburgh, Scotland, Christena had become acquainted with Philander during his training camp days in Elmira, and he had kept in periodic contact with the Walker family throughout the war. A short time later, the young couple moved to Friendship, New York, where Robert Hall Ellithorpe was born (January 1868). However, the rural agricultural community held little prospect of employment for an empty-sleeved veteran such as Philander, so his family relocated in 1869 to Buffalo, where half brother Danforth resided. Philander would make the city on Lake Erie his home for the next forty-two years. There, his family grew with the births of George (b. December 1872), Eva Pearl (b. August 1876), and John (b. May 1879).[10]

The Early Pension System

During the war, the Lincoln administration and Congress had realized that something needed to be done for the thousands of wounded and maimed

Union soldiers who would find it difficult, if not impossible, to return to prewar jobs requiring manual labor. Thus, the Pension Act of July 17, 1862, was born. The new legislation stipulated that any soldier who proved a physical disability or illness caused by a wartime event was entitled to an $8 monthly benefit. The system was based on a subjective fraction applied by a designated physician to weigh the severity of an injury or illness as it reduced the individual's ability to perform manual labor.[11]

At the end of the war, Philander, Asa, and Oliver represented three basic groups of disabled veterans: some with a total disability because of amputation (Philander), others suffering from an affliction deemed temporary (Asa), and still others showing no outward signs of illness or physical injury (Oliver). This range of conditions caused pension examiners and physicians difficulty to properly ascribe an equitable amount of compensation. Were the veterans' disabilities caused during wartime or peacetime, were they permanent or temporary, and were they incurable or treatable? Philander received the maximum grade of "total disability" from the Protective War Claim Agency of the U.S. Sanitary Commission on the day he was discharged.[12]

As an amputee, Philander was soon eligible for an artificial arm. In 1873, he had been fitted for one, but the appliance did not fit properly. The wartime surgeon who performed his amputation had removed too much of his upper arm to properly secure the prosthesis. Thus, it chafed the "irregular ganglia of the brachial nerves" and inflamed the sensitive tissue around the stump. One physician described Philander's as "an unsuccessful operation," and a second doctor who closely examined the tender and puffy cushions around his stump called his operation a completely botched job, which confirmed the amateur appraisal of Ann in 1864. Many veterans, including Philander, simply refused to accept the government's offer to procure and wear such a device.[13]

Philander and the Grand Army of the Republic

Many of the incremental pension revisions accorded to veterans were eventually overseen by an organization founded in 1866 known as the Grand Army of the Republic (GAR). The GAR hashed out a constitution, devised a ritualistic induction ceremony, and claimed to be apolitical. Its stated goals were to stress camaraderie, inspire veterans to assist each other through charitable short-term assistance, and recommend preferential treatment for veterans in the hiring process, but membership lagged for almost fifteen years.[14]

On April 1, 1870, Bidwell Post No. 9 was chartered in Buffalo, and twelve months later, a second association, J. W. Wilkeson Post No. 87, formed. Both posts followed the shortcomings of the national GAR, falling into relative inactivity for the remainder of the decade. Individual membership records are no longer extant, so it is impossible to trace whether Philander was involved in either of these brotherhoods.

Then, beginning in April 1880, a throng of former comrades in arms joined in the resurgence of the Buffalo GAR with the merger of the Bidwell and Wilkeson posts. Bidwell-Wilkeson Post No. 9 soon expanded into the largest GAR post in the state outside of New York City with 350 members. They held weekly meetings and attracted "some of the most prominent . . . commercial, manufacturing and professional men," asserted one newspaper later. Philander proudly served as the color-bearer of the combined posts, a visible role in the opening and closing of meetings.[15]

Philander and the Veterans of the 27th New York

Philander had forged deep personal relationships with comrades in his local GAR post, but he also started to reach out for other opportunities to enter fellowship and camaraderie with former comrades in arms at regimental reunions. Indeed, the formation of regimental associations and holding annual reunions had actually first appeared in the North in the mid-1870s. On May 2, 1876, the veterans of the 27th New York organized a "survivor's association" in Binghamton, the hometown of Joseph J. Bartlett. Henry Slocum, the first commander of the "Union Regiment," was elected honorary president, but the organization fell into inactivity. Then, six years later, on the twenty-first anniversary of the battle of Bull Run, Slocum hosted a banquet in Brooklyn for the purpose of revitalizing the veterans, writing a set of bylaws, electing officers, and promoting an annual reunion.[16]

The annual reunions of the former 27th New York attracted an assortment of former officers. Company I produced such notable figures as C. C. Gardner and Joseph Bodine. Regimental historians Charles B. Fairchild and William Westervelt were routinely present. These "love feasts" normally attracted more than fifty ex-servicemen. The social highlight was "the camp fire with plenty of claret, cigars, and chat." In 1887, Philander joined the association at a time when membership spiked and reunions of the 27th New York turned into two-day affairs.[17]

In 1894, Philander received a great honor at the reunion held at Cascade House in Portage Falls, where he was selected to fill in for the president, who was absent. Then, in an unexpected move, the assemblage awarded him the office of first vice president for 1895. On the second day, the revelers took an afternoon trip to Glen Iris, the beautiful country estate of William Pryor Letchworth. One unique session was slated in which only the common foot soldiers were invited to share their Civil War stories free of interruption from former officers.[18]

In 1897, Philander experienced another honor when Buffalo hosted the national GAR encampment with President William McKinley, a veteran himself, delivering the keynote address. A large contingent of veterans representing the 2nd Mounted Rifles chartered a steamer for a water excursion on the Niagara River. But Philander was not listed as one of the attendees. Instead, he opened his home on West Ferry Street to host eighteen former comrades from Company I, 27th New York.[19] Philander had made his choice regarding which former regiment held his allegiance.

The Buffalo Job Market and Family Matters

From 1870 to 1889, Philander was fortunate to secure three plum appointments to civil service positions in Buffalo. His employment résumé included stints as a letter collector with the City Post Office (1869–1873), deputy sheriff (1873–1876), and crier for the Superior Court of Buffalo (1878–1889). Securing the first position might have been aided by Philander's former colonel of the 2nd Mounted Rifles, Fisk, who had once been postmaster of Niagara Falls. The latter position of court crier was a lucrative post, paying $1,000 annually.[20]

Tragedy struck Philander's household in 1883 when Christena contracted tuberculosis. In October, the clan rushed to Colorado Springs, Colorado, hoping that the therapeutic mineral springs and climate would improve her health. Instead, she deteriorated and passed away on December 3. Philander shipped his wife's remains to Elmira for burial in the Walker family plot. Now Philander was alone with four children ranging in age from four to fifteen.[21]

On July 12, 1884, in a quick turnaround, Philander married a Welsh immigrant, Mattie Hannah James, of Centerville, New York. Philander brought his new bride from the wedding site in Pike to Buffalo, where two daughters were added to his family: Eleanor Francis (b. March 1891) and Mary Franc (b. April 1896). This completed Philander's immediate family.[22]

Philander and the Limitations of Patronage

In August 1889, two Democrats won seats on the Buffalo Superior Court bench, which spelled disaster for Philander, a Republican Party precinct captain and polling station inspector. When the new administration was installed, Philander found himself outed. He filed for reinstatement, and an embarrassing moment took place in October when both the duly appointed crier and Philander reported for work.[23]

Philander sought out allies in Buffalo's Bidwell-Wilkeson Post No. 9 who encouraged him to file a lawsuit against the City of Buffalo for violating the statutes of the Consolidation Act of 1873 and the "Veterans' Rights Act" of 1890. His lawyers argued in front of the New York State Supreme Court, and the matter dragged out for a couple of years before Philander lost his bid for restoration.[24]

Economic Hardship

Without steady income, Philander's family would struggle to remain solvent in the turbulent economic decade of the 1890s. His application for a constable's position with the City of Buffalo, a job he had once held, was rejected. The Panic of 1893 also played havoc with the family's purse strings. Philander showed no income until 1895. Two of Philander's children were teenagers, and two others were less than ten years old, and during these dark days, he relied increasingly on his meager government pension and the earnings of his grown children. Philander even resorted to subleasing rooms to boarders.[25]

Creditors were nipping at Philander's heels, too. He delayed foreclosure on the West Ferry Street home he had owned since 1883 by taking out a second mortgage, but the family was forcibly evicted in 1898 when he defaulted on that loan and declared bankruptcy. Consequently, the Ellithorpes moved into a less expensive rental house on Normal Avenue. The next ten years were highlighted by financial hardship, and he found intermittent work at odd jobs in real estate (1895–1896) and as a baker (1898–1899), a laborer (1901–1904), and a watchman (1905–1908). The Ellithorpes of Buffalo were living on a shoestring.[26]

To California

Beginning in 1898, the Ellithorpe family underwent a seismic geographic shift. First, Philander's son, George, enlisted in the U.S. Army in Elmira in May 1898 in response to the outbreak of war with Spain. Then, in October 1902, Philander's oldest son, Robert, moved to Fresno, California, where he became the city plumbing inspector for the next thirty years. George and his family followed Robert in January 1904, finding employment as a plumber with the Southern Pacific Railroad.[27]

In 1911, Philander, Mattie, and daughter Pearl relocated to Fresno to be closer to Robert and George. Philander believed the change in climate would offer his wife some relief from an undisclosed ailment. As it turned out, Philander's health was in jeopardy when, on February 6, 1915, he passed away at the age of seventy-five from a sudden heart attack. His funeral was held at the Congregational Church of Fresno in accordance with the GAR's *Ritual of the Grand Army of the Republic.* He is buried in Calvary Cemetery, Fresno, California.[28]

In a postmortem twist to Philander's Civil War record, Mattie filed for a widow's pension on the basis of the revised pension law of 1908. Her claim was initially denied because the clerk in charge determined that Philander

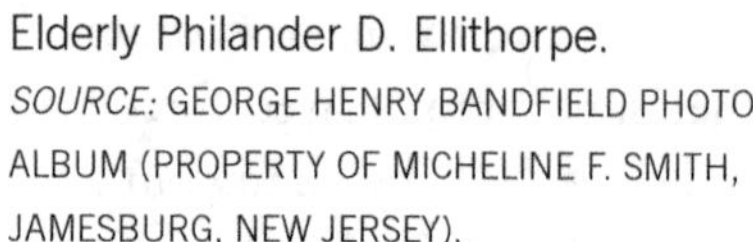

Elderly Philander D. Ellithorpe.
SOURCE: GEORGE HENRY BANDFIELD PHOTO ALBUM (PROPERTY OF MICHELINE F. SMITH, JAMESBURG, NEW JERSEY).

had died from nonmilitary causes, though that was no obstacle under current statute. Then Mattie's case turned bizarre when the Pension Bureau asserted that Philander had been receiving benefits under the name "Ellithorp" and not "Ellithorpe." The bureaucrat rejected the validity of Mattie's application because of this spelling discrepancy, an error originally made on his discharge certificate in 1865. It took more than four months to straighten out the affair, but Mattie was eventually awarded a $12 monthly widow's pension. She did not have long to spend the stipend, however. Mattie died in Buffalo in June 1918, and she is buried in Centerville Cemetery, Centerville, New York.[29]

Ann Ellithorpe Burleson

In the winter of 1872–1873, Permelia had taken an extended visit to Mary and Oliver in southern Minnesota. In a letter to Ann and Asa, the youngest Ellithorpe proposed that they, too, should journey to see the Moores in Spring Valley. Ann had been sick that winter, and a change in scenery might appeal to her, Melia reasoned.[30]

The Moores lent their support to Permelia's tender in a follow-up missive. To Asa, Oliver assured him that Mary would welcome such a visit. Furthermore, the Spring Valley school board was searching for a teacher to begin in the fall term, and Oliver offered to sell the Burlesons a vacant lot he owned across the street should they decide to stay. Since Asa had just passed the New York bar, he might welcome beginning his new career as an attorney in Minnesota. These were practical considerations.[31]

Mary supplied additional emotional reasons to Ann. She pointed out that Permelia was assisting her greatly with the care of little "Burtie," who was beginning to talk and walk. It would be good for Ann's spirits and for twelve-year-old Cora to hold the baby and assist in raising him. The clincher: "he looks so much like Phillip."[32]

The final constraint was lifted from the Burlesons on March 6, 1873, with the death of Lyman. Now freed from Rushford, there was nothing to hold back Ann and Asa, so claimed the Moores. The rationale worked. On July 17, Asa and Ann shuttered the house on Lewellan Street and departed for southern Minnesota. They left in such a hurry that Lyman's grave in Rushford Cemetery was not even marked with a headstone.[33]

To Southern Minnesota

Asa and Ann appeared in southern Minnesota just in time to experience the first of five consecutive summer grasshopper infestations in the Great Plains. One young resident of Spring Valley, Laura Ingalls, later described the natural phenomenon as "a glittering cloud." Undeterred by the horde of destructive insects, the transplanted New Yorkers were determined to make Spring Valley their new home.[34]

Asa rented office space in the Spring Valley Opera House but eventually hung out his law shingle on Jefferson Street. Ann opened a dress shop to capitalize on her skills with needle and thread. In March 1874, Asa and Ann were formally welcomed to the community in a newspaper article appearing in the *Spring Valley Western Progress.*[35]

Activities Outside the Home

Ann discovered a variety of interests to satisfy her keen intellectual curiosity. For example, in 1882, she served her community as president of the Spring Valley Board of Education, which corresponded with Cora's successful employment as a teacher.

Then, in July 1883, a national auxiliary to the GAR was chartered, the Woman's Relief Corps (WRC). At first, the WRC sought to perpetuate the patriotic goals set forth by the men's association and conduct charitable activities for the care of indigent ex-soldiers, widows, and orphans. In a few short years, however, they were undertaking the promotion and implementation of Decoration (Memorial) Day exercises, a solemn commemoration of the Federal war dead, the distribution of American flags to schoolchildren, and the promotion of local school boards to adopt "blue-penciled" history books, adopt the flag salute, institute Flag Day, and sing "The Star Spangled Banner" in schools. On November 11, 1887, Burdick Post No. 3 welcomed Woman's Relief Corps No. 38 of Spring Valley. Among the active members were Mary Moore, Ann Burleson, and Permelia Ellithorpe. In the early 1890s, chaplain Ann and treasurer Permelia would play conspicuous roles in the successful drive to erect a "soldier's monument" in the Spring Valley Cemetery.[36]

On January 14, 1916, Ann Ellithorpe Burleson, the central recipient of the Ellithorpe Civil War letters as well as their keeper and compiler, died at the age of eighty. She is buried in Spring Valley Cemetery, Spring Valley, Minnesota, beneath a granite headstone inscription that reads, "Army Nurse."[37]

Asa R. Burleson

Unlike Philander, Asa's case required more frequent interactions with the Pension Bureau, as his medical ailment was not visible to the naked eye and was open to interpretation based on whether his condition was temporary. In August 1864, Asa's medical discharge reconfirmed his condition: orchitis with "a left inguinal Hernia and varicocele with tenderness and inflammation of the left Testicle." Exactly one year later, he traveled to Warsaw, New York, to take the mandatory physical examination in order to qualify for an "invalid pension." The examiner added to the earlier findings: "a protrusion of the intestine into the Scrotal [and] a good sized rupture." The doctor concluded that Asa's condition was "temporary" and assigned a rating of one-half disability. Three days later, he submitted his original application for monthly benefits, which was accepted.[38]

By 1873, Asa began wearing a truss to control "dragging pains" in his lower abdomen, a garment made available to veterans through the latest changes to pension regulations. But his discomfort never abated. In 1886, his physical exam revealed the presence of a new growth, a right inguinal hernia. The doctor compared both bulges to the size of a walnut and subsequently to "the size of a goose egg." Over the decades, the scrotum of the

Elderly Asa and Ann Burleson (ca. 1912). *SOURCE:* GEORGE HENRY BANDFIELD PHOTO ALBUM (PROPERTY OF MICHELINE F. SMITH, JAMESBURG, NEW JERSEY).

former cavalryman remained "the size of an ordinary glass tumbler." Asa had reason to be bitter; he had paid a terrible price for his patriotism and participation in the war. The Burlesons had been denied children of their own, but their adoption of Cora had demonstrated true compassion and filled a great void.[39]

Asa and the GAR

In the 1870s, the Minnesota GAR and local posts followed the national example by descending into lethargy outside of three large cities. Then, in July 1880, the organization was revitalized, and a grassroots movement spread to large and small communities across the state. On December 4, 1880, fourteen veterans, including Oliver, convened in Asa's law office in Spring Valley and founded Burdick Post No. 3, the first of its kind in southern Minnesota. The fledgling group agreed to meet bimonthly, and soon they gathered in the prestigious Spring Valley Masonic Lodge. During its heyday in the 1890s, Burdick Post No. 3 consistently ranked ninth in statewide membership; arguably, it was one of the most vibrant rural posts in Minnesota. Over time, the post amassed "a fine War library," including a partial set of the *Official Records*.[40]

Asa was selected the first post commander, a position he held for two terms, and he frequently filled in for absent officers afterward. But Asa's true calling was at the state, or department, level. Although he missed the plenary encampment of the Minnesota Department in 1881, Asa was chosen to two-year consecutive terms on the Council of Administration, the chief oversight committee of the organization; served as junior vice commander and judge advocate; and was appointed to the Committee on Officers' Reports. He also sat on planning sessions for the national encampment scheduled for St. Paul in 1896. In 1900, Asa returned to the local level to resume an active role in Burdick Post No. 3, where he rotated the office of surgeon for the next sixteen years.[41]

Asa and the 1st New York Dragoons Survivors' Association

Asa lived remotely from most of his wartime comrades in the 1st Dragoons, but that is not to say he remained passive during the heyday of regimental reunions. Since the early 1870s, the veterans had been gathering near High

Bridge in Portage Falls, a special location on the banks of the Genesee River, where the 130th New York had first assembled and trained at Camp Williams. These "soldier picnics" attracted large crowds. Former members of the 1st Dragoons also met at national encampments to celebrate and swap stories. In 1897, during the national GAR encampment in Buffalo, more than 400 former comrades in arms supped at a banquet hosted by successful Buffalo physician and ex-Dragoon DeVillo W. Harrington. Despite Asa's transplanted upper midwestern roots, he participated in planning the reunion as a member of the national Committee on Resolutions.[42]

Accolades in Spring Valley

Asa was a pillar of the Spring Valley community almost from the first day of his arrival. Over the years, the "broadminded Democrat" had filled various positions in an otherwise Republican community, such as city attorney, town clerk, village recorder, and board president of the Fire Department. Asa's greatest achievement, however, was his intermittent terms as justice of the peace, spanning more than forty-one years.[43]

Village residents respected Asa's civic pride in the many government offices he had held over the years as well as his patriotic activities with Burdick Post No. 3. Asa was instantly identifiable on the village streets, wearing his blue army cape and thick eyeglasses. Citizens knew him as "a man of sterling worth and integrity" but also "a colorful character." Nearing the end of his life, he had forged a solid reputation in his adopted community, county, and state.

On October 4, 1917, Asa R. Burleson died from heart failure at the age of eighty-six. He is buried beside Ann in Spring Valley Cemetery, only a few steps away from the monument they had collaborated to build honoring "the boys who wore the blue." The inscription on his stone reads, "First Lieutenant, Co. H, 1st N.Y. Dragoons."[44]

Oliver Webster Moore

Oliver fared much worse than Philander and Asa in his relationships with the Pension Bureau and Veteran's Association. His postwar journey actually bucked the trend of most veterans by joining the GAR prior to making application for a pension despite having earned a medical discharge.

Oliver and the GAR

Oliver was a charter member of Burdick Post No. 3, but the post's records indicate that he did not assume any leadership role for more than a decade. Instead, he was routinely suspended (but never dropped) for failure to pay his annual dues. The exception to this indifference occurred in 1893 when he won election as quartermaster, a position that required him to fill out a quarterly financial statement for department records. He held the spot for five years. Then his official duties dropped off.[45]

In June 1885, the 1st Minnesota held its first regimental reunion in Winona, which undoubtedly attracted attention from Oliver's former Company K. There is no written record to verify Oliver's presence at any function of the 1st Minnesota Survivor's Association afterward. Still, he possessed a mahogany-framed photograph of Company K taken at the 1896 national encampment held in St. Paul. Owning such a prized heirloom might strengthen the case for Oliver's presence at such regimental conventions.[46]

Company K, 1st Minnesota, at National GAR encampment, St. Paul, Minnesota (1896).
SOURCE: COWLITZ COUNTY HISTORICAL MUSEUM, KELSO, WASHINGTON.

Battles with the Pension Bureau

Oliver struggled with his health in the postwar decades. Recall the basis for Oliver's Certificate of Disability for Discharge: "chronic diarrhea, rheumatism, and loss of teeth." The two officers who had signed his discharge papers, Dr. LeBlond and Lt. Lochren, were destined to play pivotal roles in Oliver's contentious relationship with the Pension Bureau.[47]

On October 15, 1885, Oliver filled out an application for an invalid pension, having suffered from the aforementioned illnesses and ailments since the end of the war. In the space provided on the form for additional relevant information, Oliver maintained that he had been under the care of the regimental surgeon for six months prior to his discharge and "has suffered in a severe form . . . ever since." Twelve years earlier, Oliver's personal physician deemed him completely disabled and recommended that he quit his strenuous carpentry business. It is baffling why Oliver had not filed a claim with the Pension Bureau at that time.[48]

Oliver's application hit an immediate snag. His military service file contained no evidence of his wartime medical history. Specifically, regimental muster rolls of the 1st Minnesota had never listed him on sick call. Thus, the pension examiners rejected his case on February 13, 1886.[49]

On July 2, 1886, Oliver transferred power of attorney to George M. Van Leuven Jr. of Lime Springs, Iowa. A relative of the editor of the *Spring Valley Vidette*, Van Leuven advertised his services as a successful arbiter in veteran matters through handbills strewn across southern Minnesota and northern Iowa.[50]

Undeterred by the recent decision to deny Oliver any benefits, Van Leuven understood the key piece of evidence necessary to winning an appeal would be a deposition from Dr. John Byers LeBlond, the former assistant surgeon of the 1st Minnesota. The surgeon had mustered out with the regiment; moved to Sioux Falls, Dakota Territory; and established a successful medical practice. Somehow, Van Leuven tracked down LeBlond and requested information regarding Oliver's wartime medical history. "During the time I was in the service," LeBlond replied curtly, "we had at least 1,600 men connected with the regiment. Now at this late day, to expect me to remember every man who served in the regiment, and when, and for what disease I treated him for is an impossibility."[51]

Receiving no cooperation from LeBlond, Van Leuven nonetheless ramped up the number of personal depositions in order to reboot Oliver's case. In March 1887, the attorney's efforts were rewarded when seven former comrades wrote testimonials confirming Oliver's wartime illnesses. In addition, Oliver's new petition suddenly included a list of previously undisclosed issues: heart palpitations, anemia, jaundice, and an ulcerated rectum. Since the end of the war, Oliver deposed that he had purchased over-the-counter drugs to treat his ailments, without success. As a result of Van Leuven's revised assessment of Oliver's physical condition, the pension review board overrode its previous rejection on June 7, 1887, and awarded a generous three-fourths disability.[52]

In December 1891, Van Leuven filed to change the location of Oliver's annual physical examination from Preston, Minnesota, to Cresco, Iowa. Although the distance was twice as far for Oliver to travel, the request was granted. Consequently, the Cresco pension board increased the Minnesotan's rate classification to "total disability." Van Leuven requested an outlandish benefit increase the next year, and these greedy upticks in rapid succession set off warning signals.[53]

The Van Leuven Case

Oliver's pension problems would escalate in April 1893 when President Grover Cleveland appointed a federal district court judge in Minneapolis, William Lochren, to the office of pension commissioner. Lochren, one of the officers who had signed Oliver's discharge papers thirty years earlier, was a logical choice. Once confirmed, the reform-minded Lochren tackled the growing number of fraudulent claims in the Pension Bureau. One of his special investigators, Edward F. Waite, uncovered massive evidence of fraud on applications filed by Van Leuven, including forged depositions, false medical information, exorbitant filing fees, and bribery of the Cresco Pension Board of Physicians. Oliver's case, in particular, shed light on the growing public uproar over this form of corruption as well as his role in the episode.[54]

Within one month of Lochren's appointment, Van Leuven was indicted on ninety-eight counts of defrauding the federal government. All pension cases associated with the Iowa attorney were temporarily suspended pending a full investigation by Waite's team of seven agents, called the "Van Leuven Commission." Oliver received his termination notice dated July 3, 1893.[55]

On September 11, 1893, Oliver appeared before Special Examiner Waite for an extensive interview to establish his relationship with counselor Van Leuven. Asked whether he had ever been coached by his attorney to offer a bribe to the Cresco examiners in order to secure "a good rating," Oliver flatly denied the accusation. Unknown to Oliver, Waite had already secured several items of private correspondence between Moore and Van Leuven in a raid on the attorney's office, which contradicted this sworn testimony. In his report to Pension Commissioner Lochren, Waite stated emphatically, "This witness [Oliver] is not honest." On December 5, 1893, Waite summoned Moore before a grand jury, where the Minnesotan wisely recanted his false claim of innocence and provided incriminating testimony against Van Leuven and his accomplice on the Cresco Board of Pension Examiners.[56]

Van Leuven's trial was scheduled for April 1894 in the U.S. District Court for Northern Iowa, but it was postponed until December because of the alleged illness of the defendant. In the meantime, the citizens of Cresco and Lime Springs rallied in support of their neighbor and friend. The *Howard County Times* spearheaded the offensive and accused Special Examiner Waite of employing unethical tactics to gather incriminating evidence from innocent pensioners and of inflicting "a reign of terror in northeastern Iowa." As a result, the county prosecutor indicted Waite on one count of tampering, threatening, and intimidating potential witnesses in the Van Leuven case.[57]

Meanwhile, on December 14, 1894, a packed courtroom in Dubuque observed the opening and closing arguments of the Van Leuven case. The jury deliberated only one hour, and "the suddeness [of the guilty verdict] stunned some present." The shamed attorney was sentenced to two years in Anamosa State Penitentiary and ordered to pay a $3,000 fine. He was disbarred three months later. The citizens of Howard County were outraged.[58]

Public attention now shifted to Commissioner Lochren, who had defended Waite in two Minneapolis interviews as "a thoroughly honest and reliable pension agent." The *Howard County Times* fumed in self-righteous partisanship and responded with an attack on Lochren's character. The Iowa broadsheet called the commissioner "a contemptible screed against the people of northeastern Iowa," claiming he was "a knave, fool, or liar." The contentious nature of the entire affair was about to burst onto the national stage. *Harper's Weekly* picked up the Van Leuven–Waite stories in a cogent article, using the court cases as a springboard into a broader discussion of pension fraud in general.[59]

Lochren, Waite, and the Van Leuven Commission were not coldhearted when it came to punishing the ex-pensioners. In fact, they offered these veterans an opportunity to reestablish their benefit status by supplying unvarnished, reliable depositions from former comrades, undergoing new physical examinations at locations approved by the commission, and accepting adjustments to the rate of benefit. Even before Van Leuven's case reached trial, Oliver had been examined in nearby Houston, Minnesota, and his file soon contained fresh and legitimate depositions. On March 1, 1894, Oliver had been reinstated at the base rate. Meanwhile, Commissioner Lochren had purged almost 2,300 names from the national rolls and reduced the ratings of more than 3,300. Oliver fit into the latter category, but it could have been much worse for him.[60]

Living the Private Life

Unlike Asa, Oliver was a lifelong Republican, and he never sought public office, although he was "a highly respected citizen in Spring Valley." When the first "horseless carriage" rumbled down the town's dirt streets, Oliver's days as a wagon maker were numbered. Although he had been semiretired for several years, Oliver continued to tinker in his carpentry shop largely to repair broken farm conveyances. He formally retired in 1906.

Oliver loved the outdoor life. He was an ardent duck hunter and fisherman and thus a member of the Izaak Walton League, a conservation society dedicated to the preservation of fish and wildlife. "Living life simply" was one of his mottoes, and Spring Valley residents cherished his down-to-earth philosophy. For physical exercise, he walked to the village post office from his house twice a day, a distance of half a mile.[61]

Oliver was a thoughtful person who spent a great deal of time cogitating about scientific principles of hybridization. He was a charter member of the Fillmore County Horticultural Society, founded in Asa's law office in 1895, and he held several upper-level offices in the club. An avid orchardist with a specialty in plum tree varieties, Oliver grew 100 fruit trees on his four-acre property. Later, he contributed an essay titled "Fillmore County Horticulture" to Willford and Curtiss-Wedge's *The History of Fillmore County, Minnesota*. Four years later, he drafted an unpublished piece to commemorate the fiftieth anniversary of the founding of the Minnesota Horticultural Society. Over time, Oliver garnered a reputation around the state as a knowledge-

Elderly Oliver Webster Moore.
SOURCE: WILLFORD AND CURTISS-WEDGE, *HISTORY OF FILLMORE COUNTY, MINNESOTA* (1912), 1:177.

able horticulturalist and was highly sought after as a public speaker. He also judged at the Fillmore County Fair. In nonagricultural pursuits, Oliver was inducted into the Minnesota Territorial Pioneers Association in 1899, and he achieved the rank of thirty-third-degree Mason.[62]

Decline

Between 1914 and 1918, Oliver was confronted with the passing of four close family members: his wife, two brothers-in-law, and one sister-in-law. Furthermore, he was beginning to exhibit serious mental issues. After Mary had died, his youngest daughter, Fannie, quit her job in Minneapolis and returned to Spring Valley to care for her father, who was becoming increasingly housebound. Winter was his worst season, spending long stints in bed. By 1915, Fannie deposed to the Pension Board that her father required attention "a good deal of the time" and needed daily assistance to dress himself.[63]

Other problems surfaced. He suffered from cataracts, and his oldest daughter, Verna, claimed that he had been blind in one eye since 1911. Although the troublesome cataract was removed ten years later, Oliver still required powerful reading glasses. At the same time, the octogenarian suffered from bouts of delirium.[64]

In September 1924, the *Spring Valley Mercury* interviewed Oliver on his ninety-fourth birthday. He told the reporter he planned to celebrate the occasion by burnishing his shotgun and going duck hunting, perhaps a quixotic statement in light of his poor vision. In 1925, Oliver drafted an eight-page reminiscence of pioneer life on the Minnesota plains at the request of his daughter. Titled "A Hark Backwards," the discourse was a personal epitaph of sorts.[65]

At the end of July 1926, Oliver was bedridden again, and Fannie took him to the Mayo Clinic in Rochester. But clinicians determined that he was "beyond medical aid." They recommended that he be placed on a liquid diet and made to rest as comfortably as possible. At his last physical examination in October, the doctors noted that their patient was "out of his head most of the time" and had developed a case of bronchitis.

On November 22, 1926, "one of the oldest residents of southeastern Minnesota died at his Spring Valley home." Three days later, on Thanksgiving Day, a small service was conducted by the local GAR and WRC at his house, where friends and neighbors said good-bye to one of Minnesota's last Civil War veterans. Oliver and Mary Moore are interred in the Spring Valley Cemetery Mausoleum, Spring Valley, Minnesota.[66]

Permelia Ellithorpe Spencer

Permelia had lived in the Burlesons' household since 1862, excluding her occasional visits to relatives in western New York. Then, on October 16, 1900, she married widower John F. Spencer of Pike, the village of her ancestors and her youth. The Spencers were a well-known family in southern Wyoming County. On January 11, 1931, she died there at the age of eighty-five and is buried in the Spencer family plot in Pike Cemetery. Close by are the graves of her maternal grandparents, aunts, uncles, cousins, nieces, and nephews.[67]

Phillip Griggs Ellithorpe

On October 11, 1901, a solemn memorial service was conducted by the Regimental Association of the Bucktails during their annual reunion at Gettysburg. There, the survivors met on the slope of Little Round Top to conduct a Sunset Ceremony to honor fallen comrades in the battle. Throngs of spectators gathered and listened to an oration glorifying the bravery and sacrifices of Pennsylvania leaders during the battle, such as Reynolds, Vincent, Crawford, Taylor, and McCandless. At the close of the address, three drum taps were followed by a roll call for each of the seven Bucktails who had lost their lives. Then a bugler played "Taps" as the sun set behind Houck's Ridge. One attendee described the benediction as "inspiring," and another called it "impressive and touching." Perhaps the sole fatality of Company I had finally received some measure of appreciation, a fitting requiem to Phillip G. Ellithorpe.[68]

* * * * * * *

The war had cast an inescapable long shadow over the lives of Philander, Asa, and Oliver. Each one of them suffered distinctive ailments that became problematic over a lifetime. "For soldiers who survived their wounds, recovery could be lengthy and incomplete," notes one historian of the war. Another points out that these posttraumatic ailments created psychological difficulties that only intensified over time. Thus, the triumvirate shared more than combat experience; they suffered long-term pain, both physical and mental. "The consequences of wars do not dissipate when generals proffer dress swords in surrender and statesmen sign official papers ending formal hostilities," states a third scholar. "History never becomes simply a thing of the past. The consequences of wars, their impact on all areas of human life, remain with us long after the textbooks close the chapter on this or that armed conflict." The Ellithorpes of western New York were living proof of these axioms.[69]

It is unfair, injudicious, and imprudent, however, to assert that the war was omnipresent in the lives of Philander, Asa, and Oliver. Veteranhood did not define their total identity; it merely constituted a portion of their being. So they did what most Civil War veterans did: they raised families, found suitable employment, contributed to their local communities, joined the largest fraternal veteran's organization of their time, and received modest military pensions. Each one led meaningful lives beyond—as well as in—the reaches of battlefield remembrance. One scholar remarked, "Historians have not done an outstanding job of tracing the consequences of wartime loss over the generations."[70] This book is an effort to address this void.

Appendix A

Order of Battle for the Ellithorpes

At First Bull Run

Philander/27th New York:

No corps organization

Second Division: Brigadier General David Hunter

First Brigade: Colonel Andrew Porter

27th New York: Colonel Henry W. Slocum

Other units:	8th New York Militia
	14th New York Militia
	5th U.S. Artillery, Company D

At Yorktown

Asa/5th Vermont:

IV Corps: Brigadier General Erasmus D. Keyes

Second Division: Brigadier General William F. "Baldy" Smith

Second Brigade: Brigadier General William T. H. Brooks

5th Vermont: Lieutenant Colonel Henry A. Smalley

Other units:	2nd Vermont	3rd Vermont
	4th Vermont	6th Vermont

Philander/27th New York:

I Corps: Major General Irwin McDowell

First Division: Brigadier General William B. Franklin

Second Brigade: Brigadier General Henry W. Slocum

27th New York: Colonel Joseph J. Bartlett

Other units: 16th New York 5th Maine
96th Pennsylvania

At Fair Oaks

Philander/27th New York:
VI Corps: Brigadier General William B. Franklin
First Division: Brigadier General Henry W. Slocum
Second Brigade: Colonel Joseph J. Bartlett
27th New York: Lieutenant Colonel Alexander D. Adams
Other units: 16th New York 5th Maine
96th Pennsylvania

At The Seven Days

Philander/27th New York:
VI Corps: Brigadier General William B. Franklin
First Division: Brigadier General Henry W. Slocum
Second Brigade: Colonel Joseph J. Bartlett
27th New York: Lieutenant Colonel Alexander D. Adams
Other units: 16th New York 5th Maine
96th Pennsylvania

Phillip/13th Pennsylvania Reserves:
V Corps: Brigadier General Fitz John Porter
Third Division: Brigadier General George A. McCall
First Brigade: Brigadier General John F. Reynolds
13th Pennsylvania Reserves: Major Roy Stone
Other units: 1st, 2nd, 5th, 8th
Pennsylvania Reserves

At Second Bull Run

Phillip/13th Pennsylvania Reserves:
[Kane's four detached companies at McDowell's headquarters]
III Corps: Major General Irwin McDowell
Pennsylvania Reserve Division: Brigadier General John F. Reynolds
First Brigade: Brigadier General George G. Meade
13th Pennsylvania Reserves: Colonel Hugh W. McNeil

Other units: 3rd, 4th, 7th, 8th
Pennsylvania Reserves

At South Mountain

Philander/27th New York:
VI Corps: Major General William B. Franklin
First Division: Major General Henry W. Slocum
Second Brigade: Colonel Joseph J. Bartlett
27th New York: Lieutenant Colonel Alexander D. Adams
Other units: 5th Maine 16th New York
96th Pennsylvania 121st New York

Phillip/13th Pennsylvania Reserves:
I Corps: Major General Joseph Hooker
Third Division: Brigadier General George G. Meade
First Brigade: Brigadier General Truman Seymour
13th Pennsylvania Reserves: Colonel Hugh W. McNeil
Other units: 1st, 2nd, 5th, 6th Pennsylvania Reserves

At Antietam

Philander/27th New York:
VI Corps: Major General William B. Franklin
First Division: Major General Henry W. Slocum
Second Brigade: Colonel Joseph J. Bartlett
27th New York: Lieutenant Colonel Alexander D. Adams
Other units: 5th Maine 16th New York
96th New York

Phillip/13th Pennsylvania Reserves:
I Corps: Major General Joseph Hooker
Third Division: Brigadier General George G. Meade
First Brigade: Brigadier General Truman Seymour
13th Pennsylvania Reserves: Colonel Hugh W. McNeil
(Captain Dennis McGee)
Other units: 1st, 2nd, 5th, 6th Pennsylvania Reserves

At Fredericksburg

Philander/27th New York:

- Left Grand Division: Major General William B. Franklin
  - VI Corps: Major General William F. "Baldy" Smith
    - First Division: Brigadier General William T. H. Brooks
      - Second Brigade: Brigadier General Joseph J. Bartlett
        - 27th New York: Colonel Alexander D. Adams
          - Other units: 5th Maine, 16th New York, 121st New York, 96th Pennsylvania

Phillip/13th Pennsylvania Reserves:

- Left Grand Division: Major General William B. Franklin
  - I Corps: Major General General John F. Reynolds
    - Third Division: Major General George Meade
      - First Brigade: Colonel William Sinclair (Col. William McCandless)
        - 13th Pennsylvania Reserves: Captain Charles F. Taylor
          - Other units: 1st, 2nd, 6th Pennsylvania Reserves, 121st Pennsylvania

At Suffolk Campaign

Asa/130th New York:

- VII Corps: Major General John A. Dix
  - Suffolk Garrison: Major General John J. Peck
    - First Division: Brigadier General Michael Corcoran
      - First Brigade: Brigadier General Henry Dwight Terry
        - 130th New York: Colonel Alfred Gibbs
          - Other units: 26th Michigan, 99th New York, 152nd New York, 167th Pennsylvania, 11th Rhode Island, 1st New York Sharpshooters, 1st New York Mounted Rifles

At Department of Washington (February–June 1863)

(stationed in Fairfax, Virginia)
Phillip/13th Pennsylvania Reserves:
XXII Corps: Major General Samuel P. Heintzelman
Third Division: Brigadier General Horatio G. Sickel
First Brigade: Colonel William McCandless
13th Pennsylvania Reserves: Colonel Charles F. Taylor
Other units: 1st, 2nd, 6th Pennsylvania Reserves

At Second Fredericksburg and Salem Church

Philander/27th New York:
VI Corps: Major General John Sedgwick
First Division: Brigadier General William T. H. Brooks
Second Brigade: Brigadier General Joseph J. Bartlett
27th New York: Colonel Alexander D. Adams
Other units: 5th Maine, 16th New York, 121st New York, 96th Pennsylvania

At Gettysburg

Phillip/13th Pennsylvania Reserves:
V Corps: Major General George Sykes
Third Division: Major General Samuel W. Crawford
First Brigade: Colonel William McCandless
13th Pennsylvania Reserves: Captain Charles F. Taylor
Other units: 1st, 2nd, 6th Pennsylvania Reserves

At Bristoe Station and Mine Run

Asa/19th New York Cavalry/1st New York Dragoons:
Cavalry Corps: Major General Alfred Pleasonton
First Division: Brigadier General John Buford
Reserve (Cavalry) Brigade:
Brigadier General Wesley Merritt
19th New York Cavalry/1st New York Dragoons:
Colonel Alfred Gibbs
Other units: 6th Pennsylvania Cavalry, 1st U.S. Cavalry, 2nd U.S. Cavalry, 5th U.S. Cavalry

At Washington, D.C. (March–May 1864)

Philander/2nd New York Mounted Rifles:
- XXII Corps: Major General Samuel Heintzelman
  - 2nd New York Mounted Rifles (dismounted): Colonel John Fisk

At the Overland Campaign

Asa/19th New York Cavalry/1st New York Dragoons:
- Cavalry Corps: Major General Philip H. Sheridan
  - First Division: Brigadier General Wesley Merritt (for Brig. Gen. Alfred T. A. Tolbert)
    - Reserve Brigade: Colonel Alfred Gibbs
      - 19th Cavalry: Lieutenant Colonel Thomas Jones Thorp
        - Other units: 6th Pennsylvania, 1st, 2nd, and 5th U.S. Cavalry

Philander/2nd New York Mounted Rifles:
- IX Corps: Major General Ambrose Burnside
  - First Division: Major General Thomas L. Crittenden
    - Provisional Brigade: Colonel Elisha G. Marshall
      - 2nd New York Mounted Rifles (dismounted): Colonel John Fisk
        - Other units: 24th New York Cavalry (dismounted); 14th New York Heavy Artillery; 2nd Pennsylvania Heavy Artillery

At Second Petersburg

Philander/2nd New York Mounted Rifles:
- IX Corps: Major General Ambrose Burnside
  - Second Division: Brigadier General Robert B. Potter
    - First Brigade: John Irvin Curtin
      - 2nd New York Mounted Rifles: Colonel John Fisk
        - Other units: 36th Massachusetts; 58th Massachusetts; 45th Pennsylvania; 48th Pennsylvania; 7th Rhode Island

Appendix B

Bucktail Requiem

Naturally, Phillip was not present for postwar reunions and other veteran activities of the former 13th Pennsylvania Reserves, and it is perhaps expected that his memory had become an afterthought, one of thousands of the faceless casualties of war. It seems the burial snafu at Gettysburg had been a harbinger regarding Phillip's legacy, but the postwar actions of the ex-Bucktails impacted his remembrance, nonetheless, in various ways.

The Bucktails Reunite

The formation of a Grand Army of the Republic (GAR) post in Smethport developed more slowly than in Spring Valley and Buffalo, but on June 21, 1883, McKean Post No. 347 was chartered. Of course, the members included ex-soldiers from a range of units, and familiar names to Phillip's Company I included James Landregan, Dr. S. D. Freeman, Frank Bell, William T. Blanchard, and Joe Barnes, who filled the rank of surgeon. Actually, the formation of a statewide society of Bucktails postdated the establishment of the Smethport post. On August 2, 1887, W. Ross Hartshorne and William H. Rauch invited interested ex-comrades to a plenary meeting in Harrisburg to form the "Regimental Association of the Bucktail or First Rifle Regiment."[1]

Ten weeks later, those surviving Bucktails reported to the first reunion in Williamsport, where they approved a set of bylaws and elected permanent officers. The duly installed leaders bore familiar names to the wartime command structure: W. Ross Hartshorne (president), Alanson E. Niles (vice president), Edward A. Irvin (treasurer), and William H. Rauch (secretary).

Rauch, an orderly sergeant in wartime, pandered this new clerical role into his 1906 classic *The History of the "Bucktails."*[2]

The Regimental Association of the Bucktails made a point of holding their annual reunions in towns where the soldiers had been originally recruited or in places of historical importance to the men. Gatherings were usually colorful affairs, and the former wildcats never went anywhere without their centerpiece: a stuffed stag known affectionately as "Bucky," who customarily guarded the entrance to the reunion hall and the tattered regimental battle flag on the dais.[3]

"Old Bucktail" proceedings were dominated by former officers, a regrettable feature of most Civil War regimental gatherings, but the rank and file typically shined during campfire sessions, excursions, and the parade. One enlisted man who managed to break the barrier of leadership was James Landregan. By 1890, Landregan had evolved into something of a cult hero at Bucktail reunions. Forever immortalized as the originator of the bucktailed headgear, he now officiated in ceremonies normally reserved for former officers. Consequently, in 1898, Landregan was chosen at the annual reunion to "lay the tattered and blood stained banner of the Bucktails on the tomb of the dead Colonel [Charles F.] Taylor." Then a procession of former comrades tossed flowers on the flag "in one of the most emotional memorial services ever held by the Bucktail survivors."[4]

Passing the Torch

As the aging Bucktails dealt with increasing infirmities, a number of comrades who were important in Phillip's life were "crossing the river to the other side." Those leaders on the list of the dying included Fent Ward (1884), Langhorne Wister, Alanson E. Niles, Leander W. Gifford (1891), and Samuel W. Crawford (1892). But the heaviest blow with closer ties to Phillip came with the passing of Joseph D. Barnes (1893), Frank Bell, and Dr. S. D. Freeman (1894). The twentieth century witnessed the additional losses of Roy Stone and W. Ross Hartshorne (1905), and the passing of legendary James Landregan (1907) marked the end of an era. Thereafter, McKean Post No. 347 and the Regimental Association of Bucktails rapidly dwindled.[5]

Officers of the Regimental Association of "Old Bucktails" at 1st Annual Reunion (1887). Surrounding the mascot, Bucky, are President W. Ross Hartshorne, Vice President Alanson E. Niles, Treasurer Edward A. Irvin, and Secretary William H. Rauch.

SOURCE: MCKEAN COUNTY HISTORICAL SOCIETY AND OLD JAIL MUSEUM, SMETHPORT, PENNSYLVANIA.

Last reunion of the Regimental Association of the Bucktails, Smethport (1916).
SOURCE: MCKEAN COUNTY HISTORICAL SOCIETY, SMETHPORT, PENNSYLVANIA.

Bucktails in Granite

During their years of activity, the Regimental Association of the Bucktails had been energized in constructing monuments to commemorate their own heroic past. On June 15, 1887, the state General Assembly apportioned $125,000 to mark the position of every Pennsylvania command on the Gettysburg battlefield. Two years later, the reunion attendees voted to assist the Commonwealth in funding "a Bucktail Memorial Pavilion" to be located in Rose's Grove on Houck's Ridge. A special treat for Company I veterans occurred when Frank Bell spoke at the Camp Fire, when he read an original poem about the Bucktails' feverish race on July 2, 1863, to reach Gettysburg. On September 2, 1890, the monument dedicated to Bucktail valor was unveiled on Pennsylvania Reserves Day.[6]

The statewide effort to fund and erect Civil War monuments at Gettysburg had inspired the Regimental Association of the Bucktails to construct a special granite testimonial to those who hailed from the wildcat district of

Bucktails monument on Houck's Ridge.

SOURCE: NATIONAL PARK SERVICE, GETTYSBURG NATIONAL MILITARY PARK, GETTYSBURG, PENNSYLVANIA.

Dedication of monument to the Bucktails, Driftwood, Pennsylvania (1908).
SOURCE: CAMERON COUNTY HISTORICAL SOCIETY, EMPORIUM, PENNSYLVANIA.

northwestern Pennsylvania and place it in a location holding special meaning. In April 1861, Driftwood, Pennsylvania, marked the place where the bucktailed recruits had built their log rafts to carry them downriver to Camp Curtin. In 1906, the association discussed the importance of the site to regimental history, and the Pennsylvania House of Representatives allocated $2,500 for the project the following year. On April 27, 1908, twenty-five "old" Bucktails attended the dedication, where the granddaughter of William H. Rauch unveiled the ten-foot-high monument.[7]

A Patchwork Remembrance

The first evidentiary material to be published on the men from Rushford who had been killed in action during the war appeared in a county-by-county report in the 1865 New York State Census. The tabulation laid bare discrepancies in wartime sacrifice when it listed Charles Van Dusen and eighteen others from Rushford, while Phillip's name was excluded. After all, Phillip, a New Yorker, had served in a Pennsylvania regiment. This kind of omission established a pattern that would be repeated frequently in future tributes.[8]

In 1865 and 1869, two monumental reference works were published, covering the history and rosters of the Pennsylvania Reserves and the histories and rosters of every regiment in the Commonwealth. Josiah R. Sypher published a single volume titled *History of the Pennsylvania Reserves* (1865). Sypher had read law under Thaddeus Stevens before the war, but he worked as a military correspondent for the *New York Tribune* during the hostilities. His *History* provided a narrative overview of the Pennsylvania Reserves from enlistment through discharge, complete with company rosters in every regiment. Samuel Perriman Bates, the Pennsylvania state historian, published a five-volume set titled *History of the Pennsylvania Volunteers* (1869–1871). Bates's scholarly approach differed from Sypher's by focusing on each regiment's unique history. In their coverages of the Bucktails, both authors identified Phillip with an asterisk for having "died of wounds received at Gettysburg."[9]

Philander had played a key role in keeping Phillip's sacrifice alive in Rushford and Allegany County through two local publications. In June 1895, the village of Wellsville hosted the Allegany County Centennial Celebration, a two-day event that focused on early pioneer history and local institutions, such as churches, schools, the press, business, and genealogy. Philander assisted in compiling an impressive list of Civil War fatalities from Allegany County, a compilation that included Phillip's name. In 1896, Minard and Merrill incorporated Philander's data into *Allegany County and Its People.*[10]

The town of Rushford picked up on the Allegany County celebration and its consequential publication. On August 16–21, 1908, the Rushford community held a similar centennial observance of its own under the direction of Philander's friend, former company commander in the 2nd Mounted Rifles, and town clerk, Watson W. Bush. Helen Josephine White Gilbert assembled the materials from the event for inclusion in her book *Rushford and Rushford People* (1910). The section describing Rushfordite participation in the war was exhaustive, again because of Philander's welcome assistance. Gilbert's accounts included the name and rank of the soldier, regiment and company designation, age and place of enlistment, promotions, wounds, date and place of discharge or death, and information on all three branches of the military, including local boys who had enlisted in Ohio and Pennsylvania regiments. In this manner, Phillip's name was recorded, although he was erroneously credited with having undergone three leg amputations.[11]

A Missed Opportunity

One final opportunity presented itself to publicly recognize Phillip's ultimate sacrifice at Gettysburg. In the late 1880s, ex-Gov. Curtin envisioned a

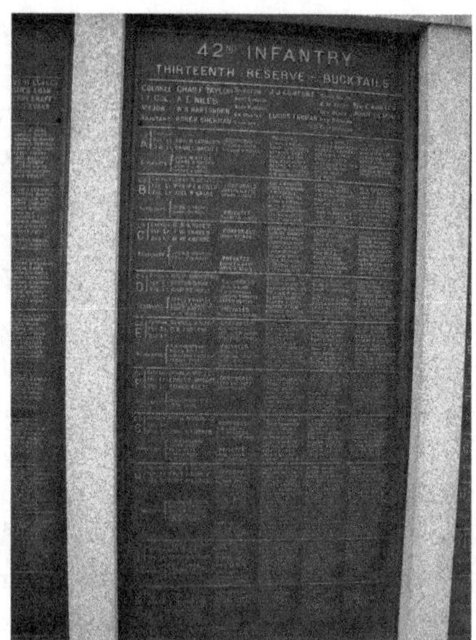

Pennsylvania monument and bronze panel of the 13th Pennsylvania Reserves on Cemetery Ridge.
SOURCE: NATIONAL PARK SERVICE, GETTYSBURG NATIONAL MILITARY PARK, GETTYSBURG, PENNSYLVANIA.

Pennsylvania Monument on Little Round Top, and twenty-five years later, the project reached fruition at, arguably, the most well-known place on the battlefield—Cemetery Ridge. In 1914, the largest state monument within the bounds of Gettysburg National Military Park was completed, and bronze regimental panels were placed along its base, listing the names of 34,500 Pennsylvania soldiers who participated in the liberation of the Commonwealth and subsequent preservation of the Union. Phillip's name appears on the plaque depicting Company I, 42nd Pennsylvania, and yet it lacks the embossed asterisk signifying a soldier who had been mortally wounded or killed in the line of duty. Although honored in name, his loss went overlooked.

* * * * * * *

Whatever became of other key characters who impacted the life of Phillip during the war? Brief postwar biographical sketches of eight individuals are provided below.

Frank J. Bell

Frank J. Bell was born to English Quakers on April 14, 1836, in Ceres, a village on the New York–Pennsylvania line. Shot through the lung at Antietam, he came back to lead Company I at Gettysburg. In October 1863, he captained Company K, 17th Regiment in the Invalid Corps, a unit sent to Indianapolis to guard the state arsenal and patrol the city streets. Understaffed, the regiment was "severely pressed" and frequently worked sixty-hour shifts. The 17th Regiment was given a second classification rating, allowing these partially disabled men to serve as cooks, orderlies, nurses, and guards. On April 25, 1864, Bell's regiment was redesignated the 94th Company, 2nd Battalion, during the reconstitution of the Invalid Corps into the Veteran Reserve Corps, and it is conceivable that he manned the trenches with Meigs's Emergency Division in the defense of Fort Stevens against Jubal Early's raiders. Promoted to brevet major a year later, Bell was discharged in June 1866.[13]

After the war, Bell studied law in Washington and continued to work in the War Department. He also worked for a number of years as a special field examiner for the Pension Bureau in Kansas, Florida, New York, and Pennsylvania. He was a steadfast champion for Civil War pensions. Frank Bell, the man who recruited Phillip into the Bucktails and lost a leg on Houck's Ridge, died in Washington on April 1, 1894.[14]

William Thomas Blanchard

Born in Palmer, Massachusetts, on March 23, 1838, William T. Blanchard belonged to an influential family. His grandfather, John B. Blanchard, moved to the area in 1824, built a scythe factory near the falls of Quabaug River, and raised six children. In civic affairs, the Blanchards served the local government as selectmen and town clerk and won seats to the state legislature. The village of Blanchardville, two miles south of Palmer, bears witness to the family's social, political, and economic successes.[15]

In the mid-1850s, William's relatives were expanding into the realm of railroad construction with the Springfield & Farmington Valley Railroad in Massachusetts. In keeping with his family's recent pursuits, William secured employment as a promoter for the Bradford & Pittsburg Railroad in McKean County shortly before the war. After the firing on Fort Sumter, Blanchard emerged as a leading recruiter in Bradford for Kane's new company of Bucktails. From this point forward, the lives of Blanchard and Phillip were intertwined in intrigue.

In the spring of 1863, Phillip had run into Blanchard at Convalescent Camp, where he plied the trade of a sutler and unequivocally refused to repay his loan. On September 5, 1863, while still residing at the camp, Blanchard enlisted in the 22nd Regiment of the Invalid Corps. Chosen captain of Company G, Blanchard's regiment was sent to Kendallville, Indiana, where they served in one of the state's rendezvous (training) sites, Camp Mitchell. Blanchard was discharged on November 23, 1865.[16]

After the war, Blanchard worked in life insurance and the coke industry, but he suffered greatly from his wartime leg wounds. Crippled since 1899, friends of the former captain of Company I petitioned the Regimental Association of the Old Bucktails to collect a small monetary gift in behalf of Blanchard because he was suffering from a painful bacterial skin infection (erysipelas) and rheumatism. In later years, he supplied helpful information about the early Bucktails to coauthors Thomson and Rauch for their *History of the "Bucktails"* (1906).

At the end of his life, Blanchard resided in the Dayton Soldiers' Home for six months and then died of chronic dementia on September 6, 1918. He is buried in Dayton National Cemetery, Dayton, Ohio.[17]

Joseph D. Barnes

After the war, Joe Barnes returned to McKean County, married, and raised three children in Kasson, Pennsylvania. Over the years, he found employment as a Kasson constable, managed a boardinghouse in Kushequa, and labored in the lumber trade. Socially, he was a fixture at gatherings of McKean Post No. 347 in Smethport.

On May 25, 1893, Barnes was found dead after splitting wood for his longtime Bucktail comrade James Landregan, who lived in Turtlepoint, Pennsylvania. Known to his comrades as a brave soldier and large-hearted man, Barnes was laid to rest in Kasson Cemetery in accordance with the GAR *Ritual of the Grand Army of the Republic*. Today, his Civil War musket and other wartime accoutrements are the centerpiece exhibit in the McKean County Historical Society and Old Jail Museum, Smethport, Pennsylvania.[18]

James Beach Clow

James Beach Clow, Phillip's supervisor in the Commissary Department, was born on March 17, 1832, in North Sewickley, Pennsylvania. Before the war, he lived for a short time in New Castle, a community known for its many iron foundries and machine shops. After the war, Clow relocated to Pittsburg and began manufacturing cast-iron water pipes.

In 1875, Clow moved to Chicago, where he formed James B. Clow & Sons, a firm that produced heating fixtures and marketed general plumbing supplies. The company was known particularly for its cast-iron "Gastream Radiator." A millionaire with a flair for reading, music, and philanthropy, Clow was an entrepreneurial giant in the Windy City. As his business thrived, branch offices were opened in New York, San Francisco, and Havana. Today, the operation is known as Clow Valve Company.

On January 7, 1908, Clow died from pneumonia. He is buried in Rosehill Cemetery, Chicago, Illinois.[19]

Jonathan J. Comfort

Jonathan J. Comfort, the new regimental surgeon of the Bucktails who ordered Phillip to accompany the most severely wounded at Fredericksburg to hospitals in Washington, was born in Fallsington, Bucks County, Pennsylvania, on January 9, 1830. Shortly after completing his education at the Jefferson School of Medicine in Philadelphia in 1859, he moved to Conshohocken, Pennsylvania, on the banks of the Schuylkill River, fifteen miles northwest of Philadelphia. Enlisting as an assistant surgeon of the 121st Pennsylvania in August 1862, Dr. Comfort was promoted to surgeon of the 13th Pennsylvania Reserves on the field of Fredericksburg. He remained a Bucktail until the regiment mustered out in May 1864, after which he transferred to the 190th Pennsylvania and served until the end of the war.

Afterward, Comfort practiced medicine in Haddonfield, New Jersey, a small community about twelve miles southeast of Philadelphia. In 1868, he was selected principal physician of Haddon township and later moved to Blackwood, New Jersey, to serve as resident physician at the Camden County Insane Asylum. He presided over the Camden County Medical Association, too.

Comfort died on March 22, 1906, at Old Point Comfort (Virginia) National Soldier's Home. He is buried in the Hampton National Cemetery, Hampton, Virginia.[20]

John Keenan Haffey

Phillip's tent mate and spiritual adviser lived an interesting life. Born on April 27, 1830, in County Armagh, Ireland, he received a formal education and immigrated to Canada when he was fourteen years old. He briefly taught school in New York for several years before being ordained in 1851. He served the Bradford (Pennsylvania) Baptist Church a short time before turning to Universalism while operating a farm. Haffey must have been inspired by the oil discoveries taking place along with the coal industry in northwestern Pennsylvania. In 1858, he turned to journalism as copublisher of the *Bradford Miner*.

Enlisting in Company I at the rank of sergeant, the former chaplain provided Phillip with much-needed spiritual guidance. He suffered poor health, however, and resigned from the 13th Pennsylvania Reserves after the Seven Days battles. Later in the war, he returned to serve as aide-de-camp for Brig. Gen. John F. Hartranft.

After the war, Haffey resumed his interest in petroleum. In 1871, he presided over an oil company in Bradford, Pennsylvania, but the lure of new discoveries in New Jersey lured him away. In 1875, he came back to establish the *Bradford New Era*, a broadsheet devoted to the petroleum industry. He returned to Beverly, New Jersey, in 1878 to run the *Beverly Banner*. He died there on November 7, 1881.[21]

Ellis P. Townsend

On May 25, 1835, Ellis P. "Snap" Townsend was born into a physician's family. In March 1863, he graduated from the University of Pennsylvania Medical School in Philadelphia, one of the most prestigious institutions in the country. Answering Letterman's emergency decree for contract physicians, Townsend tended to Phillip at Camp Letterman until near the end of the Alleganian's life. The physician served for another year in the Army of the Potomac before receiving his discharge.

In 1864, Townsend opened a practice in Beverly, New Jersey, about fifteen miles north of Philadelphia, where he established a solid reputation as a general practitioner. Then, in 1877, he headed a small medical staff in a construction company that had been contracted by the government of Brazil to build a railroad around the falls of the Madeira River, a tributary of the mighty Amazon. Such a railroad was needed to tap the rich rubber reserves in the jungle near the Bolivian border. The exotic adventure included 200 laborers from New Jersey, Pennsylvania, and New York. The "Madeira Mamore Expedition" was eventually referred to as "the railroad of death" in the press because a massive outbreak of malaria killed one-fourth of the work party in six months.

On his return to Beverly, Townsend engaged in writing a two-year series of pamphlets called *The Country Practitioner*, a collection of medical essays and advice to doctors plying their profession in rural America. In 1884, he moved to Camden, New Jersey, and shortly thereafter to Billings, Montana, where he opened a private practice and moonlighted as a surgeon for the Burlington Northern Railroad.

In 1901, Townsend was appointed chief physician for the Crow Indian Agency and the Lame Deer Agency of the Northern Cheyenne, sixty miles and 100 miles away, respectively. In 1906, while traveling to the distant Lame Deer Agency during a winter blizzard, he contracted a severe case of frostbite in both feet. For months, Townsend suffered from chronic infections that spread to both legs. His limbs turned gangrenous, resulting in a double amputation. Ironically, the physician who had reluctantly delayed in amputating Phillip's shattered knee had succumbed to a similar fate.

On July 30, 1907, "Snap" Townsend died on July 30, 1907. He is buried in Mountainview Cemetery, Billings, Montana.[22]

R. Fent Ward

Before the war, Robert Fenton Ward worked as a printer in his father's newspaper, the *Clearfield Republican*. In April 1861, he joined Company I of the Bucktails in Smethport. He was assigned the hospital stewardship of the company, a position responsible for reporting the daily list of sick soldiers to the captain. Thus, Ward and Blanchard were fully aware of Phillip's frequent visits to "Company Q" in the early months of the war. A proven warrior, Ward was promoted to lieutenant after Antietam.[23]

When the Pennsylvania Reserves were discharged after the battle of Bethesda Church, Ward transferred with other Bucktail officers, including Maj. Ross Hartshorne, Capt. Neri B. Kinsey, Capt. John Kratzner, and Capt. John Wolfe, to join the 190th Pennsylvania. On June 6, 1864, after the battle of Cold Harbor, Ward became captain of Company I.[24]

Although the 190th Pennsylvania were minimally involved at Cold Harbor, Second Petersburg, and the Crater, the Weldon Railroad fight deserves closer scrutiny, the target of Grant's fourth major attempt to break the siege at Petersburg. On August 18, the 190th and 191st Pennsylvania made up a small brigade under the temporary command of Hartshorne, and they had been sent with Crawford's division to break up railroad tracks south of Richmond. They probed the area around the Weldon Railroad and skirmished with the enemy on terrain covered by dense thickets and swampland. Heavy rainfall contributed to low visibility as Hartshorne's troops dug breastworks on the extreme right of Crawford's advance position.

On August 19, the Rebels launched an attack in the early afternoon, driving a wedge between Hartshorne's two regiments and gaining their rear. Federal artillerists lobbed shells into the battle zone, killing northerners and southerners alike. The rout was on, but not before 600 Yankees had surrendered, including most of the officers of the 190th and 191st Pennsylvania. Where was Ward?[25]

The enigma surrounding Ward's whereabouts deepens on checking company rosters of the 190th Pennsylvania listed in Bates's *History of the Pennsylvania Volunteers, 1861–1865*. The contents raise several concerns. First, most of the Company I muster roster was never filed with the adjutant general and presumably lost. Second, Ward's soldier's index card shows August 19, 1864, as his date of discharge, the day of the debacle at Weldon Railroad. Yet there is no record of his mustering out or incarceration in any Confederate prisoner-of-war camp (Salisbury, Danville, or Richmond). So, did Ward desert? Wounded five times during the war, Ward had built a reputation as a hard-nosed, no-nonsense company officer in tested combat situations at Antietam, Fredericksburg, and Gettysburg. It seems out of character for him to have taken French leave, but, curiously, he never applied for a military pension afterward.[26]

After the war, Fent's widowed mother and his brother moved to a farm in Grahampton, Pennsylvania, but Fent had disappeared. Later, in the early 1880s, he surfaced as a compositor for the *New York Times*. On June 9, 1884, R. Fenton Ward died of consumption in Hoboken, New Jersey. The former commander of two Company I's was buried in a pauper's grave in Holy Name Cemetery, Jersey City, New Jersey, a sad end to a promising life.[27]

Notes

Chapter 1: In Search of the Ellithorpes of Western New York

1. John S. Minard and Georgia Drew Merrill, *Allegany County and Its People: A Centennial Memorial History* (Alfred, NY: W. A. Ferguson, 1896), 1, 17–18, 137–38; F. W. Beers, *History of Allegany County, New York: With Illustrations and Portraits of Old Pioneers and Prominent Residents* (Boston: F. W. Beers, 1879), 254; Orsamus Turner, *Pioneer History of the Holland Land Purchase of Western New York* (Buffalo, NY: Jewett, Thomas & Co., 1850), 40–70; Anthony F. C. Wallace, *The Death and Rebirth of the Senecas* (New York: Vintage Books, 1972), 21–23, 49–107; Arthur C. Parker, *The History of the Seneca Indians* (Port Washington, NY: Ira J. Friedman, 1967 reprint), 28–30, 71–84.

2. See Joseph A. Conforti, *Imagining New England: Explorations of Regional Identity from the Pilgrims to the Mid-Twentieth Century* (Cambridge, MA: Harvard University Press, 2003), and David M. Ellis, "The Yankee Invasion of New York, 1783–1850," *New York History* 32 (1951): 1–17.

3. The author standardizes the spelling of "Ellithorpe," being mindful of the multiple range of spellings in colonial documents. Early examples include Ellithorp, Ellethorp, Elitharp, Elitrop, Ellisthorp, Ettithorp, and Lathrop. For Puritan passenger lists, see www.olivetreegenealogy.com and www.winthropsociety.com.

4. For the Ellithorpes in Rowley, see George B. Blodgett and Amos Everett Jewett, *Early Settlers of Rowley, Massachusetts: A Genealogical Record of Families* (Rowley, MA: A. E. Jewett, 1933 reprint); Thomas Gage, *History of Rowley, Massachusetts* (Boston: Ferdinand Andrews, Pub., 1840), 117–33.

5. For the Ellithorpes of colonial Thompson, Connecticut; Worthington, Massachusetts; and Hungerford, Vermont, see Richard M. Bayles, ed., *History of Windham County, Connecticut, with Illustrations* (New York: W. W. Preston & Co., 1889), 624–83; Grace Olive Chapman, *Ellithorpes of Killingly, Connecticut* (Boston: self-published, 1944): 3–7, 14–17; Louis H. Everts, *History of the Connecticut Valley in Massachusetts*, 2 vols. (Philadelphia: J. B. Lippincott and Co., 1879), 2:1003, 1008; James C. Rice and C. K. Brewster, *History of the Town of Worthington, from Its First Settlement to 1874* (Springfield, MA: Clark W. Bryan and Co., 1874): 2, 11–13, 95; and Henry Perry Smith, *A History of Addison County, Vermont: With Illustrations and Biographical Sketches of Some of Its Prominent Men and Pioneers* (Syracuse, NY: D. Mason & Co., 1886), 392. See also Town of Bridport, Vermont, Land Deeds, Book 1: 381, 389; Town of Sheldon, Vermont, Land Deeds, Book 1: 70A.

6. The four sons were Danforth (b. 1797), William (b. 1798), Charles (b. 1805), and Lyman (b. February 20, 1806). See also Smith, *History of Addison County, Vermont*, 380–96,

555–75; Doris S. Bishop, *A History of the Town of Orwell, Vermont* (Poultney, VT: Journal Press, 1963), 1–13, 84–88; Town of Orwell, Vermont, Land Deeds, Book 4: 279–80; Book 5: 199–200, 365, 500; and 2nd U.S. Census, 1800, Orwell, Addison County, VT.

7. Lewis D. Stilwell, *Migration from Vermont* (Montpelier: Vermont Historical Society, 1948), 119. See also Charles E. Brooks, *Frontier Settlement and Market Revolution: The Holland Land Purchase* (Ithaca, NY: Cornell University Press, 1996), 106–7, 154, and Harold Fisher Wilson, *The Hill Country of Northern New England: Its Social and Economic History, 1790–1830* (New York: Columbia University Press, 1936), 25–26.

8. Town Clerk's Office, Orwell, Vermont, Land Deeds: Book 8: 54, 100, 411; Town Clerk's Office, Sheldon, Vermont, Land Deeds, Book 1: 70A; Office of County Clerk, St. Lawrence County, Canton, New York, Land Deeds, Book 10: 155–56, Book 25: 534–35, Book 41C: 337–40, Book 46C: 120–21, Book 51A: 464–64, Book 67A: 99–102; Stilwell, *Migration from Vermont*, 139; Carlton E. Sanford, *Early History of the Town of Hopkinton* (Boston: Bartlett Press, 1903), 219–20; Map of St. Lawrence County, New York (Philadelphia: J. B. Shields Pub., 1858); E. A. Wood, "Nicholville, 1892–1893," *Potsdam (N.Y.) Courier-Freeman*, September 26, 1892, in St. Lawrence County Historical Association, Scrapbook #16; 5th U.S. Census, 1830, Nicholville, St. Lawrence County, NY.

9. See L. H. Everts, *History of St. Lawrence County, New York: With Illustrations and Biographical Sketches of Some of Its Prominent Men and Pioneers* (Philadelphia: L. H. Everts and Co., 1878), 318–26, 570; Gates Curtis, *Our County and Its People* (Syracuse, NY: D. Mason and Co., 1894); Map of Nicholville, St. Lawrence County, New York (1869); Sanford, *Early History of the Town of Hopkinton*, 219–20; E. A. Wood, "Nicholville, 1892–1893"; and Arthur Thornton, "A History of Nicholville," MA thesis, School of Education, State University of New York, Potsdam, 1999, 38. Today, a sizable number of Ellithorpes are buried in Mound Hill Cemetery, Nicholville, including Danforth, William, and Huldah.

10. The close proximity of the Samuel Sanford household to the Ellithorpes raises an interesting question. It might explain the unsubstantiated union of Lyman and Marinda as well as Danforth's middle name, Sanford. See 5th U.S. Census, 1830, Nicholville, St. Lawrence County, NY.

11. See *Vital Records of Roxbury, Massachusetts, to the End of 1849*, 2 vols. (Salem, MA: Essex Institute, 1925), 2:540; *Commemorative Biographical Record of Tolland and Windham Counties, Connecticut: Biographical Sketches of Prominent and Representative Citizens and Many of the Early Settled Families* (Chicago: J. H. Beers & Co., 1903), 440; Walter S. Griggs, *Genealogy of the Griggs Family* (Pompton Lakes, NJ: Biblio Co., 1926); and Bayles, *History of Windham County, Connecticut*, 754, 837–42, 924, 1007, 1034. Many Griggs descendants are buried in the prestigious King's Chapel Burying Ground in Boston as well as Woodstock Hill Cemetery, Woodstock, Connecticut, and South Cemetery, Pomfret, Connecticut.

12. In 1638, Roger Eastman boarded the *Confidence* in Southhampton, England; landed in Massachusetts Bay Colony; and established the family line in America. A "first grantor" of Salisbury, Roger's progeny pushed westward to Haverhill, Massachusetts, and Ashford, Connecticut. See Timothy S. Rix, *History and Genealogy of the Eastman Family of America* (Concord, NH: Ira C. Evans, 1901), 26, 80; David W. Hoyt, *Old Families of Salisbury and Amesbury, Massachusetts* (Providence, RI: Snow and Farnham Printers, 1897), 8–14, 141–47; George Wingate Chase, *The History of Haverhill, Massachusetts: From Its First Settlement in 1640 to the Year 1860* (Haverhill: Stone & Huse, 1861), 113–23, 128–29; Royal R. Hinman, *A Catalogue of the First Puritan Settlers of the Colony of Connecticut* (Hartford, CT: Case,

Tiffany & Co., 1852), 94, 125; and Charles Edward Banks, *Topographical Dictionary of 2885 English Emigrants to New England, 1620–1650* (Philadelphia: Elijah Ellsworth Brownell, Pub., 1937), 62, 178.

13. Stilwell, *Migration from Vermont*, 66, 95–95, 103–4; Wilson, *The Hill Country of Northern New England*, 15–19.

14. Town of Bridgewater, Vermont, Land Deeds, Book 3: 434, 493–94, 612–13; Book 5: 165; Book 6: 185–86, 280–81; 2nd U.S. Census, 1800, Bridgewater, Windsor County, VT. See also Lewis Cass Aldrich and Frank R. Holmes, *History of Windsor County, Vermont: With Illustrations and Biographical Sketches of Some of Its Prominent Men and Pioneers* (Syracuse, NY: D. Mason & Co., 1889), 601–26, and Gladys S. Adams, *Bridgewater, Vermont: 1779–1976* (Bridgewater, VT: Bridgewater Cemetery Commission, 2005), 16–23. The original spelling was "Bridgwater."

15. For the children born to Philip and Rebecca in Bridgewater/Barnard, see Griggs, *Genealogy of the Griggs Family*, 89.

16. Town of Bridgewater, Vermont, Land Deeds, Book 5: 256–57; Book 6: 187–92, 309. See also Stilwell, *Migration from Vermont*, 98, 108, 124–30, 140, 152–53, 160, and Wilson, *The Hill Country of Northern New England*, 20–26.

17. Adams, *Bridgewater, Vermont, 1779–1976*, 26, 118.

18. See William Wycoff, *The Developer's Frontier: The Making of the Western New York Landscape* (New Haven, CT: Yale University Press, 1988), 2–18; James H. Hotchkin, *A History of the Purchase and Settlement of Western New York, and of the Rise, Progress and Present State of the Presbyterian Church in That Section* (New York: M. W. Dodd, 1848), 3–10, 24; Brooks, *Frontier Settlement and Market Revolution*, 4–45; and Minard and Merrill, *Allegany County and Its People*, 46–47. For a Native American perspective, see Parker, *The History of the Seneca Indians*, 133–42.

19. Ellicott divided each township into sixty-four parcels of roughly 120 acres with boundaries often shaped by contours, such as waterways, in order to promote the erection of grist and saw mills. See Robert W. Silsby, "The Holland Land Company in Western New York," *Adventures in Western New York History Magazine* 8 (1961): 1–16; Wycoff, *The Developer's Frontier*, 24–26, 134–38; and Brooks, *Frontier Settlement and Market Revolution*, 4, 19, 28.

20. William Chazanof, *Joseph Ellicott and the Holland Land Company* (Syracuse, NY: Syracuse University Press, 1970), 1–75.

21. The classifications were bottomland, intervale, upland, swamp, or barren. The grades were 1st Quality and 2nd Quality. See Brooks, *Frontier Settlement and Market Revolution*, 14–15, 53–54, and Wycoff, *The Developer's Frontier*, 20–22, 39.

22. Brooks, *Frontier Settlement and Market Revolution*, 46; Stilwell, *Migration from Vermont*, 118, 139; McNall, *An Agricultural History of the Genesee Valley , 1790–1860* (Philadelphia: University of Pennsylvania Press, 1952), 108, 184–87; Minard and Merrill, *Allegany County and Its People*, 17–22, 137–39, 160; James Sullivan, ed., *The History of New York State, 1523–1927*, 5 vols. (New York: Lewis Historical Publishing Company, 1927), 5:1–121; Hotchkin, *A History of the Purchase and Settlement of Western New York*, 17; Wycoff, *The Developer's Frontier*, 56–61, 65–68, 78–81, 91, 104–10, 122–23, 127–28, 157, 169; F. W. Beers, *History of Wyoming County, New York: With Illustrations and Biographical Sketches and Portraits of Some Pioneers and Prominent Residents* (New York: F. W. Beers, 1880), 183.

23. Wycoff, *The Developer's Frontier*, 59–61, 106–7; Brooks, *Frontier Settlement and Market Revolution*, 46; Stilwell, *Migration from Vermont*, 127–30.

24. Town of Bridgewater, Vermont, Land Deeds, Book 6: 307–11. In July 1799, Ellicott's crew had surveyed Eagle township and given it an upland grade with a quality index of "2," a mediocre score. Generally, they found the soil hard and stony, heavily forested, and etched by a large number of "runs," swamps, marshes, and waterfalls. Ellicott held out promise for future potash production, lumber manufacturing, grazing livestock, and eventually winter wheat cultivation. See Holland Land Company Collection, Field Notes, Range 1, Township 7, Archives and Special Collections, Daniel A. Reed Library, State University of New York, Fredonia.

25. Town Clerk of Nunda, New York, Record Book, 1813–1816; Wycoff, *The Developer's Frontier*, 89; H. Wells Hand, *Centennial History of the Town of Nunda, 1808–1908* (Rochester: NY: Rochester Herald Press, 1908), 95–112; Lockwood R. Doty, *History of Livingston County, New York: From Its Earliest Traditions to the Present*, 2 vols. (Jackson, MI: W. J. Van Deusen, 1905), 2:888; John Warner Barber, *Historical Collections of the State of New York* (New York: S. Tuttle, 1846), 60–61.

26. See McNall, *An Agricultural History of the Genesee Valley*, 107–8, 183–93; Wycoff, *The Developer's Frontier*, 158–61; Minard and Merrill, *Allegany County and Its People*, 22, 160; and Stilwell, *Migration from Vermont*, 80–84, 121.

27. Minard and Merrill, *Allegany County and Its People*, 22, 27, 35, 159–60; Brooks, *Frontier Settlement and Market Revolution*, 51–52, 62, 71–73, 82, 111; Wycoff, *The Developer's Frontier*, 21–23; Beers, *History of Wyoming County*, 182.

28. Karen E. Livsey, *Western New York Land Transactions, 1804–1824* (Baltimore, MD: Genealogical Publishing Company, 1991), 250; Holland Land Company Collection, Land Transactions Ledger, Archives and Special Collections, Daniel A. Reed Library, State University of New York, Fredonia.

29. See Turner, *Pioneer History of the Holland Land Purchase of Western New York*, 537, and Brooks, *Frontier Settlement and Market Revolution*, 71–73, 82, 111.

30. See Wycoff, *The Developer's Frontier*, 60–61; McNall, *An Agricultural History of the Genesee Valley*, 75; and Brooks, *Frontier Settlement and Market Revolution*, 82–92, 99, 106, 116–17, 138.

31. Karen E. Livsey, *Western New York Land Transactions, 1825–1835* (Baltimore, MD: Genealogical Publishing Company, 1991), 25, 106, 358, 615. See also Brooks, *Frontier Settlement and Market Revolution*, 93, 97, 106, 121, 142, and McNall, *An Agricultural History of the Genesee Valley*, 27, 33, 52–53.

32. See Brooks, *Frontier Settlement and Market Revolution*, 6–10, 114, 176–80, 191–232; McNall, *Agricultural History of the Genesee Valley*, 35–37, 225–27; Minard and Merrill, *Allegany County and Its People*, 121, 736–49, 780–81; Beers, *History of Wyoming County*, 182–88, 254–56; Barber, *Historical Collections of the State of New York*, 60–61; and Wycoff, *The Developer's Frontier*, 2.

33. Minard and Merrill, *Allegany County and Its People*, 736–39; Sullivan, *History of New York State*, 5:525.

34. Lyman purchased lot 13 on Range 1, township 7. See Office of County Clerk, Allegany County, Belmont, New York, Land Deeds, Book K: 188–89, Book L: 447–48. See also McNall, *Agricultural History of the Genesee Valley*, 221–26.

35. The children of Lyman and Fannie Ellithorpe were Ann (b. August 13, 1835), Mary (b. February 9, 1837), Philander Doty (b. October 8, 1840), Phillip Griggs (b. April 8, 1843), and Permelia (b. October 5, 1845).

36. Brooks, *Frontier Settlement and Market Revolution*, 6–10, 114, 176–80, 191–232; McNall, *Agricultural History of the Genesee Valley*, 35–37, 225–27.

37. For a history of the secret society, which grew to an estimated 40,000 members, see Oscar A. Kinchen, *The Rise and Fall of the Patriot Hunters* (New York: Bookman Associates, 1956), 5–35, 42–49, 63.

38. Kinchen, *The Rise and Fall of the Patriot Hunters*, 65–84, 101, 117. For Lyman's membership, see Beers, *History of Wyoming County*, 257.

39. In 1634, Rowland "The Emigrant" Stebbins had arrived in Massachusetts Bay Colony aboard the *Francis*. Rowland lived briefly in Roxbury and Springfield, Massachusetts, where generations of his scions served their communities as selectmen, surveyors, magistrates, and church elders. See Robert Charles Anderson, *The Great Migration: Immigrants to New England, 1634–1635*, vol. 6 (Boston: New England Historic Genealogical Society, 2009), 494–96; Willis Merrill Stebbins, *Genealogy of the Stebbins Family* (Lincoln, NE: Brown Printing, 1949), 11, 14, 21–23; *Biographical Sketches of the Leading Citizens of Livingston and Wyoming Counties, New York* (Boston: Biographical Review Publishing Co., 1895), 241–42; and Office of the County Clerk, Allegany County, Belmont, New York, Land Deeds, Book 2: 541, 543, 545–46, 560.

40. See Robert M. French, "Carlos Leonard Stebbins," *Historical Wyoming* 17 (October 1963): 1–9; Ralph Stebbins Greenlee and Robert Lemuel Greenlee, *The Stebbins Genealogy*, 2 vols. (Chicago: M. A. Donohue and Co., 1904), 1:471, 476; Livsey, *Western New York Land Transactions, 1825–1835*, 23, 168, 315, 553, 575, 615; Beers, *History of Wyoming County*, 185, 262; *New Topographical Atlas of Genesee and Wyoming Counties, New York* (Philadelphia: Stone and Stewart Publishers, 1866), 83; *Biographical Sketches of the Leading Citizens of Livingston and Wyoming Counties, New York*, 242; and *Wyoming County Gazette*, February 6, 1914.

41. For treatments of these crusades beginning in the 1840s, see Alice Felt Tyler, *Freedom's Ferment: Phases of American Social History from the Colonial Period to the Outbreak of the Civil War* (1962; repr., New York: Harper Torchbooks, 1962); Whitney R. Cross, *The Burned-Over District: The Social and Intellectual History of Enthusiastic Religion in Western New York, 1800–1850* (Ithaca, NY: Cornell University Press, 1950); Michael Barkun, *Crucible of the Millennium: The Burned-Over District of New York in the 1840s* (Syracuse, NY: Syracuse University Press, 1986); and Beers, *History of Wyoming County*, 182–88.

42. For revivalism in western New York, see Hotchkin, *A History of the Purchase and Settlement of Western New York*, 115, 560, 589–91; Cross, *The Burned-Over District*, 4–9, 24–30; and Helen Josephine White Gilbert, *Rushford and Rushford People* (Chautauqua, NY: Chautauqua Print Shop, 1910), 545–48, 566.

43. For the democratization of education in the 1840s, see Frederick Jackson Turner, *The United States, 1830–1850: The Nation and Its Sections* (1935; reprint, New York: Norton & Co., 1962), 135; Cross, *The Burned-Over District*, 89; and Conforti, *Imagining New England*, 90, 97–98, 123.

44. Minard and Merrill, *Allegany County and Its People*, 169, 793–97. See also Gilbert, *Rushford and Rushford People*, 259, and Beers, *History of Wyoming County*, 182–88.

45. Gilbert, *Rushford and Rushford People*, 259–63. In 1863, the Mystic Association folded, but it resumed after the war and offered programs into the twentieth century.

46. The first mention of Permelia's medical condition appeared in Asa R. Burleson to Phillip G. Ellithorpe, August 13, 1863, in Ellithorpe Family Collection, Cowlitz County

Historical Museum, Kelso, Washington (hereafter, the collection and its location will be referenced as CCHM).

47. Minard and Merrill, *Allegany County and Its People*, 101, 794–98; McNall, *An Agricultural History of the Genesee Valley*, 6–7, 17–18, 22–24.

48. 7th U.S. Census, Agricultural Schedule, 1850, Wyoming County, NY. See also Wycoff, *The Developer's Frontier*, 158–61; Brooks, *Frontier Settlement and Market Revolution*, 68, 114; Minard and Merrill, *Allegany County and Its People*, 97–102, 159–61; Sullivan, *History of New York State*, 5:525; and McNall, *An Agricultural History of the Genesee Valley*, 59–69, 75–76, 85, 107–8, 116, 154, 184–93, 248–50.

49. Production averages were calculated by dividing the cumulative Wyoming County production figures by the total number of farms listed. See J. D. B. DeBow, *Statistical View of the United States: Compendium to the Seventh Census* (Washington, DC: Senate Printer, 1854), 278–83, and 7th U.S. Census, Agricultural Schedule, 1850, Wyoming County, NY.

50. On a county-by-county comparison of farm output in the other counties in the lower Genesee Valley, Wyoming fell in the median range. See McNall, *An Agricultural History of the Genesee Valley*, 248–56.

51. Labor laws at the time viewed children under age twenty-one as property and owned by their father. For the system of binding out, see Stilwell, *Migration from Vermont*, 169–70, and McNall, *An Agricultural History of the Genesee Valley*, 232–34. See also 8th U.S. Census, 1860, Wyoming County, NY; 7th U.S. Census, 1850, North Danville, Livingston County, NY.

52. Office of County Clerk, Allegany County, Belmont, New York, Land Deeds, Book 41: 613–14, Book 66: 361–62. See also 8th U.S. Census, 1860, Agricultural Schedule, Allegany County, NY; Minard and Merrill, *Allegany County and Its People*, 792–93; Gilbert, *Rushford and Rushford People*, 560, back matter; and G. Bechler, *Map of Allegany County, from actual surveys* (Philadelphia: Gillette, Matthews and Co., 1856), village of Rushford.

53. Another version of the village's name stems from the abundance of rushes that lined the local creek. See Minard and Merrill, *Allegany County and Its People*, 789–812, and Gilbert, *Rushford and Rushford People*, 2.

54. Minard and Merrill, *Allegany County and Its People*, 789–812; Barber, *Historical Collections of the State of New York*, 60–61, 65.

55. Phillip G. Ellithorpe to Ann and Permelia, April 1, 1860, CCHM; 8th U.S. Census, 1860, Smethport, McKean County, PA. See also J. H. Beers, *History of the Counties of McKean, Elk, Cameron, and Potter, Pennsylvania: With Biographical Selections* (Chicago: John Morris Publisher, 1890), 1014, 1059, 1062.

56. Phillip G. Ellithorpe to Ann and Permelia, April 1, 1860, CCHM.

57. Phillip G. Ellithorpe to Ann and Permelia, April 1, 1860, CCHM.

58. Phillip G. Ellithorpe to Ann, October 9, 1860, CCHM; *McKean County Miner*, June 2, 1893.

59. Phillip G. Ellithorpe to Ann, October 9, 1860, CCHM.

60. Phillip G. Ellithorpe to Ann and Permelia, April 1, 1860, CCHM.

61. Phillip G. Ellithorpe to Ann, October 9, 1860, CCHM.

62. Phillip G. Ellithorpe to Ann, October 9, 1860, CCHM; Phillip G. Ellithorpe to Permelia, March 11, 1861, CCHM.

63. Phillip G. Ellithorpe to Permelia, March 11, 1861, CCHM.

64. In 1851, the first pineapple cheese factory appeared in Rushford. The casings hung and cured in twine netting that dug into the soft outer skin of the cheddar, giving the

appearance of a pineapple. By 1856, the factory had perfected a packaging and delivery system of "boxes" to markets across the country. Pineapple cheese became a prized housewarming holiday gift in 1850s America, and Rushford was one of its principal suppliers. See Minard and Merrill, *Allegany County and Its People*, 792–93; Gilbert, *Rushford and Its People*, 560; and McNall, *An Agricultural History of the Genesee Valley*, 191–92.

65. Phillip G. Ellithorpe to Permelia, December 26, 1861, CCHM; Henry Hyde to Phillip G. Ellithorpe, January 17, 1863, CCHM.

66. Office of County Clerk, Allegany County, Belmont, New York, Land Deeds, Book 41: 613–14, Book 66: 361–62; Phillip G. Ellithorpe to Sisters, July 9, 1862, CCHM; 8th U.S. Census, 1860, Rushford, Allegany County, NY.

67. French, "Carlos Leonard Stebbins," 1–9; *Biographical Sketches of the Leading Citizens of Livingston and Wyoming Counties, New York*, 241–42; Greenlee and Greenlee, *The Stebbins Genealogy*, 2:753; Beers, *History of Wyoming County*, 257–58, 262. Many of Carlos's portraits hung in Wyoming and Allegany County residences for decades after the war. In 2016, three original Stebbins canvases were discovered in county storage. See the *Daily News* (Warsaw, Wyoming County, NY), March 25, 2016.

Chapter 2: Duty, Honor, Country: The Ellithorpe Brothers Prepare for War

1. For an examination of these powerful motivations, see James M. McPherson, *For Cause and Comrades: Why Men Fought in the Civil War* (New York: Oxford University Press, 1997), 5, 13, 21–25, 36, 44, 114, and M. Keith Harris, *Across the Bloody Chasm: The Culture of Commemoration among Civil War Veterans* (Baton Rouge: Louisiana State University Press, 2014), 12.

2. Consider the following events of the 1850s: the Compromise of 1850, the publication of *Uncle Tom's Cabin* (1852), the passage of the Kansas-Nebraska Act and birth of the Republican Party (1854), the outbreak of violence in "Bleeding Kansas" (1856), the *Dred Scott* decision and controversy over the Lecompton Constitution (1857–1858), the Lincoln–Douglas debates (1858), and John Brown's raid on Harpers Ferry (1859). To examine these causes of the Civil War, see James M. McPherson, *Battle Cry of Freedom* (New York: Ballantine Books, 1988), 6–201, and David M. Potter, *The Impending Crisis, 1848–1861* (New York: Harper & Row, 1976). See also Michael J. Dubin, *United States Presidential Elections, 1788–1860: The Official Results by County and State* (Jefferson, NC: McFarland, 2002); Kenneth M. Stampp, *The Peculiar Institution: Slavery in the Ante-Bellum South* (New York: Alfred A. Knopf, 1968); and Peter Kolchin, *American Slavery, 1619–1877* (New York: Hill and Wang, 1993).

3. See McPherson, *Battle Cry of Freedom*, 264–75; Potter, *The Impending Crisis*, 555–83; and Stephen W. Sears, *Lincoln's Lieutenants: The High Command of the Army of the Potomac* (Boston: Houghton Mifflin Harcourt, 2017), 1–7, 27–30. For an example of how this spirit of volunteerism played out in the South, see John A. Simpson, *S. A. Cunningham and the Confederate Heritage* (Athens: University of Georgia Press, 1994), 9–13.

4. For motivations for enlisting, see Bell Irvin Wiley, *The Life of Billy Yank: The Common Soldier of the Union* (1952; repr., Baton Rouge: Louisiana State University Press, 1971), 17–18, 39–40, 275; McPherson, *For Cause and Comrades*, 1–178; McPherson, *Battle Cry of Freedom*, 309, 322; Gerald F. Linderman, *Embattled Courage: The Experience of Combat in the American Civil War* (New York: Free Press, 1987); Reid Mitchell, *Civil War Soldiers: Their Expectations and Their Experiences* (New York: Touchstone, 1988); and Harris, *Across the Bloody Chasm*, 12.

5. For recruitment in northwestern Pennsylvania, see Josiah R. Sypher, *History of the Pennsylvania Reserves: A Complete Record* (Lancaster, PA: Elias Barr and Co., 1865), 17, 38, 48, 51; Uzal W. Ent, *The Pennsylvania Reserves in the Civil War: A Comprehensive History* (Jefferson, NC: McFarland, 2014), 1, 350; Samuel Penniman Bates, *History of the Pennsylvania Volunteers, 1861–1865*, 5 vols. (Harrisburg, PA: State Printing Office, 1869–1871), 1:907; Edwin A. Glover, *Bucktailed Wildcats: A Regiment of Civil War Volunteers* (New York: Thomas Yoseloff, 1960), 17–19; and Osmund Thomson and William H. Rauch, *History of the "Bucktails": Kane's Rifle Regiment of the Pennsylvania Reserve Corps, 42nd of the Line* (Philadelphia: Electric Printing Company, 1906), 5–19.

6. For the formation of the 13th Pennsylvania Reserves, see Thomson and Rauch, *History of the "Bucktails,"* 5–12, 29; Bates, *History of the Pennsylvania Volunteers*, 1:907–43; Sypher, *History of the Pennsylvania Reserves*, 90; Glover, *Bucktailed Wildcats*, 15–20; and Ent, *The Pennsylvania Reserves in the Civil War*, 4.

7. Original muster records in Phillip G. Ellithorpe, Military Service Record, 13th Pennsylvania Reserves, National Archives and Records Administration (Record Group 94), Washington, DC (hereafter cited as Phillip G. Ellithorpe Military Service Record, NARA); Pennsylvania State Archive, Civil War Veterans' Card File, 1861–6186, E. The solid beechwood traveling desk that served as the surface to enlist Smethportians into the Civil War is on display in the McKean County Historical Society and Old Jail Museum, Smethport, Pennsylvania.

8. Thomson and Rauch, *History of the "Bucktails,"* 5–12, 29; Bates, *History of the Pennsylvania Volunteers, 1861–1865*, 1:907–43; Sypher, *History of the Pennsylvania Reserves*, 90; Glover, *Bucktailed Wildcats*, 15–20; Ent, *The Pennsylvania Reserves in the Civil War*, 4. The Smethport experience was repeated in other communities throughout the North. See John D. Billings, *Hardtack and Coffee or the Unwritten Story of Army Life* (1888; repr., Williamstown, MA: Corner House Publishers, 1990), 34–44; Wiley, *The Life of Billy Yank*, 24–25, 38; and Mitchell, *Civil War Soldiers*, 16–19.

9. Phillip G. Ellithorpe to Mother, June 18, 1861, CCHM.

10. Phillip G. Ellithorpe to Sister, April 26, 1861, CCHM. At least one other Rushford boy joined Phillip's Smethport company: William A. Lafferty. See a list of all Rushford enlistees on the Allegany County Historical Society (New York) website at www.alleganyhistory.org.

11. Phillip G. Ellithorpe to Sister, April 26, 1861, CCHM; see also Ent, *The Pennsylvania Reserves in the Civil War*, 4; Glover, *Bucktailed Wildcats*, 20–21, 271; Thomson and Rauch, *History of the "Bucktails,"* 11; Bates, *History of the Pennsylvania Volunteers*, 1:907–8; Sypher, *History of the Pennsylvania Reserves*, 90; McPherson, *For Cause and Comrades*, 82–83; Wiley, *The Life of Billy Yank*, 23–25; and Mitchell, *Civil War Soldiers*, 16–19.

12. Phillip G. Ellithorpe to Sister, April 26, 1861, CCHM.

13. Glover, *Bucktailed Wildcats*, 21; Thomson and Rauch, *History of the "Bucktails,"* 11–12; *McKean County Democrat*, May 2, 1861.

14. Phillip G. Ellithorpe to Sister, April 26, 1861, CCHM.

15. Glover, *Bucktailed Wildcats*, 21–23; Thomson and Rauch, *History of the "Bucktails,"* 12–13; Bates, *History of the Pennsylvania Volunteers*, 1:907; Ent, *The Pennsylvania Reserves in the Civil War*, 2, 21.

16. Phillip G. Ellithorpe to Sister, April 26, 1861, CCHM. See also Glover, *Bucktailed Wildcats*, 13–14.

17. For problems associated with rapid recruitment nationally and statewide, see Sears, *Lincoln's Lieutenants*, 37–38, and William J. Miller, *The Training of an Army: Camp Curtin and the North's Civil War* (Shippensburg, PA: White Mane Publishing Company, 1990), v, 3, 14.

18. Glover, *Bucktailed Wildcats*, 16, 23; Thomson and Rauch, *History of the "Bucktails,"* 15; Bates, *History of the Pennsylvania Volunteers*, 1:908; Ent, *The Pennsylvania Reserves in the Civil War*, 1, 3; Sypher, *History of the Pennsylvania Reserves*, 50; Miller, *The Training of an Army*, 5, 18, 23.

19. Glover, *Bucktailed Wildcats*, 25–27; Ent, *The Pennsylvania Reserves in the Civil War*, 3.

20. Miller, *The Training of an Army*, 3–11; Glover, *Bucktailed Wildcats*, 25–27; Ent, *The Pennsylvania Reserves in the Civil War*, 1–3.

21. Phillip G. Ellithorpe to Sister, May 10, 1861, CCHM.

22. Phillip G. Ellithorpe to Ann, May 10, 17, and 19, 1861, CCHM. For forging of camaraderie, see Earl J. Hess, *The Union Soldier in Battle: Enduring the Ordeal of Combat* (Lawrence: University Press of Kansas, 1997), 117–19.

23. Phillip G. Ellithorpe to Unknown, May 4, 1861, CCHM; Phillip G. Ellithorpe to Ann, June 11, 1861, CCHM; *Harrisburg Patriot and Union*, May 18, 21, 1861. "Military regimentation was hard [for raw recruits] to accept" because individualism ran counter to military communality. See Mitchell, *Civil War Soldiers*, 57; McPherson, *For Cause and Comrades*, 47; Peter S. Carmichael, *The War for the Common Soldier: How Men Thought, Fought, and Survived in Civil War Armies* (Chapel Hill: University of North Carolina Press, 2018), 22–24; and Linderman, *Embattled Courage*, 36–37.

24. Phillip G. Ellithorpe to Sister Ann, May 17, 1861, CCHM; *Harrisburg Patriot and Union*, May 18, 21, 1861. See also Miller, *The Training of an Army*, 18–26.

25. Miller, *The Training of an Army*, 15–17; Glover, *Bucktailed Wildcats*, 25–26; Ent, *The Pennsylvania Reserves in the Civil War*, 7.

26. Phillip G. Ellithorpe to Ann, June 11, 1861, CCHM.

27. Phillip G. Ellithorpe to Unknown, May 4, 1861, CCHM; Phillip G. Ellithorpe to Mother, June 18, 1861, CCHM; Phillip G. Ellithorpe Muster Rolls, Military Service Record, NARA. See also Miller, *The Training of an Army*, 18–26, and *Harrisburg Patriot and Union*, May 18, 21, 1861.

28. Phillip G. Ellithorpe to Ann, May 17 and 19, 1861, CCHM.

29. Phillip G. Ellithorpe to Unknown, May 10, 1861, CCHM; Phillip G. Ellithorpe to Ann, May 17, 1861, CCHM. The game Phillip described was likely a precursor of kickball called "Kick the Ball." See Project Protoball at https://protoball.org/kickball, and Wiley, *The Life of Billy Yank*, 169–71.

30. Phillip G. Ellithorpe to Ann, May 19, 1861, CCHM.

31. For soldiers' homesickness, nostalgia, and sentimentality and the power of letter writing as a validation tool, see Carmichael, *The War for the Common Soldier*, 17–131; McPherson, *For Cause and Comrades*, 131–32; Hess, *The Union Soldier in Battle*, 114–18; and Wiley, *The Life of Billy Yank*, 183–85.

32. Phillip G. Ellithorpe to Ann, May 17, 1861, CCHM.

33. See Thomson and Rauch, *History of the "Bucktails,"* 31. For competitive shooting matches held in camp, see Wiley, *The Life of Billy Yank*, 174.

34. Sypher, *History of the Pennsylvania Reserves*, 15–19, 50–53, 57–60; Thomson and Rauch, *History of the "Bucktails,"* 14–17; Ent, *The Pennsylvania Reserves in the Civil War*, 1, 3; Glover, *Bucktailed Wildcats*, 25–27; Miller, *The Training of an Army*, 9, 32–33.

35. Phillip G. Ellithorpe to Ann, May 17, 1861, CCHM.

36. Phillip G. Ellithorpe to Ann, May 17, 1861, CCHM; Phillip G. Ellithorpe, Muster Roll, Military Service Record, NARA. A mess usually consisted of four to eight men, and the position of cook went to the most skilled individual. They often developed into a close-knit group. For more on this "primary group cohesion," or "band of brothers," see McPherson, *For Cause and Comrades*, 85, and Wiley, *The Life of Billy Yank*, 244–45, 340.

37. Sypher, *History of the Pennsylvania Reserves*, 68; Ent, *The Pennsylvania Reserves in the Civil War*, 3; Bates, *History of the Pennsylvania Volunteers*, 1:940; William J. Hardee, *Hardee's Rifle and Light Infantry Tactics* (Memphis, TN: E. C. Kirk & Co., 1861), 6–7. See also Archer Jones, *Civil War Command and Strategy: The Process of Victory and Defeat* (New York: Macmillan, 1992), 26, and Herman Hattaway, *Shades of Blue and Gray: An Introductory Military History of the Civil War* (Columbia: University of Missouri Press, 1997), 44.

38. For biographical information on the officers of the 13th Pennsylvania Reserves, see Sypher, *History of the Pennsylvania Reserves*, 57–84, and Thomson and Rauch, *History of the "Bucktails,"* 18–39. See also Miller, *The Training of an Army*, 18–21; Glover, *Bucktailed Wildcats*, 25, 28–31; Ent, *The Pennsylvania Reserves in the Civil War*, 1, 343–54, 362; and Sears, *Lincoln's Lieutenants*, 94.

39. Phillip G. Ellithorpe to Ann, May 17, 1861, CCHM. Regimental leaders were often father figures to young recruits. See McPherson, *For Cause and Comrades*, 54, and Hess, *The Union Soldier in Battle*, 120.

40. New enlistees required training, discipline, and leadership in the early days of 1861, but these attributes were missing because of the inexperience of "civilian" officers. See McPherson, *For Cause and Comrades*, 46–47, 53–54, 57. See also Wiley, *The Life of Billy Yank*, 26–27, 49; Jones, *Civil War Command and Strategy*, 44; Hattaway, *Shades of Blue and Gray*, 75; Linderman, *Embattled Courage*, 40–41; Jeffry D. Wert, *The Sword of Lincoln: The Army of the Potomac* (New York: Simon & Schuster, 2005), 35; Sears, *Lincoln's Lieutenants*, 125; and Carmichael, *The War for the Common Soldier*, 21.

41. Phillip G. Ellithorpe to Ann, June 11, 1861, CCHM; Phillip Ellithorpe to Mother, June 18, 1861, CCHM. See also Miller, *The Training of an Army*, 36–37; Glover, *Bucktailed Wildcats*, 35; Ent, *The Pennsylvania Reserves in the Civil War*, 6; Thomson and Rauch, *History of the "Bucktails,"* 42–43; Sypher, *History of the Pennsylvania Reserves*, 71.

42. Phillip G. Ellithorpe to Ann, May 17, 1861, CCHM. For Civil War tents, furnishings, and crowded living conditions, see Billings, *Hardtack and Coffee*, 48–53, and Wiley, *The Life of Billy Yank*, 57.

43. Hess, *The Union Soldier in Battle*, 1.

44. Phillip G. Ellithorpe to Mother, June 18, 1861, CCHM. Also see Phillip G. Ellithorpe, Muster Role (May–June 1861), Military Service Record, NARA.

45. The son of Nicholas Biddle, the former president of the Second Bank of the United States, Charles John Biddle was a Princeton-educated lawyer from Philadelphia. At the outbreak of the Mexican War, he raised a company of foot soldiers, served in a regiment led by future Confederate general Joseph E. Johnston, participated in five battles, and was breveted major for gallantry at the Battle of Chapultepec. See Miller, *The Training of an Army*, 36–37; Glover, *Bucktailed Wildcats*, 30–32, 37; Ent, *The Pennsylvania Reserves in the Civil War*, 2, 6; Thomson and Rauch, *History of the "Bucktails,"* 17, 44; Sypher, *History of the Pennsylvania Reserves*, 67–68, 71; and Bates, *History of the Pennsylvania Volunteers*, 1:908–9.

46. Phillip G. Ellithorpe to Mother, June 18, 1861, CCHM.

47. Phillip G. Ellithorpe to Father, June 18, 1861, CCHM. For discussions about hardtack, see Wiley, *The Life of Billy Yank*, 237–39, and Billings, *Hardtack and Coffee*, 113–18.

48. Phillip G. Ellithorpe to Father, June 18, 1861, CCHM. Regarding soldiers' impromptu musical gatherings and dances, see Wiley, *The Life of Billy Yank*, 38, 48–49, 157–69, 174; Billings, *Hardtack and Coffee*, 69; and Bruce C. Kelley and Mark A. Snell, eds., *Bugle Resounding: Music and Musicians of the Civil War Era* (Columbia: University of Missouri Press, 2004), 13, 209.

49. Glover, *Bucktailed Wildcats*, 38; Ent, *The Pennsylvania Reserves in the Civil War*, 7–8; Thomson and Rauch, *History of the "Bucktails,"* 41–44; Sypher, *History of the Pennsylvania Reserves*, 20, 63, 72; Bates, *History of the Pennsylvania Volunteers*, 1: 910.

50. Frederick Phisterer, *New York in the War of the Rebellion*, 2nd ed. (Albany, NY: Weed, Parsons and Co., 1890), 10.

51. Philander D. Ellithorp[e], Muster Roll, Military Service Record, NARA; Philander D. Ellithorpe to Sister, May 18, 1861, CCHM. See also Minard and Merrill, *Allegany County and Its People*, 110–12; Gilbert, *Rushford and Rushford People*, 314–15, 800; and D. E. Buell, *A Brief History of Company B, 27th New York Regiment* (Lyons, NY: Republican Press, 1874), 3.

52. See *Annual Report of the New York Adjutant-General, Roster of the 27th New York Infantry* (Albany, NY: State Printer's Office, 1900), 187; New York State Archives, Civil War Muster Roll Abstracts, 1861–1865 (Albany, NY), 516; New York State Archives, Town Clerk's Register of Men Who Served in the Civil War, 1861–1865 (Albany, NY); and *The Union Army: A History of Military Affairs in the Loyal States, 1861–1865*, 2 vols. (Madison, WI: Federal Publishing Co., 1908), 2:201. In all, Rushford supplied 156 men to serve in the Union army.

53. Philander D. Ellithorpe to Sister, May 18, 1861, CCHM.

54. For the creation of the 27th New York, see *The Union Army*, 2:201; Phisterer, *New York in the War of the Rebellion,* 394; Charles Elihu Slocum, *The Life and Services of Major-General Henry Warner Slocum* (Toledo, OH: Slocum Publishing Co., 1913), 13–14; Charles Bryant Fairchild, *History of the 27th Regiment, New York Volunteers* (Binghamton, NY: Carl and Matthews Printers, 1888), 1, 3, 237, 240, 242–43, 253–54; C. C. Gardiner, "A Reminiscence of the Civil War," paper delivered before the Missouri Commandery of the Military Order of the Loyal Legion, St. Louis, MO, April 2, 1892, 8–13; and William B. Westervelt, *Lights and Shadows of Army Life: From Bull Run to Bentonville* (1886; repr., Shippensburg, PA: White Mane Press, 1998), 1–21.

55. Philander D. Ellithorpe to Friends, June [n.d.], 1861, CCHM. Based on the letter's contents, it was probably written on June 1 or 2. See also Fairchild, *History of the 27th New York Volunteers*, 3; Westervelt, *Lights and Shadows of Army Life*, 3–5; and Henry Seymour Hall, "A Volunteer at the First Bull Run," *War Talks in Kansas, a Series of Papers Read before the Kansas Commandery of the Military Order of the Loyal Legion of the United States (MOLLUS)*, May 4, 1892, 143–59.

56. Fairchild, *History of the 27th New York Volunteers*, 3; Westervelt, *Lights and Shadows of Army Life*, 3–5.

57. Philander D. Ellithorpe to Sister, May 30, 1861, CCHM; Philander D. Ellithorp[e], Roll Call, Military Service Record, NARA; Philander D. Ellithorpe to Friends, June [n.d.], 1861, CCHM.

58. Philander D. Ellithorpe to Friends, June [n.d.], 1861, CCHM.

59. Philander D. Ellithorpe to Friends, June [n.d.], 1861, CCHM; Philander D. Ellithorpe to Sisters, June 12, 1861, CCHM. See also Fairchild, *History of the 27th New York Volunteers*, 5, and Phisterer, *New York in the War of the Rebellion*, 16.

60. Fairchild, *History of the 27th New York Volunteers*, 5. See also Phisterer, *New York in the War of the Rebellion*, 16, and Buell, *A Brief History of Company B, 27th New York Regiment*, 3–4.

61. Philander D. Ellithorpe to Sisters, June 12, 1861 CCHM; Philander D. Ellithorpe to Friends, June [n.d.], 1861, CCHM.

62. Philander D. Ellithorpe to Sister, June 21, 1861, CCHM. See also Fairchild, *History of the 27th New York Volunteers*, 5, and Westervelt, *Lights and Shadows of Army Life*, 5.

63. Philander D. Ellithorpe to Sister, June 21, 1861, CCHM ("Desertion betrayed masculine values of loyalty, honor, and courage"). See Mitchell, *Civil War Soldiers*, 42. See also McPherson, *For Cause and Comrades*, 137–38, 156, 162, 168–69; Linderman, *Embattled Courage*, 43; Hess, *The Union Soldier in Battle*, 96–98; and Carmichael, *The War for the Common Soldier*, 174–229.

64. Philander D. Ellithorpe to Sister, June 21, 1861, CCHM. See also Fairchild, *History of the 27th New York Volunteers*, 5, and Westervelt, *Lights and Shadows of Army Life*, 5.

65. For general disinterest in emancipation in 1861, see Mitchell, *Civil War Soldiers*, 14–15; Billings, *Hardtack and Coffee*, 210–14; McPherson, *For Cause and Comrades*, 117–30; and Harris, *Across the Bloody Chasm*, 90–91.

66. For descriptions of poor camp sanitation practices and rising illnesses, see Wiley, *The Life of Billy Yank*, 34–35, 45–47, 124–27, 133, 152–56, 275; Billings, *Hardtack and Coffee*, 165–95; Linderman, *Embattled Courage*, 115–19; George Washington Adams, *Doctors in Blue: The Medical History of the Union Army in the Civil War* (1952; repr., Baton Rouge: Louisiana State University Press, 1996), 9–19, 225; Paul E. Steiner, *Disease in the Civil War: Natural Biological Warfare in 1861–1865* (Springfield, IL: Charles C. Thomas, 1968), 8–12; and Stewart Brooks, *Civil War Medicine* (Springfield, IL: Charles C. Thomas, 1966), 6–11.

67. For the role of religion in camp life, see Gardiner H. Shattuck Jr., *A Shield and Hiding Place: The Religious Life of the Civil War Armies* (Macon, GA: Mercer University Press, 1987), 14, 44–98; Wiley, *The Life of Billy Yank*, 45–47, 263–74; and McPherson, *For Cause and Comrades*, 63–67.

68. See Wiley, *The Life of Billy Yank*, 275, and McPherson, *Battle Cry of Freedom*, 326.

69. Carmichael, *The War for the Common Soldier*, 101. See also Wiley, *The Life of Billy Yank*, 183–85; Billings, *Hardtack and Coffee*, 62–64; and McPherson, *For Cause and Comrades*, 132–33.

70. George C. Rable, *Fredericksburg! Fredericksburg!* (Chapel Hill: University of North Carolina Press, 2002), 110. See also Wiley, *The Life of Billy Yank*, 183–89, 289; Linderman, *Embattled Courage*, 36–37, 83; Mitchell, *Civil War Soldiers*, 66–67; McPherson, *For Cause and Comrades*, 11, 131–32; and Billings, *Hardtack and Coffee*, 62–64.

71. See McPherson, *For Cause and Comrades*, xi; Carmichael, *The War for the Common Soldier*, 128–29; and Wiley, *The Life of Billy Yank*, 27–28, 185.

72. See 8th U.S. Census, 1860, Pike, Wyoming County, NY; 9th U.S. Census, 1870, Buffalo, Erie County, NY; and *Buffalo City Directory, 1867* (Buffalo, NY: Franklin Publishing House, 1867), 231.

73. For Phillip's awareness of Mother's wishes, see Phillip G. Ellithorpe to Sister, April 26, 1861, CCHM.

74. Rable, *Fredericksburg! Fredericksburg!*, 4. See also Wiley, The *Life of Billy Yank*, 301–3; Mitchell, *Civil War Soldiers*, 56, 60; Linderman, *Embattled Courage*, 26; McPherson, *For Cause and Comrades*, 11; Hess, *The Union Soldier in Battle*, 74; Michael C. C. Adams, *Living Hell: The Dark Side of the Civil War* (Baltimore, MD: Johns Hopkins University Press, 2014), 15; and Carmichael, *The War for the Common Soldier*, 20–21.

75. See McPherson, *For Cause and Comrades*, 131. See also Harris, *Across the Bloody Chasm*, 47–48.

Chapter 3: The Road to Bull Run

1. For early war planning, see Sears, *Lincoln's Lieutenants*, 1–53, and McPherson, *Battle Cry of Freedom*, 313–32.

2. Miller, *The Training of an Army*, 36–37.

3. Jones, *Civil War Command and Strategy*, 41. See also Sypher, *History of the Pennsylvania Reserves*, 20, 63, 69–73; Ent, *The Pennsylvania Reserves in the Civil War*, 6–8; Thomson and Rauch, *History of the "Bucktails,"* 33–44; Glover, *Bucktailed Wildcats*, 33–37; and Bates, *History of the Pennsylvania Volunteers*, 1:909.

4. Phillip G. Ellithorpe to Ann, June 29, 1861, CCHM; Phillip Ellithorpe G. to Sisters, July 5, 1861, CCHM; Phillip G. Ellithorpe to Sister, July 9, 1861, CCHM.

5. See Ent, *The Pennsylvania Reserves in the Civil War*, 8; Thomson and Rauch, *History of the "Bucktails,"* 44–46; Glover, *Bucktailed Wildcats*, 38–39; and Bates, *History of the Pennsylvania Volunteers*, 1:909. For the strategic, economic, and transportation importance of Maryland, see McPherson, *Battle Cry of Freedom*, 284, 287, 297–98.

6. Phillip G. Ellithorpe to Ann, June 29, 1861, CCHM. Also see Ent, *The Pennsylvania Reserves in the Civil War*, 8; Thomson and Rauch, *History of the "Bucktails,"* 44–45; Glover, *Bucktailed Wildcats*, 38; and Sypher, *History of the Pennsylvania Reserves*, 73.

7. Phillip G. Ellithorpe to Ann, June 29, 1861, CCHM; Phillip G. Ellithorpe to Sister, July 19, 1861. For the difficulties in letter writing in the field, see Wiley, *The Life of Billy Yank*, 183–85.

8. Phillip G. Ellithorpe to Ann, June 29, 1861, CCHM; Phillip G. Ellithorpe to Sisters, July 5, 1861, CCHM. Phillip's shabby appearance contradicts the general observation posited by John D. Billings, who stated, "The neatest and most soldierly appearing guardsman was selected as captain's orderly." See Billings, *Hardtack and Coffee*, 189.

9. Glover, *Bucktailed Wildcats*, 40–41; Thomson and Rauch, *History of the "Bucktails,"* 46; Sypher, *History of the Pennsylvania Reserves*, 74–75; Ent, *The Pennsylvania Reserves in the Civil War*, 8; Bates, *History of the Pennsylvania Volunteers*, 1:909; Wert, *The Sword of Lincoln*, 12.

10. Phillip G. Ellithorpe to Sister, July 9, 1861, CCHM.

11. The North commonly named Civil War battles after a physical feature. The South, however, usually named engagements after the nearest town. For battle preparations, see Sears, *Lincoln's Lieutenants*, 40–52; McPherson, *Battle Cry of Freedom*, 347; Ethan S. Rafuse, *A Single Grand Victory: The First Campaign and Battle of Manassas* (Wilmington, DE: Scholarly Resources, 2002): 55, 61–64; John Hennessy, *The First Battle of Manassas: An End to Innocence, July 18–21, 1861* (Lynchburg, VA: H. E. Howard, 1989): 1–5, 10; Edward G. Longacre, *The Early Morning of War: Bull Run, 1861* (Norman: University of Oklahoma Press, 2014), 93–102; and William C. Davis, *Battle of Bull Run: A History of the First Major Campaign of the Civil War* (Baton Rouge: Louisiana State University Press, 1977), 138–46.

12. Phillip G. Ellithorpe to Sister, July 9, 1861, CCHM.

13. Phillip G. Ellithorpe to Sister, July 9, 1861, CCHM.

14. Phillip G. Ellithorpe to Sister, July 19, 1861, CCHM. See also Glover, *Bucktailed Wildcats*, 43; Thomson and Rauch, *History of the "Bucktails,"* 46–54; Sypher, *History of the Pennsylvania Reserves*, 74–77; Ent, *The Pennsylvania Reserves in the Civil War*, 8–9; and Bates, *History of the Pennsylvania Volunteers*, 1:909–10.

15. Phillip G. Ellithorpe to Sister, July 19, 1861, CCHM.

16. Phillip G. Ellithorpe to Sister, July 19, 1861, CCHM.

17. Thomson and Rauch, *History of the "Bucktails,"* 46–47; Sypher, *History of the Pennsylvania Reserves*, 74–76.

18. Phillip G. Ellithorpe to Sister, July 19, 1861, CCHM; Phillip G. Ellithorpe to Cousin Ell, July 23, 1861, CCHM. Ell (Ellisif) Griggs was the oldest child of Oliver Hazard Perry and Lovina Kelley Griggs.

19. Glover, *Bucktailed Wildcats*, 43–45; Sypher, *History of the Pennsylvania Reserves*, 74–76.

20. Phillip G. Ellithorpe to Sister, July 19, 1861, CCHM; Phillip G. Ellithorpe to Cousin Ell, July 23, 1861, CCHM. Phillip was acquainted with Landregan's brother from the wagon shop in Smethport.

21. Glover, *Bucktailed Wildcats*, 44–45; Thomson and Rauch, *History of the "Bucktails,"* 50–54; Sypher, *History of the Pennsylvania Reserves*, 75–77; Ent, *The Pennsylvania Reserves in the Civil War*, 9–10; Bates, *History of the Pennsylvania Volunteers*, 1:909–10.

22. Herman Hattaway and Archer Jones, *How the North Won: A Military History of the Civil War* (Urbana: University of Illinois Press, 1983), 36–39; Ethan S. Rafuse, *Manassas: A Battlefield Guide* (Lincoln: University of Nebraska Press, 2014), 3–4; Sears, *Lincoln's Lieutenants*, 42, 49; Glover, *Bucktailed Wildcats*, 47; Thomson and Rauch, *History of the "Bucktails,"* 57–58.

23. See *The War of the Rebellion: The Official Records of the Union and Confederate Armies*, 70 vols. in 128 parts and four series (Washington, DC: Government Printing Office, 1880–1901). The vast majority of notes in *All for the Union* uses material from Series 1, which includes general orders, correspondence, and reports from officers of all ranks in the field of both armies. Thus, for Biddle's reassignment to the Cheat River District, see *OR*, 2:762–63 (Brig. Gen. William S. Rosecrans). Series 1 is not mentioned because it is a given, and there are no part numbers for the first ten volumes of the *OR*. Later, this study will utilize a limited number of medical department reports and orders from the secretary of war regarding the role of regimental musicians in the Army of the Potomac taken from series 3. These citations will appear as "ser. 3" in order to differentiate them from series 1. To encapsulate, *OR*, 19, pt. 2:32 means volume 19, part 2, page 32 in series 1, and *OR*, ser. 3, 3:24 means series 3, volume 3, page 24.

24. See Rafuse, *A Single Grand Victory*, 51–54, 60–61, 65; Davis, *Battle at Bull Run*, 9–14, 42–48; Hennessy, *The First Battle of Manassas*, 1–3; and Sears, *Lincoln's Lieutenants*, 54–55.

25. Fairchild, *History of the 27th New York Volunteers*, 6; Westervelt, *Lights and Shadows of Army Life*, 5; Davis, *Battle at Bull Run*, 9, 37; Harry Smeltzer, *Bull Runnings: A Journal of the Digitization of a Civil War Battle*, https://bullrunnings.wordpress.com.

26. Philander Ellithorpe to Millie, August 1, 1861, CCHM. See also Fairchild, *History of the 27th New York Volunteers*, 7–8; Westervelt, *Lights and Shadows of Army Life*, 5; Buell, *A Brief History of Company B, 27th New York Regiment*, 4; Phisterer, *New York in the War of the Rebellion*, 394; *The Union Army*, 2:201; and Hall, "A Volunteer at the First Bull Run,"

143–59. For the physical layout of the nation's capital in 1861, see Margaret Leech, *Reveille in Washington, 1860–1865* (New York: Harper and Bros., 1941), 1–13.

27. Philander D. Ellithorpe to Friend, July 20, 1861, CCHM; Philander D. Ellithorpe to Millie, August 1, 1861, CCHM. See also Mitchell, *Civil War Soldiers*, 93.

28. Fairchild, *History of the 27th New York Volunteers*, 8; Westervelt, *Lights and Shadows of Army Life*, 5; Gardiner, "A Reminiscence of the Civil War," 13; Phisterer, *New York in the War of the Rebellion*, 394; *The Union Army*, 2:201; Hattaway, *Shades of Blue and Gray*, 38; Wiley, *The Life of Billy Yank*, 62–63.

29. See Rafuse, *A Single Grand Victory*, 74–76; Wert, *The Sword of Lincoln*, 9–12; Sears, *Lincoln's Lieutenants*, 47–48; Davis, *Battle at Bull Run*, 37–40, 76; Fairchild, *History of the 27th New York Volunteers*, 9; and Westervelt, *Lights and Shadows of Army Life*, 5–6.

30. For the three-pronged strategy, see Rafuse, *A Single Grand Victory*, 72–73, 81–92; Davis, *Battle at Bull Run*, 73–78, 90–101; Hennessy, *The First Battle of Manassas*, 7–9; Longacre, *The Early Morning of War*, 192–98; Wert, *The Sword of Lincoln*, 16; Sears, *Lincoln's Lieutenants*, 55; Hattaway and Jones, *How the North Won*, 40–49; McPherson, *Battle Cry of Freedom*, 339–49; Gardiner, "A Reminiscence of the Civil War," 10; and Hall, "A Volunteer at the First Bull Run," 143–59.

31. For the delays of July 16, see Rafuse, *A Single Grand Victory*, 81–92; Davis, *Battle at Bull Run*, 90–99; Hennessy, *The First Battle of Manassas*, 7–9; Longacre, *The Early Morning of War*, 196–200; Wert, *The Sword of Lincoln*, 116; and Jones, *Civil War Command and Strategy*, 28–32.

32. Fairchild, *History of the 27th New York Volunteers*, 9; Westervelt, *Lights and Shadows of Army Life*, 5–6; Buell, *A Brief History of Company B, 27th New York Regiment*, 4. See also Rafuse, *A Single Grand Victory*, 72; Davis, *Battle at Bull Run*, 72–77; and Sears, *Lincoln's Lieutenants*, 56.

33. See Rafuse, *A Single Grand Victory*, 72–73, 81–92; Davis, *Battle at Bull Run*, 72–78, 90–101; Hennessy, *The First Battle of Manassas*, 7–9; Longacre, *The Early Morning of War*, 192–98; McPherson, *Battle Cry of Freedom*, 335, 339–48; Jones, *Civil War Command and Strategy*, 28–32, 40–42, 58; and Sears, *Lincoln's Lieutenants*, 56.

34. See Hennessy, *The First Battle of Manassas*, 12–27; Davis, *Battle at Bull Run*, 61–131; Rafuse, *A Single Grand Victory*, 103–17; Longacre, *The Early Morning of War*, 248–88; Sears, *Lincoln's Lieutenants*, 56–59; and Wert, *The Sword of Lincoln*, 17–19.

35. Philander D. Ellithorpe to Friend, July 20, 1861, CCHM; *OR*, 2:282–83 (Col. David Hunter), 383–87 (Col. Andrew Porter), 388–89 (Maj. Joseph J. Bartlett). See also Phisterer, *New York in the War of the Rebellion*, 2:264, and *The Union Army*, 2:201.

36. Hall, "A Volunteer at the First Bull Run," 143–59. See also Sears, *Lincoln's Lieutenants*, 55–60; Davis, *Battle at Bull Run*, 152–55; Rafuse, *A Single Grand Victory*, 115–17; Hennessy, *The First Battle of Manassas*, 30–35; Longacre, *The Early Morning of War*, 288; and Wert, *The Sword of Lincoln*, 19.

37. For the flogging and branding incident, see Fairchild, *History of the 27th New York Volunteers*, 10–11; Westervelt, *Lights and Shadows of Army Life*, 6; Gardiner, "A Reminiscence of the Civil War," 11–13; Hall, "A Volunteer at the First Bull Run," 143–59; Smeltzer, *Bull Runnings*, 27th New York: "C" to Friend Black, reprinted in *Orleans (NY) Republican*, August 14, 1861; Hennessy, *The First Battle of Manassas*, 31; Wiley, *The Life of Billy Yank*, 93, 192–223; and Linderman, *Embattled Courage*, 157.

38. See Davis, *Battle at Bull Run*, 155–63; Rafuse, *A Single Grand Victory*, 121; Hennessy, *The First Battle of Manassas*, 35–40; Longacre, *The Early Morning of War*, 288–96; Wert, *The Sword of Lincoln*, 19–20; Sears, *Lincoln's Lieutenants*, 64–65, 78; and Jones, *Civil War Command and Strategy*, 59, 133.

39. *OR*, 2:388 (Maj. Joseph J. Bartlett). See also McPherson, *Battle Cry of Freedom*, 330; Sears, *Lincoln's Lieutenants*, 62–63; Hall, "A Volunteer at the First Bull Run," 143–59; and Wiley, *The Life of Billy Yank*, 66.

40. Davis, *Battle at Bull Run*, 155–59, 167–71; Rafuse, *A Single Grand Victory*, 117–23; Hennessy, *The First Battle of Manassas*, 37–39; Longacre, *The Early Morning of War*, 320–21; Wert, *The Sword of Lincoln*, 19; Sears, *Lincoln's Lieutenants*, 62–65; Gardiner, "A Reminiscence of the Civil War," 14–15; Hall, "A Volunteer at the First Bull Run," 143–59; Smeltzer, *Bull Runnings*, 27th New York: Lt. Samuel M. Harmon (Co. I), July 28, 1861, to *Holmesville (NY) Weekly Tribune*, August 23, 1861; *OR*, 2:388–89 (Col. Joseph J. Bartlett). For the chain of command as it affected Philander, see appendix A.

41. Fairchild, *History of the 27th New York Volunteers*, 11–12; Westervelt, *Lights and Shadows of Army Life*, 11–12; Buell, *A Brief History of Company B, 27th New York Regiment*, 5; Smeltzer, *Bull Runnings*, 27th New York: Charles N. Elliott, Co. I to Friend James, July 27, 1861. See also Davis, *Battle at Bull Run*, 167–69; Rafuse, *A Single Grand Victory*, 119–27; Hennessy, *The First Battle of Manassas*, 36–48; Longacre, *The Early Morning of War*, 289–90, 315–27; Wert, *The Sword of Lincoln*, 21; and Sears, *Lincoln's Lieutenants*, 67–68.

42. Smeltzer, *Bull Runnings*, 27th New York: Lt. Samuel M. Harmon (Co. I), July 28, 1861 to *Holmesville (NY) Weekly Tribune*, August 23, 1861. See also Fairchild, *History of the 27th New York Volunteers*, 11–12; Westervelt, *Lights and Shadows of Army Life*, 15–16; and Gardiner, "A Reminiscence of the Civil War," 15.

43. Fairchild, *History of the 27th New York Volunteers*, 11–12; Westervelt, *Lights and Shadows of Army Life*, 15–16; Gardiner, "A Reminiscence of the Civil War," 15; Smeltzer, *Bull Runnings*, 27th New York: Lt. Samuel M. Harmon (Co. I), July 28, 1861 to *Holmesville (NY) Weekly Tribune*, August 23, 1861; *OR*, 2:388–89 (Maj. Joseph J. Bartlett). See also Davis, *Battle at Bull Run*, 171–89; Rafuse, *A Single Grand Victory*, 129–39; Rafuse, *Manassas*, 15–27; Hennessy, *The First Battle of Manassas*, 49–60; Longacre, *The Early Morning of War*, 323–41; and Wert, *The Sword of Lincoln*, 21–22.

44. See *Tioga County Agitator*, June 26, 1861, in Glover, *Bucktailed Wildcats*, 283n1. Says Wiley, "The battle cry of the men in blue was different from that of the Rebels. The standard Yankee version was a deeply intoned hurrah or huzza" intended to relieve tension. See Wiley, *The Life of Billy Yank*, 73–74.

45. Philander D. Ellithorpe to Millie, August 1, 1861, CCHM; Gilbert, *Rushford and Rushford People*, 338; Minard and Merrill, *Allegany County and Its People*, 800. For the attack on the stone house, see *OR*, 2:388–89 (Maj. Joseph J. Bartlett); Gardiner, "A Reminiscence of the Civil War," 15; Hall, "A Volunteer at the First Bull Run," 143–59; Davis, *Battle at Bull Run*, 173–88; Rafuse, *A Single Grand Victory*, 146–47; Hennessy, *The First Battle of Manassas*, 66–67; Longacre, *The Early Morning of War*, 345–53; and Wert, *The Sword of Lincoln*, 22–23.

46. Fairchild, *History of the 27th New York Volunteers*, 12–14; Westervelt, *Lights and Shadows of Army Life*, 15–17; Hall, "A Volunteer at the First Bull Run," 143–59; Buell, *A Brief History of Company B, 27th New York Regiment*, 5–6; Gardiner, "A Reminiscence of the Civil War," 16; Smeltzer, *Bull Runnings*, 27th New York: Samuel M. Harmon (Co. I) July

28, 1861, to *Holmesville (NY) Weekly Tribune*, August 23, 1861, and Pvt. Worcester Burrows (Co. C) to *Franklin Visitor*, August 14, 1861; *OR*, 2:388–89 (Maj. Joseph J. Bartlett). See also Davis, *Battle at Bull Run*, 192–95; Hennessy, *The First Battle of Manassas*, 66–68; Rafuse, *A Single Grand Victory*, 146; Rafuse, *Manassas*, 23–39, 47–51; Longacre, *The Early Morning of War*, 342–50; Wert, *The Sword of Lincoln*, 22–23; Sears, *Lincoln's Lieutenants*, 68–69; and Slocum, *The Life and Services of Major-General Henry Warner Slocum*, 14–15.

47. Philander D. Ellithorpe to Mille, August 1, 1861, CCHM.

48. Rafuse, *A Single Grand Victory*, 144. See also Davis, *Battle at Bull Run*, 188, 203; Hennessy, *The First Battle of Manassas*, 67–74; Rafuse, *A Single Grand Victory*, 143–51; and Longacre, *The Early Morning of War*, 355–57.

49. Davis, *Battle at Bull Run*, 182–216; Hennessy, *The First Battle of Manassas*, 75–100; Rafuse, *A Single Grand Victory*, 157–63; Longacre, *The Early Morning of War*, 351–99, 402; Wert, *The Sword of Lincoln*, 23–24; Sears, *Lincoln's Lieutenants*, 60–61; Emory M. Thomas, *Bold Dragoon: The Life of J. E. B. Stuart* (New York: Harper & Row, 1986), 77–81.

50. Davis, *Battle at Bull Run*, 211–16; Hennessy, *The First Battle of Manassas*, 82–102, 126; Rafuse, *A Single Grand Victory*, 163; Longacre, *The Early Morning of War*, 377–79, 402–9; Wert, *The Sword of Lincoln*, 23–24; Sears, *Lincoln's Lieutenants*, 72–73; John A. Simpson, "The Rebel Yell in American Oral Tradition," unpublished essay, 1989.

51. *OR*, 2:389 (Maj. Joseph J. Bartlett). See also Fairchild, *History of the 27th New York Volunteers*, 14; Westervelt, *Lights and Shadows of Army Life*, 17; Smeltzer, *Bull Runnings*, 27th New York: Samuel M. Harmon (Co. I), July 28, 1861, to *Holmesville (NY) Weekly Tribune*, August 23, 1861; Hall, "A Volunteer at the First Bull Run," 143–59; Hess, *The Union Soldier in Battle*, 47, 56, 153; Davis, *Battle at Bull Run*, 217–23; Hennessy, *The First Battle of Manassas*, 102–18; Rafuse, *A Single Grand Victory*, 169–83; Longacre, *The Early Morning of War*, 409–39; Wert, *The Sword of Lincoln*, 24–25; and Sears, *Lincoln's Lieutenants*, 73.

52. One eyewitness in Philander's regiment claims that "the frantic stampede" had begun at Sudley Ford. See Fairchild, *History of the 27th New York Volunteers*, 14.

53. Fairchild, *History of the 27th New York Volunteers*, 14. See also see Smeltzer, *Bull Runnings*, 27th New York: Samuel M. Harmon (Co. I), July 28, 1861, to *Homesville (NY) Weekly Tribune*, August 23, 1861; Davis, *Battle at Bull Run*, 233–55; Hennessy, *The First Battle of Manassas*, 120–21; Rafuse, *A Single Grand Victory*, 195; Longacre, *The Early Morning of War*, 451–70, 487–89; Wert, *The Sword of Lincoln*, 25–27; and Sears, *Lincoln's Lieutenants*, 73–75.

54. Fairchild, *History of the 27th New York Volunteers*, 14; Westervelt, *Lights and Shadows of Army Life*, 17; Wiley, *The Life of Billy Yank*, 77–78, 276; Buell, *A Brief History of Company B, 27th New York Regiment*, 6; Gardiner, "A Reminiscence of the Civil War," 17–18; Hall, "A Volunteer at the First Bull Run," 143–59.

55. This study will list casualty figures as "k/w/m/c." For casualty figures, see *OR*, 2:387 (casualties); Rafuse, *A Single Grand Victory*, 203; Davis, *The Battle at Bull Run*, 245–46; Hennessy, *The First Battle of Manassas*, 81, 131; Jones, *Civil War Command and Strategy*, 34; Longacre, *The Early Morning of War*, 395; Wert, *The Sword of Lincoln*, 26–27; and Sears, *Lincoln's Lieutenants*, 76.

56. Fairchild, *History of the 27th New York Volunteers*, 14.

57. Fairchild, *History of the 27th New York Volunteers*, 14.

58. Philander D. Ellithorpe to Millie, August 1, 1861, CCHM; Smeltzer, *Bull Runnings*, 27th New York: Pvt. Charles N. Elliot (Co. D) to Friend James, July 27, 1861, in *Chenango (N.Y.) American*, August 8, 1861. See also Wiley, *The Life of Billy Yank*, 7–82;

Rable, *Fredericksburg! Fredericksburg!*, 107; and John R. Neff, *Honoring the Civil War Dead: Commemoration and the Problem of Reconciliation* (Lawrence: University Press of Kansas, 2005), 26–28.

59. See Wert, *The Sword of Lincoln*, 28–37; Stephen W. Sears, *George B. McClellan: The Young Napoleon* (New York: Ticknor and Fields, 1988), 92–95, 103; McPherson, *Battle Cry of Freedom*, 349, 359; Jones, *Civil War Command and Strategy*, 43; and Sears, *Lincoln's Lieutenants*, 79–81. On November 1, 1861, the Federals' cause suffered one other command loss when General in Chief Winfield Scott resigned. President Lincoln eventually replaced him with Maj. Gen. Henry W. Halleck the following March.

60. The reputation of officers was always being scrutinized by their men on a sliding scale depending on their most recent army performance on the battlefield. See McPherson, *For Cause and Comrades*, 60, and Wiley, *The Life of Billy Yank*, 67–68.

61. Fairchild, *History of the 27th New York Volunteers*, 21–22; Westervelt, *Lights and Shadows of Army Life*, 13, 17, 21.

62. Wiley, *The Life of Billy Yank*, 333; McPherson, *For Cause and Comrades*, 6; Carmichael, *The War for the Common Soldier*, 33, 44–45, 52, 61–65.

63. Philander D. Ellithorpe to Millie, August 1, 1861, CCHM; Philander D. Ellithorpe to Friend, August 7, 1861, CCHM. See also Wiley, *The Life of Billy Yank*, 82, and Carmichael, *The War for the Common Soldier*, 81–82, 128–29.

64. Phillip G. Ellithorpe to Sister, July 9, 1861, CCHM. See also McPherson, *For Cause and Comrades*, 139, and Hess, *The Union Soldier in Battle*, 124–25.

65. Philander D. Ellithorpe to Sister, August 7, 1861, CCHM.

66. Bad news from home led to demoralization since soldiers could not play the role of family protector while serving in the army. See Wiley, *The Life of Billy Yank*, 289; Rable, *Fredericksburg! Fredericksburg!*, 97; Mitchell, *Civil War Soldiers*, 67; McPherson, *For Cause and Comrades*, 133; and Hess, *The Union Soldier in Battle*, 124–25, 195.

67. Rable, *Fredericksburg! Fredericksburg!*, 400. See also McPherson, *For Cause and Comrades*, 148.

Chapter 4: Retooling the Army of the Potomac

1. Wert, *The Sword of Lincoln*, 32–38, 45; Sears, *Lincoln's Lieutenants*, 91, 108, 125; Sears, *The Young Napoleon*, 112, 118. See also Phillippe, Comte de Paris, "McClellan Organizing the Grand Army," in Robert Underwood Johnson and Clarence Clough Buel, eds., *Battles and Leaders of the Civil War*, 4 vols. (New York: Century, 1884–1888), 2:112–22.

2. Ent, *The Pennsylvania Reserves in the Civil War*, 9. See also Glover, *Bucktailed Wildcats*, 45–47; Thomson and Rauch, *History of the "Bucktails,"* 54–57; Sypher, *History of the Pennsylvania Reserves*, 77, 101; and Bates, *History of the Pennsylvania Volunteers*, 1:910.

3. See Ent, *The Pennsylvania Reserves in the Civil War*, 11–13; Glover, *Bucktailed Wildcats*, 49; Thomson and Rauch, *History of the "Bucktails,"* 59–60; Sypher, *History of the Pennsylvania Reserves*, 77; and Miller, *The Training of an Army*, 44–49.

4. Phillip G. Ellithorpe to Father, Mother, Sisters, August 1, 1861, CCHM.

5. Despite various spellings of this neighborhood, this study will utilize the standard usage during the Civil War: Tenallytown.

6. The all-Pennsylvania Reserves was the only division in the Army of the Potomac with volunteers entirely from one state. See Wert, *The Sword of Lincoln*, 38. Ent, *The*

Pennsylvania Reserves in the Civil War, 11–12, 16–17; Glover, *Bucktailed Wildcats*, 48–50; Thomson and Rauch, *History of the "Bucktails,"* 56–60; Sypher, *History of the Pennsylvania Reserves*, 92–93, 103; Bates, *History of the Pennsylvania Volunteers*, 1:910; Benjamin Franklin Cooling, *Symbol, Sword, and Shield* (Hamden, CT: Archon Books, 1975), 85; and Evan Morrison Woodward, *Our Campaigns; or, The Marches, Bivouacs, Battles, and Incidents of Camp Life and History of Our Regiment* [2nd Pennsylvania Reserves] (Philadelphia: John E. Potter and Co., 1865), 44–61.

7. Ent, *The Pennsylvania Reserves in the Civil War*, 15–19; Glover, *Bucktailed Wildcats*, 51; Sypher, *History of the Pennsylvania Reserves*, 20, 114; Thomson and Rauch, *History of the "Bucktails,"* 57. See also Wert, *The Sword of Lincoln*, 32–38, 45; Sears, *Lincoln's Lieutenants*, 91, 108, 125; and Sears, *The Young Napoleon*, 112, 118.

8. Ent, *The Pennsylvania Reserves in the Civil War*, 15–16; Glover, *Bucktailed Wildcats*, 50; Thomson and Rauch, *History of the "Bucktails,"* 62–63; Sypher, *History of the Pennsylvania Reserves*, 103; Bates, *History of the Pennsylvania Volunteers*, 1:910.

9. Phillip G. Ellithorpe to Father, Mother, Sisters, August 1, 1861, CCHM.

10. Phillip G. Ellithorpe to Sister, August 4, 1861, CCHM. For the soldier's use of cheerfulness as a letter-writing tool, see Carmichael, *The War for the Common Soldier*, 66–99.

11. Phillip G. Ellithorpe to Sister, September 13, 1861, CCHM. See also Glover, *Bucktailed Wildcats*, 51; Thomson and Rauch, *History of the "Bucktails,"* 64–65; Sypher, *History of the Pennsylvania Reserves*, 103; and Ent, *The Pennsylvania Reserves in the Civil War*, 16.

12. Phillip Ellithorpe to unknown, ca. August 20, 1861, CCHM; Phillip Ellithorpe to Sister, September 13, 1861, CCHM. See also *McKean County Democrat*, August 21, 30, 1861; Pennsylvania State Archive, Civil War Veterans' Card File, 1861-66, File B.

13. Philander D. Ellithorpe to Sister, August 7, 1861, CCHM. See also Fairchild, *History of the 27th New York Volunteers*, 19, and Westervelt, *Lights and Shadows of Army Life*, 13–17.

14. Cooling, *Symbol, Sword, and Shield*, 42–45; Benjamin Franklin Cooling, *Mr. Lincoln's Forts: A Guide to the Civil War Defenses of Washington* (Lanham, MD: Scarecrow Press, 2010), 38–43; Hattaway, *Shades of Blue and Gray*, 81; Leech, *Reveille in Washington*, 80, 112.

15. Fairchild, *History of the 27th New York Volunteers*, 19–20; Westervelt, *Lights and Shadows of Army Life*, 16–17, 21. See also *The Union Army*, 2:201, and Slocum, *The Life and Services of Major-General Henry Warner Slocum*, 16–18.

16. Fairchild, *History of the 27th New York Volunteers*, 21–22; Westervelt, *Lights and Shadows of Army Life*, 24. See also Cooling, *Symbol, Sword, and Shield*, 83, 85, and Cooling, *Mr. Lincoln's Forts*, 68–69.

17. Philander D. Ellithorpe to Sister, September 29, 1861, CCHM.

18. See Conforti, *Imagining New England*, 31–78. Following the northern branch of the Burleson family in Connecticut, Vermont, and New York, see Hezekiah Spencer Sheldon, *Documentary History of Suffield in the Colony and Province of the Massachusetts Bay in New England, 1660–1749*, 3 vols. (Springfield, MA: Clark W. Bryan, 1879), 1:5–7, 14, 24, 27–31, 71–72; Hinman, *A Catalogue of the First Puritan Settlers of the Colony of Connecticut*, 409; D. Hamilton Hurd, *History of New London County, Connecticut: With Biographical Sketches of Many of Its Pioneers and Prominent Men* (Philadelphia: J. W. Lewis & Co., 1882), 404–18, 595–604; Daniel Lyon Phillips, *A History: Being a History of the Town of Griswold, Connecticut* (New Haven, CT: Tuttle, Morehouse & Taylor Co., 1929); Lewis Cass Aldrich, *History of Franklin and Grand Isle Counties, Vermont* (Syracuse, NY: D. Mason and Co., 1891), 501–12, 525–40; Henry Francis Walling, *Map of the Counties of Franklin and Grand Isle,*

Vermont (Boston: Baker, Tilden and Co., 1857); Lewis Cass Aldrich, *History of Bennington County, Vermont: With Illustrations and Biographical Sketches of Some of Its Prominent Men and Pioneers* (Syracuse, NY: D. Mason and Co., 1889), 429–36; and D. Hamilton Hurd, *History of Otsego County, New York: With Illustrations and Biographical Sketches of Some of Its Prominent Men and Pioneers* (Philadelphia: Everts and Fariss, 1878), 97–108.

19. See William Adams, ed., *Historical Gazetteer and Biographical Memorial of Cattaraugus County, New York* (Syracuse, NY: Lyman, Horton Co., 1893), 673–78; L. H. Everts, *History of Cattaraugus County, New York: With Illustrations and Biographical Sketches of Some of Its Prominent Men and Pioneers* (Philadelphia: Everts and Co., 1879), 395; 6th U.S. Census, Freedom, Cattaraugus County, NY, 1830; Office of County Clerk, Cattaraugus County, Little Valley, NY, *Land Deeds, 1824–1830*; and Livsey, *Western New York Land Transactions, 1825–1835*, 137, 169.

20. For Asa's acknowledgment of an antebellum romantic interest, see Asa R. Burleson to Ann Ellithorpe, October 10, 1861, CCHM. See also William Willford and Franklyn Curtiss-Wedge, *History of Fillmore County, Minnesota*, 2 vols. (Chicago: H. C. Cooper and Co., 1912), 2:774.

21. Asa R. Burleson, Military Service Record, NARA; G. G. Benedict, *Vermont in the Civil War: A History*, 2 vols. (Burlington, VT: The Free Press, 1886), 1:180–82, 235; Theodore S. Peck, *Revised Roster of Vermont during the War of the Rebellion, 1861-66* (Montpelier, VT: Watchman Publishing Co., 1892), 142–76; *The Union Army*, 1:110–11. The "Old Brigade" numbered the 2nd, 3rd, 4th, 5th, and 6th Vermont and the 26th New Jersey.

22. On May 4, 1861, the War Department issued General Order No. 15, permitting each regiment one full brass band comprising a principal conductor and twenty-four musicians. See Kenneth E. Olson, *Music and Musket: Bands and Bandsmen of the American Civil War* (Westport, CT: Greenwood Press, 1981), 61–71, and Kelley and Snell, *Bugle Resounding*, 13, 30. See also Asa R. Burleson, Military Service Record, Muster Rolls, NARA; Peck, *Revised Roster of Vermont during the War of the Rebellion*, 145; Benedict, *Vermont in the Civil War*, 1:182.

23. Jonathan Remington to E. O. Eddy, November 1, 26, 1861, in Jonathan Remington Papers, Special Collections, University of Vermont, Montpelier, VT. See also Olson, *Music and Musket*, 61–71, and Kelley and Snell, *Bugle Resounding*, 13, 30.

24. Asa R. Burleson, Military Service Record, Muster Rolls, NARA; Willford and Curtiss-Wedge, *History of Fillmore County, Minnesota*, 2:774–75; Benedict, *Vermont in the Civil War*, 1:181–83; *The Union Army*, 1:110–11.

25. Philander D. Ellithorpe to Sister, August 7, 1861, CCHM; Phillip G. Ellithorpe to Sister Ann, September 13, 1861, CCHM.

26. Phillip G. Ellithorpe to Sister Ann, September 19, 1861, CCHM. A "wrong letter" was one that notified soldiers on the war front about troubles at home that left them powerless to act, lend assistance, or offer comfort to distressed family members. News of such events struck a blow to soldier morale and posed a threat to masculine sensibilities as defenders of the family. See McPherson, *For Cause and Comrades*, 13, and Hess, *The Union Soldier in Battle*, 124–25.

27. Phillip G. Ellithorpe to Sister Ann, September 19, 1861, CCHM.

28. The lyrics were unattached in the Ellithorpe Family Collection, but they were likely included in the heartfelt missive, Phillip G. Ellithorpe to Sister Ann, September 19, 1861, CCHM.

29. Phillip G. Ellithorpe to Sister Ann, September 19, 1861, CCHM.

30. Philander D. Ellithorpe to Sisters, September 29, 1861, CCHM.
31. Asa R. Burleson to Ann, October 9, 1861, CCHM.
32. Asa R. Burleson to Ann, October 10, 1861, CCHM.
33. For a similar case study, see Carmichael, *The War for the Common Soldier*, 103–13.
34. Asa R. Burleson to Ann, October 10, 1861, CCHM.
35. Philander D. Ellithorpe to Sisters, September 29, 1861, CCHM; Fairchild, *History of the 27th New York Volunteers*, 22. See also Jonathan Remington to E. O. Eddy, November 1, 26, 1861, in Jonathan Remington Papers, Special Collections, University of Vermont, Montpelier VT; Benedict, *Vermont in the Civil War*, 1:239–40.
36. Fairchild, *History of the 27th New York Volunteers*, 22. See also Benedict, *Vermont in the Civil War*, 1:183, 2:237–40.
37. Glover, *Bucktailed Wildcats*, 53–54; Thomson and Rauch, *History of the "Bucktails,"* 66–68; Sypher, *History of the Pennsylvania Reserves*, 123–24; Ent, *The Pennsylvania Reserves in the Civil War*, 27.
38. *OR*, 5:473–74, 480–81 (Brig. Gen. George A. McCall); Ent, *The Pennsylvania Reserves in the Civil War*, 27–29; Glover, *Bucktailed Wildcats*, 53; Thomson and Rauch, *History of the "Bucktails,"* 68–69; Sypher, *History of the Pennsylvania Reserves*, 124–26.
39. For the disastrous Ball's Bluff campaign, see Wert, *The Sword of Lincoln*, 45–48; Sears, *Lincoln's Lieutenants*, 112–19; Sears, *The Young Napoleon*, 119–22; and McPherson, *Battle Cry of Freedom*, 361.
40. Wert, *The Sword of Lincoln*, 52–53; Sears, *Lincoln's Lieutenants*, 131–32, 146. See also Glover, *Bucktailed Wildcats*, 56; Thomson and Rauch, *History of the "Bucktails,"* 69, 72; Sypher, *History of the Pennsylvania Reserves*, 121, 126; Ent, *The Pennsylvania Reserves in the Civil War*, 28–29; and Bates, *History of the Pennsylvania Volunteers*, 1:910.
41. Phillip G. Ellithorpe, Hospital Muster Roll (August 25, 1861), Military Service Record, NARA; Phillip G. Ellithorpe, Company I Muster Roll (October 31, 1861), Military Service Record, NARA. See also Phillip G. Ellithorpe to Sister, November 13, 1861, CCHM; Phillip G. Ellithorpe to Respected Friend, December 8, 1861, CCHM; J. K. Haffey to Ann, October 21, 1861, CCHM; and Philander D. Ellithorpe to Sisters, November 17, 1861, CCHM. See also Ent, *The Pennsylvania Reserves in the Civil War*, 28–29, 41, and Sypher, *History of the Pennsylvania Reserves*, 121.
42. Phillip G. Ellithorpe to Friend Nell, December 22, 1861, CCHM.
43. See Phillip G. Ellithorpe to Sister, November 13, 1861, CCHM; Sypher, *History of the Pennsylvania Reserves*, 123; and *Pennsylvania Civil War Index Cards*, C.
44. Phillip G. Ellithorpe to Sister, November 13, 1861, CCHM. See also Benedict, *Vermont in the Civil War*, 1:184, 237–39.
45. Phillip G. Ellithorpe to Sister Permelia, December 26, 1861, CCHM; Phillip G. Ellithorpe to Sister Ann, December 27, 1861, CCHM. For holiday boxes, see Billings, *Hardtack and Coffee*, 217–20; Ent, The *Pennsylvania Reserves in the Civil War*, 39; and Rable, *Fredericksburg! Fredericksburg!*, 102.
46. Phillip G. Ellithorpe to Sister Permelia, December 26, 1861, CCHM; Phillip G. Ellithorpe to Sister Ann, December 27, 1861, CCHM; Phillip G. Ellithorpe to Sisters, January 6, 1862, CCHM. "Civil War soldiers were notorious for straying from quarters." See Carmichael, *The War for the Common Soldier*, 41.
47. Phillip G. Ellithorpe to Sister Permelia, December 31, 1861, January 6 and 19, 1862, CCHM.

48. Glover, *Bucktailed Wildcats*, 66–70, 82; Thomson and Rauch, *History of the "Bucktails,"* 69–72; Sypher, *History of the Pennsylvania Reserves*, 143; Ent, *The Pennsylvania Reserves in the Civil War*, 30, 39. A similar two-hour snowball fight broke out among the 27th New York under the direction of Bartlett. See Buell, *A Brief History of Company B, 27th New York Regiment*, 8.

49. Philander D. Ellithorpe to Sisters, September 29, 1861, CCHM.

50. Philander D. Ellithorpe to Sisters, November 17, 1861, CCHM. See also Fairchild, *History of the 27th New York Volunteers*, 23, and Westervelt, *Lights and Shadows of Army Life*, 24.

51. Philander D. Ellithorpe to Sister, January 20, 1862, CCHM.

52. Philander D. Ellithorpe to Sisters, September 29, 1861, November 17, 1861, December 8, 1861, January 20, 1862, and May 1, 1862, CCHM; Philander D. Ellithorpe, Military Service Record, NARA. See also Fairchild, *History of the 27th New York Volunteers*, 27–28, and Westervelt, *Lights and Shadows of Army Life*, 24.

53. Glover, *Bucktailed Wildcats*, 56–57; Thomson and Rauch, *History of the "Bucktails,"* 70; Sypher, *History of the Pennsylvania Reserves*, 70; Ent, *The Pennsylvania Reserves in the Civil War*, 38; Fairchild, *History of the 27th New York Volunteers*, 24–26; Westervelt, *Lights and Shadows of Army Life*, 24. See also Wert, *The Sword of Lincoln*, 49–51; Sears, *Lincoln's Lieutenants*, 126; and Sears, *The Young Napoleon*, 134.

54. Philander D. Ellithorpe to Sisters, November 17, 23, and 30, 1861, CCHM.

55. Phillip G. Ellithorpe to Sisters, January 6, 1862, CCHM; Phillip G. Ellithorpe to Ann, March 14, 1862, CCHM. Unfortunately, Phillip's photograph did not survive the war.

56. For the corps system, see Wert, *The Sword of Lincoln*, 49–57; Sears, *Lincoln's Lieutenants*, 121–22, 139–40, 151, 168–69; Sears, *The Young Napoleon*, 125–26, 160; Clifford Dowdey, *The Seven Days: The Emergence of Lee* (1964; repr., Lincoln: University of Nebraska Press, 1993), 31–38; and Ent, *The Pennsylvania Reserves in the Civil War*, 37–38. For the chain of command as it affected the Ellithorpe brothers, see appendix A.

57. Glover, *Bucktailed Wildcats*, 68; Thomson and Rauch, *History of the "Bucktails,"* 81–85; Sypher, *History of the Pennsylvania Reserves*, 148; Ent, *The Pennsylvania Reserves in the Civil War*, 40; Bates, *History of the Pennsylvania Volunteers*, 1:910–11.

58. *OR*, 5:32, 290–92 (Maj. Gen. George B. McClellan), 455–56, 474–47 (Brig. Gen. George A. McCall), 477–80 (Brig. Gen. E. O. C. Ord), 481–82 (Col. Thomas L. Kane). See also Glover, *Bucktailed Wildcats*, 59–60; Thomson and Rauch, *History of the "Bucktails,"* 73–74; Sypher, *History of the Pennsylvania Reserves*, 128–29; Ent, *The Pennsylvania Reserves in the Civil War*, 30–36; and Bates, *History of the Pennsylvania Volunteers*, 1:911.

59. Glover, *Bucktailed Wildcats*, 60–62; Thomson and Rauch, *History of the "Bucktails,"* 74–77; Sypher, *History of the Pennsylvania Reserves*, 130–35; Ent, *The Pennsylvania Reserves in the Civil War*, 31–33; Bates, *History of the Pennsylvania Volunteers*, 1:911.

60. Sears, *Lincoln's Lieutenants*, 146. See also *OR*, 5:474–76 (Brig. Gen. George A. McCall), 477–80 (Brig. Gen. E. O. C. Ord), 481–82 (Col. Thomas L. Kane), 488–89 (Capt. Hezekiah Easton), 489 (casualties); Glover, *Bucktailed Wildcats*, 64–65; Thomson and Rauch, *History of the "Bucktails,"* 79–80; Sypher, *History of the Pennsylvania Reserves*, 133–39; Ent, *The Pennsylvania Reserves in the Civil War*, 35–36; and Bates, *History of the Pennsylvania Volunteers*, 1:911.

61. Phillip G. Ellithorpe to Friend Nell, December 22, 1861, CCHM; Phillip G. Ellithorpe to Sister Ann, December 27, 1861, CCHM; Phillip G. Ellithorpe to Sister Permelia, December 31, 1861, CCHM.

62. Phillip G. Ellithorpe to Sisters, January 19, 1862, CCHM.

63. Phillip G. Ellithorpe to Sisters, December 27, 1861, January 19, 1862, and February 2, 1862, CCHM. For similar nefarious activities in Asa's 5th Vermont, see Jonathan Remington to E. O. Eddy, January 24, 1862, and Jonathan Remington to Brother Thill, February 1, 1862, March 19, 1862, March 21, 1862, in Jonathan Remington Papers, Special Collections, University of Vermont, Montpelier VT.

64. Phillip G. Ellithorpe to Sisters, January 19, 1862, CCHM; Phillip G. Ellithorpe to Father, March 20, 1862, CCHM. See also Glover, *Bucktailed Wildcats*, 68; Thomson and Rauch, *History of the "Bucktails,"* 81–85, 215–16; Sypher, *History of the Pennsylvania Reserves*, 148, 392–95; Ent, *The Pennsylvania Reserves in the Civil War*, 40; and Bates, *History of the Pennsylvania Volunteers*, 1:910–11.

65. Phillip G. Ellithorpe to Sisters, February 16, 21, and 23, 1862, CCHM. See also Benedict, *Vermont in the Civil War*, 2:184.

66. For the Urbanna Plan, see Wert, *The Sword of Lincoln*, 59–60; Sears, *Lincoln's Lieutenants*, 148–54, 160–64 ; Stephen W. Sears, *To the Gates of Richmond: The Peninsula Campaign* (Boston: Houghton Mifflin, 1992): 5, 13–14; Sears, *The Young Napoleon*, 147–51, 163–64; Dowdey, *The Seven Days*, 34; and Bryan K. Burton, *Extraordinary Circumstances: The Seven Days Battles* (Bloomington: Indiana University Press, 2001), 3–4.

67. Glover, *Bucktailed Wildcats*, 70–72; Thomson and Rauch, *History of the "Bucktails,"* 87–90; Sypher, *History of the Pennsylvania Reserves*, 159–60, 167–70; Ent, *The Pennsylvania Reserves in the Civil War*, 38–41; Bates, *History of the Pennsylvania Volunteers*, 1:911.

68. Phillip G. Ellithorpe to Ann, March 15, 1862, CCHM; Phillip G. Ellithorpe to Father, March 16 and 20, 1862, CCHM.

69. Philander D. Ellithorpe to Cousin Ell, March 9, 1862, CCHM; Philander D. Ellithorpe, Muster Rolls, Military Service Record, NARA. See also Fairchild, *History of the 27th New York Volunteers*, 28–29, and Westervelt, *Lights and Shadows of Army Life*, 36.

70. Benedict, *Vermont in the Civil War*, 1:240–43.

71. Philander D. Ellithorpe to Sisters, November 19, 1861, CCHM; Philander D. Ellithorpe to Sister, January 20, 1862, CCHM.

72. See Phillip G. Ellithorpe to Sisters, November 19, 1861, January 19, 1862, and February 2, 11, 21, and 23, 1862, CCHM.

73. Phillip G. Ellithorpe, Muster Record (January–February 1862), Military Service Record, NARA.

74. Wiley, *The Life of Billy Yank*, 293; McPherson, *For Cause and Comrades*, 58.

75. For living arrangements, see New York State Census of 1855, Wyoming County and Allegany County, and 8th U.S. Census, 1860, Pike, Wyoming County and Rushford, Allegany County, NY.

76. The quote is taken from the title of Sears's book for the upcoming campaign, *To the Gates of Richmond.*

Chapter 5: The Fight for Richmond: The Peninsula Campaign and the Seven Days

1. The transfer of troops would require seventy-one side-wheelers, fifty-seven prop-driven steamers, 187 schooners, and ninety barges. Not all strategists supported the grandiose movement. High-level critics included the president, the secretary of war, and four corps commanders. For logistical considerations, see Wert, *The Sword of Lincoln*, 65–69; Sears, *Lin-*

coln's Lieutenants, 164–65, 172–77; Sears, *To the Gates of Richmond*, 23–27; Sears, *The Young Napoleon*, 167–68, 173; Dowdey, *The Seven Days*, 34–38, 43; Burton, *Extraordinary Circumstances*, 3–4; and Jones, *Civil War Command and Strategy*, 79–80.

2. The president revoked McClellan's rank of general in chief and established a War Board of top military and government advisers. See *OR*, 12, pt. 3:311 (Organization of the Department of the Rappahannock).

3. Phillip G. Ellithorpe to Sisters, February 16, 1862, CCHM; Phillip G. Ellithorpe to Ann, March 15, 1862, CCHM.

4. Born in Plattsburgh, New York, in 1836, Roy Stone moved to Warren, Pennsylvania, where he organized the Raftsman Guards (Company D) of Kane's Rifles. Chosen major in the first regimental election, Stone would later recruit and lead the 149th Pennsylvania. See Thomson and Rauch, *History of the "Bucktails,"* 22–24, 92.

5. The original copy of Kane's "Instructions for Skirmishers" has never been found. For Phillip's perspective of the fighting style and bugle calls, see Phillip G. Ellithorpe to Father, March 16, 1862, CCHM, and Phillip G. Ellithorpe to Cousin Ell, ca. July 1862, CCHM. See also Thomson and Rauch, *History of the "Bucktails,"* 64, 84–85, 92, 145–46; Sypher, *History of the Pennsylvania Reserves*, 181–82; and Bates, *History of the Pennsylvania Volunteers*, 1:911.

6. Phillip G. Ellithorpe to Father, March 16 and 20, 1862, CCHM. See also Phillip G. Ellithorpe to Sisters, April 3, 5, 6, and 10, 1862, CCHM.

7. Benedict, *Vermont in the Civil War*, 1:185, 240–45.

8. Phillip G. Ellithorpe to Sisters, April 10, 1862, CCHM. See also Thomson and Rauch, *History of the "Bucktails,"* 91–92, and Sypher, *History of the Pennsylvania Reserves*, 172–74.

9. Phillip G. Ellithorpe to Sister Ann and Friend Asa, July 8 and 26, 1862, CCHM.

10. See Philander D. Ellithorpe to Ann, April 20, 1862, CCHM, and Phillip G. Ellithorpe to Sisters, April 21 and 25, 1862, CCHM.

11. Philander D. Ellithorpe to Ann, April 20, 1862, CCHM; Phillip G. Ellithorpe to Sisters, April 21 and 25, 1862, CCHM. See also Thomson and Rauch, *History of the "Bucktails,"* 91–92, and Sypher, *History of the Pennsylvania Reserves*, 172–74, 177, 180.

12. See U.S. Sanitary Commission, *Report to the Secretary of War: Operations of the Sanitary Commission in the Volunteer Army—Month of September and October, 1861*, 37, and *Report of the Paymaster General*, 3. On July 17, 1862, the War Department disbanded regimental bands altogether and replaced them with brigade bands of sixteen members, each of whom would continue to double as stretcher bearers. See *OR*, 3, pt. 1:43, 803; 3, pt. 2:278; 1, pt. 5:89, 94 (General Order No. 91); Olson, *Music and Musket*, 72–74; and Kelley and Snell, *Bugle Resounding*, 96, 206.

13. Asa R. Burleson, Military Service Record, NARA; Asa R. Burleson, Application for Pension, Military Pension Record, NARA. See also E. H. R. to H. J. Sedgwick, April 30, 1862, CCHM; *OR*, 11, pt. 1:377–78 (Col. Henry A. Smalley); and Willford and Curtiss-Wedge, *History of Fillmore County, Minnesota*, 2:774.

14. Fairchild, *History of the 27th New York Volunteers*, 32–40. See also Westervelt, *Lights and Shadows of Army Life*, 35–37; Buell, *A Brief History of Company B, 27th New York Regiment*, 9; and Slocum, *The Life and Services of Major-General Henry Warner Slocum*, 21.

15. *OR*, 11, pt. 1:622 (Brig. Gen. Henry W. Slocum). For the chain of command as it affected Philander, see appendix A. See also Fairchild, *History of the 27th New York Volunteers*, 43–44, and Westervelt, *Lights and Shadows of Army Life*, 38–39.

16. Westervelt, *Lights and Shadows of Army Life*, 52; Slocum, *The Life and Services of Major-General Henry Warner Slocum*, 26–27; *OR*, 11, pt. 1:622 (Brig. Gen. Henry W. Slocum).

17. Westervelt, *Lights and Shadows of Army Life*, 23. See also Philander D. Ellithorpe to Ann, September 9, 1862, CCMH.

18. Philander D. Ellithorpe to Melia, May 26, 1862, CCHM. See also Fairchild, *History of the 27th New York Volunteers*, 44, and Westervelt, *Lights and Shadows of Army Life*, 38–39.

19. Philander D. Ellithorpe to Melia, May 26 and June 4, 1862, CCHM. See also Fairchild, *History of the 27th New York Volunteers*, 44–49; Westervelt, *Lights and Shadows of Army Life*, 40, 43, 47; Sypher, *History of the Pennsylvania Reserves*, 180–81; and Buell, *A Brief History of Company B, 27th New York Regiment*, 10.

20. Philander D. Ellithorpe to Sisters Ann and Melia, June 4, 17, and 19, 1862, CCHM. See also Fairchild, *History of the 27th New York Volunteers*, 44–51.

21. Phillip G. Ellithorpe to Ann, June 13 and 21, 1862, CCHM; Philander D. Ellithorpe to Melia, June 17, 1862, CCHM.

22. Phillip G. Ellithorpe to Sister, April 30, 1862, CCHM; Phillip G. Ellithorpe to Sister, May 7, 1862, CCHM; Phillip G. Ellithorpe to Melia, June 1, 1862, CCHM.

23. Thomson and Rauch, *History of the "Bucktails,"* 92–93; Sypher, *History of the Pennsylvania Reserves*, 182; Bates, *History of the Pennsylvania Volunteers*, 1:911.

24. Thomson and Rauch, *History of the "Bucktails,"* 145; Sypher, *History of the Pennsylvania Reserves*, 183–86; Bates, *History of the Pennsylvania Volunteers*, 1:911–12.

25. Thomson and Rauch, *History of the "Bucktails,"* 157–67; Sypher, *History of the Pennsylvania Reserves*, 183–86; Ent, *The Pennsylvania Reserves in the Civil War*, 49–51; Bates, *History of the Pennsylvania Volunteers*, 1:912–13.

26. Phillip G. Ellithorpe to Sister Ann and Friend Asa, June 13, 1862, CCHM; *OR*, 12, pt. 1:675–76 (Capt. Hugh McDonald), 676–77 (Brig. Gen. George D. Bayard).

27. Thomson and Rauch, *History of the "Bucktails,"* 95. See also Sypher, *History of the Pennsylvania Reserves*, 191–96, and Bates, *History of the Pennsylvania Volunteers*, 1:913–14.

28. Phillip G. Ellithorpe to Sister Ann and Friend Asa, June 13, 1862, CCHM; Phillip G. Ellithorpe to Ann, June 21, 1862, CCHM. See also Thomas, *Bold Dragoon*, 108–29.

29. Phillip G. Ellithorpe to Ann, June 13 and 21, 1862, CCHM; Philander D. Ellithorpe to Melia, June 17, 1862, CCHM.

30. Phillip G. Ellithorpe to Ann, June 21, 1862, CCHM; Philander D. Ellithorpe to Melia, June 17, 1862, CCHM.

31. *OR*, 11, pt. 2:414–19 (Maj. Roy Stone), 384–92 (Brig. Gen. George A. McCall).

32. *OR*, 11, pt. 2:414 (Col. Roy Stone). See also Ent, *The Pennsylvania Reserves in the Civil War*, 55–58; Burton, *Extraordinary Circumstances*, 49, 67; and Sypher, *History of the Pennsylvania Reserves*, 197–99, 206–9.

33. *OR*, 11, pt. 2:414 (Col. Roy Stone).

34. *OR*, 11, pt. 2:414 (Col. Roy Stone). See also Sypher, *History of the Pennsylvania Reserves*, 206–9.

35. *OR*, 11, pt. 2:384–92 (Brig. Gen. George A. McCall).

36. *OR*, 11, pt. 2:386 (Brig. Gen. George A. McCall).

37. *OR*, 11, pt. 2:385–87 (Brig. Gen. George A. McCall), 410 (Capt. James H. Cooper), 415–16 (Maj. Roy Stone). See also Bates, *History of the Pennsylvania Volunteers*, 1:914; Ent, *The Pennsylvania Reserves in the Civil War*, 57–61, 66; Sypher, *History of the Pennsylvania Reserves*, 209–14; and Thomson and Rauch, *History of the "Bucktails,"* 106–9.

38. *OR*, 11, pt. 2:416 (Maj. Roy Stone), 387 (Brig. Gen. George A. McCall). See also Glover, *Bucktailed Wildcats*, 89–95; Thomson and Rauch, *History of the "Bucktails,"* 112–21; Sypher, *History of the Pennsylvania Reserves*, 223–33; Ent, *The Pennsylvania Reserves in the Civil War*, 66–80; and Bates, *History of the Pennsylvania Volunteers*, 1:913–14.

39. *OR*, 11, pt. 2:432–36 (Brig. Gen. Henry W. Slocum), 446–50 (Col. Joseph J. Bartlett), 453–54 (Lt. Col. Alexander D. Adams).

40. *OR*, 11, pt. 2:416 (Maj. Roy Stone), 386 (Brig. Gen. George A. McCall).

41. Philander D. Ellithorpe to Ann, July 6, 1862, CCHM. See also *OR*, 11, pt. 2:432–33 (Brig. Gen. Henry W. Slocum), 447 (Col. Joseph J. Bartlett), 453 (Lt. Col. Alexander D. Adams).

42. *OR*, 11, pt. 2:432 (Brig. Gen. Henry W. Slocum), 447 (Col. Joseph J. Bartlett), 453 (Lt. Col. Alexander D. Adams). See also Slocum, *The Life and Services of Major-General Henry Warner Slocum*, 26–28, and Buell, *A Brief History of Company B, 27th New York Regiment*, 10.

43. Fairchild, *History of the 27th New York Volunteers*, 48. Soldiers often used natural events, such as rain, hail, and wind, as metaphors to describe certain battle situations.

44. Fairchild, *History of the 27th New York Volunteers*, 52–53. See also Westervelt, *Lights and Shadows of Army Life*, 48, and *OR*, 11, pt. 2:432–34 (Brig. Gen. Henry W. Slocum), 449–50 (Col. Joseph J. Bartlett); 453 (Lt. Col. Alexander D. Adams).

45. Philander D. Ellithorpe to Ann, July 6, 1862, CCHM. See also *OR*, 11, pt. 2:432–34 (Brig. Gen. Henry W. Slocum), 449–50 (Col. Joseph J. Bartlett), 453 (Lt. Col. Alexander D. Adams); Fairchild, *History of the 27th New York Volunteers*, 52; Westervelt, *Lights and Shadows of Army Life*, 48; and Slocum, *The Life and Services of Major-General Henry Warner Slocum*, 29.

46. *OR*, 11, pt. 2:417 (Col. Roy Stone). See also Sypher, *History of the Pennsylvania Reserves*, 246–48, and Thomson and Rauch, *History of the "Bucktails,"* 122–23.

47. Fairchild, *History of the 27th New York Volunteers*, 70–72; Westervelt, *Lights and Shadows of Army Life*, 49–50; Buell, *A Brief History of Company B, 27th New York Regiment*, 10.

48. Fairchild, *History of the 27th New York Volunteers*, 71.

49. *OR*, 11, pt. 2:389 (Brig. Gen. George A. McCall), 417 (Col. Roy Stone).

50. Philander D. Ellithorpe to Ann, July 6, 1862, CCHM; Philander D. Ellithorpe to Asa, August 8, 1862, CCHM. See also Buell, *A Brief History of Company B, 27th New York Regiment*, 10, and Fairchild, *History of the 27th New York Volunteers*, 72–78.

51. Glover, *Bucktailed Wildcats*, 97–105; Thomson and Rauch, *History of the "Bucktails,"* 122–35; Sypher, *History of the Pennsylvania Reserves*, 255–99; Ent, *The Pennsylvania Reserves in the Civil War*, 85–100; Bates, *History of the Pennsylvania Volunteers*, 1:915.

52. *OR*, 11, pt. 2:417 (Col. Roy Stone), 390 (Brig. Gen. George A. McCall). See also Sears, *Lincoln's Lieutenants*, 259–69; Wert, *The Sword of Lincoln*, 109–16, 125; Sears, *To the Gates of Richmond*, 282–96; Sears, *The Young Napoleon*, 218–21; Dowdey, *The Seven Days*, 285, 293; Burton, *Extraordinary Circumstances*, 197–200, 227, 237–41, 249–50; Ent, *The Pennsylvania Reserves in the Civil War*, 85–89; Thomson and Rauch, *History of the "Bucktails,"* 122–27; Sypher, *History of the Pennsylvania Reserves*, 255, 260–64; and Bates, *History of the Pennsylvania Volunteers*, 1:915.

53. Temporary brigade replacements in July 1862 included Col. Hugh W. McNeil (Bucktails) to the 1st Brigade, Col. Albert L. Magilton (4th Pennsylvania Reserves) to the 2nd Brigade, and Col. Conrad F. Jackson (9th Pennsylvania Reserves) to the 3rd Brigade.

54. *OR*, 11, pt. 2:81, 87 (Brig. Gen. John Sedgwick), 81 (Brig. Gen. John Sedgwick), 434–35 (Lt. Col. Alexander D. Adams). See also Sears, *To the Gates of Richmond*, 281–88, 296–97; Burton, *Extraordinary Circumstances*, 165–66, 236, 246, 258–59, 265, 284; and Dowdey, *The Seven Days*, 285, 292.

55. Glover, *Bucktailed Wildcats*, 104–5; Thomson and Rauch, *History of the "Bucktails,"* 127–28; Sypher, *History of the Pennsylvania Reserves*, 265–68; Ent, *The Pennsylvania Reserves in the Civil War*, 91–92, 99–100; and Bates, *History of the Pennsylvania Volunteers*, 1:915.

56. *OR*, 11, pt. 2:391–92 (Brig. Gen. George A. McCall), 418–19 (Maj. Roy Stone), 113–14 (Maj. Gen. Joseph Hooker), 228–31 (Maj. Gen. Fitz John Porter). See also Sears, *To the Gates of Richmond*, 300–309; Ent, *The Pennsylvania Reserves in the Civil War*, 103, 345–50; Sypher, *History of the Pennsylvania Reserves*, 275, 287–300; and Thomson and Rauch, *History of the "Bucktails,"* 128.

57. Glover, *Bucktailed Wildcats*, 106–7; Thomson and Rauch, *History of the "Bucktails,"* 134–35; Sypher, *History of the Pennsylvania Reserves*, 300–305; Ent, *The Pennsylvania Reserves in the Civil War*, 101–2; Bates, *History of the Pennsylvania Volunteers*, 1:915.

58. Buell, *A Brief History of Company B, 27th New York Regiment*, 10; Fairchild, *History of the 27th New York Volunteers*, 72–73; Westervelt, *Lights and Shadows of Army Life*, 52–54.

59. For charges of treason against McClellan based on his absence from most of the battles in the Seven Days, see Doris Kearns Goodwin, *Team of Rivals: The Political Genius of Abraham Lincoln* (New York: Simon and Schuster, 2005), 474–80.

60. Sypher, *History of the Pennsylvania Reserves*, 305. See also Wert, *The Sword of Lincoln*, 117–21; Sears, *Lincoln's Lieutenants*, 267–71; Sears, *To the Gates of Richmond*, 337–38; Sears, *The Young Napoleon*, 223; Burton, *Extraordinary Circumstances*, 366–71; Glover, *Bucktailed Wildcats*, 106–7; Thomson and Rauch, *History of the "Bucktails,"* 134–35; Ent, *The Pennsylvania Reserves in the Civil War*, 102; Fairchild, *History of the 27th New York Volunteers*, 72–74; and Westervelt, *Lights and Shadows of Army Life*, 55–56.

61. Quoted in Wert, *The Sword of Lincoln*, 125. See also Phillip G. Ellithorpe, Philander D. Ellithorpe, Muster Rolls, Military Service Records, NARA.

62. Casualty figures for the Army of the Potomac vary depending on the source. This study utilizes the following statistics: Mechanicsville (361k/207w/105m), Gaines' Mill (894k/3,114w/2,829m), Savage Station (919k, w/2,500m, c), Glendale (297k/1,696w/1,804m, c), and Malvern Hill (314k/1,875w/818m). See William F. Fox, *Regimental Losses in the American Civil War, 1861–1865* (Albany, NY: Albany Publishing Company, 1889), 556–58; *OR*, 11, pt. 2:24–41 (casualties). See also Glover, *Bucktailed Wildcats*, 291; Sypher, *History of the Pennsylvania Reserves*, 309–11; Thomson and Rauch, *History of the "Bucktails,"* 135–36; Ent, *The Pennsylvania Reserves in the Civil War*, 71–74, 78–82, 102; Fairchild, *History of the 27th New York Volunteers*, 55; and Westervelt, *Lights and Shadows of Army Life*, 48.

63. Philander D. Ellithorpe to Melia, June 17, 1862, CCHM; Philander D. Ellithorpe to Sister Ann, July 6, 1862, CCHM; Philander D. Ellithorpe to Ann, January 6, 1863, CCHM.

64. Office of County Clerk, Allegany County, Belmont, N.Y., *Land Deeds*, Book 66: 361–62.

65. Phillip G. Ellithorpe to Friend Asa, May 20, 1862, CCHM.

66. Philander D. Ellithorpe to Sister, May 1 and 13 and July 6, 1862, CCHM; Phillip G. Ellithorpe to Sister Ann and Friend Asa, July 26, 1862, CCHM.

67. Philander D. Ellithorpe to Melia, May 26, 1862, CCHM; Phillip G. Ellithorpe to Sister Ann and Friend Asa, June 13, 1862, CCHM; Philander D. Ellithorpe to Melia, June 17, 1862, CCHM.

68. Philander D. Ellithorpe to Melia, June 17, 1862, CCHM.

69. Phillip G. Ellithorpe to Sister Ann and Friend Asa, June 13, 1862, CCHM.

70. Phillip G. Ellithorpe to Father, March 20, 1862, CCHM. Stebbins's invention provides a necessary function in modern sewing machines. In sewing, it is important to maintain a proper amount of tension on the fabric. Otherwise, if the tension is too loose, there will be gaps, and stitches will not be strong. If the tension is too tight, it will create "puckering" and could cause thread to break. The author thanks Pam Stewart of "Pictured in Quilts," Kelso, Washington, for her sewing expertise and explanation on the importance of Stebbins's invention.

71. Phillip G. Ellithorpe to Sister Ann and Friend Asa, July 8, 1862, CCHM.

72. Phillip G. Ellithorpe to Sister Ann and Friend Asa, July 8, 1862, CCHM; Phillip G. Ellithorpe to Permelia, July 1, 1862, CCHM.

73. Philander D. Ellithorpe to Ann, July 6, 1862, CCHM; Philander D. Ellithorpe to Asa, August 8, 1862, CCHM; Phillip G. Ellithorpe to Sister Ann, September 2, 1862, CCHM.

74. Phillip G. Ellithorpe to Sisters, July 9, 1862, CCHM.

75. Philander D. Ellithorpe to Ann, July 6, 1862, CCHM.

76. Philander D. Ellithorpe to Sister, May 1 and 13 and July 6, 1862, CCHM; Philander D. Ellithorpe to Asa R. Burleson, July 26 and August 8, 1862, CCHM; Phillip G. Ellithorpe to Ann, September 2, 1862, CCHM.

77. Phillip G. Ellithorpe to Asa R. Burleson, July 26, 1862, CCHM.

Chapter 6: Watchful Waiting and Second Bull Run

1. For the ill preparedness of Army medical practices, see Adams, *Living Hell*, 85; Frank R. Freemon, *Gangrene and Glory: Medical Care during the American Civil War* (Cranbury, NJ: Associated University Presses, 1998), 41, 44; Leech, *Reveille in Washington*, 208, 216; Adams, *Doctors in Blue*, 3–4, 9–10, 22, 31–32, 45, 60–62, 66–67; Alfred Jay Bollet, *Civil War Medicine: Challenges and Triumphs* (Tucson, AZ: Galen Press, 2010), 9–16; Ira M. Rutkow, *Bleeding Blue and Gray: Civil War Surgery and the Evolution of American Medicine* (New York: Random House, 2005), 3–38, 119–20; Wiley, *The Life of Billy Yank*, 129, 147; Billings, *Hardtack and Coffee*, 298–303; McPherson, *Battle Cry of Freedom*, 486–87; Rable, *Fredericksburg! Fredericksburg!*, 312; and Linderman, *Embattled Courage*, 128.

2. Charles J. Stillé, *History of the United States Sanitary Commission* (Philadelphia: J. B. Lippincott & Co., 1866), 94–100.

3. McPherson, *Battle Cry of Freedom*, 480–84; Bollet, *Civil War Medicine*, 103, 225–29; Adams, *Doctors in Blue*, 23–25, 71–73; Rutkow, *Bleeding Blue and Gray*, 66–73, 83, 91–92, 97, 188; Freemon, *Gangrene and Glory*, 75; Leech, *Reveille in Washington*, 214–15; Stillé, *History of the United States Sanitary Commission*, 88–93, 111–37; Frederick Law Olmsted, *Hospital Transports: A Memoir of the Sick and Wounded from the Peninsula of Virginia in the Summer of 1862* (Boston: Ticknor and Fields, 1863), 1–156.

4. For the medical crisis at Harrison's Landing, see Wert, *The Sword of Lincoln*, 126; Sears, *Lincoln's Lieutenants*, 274; Sears, *To the Gates of Richmond*, 347; Dowdey, *The Seven Days*, 348; Wiley, *The Life of Billy Yank*, 140–42, 150; Adams, *Doctors in Blue*, 5, 9; Leech, *Reveille in*

Washington, 212–14; McPherson, *Battle Cry of Freedom*, 486–88; and James M. McPherson, *Crossroads of Freedom—Antietam: The Battle That Changed the Course of the Civil War* (New York: Oxford University Press, 2002), 78.

5. See Rutkow, *Bleeding Blue and Gray*, 41–49, 57, 66–73, 91–92; Bollet, *Civil War Medicine*, 57–60, 232–33, 259; and Stillé, *History of the United States Sanitary Commission*, 94–100.

6. Phillip G. Ellithorpe to Sisters, July 9, 1862, CCHM. The medical and combat half-life of a Civil War regiment was typically one year of service. See Steiner, *Disease in the Civil War*, 8–12, and Brooks, *Civil War Medicine*, 6–11, 108.

7. Philander D. Ellithorpe to Asa, August 8, 1862, CCHM. See also Wert, *The Sword of Lincoln*, 131; Sears, *Lincoln's Lieutenants*, 274–76; Sears, *To the Gates of Richmond*, 347; and Sears, *The Young Napoleon*, 226.

8. Bates, *History of the Pennsylvania Volunteers*, 1:915–16; Ent, *The Pennsylvania Reserves in the Civil War*, 104; Thomson and Rauch, *History of the "Bucktails,"* 138; Sypher, *History of the Pennsylvania Reserves*, 327.

9. Philander D. Ellithorpe to Ann, July 6, 1862, CCHM; Philander D. Ellithorpe to Asa, August 8, 1862, CCHM. See also Fairchild, *History of the 27th New York Volunteers*, 82–83; Westervelt, *Lights and Shadows of Army Life*, 56; and Buell, *A Brief History of Company B, 27th New York Regiment*, 11–12.

10. Fairchild, *History of the 27th New York Volunteers*, 82–83. Once the old values of courage proved to be invalid, the meaninglessness of the war began to manifest itself in despondency and apathy. See Linderman, *Embattled Courage*, 159–61, 234, and Hess, *The Union Soldier in Battle*, 78, 81.

11. Philander D. Ellithorpe to Ann, July 6, 1862, CCHM. See also George L. Kilmer, "The Army of the Potomac at Harrison's Landing" [Company D, 27th New York], in Johnson and Buel, *Battles and Leaders*, 2:427–28, and Buell, *A Brief History of Company B, 27th New York Regiment*, 10–11.

12. Phillip G. Ellithorpe to Asa R. Burleson, July 26, 1862, CCHM.

13. See Philander D. Ellithorpe, Military Pension Record, NARA, and *Report of the Adjutant General for the State of New York, Roster of 27th New York*, 187. For the chain of command as it affected Phillip and Philander, see appendix A.

14. Asa R. Burleson, Muster Rolls, Military Service Record, NARA; James R. Bowen, *Regimental History of the First New York Dragoons* [130th New York] (Lyons, MI: Bowen Publisher, 1900), 8–9, 21; Phisterer, *New York in the War of the Rebellion*, 2:21, 323.

15. See Glover, *Bucktailed Wildcats*, 107–10; Thomson and Rauch, *History of the "Bucktails,"* 19–23, 137–41; Sypher, *History of the Pennsylvania Reserves*, 312–13; Ent, *The Pennsylvania Reserves in the Civil War*, 103–4; Bates, *History of the Pennsylvania Volunteers*, 1:916; and *OR*, 19, pt. 2:32 (casualties).

16. Phillip G. Ellithorpe to Sisters, April 21, 1862, CCHM; Phillip G. Ellithorpe to Sister, May 7, 1862, CCHM.

17. Phillip G. Ellithorpe to Sisters, May 7, 1862, CCHM.

18. For the role of corrupt practices in the commissary, see Rable, *Fredericksburg! Fredericksburg!*, 103, 141; Wiley, *The Life of Billy Yank*, 225, 359; and Billings, *Hardtack and Coffee*, 224–27.

19. Phillip G. Ellithorpe to Friend Asa, May 20, 1862, CCHM.

20. Phillip G. Ellithorpe to Asa R. Burleson, July 26, 1862, CCHM.

21. Ambulance supply boxes contained three bed sheets, six two-pound cans of beef stock, one leather bucket, three camp kettles, one candle lantern, six tin plates with eating utensils and tumblers, and ten pounds of hardtack. See Adams, *Doctors in Blue*, 33–34, 76, 190–91; Bollet, *Civil War Medicine*, 219; Wiley, *The Life of Billy Yank*, 140–42, and Billings, *Hardtack and Coffee*, 305.

22. Phillip G. Ellithorpe, Military Service Record, NARA. For details on the new corps, see *OR*, 11, pt. 1:210–20 (Dr. Jonathan K. Letterman); Rutkow, *Bleeding Blue and Gray*, 142–46; Billings, *Hardtack and Coffee*, 303–4, 313; Adams, *Doctors in Blue*, 76, 92; Bollet, *Civil War Medicine*, 105; and Wiley, *The Life of Billy Yank*, 145.

23. Phillip G. Ellithorpe, Military Service Record, NARA; Phillip G. Ellithorpe to Sisters, September 3 and 4, 1862, CCHM. For the use of transport steamers to evacuate wounded and sick from the James Peninsula, see Bollet, *Civil War Medicine*, 9–12, 112, 318; Rutkow, *Bleeding Blue and Gray*, 3–38, 126, 131–39, 148; Stillé, *History of the United States Sanitation Commission*, 63–67, 76, 144–45, 153–62; and Olmsted, *Hospital Transports*, 1–43, 81–84.

24. Phillip G. Ellithorpe, Military Service Record, NARA; Phillip G. Ellithorpe to Sisters, September 3 and 4, 1862, CCHM; *OR*, 19, pt. 1:106–7 (Dr. Jonathan Letterman).

25. Phillip G. Ellithorpe to Sisters, September 3 and 4, 1862, CCHM.

26. Wert, *The Sword of Lincoln*, 129–33; Sears, *Lincoln's Lieutenants*, 278–99; John J. Hennessy, *Return to Bull Run: The Campaign and Battle of Second Bull Run* (New York: Simon & Schuster, 1993), 70–79; McPherson, *Crossroads of Freedom*, 53–54, 78–79; Stephen W. Sears, *Landscape Turned Red: The Battle of Antietam* (Boston: Houghton Mifflin, 1983), 2; Sears, *The Young Napoleon*, 242; McPherson, *Battle Cry of Freedom*, 524–33; Glover, *Bucktailed Wildcats*, 122; Bates, *History of the Pennsylvania Volunteers*, 1:916; Ent, *The Pennsylvania Reserves in the Civil War*, 105–10; Sypher, *History of the Pennsylvania Reserves*, 329–35; and *OR*, 12, pt. 3:584–85 (Organization of Army of Virginia).

27. Glover, *Bucktailed Wildcats*, 112; Sypher, *History of the Pennsylvania Reserves*, 329, 334; Thomson and Rauch, *History of the "Bucktails,"* 142–44, 188; *OR*, 12, pt. 2:345 (Maj. Gen. Irvin McDowell).

28. Ent, *The Pennsylvania Reserves in the Civil War*, 110–13; Glover, *Bucktailed Wildcats*, 123–26, 136; Thomson and Rauch, *History of the "Bucktails,"* 171–78; Sypher, *History of the Pennsylvania Reserves*, 360–61; Bates, *History of the Pennsylvania Volunteers*, 1:916. See also Sears, *Lincoln's Lieutenants*, 288–89, 299–302; Hennessy, *Return to Bull Run*, 1–80; and Rafuse, *Manassas*, 175–77.

29. Philander D. Ellithorpe to Ann, September 9, 1862, CCHM. See also Fairchild, *History of the 27th New York Volunteers*, 84–89; Westervelt, *Lights and Shadows of Army Life*, 32, 56; Buell, *A Brief History of Company B, 27th New York Regiment*, 12–13; and Slocum, *The Life and Services of Major-General Henry Warner Slocum*, 38–42.

30. For the Bucktails' involvement at Second Bull Run, see Glover, *Bucktailed Wildcats*, 122–38; Thomson and Rauch, *History of the "Bucktails,"* 184–95; Sypher, *History of the Pennsylvania Reserves*, 334–56; Ent, *The Pennsylvania Reserves in the Civil War*, 105–28; Bates, *History of the Pennsylvania Volunteers*, 1:917–18; *OR*, 51, pt. 1:131 (Col. Hugh McNeil); *OR*, 12, pt. 2:325–46 (Maj. Gen. Irvin McDowell), 392–95 (Brig. Gen. John F. Reynolds), 399 (Brig. Gen. George G. Meade).

31. *OR*, 51, pt. 1:131 (Col. Hugh McNeil); *OR*, 112, pt. 2:399 (Brig. Gen. George G. Meade). See also Glover, *Bucktailed Wildcats*, 126–28, 136–37; Thomson and Rauch, *History of the "Bucktails,"* 184–85; Sypher, *History of the Pennsylvania Reserves*, 334–38; Ent,

The Pennsylvania Reserves in the Civil War, 113–17; and Bates, *History of the Pennsylvania Volunteers*, 1:915.

32. Glover, *Bucktailed Wildcats*, 130–31; Ent, *The Pennsylvania Reserves in the Civil War*, 117–18; Thomson and Rauch, *History of the "Bucktails,"* 184–85; Sypher, *History of the Pennsylvania Reserves*, 336–39; *OR*, 51, pt. 1:131–32 (Col. Hugh McNeil).

33. Glover, *Bucktailed Wildcats*, 132–33; Ent, *The Pennsylvania Reserves in the Civil War*, 118–21. See also Hennessy, *Return to Bull Run*, 259, 293; Sears, *Lincoln's Lieutenants*, 324–26; and Rafuse, *Manassas*, 94, 100, 103.

34. *OR*, 51, pt. 1:132 (Col. Hugh McNeil); Glover, *Bucktailed Wildcats*, 133; Ent, *The Pennsylvania Reserves in the Civil War*, 121–22; Thomson and Rauch, *History of the "Bucktails,"* 189–92; Sypher, *History of the Pennsylvania Reserves*, 345–47; Hennessy, *Return to Bull Run*, 319.

35. *OR*, 12, pt. 1:399 (Brig. Gen. George G. Meade); Glover, *Bucktailed Wildcats*, 134–35; Ent, *The Pennsylvania Reserves in the Civil War*, 122–26. See also McPherson, *Battle Cry of Freedom*, 529–31; Rafuse, *Manassas*, 94–135; and Hennessy, *Return to Bull Run*, 407–8, 463.

36. Ent, *The Pennsylvania Reserves in the Civil War*, 127–28; Glover, *Bucktailed Wildcats*, 135–36; Thomson and Rauch, *History of the "Bucktails,"* 195–97; Sypher, *History of the Pennsylvania Reserves*, 355–60; Bates, *History of the Pennsylvania Volunteers*, 1:917–18. See also Wert, *The Sword of Lincoln*, 136–37; Sears, *Lincoln's Lieutenants*, 309, 316–27, 331; Sears, *The Young Napoleon*, 255–58; and Hennessy, *Return to Bull Run*, 436–39.

37. Philander D. Ellithorpe to Ann, September 9, 1862, CCHM. See also Fairchild, *History of the 27th New York Volunteers*, 84–89; Westervelt, *Lights and Shadows of Army Life*, 32, 56; Buell, *A Brief History of Company B, 27th New York Regiment*, 12–13; and Slocum, *The Life and Services of Major-General Henry Warner Slocum*, 38–42.

38. Phillip G. Ellithorpe to Sisters, September 4, 1862, CCHM; Phillip G. Ellithorpe to Father, September 10, 1862, CCHM. For these last evacuees to leave the James Peninsula, see McPherson, *Crossroads of Freedom*, 79, and Leech, *Reveille in Washington*, 205, 208.

39. Hennessy, *Return to Bull Run*, 463.

40. Philander D. Ellithorpe to Ann, September 9, 1862, CCHM. See also Hennessy, *Return to Bull Run*, 452, 471; Wert, *The Sword of Lincoln*, 139–43; Sears, *Lincoln's Lieutenants*, 332–34; Sears, *The Young Napoleon*, 259–62; McPherson, *Battle Cry of Freedom*, 528–34; Goodwin, *Team of Rivals*, 474–80; McPherson, *Crossroads of Freedom*, 84–86; and Sears, *Landscape Turned Red*, 4–15.

41. See Hattaway, *Shades of Blue and Gray*, 98; Michael Clodfelter, *The Dakota War: The United States Army versus the Sioux, 1862–1865* (Jefferson, NC: McFarland, 1998), 9–70; Paul N. Beck, *Columns of Vengeance: Soldiers, Sioux, and the Punitive Expeditions, 1863–1864* (Norman: University of Oklahoma Press, 2013), 1–50; and Kenneth Carley, *The Dakota War of 1862: Minnesota's Other Civil War* (St. Paul: Minnesota Historical Society Press, 1976), 7–86.

42. Phillip G. Ellithorpe to Sisters, September 24, 1862, CCHM.

43. Glover, *Bucktailed Wildcats*, 137; Thomson and Rauch, *History of the "Bucktails,"* 173–76; Sypher, *History of the Pennsylvania Reserves*, 361, 368; Ent, *The Pennsylvania Reserves in the Civil War*, 130–31; Bates, *History of the Pennsylvania Volunteers*, 1:918. The primary function of the hospital steward was to prepare the sick list for the regimental commander. See Freemon, *Gangrene and Glory*, 41.

44. Glover, *Bucktailed Wildcats*, 109–10; Thomson and Rauch, *History of the "Bucktails,"* 19–23, 137–41, 246; Sypher, *History of the Pennsylvania Reserves*, 313; Ent, *The Pennsylvania*

Reserves in the Civil War, 103–4. For the "bogus" comment, see Bates, *History of the Pennsylvania Volunteers*, 1:916.

45. Phillip G. Ellithorpe to Asa, July 26, 1862, CCHM; Phillip G. Ellithorpe to Ann, September 4, 1862, CCHM; Philander D. Ellithorpe to Ann, July 6, 1862, CCHM; Philander D. Ellithorpe to Asa, August 8, 1862, CCHM.

46. Phillip G. Ellithorpe to Sisters, July 9, 1862, CCHM. For the role played by pragmatism in the lives of Civil War soldiers, see Carmichael, *The War for the Common Soldier*, 50, 134–35, 229.

47. Thomson and Rauch, *History of the "Bucktails,"* 246; Phillip G. Ellithorpe to Sisters, November 23, 1861, CCHM.

48. Phillip G. Ellithorpe to Sisters, September 10, 1862, CCHM. For Phillip's transfer to the ambulance corps, see Phillip G. Ellithorpe, Military Service Record, NARA.

49. For dangers faced by ambulance men, see Adams, *Living Hell*, 111, 118, 127; Linderman, *Embattled Courage*, 134; Mitchell, *Civil War Soldiers*, 81; and Adams, *Doctors in Blue*, 81.

50. Adams, *Living Hell*, 13, 60.

Chapter 7: The Loss of Innocence in Maryland

1. Wert, *The Sword of Lincoln*, 142–43; Sears, *Lincoln's Lieutenants*, 344, 351–53; Sears, *The Young Napoleon*, 263–65; Sears, *Landscape Turned Red*, 82–111; Ethan S. Rafuse, *Antietam, South Mountain & Harpers Ferry: A Battlefield Guide* (Lincoln: University of Nebraska Press, 2008), 3–4.

2. Philander D. Ellithorpe to Ann, September 9, 1862, CCHM. See also Fairchild, *History of the 27th New York Volunteers*, 89.

3. *OR*, 19, pt. 1:106–13 (Dr. Jonathan K. Letterman); Phillip G. Ellithorpe to Ann, September 4, 10, and 24, 1862, CCHM.

4. For the chain of command as it affected Phillip, see appendix A. See also John David Hoptak, *The Battle of South Mountain* (Charleston, SC: The History Press, 2011), 75–76, 89–91; Sears, *Landscape Turned Red*, 100–101, 137; Ent, *The Pennsylvania Reserves in the Civil War*, 130–31; Glover, *Bucktailed Wildcats*, 141–42; Thomson and Rauch, *History of the "Bucktails,"* 200–202; Sypher, *History of the Pennsylvania Reserves*, 361–65; and Bates, *History of the Pennsylvania Volunteers*, 1:918.

5. Bowen, *Regimental History of the First New York Dragoons*, 8–9, 21. See also Phisterer, *New York in the War of the Rebellion*, 2:208–11, 323; *Annual Report of the Adjutant-General of the State of New York for 1895* (Albany, NY: State Printers, 1895): 25, 65, 169; Willford and Curtiss-Wedge, *History of Fillmore County, Minnesota*, 2:774; and Mrs. Robert Stevens, "Memoirs of 1st New York Dragoons, E. Randolph Robinson," *Historical Wyoming* 36 (October 1982): 39–43, 49.

6. Bowen, *Regimental History of the First New York Dragoons*, 8.

7. The "very raw" assessment of the 130th New York was voiced by Maj. Gen. John A. Dix, commander of the Department of Virginia stationed in Fortress Monroe. See *OR*, 18:392 (Maj. Gen. John A. Dix). For the chain of command as it affected Asa, see appendix A. See also Bowen, *Regimental History of the First New York Dragoons*, 10–14, 21, and Steven A. Cormier, *The Siege of Suffolk: The Forgotten Campaign, April 11–May 4, 1863* (Lynchburg, VA: H. E. Howard, 1989), 33.

8. For geographic descriptions, see Cormier, *The Siege of Suffolk*, 5–8, and Brian Steel Wills, *The War Hits Home: The Civil War in Southeastern Virginia* (Charlottesville: University of Virginia Press, 2001), 5–17, 172. During the war, vegetation often interfered with troop movements, communication, and actual combat. See Hess, *The Union Soldier in Battle*, 6, 48.

9. Wills, *The War Hits Home*, 66–69; Cormier, *The Siege of Suffolk*, 76, 82, 310; Bowen, *The Regimental History of the First New York Dragoons*, 15, 19, 25, 29; Asa R. Burleson, Military Service Record, NARA.

10. Bowen, *The Regimental History of the First New York Dragoons*, 29–30.

11. Bowen, *The Regimental History of the First New York Dragoons*, 16, 19–21.

12. Sears, *Lincoln's Lieutenants*, 365–66; Hoptak, *The Battle of South Mountain*, 36, 168; Sears, *The Young Napoleon*, 272–73; Sears, *Landscape Turned Red*, 82, 128–29; Wert, *The Sword of Lincoln*, 81–83, 148–51; McPherson, *Crossroads of Freedom*, 111–13.

13. The discovery of the lost dispatch was an "intelligence Coup unrivaled in all the war." See Sears, *Lincoln's Lieutenants*, 358. See also Wert, *The Sword of Lincoln*, 148–50; Sears, *Landscape Turned Red*, 90–99, 112–16; Sears, *The Young Napoleon*, 280–83 ; Hoptak, *The Battle of South Mountain*, 33–34; McPherson, *Crossroads of Freedom*, 104–9; Rafuse, *Antietam, South Mountain & Harpers Ferry*, 5–6, 173–74; and John Michael Priest, *Before Antietam: The Battle for South Mountain* (New York: Oxford University Press, 1992), 109–13.

14. Sears, *Lincoln's Lieutenants*, 259–60; Sears, *The Young Napoleon*, 285–89; Sears, *Landscape Turned Red*, 129–34; Hoptak, *The Battle of South Mountain*, 87–91, 130, 170; Priest, *Before Antietam*, 223.

15. *OR*, 19, pt. 1:267 (Brig. Gen. George G. Meade), 272 (Brig. Gen. Truman Seymour). See also Glover, *Bucktailed Wildcats*, 139–41; Ent, *The Pennsylvania Reserves in the Civil War*, 131–32; Rafuse, *Antietam, South Mountain & Harpers Ferry*, 8, 16, 175–84; Priest, *Before Antietam*, 129–219; Wert, *The Sword of Lincoln*, 151; Sears, *Lincoln's Lieutenants*, 359–64; and Sears, *Landscape Turned Red*, 130–35.

16. Priest, *Before Antietam*, 220–24; Rafuse, *Antietam, South Mountain & Harpers Ferry*, 186–88; Ent, *The Pennsylvania Reserves in the Civil War*, 131–37; Glover, *Bucktailed Wildcats*, 143–45; Thomson and Rauch, *History of the "Bucktails,"* 201–3; Sypher, *History of the Pennsylvania Reserves*, 362–68; Hoptak, *The Battle of South Mountain*, 90–93; D. Scott Hartwig, *To Antietam Creek: The Maryland Campaign of 1862* (Baltimore, MD: Johns Hopkins University Press, 2012), 377–79, 384, 619–20; Sears, *Lincoln's Lieutenants*, 365–66.

17. Glover, *Bucktailed Wildcats*, 145–49; Thomson and Rauch, *History of the "Bucktails,"* 204–5; Sypher, *History of the Pennsylvania Reserves*, 364–68; Ent, *The Pennsylvania Reserves in the Civil War*, 133–37; Bates, *History of the Pennsylvania Volunteers*, 1:918. See also Hoptak, *The Battle of South Mountain*, 91–99; Hartwig, *To Antietam Creek*, 377–79; Priest, *Before Antietam*, 224–50; and Rafuse, *Antietam, South Mountain & Harpers Ferry*, 186–88, 193.

18. Priest, *Before Antietam*, 234–39; Rafuse, *Antietam, South Mountain & Harpers Ferry*, 188; Sears, *Landscape Turned Red*, 139–40; Ent, *The Pennsylvania Reserves in the Civil War*, 137–38; Hoptak, *The Battle of South Mountain*, 94; Hartwig, *To Antietam Creek*, 384–89; Sears, *Landscape Turned Red*, 139.

19. *OR*, 19, pt. 1:107 (Dr. Jonathan K. Letterman), 185 (casualties); Phillip G. Ellithorpe to Ann, September 24, 1862, CCHM. See also Hartwig, *To Antietam Creek*, 389–95; Hoptak, *The Battle of South Mountain*, 101–5; Ent, *The Pennsylvania Reserves in the Civil War*, 141; Priest, *Before Antietam*, 247; *Pennsylvania Civil War Index Cards*, K. There was an

inordinately large number of fatal head wounds at Turner's Gap as the Confederates fired downhill. Lt. Col. Irvin of the Bucktails was seriously wounded in this manner. See Sears, *Landscape Turned Red*, 139, and Glover, *Bucktailed Wildcats*, 150.

20. Hoptak, *The Battle of South Mountain*, 94–100, 129–30; Hartwig, *To Antietam Creek*, 433; Priest, *Before Antietam*, 244–47; Rafuse, *Antietam, South Mountain & Harpers Ferry*, 188, 192–95; Glover, *Bucktailed Wildcats*, 147–49; Thomson and Rauch, *History of the "Bucktails,"* 205–6; Sypher, *History of the Pennsylvania Reserves*, 374; Ent, *The Pennsylvania Reserves in the Civil War*, 135–38; Bates, *History of the Pennsylvania Volunteers*, 1:918.

21. Sears, *Landscape Turned Red*, 146–49; Priest, *Before Antietam*, 272–76; Hoptak, *The Battle of South Mountain*, 132–34, 175–78; Rafuse, *Antietam, South Mountain & Harpers Ferry*, 197; Hartwig, *To Antietam Creek*, 438–39; Wert, *The Sword of Lincoln*, 153–54; Sears, *Lincoln's Lieutenants*, 366–67; Sears, *The Young Napoleon*, 285–89. For the chain of command as it affected Philander, see appendix A.

22. *OR*, 19, pt. 1:380–82 (Maj. Gen. Henry W. Slocum), 388–90 (Col. Joseph J. Bartlett), 392–93 (Col. Henry L. Lake). See also Priest, *Before Antietam*, 273–76; Hoptak, *The Battle of South Mountain*, 136–40; Rafuse, *Antietam, South Mountain & Harpers Ferry*, 199–203; and Hartwig, *To Antietam Creek*, 440–41.

23. Priest, *Before Antietam*, 275–78; Hoptak, *The Battle of South Mountain*, 140–43; Rafuse, *Antietam, South Mountain & Harpers Ferry*, 202–3; Hartwig, *To Antietam Creek*, 441–47; Slocum, *The Life and Services of Major-General Henry Warner Slocum*, 46–48.

24. Fairchild, *History of the 27th New York Volunteers*, 91–92. See also Westervelt, *Lights and Shadows of Army Life*, 66.

25. Priest, *Before Antietam*, 280–82; Hoptak, *The Battle of South Mountain*, 143–45; Hartwig, *To Antietam Creek*, 441, 447–50, 451–52; Buell, *A Brief History of Company B, 27th New York Regiment*, 13.

26. Sears, *Landscape Turned Red*, 156, 363; Priest, *Before Antietam*, 282–86; Hoptak, *The Battle of South Mountain*, 147–48; Rafuse, *Antietam, South Mountain & Harpers Ferry*, 201–3; Hartwig, *To Antietam Creek*, 451–54, 459.

27. Fairchild, *History of the 27th New York Volunteers*, 92–93; Westervelt, *Lights and Shadows of Army Life*, 62, 67, 75; *OR*, 19, pt. 1:183 (casualties); Phisterer, *New York in the War of the Rebellion*, 2:182. See also Priest, *Before Antietam*, 288–301; Hoptak, *The Battle of South Mountain*, 145–52, 157, 163; Hartwig, *To Antietam Creek*, 451, 458–63, 469, 473; and Sears, *Landscape Turned Red*, 149.

28. Wert, *The Sword of Lincoln*, 156; Sears, *Lincoln's Lieutenants*, 368–78; Sears, *Landscape Turned Red*, 159–70; Glover, *Bucktailed Wildcats*, 149–51; Ent, *The Pennsylvania Reserves in the Civil War*, 143–44.

29. Rafuse, *Antietam, South Mountain & Harpers Ferry*, 23–27; Ent, *The Pennsylvania Reserves in the Civil War*, 144–48; Sears, *Landscape Turned Red*, 170–73; McPherson, *Crossroads of Freedom*, 115–16; Wert, *The Sword of Lincoln*, 156–58; Sears, *Lincoln's Lieutenants*, 379; Sears, *The Young Napoleon*, 303–5; Glover, *Bucktailed Wildcats*, 153–58; Hartwig, *To Antietam Creek*, 639–41; Thomson and Rauch, *History of the "Bucktails,"* 209; Sypher, *History of the Pennsylvania Reserves*, 375–78; Bates, *History of the Pennsylvania Volunteers*, 1:918.

30. *OR*, 19, pt. 1:268–71 (Brig. Gen George G. Meade); Glover, *Bucktailed Wildcats*, 153–54; Rafuse, *Antietam, South Mountain & Harpers Ferry*, 15, 23–37; Ent, *The Pennsylvania Reserves in the Civil War*, 143–44; Bates, *History of the Pennsylvania Volunteers*, 1:918. See also Sears, *Landscape Turned Red*, 176–81; John Michael Priest, *Antietam: The Soldiers' Battle*

(New York: Oxford University Press, 1989), 15–17, 31; Hartwig, *To Antietam Creek*, 617–21; Sears, *Lincoln's Lieutenants*, 379–81; Sears, *The Young Napoleon*, 297; and Miller, *The Training of an Army*, 117–18.

31. *OR*, 51, pt. 1:155–56 (Capt. Dennis McGee); Glover, *Bucktailed Wildcats*, 156; Ent, *The Pennsylvania Reserves in the Civil War*, 145; Sypher, *History of the Pennsylvania Reserves*, 377–78; Thomson and Rauch, *History of the "Bucktails,"* 209; Bates, *History of the Pennsylvania Volunteers*, 1:918. See also Priest, *Antietam*, 15–17; Rafuse, Antietam, *South Mountain & Harpers Ferry*, 17, 27; Hartwig, *To Antietam Creek*, 617–21; and Miller, *The Training of an Army*, 118.

32. The following lyrics were sung to the tune of "The Boys of Kilkenny," which appeared in the *Tioga County (Wellsboro) Agitator* on December 10, 1862, and reprinted in Glover, *Bucktailed Wildcats*, 169:

> Here's a tear for our Colonel [McNeil]; he was one of the best,
> Here's a sigh for the Bucktails that have gone to their rest;
> Glorious was their death—they fell fighting like men.
> Let us drink now, in silence, in memory of them.

33. *OR*, 51, pt. 1:155–56 (Capt. Dennis McGee); Glover, *Bucktailed Wildcats*, 156; Thomson and Rauch, *History of the "Bucktails,"* 210; Ent, *The Pennsylvania Reserves in the Civil War*, 145–46. See also Priest, *Antietam*, 15–16, 18–20; Sears, *Landscape Turned Red*, 184, 205; and Hartwig, *To Antietam Creek*, 617–21.

34. See *OR*, 51, pt. 1:155–56 (Capt. Dennis McGee); Glover, *Bucktailed Wildcats*, 154–58; Thomson and Rauch, *History of the "Bucktails,"* 209–10; Sypher, *History of the Pennsylvania Reserves*, 378–80, 390–92; Ent, *The Pennsylvania Reserves in the Civil War*, 144–46; Bates, *History of the Pennsylvania Volunteers*, 1:918; Oliver C. Bosbyshell, *Pennsylvania at Antietam* (Harrisburg, PA: State Printer, 1906), 134. See also Rafuse, *Antietam, South Mountain & Harpers Ferry*, 23–27; Sears, *Landscape Turned Red*, 176–77; Sears, *Lincoln's Lieutenants*, 382–83; Wert, *The Sword of Lincoln*, 158–59; Hartwig, *To Antietam Creek*, 620–21; Priest, *Antietam*, 15–29; and McPherson, *Crossroads of Freedom*, 116–18.

35. Rafuse, *Antietam, South Mountain & Harpers Ferry*, 27, 32–33, 37–39; Sears, *Lincoln's Lieutenants*, 381–82; Ent, *The Pennsylvania Reserves in the Civil War*, 147–48; Sears, *Landscape Turned Red*, 180–81; Hartwig, *To Antietam Creek*, 639–41; Priest, *Antietam*, 22–31; Wert, *The Sword of Lincoln*, 158–59; Sears, *The Young Napolean*, 303; McPherson, *Crossroads of Freedom*, 116–18; McPherson, *Battle Cry of Freedom*, 540–41; Glover, *Bucktailed Wildcats*, 154–58; Thomson and Rauch, *History of the "Bucktails,"* 209–11; Sypher, *History of the Pennsylvania Reserves*, 378–83, 390–92; Ent, *The Pennsylvania Reserves in the Civil War*, 144–48; Bates, *History of the Pennsylvania Volunteers*, 1:918; Miller, *The Training of an Army*, 119; Bosbyshell, *Pennsylvania at Antietam*, 134.

36. See Rafuse, *Antietam, South Mountain & Harpers Ferry*, 32–39; Sears, *Landscape Turned Red*, 185–90, 197–201; Priest, *Antietam*, 29–31, 46, 55, 60–63; and Wert, *The Sword of Lincoln*, 160.

37. For the "whisper" quote, see Wert, *The Sword of Lincoln*, 159, 448n63. See also Sears, *Landscape Turned Red*, 181; Priest, *Antietam*, 59–69; Rafuse, *Antietam, South Mountain & Harpers Ferry*, 27–28, 45–46; McPherson, *Crossroads of Freedom*, 116–18; McPherson, *Battle Cry of Freedom*, 540–41; Wert, *The Sword of Lincoln*, 157–71; Sears, *Lincoln's Lieutenants*, 384–85; and Sears, *The Young Napolean*, 296–317.

38. Thomson and Rauch, *History of the "Bucktails,"* 211–18; Sypher, *History of the Pennsylvania Reserves*, 380–86; Ent, *The Pennsylvania Reserves in the Civil War*, 149, 155, 344. See also Sears, *Landscape Turned Red*, 184–85, 215; Sears, *Lincoln's Lieutenants*, 388–89; Rafuse, *Antietam, South Mountain & Harpers Ferry*, 27–28; and Wert, *The Sword of Lincoln*, 159.

39. See Priest, *Antietam*, 66, 69, 91, 93, and Sears, *Landscape Turned Red*, 213.

40. Phillip G. Ellithorpe to Sisters, September 24, 1862, CCHM.

41. *OR*, 19, pt. 1:275–77 (Maj. Gen. Edwin V. Sumner), 310–12 (Brig. Gen. Willis A. Gorman), 314–15 (Col. Alfred Sully). See also Wert, *The Sword of Lincoln*, 160–63; Sears, *Lincoln's Lieutenants*, 383–84, 390–93; Sears, *Landscape Turned Red*, 197–202, 216–29, 235–54; Priest, *Antietam*, 46–57, 71–77, 96–98, 106–33, 150–51; Rafuse, *Antietam, South Mountain & Harpers Ferry*, 61, 65–66, 68–73; and McPherson, *Crossroads of Freedom*, 119–20.

42. Fairchild, *History of the 27th New York Volunteers*, 95; Westervelt, *Lights and Shadows of Army Life*, 75; Buell, *A Brief History of Company B, 27th New York Regiment*, 13; Phisterer, *New York in the War of the Rebellion*, 2:183–87. See also Wert, *The Sword of Lincoln*, 163–66, 171; Sears, *Landscape Turned Red*, 256–57, 272–73; Sears, *Lincoln's Lieutenants*, 410; Priest, *Antietam*, 165–67, 338; and Slocum, *The Life and Services of Major-General Henry Warner Slocum*, 49–50.

43. *OR*, 19, pt. 1:183–93 (casualties). See also Wert, *The Sword of Lincoln*, 163–69; Rafuse, *Antietam, South Mountain & Harpers Ferry*, 80–114; Sears, *Lincoln's Lieutenants*, 393–405; Sears, *The Young Napolean*, 298–309; Priest, *Antietam*, 138–315; Sears, *Landscape Turned Red*, 257–98; and McPherson, *Battle Cry of Freedom*, 543–45.

44. Fairchild, *History of the 27th New York Volunteers*, 96. See also Westervelt, *Lights and Shadows of Army Life*, 77; Hess, *The Union Soldier in Battle*, 37–41, 149, 156; Linderman, *Embattled Courage*, 125; Sears, *Lincoln's Lieutenants*, 414; Wert, *The Sword of Lincoln*, 171; Sears, *Landscape Turned Red*, 293–94, 305, 314; Rafuse, *Antietam, South Mountain & Harpers Ferry*, 119–20; McPherson, *Crossroads of Freedom*, 6; and Priest, *Antietam*, 314.

45. Sears, *Lincoln's Lieutenants*, 424–27; Wert, *The Sword of Lincoln*, 174–75; Sears, *The Young Napolean*, 332–33; Rafuse, *Antietam, South Mountain & Harpers Ferry*, 230–31; Sears, *Landscape Turned Red*, 323–32; Priest, *Antietam*, 334–35.

46. Glover, *Bucktailed Wildcats*, 160; Thomson and Rauch, *History of the "Bucktails,"* 218; Sypher, *History of the Pennsylvania Reserves*, 386; Ent, *The Pennsylvania Reserves in the Civil War*, 148–49; *OR*, 51, pt. 1:155–56 (Capt. Dennis McGee).

47. Phillip G. Ellithorpe to Sister, October 19, 1862, CCHM; *OR*, 51, pt. 1:155–56 (Capt. Dennis McGee). See also Glover, *Bucktailed Wildcats*, 158, 162–63; Thomson and Rauch, *History of the "Bucktails,"* 211, 215–21; Sypher, *History of the Pennsylvania Reserves*, 404; Ent, *The Pennsylvania Reserves in the Civil War*, 157–61; Bates, *History of the Pennsylvania Volunteers*, 1:918; Sears, *Lincoln's Lieutenants*, 417, 428–29; Wert, *The Sword of Lincoln*, 169; Sears, *The Young Napolean*, 331; Sears, *Landscape Turned Red*, 294; and McPherson, *Crossroads of Freedom*, 129, 177.

48. Phillip G. Ellithorpe to Sisters, September 24, 1862, CCHM.

49. Glover, *Bucktailed Wildcats*, 163–64; Thomson and Rauch, *History of the "Bucktails,"* 220–22; Sypher, *History of the Pennsylvania Reserves*, 396–99; Ent, *The Pennsylvania Reserves in the Civil War*, 160–61; Wiley, *The Life of Billy Yank*, 286.

50. Phillip G. Ellithorpe to Ann, October 19, 1862, CCHM; Philander D. Ellithorpe to Ann, October 3–7, 1862, CCHM. See also Phillip G. Ellithorpe to Sisters, September 24, 1862, CCHM; Phillip G. Ellithorpe to Permelia, October 19, 1862, CCHM; Philander D. Ellithorpe to Ann, November 3, 1862, CCHM; Hess, *The Union Soldier in Battle*,

33; Sypher, *History of the Pennsylvania Reserves*, 404–5; and Thomson and Rauch, *History of the "Bucktails,"* 219.

51. Philander D. Ellithorpe to Ann and Permelia, September 29, 1862, and October 3, 1863, CCHM. See also Phisterer, *New York in the War of the Rebellion*, 2:188–94, and Westervelt, *Lights and Shadows of Army Life*, 23, 80.

52. Philander D. Ellithorpe to Ann, November 3, 1862, CCHM.

53. Buell, *A Brief History of Company B, 27th New York Regiment*, 14.

54. Philander D. Ellithorpe to Ann, November 3, 1862, CCHM. See also Fairchild, *History of the 27th New York Volunteers*, 97–110; Westervelt, *Lights and Shadows of Army Life*, 78–86; Buell, *A Brief History of Company B, 27th New York Regiment*, 14–15; Sears, *Landscape Turned Red*, 327–28; Wert, *The Sword of Lincoln*, 174–78; Sears, *Lincoln's Lieutenants*, 427; Hattaway, *Shades of Blue and Gray*, 95–99; Sears, *The Young Napolean*, 328–29, 332–33, 337; Rafuse, *Antietam, South Mountain & Harpers Ferry*, 230–31; and McPherson, *Crossroads of Freedom*, 149.

55. Phillip G. Ellithorpe to Sister, November 2, 1862, CCHM.

56. Phillip G. Ellithorpe to Sister, November 29, 1862, CCHM. See also Fairchild, *History of the 27th New York Volunteers*, 97–110, and Westervelt, *Lights and Shadows of Army Life*, 78–86.

57. Philander D. Ellithorpe to Cousin Ell, November 29, 1862, CCHM. See also Fairchild, *History of the 27th New York Volunteers*, 108–12, and Westervelt, *Lights and Shadows of Army Life*, 86. For McClellan's removal, see Wert, *The Sword of Lincoln*, 174–75, 180–82; Sears, *Lincoln's Lieutenants*, 433–36; Sears, *Landscape Turned Red*, 337–44; Sears, *The Young Napolean*, 338–41; Rafuse, *Antietam, South Mountain & Harpers Ferry*, 230–31; and McPherson, *Crossroads of Freedom*, 152.

58. Phillip G. Ellithorpe to Sisters, November 13, 1862, CCHM; Philander D. Ellithorpe to Cousin Ell, November 29, 1862, CCHM.

59. Philander D. Ellithorpe to Ann, October 7, 1862, CCHM.

60. See Bowen, *The Regimental History of the First New York Dragoons*, 22, 25–26, 48–50; *OR*, 18, pt. 2:15–16, 19–20 (Maj. Gen. John A. Dix), 16–18, 20–21 (Maj. Gen. John J. Peck); and Wills, *The War Hits Home*, 71.

61. McPherson, *Battle Cry of Freedom*, 484–85. See also Adams, *Doctors in Blue*, 69, 190–91; Freemon, *Gangrene and Glory*, 43–44; and Bollet, *Civil War Medicine*, 2, 123–24.

62. Quoted in Hartwig, *To Antietam Creek*, 470–71.

63. Phillip G. Ellithorpe to Sisters, September 24, 1862, CCHM.

Chapter 8: The Saddest Hour at Fredericksburg

1. The "saddest hour" quote is attributed to Lt. Col. St. Clair A. Mulholland of the 116th Pennsylvania. See Wert, *The Sword of Lincoln*, 204.

2. For the chain of command as it affected Phillip and Philander, see appendix A. For Burnside's Grand Division design, see Wert, *The Sword of Lincoln*, 183–85; Sears, *Lincoln's Lieutenants*, 441–43; Rable, *Fredericksburg! Fredericksburg!*, 59–60; Francis Augustin O'Reilly, *The Fredericksburg Campaign: Winter War on the Rappahannock* (Baton Rouge: Louisiana State University Press, 2003), 21–24; Hattaway, *Shades of Blue and Gray*, 106–11; Glover, *Bucktailed Wildcats*, 165; Thomson and Rauch, *History of the "Bucktails,"* 223; Sypher, *History of the Pennsylvania Reserves*, 407–9; Ent, *The Pennsylvania Reserves in the Civil War*, 164;

Daniel E. Sutherland, *Fredericksburg and Chancellorsville: The Dare Mark Campaign* (Lincoln: University of Nebraska Press, 1998), 1–14; Chris Mackowski and Kristopher D. White, *Simply Murder: The Battle of Fredericksburg, December 13, 1862* (El Dorado Hills, CA: Savas Beatie, 2013), 5; Fairchild, *History of the 27th New York Volunteers*, 113–14; and Westervelt, *Lights and Shadows of Army Life*, 85–88.

3. Wert, *The Sword of Lincoln*, 185; Sears, *Lincoln's Lieutenants*, 443–44; Rable, *Fredericksburg! Fredericksburg!*, 30–32; O'Reilly, *The Fredericksburg Campaign*, 3–7, 23–25; Sutherland, *The Dare Mark Campaign*, 1–12; Jones, *Civil War Command and Strategy*, 100–103.

4. Phillip G. Ellithorpe to Sisters, November 13, 1862, CCHM. For the concept of concentration in time, see Jones, *Civil War Command and Strategy*, 100–103.

5. Wert, *The Sword of Lincoln*, 186; Sears, *Lincoln's Lieutenants*, 445; Rable, *Fredericksburg! Fredericksburg!*, 66–70, 81; O'Reilly, *The Fredericksburg Campaign*, 26–27, 44–45; Mackowski and White, *Simply Murder*, 5; Sutherland, *The Dare Mark Campaign*, 23–36; McPherson, *Battle Cry of Freedom*, 570–71; Glover, *Bucktailed Wildcats*, 166–68; Thomson and Rauch, *History of the "Bucktails,"* 223–26; Sypher, *History of the Pennsylvania Reserves*, 408–10; Ent, *The Pennsylvania Reserves in the Civil War*, 165–66.

6. Wert, *The Sword of Lincoln*, 186–87; Sears, *Lincoln's Lieutenants*, 436, 441–46, 451; Rable, *Fredericksburg! Fredericksburg!*, 64, 78, 82–85, 103; O'Reilly, *The Fredericksburg Campaign*, 32, 45, 49, 53, 59–65; Mackowski and White, *Simply Murder*, 6, 15; Sutherland, *The Dare Mark Campaign*, 16–17, 23, 31.

7. Phillip G. Ellithorpe to Sisters, September 24, 1862, CCHM.

8. Phillip G. Ellithorpe to Sister, November 9, 1862, CCHM.

9. Phillip G. Ellithorpe to Sisters, November 9, 13, and 15, 1862, CCHM.

10. Phillip G. Ellithorpe to Sisters, November 15 and 16, 1862, CCHM.

11. Phillip G. Ellithorpe to Sisters, November 9, 1862, CCHM.

12. See the composite letter of Phillip G. Ellithorpe to Sisters and Father, November 20–22, 1862, CCHM.

13. Phillip G. Ellithorpe to Sisters, November 16 and 20, 1862, in Ellithorpe Family Collection, CCHM.

14. Wert, *The Sword of Lincoln*, 187–88; Sears, *Lincoln's Lieutenants*, 449; Rable, *Fredericksburg! Fredericksburg!*, 100–103; Ent, *The Pennsylvania Reserves in the Civil War*, 166; Thomson and Rauch, *History of the "Bucktails,"* 224–28; Sypher, *History of the Pennsylvania Reserves*, 410.

15. Philander D. Ellithorpe to Cousin Ell, November 29, 1862, CCHM. See also Fairchild, *History of the 27th New York Volunteers*, 114; Westervelt, *Lights and Shadows of Army Life*, 86; and Buell, *A Brief History of Company B, 27th New York Regiment*, 14.

16. Phillip G. Ellithorpe to Sisters and Father, November 20, 1862, CCHM; Philander D. Ellithorpe to Cousin Ell, November 29, 1862, CCHM.

17. Ent, *The Pennsylvania Reserves in the Civil War*, 166; Glover, *Bucktailed Wildcats*, 167; Thomson and Rauch, *History of the "Bucktails,"* 224–25; Sypher, *History of the Pennsylvania Reserves*, 410; Bates, *History of the Pennsylvania Volunteers*, 1:933.

18. Fairchild, *History of the 27th New York Volunteers*, 114. See also Westervelt, *Lights and Shadows of Army Life*, 86; Buell, *A Brief History of Company B, 27th New York Regiment*, 14; Ent, *The Pennsylvania Reserves in the Civil War*, 166; Glover, *Bucktailed Wildcats*, 167; Thomson and Rauch, *History of the "Bucktails,"* 224–25; Sypher, *History of the Pennsylvania Reserves*, 410; and Bates, *History of the Pennsylvania Volunteers*, 1:933.

19. Phillip G. Ellithorpe to Sister and Father, November 22, 1862, CCHM. For the use of music and nature as metaphor, see Hess, *The Union Soldier in Battle*, 15.

20. Phillip G. Ellithorpe to Sister and Father, November 22, 1862, CCHM. Officers like Ward had grown weary of dealing with soldiers who exhibited questionable characteristics, such as malingering, suspicious illness, and unexplained absenteeism. See Carmichael, *The War for the Common Soldier*, 134–35, 143, 160, 164, 179.

21. Phillip G. Ellithorpe to Sisters, December 6, 1862, CCHM. An observer in Philander's 27th New York confirms that the lunar eclipse "attracted a great deal of attention" in the Army of the Potomac. See Fairchild, *History of the 27th New York Volunteers*, 116.

22. Buell, *A Brief History of Company B, 27th New York Regiment*, 14. See also Rable, *Fredericksburg! Fredericksburg!*, 136–38; O'Reilly, *The Fredericksburg Campaign*, 51–52; Sutherland, *The Dare Mark Campaign*, 28–30; Glover, *Bucktailed Wildcats*, 172–73; Ent, *The Pennsylvania Reserves in the Civil War*, 167; Thomson and Rauch, *History of the "Bucktails,"* 227–28; Sypher, *History of the Pennsylvania Reserves*, 410; Fairchild, *History of the 27th New York Volunteers*, 115–17; and Westervelt, *Lights and Shadows of Army Life*, 88.

23. Wert, *The Sword of Lincoln*, 188–90; Sears, *Lincoln's Lieutenants*, 450–52; Rable, *Fredericksburg! Fredericksburg!*, 158–59; O'Reilly, *The Fredericksburg Campaign*, 52–57; Sutherland, *The Dare Mark Campaign*, 28–32; Glover, *Bucktailed Wildcats*, 172–73; Ent, *The Pennsylvania Reserves in the Civil War*, 166–67; McPherson, *Battle Cry of Freedom*, 570–71; Miller, *The Training of an Army*, 140.

24. Wert, *The Sword of Lincoln*, 188–89, 194–95; Sears, *Lincoln's Lieutenants*, 450–55; Rable, *Fredericksburg! Fredericksburg!*, 154–55; O'Reilly, *The Fredericksburg Campaign*, 52–54; Mackowski and White, *Simply Murder*, 10; Sutherland, *The Dare Mark Campaign*, 28–32, 42.

25. *OR*, 21:509–10 (Maj. Gen. George G. Meade).

26. *OR*, 21:180–83 (Brig. Gen. Henry J. Hunt), 225 (Lt. Edmund Kirby), 513–14 (Lt. John G. Simpson), 515–16 (Capt. James H. Cooper). See also O'Reilly, *The Fredericksburg Campaign*, 57, 65–67; Rable, *Fredericksburg! Fredericksburg!*, 156–60; and Mackowski and White, *Simply Murder*, 19–22, 27–28.

27. See Fairchild, *History of the 27th New York Volunteers*, 118–19, and Westervelt, *Lights and Shadows of Army Life*, 84–88. For general events of December 10–11, see Sutherland, *The Dare Mark Campaign*, 38; Rable, *Fredericksburg! Fredericksburg!*, 190; Sears, *Lincoln's Lieutenants*, 450–56; O'Reilly, *The Fredericksburg Campaign*, 57, 71–76; and Mackowski and White, *Simply Murder*, 21–22.

28. Rable, *Fredericksburg! Fredericksburg!*, 191–95; O'Reilly, *The Fredericksburg Campaign*, 112–13, 137–39, 142; Wert, *The Sword of Lincoln*, 195–97; Sears, *Lincoln's Lieutenants*, 457; Mackowski and White, *Simply Murder*, 67; Glover, *Bucktailed Wildcats*, 171–74; Thomson and Rauch, *History of the "Bucktails,"* 227–31; Sypher, *History of the Pennsylvania Reserves*, 411–13; Ent, *The Pennsylvania Reserves in the Civil War*, 167–71; *OR*, 21:452–53 (Maj. Gen. John F. Reynolds), 509–10 (Maj. Gen. George G. Meade), 513–14 (Lt. John G. Simpson), 515–16 (Capt. James H. Cooper).

29. Fairchild, *History of the 27th New York Volunteers*, 120–28; Westervelt, *Lights and Shadows of Army Life*, 98–103; Buell, *A Brief History of Company B, 27th New York Regiment*, 14–15. See also Wert, *The Sword of Lincoln*, 193–95; Sears, *Lincoln's Lieutenants*, 457, 470; Ent, *The Pennsylvania Reserves in the Civil War*, 170; Rable, *Fredericksburg! Fredericksburg!*, 176–77, 194–95; O'Reilly, *The Fredericksburg Campaign*, 111–12, 137–41; Mackowski and

White, *Simply Murder*, 41–42; Sutherland, *The Dare Mark Campaign*, 43–47; McPherson, *Battle Cry of Freedom*, 572; and Hattaway, *Shades of Blue and Gray*, 106–11.

30. *OR*, 21:510–11 (Maj. Gen. George G. Meade), 513–14 (Lt. John G. Simpson), 515–16 (Capt. James H. Cooper).
See also Glover, *Bucktailed Wildcats*, 172–74; Thomson and Rauch, *History of the "Bucktails,"* 227–31, 275; Ent, *The Pennsylvania Reserves in the Civil War*, 172–74; and Sypher, *History of the Pennsylvania Reserves*, 411–12, 472–73.

31. Sypher, *History of the Pennsylvania Reserves*, 420; Bates, *History of the Pennsylvania Volunteers*, 1:935; *Pennsylvania Civil War Soldier's Index Cards*, O. Lieutenant Patrick J. O'Rourke was serving in Company E, 1st Pennsylvania Reserves, when he was promoted to captain in Meade's ambulance corps on August 8, 1862.

32. *OR*, 21:510–11 (Maj. Gen. George G. Meade), 518–19 (Col. William McCandless); Glover, *Bucktailed Wildcats*, 174; Thomson and Rauch, *History of the "Bucktails,"* 231–32; Sypher, *History of the Pennsylvania Reserves*, 420–21; Ent, *The Pennsylvania Reserves in the Civil War*, 174–76. See also Wert, *The Sword of Lincoln*, 195–96; Sears, *Lincoln's Lieutenants*, 457–58; Rable, *Fredericksburg! Fredericksburg!*, 196–202; O'Reilly, *The Fredericksburg Campaign*, 143–60; Mackowski and White, *Simply Murder*, 43–45, 51–52; and Sutherland, *The Dare Mark Campaign*, 47–49.

33. *OR*, 21:514–15 (Lt. John G. Simpson). See also Miller, *The Training of an Army*, 141–42, and Ent, *The Pennsylvania Reserves in the Civil War*, 176. So many horses were killed in Meade's assault that some of the Federals nicknamed Prospect Hill "Dead Horse Hill."

34. Glover, *Bucktailed Wildcats*, 174–76; Thomson and Rauch, *History of the "Bucktails,"* 233; Ent, *The Pennsylvania Reserves in the Civil War*, 176. See also Rable, *Fredericksburg! Fredericksburg!*, 204; O'Reilly, *The Fredericksburg Campaign*, 166–67; and Sutherland, *The Dare Mark Campaign*, 49.

35. Phillip G. Ellithorpe to Sister, December 22, 1862, CCHM. Another colorful member of the 1st Rifles was wounded in the attack, Francis "French Frank" Gruay. The forty-five-year-old soldier of fortune had fought in several European wars, and he was especially skilled in the use of the bayonet, a skill he imparted to bucktailed comrades at Camp Curtin. Later, Gruay worked as a sutler in Washington. See Thomson and Rauch, *History of the "Bucktails,"* 239.

36. Sypher, *History of the Pennsylvania Reserves*, 421. See also Glover, *Bucktailed Wildcats*, 176; Thomson and Rauch, *History of the "Bucktails,"* 232–36; Sypher, *History of the Pennsylvania Reserves*, 415, 442; Ent, *The Pennsylvania Reserves in the Civil War*, 177–81; *OR*, 21:510–11 (Maj. Gen. George G. Meade), 518–19 (Col. William McCandless); Sears, *Lincoln's Lieutenants*, 458; Rable, *Fredericksburg! Fredericksburg!*, 205–9; O'Reilly, *The Fredericksburg Campaign*, 165–67, 171–74, 184–85; Mackowski and White, *Simply Murder*, 45; and Sutherland, *The Dare Mark Campaign*, 49.

37. Wert, *The Sword of Lincoln*, 196; Sears, *Lincoln's Lieutenants*, 458; Rable, *Fredericksburg! Fredericksburg!*, 193–98, 205–7; O'Reilly, *The Fredericksburg Campaign*, 129, 172–82, 187–98; Mackowski and White, *Simply Murder*, 55–59; Sutherland, *The Dare Mark Campaign*, 49; Glover, *Bucktailed Wildcats*, 176; Thomson and Rauch, *History of the "Bucktails,"* 233–36; Ent, *The Pennsylvania Reserves in the Civil War*, 179–81, 184–85; Miller, *The Training of an Army*, 142.

38. Wert, *The Sword of Lincoln*, 196; Sears, *Lincoln's Lieutenants*, 458; Rable, *Fredericksburg! Fredericksburg!*, 214–15, 244–48; O'Reilly, *The Fredericksburg Campaign*, 198–245, 343, 355; Mackowski and White, *Simply Murder*, 65; Sutherland, *The Dare Mark Campaign*, 50–51; Ent, *The Pennsylvania Reserves in the Civil War*, 181–82; Glover, *Bucktailed Wildcats*, 177; Thomson and Rauch, *History of the "Bucktails,"* 238–39; Sypher, *History of the Pennsylvania Reserves*, 415; *OR*, 21:139 (casualties).

39. Fairchild, *History of the 27th New York Volunteers*, 119. See also *OR*, 21:522–24 (Maj. Gen. William F. Smith), 526–27 (Brig. Gen. William T. H. Brooks); O'Reilly, *The Fredericksburg Campaign*, 113, 141, 356; Sutherland, *The Dare Mark Campaign*, 51; and Rable, *Fredericksburg! Fredericksburg!*, 250–51.

40. Philander D. Ellithorpe to Friends, December 14, 1862, CCHM.

41. Fairchild, *History of the 27th New York Volunteers*, 119–22.

42. Federal casualties reported were as follows: Right Grand Division (5,444), Center Grand Division (3,355), and Left Grand Division (3,787). See *OR*, 21:142 (casualties); Wert, *The Sword of Lincoln*, 203; Sears, *Lincoln's Lieutenants*, 465–67; Rable, *Fredericksburg! Fredericksburg!*, 255–67, 271–87, 309–10; O'Reilly, *The Fredericksburg Campaign*, 397, 412, 430–45, 452; Mackowski and White, *Simply Murder*, 87; Sutherland, *The Dare Mark Campaign*, 56–63; Hattaway, *Shades of Blue and Gray*, 108–11; and McPherson, *Battle Cry of Freedom*, 572.

43. Philander D. Ellithorpe to Sister Ann, December 24, 1862, CCHM.

44. Philander D. Ellithorpe to Sister Ann, December 24, 1862, CCHM. On fraternization, see Fairchild, *History of the 27th New York Volunteers*, 122–28; Westervelt, *Lights and Shadows of Army Life*, 101–3; Buell, *A Brief History of Company B, 27th New York Regiment*, 15; Wiley, *The Life of Billy Yank*, 352–53; and Linderman, *Embattled Courage*, 67–70.

45. Phillip G. Ellithorpe to Ann, December 19, 1862, CCHM. See also Thomson and Rauch, *History of the "Bucktails,"* 240; Rable, *Fredericksburg! Fredericksburg!*, 281, 307–22; O'Reilly, *The Fredericksburg Campaign*, 446–47, 453; and Sutherland, *The Dare Mark Campaign*, 59. Letterman's system operated efficiently in this casualty-laden engagement. Medical supplies had been stockpiled at Aquia Landing beforehand, field and division hospitals had been erected, and 500 canvas hospital tents with a twenty-patient capacity were on the scene before the battle. The stretcher bearers had performed admirably, too. On December 15, more than 1,000 deliveries had been made to eighteen division hospitals in Falmouth. As a result, the mortality ratio of men collected dropped from one in four at Antietam to one in seven at Fredericksburg. Phillip could take some credit for this resounding success. Despite numerous delays, most patients were quartered in northern hospitals within twenty-four hours of leaving Falmouth. See Rutkow, *Bleeding Blue and Gray*, 214, 222–23.

46. Phillip G. Ellithorpe to Ann, December 19, 1862, CCHM; *OR*, 21:139, 142 (casualties). In 1859, Comfort graduated from the Jefferson Medical College in Philadelphia and enlisted in the 121st Pennsylvania on August 18, 1862. See Bates, *History of the Pennsylvania Volunteers*, 1:923; William H. Strong, *History of the 121st Regiment, Pennsylvania Volunteers* (Philadelphia: Burk and McFetridge Co., 1893), 23, 30, 239; N. A. Strait, *Roster of All Regimental Surgeons and Assistant Surgeons in the Late War* (Washington, DC: U.S. Pension Office, 1882), 232; and George R. Prowell, *The History of Camden County, New Jersey* (Philadelphia: L. J. Richards and Co., 1886), 249–52.

47. Phillip G. Ellithorpe to Ann, December 19, 1862, CCHM.

48. Phillip G. Ellithorpe to Sister, December 22, 1862, CCHM.

49. Phillip G. Ellithorpe to Sisters, December 31, 1862, CCHM.

50. Phillip G. Ellithorpe to Sister, December 22, 1862, CCHM.

51. Phillip G. Ellithorpe to Sister Ann, December 18, 19, 22, and 31, 1862, and January 1, 1863, CCHM. For more on the difficult decision of desertion, see Carmichael, *The War for the Common Soldier*, 177–79, 227.

52. For an account of Trinity Episcopal Church during the Civil War, see John Kelly, "James Renwick's Trinity Episcopal Church," *Washington Post*, January 4, 2014.

53. Phillip G. Ellithorpe to Ann, December 31, 1862, and January 1, 1863, CCHM; Phillip G. Ellithorpe to Sister Mary, January 5, 1863, CCHM; Phillip G. Ellithorpe, Roll Call, Military Service Record, NARA. See also Rable, *Fredericksburg! Fredericksburg!*, 317, 357, 367, and Adams, *Doctors in Blue*, 54. For the pragmatic requests for items such as fruit and warm clothing, see Carmichael, *The War for the Common Soldier*, 33, 49.

54. Phillip G. Ellithorpe to Sisters, January 4, 17, and 20, 1863, CCHM.

55. Phillip G. Ellithorpe to Sister, January 20, 1863, CCHM. For soldiers' use of poetry to lessen the brutal realities of war in family correspondence, see Wiley, *The Life of Billy Yank*, 185–87.

56. Phillip G. Ellithorpe to Sister, January 20, 1863, CCHM.

57. *Pennsylvania Civil War Veteran's Index Card File*, P and S; Bates, *History of the Pennsylvania Volunteers*, 1:935. This undated and unattached handwritten acrostic poem is found in Ellithorpe Family Collection, CCHM. Steiner survived the war, but Pardeye was not present when his regiment mustered out in 1865.

58. Sutherland, *The Dare Mark Campaign*, 79–81, 85; Rable, *Fredericksburg! Fredericksburg!*, 354–55, 403; Ent, *The Pennsylvania Reserves in the Civil War*, 187–88; Glover, *Bucktailed Wildcats*, 180–81; Thomson and Rauch, *History of the "Bucktails,"* 241; Sypher, *History of the Pennsylvania Reserves*, 427; Mackowski and White, *Simply Murder*, 104–5; O'Reilly, *The Fredericksburg Campaign*, 462–65; Wiley, *The Life of Billy Yank*, 290–91.

59. Linderman, *Embattled Courage*, 163, 187. See also Rable, *Fredericksburg! Fredericksburg!*, 304; Hess, *The Union Soldier in Battle*, 75; and Carmichael, *The War for the Common Soldier*, 134–40.

60. Henry Hyde to Phillip G. Ellithorpe, January 17, 1863, CCHM. For civilian defeatism, see Sutherland, *The Dare Mark Campaign*, 78, 87; Linderman, *Embattled Courage*, 159, 216, 222, 245; Wiley, *The Life of Billy Yank*, 278; Carmichael, *The War for the Common Soldier*, 77–79; and McPherson, *For Cause and Comrades*, 121–22.

61. See Carmichael, *The War for the Common Soldier*, 77–79, 144–49, 174–79; McPherson, *Battle Cry of Freedom*, 574; Wert, *The Sword of Lincoln*, 211; and Adams, *Living Hell*, 126.

62. Philander D. Ellithorpe to Ann, January 6, 1863, CCHM.

63. Phillip G. Ellithorpe to Sister, January 31, 1863, CCHM.

64. Philander D. Ellithorpe to Ann, January 6 and 15, 1863, CCHM.

65. See Phillip G. Ellithorpe to Sisters, December 6, 1862, CCHM; Phillip G. Ellithorpe to Asa R. Burleson, July 26, 1862, CCHM.

66. Westervelt, *Lights and Shadows of Army Life*, 96; Fairchild, *History of the 27th New York Volunteers*, 119. See also Carmichael, *The War for the Common Soldier*, 30–32; Rable, *Fredericksburg! Fredericksburg!*, 4, 252; Hess, *The Union Soldier in Battle*, 78–81, 159; and Eric

Dean, "Post Traumatic Stress," in *The Civil War Veteran: A Historical Reader*, ed. Larry M. Logue and Michael Barton (New York: New York University Press, 2007), 126–45.

67. Adams, *Doctors in Blue*, 86–89; Rable, *Fredericksburg! Fredericksburg!*, 307–22.

68. Dean, "Post Traumatic Stress," in Logue and Barton, *The Civil War Veteran*, 126–45.

69. *OR*, 21:139, 142 (casualties). See also Thomson and Rauch, *History of the "Bucktails,"* 240; Glover, *Bucktailed Wildcats*, 180; Sypher, *History of the Pennsylvania Reserves*, 420; Ent, *The Pennsylvania Reserves in the Civil War*, 184; Miller, *The Training of an Army*, 143; Rable, *Fredericksburg! Fredericksburg!*, 194–95, 288; O'Reilly, *The Fredericksburg Campaign*, 139; Wert, *The Sword of Lincoln*, 204; Mackowski and White, *Simply Murder*, 98; Sutherland, *The Dare Mark Campaign*, 68; and Fox, *Regimental Losses*, 41.

70. Phillip G. Ellithorpe to Sister, January 1, 1863, CCHM; Phillip G. Ellithorpe to Sisters, January 17, 1863, CCHM. An offense similar to Blanchard's took place in the 27th New York when Capt. William B. Brainerd (Company F) absconded with a sizable amount of cash he had borrowed from enlisted men as well as tills from the company hospital and commissary fund. See Westervelt, *Lights and Shadows of Army Life*, 99.

Chapter 9: "I Have Seen Enough of This Unjust War": The Ellithorpe Brothers and the Limits of Patriotism

1. For the source of the quotation in the chapter title, see Phillip G. Ellithorpe to Sisters, February 21, 1863, CCHM.

2. For the Mud March (January 20–23, 1863), see Wert, *The Sword of Lincoln*, 206–14; Sears, *Lincoln's Lieutenants*, 472–83; Rable, *Fredericksburg! Fredericksburg!*, 409–13; O'Reilly, *The Fredericksburg Campaign*, 461–76; Mackowski and White, *Simply Murder*, 98–99; and Sutherland, *The Dare Mark Campaign*, 84–91.

3. Philander D. Ellithorpe to Sisters, January 15, 1863, CCHM.

4. Philander D. Ellithorpe to Sisters, January 15, 1863, CCHM; Phillip G. Ellithorpe to Sisters, November 2, 1862, and February 21, 1863, CCHM.

5. O'Reilly, *The Fredericksburg Campaign*, 488–89; Fairchild, *History of the 27th New York Volunteers*, 129–34; Westervelt, *Lights and Shadows of Army Life*, 104–8.

6. Glover, *Bucktailed Wildcats*, 182; Thomson and Rauch, *History of the "Bucktails,"* 242–43; Sypher, *History of the Pennsylvania Reserves*, 427; Ent, *The Pennsylvania Reserves in the Civil War*, 189–90; Fairchild, *History of the 27th New York Volunteers*, 137–40; Westervelt, *Lights and Shadows of Army Life*, 106–10.

7. Hooker immediately disbanded the grand divisions and reinstated the eight corps system, created an independent cavalry corps, and returned the artillery to corps-level control.

8. For the chain of command as it affected Phillip and Philander, see appendix A.

9. Thomson and Rauch, *History of the "Bucktails,"* 241–45; Sypher, *History of the Pennsylvania Reserves*, 427–33; Ent, The *Pennsylvania Reserves in the Civil War*, 190–91; Bates, *History of the Pennsylvania Volunteers*, 1:919.

10. Ent, *The Pennsylvania Reserves in the Civil War*, 191; Leech, *Reveille in Washington*, 263; Glover, *Bucktailed Wildcats*, 187–88; Thomson and Rauch, *History of the "Bucktails,"* 246.

11. For placement of the three brigades of Pennsylvania Reserves around the capital, see *OR*, 51, pt. 1:985 (Special Order No. 2). See also Glover, *Bucktailed Wildcats*, 183–84; Thomson and Rauch, *History of the "Bucktails,"* 243–44; Sypher, *History of the Pennsylvania*

Reserves, 427–34; Ent, *The Pennsylvania Reserves in the Civil War*, 190–91; and Bates, *History of the Pennsylvania Volunteers*, 1:919.

12. Phillip G. Ellithorpe to Sister, February 6, 1863, CCHM. Pvt. Lewis Gibble of Co. F, 93rd Pennsylvania, was wounded at Fredericksburg and discharged on February 14, 1863. See *Pennsylvania Civil War Veterans Index*, G, and Penrose G. Mark, *Red, White, and Blue Badge: A History of the 93rd Regiment, Known as the "Lebanon Infantry"* (Harrisburg, PA: Aughinbaugh Press, 1911), 75, 191–92.

13. Asa R. Burleson to Ann, January 27, 1863, CCHM; Asa R. Burleson to Phillip G. Ellithorpe, March 14, 1863, CCHM; Bowen, *Regimental History of the First New York Dragoons*, 35–38, 43. For the chain of command as it affected Asa, see appendix A.

14. Bowen, *Regimental History of the First New York Dragoons*, 52–57.

15. *OR*, 18:132–35 (Maj. Gen. John J. Peck), 136–40 (Brig. Gen. Michael Corcoran). See also Bowen, *Regimental History of the First New York Dragoons*, 58–64.

16. *OR*, 18:134–35 (Maj. Gen. John J. Peck), 139–40 (Brig. Gen. Michael Corcoran). See also Levi D. Green to Mother, April 23, 1863, in Green Family Collection, Allegany County Historical Society, Andover, NY.

17. Asa R. Burleson to Phillip G. Ellithorpe, March 14, 1863, CCHM. See also Bowen, *Regimental History of the First New York Dragoons*, 69–71, and Phisterer, *New York in the War of the Rebellion*, 2:324.

18. Wills, *The War Hits Home*, 70–71, 95–122.

19. Asa R. Burleson to Ann, January 26, 1863, CCHM; Asa R. Burleson to Phillip G. Ellithorpe, March 23, 1863, CCHM.

20. For Hooker's reforms, see Wert, *The Sword of Lincoln*, 211, 225–26; Sears, *Lincoln's Lieutenants*, 488–89; Sutherland, *The Dare Mark Campaign*, 96–107; John Hennessy, "The Army of the Potomac on the Eve of Chancellorsville," in *Chancellorsville: The Battle and Its Aftermath*, ed. Gary W. Gallagher (Chapel Hill: University of North Carolina Press, 1996), 9–11; and Stephen W. Sears, *Chancellorsville* (Boston: Houghton Mifflin, 1996), 17, 70–73.

21. Wiley, *The Life of Billy Yank*, 226–27, 282–85; Billings, *Hardtack and Coffee*, 257–68.

22. See Phillip G. Ellithorpe to Sisters, January 31, February 17, March 21 and 25, and May 9, 1863, CCHM. See also Thomson and Rauch, *History of the "Bucktails,"* 246, and Stillé, *History of the United States Sanitary Commission*, 301–2.

23. Phillip G. Ellithorpe to Sisters, February 17 and March 25, 1863, CCHM.

24. For the Mosby incident, see Glover, *Bucktailed Wildcats*, 183–85; Thomson and Rauch, *History of the "Bucktails,"* 245–47; Sypher, *History of the Pennsylvania Reserves*, 427–34; Ent, *The Pennsylvania Reserves in the Civil War*, 190–92; Bates, *History of the Pennsylvania Volunteers*, 1:919; Sutherland, *The Dare Mark Campaign*, 116; Sears, *Lincoln's Lieutenants*, 439; and Cooling, *Symbol, Sword, and Shield*, 149.

25. Phillip G. Ellithorpe to Sisters, January 27, 1863, CCHM; Phillip G. Ellithorpe to Ann, February 17 and 21, 1863, CCHM.

26. Asa R. Burleson to Phillip G. Ellithorpe, March 14, 1863, CCHM.

27. Asa R. Burleson to Phillip G. Ellithorpe, March 23, 1863, CCHM.

28. Phillip G. Ellithorpe to Sister, March 25 and April 25, 1863, CCHM. Convalescent Camp was later known as Rendezvous of Distribution.

29. Phillip G. Ellithorpe to Sister, April 25 and May 9, 1863, CCHM.

30. Bowen, *Regimental History of the First New York Dragoons*, 70–72; *OR*, 18:268–72 (Maj. Gen. John A. Dix), 274–81 (Maj. Gen. John J. Peck), 288–91 (Brig. Gen. Michael

Corcoran), 292–93 (Brig. Gen. Henry D. Terry). See also Wills, *The War Hits Home*, 123–36; Cormier, *The Siege of Suffolk*, 130–37; and Bowen, *Regimental History of the First New York Dragoons*, 70–72.

31. Bowen, *Regimental History of the First New York Dragoons*, 71–72.

32. See Cormier, *The Siege of Suffolk*, 202.

33. *OR*, 18:289 (Brig. Gen. Michael Corcoran), 292 (Brig. Gen. Henry D. Terry), 277, 280 (Maj. Gen. John J. Peck); Bowen, *Regimental History of the First New York Dragoons*, 71–72; Willford and Curtiss-Wedge, *History of Fillmore County, Minnesota*, 2:973. See also Wills, *The War Hits Home*, 149–57, and Cormier, *The Siege of Suffolk*, 134, 188–93, 228.

34. Bowen, *Regimental History of the First New York Dragoons*, 75–79.

35. Bowen, *Regimental History of the First New York Dragoons*, 78–79; Fairchild, *History of the 27th New York Volunteers*, 153; Westervelt, *Lights and Shadows of Army Life*, 116; Sutherland, *The Dare Mark Campaign*, 97, 101–3; Sears, *Chancellorsville*, 16–18; Hennessy, "The Army of the Potomac on the Eve of Chancellorsville," 10.

36. Fairchild, *History of the 27th New York Volunteers*, 155–75; Westervelt, *Lights and Shadows of Army Life*, 115–28; Buell, *A Brief History of Company B, 27th New York Regiment*, 20–21; Phisterer, *New York in the War of the Rebellion*, 2:195–98.

37. Fairchild, *History of the 27th New York Volunteers*, 153, 163; Westervelt, *Lights and Shadows of Army Life*, 118; Buell, *A Brief History of Company B, 27th New York Regiment*, 19.

38. For Hooker's battle plan, see Sears, *Lincoln's Lieutenants*, 494–503; Wert, *The Sword of Lincoln*, 225–26, 232–33; Sutherland, *The Dare Mark Campaign*, 130–36; Hattaway, *Shades of Blue and Gray*, 115–20; Hennessy, "The Army of the Potomac on the Eve of Chancellorsville," 14; Chris Mackowski and Kristopher D. White, *Chancellorsville's Forgotten Front: The Battles of Second Fredericksburg and Salem Church, May 3, 1863* (El Dorado Hills, CA: Savas Beatie, 2013), 24–30, 45–50; and Phillip W. Parsons, *The Union Sixth Army Corps in the Chancellorsville Campaign: A Study of the Engagements of Second Fredericksburg, Salem Church and Banks' Ford, May 3–4, 1863* (Jefferson, NC: McFarland, 2006), 9–20, 34–38.

39. Philander D. Ellithorpe to Phillip G. Ellithorpe, April 14, 1863, CCHM. See also Fairchild, *History of the 27th New York Volunteers*, 154–55; Westervelt, *Lights and Shadows of Army Life*, 114–18; and Buell, *A Brief History of Company B, 27th New York Regiment*, 20–21.

40. See Philander D. Ellithorpe, Military Service Record, NARA. See also Fairchild, *History of the 27th New York Volunteers*, 285–288, and Adjutant General's Report for the State of New York, 27th New York, 192, 201.

41. Philander D. Ellithorpe to Phillip G. Ellithorpe, April 14, 1863, CCHM.

42. Philander D. Ellithorpe, Military Service Record, NARA; Fairchild, *History of the 27th New York Volunteers*, 163–64, 285. See also Sutherland, *The Dare Mark Campaign*, 132; Sears, *Chancellorsville*, 130–33; and *Parsons, The Union Sixth Army Corps in the Chancellorsville Campaign*, 41, 54.

43. Philander D. Ellithorpe to Phillip G. Ellithorpe, April 14, 1863, CCHM. See also Fairchild, *History of the 27th New York Volunteers*, 155.

44. Fairchild, *History of the 27th New York Volunteers*, 163; Westervelt, *Lights and Shadows of Army Life*, 115–18; Buell, *A Brief History of Company B, 27th New York Regiment*, 19; Phisterer, *New York in the War of the Rebellion*, 2:195–98.

45. Philander D. Ellithorpe to Sister Ann, April 27, 1863, CCHM; Philander D. Ellithorpe, Muster (Hospital) Records, Military Service Record, NARA.

46. Fairchild, *History of the 27th New York Volunteers*, 163–65; Westervelt, *Lights and Shadows of Army Life*, 120; Buell, *A Brief History of Company B, 27th New York Regiment*, 19; *OR*, 25, pt. 1:579–80 (Brig. Gen. Joseph J. Bartlett), 566 (Brig. Gen. William H. T. Brooks).

47. Fairchild, *History of the 27th New York Volunteers*, 165–66. See also Westervelt, *Lights and Shadows of Army Life*, 120–23; Buell, *A Brief History of Company B, 27th New York Regiment*, 19–20; Phisterer, *New York in the War of the Rebellion*, 2:195–98; and *OR*, 25, pt. 1:579–80 (Brig. Gen. Joseph J. Bartlett), 566 (Brig. Gen. William H. T. Brooks), 587 (Col. Alexander D. Adams).

48. Fairchild, *History of the 27th New York Volunteers*, 167; Westervelt, *Lights and Shadows of Army Life*, 124; *OR*, 25, pt. 1:580 (Brig. Gen. Joseph J. Bartlett), 566 (Brig. Gen. William H. T. Brooks), 587 (Col. Alexander D. Adams).

49. Wert, *The Sword of Lincoln*, 244–46; Sears, *Lincoln's Lieutenants*, 507; Sutherland, *The Dare Mark Campaign*, 140–63; Sears, *Chancellorsville*, 304, 329–33, 357–58; Parsons, *The Union Sixth Army Corps in the Chancellorsville Campaign*, 62; Mackowski and White, *Chancellorsville's Forgotten Front*, 225–28; McPherson, *Battle Cry of Freedom*, 640–42.

50. Fairchild, *History of the 27th New York Volunteers*, 167; *OR*, 25, pt. 1:587 (Col. Alexander D. Adams).

51. Fairchild, *History of the 27th New York Volunteers*, 167–69; Westervelt, *Lights and Shadows of Army Life*, 127; *OR*, 25, pt. 1:580–81 (Brig. Gen. Joseph J. Bartlett), 567 (Brig. Gen. William H. T. Brooks), 588 (Col. Alexander D. Adams).

52. Fairchild, *History of the 27th New York Volunteers*, 169–70; Westervelt, *Lights and Shadows of Army Life*, 126–27; *OR*, 25, pt. 1:581 (Brig. Gen. Joseph J. Bartlett), 567 (Brig. Gen. William H. T. Brooks), 588 (Col. Alexander D. Adams). See also Sutherland, *The Dare Mark Campaign*, 165–68; Sears, *Chancellorsville*, 349–57; and Parsons, *The Union Sixth Army Corps in the Chancellorsville Campaign*, 65–80.

53. *OR*, 25, pt. 1:588 (Col. Alexander D. Adams).

54. Sutherland, *The Dare Mark Campaign*, 168–69; Sears, *Chancellorsville*, 377–79; Mackowski and White, *Chancellorsville's Forgotten Front*, 232–37, 242–48, 254–58; Parsons, *The Union Sixth Army Corps in the Chancellorsville Campaign*, 81–98; Sears, *Chancellorsville*, 372–77.

55. Fairchild, *History of the 27th New York Volunteers*, 170–72; Westervelt, *Lights and Shadows of Army Life*, 121; *OR*, 25, pt. 1:189 (casualties), 588 (Col. Alexander D. Adams), 581 (Brig. Gen. Joseph J. Bartlett), 568 (Brig. Gen. William H. T. Brooks).

56. *OR*, 25, pt. 1:568 (Brig. Gen. William H. T. Brooks). See also Fairchild, *History of the 27th New York Volunteers*, 171; Westervelt, *Lights and Shadows of Army Life*, 126–27; Sutherland, *The Dare Mark Campaign*, 170–76; Mackowski and White, *Chancellorsville's Forgotten Front*, 240, 247, 268, 277, 280–82; Parsons, *The Union Sixth Army Corps in the Chancellorsville Campaign*, 100–109, 115–19, 127–30; and Sears, *Chancellorsville*, 380–95.

57. *OR*, 25, pt. 1:588 (Col. Alexander D. Adams), 581–83 (Brig. Gen. Joseph J. Bartlett), 568 (Brig. Gen. William H. T. Brooks). See also Fairchild, *History of the 27th New York Volunteers*, 171–75, and Westervelt, *Lights and Shadows of Army Life*, 126–27.

58. Fairchild, *History of the 27th New York Volunteers*, 173.

59. Federal losses in the Chancellorsville campaign exceeded 11,000 killed or wounded with 6,000 temporarily missing. Bartlett's casualties (612) were the highest in Brooks's division and second highest in Sedgwick's corps. See *OR*, 25, pt. 1:172–92 (casualties).

60. Fairchild, *History of the 27th New York Volunteers*, 175; Newton Martin Curtis, *From Bull Run to Chancellorsville: The Story of the 16th New York Infantry* (New York: Putnam's Sons, 1906), 304, 307, 312.

61. *OR*, 25, pt. 1:583 (Brig. Gen. Joseph J. Bartlett).

62. Fairchild, *History of the 27th New York Volunteers*, 176–79; Westervelt, *Lights and Shadows of Army Life*, 129–33; Buell, *A Brief History of Company B, 27th New York Regiment*, 20–21.

63. For news of the banquet, see H. L. Wesley to Phillip G. Ellithorpe, June 7, 1863, CCHM.

64. Phillip G. Ellithorpe to Sisters, March 17 and 25, 1863, CCHM.

65. Phillip G. Ellithorpe to Sisters, May 14, 1863, CCHM.

66. Phillip G. Ellithorpe to Sister, March 17 and 25, April 25, and May 14, 1863, CCHM.

67. Carmichael, *The War for the Common Soldier*, 50, 134–35, 229.

68. See Hattaway, *Shades of Blue and Gray*, 239–40.

Chapter 10: "Death before Dishonor": Gettysburg

1. For the chain of command as it affected Phillip, see appendix A. See also *OR*, 25, pt. 2:182 (Organization of Department of Washington); Glover, *Bucktailed Wildcats*, 183–89; Sypher, *History of the Pennsylvania Reserves*, 443–44; Thomson and Rauch, *History of the "Bucktails,"* 246, 249–50, 260; Ent, *The Pennsylvania Reserves in the Civil War*, 193–94; and Bates, *History of the Pennsylvania Volunteers*, 1:919.

2. Phillip G. Ellithorpe to Sisters, May 14, 1863, CCHM.

3. Dealing with deserters and malingerers had become such a problem by 1863 that Dr. Roberts Bartholow published a manual for officers with practical steps on how to identify ailments that could be easily feigned. The tome even included a profile of the reluctant warrior: "The typical malingerer has dark brown or hazel eyes, dark hair, dark complexion," and shifty, suspicious eyes and a downward tilt to his head. See Roberts Bartholow, *Manual for Instructions for Enlisting and Discharging Soldiers* (Philadelphia: J. B. Lippincott, 1863), 95–96, cited in Carmichael, *The War for the Common Soldier*, 143, 340n31. See also Ella Lonn, *Desertion during the Civil War* (New York: Century, 1928).

4. Phillip G. Ellithorpe to Cousin Ell, May 15, 1863, CCHM. See also Phillip G. Ellithorpe to Sisters, June 18, 1863, CCHM; Glover, *Bucktailed Wildcats*, 187–89; Thomson and Rauch, *History of the "Bucktails,"* 249–50; Sypher, *History of the Pennsylvania Reserves*, 443; Ent, *The Pennsylvania Reserves in the Civil War*, 194; Bates, *History of the Pennsylvania Volunteers*, 1:919; and Richard Wagner, *For Honor, Flag, and Family: Civil War Major General Samuel W. Crawford, 1827–1892* (Shippensburg, PA: White Mane Press, 2005), 152–56.

5. Wert, *The Sword of Lincoln*, 259–62; Sears, *Lincoln's Lieutenants*, 532–34, 540; Harry W. Pfanz, *Gettysburg: The Second Day* (Chapel Hill: University of North Carolina Press, 1987), 8; Stephen W. Sears, *Gettysburg* (Boston: Houghton Mifflin, 2003), 59, 74, 84.

6. Bowen, *Regimental History of the First New York Dragoons*, 80–81. See also *OR*, 27, pt. 2:817–37 (Maj. Gen. John A. Dix), 854–57 (Maj. Gen. Erasmus D. Keyes).

7. Bowen, *Regimental History of the First New York Dragoons*, 81–84; Wills, *The War Hits Home*, 193; E. Marshall to Parents, June 28, 1863, Charley to Dear Ones at Home, June 28, 1863, A. W. T. to Editor, June 30, 1863, and L. A. C. to *New Yorker*, July 1, 1863, in *1st*

Regiment of Dragoons, New York Volunteers, Civil War Newspaper Clippings, New York State Military Museum and Veteran's Research Center, Albany, NY.

8. Phillip G. Ellithorpe to Sisters, June 18, 1863, CCHM.

9. For three recollections of Company I and the Bucktails in the Gettysburg campaign, see Frank J. Bell, *Recollection*, 1–6, Gettysburg National Military Park Library and Research Center, Gettysburg, PA (hereafter referred to as GNMPLRC); Capt. John P. Bard, "The 'Old Bucktails,' 42nd Regt., P. V., at the Battle of Gettysburg," in *Philadelphia Weekly Press*, May 19, 1886; and William C. Weidner Jr., "A Memoir of the Thirteenth Infantry Regiment of the Pennsylvania Reserve Corps," 3, in drawer 6-PA 42, GNMPLRC. See also Glover, *Bucktailed Wildcats*, 189–91; Thomson and Rauch, *History of the "Bucktails,"* 255–60; Sypher, *History of the Pennsylvania Reserves*, 448; Ent, *The Pennsylvania Reserves in the Civil War*, 199; and Bates, *History of the Pennsylvania Volunteers*, 1:919.

10. Phillip G. Ellithorpe to Ann, June 25, 1863, CCHM.

11. For the chain of command at it affected Phillip, see appendix A. See also Bard, "The 'Old' Bucktails," *Philadelphia Weekly Press*, May 19, 1886; Weidner, "A Memoir of the Thirteenth Infantry Regiment of the Pennsylvania Reserve Corps," 3, GNMPLRC; and *OR*, 25, pt. 2:182 (Organization of Department of Washington). See also Glover, *Bucktailed Wildcats*, 192; Thomson and Rauch, *History of the "Bucktails,"* 260; Sypher, *History of the Pennsylvania Reserves*, 449; and Ent, *The Pennsylvania Reserves in the Civil War*, 200–202.

12. Bell, *Recollection*, 1 (GNMPLRC); Bard, "The 'Old' Bucktails."

13. *OR*, 27, pt. 1:592–95 (Maj. Gen. George Sykes); Phillip G. Ellithorpe, Military Service Record, NARA; Weidner, "A Memoir of the Thirteenth Infantry Regiment of the Pennsylvania Reserve Corps," 1–2, GNMPLRC.

14. For Crawford's remarks, see Wagner, *For Honor, Flag, and Family*, 160–61. See also Ent, *The Pennsylvania Reserves in the Civil War*, 208; Glover, *Bucktailed Wildcats*, 191–94; and Thomson and Rauch, *History of the "Bucktails,"* 261–62.

15. Wert, *The Sword of Lincoln*, 275–83; Sears, *Lincoln's Lieutenants*, 551–58; Pfanz, *Gettysburg*, 31–42; Sears, *Gettysburg*, 158–225; Glenn W. LaFantasie, *Twilight at Little Round Top, July 2, 1863—The Tide Turns at Gettysburg* (Hoboken, NJ: John Wiley & Sons, 2004), 14–20; McPherson, *Battle Cry of Freedom*, 654–55; Ent, *The Pennsylvania Reserves in the Civil War*, 206–7.

16. Bell, *Recollection*, 1, GNMPLRC. See also Weidner, "A Memoir of the Thirteenth Infantry Regiment of the Pennsylvania Reserve Corps," 3, GNMPLRC; Thomson and Rauch, *History of the "Bucktails,"* 260–64; and Sypher, *History of the Pennsylvania Reserves*, 448–50.

17. See *OR*, 27, pt. 1:652–53 (Brig. Gen. Samuel W. Crawford); Weidner, "A Memoir of the Thirteenth Infantry Regiment of the Pennsylvania Reserve Corps," 6; Glover, *Bucktailed Wildcats*, 195–97; Thomson and Rauch, *History of the "Bucktails,"* 262–63; Sypher, *History of the Pennsylvania Reserves*, 450–59; Ent, *The Pennsylvania Reserves in the Civil War*, 208–9; and Bates, *History of the Pennsylvania Volunteers*, 1:919.

18. Thomson and Rauch, *History of the "Bucktails,"* 264–65; Sypher, *History of the Pennsylvania Reserves*, 458–60; Bard, "The 'Old' Bucktails"; Wert, *The Sword of Lincoln*, 286–88; Sears, *Gettysburg*, 249–50; Pfanz, *Gettysburg*, 124–47; Glover, *Bucktailed Wildcats*, 198–200; Ent, *The Pennsylvania Reserves in the Civil War*, 208; Sears, *Lincoln's Lieutenants*, 559–60; LaFantasie, *Twilight at Little Round Top*, 56–58.

19. *OR*, 27, pt. 1:593 (Maj. Gen. George Sykes). See also Jay Jorgensen, *Gettysburg's Bloody Wheatfield* (Shippensburg, PA: White Mane Press, 2002), 49–131.

20. Weidner, "A Memoir of the Thirteenth Infantry Regiment of the Pennsylvania Reserve Corps," 7, GNMPLRC; Thomson and Rauch, *History of the "Bucktails,"* 265; Sypher, *History of the Pennsylvania Reserves*, 460; Bates, *History of the Pennsylvania Volunteers*, 1:919; Bell, *Recollection*, 1, GNMPLRC; Bard, "The 'Old' Bucktails." See also Wert, *The Sword of Lincoln*, 290; Pfanz, *Gettysburg*, 392; Ent, *The Pennsylvania Reserves in the Civil War*, 211–12; and Glover, *Bucktailed Wildcats*, 201–2.

21. *OR*, 27, pt. 1:662 (Capt. Frank C. Gibbs).

22. *OR*, 27, pt. 1:662 (Capt. Frank C. Gibbs); Weidner, "A Memoir of the Thirteenth Infantry Regiment of the Pennsylvania Reserve Corps," 7, GNMPLRC.

23. *OR*, 27, pt. 1:657 (Col. William McCandless), 653 (Brig. Gen. Samuel W. Crawford); Weidner, "A Memoir of the Thirteenth Infantry Regiment of the Pennsylvania Reserve Corps," 3, 7, GNMPLRC.

24. Quoted in Wagner, *For Honor, Flag, and Family*, 163. See also Bell, *Recollection*, 1, GNMPLRC; Bard, "The 'Old' Bucktails"; *OR*, 27, pt. 1:657 (Col. William McCandless), 653 (Brig. Gen. Samuel W. Crawford); and Wagner, *For Honor, Flag, and Family*, 163–65.

25. *OR*, 27, pt. 1:597 (Capt. James A. Bates, chief ambulance officer, V Corps); Bell, *Recollection*, 1, GNMPLRC; Bard, "The 'Old' Bucktails." See also Wert, *The Sword of Lincoln*, 290; Sears, *Lincoln's Lieutenants*, 561–64; Pfanz, *Gettysburg*, 391–92; Sears, *Gettysburg*, 292–321; LaFantasie, *Twilight at Little Round Top*, 125, 179, 193–200; Jorgensen, *Gettysburg's Bloody Wheatfield*, 49–131; Wagner, *For Honor, Flag, and Family*, 163–65; Thomson and Rauch, *History of the "Bucktails,"* 266–67; Sypher, *History of the Pennsylvania Reserves*, 461; Bates, *History of the Pennsylvania Volunteers*, 1:919; Glover, *Bucktailed Wildcats*, 204–6; and Ent, *The Pennsylvania Reserves in the Civil War*, 211–14.

26. Adams, *Doctors in Blue*, 91; Gerard A. Patterson, *Debris of Battle: The Wounded of Gettysburg* (Mechanicsburg, PA: Stackpole Books, 1997), 7–10, 14, 97; Gregory A. Coco, *A Vast Sea of Misery: A History and Guide to the Union and Confederate Field Hospitals at Gettysburg, July 1–November 20, 1863* (Gettysburg, PA: Thomas Publications, 1988), 186; *OR*, 27, pt. 1:655 (Brig. Gen. Samuel W. Crawford), 597 (Capt. James A. Bates), 195–97 (Dr. Jonathan Letterman); John K. Barnes, Joseph Janvier Woodward, Charles Smart, George A. Otis, and D. L. Huntington, *The Medical and Surgical History of the War of the Rebellion, 1861–1865*, 12 vols. (Washington, DC: Government Printing Office, 1870–1888), 2:240–45, 360; Louis C. Duncan, *The Medical Department of the U.S. Army in the Civil War* (Washington, DC: Government Printing Office, 1910), 249–52.

27. *OR*, 27, pt. 1:657 (Col. William McCandless), 655 (Brig. Gen. Samuel W. Crawford). See also Pfanz, *Gettysburg*, 78, 398–400, 547; LaFantasie, *Twilight at Little Round Top*, 195–96; and Ent, *The Pennsylvania Reserves in the Civil War*, 215.

28. Bell, *Recollection*, 2, GNMPLRC. See also Bard, "The 'Old' Bucktails"; *OR*, 27, pt. 1:657 (Col. William McCandless), 662 (Capt. Frank C. Gibbs).

29. Thomson and Rauch, *History of the "Bucktails,"* 267–71; Sypher, *History of the Pennsylvania Reserves*, 461–73; Bates, *History of the Pennsylvania Volunteers*, 1:920; Bell, *Recollection*, 2, GNMPLRC; Bard, "The 'Old' Bucktails"; Weidner, "A Memoir of the Thirteenth Infantry Regiment of the Pennsylvania Reserve Corps," 9, GNMPLRC.

30. Thomson and Rauch, *History of the "Bucktails,"* 267–71; Sypher, *History of the Pennsylvania Reserves*, 461–73; Bates, *History of the Pennsylvania Volunteers*, 1:920; Bell, *Recollection*, 2, GNMPLRC; Bard, "The 'Old' Bucktails"; Weidner, "A Memoir of the Thirteenth Infantry Regiment of the Pennsylvania Reserve Corps," 9, GNMPLRC.

31. Bell, *Recollection*, 2, GNMPLRC; Bard, "The 'Old' Bucktails"; Weidner, "A Memoir of the Thirteenth Infantry Regiment of the Pennsylvania Reserve Corps," 10, GNMPLRC; Thomson and Rauch, *History of the "Bucktails,"* 268–69; *OR*, 27, pt. 1:654 (Brig. Gen. Samuel W. Crawford); Travis W. Busey and John W. Busey, *Union Casualties at Gettysburg: A Comprehensive Record*, 3 vols. (Jefferson, NC: McFarland, 2011), 2:815; John W. Busey, *These Honored Dead: The Union Casualties at Gettysburg* (Hightstown, NJ: Longstreet House, 1996), 243. See also Ent, *The Pennsylvania Reserves in the Civil War*, 216.

32. *OR*, 27, pt. 1:654 (Brig. Gen. Samuel W. Crawford), 593 (Maj. Gen. George Sykes); Bell, *Recollection*, 2, GNMPLRC; Bard, "The 'Old' Bucktails"; Thomson and Rauch, *History of the "Bucktails,"* 268–69; Weidner, "A Memoir of the Thirteenth Infantry Regiment of the Pennsylvania Reserve Corps," 9–10, GNMPLRC.

33. Phillip G. Ellithorpe, Record of Superintendent of Hospitals (Camp Letterman), Gettysburg, PA, Military Service Record, NARA. See also Coco, *A Vast Sea of Misery*, 188; Gregory A. Coco, *A Strange and Blighted Land, Gettysburg: The Aftermath of a Battle* (Gettysburg, PA: Thomas Publications, 1995), 204–5; Busey and Busey, *Union Casualties at Gettysburg*, 3:1349; Bollet, *Civil War Medicine*, 3, 218; Adams, *Living Hell*, 86–89; and Barnes et al., *The Medical and Surgical History of the War of the Rebellion*, 2:240–45.

34. Bell, *Recollection*, 3–4, GNMPLRC. See also Thomson and Rauch, *History of the "Bucktails,"* 272–73; Sypher, *History of the Pennsylvania Reserves*, 468–70; Ent, *The Pennsylvania Reserves in the Civil War*, 219; Bates, *History of the Pennsylvania Volunteers*, 1:920; Bard, "The 'Old' Bucktails."

35. Coco, *A Vast Sea of Misery*, 89; Coco, *A Strange and Blighted Land*, 205.

36. Bell, *Recollection*, 4, GNMPLRC; Coco, *A Strange and Blighted Land*, 205; Barnes et al., *The Medical and Surgical History of the War of the Rebellion*, 2:240–45.

37. Wert, *The Sword of Lincoln*, 297–300; Sears, *Lincoln's Lieutenants*, 572–78; Ent, *The Pennsylvania Reserves in the Civil War*, 220–21; Glover, *Bucktailed Wildcats*, 211–12; Thomson and Rauch, *History of the "Bucktails,"* 272–73; Sypher, *History of the Pennsylvania Reserves*, 469–70.

38. Thomson and Rauch, *History of the "Bucktails,"* 273–83; Sypher, *History of the Pennsylvania Reserves*, 470–71; Bates, *History of the Pennsylvania Volunteers*, 1:920; Sears, *Gettysburg*, 496–97; Busey and Busey, *Union Casualties at Gettysburg*, 2:815; Wagner, *For Honor, Flag, and Family*, 167; *OR*, 27, pt. 1:198 (Dr. Johnathan K. Letterman), 658 (Col. William McCandless), 655 (Brig Gen. Samuel W. Crawford); Bard, "The 'Old' Bucktails."

39. Bell, *Recollection*, 4–5, GNMPLRC.

40. *Journal of Dr. Henry Janes, Camp Letterman General Hospital Orders and Correspondence*, July 26–September 9, 1863, Henry J. Janes Collection, GNMPLRC. See also Patterson, *Debris of Battle*, 81, 96; Adams, *Doctors in Blue*, 91; Bollet, *Civil War Medicine*, 125; Thomson and Rauch, *History of the "Bucktails,"* 277; and Sypher, *History of the Pennsylvania Reserves*, 490–94.

41. Phillip G. Ellithorpe to Ann, August 8, 1863, CCHM. See also Patterson, *Debris of Battle*, 5, 46–69, 124, 150–63; Duncan, *The Medical Department of the U.S. Army in the Civil War*, 252; and Bollet, *Civil War Medicine*, 127.

42. Patterson, *Debris of Battle*, 74; Rutkow, *Bleeding Blue and Gray*, 30, 217–20; Adams, *Living Hell*, 91; Bollet, *Civil War Medicine*, 4, 99, 147–54.

43. *Journal of Dr. Henry Janes, Camp Letterman General Hospital Orders and Correspondence*, July 26–September 9, 1863, Henry J. Janes Collection, GNMPLRC; List of United

States Medical Officers at Camp Letterman, Camp Letterman Papers, Gregory Coco Collection, GNMPLRC; Ellerslie Wallace, *The Graduating Class of Jefferson Medical College of Philadelphia, Delivered March 10, 1863* (Philadelphia: n. p., 1863), 19; Ewing Jordan, *University of Pennsylvania Men Who Served in the Civil War, 1861–1865; Department of Medicine* (Philadelphia: n.p., 1900), 478; Barnes et al., *The Medical and Surgical History of the War of the Rebellion*, 2:66, 92, 372, 11:79, 186, 12:436, 530. See also Coco, *A Vast Sea of Misery*, 180–86; Sandra Moss, "The Country Practitioner: A Medical Journal with "Snap," *Garden State Legacy* 12 (June 2011): 1–17; Bollet, *Civil War Medicine*, 31; Rutkow, *Bleeding Blue and Gray*, 282, 307; and Adams, *Doctors in Blue*, 38, 56–57, 115–19.

44. Phillip G. Ellithorpe, Camp Letterman Medical Chart, Military Service Record, NARA; Phillip G. Ellithorpe, Final Medical Record, Military Pension Record, NARA. Postwar research claimed that 57 percent of knee amputations resulted in death. See Busey and Busey, *Union Casualties at Gettysburg*, 3:1358.

45. Phillip G. Ellithorpe to Ann, August 8, 1863, CCHM; Phillip G. Ellithorpe, Camp Letterman Medical Chart, Military Service Record, NARA; Phillip G. Ellithorpe, Final Medical Record, Military Pension Record, NARA; Busey and Busey, *Union Casualties at Gettysburg*, 3:1358.

46. Phillip G. Ellithorpe to Ann, August 8, 1863, CCHM. It was not uncommon for loved ones to travel to military hospitals and care for wounded family members. See Adams, *Doctors in Blue*, 69, 163, 178; Neff, *Honoring the Civil War Dead*, 52; Hess, *The Union Soldier in Battle*, 150; and Bollet, *Civil War Medicine*, 231.

47. Phillip G. Ellithorpe, Camp Letterman Medical Chart, Military Service Record, NARA; Phillip G. Ellithorpe, Final Medical Record, Military Pension Record, NARA. For accounts of the celebration, see Justus Sillman to Mother, August 11, 19, 1863, Camp Letterman Papers, Gregory Coco Collection, GNMPLRC; *Gettysburg Compiler*, August 23, 28, 1863; and Patterson, *Debris of Battle*, 171–73.

48. See Phillip G. Ellithorpe, Camp Letterman Medical Chart, Military Service Record, NARA; Phillip G. Ellithorpe, Final Medical Record, Military Pension Record, NARA; Phillip G. Ellithorpe, Surgeon General's Report, Military Pension Record, NARA. Dr. Cordon Bittner of Longview, Washington, offered valuable medical expertise to the author in analyzing Phillip's treatments.

49. Duncan, *The Medical Department of the U.S. Army in the Civil War*, 264–66; Drew Gilpin Faust, *This Republic of Suffering: Death and the American Civil War* (New York: Vintage Books, 2008), 86–87; Neff, *Honoring the Civil War Dead*, 110–11.

50. For various accounts of the friendly fire incident, see Bell, *Recollection*, 4–5, GNMPLRC; Weidner, "A Memoir of the Thirteenth Infantry Regiment of the Pennsylvania Reserve Corps," 9–10, GNMPLRC; Bard, "The 'Old' Bucktails"; Glover, *Bucktailed Wildcats*, 207; Thomson and Rauch, *History of the "Bucktails,"* 268; Sypher, *History of the Pennsylvania Reserves*, 461–64; and Ent, *The Pennsylvania Reserves in the Civil War*, 215–16.

51. See Bollet, *Civil War Medicine*, 283–86, and Andrew B. Cross, *The Battle of Gettysburg and the Christian Commission* (Baltimore, MD: n.p., 1865), 122.

52. Rutkow, *Bleeding Blue and Gray*, 26, 238.

53. Kathleen G. Harrison, "Unresolved Burial Sites," 43, Camp Letterman Papers, Gregory Coco Collection, drawer 14A, GNMPLRC.

54. Report of Henry J. Janes, *List of Deaths in the Letterman Hospital, Gettysburg, PA*, drawer V7-12-3, GNMPLRC; *Detailed Soldier Information of Men Buried at Camp Letter-*

man Cemetery and Disposition after Removal, Camp Letterman Collection, GNMPLRC; Camp Letterman Papers, Gregory Coco Collection, drawer 14A, GNMPLRC.

55. A. Gilman Foster to Permelia Ellithorpe, October 30, 1863, CCHM. See also U.S. Sanitary Commission to Philander D. Ellithorpe, September 21, October 30, and December 21, 1863, in United States Sanitary Commission Collection, Brooke Russell Astor Reading Room, New York Public Library, New York, NY, box 14, folder 17. See also Kathleen G. Harrison, *Camp Letterman, U.S. General Hospital*, 43, Camp Letterman Papers, Gregory Coco Collection, GNMPLRC.

56. See Faust, *This Republic of Suffering*, 6–109. See also Freemon, *Gangrene and Glory*, 152; Adams, *Living Hell*, 152; and Neff, *Honoring the Civil War Dead*, 11, 19–23.

57. Faust, *This Republic of Suffering*, 6–11; Neff, *Honoring the Civil War Dead*, 11, 19–23, 43–45.

58. Faust, *This Republic of Suffering*, 14–15, 22–25.

59. A. Gilman Foster to Permelia Ellithorpe, October 30, 1863, CCHM. See also Faust, *This Republic of Suffering*, 106–9.

60. See undated envelope indicating a $20 bill from the Adams Express Company to Ann in Ellithorpe Family Collection, CCHM. See also Faust, *This Republic of Suffering*, 85–92, and Neff, *Honoring the Civil War Dead*, 46–51. Ann's trip to Gettysburg to nurse Phillip is mentioned in Asa's autobiography in Wilford and Curtiss-Wedge, *History of Fillmore County, Minnesota*, 2:775.

61. Garry Wills, *Lincoln at Gettysburg: The Words That Remade America* (New York: Simon & Schuster, 1992), 19–176.

62. See McPherson, *For Cause and Comrades*, 77, and Carmichael, *The War for the Common Soldier*, 7–9, 134–35. For vignettes of other nonfamily characters who were important to Phillip Ellithorpe during the Civil War, see appendix B.

Chapter 11: In and Out of the Saddle: The Overland Campaign

1. Noah Andre Trudeau, *Bloody Roads South: The Wilderness to Cold Harbor, May–June 1864* (Boston: Little, Brown, 1989), vii.

2. Asa R. Burleson to Phillip G. Ellithorpe, August 13, 1863, CCHM.

3. For firsthand descriptions of the transformation of the 130th New York into the 19th New York Cavalry, see Levi D. Green to Mother, September 20, 1863, and Marvin W. Green to Brother John, August 4, 1863, in Green Family Collection, Allegany County Historical Society, Andover, New York. See also Bowen, *Regimental History of the First New York Dragoons*, 83–89; Stephen Z. Starr, *The Union Cavalry in the Civil War*, 2 vols. (Baton Rouge: Louisiana State University Press, 1979), 2:6, 11; and Frederick H. Dyer, *A Compendium of the War of the Rebellion*, 3 vols. (New York: Yoselof, 1959), 3:1369–70.

4. See General Order No. 236, *OR*, ser. 3, 3:580. See also Starr, *The Union Cavalry in the Civil War*, 2:4–5, 12–16; Charley to Sister, August 5, 1863, in *1st Regiment of Dragoons, New York Volunteers*, Civil War Newspaper Clippings, New York State Military Museum and Veteran's Research Center, Albany, NY; and *Geneseo Republican*, August 10, 1863.

5. Starr, *The Union Cavalry in the Civil War*, 2:12–16; Adams, *Living Hell*, 39.

6. See Asa R. Burleson, Military Service Record, 1st New York Dragoons, NARA; Willford and Curtiss-Wedge, *History of Fillmore County, Minnesota*, 2:774; Bowen, *Regimen-*

tal History of the First New York Dragoons, 96–99; and Phisterer, *New York in the War of the Rebellion*, 2:208–10. For the chain of command as it affected Asa, see appendix A.

7. Bowen, *Regimental History of the First New York Dragoons*, 96–104. See also Gordon C. Rhea, *The Battle of the Wilderness, May 5–6, 1864* (Baton Rouge: Louisiana State University Press, 1994), 40.

8. *OR*, 29, pt. 1:145 (Col. Alfred Gibbs); Phisterer, *New York in the War of the Rebellion*, 2: 208–10.

9. See Asa R. Burleson, Pension Applications (1866–1916), Military Pension Records, NARA; Asa R. Burleson, Muster Record (September–October 1863), Military Service Record, Co. H, 1st New York Dragoons, NARA; and Deposition of Charles W. McIntosh, in Asa R. Burleson, Military Service Record, NARA. See also Willford and Curtiss-Wedge, *History of Fillmore County, Minnesota*, 2:774, and Bowen, *Regimental History of the First New York Dragoons*, 10.

10. See Dr. W. R. DeWitt to Asa R. Burleson, October 12, 1863, in Asa R. Burleson, Muster Records, Military Service Record, NARA, and Testimony of Asa R. Burleson to Medical Examining Board, August 15, 1864, in Asa R. Burleson, Military Service Record, NARA. See also Albert Swift to *Geneseo Republican*, October 22, 1863, in *1st Regiment of Dragoons, New York Volunteers*, Civil War Newspaper Clippings, New York State Military Museum and Veteran's Research Center, Albany, NY, and Bowen, *Regimental History of the First New York Dragoons*, 101–4.

11. Phisterer, *New York in the War of the Rebellion*, 2:212–13; *OR*, 29, pt. 1:675, 805–6 (Col. Alfred Gibbs). See also Steven E. Sodergren, *The Army of the Potomac in the Overland and Petersburg Campaign* (Baton Rouge: Louisiana State University Press, 2017), 1–2, and A. Wilson Greene, *A Campaign of Giants—The Battle of Petersburg*, vol. 1, *From the Crossing of the James to the Crater* (Chapel Hill: University of North Carolina Press, 2018), 13.

12. Bowen, *Regimental History of the First New York Dragoons*, 104–15.

13. See E. Walter Lowe to Editor of *Express*, February 5, 1864, in *1st Regiment of Dragoons, New York Volunteers*, Civil War Newspaper Clippings, New York State Military Museum and Veteran's Research Center, Albany, NY; Phisterer, *New York in the War of the Rebellion*, 2:214; and Bowen, *Regimental History of the First New York Dragoons*, 118.

14. Asa R. Burleson to Ann, March 22 and April 2 and 6, 1864, CCHM. See also Asa's handwritten request for furlough in Asa R. Burleson to Capt. E. B. Parsons, January 14, 1864, in Asa R. Burleson, Military Service Record, NARA, and Asa R. Burleson, Roll Call (January–February 1863), Military Service Record, NARA.

15. Asa R. Burleson to Ann, March 22, 1864, CCHM. See also Bowen, *Regimental History of the First New York Dragoons*, 111–13; Albert Swift to *Geneseo Republican*, February 25, 1864, in *1st Regiment of Dragoons, New York Volunteers*, Civil War Newspaper Clippings, New York State Military Museum and Veteran's Research Center, Albany, NY; and Joseph Wheelan, *Bloody Spring: Forty Days That Sealed the Confederacy's Fate* (Boston: Da Capo Press, 2014), 23.

16. Asa R. Burleson to Ann, March 22 and April 2 and 6, 1864, CCHM.

17. Gilbert, *Rushford and Rushford People*, 500–502; *Rushford Spectator*, August 24, 1911; Phisterer, *New York in the War of the Rebellion*, 2:221, 321.

18. Philander D. Ellithorpe, Military Service Record, NARA. See also Phisterer, *New York in the War of the Rebellion*, 2:220–21, 321; *Annual Report of the Adjutant General of the*

State of New York, 2nd Mounted Rifles, 876, 993, 1010; *New York, Town Clerk's Registers of Men Who Served in the Civil War, 1861–1865 (Gainesville)*. For the manpower shortage, see Mark Grimsley, *And Keep Moving On: The Virginia Campaign, May–June 1864* (Lincoln: University of Nebraska Press, 2002), 8–9; Ron Chernow, *Grant* (New York: Penguin Press, 2017), 356–60; and William S. McFeely, *Grant: A Biography* (New York: Norton, 1981), 175–76.

19. See Watson W. Bush to Father, April 4, 1864, in Watson W. Bush Papers, New York State Library, Cultural Education Center, Albany, New York; Philander D. Ellithorpe, Military Service Record, NARA; Dyer, *A Compendium of the War of the Rebellion*, 3:1372; and Nahum Ward Cady, *Court Martial of Major N. Ward Cady, 2nd Mounted Rifles, New York Volunteers: Including the Offense, Defense, Sentence, Correspondence* (Yates, NY: n.p., 1864).

20. Bowen, *Regimental History of the First New York Dragoons*, 131. See also John J. Hennessy, "I Dread the Spring: The Army of the Potomac Prepares for the Overland Campaign," in *The Wilderness Campaign*, ed. Gary W. Gallagher (Chapel Hill: University of North Carolina Press, 1997), 66–96; Sean Michael Chick, *The Battle of Petersburg, June 15–18, 1864* (Lincoln, NE: Potomac Books, 2015), 28–39; and Ernest B. Furgurson, *Not War but Murder: Cold Harbor 1864* (New York: Vintage Books, 2000), 5–6, 14.

21. Wert, The *Sword of Lincoln*, 324, 330; Sears, *Lincoln's Lieutenants*, 624–25; Rhea, *The Battle of the Wilderness*, 40, 106–9; Hennessy, "I Dread the Spring," 85; Chernow, *Grant*, 361; Starr, *The Union Cavalry in the Civil War*, 2:68–74.

22. Bowen, *Regimental History of the First New York Dragoons*, 148.

23. Bowen, *Regimental History of the First New York Dragoons*, 135–36.

24. *OR*, 33:891–93 (Capt. F. C. Newhall); Starr, *The Union Cavalry in the Civil War*, 2:79–82; Bowen, *Regimental History of the First New York Dragoons*, 139.

25. Asa R. Burleson to Ann, April 28, 1863, CCHM. See also Bowen, *Regimental History of the First New York Dragoons*, 136–39.

26. Rhea, "Union Cavalry in the Wilderness," in Gallagher, *The Wilderness Campaign*, 106–30; Bowen, *Regimental History of the First New York Dragoons*, 134–54.

27. See J. F. C. Fuller, *Grant and Lee: A Study in Personality and Generalship* (Bloomington: Indiana University Press, 1982), 208–26.

28. Asa R. Burleson, Roll Call, Military Service Record, NARA. See also Bowen, *Regimental History of the First New York Dragoons*, 139–42.

29. See Starr, *The Union Cavalry in the Civil War*, 2:91, and *OR*, 36, pt. 1:773 (Maj. Gen. Philip H. Sheridan).

30. For details of the Todd's Tavern cavalry engagement, see *OR*, 36, pt. 1:846 (Col. Alfred Gibbs), 811 (Brig. Gen. Wesley Merritt), 466, 773–76 (Maj. Gen. Philip H. Sheridan), 466 (Brig. Gen. George A. Custer); Bowen, *Regimental History of the First New York Dragoons*, 142–45; Gordon C. Rhea, *The Battles for the Spotsylvania Court House and the Road to Yellow Tavern, May 7–12, 1864* (Baton Rouge: Louisiana State University Press, 1997), 14–20, 30–36; Starr, *The Union Cavalry in the Civil War*, 2:89, 93–95; and Edward G. Longacre, *Lincoln's Cavalrymen: A History of the Mounted Forces of the Army of the Potomac* (Mechanicsburg, PA: Stackpole Books, 2000), 259–60.

31. See *OR*, 36, pt. 1:124 (casualties); Bowen, *Regimental History of the First New York Dragoons*, 150–52; and Phisterer, *New York in the War of the Rebellion*, 2:218, 324.

32. *OR*, 36. pt. 1:846 (Col. Alfred Gibbs), 811 (Brig. Gen. Wesley Merritt).

33. See Starr, *The Union Cavalry in the Civil War*, 2:93–96.

34. For Sheridan's Raid, see *OR*, 36, pt. 1:812–13 (Brig. Gen. Wesley Merritt), 847 (Col. Alfred Gibbs), and Theodore F. Rodenbaugh, "Sheridan's Richmond Raid," in *Battles and Leaders of the Civil War*, 4 vols., ed. Robert Underwood Johnson and Clarence Clough Buel (New York: Century, 1887), 4:189–90. See also Bowen, *Regimental History of the First New York Dragoons*, 153–54; Phisterer, *New York in the War of the Rebellion*, 2:223–25; Starr, *The Union Cavalry in the Civil War*, 2:97–107; and Longacre, *Lincoln's Cavalrymen*, 264–65.

35. For the cavalry engagement at Yellow Tavern to Haxall's Landing, see *OR*, 36, pt. 1:847 (Col. Alfred Gibbs), 812–13 (Brig. Gen. Wesley Merritt). See also Gordon C. Rhea, *To the North Anna River: Grant and Lee, May 13–25, 1864* (Baton Rouge: Louisiana State University Press, 2000), 35–63, 162, 195, 282, 330, 350; Bowen, *Regimental History of the First New York Dragoons*, 155–64; Starr, *The Union Cavalry in the Civil War*, 2:109–13; Thomas, *Bold Dragoon*, 290–94; Longacre, *Lincoln's Cavalrymen*, 266–67; and Rodenbaugh, "Sheridan's Richmond Raid," 190–92.

36. *OR*, 36, pt. 1:410 (Brig. Gen. John R. Brooke). By the time Brooke submitted his report in November 1864, he had been promoted to brigadier general.

37. *OR*, 36, pt. 1:410–15 (Brig. Gen. John R. Brooke), 415–18 (Lt. Col. William Glenny). Charles Van Dusen is buried in the family's plot in White Cemetery, the graveyard of many prominent settlers of early Rushford.

38. *OR*, 36, pt. 1:137 (casualties); *OR*, 36, pt. 2:696–97 (Maj. Gen. Henry W. Halleck). See also Phisterer, *New York in the War of the Rebellion*, 2:221–22; Cooling, *Symbol, Sword, and Shield*, 183; and Benjamin Franklin Cooling, *Jubal Early's Raid on Washington, 1864* (Tuscaloosa: University of Alabama Press, 1989), 7.

39. Phisterer, *New York in the War of the Rebellion*, 2:1133; Keith T. McKenzie to Unknown, July 20, 1864, in *2nd New York Mounted Rifles*, Civil War Newspaper Clippings, New York State Military Museum and Veteran's Center, Albany, NY (hereafter cited as McKenzie letter); *OR*, 36, pt. 1:924 (Col. Elisha G. Marshall), 909 (Maj. Gen. Ambrose E. Burnside). For the chain of command as it affected Philander, see appendix A.

40. See Theodore Lyman, *Meade's Headquarters, 1863–1865: The Letters of Colonel Theodore Lyman from the Wilderness to Appomattox* (Boston: Massachusetts Historical Society, 1881), 199. In November 1863, Marshall's artillerists were assigned to garrison duty in New York Harbor until they were summoned by Halleck to report to Grant. See W. H. McIntosh, *History of Monroe County, New York* (Rochester, NY: W. E. Morrison, 1877), 48–50, 65–68; Samuel W. Durant and Henry B. Peirce, *History of St. Lawrence County, New York: With Illustrations and Biographical Sketches of Some of Its Prominent Men and Pioneers* (Philadelphia: L. H. Everts, 1878), 481; and *OR*, ser. 3, 3:527, 586, 693, 715.

41. *OR*, 36, pt. 1:114 (organization of army), 924 (Col. Elisha G. Marshall), 909 (Maj. Gen. Ambrose E. Burnside).

42. Cady Court Martial, October 26, 1864, transcript. Cady complained to the adjutant general of the army, the secretary of war, his state congressman, and Burnside, Meade, and Grant.

43. *OR*, 36, pt. 1:910 (Maj. Gen. Ambrose E. Burnside), 133, 148 (casualties); McKenzie letter, July 20, 1864. See also Rhea, *To the North Anna River*, 125–88.

44. Bowen, *Regimental History of the First New York Dragoons*, 169–70; *OR*, 36, pt. 1:813–14, 848–52 (Brig. Gen. Wesley Merritt), 847 (Col. Alfred Gibbs), 910–11 (Maj. Gen. Ambrose E. Burnside), 924–26 (Brig. Gen. Elisha G. Marshall), 161 (casualties), 804, 848–49 (Brig. Gen. Alfred T. A. Torbert).

45. Rodenbaugh, "Sheridan's Richmond Raid," 192–93; Bowen, *Regimental History of the First New York Dragoons*, 169–70; *OR*, 36, pt. 1:804 (Col. Alfred Gibbs), 848–49 (Brig. Gen. Wesley Merritt), 815–25 (Brig. Gen. George A. Custer). See also Gordon C. Rhea, *Cold Harbor: Grant and Lee, May 26–June 3* (Baton Rouge: Louisiana State University Press, 2002), 27–50, 61–91.

46. Asa R. Burleson, Roll Call, Military Service Record, NARA.

47. Asa R. Burleson, Roll Call, Military Service Record, NARA; Asa R. Burleson, Hospital Muster Roll, Annapolis, Military Service Record, NARA; Deposition of C. W. McIntosh (September 22, 1866), in Asa R. Burleson, Military Pension Record, NARA; *The Crutch* (Annapolis), June 18, 1864. See also Adams, *Doctors in Blue*, 171–72; Bollet, *Civil War Medicine*, 5, 134; Rutkow, *Bleeding Blue and Gray*, 313–14; and Freemon, *Gangrene and Glory*, 50.

48. Ann to Asa R. Burleson, June 2, 1864, CCHM.

49. Ann to Asa R. Burleson, July 3, 1864, CCHM.

50. Asa R. Burleson to Ann, July 21 and August 4, 1864, CCHM.

51. Asa R. Burleson to Ann, August 4, 1864, CCHM.

52. See McKenzie letter, July 20, 1864; *OR*, 36, pt. 1:913–17 (Maj. Gen. Ambrose E. Burnside), and Phisterer, *New York in the War of the Rebellion*, 2:226. On May 30, Phillip's bucktailed comrades fought with tenacity and sustained casualties at Bethesda Church, the same day they were scheduled for discharge. See Glover, *Bucktailed Wildcats*, 261–64; Ent, *The Pennsylvania Reserves in the Civil War*, 274–84; Thomson and Rauch, *History of the "Bucktails,"* 311–21; and Sypher, *History of the Pennsylvania Reserves*, 546–47.

53. Phisterer, *New York in the War of the Rebellion*, 2:228; *OR*, 36, pt. 1:913–17 (Maj. Gen. Ambrose E. Burnside), 572 (Brig. Gen. Joseph J. Bartlett).

54. Capt. Runyan was eventually reinstated. See Watson W. Bush to Father, May 30, 1864, in Watson W. Bush Papers, New York State Library and Cultural Center, Albany, NY. See also McKenzie letter, July 20, 1864, and *OR*, 36, pt. 1:926–27 (Brig. Gen. Elisha G. Marshall).

55. Hattaway and Jones, *How the North Won*, 577–78.

56. *OR*, 36, pt. 1:188 (casualties). See also Gordon C. Rhea, *On to Petersburg, Grant and Lee, June 4–15* (Baton Rouge: Louisiana State University Press, 2017), 30–197.

57. McKenzie letter, July 20, 1864; *OR*, 36, pt. 1:914 (Maj. Gen. Ambrose E. Burnside), 917 (Maj. Gen. Ambrose E. Burnside), 930–31 (Brig. Gen. Robert B. Potter). See also Chick, *The Battle of Petersburg*, 191–93.

58. A competent subordinate with close ties to Burnside, Potter earned a reputation as an aggressive general. See Rhea, *On to Petersburg*, 45–47, 111; Wheelan, *Bloody Spring*, 28; *OR*, 36, pt. 1:915–16 (Maj. Gen. Ambrose E. Burnside), 196 (Special Order No. 30); and *Annual Report of the Adjutant General of the State of New York, 51st New York*, 179. For Philander's revised chain of command, see appendix A.

59. For Potter's unflattering remarks, see Brig. Gen. Robert B. Potter to Maj. Gen. George G. Meade, September 13, 1864, and Brig. Gen. Robert B. Potter to Maj. Gen. John G. Parke, September 13, 1864, in Court Martial of Major N. Ward Cady, transcript.

60. *OR*, 40, pt. 1:544–45 (Brig. Gen. Robert B. Potter), 521–22 (Maj. Gen. Ambrose E. Burnside); McKenzie letter, July 20, 1864. See also Rhea, *On to Petersburg*, 139–223, 238–50, 294–301, and Greene, *A Campaign of Giants*, 147–49.

61. McKenzie letter, July 20, 1864. See also Chick, *The Battle of Petersburg*, 160–62.

62. McKenzie letter, July 20, 1864; Philander D. Ellithorpe, Military Service Record, NARA; Philander D. Ellithorpe, Military Pension Record, NARA. See also Phisterer, *New York in the War of the Rebellion*, 2:232; Greene, *A Campaign of Giants*, 150–68; Chick, *The Battle of Petersburg*, 197–202, 243–90; and *OR*, 40, pt. 1:181 (casualties), 545 (Brig. Gen. Robert B. Potter).

63. See Cooling, *Jubal Early's Raid on Washington, 1864*, 10–127; Leech, *Reveille in Washington*, 329–46; and Cooling, *Symbol, Sword, and Shield*, 187–210.

64. Ann to Asa R. Burleson, June 28 and July 3, 1864, CCHM. See also Cooling, *Jubal Early's Raid on Washington, 1864*, 53–95, 157–76, 240; Leech, *Reveille in Washington*, 331–33; *OR*, 37, pt. 1:464 (Maj. Gen. Henry W. Halleck); and Asa R. Burleson, Roll Call, Military Service Record, NARA. For the chain of command as it affected Asa at Annapolis, see *OR*, 37, pt. 1:704.

65. Asa R. Burleson to Ann, July 21, 1864, CCHM; Willford and Curtiss-Wedge, *History of Fillmore County, Minnesota*, 2:974. See also Leech, *Reveille in Washington*, 334–45, and Cooling, *Jubal Early's Raid on Washington, 1864*, 113–38.

66. Report of Board of Medical Examiners, Annapolis, MD, August 22, 1864, in Asa R. Burleson, Military Pension Record, NARA; Asa R. Burleson, Certificate of Medical Discharge, Company H, 1st Dragoons, Muster Roll, Military Service Record, NARA. See also Gilbert, *Rushford and Rushford People*, 514–16, and Minard and Merrill, *Allegany County and Its People*, 794–95.

67. Report of the Adjutant General, State of New York, Military Museum and Veterans Research Center, 2nd Mounted Rifles, 993; New York State Census, 1865, Rushford, NY; 9th U.S. Census (1870), Rushford, Allegany County, NY. Cora would attend Winona Normal School in the late 1870s and teach in Spring Valley. In 1883, she married a prominent businessman and Republican figure, and they raised four children. Cora died suddenly from pneumonia in April 1899, and she is buried in Oakwood Cemetery in Austin, Minnesota. See William Willford and Franklyn Curtiss-Wedge, eds., *The History of Mower County, Minnesota* (Chicago: H. C. Cooper, Jr., and Co., 1911), 716, and *Mower County Transcript*, April 19, 1899.

68. Meade's Army of the Potomac placed great emphasis on efficient ambulance service during the Overland campaign, where 46,000 wounded and 11,000 sick were expeditiously evacuated from the field in 600 wagons painted with corps and division markings. See Adams, *Doctors in Blue*, 97–98, 103–5; Rutkow, *Bleeding Blue and Gray*, 302, 311–13; and Bollet, *Civil War Medicine*, 5, 131.

69. It is not known where Philander's amputation took place: the field hospital, City Point, or Mount Pleasant Hospital in Washington. See Philander D. Ellithorpe, Medical Examinations (1864–1915), Military Pension Record, NARA.

70. Philander D. Ellithorpe, Military Service Record, Invalid Army Pension Application, NARA. See also Bollet, *Civil War Medicine*, 149, and Adams, *Doctors in Blue*, 184.

71. Ann to Asa R. Burleson, June 28, 1864, CCHM.

72. Philander D. Ellithorpe to Brother Asa, July 3, 1864, CCHM.

73. Ann to Asa R. Burleson, September 5, 1864, CCHM; Philander D. Ellithorpe to Ann, October 1, 1864, CCHM.

74. Philander D. Ellithorpe to Ann, September 26, 1864, and October 1 and 11, 1864, CCHM. See also Brian Matthew Jordan, *Marching Home: Union Veterans and Their Unending Civil War* (New York: Norton, 2014), 52–57.

75. Philander D. Ellithorpe to Ann, October 1, 1864, CCHM.

76. Philander D. Ellithorpe to Ann, December 16, 1864, CCHM.

77. Philander D. Ellithorpe to Brother Asa, January 27, 1865, CCHM.

78. See McPherson, *For Cause and Comrade*, 63–64.

79. Philander D. Ellithorpe to Ann, December 16, 1864, and Philander D. Ellithorpe to Brother Asa, January 27, 1865, CCHM; Philander D. Ellithorpe, Military Service Record, Invalid Army Pension Application, NARA.

80. Philander D. Ellithorpe to Millie, February 25, 1865, CCHM.

81. Rutkow, *Bleeding Blue and Gray*, 167; Adams, *Doctors in Blue*, 156–60, 185; Carmichael, *The War for the Common Soldier*, 7–9, 303–5.

82. Philander D. Ellithorpe, Certificate of Medical Discharge, July 22, 1865, Military Service Record, NARA; Philander D. Ellithorpe, Original Invalid Army Pension Application, October 24, 1865, Military Pension Record, NARA.

Chapter 12: A Trunkful of Letters

1. Marriage Certificate of Oliver Moore and Mary Ellithorpe, in Oliver Webster Moore, Miscellaneous file, CCHM. See also Willford and Curtiss-Wedge, *History of Fillmore County, Minnesota*, 2:775; Minnesota Territorial Census, 1857; Edward D. Neill, *History of Fillmore County* (Minneapolis: Minnesota Historical Company, 1882), 368; 9th U.S. Census, 1870, Rushford, Fillmore County, MN; Minnesota State Census, 1875, Rushford, Fillmore County, MN.

2. Willford and Curtiss-Wedge, *History of Fillmore County, Minnesota*, 2:775, 1157; Oliver Webster Moore, Muster Record, Military Service Record, NARA; Oliver Webster Moore, Military Pension Record, NARA. For accounts of the 1st Minnesota during Oliver's tenure, see Richard Moe, *The Last Full Measure: The Life and Death of the First Minnesota Volunteers* (New York: Avon Books, 1993), 1–232; Jasper Newton Searles, *History of the First Regiment, Minnesota Volunteer Infantry* (Stillwater, MN: Easton and Masterman Printers, 1916), 1–275; and William Lochren, *Minnesota in the Civil and Indian Wars, 1861–1865* (St. Paul, MN: Pioneer Press Co., 1891), 1–78.

3. Certificate of Disability for Discharge, Oliver Webster Moore, Military Pension Record, NARA. See also Declaration for Original Invalid Pension, October 15, 1885, and Deposition of O. W. Moore, October 26, 1893, and January 25, 1894, in Oliver Webster Moore, Military Pension Record, NARA; Oliver Webster Moore, Muster Roll, Military Service Record, NARA; and multiple depositions from ex-comrades, Oliver Webster Moore, Military Pension Record, NARA.

4. See Oliver Webster Moore, Muster Record, Military Service Record, NARA; and multiple depositions, Oliver Webster Moore, Military Pension Record, NARA.

5. Depositions and Original Pension Application, Oliver Webster Moore, Military Pension Record, NARA. See also *OR*, 19, pt. 1:310–11 (Lt. George A. Woodruff); Curt Johnson and Richard C. Anderson Jr., *Artillery Hell: The Employment of Artillery at Antietam* (College Station: Texas A&M University Press, 1995); Moe, *The Last Full Measure*, 179–203; and Searles, *History of the First Regiment, Minnesota Volunteer Infantry*, 191–222.

6. See Certificate of Disability for Discharge, Oliver Webster Moore, Military Service Record; Oliver Webster Moore to Pension Bureau, October 26, 1893, Oliver Webster

Moore, Military Pension Record, NARA. For modern studies of gastrointestinal diseases during the Civil War, see Bollet, *Civil War Medicine*, 365–69; Adams, *Living Hell*, 25; McPherson, *Battle Cry of Freedom*, 584; and Rable, *Fredericksburg! Fredericksburg!*, 284, 395.

7. O. W. Moore, "A Hark Backward" (1926), in Oliver Webster Moore, Miscellaneous file, CCHM; Mortgage Deeds, Spring Valley, MN, in Oliver Webster Moore, Miscellaneous file, CCHM. See also Willford and Curtiss-Wedge, *History of Fillmore County, Minnesota*, 2:775, 1157; Minnesota Territorial Census, 1857; and Neill, *History of Fillmore County*, 368. John L. Moore is buried in Oak Grove Cemetery, Rushford, Minnesota.

8. Willford and Curtiss-Wedge, *History of Fillmore County, Minnesota*, 2:776, 1157; Mortgage Deeds, Spring Valley, MN, in Oliver Webster Moore, Miscellaneous file, CCHM.

9. Neill, *History of Fillmore County*, 540–44; Mary Jo Dathe and Sharon Jahn, *Tales of Our Town: Spring Valley Sesquicentennial, 1855–2005* (Spring Valley, MN: Spring Valley Historical Society, 2005), 1–6, 11, 39; Willford and Curtiss-Wedge, *History of Fillmore County, Minnesota*, 2:776.

10. Ronald Prinz Moore (b. April 22, 1897) and Maxwell Clayton Moore (b. October 4, 1902). In June 1918, Ronald registered for the draft, and by Armistice Day, he was training at the naval training center in Camp Farragut, Illinois. See Ronald Moore to O. W. Moore, November 6, 1918 (postcard), in Oliver Webster Moore, Miscellaneous file, CCHM. See also *Longview Daily News*, February 7 and 8, 1968, and June 22, 1991; Carlton Graduation Announcement for Ronald Moore, Miscellaneous file, Ellithorpe Family Collection, CCHM.

11. Virginia Urrutia, *They Came to Six Rivers: The Story of Cowlitz County* (Kelso, WA: Cowlitz County Historical Society, 1998), 8–73, 204.

12. Urrutia, *They Came to Six Rivers*, 126.

13. For a biography of R. A. Long, see John B. McClelland Jr., *R. A. Long's Planned City: The Story of Longview* (Longview, WA: Westmedia, 1998), 1–10, 218–30. See also Urrutia, *They Came to Six Rivers*, 132–34.

14. Urrutia, *They Came to Six Rivers*, 134–36; McClelland, *R. A. Long's Planned City*, 4–10.

15. Urrutia, *They Came to Six Rivers*, 144–50; McClelland, *R. A. Long's Planned City*, 11–43, 65–85, 111–14.

16. Ronald Moore to Oliver W. Moore, September 4, 1926, CCHM; Urrutia, *They Came to Six Rivers*, 107, 143–44; McClelland, *R. A. Long's Planned City*, 44–47, 262; *Kelsonian-Tribune*, September 1–3, 1926; *Longview Daily News*, September 1–2, 1926, and February 7, 1968; *Polk's Kelso, Longview, Woodland, and Cowlitz County Directory, 1926* (Seattle, WA: R. L. Polk, 1926), 67, 127, 489. Ronald was involved in a number of local organizations, including the Kelso B.P.O.E, Masonic Lodge, Scottish Rite, Columbia River Shriners, and Guy Rathbun American Legion Post No. 25, and was founding president of Kelso Kiwanis. In 1933, he sat one term in the Washington State Legislature.

17. *Minneapolis City Directory, 1925* (Minneapolis: Minneapolis Directory Company, 1925), 1538. See also directories for *1926*, 1604; *1927*, 1608; *1928*, 1640; *1929*, 1608–9; *1930*, 1128–29; *1932*, 853–54; *1933*, 888–89; *1934*, 890; *1935*, 925; *1936*, 953–54; and *1937*, 1022. *Hopkins City Directory, 1939* (Hopkins, MN: Hennepin County Review, 1939), 31. See also directories for *1941*, 64–65; *1943*, 140; and *1944*, 97.

18. *Kelsonian-Tribune*, August 30, 1945, March 7, 1946, and May 7, 1953; *Longview Daily News*, May 5, 1953, and June 22, 1991; *Polk's Kelso and Longview City Directory, 1940*, 91; *Polk's Kelso and Longview City Directory, 1946*, 283; *Polk's Kelso and Longview City*

Directory, 1948, 446; *Kelso-Longview Telephone Directory, February 1945*, 22; *Kelso-Longview Telephone Directory, February 1948*, 15, 35.

19. *Longview Daily News*, February 7 and 8, 1968, and June 22, 1991.

Postscript: Bivouac of the Dead

1. Asa R. Burleson to Commissioners of Pensions, March 4, 1871, CCHM. See Depositions of Dr. Jesse P. Bixby and DeWitt McDonald, in Phillip G. Ellithorpe, Military Pension Record, NARA.

2. Mary Ellithorpe Moore to Ann Burleson (ca. March 23, 1873), CCHM.

3. Danforth's employment history with Watson Elevator, Tifft Elevator, and Plympton Elevator spanned the years between 1866 and 1880 and 1891–1892. See *City Directory of Buffalo, 1867*, 231; *1877*, 345; *1880*, 350; *1891*, 459; and *1892*, 459. See also *Buffalo Address Book and Family Directory, 1883–1912* (various publishers), and New York State Census, 1865.

4. *City Directory of Buffalo, 1867*, 231, and *1870*, 348. See also Deposition of Robert H. Walker, November 26, 1909, in Philander D. Ellithorpe, Military Pension Record, NARA; *Friendship Weekly Register*, January 30, 1890; and Martha Ellithorpe census card in 1905 South Dakota State Census, Spink County, South Dakota.

5. Doane Robinson, *History of South Dakota* (Logansport, IN: B. F. Bowen and Co., 1904), 285, 294, 299–300; Dana D. Harlow, *Prairie Echoes: Spink County in the Making* (Aberdeen, SD: Hayes Brothers Printers, 1961), 8–17, 42–48.

6. See South Dakota Territorial Census, 1885; *City Directory of Buffalo, 1881*, 354; Census card for Martha Ellithorpe, 1905 South Dakota State Census, Spink County, South Dakota; U.S. Department of the Interior, Bureau of Land Management, General Land Office Records, Danforth Ellithorp, accession #SDMTAA, document #1320; and E. Frank Peterson, *Map of Spink County, South Dakota: Compiled and Drawn from a Special Survey and Official Records* (Vermillion, SD: E. Frank Peterson, 1899).

7. French, "Carlos Leonard Stebbins," 1–9; *Wyoming County Gazette*, February 6, 1914; Greenlee and Greenlee, *The Stebbins Genealogy*, 2:753–54; *Biographical Sketches of the Leading Citizens of Livingston and Wyoming Counties, New York*, 241–42. In 1937, Stebbins was still remembered fondly by the people of Wyoming County "as a person presenting the qualities of a gentleman of the finer instincts." See *Wyoming County Times*, December 16, 1937.

8. *Spring Valley Mercury*, May 1, 1914. See also Depositions of Verna Moore Tretheway and Frances Moore (1914–1927), Military Pension Record, NARA.

9. Philander D. Ellithorpe, Certificate of Medical Discharge, July 22, 1865, Military Pension Record, NARA. See also Jordan, *Marching Home*, 16, 24, 29–31, 36, 60–62; Dixon Wecter, *When Johnny Comes Marching Home* (Cambridge, MA: Riverside Press, 1944), 138–41, 182–207; Mary R. Dearing, *Veterans in Politics: The Story of the GAR* (Baton Rouge: Louisiana State University Press, 1952), 50–54; Stuart McConnell, *Glorious Contentment: The Grand Army of the Republic, 1865–1900* (Chapel Hill: University of North Carolina Press, 1992), 10–13, 31; Neff, *Honoring the Civil War Dead*, 103–4; M. Keith Harris, *Across the Bloody Chasm: The Culture of Commemoration among Civil War Veterans* (Baton Rouge: Louisiana State University Press, 2014), 15–18; and Dearing, "Veterans in Politics," in *The Civil War Veteran: A Historical Reader*, ed. Larry M. Logue and Michael Barton (New York: New York University Press, 2007), 278–82.

10. In August 1870, Philander transferred his Civil War pension from the Canandaigua Agency to the Buffalo Agency. See Philander D. Ellithorpe, Transfer of Agency, Military Pension Record, NARA. See also *City Directory of Buffalo, 1867*, 231, and *1870*, 348; Deposition of Robert H. Walker, November 26, 1909, in Philander D. Ellithorpe, Military Pension Record, NARA; and *Friendship Weekly Register*, January 30, 1890.

11. Certificate of Medical Discharge, July 22, 1865; Philander D. Ellithorpe, Military Service Record, Pension Record, Invalid Army Pension application, NARA. See also Claire Prechtel-Kluskens, "A Reasonable Degree of Promptitude: Civil War Pension Application Processing, 1861–1865," *Prologue* 42 (Spring 2010): 26–35; Theda Skocpol, "America's First Social Security System," in Logue and Barton, *The Civil War Veteran*, 181–82; Jordan, *Marching Home*, 57, 152–55; Dearing, *Veterans in Politics*, 52; and McConnell, *Glorious Contentment*, 143–47.

12. Philander D. Ellithorpe, Certificate of Medical Discharge, Examining Surgeon's Certificate, Oath of Allegiance, Application for Invalid Army Pension, Application for Increase, Military Pension Record, NARA. See also Prechtel-Kluskens, "A Reasonable Degree of Promptitude," 27–29.

13. Philander D. Ellithorpe, Examining Surgeon's Certificate, November 4, 1874, November 4 and 13, 1888, and May 20, 1903, in Military Pension Record, NARA. See also Wecter, *When Johnny Comes Marching Home*, 212–14.

14. Dearing, *Veterans in Politics*, 81–112, 185–250; Jordan, *Marching Home*, 69, 79; Wecter, *When Johnny Comes Marching Home*, 245; *Ritual of the Grand Army of the Republic* (Washington, DC: Headquarters of the Grand Army of the Republic, 1869), 1–40; McConnell, *Glorious Contentment*, 20–33, 79–128, 167–205; Dearing, *Veterans in Politics*, 86; Dearing, "Veterans in Politics," 286–89; Nina Silber, *The Romance of Reunion: Northerners and the South, 1865–1900* (Chapel Hill: University of North Carolina Press, 1993), 15, 169.

15. *Buffalo Courier*, May 30, 1903.

16. *Proceedings of the Annual Reunions and Banquets of the Survivor's Association, 27th Regiment, New York State Volunteers* (Binghamton, NY: Carl and Spaulding, 1889), 3–36. At first, reunion organizers selected the anniversary of Bull Run for its meeting date, and the sitting president chose the site of the next meeting. Reunion locations of the 27th New York Veteran's Association include Binghamton (1876), Brooklyn (1882), New York City (1883), Binghamton (1884), Elmira (1885), Rochester (1886), Mount Morris (1887), Deposit (1888), Seneca Falls (1889), Portage Falls (1894), Binghamton (1895), Elmira (1896), Buffalo (1897), and Binghamton (1898).

17. *Proceedings of the Annual Reunions and Banquets of the Survivor's Association, 27th Regiment*, 33, 75–76.

18. *Eleventh Annual Reunion of the Survivor's Association, 27th Regiment, New York Volunteers; Held at Portage Falls, New York, August 28–29, 1894*, 6, 10, 29, 38–42. Cascade House became a popular gathering spot for reunions of the 27th New York, 2nd New York Mounted Rifles, and 1st New York Dragoons in the 1880s and 1890s.

19. *Fourteenth Annual Reunion of the Survivor's Association, 27th Regiment, New York Volunteers; Held at Buffalo, New York, August 24, 1897*, 100, 105–7.

20. City Directory of Buffalo, *1870*, 348; *1871*, 328; *1872*, 313; *1873*, 318; *1874*, 38, 323; *1875*, 348; *1876*, 365; *1877*, 345; *1878*, 338; *1879*, 44, 345; *1880*, 350; *1881*, 354; *1882*, 361; *1883*, 353; *1884*, 412; *1885*, 406; *1886*, 418; *1887*, 433; *1888*, 429; *1889*, 437; *1890*, 428; *1891*, 450; *1892*, 459; *1893*, 475; *1894*, 511; *1896*, 569; *1897*, 416; *1898*, 467; *1899*, 456;

1900, 453; *1901*, 461; *1902*, 411–12; *1903*, 519; *1904*, 568; *1905*, 441; *1906*, 450; *1907*, 453; *1908*, 419; *1909*, 422; *1910*, 425; *1911*, 420; *1912*, 407. See also *Buffalo Address Book and Family Directory, 1883–1912*.

21. See Philander D. Ellithorpe, Depositions of Robert and George Ellithorpe, Military Pension Record, NARA; *Buffalo Morning Express*, December 5, 1883.

22. See Marriage Record, Depositions of Thomas James, Robert H. Walker, Robert H. Ellithorpe, and George T. Ellithorpe, in Philander D. Ellithorpe, Military Pension Record, NARA.

23. *Buffalo Courier*, September 17, 1889, and January 25 and October 5, 1890; *Buffalo Morning Express*, October 2, 1889; *Utica Weekly Herald*, September 21 and 24, 1889.

24. *Buffalo Morning Express*, November 16 and December 20 and 25, 1889; *Buffalo Courier*, January 25, 1890; *Buffalo Evening News*, March 10, 1891; *Troy Daily Times*, March 10, 1891; *Albany Evening Times*, March 11, 1891; *Buffalo Evening News*, September 9, 1895.

25. In the late 1890s, his sons, George and Robert, had secured jobs as a plumber and a lumber inspector, respectively, and his daughter, Pearl, earned a wage as a piano teacher and stenographer. See Ellithorpe family entries in *City Directory of Buffalo, 1890–1908*.

26. Philander D. Ellithorpe, Military Pension Records, NARA; *Buffalo Courier*, December 13, 1892, and May 2, 1901; *Buffalo Evening News*, October 20, 1896, and January 10 and 12, 1899; *Buffalo Morning Express*, January 13, 1899; *Buffalo Courier*, May 2, 1901; *City Directory of Buffalo, 1890–1908*; *Buffalo Address Book and Family Directory, 1883–1912*.

27. See *Buffalo Commercial*, September 13, 1902; *Buffalo Inquirer*, January 20, 1904; *Fresno City Directory, 1904*, 122, and *1906*, 139; and *Fresno Bee*, April 12, 1935. For George's six-month military service, see *New York in the Spanish-American War: Part of the Report of the Adjutant General of the State for 1900*, 3 vols. (Albany, NY: James B. Lyon, State Printer, 1900), 1:715.

28. See *Fresno City Directory, 1912*, 126; California State Board of Health, Bureau of Vital Statistics, Certificate of Death, Philander D. Ellithorpe; *Buffalo Evening News*, February 19, 1915; and *Fresno Bee*, February 8, 1915. Philander's grave is in the Ellithorpe family plot, accompanied by his two sons and their wives.

29. See Declaration of a Widow for Original Pension, February 25, 1915, in Philander D. Ellithorpe, Military Pension Record, NARA; correspondence regarding Mattie's pension claim (February–July 1915), in Philander D. Ellithorpe, Military Pension Record, NARA; *Index to Death Records, City of Buffalo, 1918*, vol. 288, #3575 (Mattie Ellithorpe).

30. Permelia to Ann and Asa R. Burleson, February 27, 1873, CCHM.

31. Oliver Moore to Asa Burleson, March 23, 1873, CCHM.

32. Mary Ellithorpe Moore to Ann Burleson (ca. March 23, 1873), CCHM.

33. Oliver Moore to Asa Burleson, March 23, 1873, Mary Ellithorpe Moore to Ann Burleson (ca. March 23, 1873), CCHM; Willford and Curtiss-Wedge, *History of Fillmore County, Minnesota*, 2:774–75; Asa R. Burleson, Military Pension Records, NARA.

34. Laura Ingalls Wilder, *On the Banks of Plum Creek* (New York: HarperTrophy, 2004 reprint). See also R. L. Cartwright, "Grasshopper Plagues, 1873–1877," www.MNopedia.org, and Frank H. Heck, "The Grand Army of the Republic in Minnesota, 1866–1880," *Minnesota History* 16 (December 1935): 432–33.

35. Dathe and Jahn, *Tales of Our Town*, 4, 6, *Spring Valley Western Progress*, March 4 and 18, 1874; *Spring Valley Vidette*, September 22, 1877.

36. The first grave commemoration in the North occurred at Waterloo, New York, in May 1866, an exercise that evolved into Memorial Day. See Harris, *Across the Bloody Chasm*, 50; Neff, *Honoring the Civil War Dead*, 136–39; McConnell, *Glorious Contentment*, 183–85, 219; William H. Ward, *Records of Members of the Grand Army of the Republic* (San Francisco: H. S. Crocker, 1886), 67; Dearing, *Veterans in Politics*, 275–76, 401–74; and *Spring Valley Sun*, October 14, 1892.

37. Neill, *History of Fillmore County*, 548; Willford and Curtiss-Wedge, *History of Fillmore County*, 2:775; *Spring Valley Mercury*, January 21, 1916.

38. See Examining Surgeon's Certificate, August 24, 1865, Declaration for Invalid Pension, August 28, 1865, Deposition of C. W. McIntosh, September 22, 1866, in Asa R. Burleson, Military Pension Record, NARA. See also Prechtel-Kluskens, "A Reasonable Degree of Promptitude," 28, and Jordan, *Marching Home*, 126.

39. Asa R. Burleson, Surgeon's Certificate, September 14, 1877, Application for Increase of Pension, October 22, 1884, Correction to Invalid Pension, February 5, 1885, February 4, 1902, March 1, 1905, Medical Pension Record, NARA ("Abdominal wounds healed incompletely and abscesses kept developing"). See George C. Rable, "It Is Well That War Is So Terrible," in *The Fredericksburg Campaign*, ed. Gary W. Gallagher (Chapel Hill: University of North Carolina Press, 1995), 60.

40. Department of Minnesota, Post Records and Descriptive Book, Burdick Post No. 3, in Grand Army of the Republic Collection, Gale Family Library, Minnesota Historical Society, St. Paul, MN; *Spring Valley Sun*, October 14, 1892. See also Richard V. Punchard, *Grand Army of the Republic: Minnesota Department* (Minneapolis: VOL Publishing, 2016), 5–6; Peter J. DeCarlo, "Grand Army of the Republic in Minnesota," www.MNopedia.org; Heck, "The Grand Army of the Republic in Minnesota, 1866–1880," 427–44; Frank H. Heck, *The Civil War Veteran in Minnesota Life and Politics* (Oxford, OH: Mississippi Valley Press, 1941), 5–14; Willford and Curtiss-Wedge, *History of Fillmore County, Minnesota*, 2:1146; Neill, *History of Fillmore County*, 545–46; and *Journal of Proceedings of the Thirty-First Annual Encampment, Department of Minnesota, Grand Army of the Republic* (St. Paul, MN: The Pioneer Press, 1897), 42. (Over the years, this source title changes from *Proceedings of* to *Journal of* to *Record of*. Hereafter, the most commonly used citation, *Proceedings of*, will be used in short-form notes.)

41. Charter of Incorporation, in Grand Army of the Republic Collection, Gale Family Library, Minnesota Historical Society, St. Paul, MN; Heck, *The Civil War Veteran in Minnesota Life and Politics*, appendix A, 5–6, 30; Post Adjutant General and Quartermaster Reports, Burdick Post No. 3 folder, in Grand Army of the Republic Collection, Gale Family Library, Minnesota Historical Society, St. Paul, MN; Punchard, *Grand Army of the Republic*, 11; *Proceedings of the First Encampment, Stillwater, August 17, 1881*, 5–6; *Proceedings of the Second Encampment, Minneapolis, January 18, 1882*, 20–21, 24, 32; *Proceedings of the Third Encampment, St. Paul, January 17, 1883*, 39–41; *Proceedings of the Fifth Encampment, Mankato, January 28–29, 1885*, 104; *Proceedings of the Sixth Encampment, Faribault, February 10–11, 1886*, 7, 54–55; *Proceedings of the Sixteenth Encampment, Minneapolis, March 11–12, 1896*, 79; *Proceedings the Seventeenth Encampment, St. Paul, February 23, 1897*, 241, 262. After 1920, Burdick Post No. 3 was challenged by a new organization that appealed to a younger veteran population, the American Legion. Shortly thereafter, the post fell into obscurity.

42. Bowen, *Regimental History of the First New York Dragoons*, 301, 313; *Buffalo Commercial*, September 4, 1897; *Buffalo Evening News*, August 26, 1897.

43. Dathe and Jahn, *Tales of Our Town*, 7; Willford and Curtiss-Wedge, *History of Fillmore County, Minnesota*, 1:301, 2:775; *Spring Valley Vidette*, September 22, 1877; *Spring Valley Mercury*, May 19, 1887, and October 12, 1917.

44. Willford and Curtiss-Wedge, *History of Fillmore County, Minnesota*, 2:774–75; *Wyoming County Herald*, October 19, 1917.

45. Post Adjutant General and Quartermaster Reports, Burdick Post No. 3 folder, in Grand Army of the Republic Collection, Gale Family Library, Minnesota Historical Society, St. Paul, MN; Punchard, *Grand Army of the Republic*, 8–11.

46. Punchard, *Grand Army of the Republic*, 66; Moe, *The Last Full Measure*, 311–12.

47. Certificate of Disability for Discharge, March 25, 1863, Oliver Webster Moore, Military Pension Record, NARA.

48. Declaration for Original Invalid Pension, October 15, 1885, Oliver Webster Moore, Military Pension Record, NARA; Deposition of Dr. C. H. Wagner, July 21, 1886, Oliver Webster Moore, Military Pension Record, NARA.

49. Physicians Affidavits, Dr. R. L. Moore, July 21, 1886, and January 12, 1887, Dr. Henry C. Grover, April 6, 1887, Oliver Webster Moore, Military Pension Record, NARA; War Department, Adjutant General's Office, Report on Case of Oliver W. Moore, March 15, 1886, Oliver Webster Moore, Military Pension Record, NARA.

50. R. E. Thompson to Hon. John C. Polock, July 2, 1886, Oliver Webster Moore, Military Pension Record, NARA.

51. J. B. LeBlond to George M. Van Leuven, December 13, 1886, Oliver Webster Moore, Military Pension Record, NARA. This kind of proof was very difficult to obtain twenty-one years after the war. See Prechtel-Kluskens, "A Reasonable Degree of Promptitude," 31; Jordan, *Marching Home*, 155–56; and Dana R. Bailey, *History of Minnehaha County, South Dakota* (Sioux Falls, SD: Brown & Saenger, 1899), 601.

52. Original Invalid Form, June 20, 1887, Oliver Webster Moore, Military Pension Record, NARA; Surgeon's Report, February 2 and July 3, 1888, and May 28, 1890, Oliver Webster Moore, Military Pension Record, NARA.

53. Surgeon's Report, July 3, 1888, and May 28, 1890, Oliver Webster Moore, Military Pension Record, NARA; Increase of Invalid Pension, May 28, 1890, and March 30, 1892, Oliver Webster Moore, Military Pension Record, NARA; George W. Van Leuven to O. W. Moore, December 4, 1891, Oliver Webster Moore, Military Pension Record, NARA; O. W. Moore to George W. Van Leuven, February 3, 1892, Oliver Webster Moore, Military Pension Record, NARA.

54. Reports of E. F. Waite, Van Leuven Case File, Oliver Webster Moore, Military Pension Record, NARA. See also Dearing, *Veterans in Politics*, 448.

55. *Howard County (IA) Times*, December 28, 1893, January 4, 1894, and April 26, 1894; *Omaha Daily Bee*, June 2, 1893; Reports of E. F. Waite, Van Leuven Case File, Oliver Webster Moore, Military Pension Record, NARA. Two trials were eventually held: one in Minneapolis stemming from sixty-four indictments in southern Minnesota and the other in Dubuque stemming from thirty-four cases in northern Iowa.

56. See the transcript of Moore's eight-page interview in Oliver Webster Moore, Van Leuven Case File, Military Pension Record, NARA. See also Edward F. Waite to Commissioner William Lochren, October 6, 1893; George W. Van Leuven to O. W. Moore,

December 30, 1891; and Oliver W. Moore to George M. Van Leuven, February 3, 1892, Oliver Webster Moore, Military Pension Record, NARA; *Spring Valley Mercury*, September 29, 1893; Records of the United States District Court for the Eastern (Dubuque) Division of the Northern District of Iowa, Criminal Case file #3517, *U.S. v. G. M. Van Leuven, Jr.*

57. *Howard County (IA) Times*, January 4 and 19, 1894, April 5, 1894, and December 18 and 25, 1894; *Sioux City (IA) Journal*, January 13, 1895; *Spring Valley Mercury*, April 20, 1894.

58. *Howard County (IA) Times*, December 18 and 25, 1894, and March 12, 1895; *Dubuque Herald*, December 19, 1894; *Lime Springs Sun*, January 1, 1897.

59. "The Pension Poison" (editorial), *Harper's Weekly*, July 27, 1895. See also *Minneapolis Tribune*, July 7, 1895; *Minneapolis Journal*, June 22, 1895; *Howard County (IA) Times*, April 23, June 11 and 25, July 16, and August 20, 1895.

60. H. R. Arnold to Commissioner William Lochren, October 12, 1893, and January 27, 1894, in Oliver W. Moore, Military Pension Record, NARA. See also Dearing, *Veterans in Politics*, 436. In October 1895, President Cleveland pardoned Van Leuven, after a second petition, because of illness. In 1897, Waite's conviction was overturned.

61. Willford and Curtiss-Wedge, *History of Fillmore County, Minnesota*, 1:176–85, 2:776; *Spring Valley Mercury*, November 26, 1926.

62. Willford and Curtiss-Wedge, *History of Fillmore County, Minnesota*, 1:176–85, 2:776; "The Nobility of Service of Our Past and Present [Horticultural] Veterans," O. W. Moore (unpublished address, 1916); Spring Valley (MN), *Cemetery Records*, 182; Minnesota Territorial Pioneer's Association Papers, Minnesota Historical Society, St. Paul, MN; Certificate of Membership, June 6, 1899, Oliver Webster Moore, Miscellaneous file, CCHM; *Spring Valley Mercury*, November 26, 1926.

63. Fannie Moore Affidavit, June 2 and August 25, 1915; Surgeon's Certificate, Dr. J. D. Utley, June 2, 1915, Oliver W. Moore, Military Pension Record, NARA.

64. Surgeon's Certificate, December 1, 1915, and January 4, 1916; Fannie Moore Affidavit, August 21, 1926; Verna Tretheway Affidavit, August 25, 1926, Oliver W. Moore, Military Pension Record, NARA.

65. See the interview referenced in the *Spring Valley Mercury-Vidette*, November 27, 1926. See also *Tri-County Record*, December 2, 1926, and *Winona Republican-Herald*, August 6 and November 26, 1926. A handwritten copy and typescript of Oliver's reminiscence is found in Oliver Webster Moore, Miscellaneous file, CCHM.

66. *Tri-County Record*, December 2, 1926; *Winona Republican-Herald*, November 26, 1926; *Spring Valley Mercury-Vidette*, November 27, 1926.

67. Ronald Moore to Verna [Moore] Tretheway, February 2, 1931, and John W. Ellithorpe to Frances M. Moore, February 11, 1933, in Oliver Webster Moore, Miscellaneous file, CCHM; New York State Death Index, 1880–1956. See also all U.S. census reports for Fillmore County, Minnesota, 1880, 1900; Minnesota State Census, 1875–1895.

68. *Fifteenth Annual Reunion, Regimental Association of the Bucktails*, unnumbered pages. See the oration delivered at the Sunset Service. Unfortunately, the account does not list the announced names of the seven honorees.

69. Rable, "It Is Well That War Is So Terrible," 60. See also Rable, *Fredericksburg! Fredericksburg!*, 432; Dean, "Post Traumatic Stress," in Logue and Barton, *The Civil War Veteran*, 126–45; Adams, *Living Hell*, 181, 205; and Hess, *The Union Soldier in Battle*, 159.

70. Adams, *Living Hell*, 202.

Appendix B: Bucktail Requiem

1. Beers, *History of the Counties of McKean, Elk, Cameron, and Potter, Pennsylvania*, 270–71; Thomson and Rauch, *History of the "Bucktails,"* 449–52; *Third Annual Reunion, Regimental Association of the Bucktails or First Rifle Regt., P. R. V. C., Philipsburg, PA, August 21–22, 1889* (Philadelphia: Electric Print Co., 1889), 12.

2. Thomson and Rauch, *History of the "Bucktails,"* 439; *First Annual Reunion, Regimental Association of the Bucktails or First Rifle Regt., P. R. V. C., Williamsport, PA, October 21–22, 1887*; *Third Annual Reunion, Regimental Association of the Bucktails*, 7, 30–31.

3. Bucktail regimental reunions were held in Williamsport (1887), Bradford (1888), Philipsburg (1889), Wellsboro (1890), Mauch Chunk (1891), Washington, DC (1892), Williamsport (1894), Lock Haven (1895), Emporium (1896), Smethport (1897), Kennett Square (1898), Philadelphia (1899), Ridgway (1900), Gettysburg (1901), Dubois (1902), Harrisburg (1903), Lock Haven (1904), Curwensville (1905), Driftwood (1906), Driftwood (1908), Richmond, VA (1909), Gettysburg (1910), Rochester, NY (1911), Gettysburg (1913), Wellsboro (1914), Washington, DC (1915), Smethport (1916). See Bucktail Reunions, Vertical File, McKean County Museum Library, Smethport, PA.

4. *Twelfth Annual Reunion, Regimental Association of the Bucktails*, 30; *Fourteenth Annual Reunion, Regimental Association of the Bucktails*, 25.

5. *Fifth Annual Reunion, Regimental Association of the Bucktails*, 14–15; *Seventh Annual Reunion, Regimental Association of the Bucktails*, 30–31; Thomson and Rauch, *History of the "Bucktails,"* 239; *McKean County Democrat*, May 30, 1929, and December 28, 1939.

6. *Third Annual Reunion, Regimental Association of the Bucktails*, 30–31; John P. Nicholson, ed., *Pennsylvania at Gettysburg: Ceremonies at the Dedication of the Monuments Erected by the Commonwealth of Pennsylvania*, 2 vols. (Harrisburg, PA: William Stanley Ray, 1893), v–viii, 1:276–83.

7. *Twentieth Annual Reunion, Regimental Association of the Bucktails*; *Driftwood (PA) Weekly Gazette*, April 30, 1908.

8. 1865 New York State Census, Allegany County, NY. See also Gilbert, *Rushford and Rushford People*, 307–37, and Minard and Merrill, *Allegany County and Its People*, 800.

9. Sypher and Bates drew their roster information from the three-by-five-inch index card file of every soldier who fought in a Pennsylvania unit. For focus on the 13th Pennsylvania Reserves, see Sypher, *History of the Pennsylvania Reserves*, 710–23, and Bates, *History of the Pennsylvania Volunteers*, 1:907–43.

10. See *The Rushford Centennial, August 16–21, 1908* (Rushford, NY: Centennial Committee, 1908), 169, 188, 363, 399–402. See also Minard and Merrill, *Allegany County and Its People*, 297–313, 800, and *Rushford Spectator*, June 27, 1907.

11. For Ellithorpe biographies, see Gilbert, *Rushford and Rushford People*, 315, 324, 335. See also *Rushford Centennial, August 16–21, 1908,* 146, 156–82.

12. For the only modern secondary reference to Phillip's death, see Ent, *The Pennsylvania Reserves in the Civil War*, 216.

13. See *Official Army Register of the Volunteer Forces, U.S. Army, pt. VIII, Veteran's Reserve Corps* (Washington, DC: Adjutant General's Office, 1867), 58, 62, 97, and *OR*, 3, pt. 5:546–52, 564. On April 25, 1864, Bell's regiment was redesignated the 94th Company, 2nd Battalion, Veteran Reserve Corps, and assigned to the Surgeon General's Department.

14. Thomson and Rauch, *History of the "Bucktails,"* 255; Bell, *Recollection*, 5 (GNMPLRC).

15. See Alfred Minott Copeland, *"Our Country and Its People": A History of Hampden County, Massachusetts*, 3 vols. (Boston: Century Memorial Publishing Co., 1902), 1:134, 187, 191, 3:145, 149, 150, 157, 160–61, 164, and Josiah Howard Temple, *History of the Town of Palmer, Massachusetts, Early Known as the Elbow Tract* (Springfield, MA: Clark W. Bryan and Co., 1889), 11, 260–61, 429.

16. *OR*, 3, pt. 5:565; *Official Army Register of the Volunteer Forces, U.S. Army, pt. VIII, Veteran's Reserve Corps*, 66; Thomson and Rauch, *History of the "Bucktails,"* 29. On March 26, 1864, Blanchard's regiment was redesignated the 96th Company, 2nd Battalion, Veteran Reserve Corps, and assigned to the Surgeon General's Department.

17. Thomson and Rauch, *History of the "Bucktails,"* viii, 10, 157, 255, 449; *U.S. National Homes for Disabled Volunteer Soldiers, Dayton, Ohio, Patient Ledger Book, 1918*.

18. *McKean County Miner*, June 2, 1893; Thomson and Rauch, *History of the "Bucktails,"* 449, 452.

19. John W. Leonard, ed., *The Book of Chicagoans: A Biographical Dictionary of Leading Men & Women* (Chicago: A. N. Marquis, 1908), 127.

20. *Pennsylvania Civil War Index Cards*, C; Strait, *Roster of All Regimental Surgeons and Assistant Surgeons in the Late War*, 232; Prowell, *The History of Camden County, New Jersey*, 249, 251–52; Bates, *History of the Pennsylvania Volunteers*, 2:923, 4:37; *West Jersey Press*, October 25, 1865; *Camden Democrat*, March 21, 1868; *Tecumseh (MI) Daily Telegram*, November 3, 1905; Ancestry.com, *Quaker Meeting Records for Jonathan J. Comfort, 1681–1935*; *The American Friend*, January–December 1907, 13–14.

21. Vernelle A. Hatch, *Illustrated History of Bradford, McKean County, PA* (Bradford, PA: Burk Brothers, 1901), 104, 106; Michael A. Leeson, *History of the Counties of McKean, Elk, and Forest, Pennsylvania* (Chicago: J. H. Beers, 1890), 63, 146–47, 186, 360; *Pennsylvania Civil War Soldiers' Index Cards*, H.

22. For a biography of Townsend, see Sandra Moss, "The Country Practitioner: A Medical Journal with "Snap," *Garden State Legacy* 12 (June 2011): 1–17.

23. For information on the Ward family, see Lewis Cass Aldrich and Frank R. Holmes, eds., *History of Clearfield County, Pennsylvania: With Illustrations and Biographical Sketches of Some of Its Prominent Men and Pioneers* (Syracuse, NY: D. Mason Publisher, 1887), 245, 344.

24. See Thomson and Rauch, *History of the "Bucktails,"* 416; R. Fenton Ward, 190th Pennsylvania, Military Service Record, NARA; *Pennsylvania Civil War Soldier's Index Card*; and Patrick A. Schroeder, *Pennsylvania Bucktails: A Photographic Album of the 42nd, 149th & 150th Pennsylvania Regiments from the Collection of Ronn Palm* (Daleville, VA: Schroeder Publications, 2001), 105.

25. Crawford initially reported that his losses exceeded 750 men. *OR*, 42, pt. 1:491–94 (Brig. Gen. Samuel W. Crawford), 505–6 (Col. Thomas F. McCoy), 124 (casualties for Weldon Railroad); R. E. McBride, *In the Ranks: From the Wilderness to Appomattox Court House* (Online Pantianos Classics, 2018 reprint), 40. After the debacle at Weldon Railroad, two former Bucktails, Maj. John Wolfe and Capt. Neri B. Kinsey, assumed temporary command of the decimated regiments.

26. Company I did not select a captain until December 1864. *Pennsylvania Civil War Soldier's Index Card*, R. Fenton Ward; Bates, *History of the Pennsylvania Volunteers*, 5:299.

27. See *Raftsman's Journal* (Clearfield, PA), June 18, 1884, and February 27, 1889.

Bibliography

Primary Sources

Public Records

Annual Report of the Adjutant-General of the State of New York, 1895–1900. Albany, NY: James B. Lyon, State Printer, 1900.

Barnes, Joseph K., Joseph Janvier Woodward, Charles Smart, George A. Otis, and D. L. Huntington. *The Medical and Surgical History of the War of the Rebellion, 1861–1865.* Washington, DC: Government Printing Office, 1870–1888.

Buffalo City Directory, 1866–1912. (various publishers).

DeBow, J. D. B. *Statistical View of the United States: Compendium to the Seventh Census, 1850.* Washington, DC: Beverly Tucker, Senate Printer, 1854.

Fresno City Directory, 1904–1906, 1912–1915. (various publishers).

Minneapolis City Directory, 1924–1938. Minneapolis: Minneapolis Directory Company, 1924–1938.

Minnesota State Population Schedules, 1865–1905. St. Paul: Minnesota Historical Society, n.d.

New York in the Spanish-American War: Part of the Report of the Adjutant General of the State for 1900. 3 vols. Albany, NY: James B. Lyon, State Printer, 1900.

Office of the County Clerk, Allegany County, Belmont, NY. *Land Deeds.*

Office of the County Clerk, Genesee County, Batavia, NY. *Land Deeds.*

Office of the County Clerk, Livingston County, Geneseo, NY. *Land Deeds.*

Office of the County Clerk, St. Lawrence County, Canton, NY. *Land Deeds.*

Office of the County Clerk, Wyoming County, Warsaw, NY. *Land Deeds.*

Report of the Paymaster General. Washington, DC: Government Printing Office, 1861.

Report of the Pennsylvania Commission. *Fiftieth Anniversary of the Battle of Gettysburg.* Harrisburg, PA: State Printing Office, 1914.

Roster and Record of Iowa Soldiers in the War of the Rebellion, 1861–1865. 4 vols. Des Moines, IA: E. H. English, 1908–1911.

Spring Valley (MN) Cemetery Records.

State of Connecticut. *Birth, Death and Burial Records, 1649–1906.*

State of Minnesota. *Death Records, Fillmore County, Minnesota*, 1926.

———. *Minnesota Marriage Index*, 1849–1950.

———. *Minnesota Death Index*, 1908–2002.

State of New York. Census, *Population*, 1835, 1845, 1855, 1865, 1875, 1885.

State of Vermont. *Births and Christenings*, 1765–1908.

———. *Census*, 1785.

Town Clerk of Bridgewater, VT. *Land Deeds.*

Town Clerk of Bridport, VT. *Land Deeds.*
Town Clerk of Nunda, NY. *Record Book.*
Town Clerk of Orwell, VT. *Land Deeds.*
Town Clerk of Sheldon, VT. *Land Deeds.*
U.S. Census. Agricultural Schedule, Allegany County, New York, 1850–1860.
———. *Agricultural Schedule, Wyoming County, New York*, 1850–1870.
———. *Population, Allegany County, New York*, 1830–1870.
———. *Population, Bennington County, Vermont*, 1790–1810.
———. *Population, Cattaraugus County, New York*, 1830–1860.
———. *Population, Chittenden County, Vermont*, 1860.
———. *Population, Erie County, New York*, 1870–1910.
———. *Population, Fillmore County, Minnesota*, 1880–1920.
———. *Population, Montgomery County, New York*, 1830.
———. *Population, Oneida County, New York*, 1840.
———. *Population, Otsego County, New York*, 1810–1820.
———. *Population, St. Lawrence County, New York*, 1820–1870.
———. *Population, Windham County, Connecticut*, 1790–1830.
———. *Population, Windsor County, Vermont*, 1790–1820.
———. *Population, Wyoming County, New York*, 1850–1910.
U.S. Civil War Pension Index: General Index to Pension Files, 1861–1934. Washington, DC: National Archive and Records Administration.
U.S. Congress. House Committee on Veteran Affairs. *Historical Statistics of the Veteran Population, 1865–1960; A Compendium of Facts about Veterans.* House Committee Report no. 69, 87th Congress, 1st session, 1961.
U.S. Sanitary Commission. *Report to the Secretary of War: Operations of the Sanitary Commission in the Volunteer Army—Month of September and October, 1861.* New York: U.S. Sanitation Commission, 1866.
War of the Rebellion: A Compilation of the Official Records of the Union and Confederate Armies. 128 vols. Washington, DC: Government Printing Office, 1880–1901.

Proceedings

Journal of the Proceedings of the Annual Sessions of the Minnesota Department, Grand Army of the Republic, 1881–1920.

Newspapers and Periodicals

Albany Evening Times, 1891.
The American Friend, 1907.
Batavia Republican Advocate, 1833.
Batavia Spirit of the Times, 1840.
Buffalo Commercial, 1902.
Buffalo Courier, 1889–1890.
Buffalo Evening News, 1891–1895.
Buffalo Inquirer, 1904.
Buffalo Morning Express, 1883–1890.
Camden Democrat, 1868.

Confederate Veteran, 1893–1932.
Corvallis (OR) Daily Gazette Times, 1915.
The Daily News (Longview, WA), 2014–2015.
Driftwood (PA) Weekly Gazette, 1908.
Fresno (CA) Bee, 1915, 1935.
Friendship (NY) Weekly Register, 1890.
Harrisburg Patriot and Union, 1861.
Howard County (IA) Times, 1893–1897.
Lime Springs (IA) Sun, 1897.
McKean County Democrat, 1861, 1900–1939.
Minneapolis Journal, 1895.
Minneapolis Tribune, 1895.
Mower County Transcript, 1899.
New York Times, 1861.
Philadelphia Weekly Press, 1886.
Potsdam (NY) Courier-Freeman, 1892.
Rushford (MN) Tri-County Record, 1926.
Spring Valley (MN) Mercury, 1887–1917.
Spring Valley (MN) Vidette, 1877–1890.
Spring Valley (MN) Sun, 1891–1892.
Tecumseh (MI) Daily Telegram, 1905.
Troy (NY) Daily Times, 1891.
Utica (NY) Weekly Herald, 1889.
Washington Post, 2014.
West Jersey Press, 1865.
Wyoming County (NY) Gazette, 1914.

Manuscripts

Allegany County Historical Society, Andover, NY
Green Family Collection
Bailey/Howe Library, University of Vermont, Burlington, VT
Jonathan Remington Papers
Cowlitz County Historical Museum, Kelso, WA
- Ellithorpe Family Collection
  - Phillip Griggs Ellithorpe Letters
  - Philander Doty Ellithorpe Letters
  - Asa R. Burleson Letters
  - Oliver Webster Moore Letters
  - Miscellaneous Documents

Daniel A. Reed Library, Archives and Special Collections, State University of New York, Fredonia
- Holland Land Company Collection
  - Land Transactions Ledger
  - Field Notes
  - Maps

Gale Family Library, Minnesota History Center, St. Paul, MN
Grand Army of the Republic
Department of Minnesota
Charters of Incorporation
Post Records, Descriptive Book, 1880–1890
Post Adjutant and Quartermaster Reports, 1880–1940
Minnesota Territorial Pioneer's Association Papers
Correspondence, 1898–1941
George Henry Bandfield Photo Album (Property of Micheline F. Smith, family genealogist, Jamesburg, New Jersey)
Gettysburg National Military Park Library and Research Center (GNMPLRC), Gettysburg, PA
Frank J. Bell, *Recollection*
Camp Letterman Papers
Gregory Coco Collection (drawer 14 A)
Detailed Soldier Information of Men Buried at Camp Letterman Cemetery and Disposition after Removal
Index Cards
List of U.S. Medical Officers at Camp Letterman
Weather Reports, June 25–July 8 (box B-75-2/item O 260, O 314, O 325)
Map of Hospitals at Gettysburg, in Andrew B. Cross, *Battle of Gettysburg and the Christian Commission, 1865* (drawer V7-12-3, 7-10)
Henry J. Janes Collection
Journal of Dr. Henry Janes, Camp Letterman General Hospital Orders and Correspondence, July 26–September 9, 1863
Report of Henry J. Janes, *List of Deaths in the Letterman Hospital* (drawer V7-12-3)
Union Field Hospital Records, Gettysburg (drawer 7)
William C. Weidner Jr., "A Memoir of the Thirteenth Infantry Regiment of Pennsylvania Reserve Corps" (drawer 6-PA 42)
Missouri History Museum, St. Louis, MO
C. C. Gardiner, "A Reminiscence of the Civil War." Paper delivered before the Missouri Commandery of the Military Order of the Loyal Legion, St. Louis, MO, April 2, 1892.
National Archives and Records Administration (NARA), Washington, DC
Military Service Records
Phillip Griggs Ellithorpe
Philander Doty Ellithorpe
Asa R. Burleson
Oliver Webster Moore
Federal Military Pension Records
Phillip Griggs Ellithorpe
Philander Doty Ellithorpe
Asa R. Burleson
Oliver Webster Moore
New York Public Library, New York, NY

United States Sanitation Commission Collection
Phillip G. Ellithorpe file, box 14, folder 17
New York State Military Museum and Veteran's Research Center, Albany, NY
Civil War Newspaper Clippings
1st Regiment of Dragoons, New York Volunteers
2nd New York Mounted Rifles
Pennsylvania State Archive, Harrisburg, PA
Civil War Veterans Index Card File, 1861–1866

Maps

New Topographical Atlas of Genesee and Wyoming Counties, New York. Philadelphia: Stone and Stewart Publishers, 1866.

Theses, Dissertations, and Unpublished

Hunter, Lloyd Arthur. "The Sacred South: Postwar Confederates and the Sacralization of Southern Culture." PhD diss., St. Louis University, 1978.
Simpson, John A. "The Rebel Yell in American Oral Tradition." Unpublished essay, 1989.
Thornton, Arthur. "A History of Nicholville." MA thesis, State University of New York, Potsdam, 1999.

Articles

Bard, Capt. John P. "The 'Old Bucktails,' 42nd Regt., P. V., at the Battle of Gettysburg." *Philadelphia Weekly Press*, May 19, 1886.
Gardiner, Curtiss Crane. "A Reminiscence of the Civil War." Paper delivered before the Missouri Commandery of the Military Order of the Loyal Legion, St. Louis, MO, April 2, 1892.
Hall, Henry Seymour. "A Volunteer at the First Bull Run." In *War Talks in Kansas; A Series of Papers Read before the Kansas Commandery of the Military Order of the Loyal Legion of the United States (MOLLUS)*, May 4, 1892, 143–59.
Wood, E. A. "Nicholville, 1892–1893." In St. Lawrence County Historical Association Scrapbook Collection, Scrapbook #16.

Books (Pre-1910)

Adams, William, ed. *Historical Gazetteer and Biographical Memorial of Cattaraugus County, New York.* Syracuse, NY: Lyman, Horton Co., 1893.
Aldrich, George. *Walpole As It Was and As It Is.* Claremont, NH: Claremont Co., 1880.
Aldrich, Lewis Cass, and Frank R. Holmes, eds., *History of Bennington County, Vermont: With Illustrations and Biographical Sketches of Some of Its Prominent Men and Pioneers.* Syracuse, NY: D. Mason & Co., 1889.
———. *History of Clearfield County, Pennsylvania: With Illustrations and Biographical Sketches of Some of Its Prominent Men and Pioneers.* Syracuse, NY: D. Mason & Co., 1887.
———. *History of Franklin and Grand Isle Counties, Vermont: With Illustrations and Biographical Sketches of Some of Its Prominent Men and Pioneers.* Syracuse, NY: D. Mason & Co., 1891.

———. *History of Windsor County, Vermont: With Illustrations and Biographical Sketches of Some of Its Prominent Men and Pioneers*. Syracuse, NY: D. Mason & Co., 1891.

Atlas of Allegany County, New York. New York: D. G. Beers, 1869.

Bailey, Dana R. *History of Minnehaha County, South Dakota*. Sioux Falls, SD: Brown & Saenger, 1899.

Barber, John Warner. *Historical Collections of the State of New York*. New York: S. Tuttle, 1846.

Bates, Samuel Penniman. *History of the Pennsylvania Volunteers, 1861–1865*. 5 vols. Harrisburg, PA: State Printing Office, 1869–1871.

Bayles, Richard M. *History of Windham County, Connecticut, with Illustrations*. New York: W. W. Preston & Co., 1889.

Beauchamp, William M. *Past and Present of Syracuse and Onondaga County: From Its Prehistoric Times to the Beginning of 1908*. New York: S. J. Clarke Publishing Co., 1908.

Bechler, G. *Map of Allegany County, from Actual Surveys*. Philadelphia: Gillette, Matthews and Co., 1856.

Beers, F. W. *History of Allegany County, New York: With Illustrations and Portraits of Old Pioneers and Prominent Residents*. New York: F. W. Beers, 1879.

———. *History of Montgomery and Fulton Counties, New York: With Illustrations and Portraits of Old Pioneers*. New York: F. W. Beers and Co., 1878.

_____. *History of Wyoming County, New York: With Illustrations and Biographical Sketches and Portraits of Some Pioneers and Prominent Residents*. New York: F. W. Beers, 1880.

Beers, J. H. *History of the Counties of McKean, Elk, Cameron, and Potter, Pennsylvania: With Biographical Selections*. Chicago: John Morris Publisher, 1890.

Benedict, G. G. *Vermont in the Civil War: A History*. 2 vols. Burlington, VT: The Free Press, 1886.

Billings, John D. *Hardtack and Coffee or the Unwritten Story of Army Life*. 1888. Reprint, Williamstown, MA: Corner House Publishers, 1990.

Biographical Sketches of the Leading Citizens of Livingston and Wyoming Counties, New York. Boston: Biographical Review Publishing Co., 1895.

Blodgett, George B., and Amos Everett Jewett. *Early Settlers of Rowley, Massachusetts: A Genealogical Record of Families*. Reprint ed. Rowley, MA: A. E. Jewett, 1933.

Bodge, George M. *Soldiers in King Philip's War: Containing Lists of the Soldiers of Massachusetts Colony Who Served in the Indian War of 1675–1676*. Boston: David Clapp & Son, 1891.

Bosbyshell, Oliver C. *Pennsylvania at Antietam*. Harrisburg, PA: State Printer, 1906.

Bowen, James R. *Regimental History of the First New York Dragoons (130th New York)*. Lyons, MI: Bowen Publisher, 1900.

Bromley, Viola A. *The Bromley Genealogy*. New York: Frederick H. Hitchcock, 1911.

Buell, D. E. *A Brief History of Company B, 27th New York Regiment: Its Organization and the Part It Took in the War*. Lyons, NY: Republican Press, 1874.

Cady, Nahum Ward. *Court Martial of Major N. Ward Cady, 2nd Mounted Rifles, New York Volunteers: Including Offense, Defense, Sentence, and Correspondence*. Yates, NY: n.p., 1864.

Chapman, Grace Olive. *Ellithorpes of Killingly, Connecticut*. Boston: self-published, 1944.

Chase, George Wingate. *The History of Haverhill, Massachusetts: From Its First Settlement in 1640 to the Year 1860*. Haverhill, MA: Stone & Huse, 1861.

Commemorative Biographical Record of Tolland and Windham Counties, Connecticut: Biographical Sketches of Prominent and Representative Citizens and Many of the Early Settled Families. Chicago: J. H. Beers & Co., 1903.

Copeland, Alfred Minott. *"Our Country and Its People": A History of Hampden County, Massachusetts.* 3 vols. Boston: Century Memorial Publishing Co., 1902.

Cox, James, ed. *Notable St. Louisans in 1900.* St. Louis, MO: Benesch Art Publishing Co., 1900.

Cunningham, Sumner A. *Reminiscences of the 41st Tennessee Regiment.* Shelbyville, TN: Commercial Press, 1872.

Curtis, Gates. *Our County and Its People.* Syracuse, NY: D. Mason and Co., 1894.

Curtis, Newton Martin. *From Bull Run to Chancellorsville: The Story of the 16th New York Infantry.* New York: Putnam's Sons, 1906.

Davenport, Alfred. *Camp and Field Life of the Fifth New York Volunteers.* New York: Dick and Fitzgerald, 1879.

DeBow, J. D. *Statistical View of the United States: Compendium to the Seventh Census.* Washington, DC: Senate Printer, 1854.

Doty, Lockwood R. *History of Livingston County, New York: From Its Earliest Traditions to the Present.* 2 vols. Jackson, MI: W. J. Van Deusen, 1905.

Duncan, Louis C. *The Medical Department of the U.S. Army in the Civil War.* Washington, DC: Government Printing Office, 1910.

Durant, Samuel W., and Henry B. Peirce. *History of St. Lawrence County, New York: With Illustrations and Biographical Sketches of Some of Its Prominent Men and Pioneers.* Philadelphia: L. H. Everts, 1878.

Everts, Louis H. *History of Cattaraugus County, New York: With Illustrations and Biographical Sketches of Some of Its Prominent Men and Pioneers.* Philadelphia: Everts & Co., 1879.

———. *History of the Connecticut Valley in Massachusetts: With Illustrations and Biographical Sketches of Some of Its Prominent Men and Pioneers.* 2 vols. Philadelphia: J. B. Lippincott and Co., 1879.

———. *History of St. Lawrence County, New York: With Illustrations and Biographical Sketches of Some of Its Prominent Men and Pioneers.* Philadelphia: L. H. Everts & Co., 1878.

Fairchild, Charles Bryant. *History of the 27th Regiment, New York Volunteers.* Binghamton, NY: Carl and Matthews Printers, 1888.

Fox, William F. *Regimental Losses in the American Civil War, 1861–1865.* Albany, NY: Albany Publishing Company, 1889.

Gage, Thomas. *History of Rowley, Massachusetts.* Boston: Ferdinand Andrews Pub., 1840.

Gilbert, Helen Josephine White. *Rushford and Rushford People.* Chautauqua, NY: Chautauqua Print Shop, 1910.

Greenlee, Ralph Stebbins, and Robert Lemuel Greenlee. *The Stebbins Genealogy.* 2 vols. Chicago: M. A. Donohue and Co., 1904.

Hand, H. Wells. *Centennial History of the Town of Nunda, 1808–1908.* Rochester, NY: Rochester Herald Press, 1908.

Hardee, William J. *Hardee's Rifle and Light Infantry Tactics.* Memphis, TN: E. C. Kirk & Co., 1861.

Hardin, George Anson. *History of Herkimer County, New York.* Syracuse, NY: D. Mason and Co., 1893.

Hatch, Vernelle A. *Illustrated History of Bradford, McKean County, PA*. Bradford, PA: Burk Brothers, 1901.

Hicks, Oliver. *Rutherford County, North Carolina, Its Establishment, Early History, Topography, Soil, Products and Other Resources*. Shelby, NC: Babington Roberts and Co., 1886.

Hinman, Royal R. *A Catalogue of the First Puritan Settlers of the Colony of Connecticut*. Hartford, CT: Case, Tiffany & Co., 1852.

History of Wyoming County, New York, with Illustrations, Biographical Sketches and Portraits of Some Pioneers and Prominent Residents. New York: F. W. Beers, 1880.

Hotchkin, James H. *A History of the Purchase and Settlement of Western New York, and of the Rise, Progress and Present State of the Presbyterian Church in That Section*. New York: M. W. Dodd, 1848.

Hoyt, David W. *Old Families of Salisbury and Amesbury, Massachusetts*. Providence, RI: Snow and Farnham Printers, 1897.

Hurd, D. Hamilton. *History of Otsego County, New York: With Illustrations and Biographical Sketches of Some of Its Prominent Men and Pioneers*. Philadelphia: Everts & Fariss, 1878.

———. *History of New London County, Connecticut: With Biographical Sketches of Many of Its Pioneers and Prominent Men*. Philadelphia: J. W. Lewis & Co., 1882.

Johnson, Robert Underwood, and Clarence C. Buel, eds. *Battles and Leaders of the Civil War*. 4 vols. New York: Century, 1884–1888.

Jordan, Ewing. *University of Pennsylvania Men Who Served in the Civil War, 1861–1865; Department of Medicine*. Philadelphia: n.p., 1900.

Judd, David W. *The Story of the Thirty-Third New York Volunteers*. Rochester, NY: Benton and Andrews, 1864.

Leeson, Michael A. *History of the Counties of McKean, Elk, and Forest, Pennsylvania*. Chicago: J. H. Beers, 1890.

Leonard, John W. ed., *The Book of Chicagoans: A Biographical Dictionary of Leading Men and Women*. Chicago: A. N. Marquis, 1908.

Livermore, Thomas L. *Numbers and Losses in the Civil War in America, 1861–1865*. Boston: Houghton Mifflin, 1901.

Lochren, William. *Minnesota in the Civil and Indian Wars, 1861–1865*. St. Paul, MN: Pioneer Press Co., 1891.

Lyman, Theodore. *Meade's Headquarters, 1863–1865: The Letters of Colonel Theodore Lyman from the Wilderness to Appomattox*. Boston: Massachusetts Historical Society, 1881.

Map of St. Lawrence County, New York. Philadelphia: J. B. Shields Pub., 1858.

Mark, Penrose G. *Red, White, and Blue Badge: A History of the 93rd Regiment, Known as the "Lebanon Infantry."* Harrisburg, PA: Aughinbaugh Press, 1911.

McIntosh, W. H. *History of Monroe County, New York*. Rochester, NY: W. E. Morrison, 1877.

Miller, Francis Trevelyn, ed. *The Photographic History of the Civil War in Ten Volumes*. New York: Review of Reviews, 1911.

Minard, John S., and Georgia Drew Merrill. *Allegany County and Its People: A Centennial Memorial History*. Alfred, NY: W. A. Ferguson and Co., 1896.

Neill, Edward D. *History of Fillmore County*. Minneapolis: Minnesota Historical Company, 1882.

New Topographical Atlas of Genesee and Wyoming Counties, New York. Philadelphia: Stone and Stewart Publishers, 1866.

Nicholson, John P., ed. *Pennsylvania at Gettysburg: Ceremonies at the Dedication of the Monuments Erected by the Commonwealth of Pennsylvania*. 2 vols. Harrisburg, PA: William Stanley Ray, 1893.

Olmsted, Frederick Law. *Hospital Transports: A Memoir of the Sick and Wounded from the Peninsula of Virginia in the Summer of 1862*. Boston: Ticknor and Fields, 1863.

Peck, Theodore S. *Revised Roster of Vermont during the War of the Rebellion, 1861–66*. Montpelier, VT: Watchman Publishing Co., 1892.

Peterson, E. Frank. *Map of Spink County, South Dakota: Compiled and Drawn from a Special Survey and Official Records*. Vermillion, SD: E. Frank Peterson, 1899.

Phillips, Daniel Lyon. *A History: Being a History of the Town of Griswold, Connecticut*. New Haven, CT: Tuttle, Morehouse & Taylor Co., 1929.

Phisterer, Frederick. *New York in the War of the Rebellion*. 6 vols. Albany, NY: Weed, Parsons and Co., 1890.

Prowell, George R. *The History of Camden County, New Jersey*. Philadelphia: L. J. Richards and Co., 1886.

Rice, James C., and C. K. Brewster. *History of the Town of Worthington, from Its First Settlement to 1874*. Springfield, MA: Clark W. Bryan and Co., 1874.

Ritual of the Grand Army of the Republic. Washington, DC: Headquarters of the Grand Army of the Republic, 1869.

Roster of the Department of Missouri, Grand Army of the Republic, 1895. Kansas City, MO: Western Veteran, 1895.

Sanford, Carlton. E. *Early History of the Town of Hopkinton*. Boston: Bartlett Press, 1903.

Searles, Jasper Newton. *History of the First Regiment, Minnesota Volunteer Infantry*. Stillwater, MN: Easton and Masterman Printers, 1916.

Sheldon, Hezekiah Spencer. *Documentary History of Suffield in the Colony and Province of the Massachusetts Bay in New England, 1660–1749*. 3 vols. Springfield, MA: Clark W. Bryan, 1879.

Smith, Henry Perry. *A History of Addison County, Vermont: With Illustrations and Biographical Sketches of Some of Its Prominent Men and Pioneers*. Syracuse, NY: D. Mason & Co., 1886.

Smith, James H. *History of Livingston County, New York: With Illustrations and Biographical Sketches of Some of Its Prominent Men and Pioneers*. Syracuse, NY: D. Mason and Co., 1881.

Stillé, Charles J. *History of the United States Sanitation Commission*. Philadelphia: J. B. Lippincott & Co., 1866.

Strait, N. A. *Roster of All Regimental Surgeons and Assistant Surgeons in the Late War*. Washington, DC: U.S. Pension Office, 1882.

Strong, William H. *History of the 121st Regiment, Pennsylvania Volunteers*. Philadelphia: Burk and McFetridge Co., 1893.

Sullivan, James, ed. *History of New York State, 1523–1927*. 5 vols. New York: Lewis Historical Publishing Company, 1927.

Sypher, Josiah R. *History of the Pennsylvania Reserves: A Complete Record*. Lancaster, PA: Elias Barr and Co., 1865.

Temple, Josiah Howard. *History of the Town of Palmer, Massachusetts, Early Known as the Elbow Tract*. Springfield, MA: Clark W. Bryan and Co., 1889.

The Union Army: A History of Military Affairs in the Loyal States, 1861–1865. Madison, WI: Federal Publishing Company, 1908.

Thomson, Osmund, and William H. Rauch. *History of the "Bucktails": Kane's Rifle Regiment of the Pennsylvania Reserve Corps, 42nd of the Line*. Philadelphia: Electric Printing Co., 1906.

Turner, Orsamus. *Pioneer History of the Holland Land Purchase in Western New York*. Buffalo, NY: Jewett, Thomas & Co., 1850.

Van Schaack, Henry C. *A History of Manlius Village*. Fayetteville, NY: Recorder, 1873.

Vital Records of Roxbury, Massachusetts, to the End of 1849. Salem, MA: Essex Institute, 1925.

Wallace, Ellerslie. *The Graduating Class of Jefferson Medical College of Philadelphia, Delivered March 10, 1863*. Pamphlet, n.p., 1863.

Walling, Henry Francis. *Map of the Counties of Franklin and Grand Isle, Vermont*. Boston: Baker, Tilden and Co., 1857.

Ward, William H. *Records of Members of the Grand Army of the Republic*. San Francisco: H. S. Crocker, 1886.

Westervelt, William B. *Lights and Shadows of Army Life: From Bull Run to Bentonville*. 1886. Reprint, Shippensburg, PA: White Mane Press, 1998.

Willford, William, and Franklyn Curtiss-Wedge. *History of Fillmore County, Minnesota*. 2 vols. Chicago: H. C. Cooper, 1912.

Woodward, Evan Morrison. *Our Campaigns; or, The Marches, Bivouacs, Battles, and Incidents of Camp Life and History of Our Regiment*. Philadelphia: John E. Potter and Co., 1865.

Wright, Carroll D. *History and Growth of the United States Census*. Washington, DC: Government Printing Office, 1900.

Secondary Sources

Articles

Ellis, David M. "The Yankee Invasion of New York, 1783–1850." *New York History* 32 (1951): 1–17.

French, Robert M. "Carlos Leonardo Stebbins." *Historical Wyoming (County)* 17 (October 1963): 1–9.

Goff, Reda C. "The Confederate Veteran Magazine." *Tennessee Historical Quarterly* 31 (1972): 45–60.

Harris, Moira F., and Leo J. Harris. "St. Paul's Biggest Party: The Grand Army of the Republic's 1896 National Encampment." *Ramsey County History* 44 (Fall 2009): 13–20.

Heck, Frank H. "The Grand Army of the Republic in Minnesota, 1866–1880." *Minnesota History* 16 (December 1935): 427–44.

Moss, Sandra. "The Country Practitioner: A Medical Journal with 'Snap.'" www.GardenStateLegacy.com, 12 (June 2011): 1–17.

Prechtel-Kluskens, Claire. "A Reasonable Degree of Promptitude: Civil War Pension Application Processing, 1861–1865." *Prologue* 42 (Spring 2010): 26–35.

Sherry, Jeffrey F. "'The Terrible Impetuosity': The Pennsylvania Reserves at Gettysburg." *Gettysburg Magazine* 16: 68–80.

Silsby, Robert W. "The Holland Land Company in Western New York." *Adventures in Western New York History Magazine* 8 (1961).

Simpson, John A. "The Cult of the Lost Cause." *Tennessee Historical Quarterly* 34 (1975): 350–61.

———. "The Rebel Yell in American Oral Tradition." Unpublished paper, 1989.

Stevens, Mrs. Robert. "Memoirs of the 1st New York Dragoons, E. Randolph Robinson." *Historical Wyoming* 36 (October 1982): 39–43, 49.

Watson, Bill. "Cowlitz County's Adopted Civil War Veterans." *Cowlitz County Historical Quarterly* 55 (2013): 30–42.

Books

Adams, George Worthington. *Doctors in Blue: The Medical History of the Union Army in the Civil War*. 1952. Reprint, Baton Rouge: Louisiana State University Press, 1996.

Adams, Gladys S. *Bridgewater, Vermont: 1779–1976*. Bridgewater, VT: Bridgewater Cemetery Commission, 2005.

Adams, Michael C. C. *Living Hell: The Dark Side of the Civil War*. Baltimore, MD: Johns Hopkins University Press, 2014.

Anderson, Robert Charles. *The Great Migration: Immigrants to New England, 1634–1635*. Vol. 6. Boston: New England Historic Genealogical Society, 2009.

Arthur, John Preston. *Western North Carolina: A History, 1730 to 1913*. Raleigh, NC: Edwards and Broughton Printing Company, 1914.

Banks, Charles Edward. *Topographical Dictionary of 2885 English Emigrants to New England, 1620–1650*. Philadelphia: Elijan Ellsworth Brownell, Pub., 1937.

Barkun, Michael. *Crucible of the Millennium: The Burned-Over District of New York in the 1840s*. Syracuse, NY: Syracuse University Press, 1986.

Beck, Paul N. *Columns of Vengeance: Soldiers, Sioux, and the Punitive Expeditions, 1863–1864*. Norman: University of Oklahoma Press, 2013.

Bishop, Doris S. *A History of the Town of Orwell, Vermont*. Poultney, VT: Journal Press, 1963.

Bollet, Alfred Jay. *Civil War Medicine: Challenges and Triumphs*. Tucson, AZ: Galen Press, 2002.

Brooks, Charles E. *Frontier Settlement and Market Revolution: The Holland Land Purchase*. Ithaca, NY: Cornell University Press, 1996.

Brooks, Stewart. *Civil War Medicine*. Springfield, IL: Charles C. Thomas, 1966.

Burton, Brian K. *Extraordinary Circumstances: The Seven Days Battles*. Bloomington: Indiana University Press, 2001.

Busey, John W. *These Honored Dead: The Union Casualties at Gettysburg*. Hightstown, NJ: Longstreet House, 1996.

Busey, Travis W., and John W. Busey. *Union Casualties at Gettysburg: A Comprehensive Record*. 3 vols. Jefferson, NC: McFarland, 2011.

Carley, Kenneth. *The Dakota War of 1862: Minnesota's Other Civil War*. St. Paul: Minnesota Historical Society Press, 1976.

Carmichael, Peter S. *The War for the Common Soldier: How Men Thought, Fought, and Survived in Civil War Armies*. Chapel Hill: University of North Carolina Press, 2018.

Chazanof, William. *Joseph Ellicott and the Holland Land Company*. Syracuse, NY: Syracuse University Press, 1970.

Chernow, Ron. *Grant*. New York: Penguin Press, 2017.

Chick, Sean Michael. *The Battle of Petersburg, June 15–18, 1864*. Lincoln, NE: Potomac Books, 2015.

Clodfelter, Michael. *The Dakota War: The United States Army versus the Sioux, 1862–1865*. Jefferson, NC: McFarland, 1998.

Coco, Gregory A. *A Strange and Blighted Land, Gettysburg: The Aftermath of a Battle*. Gettysburg, PA: Thomas Publications, 1995.

———. *A Vast Sea of Misery: A History and Guide to the Union and Confederate Field Hospitals at Gettysburg, July 1–November 20, 1863*. Gettysburg, PA: Thomas Publications, 1988.

Coles, Harry L. *The War of 1812*. Chicago: University of Chicago Press, 1971.

Conforti, Joseph A. *Imagining New England: Explorations of Regional Identity from the Pilgrims to the Mid-Twentieth Century*. Cambridge, MA: Harvard University Press, 2003.

Cooling, Benjamin Franklin. *Jubal Early's Raid on Washington, 1864*. Tuscaloosa: University of Alabama Press, 1989.

———. *Mr. Lincoln's Forts: A Guide to the Civil War Defenses of Washington*. Lanham, MD: Scarecrow Press, 2010.

———. *Symbol, Sword, and Shield*. Hamden, CT: Archon Books, 1975.

Cormier, Steven A. *The Siege of Suffolk: The Forgotten Campaign, April 11–May 4, 1863*. Lynchburg, VA: H. E. Howard, 1989.

Cozzens, Peter. *Shenandoah 1862: Stonewall Jackson's Valley Campaign*. Chapel Hill: University of North Carolina Press, 2008.

Cross, Whitney R. *The Burned-Over District: The Social and Intellectual History of Enthusiastic Religion in Western New York, 1800–1850*. Ithaca, NY: Cornell University Press, 1950.

Curtin, Jeremiah. *Seneca Indian Myths*. New York: E. P. Dutton, 1923.

Daniel, Larry J. *Soldiering in the Army of Tennessee: A Portrait of Life in a Confederate Army*. Chapel Hill: University of North Carolina Press, 1991.

Dathe, Mary Jo, and Sharon Jahn. *Tales of Our Town: Spring Valley Sesquicentennial, 1855–2005*. Spring Valley, MN: Spring Valley Historical Society, 2005.

Davidson, Theodore F. *Genesis of Buncombe County*. Ashville, NC: The Citizen Company, 1922.

Davis, William C. *Battle at Bull Run: A History of the First Major Campaign of the Civil War*. Baton Rouge: Louisiana State University Press, 1977.

Dearing, Mary R. *Veterans in Politics: The Story of the GAR*. Baton Rouge: Louisiana State University Press, 1952.

Dowdey, Clifford. *The Seven Days: The Emergence of Lee*. 1964. Reprint, Lincoln: University of Nebraska Press, 1993.

Dubin, Michael J. *United States Presidential Elections, 1788–1860: The Official Results by County and State*. Jefferson, NC: McFarland, 2002.

Dyer, Frederick H. *A Compendium of the War of the Rebellion*. 3 vols. New York: Yoselof, 1959.

Ent, Uzal W. *The Pennsylvania Reserves in the Civil War: A Comprehensive History*. Jefferson, NC: McFarland, 2014.

Faust, Drew Gilpin. *This Republic of Suffering: Death and the American Civil War*. New York: Vintage Books, 2008.

Faust, Patricia L., ed. *Historical Times Illustrated Encyclopedia of the Civil War*. New York: Harper & Row, 1986.

Foster, Gaines M. *Ghosts of the Confederacy: Defeat, the Lost Cause, and the Emergence of the New South, 1865–1913*. New York: Oxford University Press, 1987.

Freemon, Frank R. *Gangrene and Glory: Medical Care during the American Civil War*. Cranbury, NJ: Associated University Presses, 1998.

Fuller, J. F. C. *Grant and Lee: A Study in Personality and Generalship*. Bloomington: Indiana University Press, 1982.

Furgurson, Ernest B. *Not War but Murder: Cold Harbor 1864*. New York: Vintage Books, 2000.

Gallagher, Gary W., ed. *The Fredericksburg Campaign*. Chapel Hill: University of North Carolina Press, 1995.

———. *Chancellorsville: The Battle and Its Aftermath*. Chapel Hill: University of North Carolina Press, 1996.

———. *The Wilderness Campaign*. Chapel Hill: University of North Carolina Press, 1997.

Glover, Edwin A. *Bucktailed Wildcats: A Regiment of Civil War Volunteers*. New York: Thomas Yoseloff, 1960.

Goodwin, Doris Kearns. *Team of Rivals: The Political Genius of Abraham Lincoln*. New York: Simon & Schuster, 2005.

Gordon, Leslie J. *General George E. Pickett in Life and Legend*. Chapel Hill: University of North Carolina Press, 1998.

Green, A. Wilson. *A Campaign of Giants—The Battle of Petersburg*. Vol. 1, *From the Crossing of the James to the Crater*. Chapel Hill: University of North Carolina Press, 2018.

Griggs, Walter S. *Genealogy of the Griggs Family*. Pompton Lakes, NJ: Biblio Co., 1926.

Grimsley, Mark. *And Keep Moving On: The Virginia Campaign, May–June 1864*. Lincoln: University of Nebraska Press, 2002.

Harlow, Dana D. *Prairie Echoes: Spink County in the Making*. Aberdeen, SD: Hayes Brothers Printers, 1961.

Harris, M. Keith. *Across the Bloody Chasm: The Culture of Commemoration among Civil War Veterans*. Baton Rouge: Louisiana State University Press, 2014.

Hartwig, D. Scott. *To Antietam Creek: The Maryland Campaign of 1862*. Baltimore, MD: Johns Hopkins University Press, 2012.

Hattaway, Herman, and Archer Jones. *How the North Won: A Military History of the Civil War*. Urbana: University of Illinois Press, 1983.

Heck, Frank H. *The Civil War Veteran in Minnesota Life and Politics*. Oxford, OH: Mississippi Valley Press, 1941.

Hennessy, John. "The Army of the Potomac on the Eve of Chancellorsville." In *Chancellorsville: The Battle and Its Aftermath*, ed. Gary W. Gallagher. Chapel Hill: University of North Carolina Press, 1996.

———. *The First Battle of Manassas: An End to Innocence, July 18–21, 1861*. Lynchburg, VA: H. E. Howard, 1989.

———. *Return to Bull Run: The Campaign and Battle of Second Bull Run*. New York: Simon & Schuster, 1993.

Hess, Earl J. *The Union Soldier in Battle: Enduring the Ordeal of Combat*. Lawrence: University Press of Kansas, 1997.

Hopkins City Directory, 1939, 1941, 1943, 1944. Hopkins, MN: Hennepin County Review, 1939, 1941, 1943, 1944.

Hoptak, John David. *The Battle of South Mountain*. Charleston, SC: The History Press, 2011.

Howe, Daniel Walker. *The Political Culture of the American Whigs*. Chicago: University of Chicago Press, 1979.

Johnson, Curt, and Richard C. Anderson Jr. *Artillery Hell: The Employment of Artillery at Antietam*. College Station: Texas A&M University Press, 1995.

Jones, Archer. *Civil War Command and Strategy: The Process of Victory and Defeat*. New York: Macmillan, 1992.

Jordan, Brian Matthew. *Marching Home: Union Veterans and Their Unending Civil War*. New York: Norton, 2014.

Jorgensen, Jay. *Gettysburg's Bloody Wheatfield*. Shippensburg, PA: White Mane Press, 2002.

Kelley, Bruce C., and Mark A. Snell, eds. *Bugle Resounding: Music and Musicians of the Civil War Era*. Columbia: University of Missouri Press, 2004.

Kinchen, Oscar A. *The Rise and Fall of the Patriot Hunters*. New York: Bookman Associates, 1956.

Kolchin, Peter. *American Slavery, 1619–1877*. New York: Hill and Wang, 1993.

LaFantasie, Glenn W. *Twilight at Little Round Top: July 2, 1863—The Tide Turns at Gettysburg*. Hoboken, NJ: John Wiley & Sons, 2004.

Leech, Margaret. *Reveille in Washington, 1860–1865*. New York: Harper and Brothers, 1941.

Linderman, Gerald F. *Embattled Courage: The Experience of Combat in the American Civil War*. New York: Free Press, 1987.

Livsey, Karen E. *Western New York Land Transactions, 1804–1835*. 2 vols. Baltimore, MD: Genealogical Publishing Co., 1991.

Logue, Larry M., and Michael Barton, eds. *The Civil War Veteran: A Historical Reader*. New York: New York University Press, 2007.

Longacre, Edward G. *Lincoln's Cavalrymen: A History of the Mounted Soldiers of the Army of the Potomac, 1861–1865*. Mechanicsburg, PA: Stackpole Books, 2000.

———. *The Early Morning of War: Bull Run, 1861*. Norman: University of Oklahoma Press, 2014.

Lonn, Ella. *Desertion during the Civil War*. New York: Century, 1928.

Mackowski, Chris, and Kristopher D. White. *Chancellorsville's Forgotten Front: The Battles of Second Fredericksburg and Salem Church, May 3, 1863*. El Dorado Hills, CA: Savas Beatie, 2013.

———. *Simply Murder: The Battle of Fredericksburg, December 13, 1862*. El Dorado Hills, CA: Savas Beatie, 2013.

Maney, R. Wayne. *Marching to Cold Harbor: Victory and Failure, 1864*. Shippensburg, PA: White Mane Press, 1995.

Marten, James. *America's Corporal: James Tanner in War and Peace*. Athens: University of Georgia Press, 2014.

McBride, R. E. *In the Ranks: From the Wilderness to Appomattox Court House*. Online Pantianos Classics, 2018 reprint.

McClelland, John B., Jr. *R. A. Long's Planned City: The Story of Longview*. Longview, WA: Westmedia, 1998.

McConnell, Stuart. *Glorious Contentment: The Grand Army of the Republic, 1865–1900*. Chapel Hill: University of North Carolina Press, 1992.

McFeely, William S. *Grant: A Biography*. New York: Norton, 1981.

McNall, Neil Adam. *An Agricultural History of the Genesee Valley, 1790–1860*. Philadelphia: University of Pennsylvania Press, 1952.

McPherson, James M. *Battle Cry of Freedom: The Civil War Era*. New York: Ballantine Books, 1988.

———. *Crossroads of Freedom—Antietam: The Battle That Changed the Course of the Civil War*. New York: Oxford University Press, 2002.

———. *For Cause and Comrades: Why Men Fought in the Civil War*. New York: Oxford University Press, 1997.

Miller, William J. *The Training of an Army: Camp Curtin and the North's Civil War*. Shippensburg, PA: White Mane Publishing Company, 1990.

Mitchell, Reid. *Civil War Soldiers: Their Expectations and Their Experiences*. New York: Touchstone, 1988.

Moe, Richard. *The Last Full Measure: The Life and Death of the First Minnesota Volunteers*. New York: Avon Books, 1993.

Morris, Richard B. *The Forging of the Union, 1781–1789*. New York: Harper & Row, 1987.

Neff, John R. *Honoring the Civil War Dead: Commemoration and the Problem of Reconciliation*. Lawrence: University Press of Kansas, 2005.

Newton, William Monroe. *The History of Barnard, Vermont*. 2 vols. Barre: Vermont Historical Society, 1928.

Olson, Kenneth E. *Music and Musket: Bands and Bandsmen of the American Civil War*. Westport, CT: Greenwood Press, 1981.

O'Reilly, Francis Augustin. *The Fredericksburg Campaign: Winter War on the Rappahannock*. Baton Rouge: Louisiana State University Press, 2003.

Parker, Arthur C. *The History of the Seneca Indians*. Port Washington, NY: Ira J. Friedman, 1967.

Parsons, Philip W. *The Union Sixth Army Corps in the Chancellorsville Campaign: A Study of the Engagements of Second Fredericksburg, Salem Church and Bank's Ford, May 3–4, 1863*. Jefferson, NC: McFarland, 2006.

Patterson, Gerard A. *Debris of Battle: The Wounded of Gettysburg*. Mechanicsburg, PA: Stackpole Books, 1997.

Petersen, Svend. *A Statistical History of American Presidential Elections*. New York: Frederick Ungar, 1963.

Pfanz, Harry W. *Gettysburg: The Second Day*. Chapel Hill: University of North Carolina Press, 1987.

Polk's Kelso, Longview, Woodland, and Cowlitz County Directory, 1926, 1940, 1942, 1945, 1946, 1948. Seattle, WA: R. L. Polk, 1926, 1940, 1942, 1945, 1946, 1948.

Potter, David M. *The Impending Crisis, 1848–1861*. New York: Harper & Row, 1976.

Priest, John Michael. *Antietam: The Soldiers' Battle*. New York: Oxford University Press, 1989.

———. *Before Antietam: The Battle for South Mountain*. New York: Oxford University Press, 1992.

Proceedings of the Annual Reunions and Banquets of the Survivor's Association, 27th Regiment, New York State Volunteers. Binghamton, NY: Carl and Spaulding, 1889.

Punchard, Richard V. *Grand Army of the Republic: Minnesota Department*. Minneapolis: VOL Publishing, 2016.

Rable, George C. *Fredericksburg! Fredericksburg!* Chapel Hill: University of North Carolina Press, 2002.

Rafuse, Ethan S. *Antietam, South Mountain & Harpers Ferry: A Battlefield Guide*. Lincoln: University of Nebraska Press, 2008.

———. *A Single Grand Victory: The First Campaign and Battle of Manassas*. Wilmington, DE: Scholarly Resources, 2002.

———. *Manassas: A Battlefield Guide*. Lincoln: University of Nebraska Press, 2014.

———. *McClellan's War: The Failure of Modernization in the Struggle for the Union*. Bloomington: Indiana University Press, 2005.

Reardon, Carol. *Pickett's Charge in History and Memory*. Chapel Hill: University of North Carolina Press, 1997.

Rhea, Gordon C. *The Battle of the Wilderness, May 5–6, 1864*. Baton Rouge: Louisiana State University Press, 1994.

———. *The Battles for the Spotsylvania Court House and the Road to Yellow Tavern, May 7–12, 1864*. Baton Rouge: Louisiana State University Press, 1997.

———. *To the North Anna River: Grant and Lee, May 13–25, 1864*. Baton Rouge: Louisiana State University Press, 2000.

———. *Cold Harbor: Grant and Lee, May 26–June 3, 1864*. Baton Rouge: Louisiana State University Press, 2002.

———. *On to Petersburg, Grant and Lee, June 4–15*. Baton Rouge: Louisiana State University Press, 2017.

Rix, Timothy S. *History and Genealogy of the Eastman Family of America*. Concord, NH: Ira C. Evans, 1901.

Robinson, Doane. *History of South Dakota*. Logansport, IN: B. F. Bowen and Co., 1904.

Rutkow, Ira M. *Bleeding Blue and Gray: Civil War Surgery and the Evolution of American Medicine*. New York: Random House, 2005.

Schlesinger, Arthur M., Jr. *The Age of Jackson*. Boston: Little, Brown, 1945.

Schroeder, Patrick A. *Pennsylvania Bucktails: A Photographic Album of the 42nd, 149th & 150th Pennsylvania Regiments from the Collection of Ronn Palm*. Daleville, VA: Schroeder Publishers, 2001.

Sears, Stephen W. *Chancellorsville*. Boston: Houghton Mifflin, 1996.

———. *George B. McClellan: The Young Napoleon*. New York: Ticknor and Fields, 1988.

———. *Gettysburg*. Boston: Houghton Mifflin, 2003.

———. *Landscape Turned Red: The Battle of Antietam*. Boston: Houghton Mifflin, 1983.

———. *Lincoln's Lieutenants: The High Command of the Army of the Potomac*. Boston: Houghton Mifflin Harcourt, 2017.

———. *To the Gates of Richmond: The Peninsula Campaign*. Boston: Houghton Mifflin, 1992.

Shattuck, Gardiner H., Jr. *A Shield and Hiding Place: The Religious Life of the Civil War Armies*. Macon, GA: Mercer University Press, 1987.

Silber, Nina. *The Romance of Reunion: Northerners and the South, 1865–1900*. Chapel Hill: University of North Carolina Press, 1993.

Simpson, John A. *S. A. Cunningham and the Confederate Heritage*. Athens: University of Georgia Press, 1994.

Slocum, Charles Elihu. *The Life and Services of Major-General Henry Warner Slocum*. Toledo, OH: Slocum Publishing Co., 1913.

Smeltzer, Harry. *Bull Runnings; A Journal of the Digitization of a Civil War Battle*. https://bullrunnings.wordpress.com.

Sodergren, Steven E. *The Army of the Potomac in the Overland and Petersburg Campaign*. Baton Rouge: Louisiana State University Press, 2017.

Sondley, F. A. *Asheville and Buncome County*. Asheville, NC: The Citizen Company, 1922.

Stampp, Kenneth M. *The Causes of the Civil War*. Rev. ed. New York: Touchstone, 1992.

———. *The Peculiar Institution: Slavery in the Ante-Bellum South*. New York: Alfred A. Knopf, 1968.

Starr, Stephen Z. *The Union Cavalry in the Civil War*. 2 vols. Baton Rouge: Louisiana State University Press, 1979.

Stebbins, Willis Merrill. *Genealogy of the Stebbins Family*. Lincoln, NE: Brown Printing, 1949.

Steiner, Paul E. *Disease in the Civil War: Natural Biological Warfare in 1861–1865*. Springfield, IL: Charles C. Thomas, 1968.

Stilwell, Lewis D. *Migration from Vermont*. Montpelier: Vermont Historical Society, 1948.

Sutherland, Daniel E. *Fredericksburg and Chancellorsville: The Dare Mark Campaign*. Lincoln: University of Nebraska Press, 1998.

Thomas, Emory M. *Bold Dragoon: The Life of J. E. B. Stuart*. New York: Harper & Row, 1986.

Trudeau, Noah Andre. *Bloody Roads South: The Wilderness to Cold Harbor, May–June 1864*. Boston: Little, Brown, 1989.

———. *Gettysburg: A Testing of Courage*. New York: HarperCollins, 2002.

Turner, Frederick Jackson. *The United States, 1830–1850: The Nation and Its Sections*. 1935. Reprint, New York: Norton & Co., 1962.

Turner, Robert G. *Stonewall in the Valley: Thomas J. "Stonewall" Jackson's Shenandoah Valley Campaign, Spring 1862*. Garden City, NY: Doubleday and Co., 1976.

Tyler, Alice Felt. *Freedom's Ferment: Phases of American Social History from the Colonial Period to the Outbreak of the Civil War*. 1944. Reprint, New York: Harper Torchbooks, 1962.

Urrutia, Virginia. *They Came to Six Rivers: The Story of Cowlitz County*. Kelso, WA: Cowlitz County Historical Society, 1998.

Wagner, Richard. *For Honor, Flag, and Family: Civil War Major General Samuel W. Crawford, 1827–1892*. Shippensburg, PA: White Mane Press, 2005.

Wallace, Anthony F. C. *The Death and Rebirth of the Senecas*. New York: Vintage Books, 1972.

Warner, Ezra J. *Generals in Blue: Lives of the Union Commanders*. Baton Rouge: Louisiana State University Press, 1964.

Wecter, Dixon. *When Johnny Comes Marching Home*. Cambridge, MA: Riverside Press, 1944.

Wert, Jeffry D. *The Sword of Lincoln: The Army of the Potomac*. New York: Simon & Schuster, 2005.

Wheelan, Joseph. *Bloody Spring: Forty Days That Sealed the Confederacy's Fate*. Boston: Da Capo Press, 2014.

Wickman, Donald H. *"A Very Fine Appearance": The Vermont Civil War Photographs of George Houghton*. Barre: Vermont Historical Society, 2011.

Wiley, Bell I. *The Life of Billy Yank: The Common Soldier of the Union*. 1952. Reprint, Baton Rouge: Louisiana State University Press, 1971.

Willford, William, and Franklyn Curtiss-Wedge, eds. *The History of Mower County, Minnesota*. Chicago: H. C. Cooper, Jr., and Co., 1911.

Williams, T. Harry. *Lincoln and His Generals*. New York: Vintage Books, 1952.

Wills, Brian Steel. *The War Hits Home: The Civil War in Southeastern Virginia*. Charlottesville: University of Virginia Press, 2001.

Wills, Garry. *Lincoln at Gettysburg: The Words That Remade America*. New York: Simon & Schuster, 1992.

Wilson, Charles R. *Baptized in Blood: The Religion of the Lost Cause, 1865–1920*. Athens: University of Georgia Press, 1980.

Wilson, Harold Fisher. *The Hill Country of Northern New England: Its Social and Economic History, 1790–1830*. New York: Columbia University Press, 1936.

Wood, Gordon S. *The Creation of the American Republic, 1776–1787*. Chapel Hill: University of North Carolina Press, 1969.

Wycoff, William. *The Developer's Frontier: The Making of the Western New York Landscape*. New Haven, CT: Yale University Press, 1988.

Websites

http://www.alleganyhistory.org
http://www.ancestry.com
http://www.archive.org
http://www.familysearch.org
http://www.findagrave.com
http://www.MNopedia.org
http://www.olivetreegenealogy.com
http://www.protoball.org
http://www.winthropsociety.com

Index